SPORT
and
INTERNATIONAL RELATIONS

Benjamin Lowe
David B. Kanin
Andrew Strenk

SPORT
and
INTERNATIONAL RELATIONS

Edited by

Benjamin Lowe
Governors State University, Illinois

David B. Kanin
Boston College, Massachusetts

Andrew Strenk
University of Southern California

ISBN 0-87563-162-2

Published by
STIPES PUBLISHING COMPANY
10-12 Chester Street
Champaign, Illinois 61820

Preface

In April, 1976, a singular event in the world of sport took place. This event was all the more unique because it had nothing to do directly with athletic performance, coaching or officiating. In Paris, UNESCO called the "First International Conference of Ministers and Senior Officials responsible for Physical Education and Sport," the significance of which is underscored by the fact that reference can be made freely nowadays to "Ministers of Sport." The position of Minister of Sport is a contemporary development in governments; no such position obtained before World War II.

Delegates from 102 countries attended the International Conference, testifying to the role that sport plays in the lives of men and women throughout the world. If a country has not appointed a Minister of Sport in the last ten years, then the responsibility for sport usually rests with the Minister of Cultural Affairs. Sport is becoming recognized as a vital cultural force by many nations.

Unlike many forms of intercultural relations, sport is competitive in nature. Art works can be exchanged without necessarily leading to a "zero-sum" comparison of national heritages. A Frenchman can admire Beethoven and Goethe without having to denigrate the memory of Debussy or Molière. Comparisons between cultures are common, but they are not required by the mechanism of cultural activity itself.

Such comparisons are intrinsic to the nature of international sport. If the staging of a sports event can be a sign of cooperation between states, the activity itself is a direct comparison of the physical and mental abilities of the societies' human resources. States may try to use sport to represent international goodwill, but the mechanism of sport makes it a potential forum for interstate competition as well.

The field of international studies, according to Rosenau (1973):-

> consists of area specialists and discipline generalists, psychologists, and anthropologists, students of national institutions and investigators of international processes, single-discipline experts in cross-national comparison and multi-discipline experts in single-country analysis, political scientists and sociologists, case writers and quantifiers, government officials and practicing lawyers, teachers and researchers, raw empiricists and general theorists, computer scientists and language specialists, functionalists who specialize in military affairs and others who focus on economic affairs, policy-oriented analysis and mathematical model builders, specialists in public health and experts in agriculture, historians of real worlds and students of simulated worlds--to mention but a few of the foci and skills embraced by the field. (p. 23)

The sport sciences can claim an appeal of similar breadth, but further, sport can be identified as a phenomenon of international concern. To focus on sport in the assessment of international affairs might be perceived as contributory to their science by those professionals in international studies. By the same token, sport scientists are being made patently aware that élite athletic performance in the international stadia affects their assessment of sport in society. Both the sports sciences and international studies draw from a number of established disciplines. For the analysis of sport in a context of international relations, then, it is recommended that a synthesis of concepts and data be drawn from a common pool of parent disciplines.

Transnational sport phenomena, such as the international sports federations, the International Olympic Committee, and even the unspoken and unwritten appeal that international sport as a form of intercultural activity has for a mass public, need to be understood in the context of a subdiscipline drawing major strengths from both the sport sciences and international relations. This anthology of readings makes an initial attempt to synthesize knowledge towards better comprehension of such a subdiscipline, whether it be adopted by departments of sports studies, of political science, of international relations, or of communications.

Modern communications technology makes matches of national interest immediately available to anyone who wants to watch or listen. Governments are aware that such communications technology enables this mass public, which tends to identify with the athletes, to take instant notice of contests against teams or individuals from friendly or hostile states. Governments can use this identification when sports events are staged to demonstrate the temper of relations between the states represented by the athletes. The cancellation of such an activity can also be useful in "public diplomacy."[1] It is a safe way (in terms of the risk of war or diplomatic rupture) of expressing displeasure with another country and its policies. As Glass and Pinson (1972) state:

> The similarities between sports and war are superficial. The differences are significant. Wars are political contests. Sports are not. War affects the fate of entire nations, soldiers and civilians. Sports affect the destiny of relatively few people. The purpose of war is to destroy the enemy. No one in an athletic contest is out to kill anyone. Players hit hard, but they are not trying to destroy one another. The object in sports is to compete against an opponent, not annihilate him ...War causes widespread destruction. Sports cause none... War supplies are intended to kill and destroy. Sports equipment is used to play a game. Players are sometimes killed

---

[1] According to Philip Horton, Director of the Edward R. Murrow Center for Public Diplomacy, The Fletcher School of Law and Diplomacy, "Public Diplomacy" is "the exercise of open communication by word, deed, or image whether by government or private group and organization, for the purpose of influencing international relations and the formation and execution of foreign policy."

in a sporting event, but very rarely. And their deaths are accidental, not intentional. Millions die in wars--and their deaths are no accident. War is so different from sports that a comparison is silly. (p. 54)

Sport is safe because it is peripheral to the international political system. Sports activities are not as vital to the state as are economic, legal, or diplomatic relations. A defeat in a match will not normally be avenged by the use of force by the state whose athletic representatives have lost. Although sport is an activity which is organized largely into units corresponding in name and jurisdiction to the state, the state has little control over the rules, equipment, standard, and outcome of play. Yet, even without the direct involvement of state power, the public can be made aware, through sport, of state moods and policies toward other states. On the other hand, as the Final Report of the First International Conference of Ministers and Senior Officials responsible for Physical Education and Sport (UNESCO) indicates, international cooperation between states can influence the media to play a more educational role in depicting sport than typically glorifying the function of sport as spectacle. Sport, then, becomes a function of international cooperation, albeit peripheral to state political systems.

If sport is a useful instrument in public diplomacy because of its public, politically peripheral nature, and unusual in intercultural relations because of its intrinsically competitive nature, it is also important in international relations because, as an activity, it has no intrinsic political value. Sport can be used by any state to demonstrate the physical prowess of the human resources of any ideology or value system. Sport activity has no political content in itself, therefore, the sport process can be given any political interpretation imaginable. The "Gentleman Sportsman," "All-American Boy," and "New Soviet Man" can all play the same sport controlled by the same international federation. Sport provides an arena for the direct comparison of athletes representing different societies by spectators who can understand rules which are common to most of the world. This has been called the "liquid" quality of sport (Edwards, 1973), a quality which, when tested in the arena of international sports exchange, is found to be less viscous than expected. This is especially true when sport as a whole is placed in a hypothetical formula with culture and politics.

The social equation which brings the closest interrelationship between culture, sport and politics is illustrated by the example of Cuba abolishing entrance fees (tickets) to stadia for sports events. In 1967, the Cuban government announced that sport was to be seen as an inseparable element of education, culture, health, defence, happiness and the development of the people. In terms of her sports identity, Cuba has been able to show this to best effect by her efforts and results in the Pan-American Games in recent years. Most effectively Cuba has demonstrated a greater proportion of athletic successes in relation to national population figures than any of the other participant countries of the Pan-American Games.

Writing the sports-culture-politics equation another way, the People's Republic of China propounds "Friendship First, Competition Second." This slogan is politically inspired by Maoist thought, and reminds the Chinese athletes of the People's Republic of China to continue to give priority to politics in their athletic endeavors. A former Chinese table tennis champion is reputed to have said: "If you learn techniques but not politics and do not put politics in command, you will not be able to play good ping-pong." According to Goodhart and Chattaway (1968):

> Other Chinese sportsmen also seek the guidance of Mao. At the first Chinese athletic championships after the outbreak of the cultural revolution, the victorious high jumper was observed reading The Thoughts of Chairman Mao before each leap, while the Chinese weight lifters in international events would lift the same slim volume above their heads before attempting their snatches and presses. (p. 85)

Take, for purposes of comparison, the philosophy of "winning" traditionally attributed to the great American football coach, Vince Lombardi. Rightly or wrongly, Lombardi has been accused of placing a winning result over all other considerations held by his athletes (personal physical health or injury; religious convictions; pecuniary rewards; values and beliefs). Various social analysts of the role of sport in American society have vindicated Lombardi as being a product of his culture (emphasizing a competitive industrial work ethos), while others have said that his influence on the culture via the mass communications media has contributed to a debasement of values by distorting the perception of winning as a norm. In the American version of the equation, then, politics is reduced almost to insignificance.

Culture became the dominant element of the equation in Nazi Germany, when the persecution of the Jews involved their exclusion from national representation in major sports events including the Berlin Olympiad of 1936. The complexity involved in weighing the relative significance of culture and politics becomes particularly problematical in other circumstances. In 1964, for example, the Russian tennis star, Alex Metrevali, withdrew from the Wimbledon Championships for "personal reasons." The opponent he was due to play was the South African tennis ace, Abe Segal, and all Soviet tennis players had boycotted South African players that year to demonstrate their abhorrence of apartheid. Furthermore, and as if to complicate the analysis of this case, it should be noted that Segal is a Jew, and Jews have had to suffer severely due to Soviet government pressure (as in Nazi Germany).

On one occasion, Avery Brundage attempted to show that sport could be given the greatest factor loading in the equation. He instructed the West Germans and East Germans, in 1950, to resolve their post-war political division in order to enter one representative German team in the Helsinki Olympiad. Sport almost prevailed over politics when the delegates from the divided country met at the headquarters of the International Olympic Committee in Lausanne, and, after cordial discussions, agreed that one united team should represent Germany. It never came to pass for the East German Government would not hear of the proposal and the East German delegates disappeared from the sports scene. However, a second effort was made, but the East German committee was pulled out at the eleventh hour, having arrived in Copenhagen for final arrangements prior to Helsinki in 1952. Avery Brundage was now able to exert some pressure on the East Germans for their repudiation of previous agreements, and in 1954, they re-accepted the original Lausanne agreement which resulted in both West and East German athletes marching together at the 1956 Winter Olympics held in Cortina d'Ampezza. Thus, on this one occasion sport proved the greatest factor in the equation, although it can be noted that culture must have significantly loaded also in respect of the sense of Teutonic integrity that would have been felt by the German people as a whole (regardless of which side of the Iron Curtain they lived). It is not the athlete who is the most important actor in international sport, considered as a political phenomenon. It is the spectator. The public nature of sport is what makes this politically peripheral phenomenon important in world affairs. Spectators are the targets for the national and ideological comparisons which are intrinsic to the sports process. A further elaboration on the role and function of the spectator is given in the following exercise on definitions.

SPORT: There are many definitions of sport and many problems with defining it in a social context, as Talamini and Page (1973) recognized in the introduction to their anthology Sport and Society:

> Consider the following depictions of sport in current writing: a major component of the consumer or 'postindustrial' society, but [auth. ital.] merely a part of the entertainment industry; big business and big bureaucracy, but the last refuge of individual enterprise; a moral equivalent of war ('Ping-Pong Diplomacy' was recently with us), but a basis of international conflict; an important character building activity, but an arena of exploitation and degradation; a channel of opportunity for the disadvantaged, but an enterprise marked by racism and reactionary practice; an occupation in which performance counts most, but one stamped by cronyism and personal prejudice; a safety valve for tension and man's propensity for conflict, but a manifestation of collective madness; a social and psychological requirement of modern mass society, but a replacement for religion as the opiate of the masses ('the right wing theater of America'). (p. 3)

With such a plethora of considerations, there can be no surprise at the array of definitions of sport. The etymological history of the word is drawn from the French "desporter"--to divert or amuse. Traditional definitions (Hughes and Williams, 1944) limit sport to being a game or an athletic form of play engaged in for the sheer enjoyment of it; or to being a playing attitude extended from childhood. (Helanko, 1957)

The oversimplification of sport as an extension of "game" is a common one. Sport has been described as "a set of rules institutionalized in games," or in any game occurrence or event. (Weiss, 1969) More elaborate definitions take the role of sport in society into account. For Sipes (1973), sport becomes:

A physical activity (1) engaged in primarily for amusement or recreation, (2) with no ostensible religious ritual or substance-activity training significance and (3) involving at least two adult individuals. (p. 64)

This definition leaves out the necessary elements of competition and ruleboundedness. Sport is a rulebound, competitive set of activities with uncertain outcomes engaged in for non-occupational purposes (except in league franchise circumstances). While "sport" is used to describe the concept, "sports" refers to the activities themselves in the plural. Sports have histories, rituals, and traditions attached to them resulting from their organization into bureaucratic administrative structures. Agreed-upon measures of performance increase the unity of sport tradition. Statistics serve as the unity of each sport activity through time and space (Edwards, 1973). The prescription for the participants of sport is:

(1) They are always representative of a group or organization, and thus prone to group pressure.

(2) Sports require particular preparation.

(3) Individual roles are explicitly named or defined.

(4) Sports have a seriousness of purpose as social phenomena.

(5) Winning is the purpose of sport.

Edwards (1973) is especially interested in the modern American sports establishment, but his prescription is important in its emphasis of the seriousness of the sport to the participant. Even though the activities are not occupational (except in league franchises) they are important to the athlete and to the spectator.

There is sometimes the distinction made between combative and non-combative sports, depending on the acceptance of body contact or potential body contact within the framework of each particular sport. This dichotomy does not work with chess, and becomes even less meaningful when the mass media and the spectators are taken into account.

ATHLETICS: Athletics and Sports are usually considered synonymous. The word itself is from the Greek "athios," or prize, which stresses the goal of sport--winning. Keating (1964) defines the sportsman as interested in competition, and the athlete as interested only in winning.

Actually, the terms are not really synonymous. In many parts of the old British Empire, "athletics" refers specifically only to those sports which are groups, in other parts of the world, under the term "Track and Field." "Athletics" actually include those sports which involve competition through some measure of physical exertion. Chess is a game which has become a sport through organization on the local, national, and international level, and through the resulting creation of a recorded tradition. Chess has its statistics, administration, and mass appeal like any other sport. Bridge, another non-athletic activity, is developing along the same lines.

A growing phenomenon in the athletic world is that of the athletic exhibition. International tours of the Soviet gymnastic teams do not always involve competition with other athletes. Athletics are staged in such a way as to remove the competitive aspects of the event. Although still athletic, these exhibitions enter the realm of circuses and spectacles, not sport.

CONTEST: Lüschen (1970) defines contest in the following manner:

> Contest in sport occurs when at least two units (individuals or teams) compete under specific rules and agreements, for superiority in a non-representative [italics added] skill or strategy. (p. 21)

This operational definition is confused by the word "non-representative." Sport may not have anything to do with the contestant's occupations or "real life" activities, but the sport may be quite "representative" of the organizations or states in whose names they vie (Goodhart and Chattaway, 1968). International sports organizations would have people believe that contests under their jurisdiction are separate from the international political activities of the states represented in sport. Actually, the contestants in international sport activities are representative of their states and serve as conscious national symbols for their respective political systems.

COMPETITION: Competition is the mechanism of sport. It is the struggle between at least two units for the stakes of the sport or game using all methods and weapons allowed under the rules of the particular event. In this way, it is different from conflict which is the use of all means available to win-- regardless of the rules of the sport.

Competition is a relationship between two opponents (at least) who agree to play within the rules or between a human participant and a self-imposed opponent (the clock, a geographical obstacle, or his own expectations). Conflict need not be a relationship if either side or both sides struggle for their own goals, according to their own value systems. (Schelling, 1960) If the opponent is viewed as so reprehensible that his defeat is more important than the fair struggle in the sport, then discreet violation of the rules may be consciously employed. The intensity of competition and its tendency to spill over into conflict concerned Thorstein Veblen (1899), who stated:

> Modern competition is in large part a process of self-assertion on the basis of these traits of predatory human nature. (p. 262)

SPORTSMANSHIP: This concept is surrounded by connotations of honor and ethical imperative. (Lowe, 1974) Its ostensible purpose is to keep competition within bounds so that sport is contested fairly--to prevent competition from becoming conflict.

In 1926, the National Sportsmanship Brotherhood was formed. This group listed explicit rules for sportsmanship.

(1) Keep the Rules.

(2) Keep Faith with Your Comrades.

(3) Keep Yourself Fit.

(4) Keep Your Temper.

(5) Keep Your Play Free from Brutality.

(6) Keep Pride Under in Victory.

(7) Keep Stout Heart in Defeat.

(8) Keep a Sound Soul and a Clean Mind in a Healthy Body.

These categories expressed an ideal of social behavior in athletic form. Sportsmanship is the attempt to inculcate the individual with societal values through the medium of sport participation. Since the rules of sport (and the "Rights" and "Wrongs" of sport) are more clearly perceived by more people than the intricacies of legal jargon and political maneuver, principles of sportsmanship are effective weapons in the state's struggle to integrate its people and its doctrines.

SPECTATOR: A spectator is an indirect or vicarious participant in a sports event. The mass of followers of sport are even more the targets of propaganda for national integration than the athletes themselves. They are also the recipients of much international propaganda through sport. To quote Beisser, (1967):

> The fan is an athlete once removed, an athlete in spirit if not in fact. Through lack of physical capacity or psychological desire, he is a competitor without necessarily facing the dangers of competition. He is aggressive without threat of injury either to his body or his pride. Although his competition is vicarious he can enjoy the pleasure of victory, the sorrow of defeat, the tension of the climactic moment. However he can, if he wishes, express his emotion verbally and even physically without fear of censure. The fan enjoys a peculiarly luxurious position between the camaraderie and the anonymity of the crowd. He can share intense feelings with strangers who understand. (p. 139)

A **fan** is a spectator who feels partisan emotion toward one of the contestants in a sports event.[2]

Spectators must do more than just view the sport event. They must have at least a rudimentary understanding of the rules and the stakes of the event in order to induce their vicarious participation.

Spectator sports are dramatic displays of sport for the purpose of entertaining masses of people. As in all dramas, there are heroes and villains. Winning and losing are more clearly portrayed in sport than in many forms of drama, and the fact that these events are part of the real life experience of spectators can lead to a violent reaction or a somber depression resulting from the event.

Lewis Mumford defined mass sport in terms of such dramatic spectacles, (cited in Talamini and Page, 1973). The era of mass media, international sport exchange and propaganda, and of sport as big business has pushed sport into public and, therefore, governmental prominence. Spectators are the consumers of such events.

Direct sports consumption is the attendance at the sport events themselves; **Indirect sports consumption** is spectating through television, radio, or other media intermediaries. (McPherson, 1972)

According to Paul Weiss, "A public struggle entrains a public evaluation." (p. 167) Therefore, nations stage many public sports struggles to obtain prestige from the performances of athletes produced by the state and its political system. Such political motives are intrinsic to international sport, and are most especially part of the Olympic Games. Such motives and problems arising from such motives, therefore, are not exceptional or mere aberrations caused by a few misguided people.

This book explores first the interrelationship of sport and culture. The selections represent both classical and innovative statements of the relationship in "Foundations in Culture: Antecedents to Political Sport." There have been a succession of events in which sport cannot be separated from political action in one form or another. Continuity between sections 1 and 2 has been attempted by linking Weber's views on late nineteenth century European sport with an original article by the founder of the modern Olympic Games, Coubertin, whose political philosophy underpins his best hopes for

---

[2] The etymology of "fan" is grounded in "the Fancy." (Lowe, 1978) The Fancy refers to a loosely knit social subculture, the members of which were drawn from all levels of eighteenth century English society, from the destitute to the nobility. The major bonding factor for self-identification as a **bona fide** member of the Fancy rested solely as whether a person claimed a proclivity for the active support of pugilism. To be "of the Fancy," (equivalent to being "a fancier" in most respects) meant either that one participated as a pugilist (athlete) or one attended, and typically wagered at pugilistic encounters.

apolitical sport, Olympism, it might be argued, is a form of ideology--and like any ideology must suffer to be tested on many levels. In Section 3, at least three meanings of "ideology" are explored: (i) the social ideology of the athlete (in classical history); 9ii) the cultural ideology of a recently developed Commonwealth country; and (iii) the political ideology of newly-emerging nations. Section 4, "Policy and International Sport," focuses on the sharp interplay of sport and politics at the hands of government, particularly as international sport might be construed to be an effect of government policy. In the concluding section on "Sport Communication for Development and Education," (Section 5) an effort is made to recall much of what has gone before in the anthology, emphasizing the message that international sports exchange is a form of communication. The grand expectancy for sport is explored in the concept of nation building, and finally, the theme of the anthology is presented as being contributory to education resting on the motto as expressed by the I.O.C. "Sport for a World of Peace."

Contents

Section 1

FOUNDATIONS IN CULTURE: ANTECEDENTS TO POLITICAL SPORT

Introduction

As H. L. Nieburg stated in <u>Culture Storm: Politics and Ritual Order</u>, culture and politics cannot be separated. However, the argument that sport and culture are interrelated and interdependent remains open. Sport can be viewed as a function either of culture or of politics, but the purpose of Section 1, "Foundations in Culture: Antedecents to Political Sport," is to explore both functions and interactions.

Sport is a profoundly competitive activity. Its practitioners are compared as well as admired by those before whom they display their skills. For the spectator it is a short perceptual step from the comparison of athletes to that of the cultures they represent. As a cultural phenomenon, sport covers questions relating to aggression, conflict, socialization and cooperation, but the social role of sport becomes sublimated when "broader" issues are at stake. Examples which come to mind immediately are:-

a) 1956, the Hungarian revolution, occurring proximally close in time with the Melbourne Olympiad, promoted an unarmed extension of hostilities between athletes both of the Hungarian and of the Soviet water polo teams; and

b) the International Olympic Committee appears to have become inextricably involved with sports issues challenged by <u>apartheid</u>, the policy of government exercised by South Africa to the detriment of South African athletes, and more recently, by a divided China, in which only the athletes of Taiwan (the minority of the division) have official I.O.C. representation.

The social science of sport takes on new dimensions when viewed in a context of international relations. Social relations in sport can no longer be taken in microcosm, for a grander question is posed.

"Political sport" is an imprecise construct, the nature of which becomes clearer as reference is made to later Sections of this anthology. On the face of it, "political sport" may have several interpretations. In Augustan Rome (31 B.C.-A.D. 14), provincial officials seeking higher and more lucrative government office positions, such as praetor or consul, attempted to outbid each other for popular favor (future votes) by the extravagance of the "sports" spectacles (<u>ludi circenses</u>, <u>numera gladiatoria</u>, or <u>venationes</u>) which they offered to the public. The Emperor Augustus instituted the Games of Mars in association with the dedication of the great Temple of Mars in honor of the day when Antonius died and Egypt was placed under Roman rule (Rowell, 1962). When political sport is interpreted for the purpose of distinguishing social class cleavages, the tempestuous history of professionalism in sport can be examined both intra-culturally (Periclean Greece and nineteenth century England) and cross-culturally. For the purposes of Sport and International Relations, the construct "political sport" presents the parsimony of symbolic statement suggesting the broader interactions (in either direction) between "politics" and "sport." Since the majority of the anthology explores these diverse interactions, there is a fundamental requirement for establishing sources of such interactions. Political thought and action (social "movement" theory) is expressed as a function of the sport paradigm. It is stressed that the antecedents to political sport are just as politically motivated as are contemporary succeeding effects; evidence is drawn from the evolutionary progression of communications systems from newspapers to television to illustrate the spread of political sport. Examples are presented of different nationalisms using sport as a tool, and it is shown that sport is neither unique nor different from any other form of political culture. Parallels can be found in Third World exploitations of sport for purposes of prestige in international relations.

Instead, assumptions are advanced concerning the benefits of "people-to-people" contacts and of cross-cultural fertilization. But what if the transaction involves competition as well as cooperation? In such cases, how universal is the concept "Friendship First, Competition Second?"

Most states claim athletic heroes as representative of the "best" in their cultures, but what is it in culture - or in ourselves - from which such competition springs? Is sport a safety-valve designed to allow us to let off steam, a mechanism which structures inner conflict and controls vestiges of barbarism? If so, one can draw contradictory conclusions. Sport can be seen either as a triumph of human adaptation, or as evidence that we have not advanced very far on the evolutionary ladder. It can be hailed as proof of the human ability to overcome natural aggressive instincts by releasing them within the confines of the athletic field. On the other hand, the very need for this release might be a reminder that our civilization is only a veneer.

The assumption that all - or even most - of our aggression is released in sport can be challenged. Perhaps the expression of aggression in sport competition goes hand in hand with its dominance of other sectors of human contact. Rather than sublimating aggression, sport might actually be one minor expression of it. War, crime, and random violence might be linked to sport as examples of the same basic drive in our biological make-up.

A cultural approach would challenge the universality of the aggressive impulse. Aggressive behavior would be considered as a result of acculturation. Social processes, rather than biological impulses, would become the loci of investigation. "Contact" sports might flourish in those societies where aggressive behavior is approved, and not exist where it is not.

But what of those sports which do not involve a great deal of overt aggressive behavior? Is it still possible for them to reflect resentment or hostility? Sports such as croquet, badminton, and chess do not require contestants to better their opponents except in the psychology of "winning" or "losing" the event. Perhaps it is enough to demonstrate superiority of mind in order to raise feelings of aggression on the part of the defeated.

This raises another issue; perhaps sport can as easily build up aggression as dissipate it. The possibility that sport creates tension must not be overlooked in a world where representative national teams contest skill and strength before spectators who identify with victory, and who sometimes will not forgive defeat. Ten years ago, in their book War Without Weapons, Goodhart and Chattaway (1968) commented on this cultural relationship:

> Certainly, a number of Western European governments have proceeded in recent years in the belief that there is a political value in sporting success which is worth paying for. In all this, governments are almost certainly acting in accordance with the wishes of the public. Around the world, people appear to attach more and more weight to success in international sport. Their team's performance in the Olympics is increasingly seen as some sort of measure of a nation's worth. More and more athletes see themselves as engaged in an activity that is of importance to their country. (p. 17)

As far as these authors were concerned, the writing was already on the wall. During the last ten years the sports efforts both of the German Democratic Republic (East Germany) and of Cuba, to win gold medals in the Olympics, have borne out their commentary to the letter. Indeed, what Goodhart and Chattaway (1968) stated about the division of Germany later in their book is worth quoting directly for the salutory distinction it makes in respect to intracultural sport rivalry:

> Of the satellite nations, East Germany probably invests most heavily in sporting success......Some of the results were seen in the remarkable supremacy of East German athletes at the European Games in Budapest in 1966. The constant urge to do better than the West Germans has added a neurotic edge to the East German will to succeed. When the East German girl tobogganists were disqualified for heating their runners in the 1956 Winter Olympics the team manager's references to 'reactionary revanchist plots' were worthy of the hey-day of Stalinism. (p. 83)

It appears, then, that the meaning of sport can be distorted according to how the concept is to serve state interests. Can we expect to see new contradictions as the China (Peking) Question becomes focused?

What is clear about sport, whatever assumptions one might hold concerning its origins and nature, is that contemporary sport has been molded within contemporary society. Urbanization, industrialization, and revolutions in technology have made it possible for athletes to travel around the world and to reach millions of fans. Spectators can now watch matches of national (and therefore political) interest thousands of miles away without leaving their homes. Is sport a different process now that most of these concerned with it never even attend the event?

Thorstein Veblen was not wrong when he heralded the age of the leisure class. The existence of individuals who spend most of their time organizing their own recreation is unquestioned. What he did not understand was that the activities in which these people indulged would become the profession of members of other social classes ("profession" includes world class "amateurs"). The concentration of millions in urban factories meant not only that they would work in the same place; it meant that they would be at leisure at the same time. Modern sport has contributed to both the organization of that leisure and the profit some came to enjoy from it.

These situational factors are Western in orientation. The modern sport system is part of an international environment dominated by Western (Europe and its white stepchildren) institutions, laws, and diplomatic practices. Most international sports are of Western origin. In some cases they have supplanted or replaced traditional forms of recreation, contributing to the assimilation of whole societies into the politics and social structure of colonial powers. The fact that the contemporary international system is dominated by Western cultural forms and institutions is as significant for sport as for other political processes.

Of these cultural forms, the growth of European nationalism is perhaps the most important. The origins of any relationship between sport and nationalism in modern times may be traced to the words of Jean Jacques Rousseau. In 1773, Rousseau published his pamphlet Considerations on the Government of Poland, in which he stated that games should be organized so that they "make the hearts of children glow, and create a deep love for the fatherland and its laws." (cited in Goodhart and Chattaway, 1968, p. 35). Nationalism is not necessarily the same thing as patriotism; the former describes a feeling of loyalty to the political movement of one's ethnic group, while the latter means only that one is loyal to the state--even if that state is not under the control of people with whom the individual might ethnically identify. The growth of mass sport corresponded to the growth of national movements in opposition to the prevailing political order. F. L. Jahn, called "the father of gymnastics," proclaimed a doctrine that a national athletic movement would regenerate the German people, and defined his intention as "protecting youth from softness and excess in order to keep them sturdy for the coming struggle for the fatherland." (cited in Vinnai, 1973, p. 103).

Nationalism was thus a revolutionary force, and was opposed by many of the states it threatened. Habsburgs and Hohenzollerns, for example, had little use for a "German" nationalism which would replace loyalty to the dynastics with some new form of German union. The Habsburgs were particularly concerned since German nationalism might spark similar movements among Czechs, Hungarians, Slovaks, and South Slavs.

In this situation, the legacy of Father Jahn, and of the Bohemian Sokols, proved to be revolutionary in nature. It is wholly inaccurate to lump Jahn with "Prussian Militarism," or to dismiss him as an antecedent to Hitler (who was neither a Prussian nor content with the kind of movement Jahn had in mind). Jahn's form of gymnastics was devised to strengthen the muscles and cardiorespiratory physiology of German youth, as well as to serve the purpose of developing military abilities. At about this same period in time, P. H. Ling in Sweden designed a system of gymnastics that gained widespread popularity. It is not widely known today that P. H. Ling was inspired in this direction by a sense of national pride stemming from his knowledge of and love for Nordic folk mythology. In the words of Goodhart and Chattaway (1968): "The work of Jahn, and more particularly of Ling, was soon made known to Britain, but the impact of their doctrine on the British sporting revolution was negligible." (p. 35) Jahn was a Prussian patriot, yet he was jailed by the Prussian government because his Turnvereine let loose national sentiments which the dynasty could not control. His loyalty may have been to Prussia, but the effect of his organization was to enflame the kind of Pan-Germanism which would be the spirit of 1848.

This difference between ideology and organization is an important one. Just as the Olympic system would have little to do with "Olympism," Turnvereine and Burschenschaften went beyond Jahn's own conceptualisation to encompass greater German identification. Indeed, the "Turners" spread to the United States, where they served as a direct link between the Fatherland and people who would otherwise lose touch with it.

Jahn's use of sport did leave one international object lesson. The concept of "reawakening" through physical exercise took on a political meaning. In Jahn's case it meant that the Prussian people would arm themselves and throw off Napoleon (and then the Autrian hegemony which replaced him). Once the German Empire was created, the new Reich sought to make Turnvereine energy over into a medium for the creation of mass pride to the state. After 1871 nationalism became a state ideology, and took on a character more familiar to a contemporary audience.

In the meantime, other people began to "reawaken." The Sokol movement sought to both educate and invigorate a people believed to have been asleep since 1620. The Battle of White Mountain was pointed to as a national debacle, and Czechs were urged to use the meaning of national disgrace as a spur to a greater future. Physical exercise was to have a callisthenic effect. Dr. Tyrs and his followers hoped people would wake up to their own future.

When the importance of European nationalism is recognized, the "Olympic" revival can be analyzed in its political context. The creation of the Olympic Movement not only involved placing a coat of idealism around sport activity, it meant specific encouragement of Greek nationalism. Byron and the Philhellenes not only feeled study of Greek tradition, they sparked the translation of mass nationalism into the Greek context. The Philike Hetaira and allied literary societies did for Greece what Grimm's Fairy Tales did for Germany. Literary tradition was revived as a means of heightened national consciousness.

The discoveries at Troy and Olympia proved the reality of Greek tradition, Greeks and foreigners alike were made aware that Homer and Pindar had dealt in more than mythology. The glories of the Greek past, however, were in sharp contrast to the Greek present. Greece had only recently become independent of Turkish power. Europe had not even seen fit to allow

Greeks to rule themselves. Rulers were imported in order to give life to a "Greek" state.

The first Olympic revivals have been dismissed as athletic failures. In fact, however, they were political successes. The "Olympiads" of 1859 and after drew mass attention to the Greek past. The "Greek" royal family recognized this fact, and sought to use Coubertin's movement to their own advantage. Crown Prince Constantine took over the organizing committee of the First Olympiad despite protests from an economy-minded Prime Minister. The dynasty made a conscious attempt to tie itself to the Greek past by means of Olympic celebration. In addition, Philhellenes were reminded that Greece could serve as a civilized bulwark against Turkey in modern times as it had been against Persia in the Golden Age. Naming the most prestigious Olympic event the "Marathon" had significant political content (Turkey and Greece soon went to war over Crete).

The lessons of political sport were not lost on those who affored alternatives to national orientation. Social-Democrats in Germany and Austria used sport as a means to order the social lives of their constituency. The Party not only provided help on the job, it provided outlets for fun and recreation. Socialists vied with nationalists in the use of sport for the creation of mass political loyalty. Once in power, socialists (or Communists) could use sport for the cement needed to combine national feeling with loyalty to the new regime.

So many sports movements were political from their beginnings. In particular those movements dominating the contemporary sports system used their considerable political content to create mass movements out of national discontent. Even before the Olympic Games, "politics" did not intrude upon sport, but rather provided the only means by which sport could develop into an organized, popular international activity.

Perhaps sport serves an educational function in political development. But it is also possible that it is a form of cultural imperialism. Why should non-Western peoples pay homage to Olympic tradition? Why doesn't the "Third World," or several parts of it, form international sport institutions of its own? If such attitudes prevail, there could some day be a repetition of the attempt at a "Games of the New Emerging Forces."

It is, therefore, not enough to merely consider sport as a cultural phenomenon. To which culture does the investigator refer? How universal is the applicability of the findings of an individual familiar only with his or her own environment?

The fundamental point in Maheu's "Sport and Culture," that "sport and culture spring from the same source--that is, leisure" states the intent of the thesis relating sport and culture. Equal weight is given to the analysis of both sport and culture and the limitations of their interrelatedness are explored primarily on historico-philosophical grounds. Values (ethics) common to both factors are mentioned and the appeal of each to mass audiences/communication is highlighted. Many of the abstractions presented here are given substance throughout the rest of the selected readings, even from the point where Lüschen follows with his sociological analysis of the interdependence of sport and culture. Lüschen presents a general sociological statement about the structural relationship between sport and both "high" and "low" culture across several forms of society (primitive to complex). Cultural values underpinning a society, whether predominantly of industrialization or of religion, integrate the role and function of sport, and can be used for explanatory purposes. Alternatively, sport systems can be used to explain other factors in a given social system or subsystem (sex, class, age-groups and institutions). The subculture of an institution can influence sport. "Fair play" or "sportsmanship" characteristics are found in both primitive societies and complex industrial societies, but a difference remains between the physical competitive pursuits of the former groups and the sport elements of the latter.

As elaborated above, Father Jahn, in the brief reading by Hertz (from The German Public Mind in the Nineteenth Century), is considered in the light of German political philosophy in the era after the defeat of Napoleon. His nationalism is explained in the context of his peers, thus refuting simplistic conclusions concerning the relationship between Jahn's ideas and Nazism.

Veblen considers the sporting instinct to be a manifestation of male emotional immaturity, and believes sport itself to be the province of the upper classes. His neglect of mass sport is interesting, as well as indicative of turn-of-the-century cultural attitudes. Thorstein Veblen's ideas should be contrasted with what factually happened and what he failed to predict, namely, the emergence of mass sport. He should not be harshly criticized, for in his day, élite athletes dominated early European Olympics. Veblen's aristocrats, American "amateurs" and the rest of the gladiators of sport became more than heroes when seen in the light of Sipes (1972) empirical testing of aggression as a cultural (anthropological) problem against being a physical (biological) drive.

The presentation by Jandasek analyzes the Bohemian sports tradition in terms of its contribution to national revival in the last quarter of the last century. Sokol lore and organization are seen as conscious attempts to galvanize the national movement and to regain the vitality needed to create a state.

Weber discusses how the humiliation of 1870 spurred the kind of self-examination which resulted in French acceptance of sport, despite its connection with English and German culture. The sport movement had to overcome resistance in both political and educational circles which doubted the value of physical training as opposed to mental discipline.

Shinnick examines a work-play dictotomy in a contemporary context of cultural hegemony, and shows how sport serves the interest of a commodity production process. A common energy source serves both work and play; class distinctions separate worker from "player," and sport is made the object for re-affirming the inherent contradictions of urban life. The sport role, rulebound and unquestioning, ensures that both the citizen and the élite athlete comply with the dominant economic and political system. Capitalist

societies see threat in the Olympic medal accumulations of socialist societies, and nationalistic appeals are made to the code of enterprise to set this
right.

With the close of the nineteenth century, the spirit of Olympism had
been rekindled. The Olympic Games, as an institution, almost foundered,
but the message they carried was one that is easily understood by the masses. Twentieth century statesmen were well aware of this.

Sport And Culture

Rene Maheu

If we consider sport and physical training as what they are in essence --human disciplines with a social function and a role in the formation and full development of personality--we at once begin to wonder what connexions and interactions there are between athleticism and culture, seeing that both contribute to the enrichment of our human heritage, sport by the conscious and rational development of our bodies and culture by a steady pursuit of perfection which appears to enlarge progressively the range of our intellects and sensibilities.

What are the connexions between sport and culture? This question is one of the major problems of our age and I have been thinking about it for years. But in spite of this I feel I have made hardly any progress towards an understanding of it. This means that I shall not presume to offer any final answer; all I shall do is put forward a few personal observations and if my comments and speculations prompt any thoughts that may help to elucidate this extremely difficult question I shall be happy.

I do not intend to examine the relations between culture and sport from an historical angle. The problem of contemporary civilization is what matters to us and though comparisons with the past may help throw light on the subject, we must concentrate on the situation as it is today.

The first thing to be said is that if we take culture in the sense of any of its forms of expression, present contacts between it and sport are extremely slight, in fact practically non-existent. In philosophy, literature, the theatre, even the cinema, in painting, sculpture and music, works of merit based on sport either in form of substance are few indeed. It inspires only a very small number of works of the mind or of art of any aesthetic significance.

But this is not the worst. If we take France as our example (for what is true of this country appears to be broadly true of many others), we find that the few interesting works influenced by the highly idiosyncratic world of sport belong to a far distant and long-since-ended epoch when sport was still in the aggressive stage of seeking acceptance as a customary social activity. I need only name Giraudoux, Montherlant, Jean Prevost, Andre Obey and Joseph Jolinon in literature and--if I may be permitted to annex Switzerland

---

* From the International Journal of Adult and Youth Education, No. 14.
(c) UNESCO, 1962. Reproduced by permission of UNESCO.

for argument's sake--Arthur Honegger in music. And nothing connected with sport by any of them is later than 1925.

Since that date sport has steadily continued not only to make its presence felt but to gain widespread social acceptance. Yet it is noticeable that in spite of this triumph as a social phenomenon there have been hardly any worthwhile cultural works with sport as their basis. Conversely, the world of sport is less and less informed with intellect and art. Where, in the stadiums, are there statues worthy of the beauty of the contestants' movements and the artistry of the games? At Helsinki, the bronze running figure of Nurmi moved me more by its fidelity to reality than by its aesthetic value as a statue. Where are the plays, the symphonies, the songs and the ballets which should provide the counterpoint, the preludes and the codas to the struggles and drama of athletics? Where are the meditations, the exordia, the musings which should reflect and deepen the concept of balanced mastery of body and soul? Who cannot fail to deplore the lamentable mediocrity of the literature and art in the contests which Pierre de Coubertin wanted to be an integral part of the Olympic Games, as in the days of antiquity, but which, since Melbourne, have come, understandably, to be treated as the merest sideshows? All this adds up to the astounding, dismaying, infuriating and even, to be frank, scandalous situation in which sport, otherwise triumphant, is excluded from what I shall not call culture but culture's modes of expression.

It is from this that I want to start in an attempt to understand and, if possible, to find a solution to the problem of the mysterious relations between sport and culture. Of course, there is one explanation that immediately comes to mind which is accepted by many people. Sport, it is argued, is incompatible with culture or at most is still at its confines and only at a later stage in its evolution will it cross the threshold of acceptance into culture.

This opinion is still widespread in many quarters considered intellectual and among many teachers and educators. Hence it is all the more urgent to show just how far from the truth it is. In my opinion sport is far from being incompatible with culture and inferior to it but is a variety of it, and that as things stand it fulfils a cultural function for vast numbers. This is the idea I should like to develop by reviewing certain features which justify our regarding sport as a companion phenomenon to culture itself.

To begin with, sport and culture spring from the same source--that is, leisure. There can be neither culture nor sport without the luxury of leisure, without the spare time and the unspent energy left to a man after his work to use as he wishes. Now in today's civilization, leisure is constantly increasing. Over a very long period work was the essential occupation of civilization but now with the great strides made in mechanization it is leisure that is the essential, if not the most important thing, in life. In the same way, in antiquity, the free man's life, except in time of war, was all leisure.

The pursuit of culture and the cultivation of certain values do in fact imply large surpluses of energy and time for man to use as he wishes; so much so that the Greeks used the same word for leisure, schooling and education. Nowadays sport is perhaps the most widespread leisure activity. In many countries 'sport' and 'leisure activity' are practically synonymous so, if sport does not ally itself with culture, it is bound to contend with it. For, though both derive alike from leisure, we cannot but perceive that sport has a much stronger attraction for the masses than culture.

Sport, as we have seen, fulfils the same function as culture, for it too dignifies those hours and that energy not absorbed by our utilitarian work. That is why sport as a job is not really sport. The only true sport is amateur. The moment sport becomes a utilitarian activity practised for profit it loses its connexion with leisure from which it originally sprang and which gives it its essential dignity and its close affinity with culture.

Let us go a little farther. Among the various activities that fill our leisure, there is one, common to both sport and culture, that we call play. This introduces a new element, for play is indulged in for its own sake. It is a voluntary and unpaid activity of free men, valued for itself; it is its own reward and its own justification. But culture is the same: it is play, unrealistic in comparison with the purposeful activities, of life, and this is true even of the study of philosophy or the humanities. Sport, too, is essentially play: it is not by accident, for instance, that in English sports are 'games' and are 'played' not 'practised'. Physical and intellectual play are both self-justifying, gratuitous activities.

The comparison could be carried much further, to include even the details.

Thus, the gratuitous nature of 'play' is by no means exclusive of logical necessity--it may even be said to generate such necessity. The less trammelled an activity is in itself, the greater its need for rules to give it the appearance of being bound by its own arbitrary laws; thus the fictional domain in which play takes place is given the same coherence and the same realism that the laws of nature confer on the real world. And so, in sport, progress always follows increased refinement of the rules. This means, not that sport is an activity born of necessity, but quite the contrary; that, as a gratuitous activity, it must look to the rules to provide it with standards and an anatomy.

If we carry the analysis further, yet another characteristic emerges. 'Play' is divisible into two categories of game, games of chance and competitive games. On the one hand, there are the games in which man with his freedom to choose pits himself against chance (which is the absolute negation of rule and of fatality) and, on the other, there is what Roger Caillois calls the agon, the contest-game, the competitive game, where man (and this is true of all games of skill) pits himself against material objects and the forces of nature or against himself or, in competitive games, against other men. Of these two types of play, games of chance, e.g., dice and all their variants, and the contest-game, it is undoubtedly the second to which sport belongs. Now, the distinctive feature of the contest-game essentially is to awaken in the spectator an understanding born of sympathy which the game of chance in no way arouses. Take the case of a gamester, say, at roulette or dice: there is no current of sympathy (except fortuitous, born of personal links) between gamester and watcher, and the latter does not feel involved. If, on the other hand, we take a contest-game, we find a current of sympathetic participation linking watcher and player from the start.

Here we have an element common to sporting events and cultural spectacles. In the theatre, the audience involves itself in the drama being enacted before it (thus becoming, after a fashion, actor as well as spectator) and similarly in the stadium, an intense empathy develops between spectators and performer. I would even assert--and here we see how closely cultural spectacles (e.g., the theatre) and sports are parallel and comparable --I would even assert that spectator sports are the true theater of our day. Think of the tens of thousands who fall silent as the athlete prepares to jump, and shout with relief as he soars upward. In what theatre could one find an instance of comparable communion? This participation by the spectator as well as the performer, this close link generating a current of sympathy, understanding and support from the nameless crowd of watchers or listeners to the individual taking the stage and expending himself, takes us back to the very start of the theatre of antiquity, the theatre of Greece. That is why sport, because it involves this particular facet of contest-play, is able to release and, in the Aristotelian sense, to 'purge' the emotions of the spectator, just as effectively as any work of art in general and of the theatre in particular.

There is only one emotion that I know of which has absolutely no place in spectator sport and is death to it--laughter. Laughter is not for the sports ground and, if it occurs, it means that sport has turned into something else. Sport is action which expresses the lyric or dramatic and sometimes even tragic emotions; it is play of extraordinary seriousness, with a place for the smile of satisfaction but none whatever for the destructive laughter which shatters the whole atmosphere and destroys the hold of the spectacle upon its audience; such laughter is the evil genius of sport and alone is barred from the stadium. All other human feelings, all other emotions, sport can express. Like culture and the arts in general (particularly ballet and the theatre, which are the most comprehensive of the arts) sport exteriorizes those feelings and emotions in the player and, by empathy, in the spectator, thereby assuming the function of 'catharsis', of purification, which Aristotle had long ago remarked in the theatre.

It is therefore not astonishing that sport, like the theatre, like literature and like the plastic arts, should be a creator of myths. There is indeed a mythology of sport, which may at times seem somewhat childish to intellectuals, but this mythology has its legends and its heroes and, however it is expressed, it evidences a power of creation which shows the close kinship of the 'all-round' arts with sport.

Lastly, I need hardly say that sport is a creator of beauty. In the action and rhythm which testify to mastery of space and time, sport becomes akin to the arts which create beauty. No athlete can accomplish a genuine feat without such perfect physical control, in time and space, that his movements and the rhythm of their timing are not to be differentiated from the finest ballet, the most splendid passages of prose or verse, the most glorious lines in architecture or sculpture or the loveliest harmonies of light and colour. Lastly, in art as in sport, we find in the protagonist the same inimitable assertion of personality which we call style.

Several runners may well achieve the same record time for the same distance, but no two of them will do it in the same way. Two athletes, or three, may clear the same height or reach the same distance with the javelin, but each will have his own style and stand out as a different personality. Thus individuality asserts itself even, seemingly, at that highest pitch of perfection which characterizes both art and sport.

In conclusion, to end this brief review of the analogies between culture and sport, we may note that they are both vehicles for ethical values, though not to be confused with them. Art and culture uphold a moral code but are not 'identical' with it, in accord with Gide's celebrated dictum that there is more to writing true literature than having the right feelings. Both alike are the natural vehicles of moral values which they propagate and bring within the grasp of ever broader and deeper segments of the population.

Whether we consider the asceticism of training, the ideal of balanced personality, the sense of justice implicit in obedience to rules, or the brotherhood of classes, races and peoples evinced on the field and in spectator sport, these major ethical values are sustained in our modern civilization by sport more than by anything else. I know of no social, ideological or intellectual movement able to bring home the gamut of these basic values so directly to the young, to every class and, overcoming political barriers and differences of race and language, to all peoples of the world.

Thus, not only do sport and culture have a common origin in leisure, but throughout the whole development and aesthetic refinement of their respective forms of expression, they express the same ethical values and serve parallel causes. Nevertheless, the initial fact remains true: in modern civilization, the artists and the intellectuals have not yet managed to master sport and incorporate it in their work. This, as I hope I have shown, is not because of any incompatibility between sport and culture; on the contrary, it would be hard to think of two phenomena which are such near neighbours, so closely related. That notwithstanding, sport has not yet crossed the threshold of the study. In other words, sport is a culture and corresponds in its content to all that a culture is, but it has not achieved the formal expression proper to culture.

It is precisely on this point that I should like to put forward certain reflections. Why should this be so? The causes of this astounding situation, I believe, are manifold and are such as to preclude any simplification of the problem. They can be divided into three distinct categories: sociological, ethical and, finally, strictly aesthetic. To my mind, they explain why a phenomenon as important socially, and even economically, as sport and so similar in other respects to the phenomenon of culture is still without the formal expression that we normally associate with cultural things.

Let us start with the sociological causes. Here we must have the courage to admit certain defects peculiar to contemporary society which are brought out at once by comparison of it with the society of antiquity or that of the Renaissance. In those earlier ages, it was the same society, the same social class, which pursued both culture and sport. We, however, have to recognize that in many contemporary societies cultural creation is the prerogative of a minority; culture is the property of a minority, be it a ruling class or a class of professional practitioners, and the bulk of sports supporters are not to be found in this minority. In class societies, culture can be found in a particular class (for instance the bourgeoisie) which represents a relatively small proportion of the population. Let us once again take France as an example, and nobody, I think, will dispute the long standing either of its culture or of its democratic tradition. The plain fact is that nearly three-quarters of the French nation have no access directly to arts such as the theatre, painting or sculpture. How many peasants or manual workers go to the theatre or visit art exhibitions? Fifty per cent of the peasantry and 25 per cent of the working class play no direct part in the cultural movement, even if we exclude for the moment those highly refined forms of culture such as philosophy, poetry and others which have a special language of their own. In many countries, where there are class societies, it often seems as if culture were reserved for a favoured elite, and this is also true of those societies where there is not the same stratification in classes but where the differentiations arise from the fact that culture is the prerogative of professionals. For it is one of the major aberrations of our culture that the forms of cultural expression lie beyond the reach of the worker or peasant to whom we have just referred. I say 'forms of cultural expression' advisedly, for I recognize that, in fact, the same culture is shared by the theatregoers and by the peasants or workers who for obvious financial reasons do not go to the theatre. What they have not got is access to the artistic milieu in which that culture expresses itself.

Sport, on the other hand, has reached its heights in the classes which are often the least privileged; it thus represents, in class societies, a form of social advancement, just as elsewhere in the world it is a sign of a people's advance towards a status of equality or freedom. It is because the sports movement has been one of social, and sometimes even political, advance that it is a mass movement. But for this very reason its sociological roots are too often removed from those of culture. The sociologies of culture and of sport are not the same, even though, in certain circles and at certain periods, overlappings, which of course are extremely beneficial, are observable. Broadly speaking, we must recognize that if sport has not achieved cultural expression, it is to some extent because of the extreme conservatism of our culture, which remains far too much the preserve of minorities, instead of being open to all the vital influences of the country. So much for the sociological reasons or, at least, for the principal reasons in this category.

There are also causes which I shall describe as being of an ethical nature. I was saying just now that sport, like culture, is a vehicle of moral and ethical values, of which I quoted some examples. Unfortunately, what forms the basis of the ethical values of sport is not always recognized in the general culture of contemporary societies. The fact is that the ethics of sport are based on the body and, in our civilization, the body still ranks low in the scale of values. After having long been anathematized as sinful, by virtue of the teachings of certain religions, and after having long been the target for intellectual contempt, the body in our own day is faced with a formidable competitor in the machine--which either makes it useless or to all intents and purposes turns it into another machine and develops in it the very mechanical reactions which it is the purpose of sport to put to service and transcend. The result is that the ethics of sport, even when they incoporate universally accepted values, start from a principle whose dignity and validity are not universally recognized.

If sport is to cross the threshold to recognition through cultural expression, we should need to establish that humanism of the body of which the first principles only have been outlined by Jean Prevost and which still remains to be worked out in full. What, however, is the body's place in our philosophies, arts, literatures and civilization as a whole? In many philosophies (and this is the result of obvious religious traditions) the body is considered as something unclean or inferior; it represents the animal part of man which must be kept under, mastered, sometimes forgotten, and schooled. At no point is it admitted that the body may be of equal dignity with the mind, the heart and the soul. Things are no different in our literature, however far removed it may be from the philosophic or religious ideas I have just mentioned. For instance, how much does contemporary literature say about the body? The answer is quite simple: in contemporary novels, the body means sex, sexuality. For our young novelists in general, and female novelists in particular, nothing about the body appears to be of any interest except this single aspect, which I agree is extremely important but whose importance from the point of view of cultural expression may perhaps have been exaggerated. This, of course, is an intellectual prejudice: intelligence taking its vengeance on the body by only considering that aspect of physical being which is furthest from reason and intelligence, namely sexuality. But everything else about the body, particularly that marvellous coordination which in fact reaches its fullness in sport, where there is no sexual clement, is left completely untouched by our poetry, our theatre and our novels in a word, by all our literature.

As far as the serious side of life is concerned, modern man could be almost glad to be able to do without his body. Machines are taking over more and more what the body used to do and science, that essential and determining factor in modern civilization, is perhaps the most deadly enemy of any humanism of the body, for in the final count the whole teaching of science is that the body is merely a machine and can be improved by means which practically deny its humanity. I have in mind the fine physical specimens we are training for interplanetary journeys. I think of the photographs we have all seen of those splendid bodies, carefully selected and swathed in wrappings like those in which the Ancient Egyptians bound the mummies of their Pharaohs for journeys into yet more endless space. Here, we imprison bodies made for movement and the joy of living: we make machines of them and all we ask of them is to remain perfectly still and, above all, to exert no weight in those realms of space where conditions are so completely incomparable to the concrete circumstances of our normal existence.

Thus, religious ethics, intellectual literature, the utilitarian ideology of mechanization and absolute scientific positivism all have this disparagement of the body in common. The body becomes a thing that one dare not discuss, that one strives to dispense with, that one would like to reduce to a minimum, because its manifestations are only to be seen in sin, passion, sickness, error and weakness.

The ethics of sport, on the contrary, proclaim the dignity of the body and deny that there can be any possible comparison between the machine that is the human body, and a machine fashioned by man, or even any comparison, as Jean Prevost has said, between the skill and strength of an animal and the skill and strength of man.

On the ethical plane, the battle is therefore not yet won, for the whole evolution of our moral concepts tend to drive us further and further away from that respect for the body which prevailed in antiquity and still prevailed at the time of the Renaissance.

Finally, we come to the third and last category of causes--those of a strictly aesthetic nature and deriving from the very nature of art, that is to say of cultural expression. For, while it is true that sport creates beauty, the beauty it begets is immanent in the very act which creates it. There is no difference, but an identity between the act which creates the beauty and that beauty itself, immanent in the act. The beauty of sport lies in movement, in the performance of an action that is unique; it is inseparable from the fleeting moment. I have spoken of mastery over time and space--but this is a mastery which is lost at the moment of its achievement.

Art, on the other hand, expresses itself quite differently, through signs, through the stylization, not of things, the body, or living creatures, but of signs. Thus it places a distance between the object and the creation of beauty. The substance of sport is the body and life itself. Sport belongs wholly to the present, the actor merging completely with his action. The substance of art, however, is the sign, a series of signs which are bound to the object or idea they are intended to evoke purely by a relationship of meaning, a relationship which is utterly arbitrary and removed from any natural context. The man of letters and the writer do not work with emotions or ideas or passions, but with words. It is these words which provide them with the raw material for their labours and which are ordered to form phrases of beauty: this is what we mean by literary beauty and beauty of language.

Similarly, the painter works with colours and light effects which represent, or can represent, other things or objects, but for him the sign is all important. Even in sculpture and the most concrete arts, even in music, it is the sign that counts. Between the creator and the object he creates is fixed that distance which liberates art and endows it with its quality of eternity. Sport consists wholly of action; art, on the contrary, by its employment of the sign which frees it from the object and from life, moves into eternity. Thus sport and art face in opposite directions.

The very success which sport has achieved in the sphere of mass communication media offers us proof of this divergence. Not in literature or in music must we seek the image of sport, but in the press, in photography and television. All the mass communication media appear ready-made for sport and, between them and it, there exists that splendid harmony with which we are familiar.

The finest achievement in this field is clearly television, perhaps the most serious rival which the actual sporting event has ever known. At the Olympic Games in Rome, I saw many people for whom attendance at the Games meant sitting down in front of a television set. If the transmission is direct, as is often the case, the actual event and its appearance on the television screen are absolutely simultaneous. The distance between the event in which the athlete's performance takes place and the reporting, or more precisely the projection of that event throughout the world, is completely eliminated. At the same time, television, like all projection, represents an analysis and thus splits up the athletic action into its different constituent elements. This may, however, be an advantage in certain respects, for what we lose in emotion by not participating, in the stadium itself, in that communion which invests the sporting event with its nobility, we gain in intellectual understanding, thanks to the remarkable analytical effects which can be achieved by variously focused and differently angled camera-shots of specific details of the particular performance.

Mass communication and sport, which is action, fit in with each other quite naturally. Art and culture--cultural expression--on the other hand, because their substance is not the event but the sign, move in a diametrically opposite direction: they seek a representation which may remain fixed for all eternity. It must be admitted that this divergence is still further accentuated, by our present-day culture. If we consider the most enterprising forms of expression of our contemporary culture, the avant-grade arts, which one might think would be highly receptive to such modern phenomena as sport, we realize that, on the contrary, they are moving far away from them. This is true of painting and sculpture and lyric poetry, which are undergoing a real revolution at the present time.

For this revolution consists not in bringing sign and object closer together, but rather in raising the sign to the status of an object in itself. I am thinking, for instance, of abstract painting in which the sign, that is to say the colour, ceases even to be a sign since, by definition, all connexion has been removed between this colour and any object, idea or sentiment. This is the painting of colour for the sake of colour, the interplay of colour and light, the interplay of form, colour and light for their own sake, without any contextual significance whatever.

Sport is preeminently concrete action. It is bodily action, at a given moment, sufficient unto itself and never to be recaptured. How could this be expressed in the language of abstract painting? By definition there is a divorce between these two phenomena which move in opposite directions. The same applies, of course, to abstract sculpture and to what is called 'concrete music'--which is one manner of saying that it is abstract in its own way--and likewise to lyric poetry, which is now engaged in the reinvention of language is isolation from the meaning of the words.

These, then, are the aesthetic reasons, some profound, others incidental, for considering that artistic expression and sport are, despite appearances, at opposite poles. Sport and art both create beauty, but in completely different ways. Sport is immanent beauty, identified with the act which creates it. Art, especially in its most recent forms, is an art of dissociation, whereby the sign creates a universe which, at one and the same time, competes with the real universe and withdraws from it. What is lacking in sport is precisely this distance which, in art or literature, lies between the event and the sign and is the dimension of conscious awareness, that is to say, of the whole area in which significance of universal appeal finds a place. It is there that this alchemy of reflection occurs and the final spiritual transformation takes place. What precisely, for instance, is the movement of the discus thrower which we have just admired in the stadium? No more than a single moment in time, a movement which had never been seen before and will never be seen again. Apart from the photographic image which has preserved it or the mass communication medium which has transmitted it instantaneously to the four corners of the world, nothing remains of it but a memory. If, on the other hand, I compare the movement of this athlete with Myron's Discobolus, I turn from momentary action to eternal movement. The spectacle confronting me now is not that of Oerter's victory which, in a few months' or a few years' time, we may well find difficult to visualize without a certain effort. What I discover here in its universal significance, is the beauty of the movement performed by all the champions who have ever thrown a discus. I have chosen a statue as my example, but I could as easily have chosen a poem, a musical score or a painting. Sport cannot as yet give us what we are offered by artistic expression and culture, namely a meaning which enables us to transcend the temporary, to transcend all that is ephemeral, and to discover something of eternal value.

One day, nonetheless, sport will have to cross this threshold and culture will have to emerge from this somewhat too narrow circle in which, at times, it appears to be the preserve of a small and select elite. One day sport must cease to be this pointless exhaustion of youth, as in the unending series of athletic feats in which the exhilaration of the 'never before', which is the record, gives way to the sad anticlimax of the 'never again', which is the act which will never be seen a second time. One day sport, too, must rise to those eternal heights which it can reach only through culture.

It may be that certain differences, such as the ethical and aesthetic differences to which I have referred, are inherent in the nature of things and that between sport and art there will always exist this parallelism and these resemblances, but never complete identity, never the profound harmony we desire. Yet it should be possible to bridge this gulf which we have observed, at any rate in so far as it is not due to the egoism of our culture or to a certain disdain for intellectuality and beauty on the part of some of our sportsmen. It is surely incumbent upon the specialists in general and physical education, and particularly upon all the organizations concerned with this field, to work for the establishment of a closer relationship between sport and culture, between the cultivation of the body and that of the mind, which constitute—or ought to do so—the two sides, the two facets of the same humanism.

For nothing in the world today is younger or has greater potentialities than sport, and nothing is older or richer than culture, and it is of vital importance to us that there should be interpenetration and mutual understanding between the two.

The Interdependence Of Sport And Culture

Günther Lüschen

Introduction

Sport is a rational, playful activity in interaction, which is extrinsically rewarded. The more it is rewarded, the more it tends to be work; the less, the more it tends to be play.[1] If we describe it in an action system frame of reference this activity depends on the organic, personality, social, and cultural systems. By tradition, physical education has tried to explain this action system largely on the grounds of the organic system, sometimes making references to the personality system. Only on rare occasions it has been approached systematically from the social and cultural systems as well. Yet it seems obvious that any action going on in this system is to be explained with reference to all of the subsystems of the action system.

Even such a simple motor activity as walking is more than a matter of organic processes initiated by the personality system. It is determined by the social and cultural systems as well as is most evident, in the way the Israelians from the Yemen walk. Since in their former society, in the Yemen, the Jews were the outcasts, and every Yemenite could feel free to hit a Jew (whenever he could get hold of one), the Yemenitic Jew would always run in order to escape this oppression. This way of walking finally became an integrated pattern of his culture. And though the environment in Israel no longer is hostile to him, the Yemenitic Israelite still carries this pattern with him as part of his culture and walks in a shy and hasty way.

This example shows in addition that the different subsystems of action are not independent from one another, they are structurally related. Thus, in dealing with the cultural system of sport and its interdependence with general culture, we will not always be able to explain the culture of sport and that of its environment in terms of the cultural system, and therefore should refer as well to the social and personality system to describe and explain what we call culture. It was Radcliffe-Brown who stressed the point that culture should be explained through its social structure. Furthermore, one should discuss the function of a unit within general culture, as well as cultural process and change.[2]

From International Review of Sport Sociology 2, (1967):27-41. Reprinted by permission.

Concepts of Culture and Review of Results

Culture as a concept does not refer to behavior itself. It deals with those patterns and abstractions that underlie behavior or are the result of it. Thus culture exists of cognitive elements which grow out of every day or scientific experience. It consists of beliefs, values, norms, and of signs, that include symbols of verbal as well as non-verbal communication.[3]

Anthropologists have sometimes held a broader view of culture and given more attention to the material results of human behavior. Leslie White in a critique of the above-stated concept of culture has called for more attention to "acts, thoughts and things dependent upon symboling". These would include not only the study of the above-mentioned elements, but also those of art, tools, machines, fetishes, etc.[4] As attractive as White's critique may be, especially for cultural anthropology as an independent science, this approach as related to the cultural study of sports has led more to mere curiosity about things than to theoretical insights. This methodological approach has also dealt more with the cultural diffusion of sport and games than with the social structure of which they are a part. For decades we have learned about all types of games in all types of societies (especially primitive ones), which may well lead to the conclusion that we know more about the games and sports displayed by some Polynesian tribe than those of our own children and ancestors. For an understanding of sport it is less important to find the same games in different cultures as Tylor did.[5] It is more important to analyse for example the different meaning of baseball in the United States and Lybia, which in the one culture has ritualistic functions, while it has also economic functions in the other.[6]

Another concept of culture, mainly held in Central Europe, has almost led to the same results for sport. In this concept "higher" culture was separated from civilization and expressed itself significantly in the arts and sciences. On the basis of values attributed to sport a priori, it was related either to "Zivilisation" or to "Kultur".[7] Physical educationalists through Huizinga's theory on the origin of culture in play saw in the latter approach their main support.[8] Thus defining sport as a special form of play, physical educationalists felt safe in their implicit attempt to justify sport for educational purposes. Yet Huizinga's theory has not only been criticized on the basis of ethnological findings,[9] but he himself was very critical about the play-element in sport.[10] Those that believed in the role of sport within higher culture were hardly able to prove their hypothesis. So, as recently René Maheu,[11] they often expressed their hope that sport in the future would contribute to "Kultur".

One can hardly deny that sport has indeed some impact on "higher" culture, as may be shown by symbolic elements from sport to be found in script and language. In an analysis of the cultural meaning of the ball-game of the Aztecs and Maya, Krickeberg found that in their script there were elements related to this game. The symbol for movement, for example was identical with the I-shape of the ball-court.[12] "To get (take) a rain check" refers to baseball, but has now become in American English symbolic for any situation where you get another chance. "That's not cricket" refers to a dishonest procedure in everyday life. And though German is not as idiomatic as English, it contains elements which originated in sport and games as well. "Katzbalgerei", and the phrase "sich gegenseitig die Bälle zuspielen", refer to a game which today is still known in the Netherlands as "Kaatsen" and perhaps appears in the New York children's game of one-o-cat. As did football in Shakespeare's King Lear, so appeared this game and its terminology in the 16th century poetry of J. G. Fischart.[13]

How weak the relationships of sport to "higher" culture indeed are, may be shown by the relatively unsuccessful attempts to establish, through special contests in modern Olympics, a relationship between sport and the arts. Sport only rarely expresses itself in the material aspects of culture. It is, what I would like to call a momentary activity.

Just from a certain leeel on may an event have its appearance on such a short-range cultural element as the sports page of the next day's newspaper.[14] This appearance of sport in the media of mass communication, in language, poetry, and the arts is significant for the overall meaning of sport within society, but these manifestations tell us little about sport itself and its interdependence with general culture as we define it.

It may also be interesting to discuss cognitive elements such as scientific insight coming out of sport. Also religious beliefs and ritual found in sport would be an interesting point of analysis. Yet showing how sport is indeed bound to society and structured by general culture, we will mainly discuss our problem on the level of cultural values and their related social structure.

Sport as Part of Culture and Society

That sport is structurally related to culture and society has sometimes been questioned. Yet it is quite easy to show how strong this relationship is. Sport is indeed an expression of that sociocultural system in which it occurs. David Riesman and Reuel Denny describe how American Football was changed through the American culture from rugby to a completely different game. It is now well integrated and quite obviously shows in its vigor, its hard contact and greater centrality on the individual, the basic traits of the culture of American society.[15]

On the level of the so-called primitive societies we see the same dependence of sport and games on culture and its underlying social structure. The Hopi Indians had 16 different terms for foot races which nearly all referred to one aspect of the social organization of that tribe.[16] A recent sociohistorical study on three Illinois subcultures finds the same close relationship between sociocultural system and sport.[17] And Käte Hyé-Kerkdal outlines the tight structural relation between the log-races of the tribe of the Timbira in Brazil and their sociocultural system. This ritualistic competition between two teams has symbolic meaning for nearly every aspect of the dual-organization of this tribe. It refers to all kinds of religious and social polarities and is so strongly imbedded in this religious-dominated system that winning or losing does not have any effect on the status of the team or individual, nor are there any other extrinsic rewards. Yet these races are performed vigorously and with effort.[18]

Now that we have proven that there is a structural relationship between sport and culture, the first question is that of sport's dependency on culture. What factors make for the appearance of sport? Or more specifically, what are the underlying cultural values?

Cultural Values and Sport

By values we mean those general orientations in a sociocultural system that are not always obvious to its members, but are implicit in actual behavior. On the level of the personality system they are expressed partly in attitudes. Values should be separated from norms which are derived from values and are actual rules for behavior. For instance, health is a high value in the American culture as it seems to be in all young cultures, while death is higher in the hierarchy of values in old cultures like India.[19] On this continuum we may explain why sport as an expression of the evaluation of health is more important in American than Indian society. The whole emphasis on physical fitness in the United States may well be explained by this background, and the norm "run for your life" is directly related to it.

Sport, Industrialization and Technology

In comparing the uneven distribution and performance level of sport all over the world, one widely accepted hypothesis is that sport is an offspring of technology and industrialization. The strong emphasis on sport in industrialized societies seems to show that industrialization and technology are indeed a basis for sport. This would be a late confirmation of Ogburn's theory of social change, as well as of the Marxian theory that society and its structure depend on its economic basis. However there are quite a number of inconsistencies. Not all sport-oriented societies or societal subsystems show a relation to technology and industrialization, and historically games and sport have been shown to have existence prior to industrialization. Yet it can hardly be denied that certain conditions in the later process of industrialization have promoted sport; and technology has at least its parallels in modern sport. The above-stated hypothesis may, despite its obvious limitations lead us to the independent variable.

Sport, a Protestant Subculture?

In an investigation that because of its methodological procedure turned out to be a profound critique of Marxian materialism, Max Weber studied the interrelationship of what he called "The Protestant Ethic and the Spirit of Capitalism."[20] This investigation about the underlying values of capitalism in Western societies quoted data on the overrepresentation of Protestants in institutions of higher learning, their preference for industrial and commercial occupations and professions, and the stronger trend towards capitalism in Protestant-dominated countries (most obvious in the United States). Weber found not the material basis but Protestant culture, with achievement of worldly success and asceticism held as the basic values, caused industrialization and capitalism. In accordance with the Calvinistic belief in predestination the Protestant felt that he was blessed by God once he had achieved success. Thus, need for achievement became an integrated part of his personality and a basic value in Protestantism. Together with the value of asceticism this led to the accumulation of wealth and to Western capitalism. If we turn to sport, we find the same values of achievement and asceticism. Even the Puritans, generally opposed to a leisure life, could therefore justify sport as physical activity that contributed to health.[21]

Today we find significance for this relationship in the YMCA, in a group like the American Fellowship of Christian Athletes, and also in the Protestant minister who in Helsinki became an Olympic medal winner in the pole vault. He showed the consistency between Protestantism and sport in his prayer right after his Olympic winning vault. Max Weber's findings about the relationship between the Protestant ethic and the spirit of capitalism may thus well be extented to the "spirit" of sport. Not only Weber was aware of this relationship but also Thorstein Veblen who described the parallels in religious and sport ritual.[22]

The relationship between sport and Protestantism is not only to be observed in the emphasis on sport in the Scandinavian and other Protestant countries. A rough compilation of the probable religious preference of Olympic medal winners on the basis of the percentage of different religious groups in their countries also shows the dominance of Protestantism up to 1960. Protestantism accounted for more than 50% of the medal winners, while its ratio among the world population is less than 8 per cent.[23] Furthermore, in 1958 a survey of young athletes in West Germany showed the following distribution according to religious preference (in %):[24]

	Whole Population West Germany	Sport Club-Members 15-25	Track, Swimming	High Achievers Track/Swimming
Protestants	52	60	67	73
Catholics	44	37	31	26
Others	4	3	2	1
n =	universe	1,880	366	111

These figures indicate the overrepresentation of Protestants in German sport. Moreover, they indicate a higher percentage in individual sports, and an even higher percentage of Protestants among those that have achieved a higher level of performance. Thus it may be concluded that there is a correlation between Protestantism and sport and the culture of both. This was obvious for individual sports, but less for team sports where in the German sample Catholics appeared quite often. Since in Catholicism collectivity is highly regarded, this inconsistency is to be explained by the value of collectivity in team sports. It is consistent with this hypothesis that Catholic Notre Dame University has been one of the innovators of football in America. At present, it is a leading institution in this discipline. And internationally Catholic-dominated South America is overall rather poor in individual sports, but outstanding in team sports like soccer and basketball.

This result on the overall, strong relationship between sport and Protestantism is, despite support by data, theoretically insufficient. As was the case with sport in its relationship to industrialization, there are many exceptions.

The high achievement in sport of the Russians, the Poles, the Japanese, the Mandan Indians, the Sikhs in India, or the Watusi in Africa can not be related to Protestantism, though in Japanese Zen-Buddhism there are parallels.

The Centrality of the Achievement-Value

Since again Protestantism can not be specifically identified as being the independent variable, we may hopothesize that there is a more general system of values as the basis for Protestantism, capitalism, and sport. In his critique of Max Weber, D. C. McClelland has considered the ethic of Protestantism as a special case of the general achievement orientation of a system, this being the independent variable. Achievement orientation (or, as he puts in on the personality-system-level, need achievement) precedes all periods of high cultural achievement in ancient Greece, in the Protestant Reformation, in modern industrialism[25]--and, as we may conclude in modern sport. He referred in his analysis also to the related social structure of the achievement value, (such as family organization), which should also be studied in its relation to sport.

If we turn again to the cross-cultural comparison of those systems that participate and perform strongly in sport, we find that in all of these societies achievement-orientation is basic. In Russia this value is expressed in the norm that social status should depend only on achievement. The Sikhs and the Watusi are both minority groups in their environment. In order to keep their position, they have to achieve more than the other members of the societies they live in. The Japanese[26] and the Mandan Indians[27] also place a heavy emphasis on achievement.

Similar results appear in cross-cultural investigations of different types of games as related to basic orientations in the process of socialization. Roberts and Sutton-Smith find in a secondary analysis of the Human Relation Area Files of G. P. Murdock that games of chance are related to societies that emphasize routine responsibility in the socialization process. Games of strategy are found in societies where obedience, games of physical skill in those where achievement is stressed.[28] Individual sports would mainly qualify as games of physical skill and again show achievement as their basic cultural value. Team sports as well are games of strategy. Their relations to training of obedience would support exactly what we called earlier the value of collectivity.

It remains an open question, for further research into the value structure of sport, as to which other values are related to this system. It is to be expected that the structure of values will be more complex than it appears on the basis of our limited insight now. Roberts and Sutton-Smith briefly remark that games of physical skill are related to occupational groups that exert power over others.[29] Thus, power orientation may be another value supporting sport. This would cross-culturally be consistent with power oriented political systems that strongly emphasize sport. Here we could refer to countries like Russia or the United States, as well as to tribes like the Mandan Indians.

The Culture of Societal Subsystems and Its Relation to Sport

Within a society we find subsystems that have their own subculture, which will be another influence on sport. The female role in modern societies still depends on a culture that stresses obedience as the main value-orientation, while the male culture is strongly oriented towards achievement. Thus we find a disproportionately high participation of men in sport which in most of the disciplines is a male-culture. One of the most male-oriented sports however is pool, a game supported mainly by the subculture of the bachelor; it has, with the general change in the number of people marrying lost its main supporting culture.[30]

Another subsystem which in its culture shows a strong relationship to sport is that of the adolescent age-group.[31] Sport is dependent on the culture of the adolescent than on that of any other age-group. Helanko raises the point, referring to his studies of boys gangs in Turku, that sport has its origin in the gang-age and boys' gangs. The fact that there are no rules for early sports to be found is seen as one of the supporting factors.[32] Generally speaking, achievement is again more central as a value in adolescence and early adulthood than later, where the main response to sport goes not so much towards achievement but towards values of health and fitness.

The different social classes have a culture of their own. The greatest emphasis on achievement and thus the highest sport participation, is to be found in the upper middle class. It is considerably less important in the lower class where routine responsibility is valued. The notion that there is no way to gain higher status accounts for the high regard for games of chance or those sports where one may just have a lucky punch, as in boxing.[33] Loy has related the different types of games and the passive and active participation in sport to different modes of adaptation and to the members of social classes.[34] His theoretical analysis as to "innovation" found in the lower class, ritualism in the lower-middle class, and conformity in the upper-middle class is supported by data, that show the same ways of adaptation in sport.[35] However, in responding to the social class system and its culture as related to sport one should have in mind that class determined behavior may not follow the traditional class lines sport. Sport may indeed show or promote new orientations in the class system.[36]

Finally sport is organized within, or relates to different institutions, whose cultures sometimes have a profound influence on sport itself. This is especially true for physical education in schools where, with the same skills and rules, we may find a completely different culture as compared to sport in the military establishment. And while intercollegiate and interscholastic athletics are overall a surprisingly well integrated subculture within American schools and universities, the different values held by an educational (the school or university) and a solely success-oriented unit (the team) may well lead to strong value-conflicts. This could result in a complete separation of school and athletics.[37]

Functions and Dysfunctions

The Functions of Sport within Culture and Society

After we have found achievement, asceticism in individual sports, obedience (collectivity) in team sports, and exertion of power the basic value orientations that give structure to this activity, we may then proceed to the second question: How does sport influence the sociocultural system at large? Though we have little evidence through research, we may on the basis of structural-functional methodology be able to outline the basic functions of sport for pattern maintenance, integration, adaptation and goal attainment.

As in the case of the Timbira, Hye-Kerkdal states that through the log-race the basic values of that culture were learned. Furthermore, the participants were functionally integrated into the social system.[38] Thus we may hypothesize that the main functions of sport are for pattern maintenance and integration.

Since sport implies (as we saw) basic cultural values, it has the potential to pass these values on to its participants. We know at least from studies of the process of socialization that the exposure of children to competitive sport will cause these children to become achievement-motivated; the earlier this exposure occurs, the more achievement-motivated they become.[39] And the child's moral judgment may for instance, be influenced through games such as marbles. Again, according to Piaget, the child not only becomes socialized to the rules but he at a later age also gets an insight into the underlying structure and the function of the rules of a game, and thus into the structure and function of social norms and values as such.[40] Overall from the level of primitive societies to modern societies sport does not only socialize to the system of values and norms. In primitive societies it socializes towards adult and warfare skills as well.[41]

Since we mentioned that sport is also structured along such societal subsystems as different classes, mores, urban areas, schools, and communities, it functions for integration as well. This is obvious also in spectator sport, where the whole country or community identifies with its representatives in a contest. Thus, sport functions as a mean of integration, not only for the actual participants, but also for the represented members of such a system.

Sport in modern societies may as well function for goal-attainment on the national polity level. Sport in primitive societies functions besides for goal-attainment also for adaptation, since the sport skills of swimming, hunting, and fishing are used for the supply of food and mere survival.

Possible Dysfunctions of Sport and Social Control

A question that should be raised at this point is whether sport is dysfunctional for culture and society as well. Th. W. Adorno has called sport an area of unfreedom ("ein Bereich der Unfreiheit"),[42] by which he obviously referred to the differentiated code of rules which earlier led Huizinga to

his statement that excluded sport from play.[43] Both seem to overlook what
Piaget called the reciprocity and mutual agreement on which such rules
rest.[44] And they may also be considered as an expression of a highly structured system.

Another dysfunctional element for culture and for the system of sport
itself could be the centrality of achievement. It has such a high rank in the
hierarchy of values of sport that, by definition, the actual objective performance of a member of this system will decide the status he gets. In the
core of sport, in the contest on the sports field there only is achieved status.
It seems that there is no other system or any societal subsystem with the
exception of combat where achievement ranks that high. It may create conflict once this value-orientation is imposed on the whole culture, and it may
create conflict within the system of sport itself since its members bring
other values into this system as well.

Mr. Mead in an investigation of competition and cooperation (the first
concept of which is related to achievement) of primitive peoples, however,
finds that there seems to be no society where one of these principles existed
alone.[45] And on the micro-sociological level, small groups seem to control
this value by discrimination against those that deviate from the group norm
of a fair performance.[46] Thus one would notify some kind of a mechanism
built into a social system that keeps it in a state of balance. Exactly this
seems to happen within sport where the sporting groups themselves and their
differentiated organizational and institutional environment perform social
control in regard to those participants whose achievements surpass a certain
level.

In a survey of sport club members in Germany, it was found that the
norms expressed for the behavior of an athlete referred surprisingly less to
the achievement-value, but very often to a value of affiliation, which is to be
defined as a positive orientation towards other group members or opponents.
Fair play was the one mentioned most frequently. The value of affiliation
expressed by the respondents was found the more in normative statements
the higher their level of performance. On the basis of the hypothesized
mechanism of social control they are under stronger pressure to affiliate
with others.[47] Similar results were found in a field experiment with two
school classes.[48] This may explain (on the basis of this structural relationship) why in the culture of sport, we find not only the value of achievement
but also that of fair play and other affirmative orientations.

However, achievement and affiliation may not necessarily be related.
It depends on the amount of social control imposed on sport from the internal
as well as external system, whether this relationship will be strong or weak.
In professional boxing these controls are very weak, while in golf with the
handicap-rule they seem to be comparatively strong.

How much this pattern would influence the culture as such is an open
question. Yet it seems not so misoriented as Litt and Weniger thought when
Oetinger stated that sport would provide a good model for political partnership.[49] We may on the basis of our findings hypothesize that also on the political level the amount of social control will decide whether two or more
systems will co-exist or not.

Change and Evolution

Sport and Sociocultural Change

After we have discussed the culture and underlying social structure of sport and its function, we are left with Radcliffe-Brown's third programmatic point--that of social and cultural change. We know little about the role of sport in sociocultural change, though we hypothesized earlier that it may have a function of innovation, or at least structural relationship to changes in the system of social classes. Sport has also functioned as an initiator for the diffusion of technical inventions, such as the bicycle or the automobile.[50] The same holds true to a degree for conduct in regard to fashion and a healthy life. Typically, this question of change has been highly neglected so far.

Sport and Cultural Evaluation

If we finally try to explain the different cross-cultural appearance of sport on the basis of an evolutionary theory it is hard to justify on the basis of our present knowledge, about the appearance of sport that there are much things as primitive and developed cultures of sport. The Mandan Indians had a highly developed sport culture, the Australian aboriginals as perhaps the most primitive people known to us today knew quite a variety of recreational activities and physical skills, and the variety of competitive games in Europe and America in the past was probably richer than today.

An evolution can only be seen on a vertical level which on the one hand shows in a state of mechanic solidarity rather simple rules in sport and games, while in a state of organic solidarity as in modern industrialized societies the code of rules and the structure of games get more differentiated.

What we may furthermore state is, that on the level of primitive cultures sport's function is universal, often religious, collectivity oriented, and in the training of skills representative and related to adult and warfare skills, while modern sport's function may be called specific for pattern maintenance and integration, is individual oriented and in the training of skills non-representative. The rewards are more instrinsic in primitive cultures, while they are more extrinsic in the sport of modern cultures. Thus, referring to our definition at the beginning, one may well differentiate between physical and recreational activities of primitive cultures and sport in modern cultures.[51]

Footnotes

[1] I owe much of this definition to a discussion with my colleague, G. P. Stone, University of Minnesota.

[2] A. R. Radcliffe-Brown, Structure and Function in Primitive Society, III, The Free Press, Glencoe, 1952.

[3] This refers to a concept held by Kluckhohn/Kroeber and Talcott Parsons. For a general reference as to culture and the action frame of reference within structural-functionalism see H. M. Johnson, Sociology: A Systematic Introduction. Harcourt, Brace and World, New York, 1960.

[4] L. White, The Concept of Culture, in: "American Anthropologist", 61, 1959, pp. 227-251.

[5] Cf. E. B. Tylor, On American Lot-Games, in: "Internationales Archiv für Ethnographic", supplement 9, Leiden, 1896, pp. 55-67.

[6] C. Gini, Rural Ritual Games in Lybia, in: "Rural Sociology", 4, 1939, pp. 283-299.

[7] Most significantly to be found in an unpublished lecture of C. Diem, Sport und Kultur, 1942, at the University of Halle.

[8] J. Huizinga, Homo Ludens, The Beacon Press, 1955.

[9] Cf. A. E. Jensen, Spiel und Ergriffenheit, "Paideuma", 3, 1942, pp. 124-139.

[10] J. Huizinge, op. cit., p. 196.

[11] R. Maheu, Sport and Culture, in: "International Journal of Adult and Youth Education", 14, 1962, 4, pp. 169-178.

[12] W. Krickeberg, Das mittleamerikanische Ballspiel und seine religiöse Symbolik, in: "Paideuma", 3, 1944.

[13] Cf. articles Katzball and Katzenspiel, in: J. Grimm and W. Grimm. Deutsches Wörterbuch 5, Hirtz, Leipzig, 1873, pp. 279 and 302.

[14] For one of the few content-analyses of the special jargon of sport-language see P. H. Tannenbaum and J. E. Noah, Sportugese: A study of Sports Page Communication, in: Journalism Quarterly, 36, 1959, 2, pp. 163-170.

[15] D. Riesman and R. Denney, Football in America, in: D. Riesman, Individualism Reconsidered, III, Glencoe, 1954, pp. 242-251.

[16] S. Culin, Games of the North American Indians. 24th Annual Report. Bureau of American Ethnology, Washington, D. C., 1907, p. 801.

[17] Ph. J. Hill, A Cultural History of Frontier Sport in Illinois, 1673-1820. Unpublished Ph.D.-Thesis. University of Illinois, 1966.

[18] K. K. Hye-Kerkdal, Wettkampfspiel und Dualorganisation bei den Timbira Brasillens, in: J. Hackel (ed.), Die Wiener Schule der Volkerkunde. Wien, 1956, pp. 504-533.

[19] Cf. T. Parsons, Toward a Healthy Maturity, in: "Journal of Health and Human Behavior", 1, 1960, 3, pp. 163-173.

[20] M. Weber, Die protestantische Ethik und der Geist des Kapitalismus. Gesammelte Aufsätze zur Religionssoziologie. Tubingen, 1920, 1.

[21] Cf. P. C. McIntosh, Sport and Society. Watts, London, 1963, pp. 35-45.

[22] Th. Veblen, The Theory of the Leisure Class. University of Chicago Press, Chicago, 1899.

[23] G. Lüschen, Der Leistungssport in seiner Abhängigkeit vom soziokulturellen System, in: "Zentralblatt für Arbeitswissenschaft", 16, 1962, 12, pp. 186-190.

[24] Unpublished, investigation of German Sport's Youth by Lüschen, 1958. Data retained by random-sample of sportsclub members 15-25 in West Germany and West Berlin.

[25] D. C. McClelland, The Achieving Society. Van Nostrand, New York, 1961.

[26] R. N. Bellah, Tokugawa Religion: The Values of Pre-Industrial Japan, III. Free Press, Glencoe, 1957, p. 57.

[27] D. C. McClelland, op. cit., p. 491.

[28] J. M. Roberts and B. Sutton-Smith, Child Training and Game Involvement, in: "Ethnology", 1, 1962, 2, pp. 166-185.

[29] B. Sutton-Smith, J. M. Roberts and R. M. Kozelka, Game Involvement in Adults, in: "Journal of Social Psychology", 60, 1963, 1, pp. 15-30.

[30] N. Polsky, Poolrooms and Poolplayers, in: "Trans-action", 1967, 4, pp. 32-40.

[31] J. S. Coleman, The Adolescent Society. Illinois: The Free Press, Glencoe, 1961.

[32] R. Helanko, Sports and Socialization, in: "Acta Sociologica", 2, 1957, 4, pp. 229-240.

[33] S. K. Weinberg and R. Arond, The Occupational Culture of the Boxer, in: "American Journal of Sociology", 57, 1952, 5, pp. 460-463.

[34] J. W. Loy, Sport and Social Structure. Paper at the AAHPER Convention, Chicago, 1966.

[35] G. Lüschen, Soziale Schichtung und soziale Mobilität, in: "Kölner Zeitschrift für Soziologie und Sozialpsychologie", 15, 1963, 1, pp. 74-93.

[36] G. Kunz and G. Lüschen, Leisure and Social Stratification. Paper at Innational Congress for Sociology, Evian/France, 1966.

[37] This institutional influence is so strong that it may well be advisable to treat informal (recreation), formal (organized for sport purpose only) and institutional sport (physical education and athletics in school) separately.

[38] K. K. Hye-Kerkdal, op. cit.

[39] M. R. Winterbottem, The Relation of Childhood Training in Independence to Achievement Motivation. Unpublished Ph.D.-Thesis, University of Michigan, 1953.

[40] J. Piaget, The Moral Judgment of the Child. The Free Press, New York, 1965.

[41] F. Stumpf and F. W. Cozens, Some Aspects of the Role of Games, Sports and Recreational Activities in the Culture of Primitive Peoples, in: "Research Quarterly", 18, 1947, 3, pp. 198-218 and 20, 1949, pp. 7-30.

[42] Th. W. Adorno, Prismen. Suhrkamp, Frankfurt, 1957.

[43] J. Huizinga, op. cit.

[44] J. Piaget, op. cit.

[45] M. Mead, Competition and Cooperation Among Primitive Peoples. University of California Press, Berkeley, 1946.

[46] F. J. Roethlisberger and W. J. Dickson, _Management and the Worker_. Massachusetts: Harvard University Press, Cambridge, 1939.

[47] G. Lüschen, _Soziale Schichtung..., op. cit._

[48] G. Lüschen, _Leistungsorientierung und ihr Einfluß auf das soziale und personale System_, G. Luschen (ed.), _Kleingruppenforschung und Gruppe im Sport_. Köln und Opladen: Westdeutscher Verlag, 1966, pp. 209-223.

[49] Oetinger, F. Partnerschaft. Stuttgart 1954. Litt and Weniger, in: "Die Sammlung". Gottingen, 1952, attacked the concept of partnership as a mode of political conduct which would not provide a way of socialization towards political power.

[50] A. L. Kroeber, _Anthropology_. Harcourt, Brace and World, New York, 1963, pp. 163-165.

[51] Cf. H. Damm, _Vom Wesen sogenannter Leibesübungen bei Naturvölkern_, in: "Studium Generale", 13, 1960, pp. 3-10.

Friedrich Ludwig Jahn

F. Hertz

Friedrich Ludwig Jahn (1778-1852) was the son of a Prussian clergy-man in Prignitz, where the peasants were free and prosperous and there were none of the old manorial estates. Even as a boy he was distinguished for his wide knowledge of the Bible. From his youth he was a fervent patriot, and because he was born not far from where several frontiers met, he was able to see how the inhabitants of various German countries manifested towards one another a jealousy which at that time passed under the name of nationalism. Quite early on he began to travel extensively and gradually he covered wide areas of Germany and grew acquainted with the people, their dialects and customs. Out of these travels grew his yearning for German unity under the leadership of Prussia. At his grammar school his rugged, independent character often made life awkward for him. From 1796 to 1803 he attended the Universities of Halle, Jena and Greifswald, where he studied mainly history and the German language, but although he read widely, he was not the stuff of which scholars are made. Among the German students of his day conditions of incredible brutality prevailed; there were constant challenges to duels, brawls, drunkenness and immorality, and though Jahn was averse to duels he was often involved in brawls. He finally emerged as a champion of the moral reform of student life and from this the concept of the Burschenschaft (students' association) was later to develop. His main opponents were the Landsmannschaften, in which the students were grouped according to their geographical origins. During this period Jahn, who was poor, lived from hand to mouth; at times, indeed, his only shelter was a sort of cave he had made himself near a small allotment on which he grew potatoes.

When the French Revolution broke out, Jahn was fired with enthusiasm, his special hero being Danton. Later, like many other Germans, he was disillusioned by developments in France, and soon came to hate the French. He wrote pamphlets on how to promote Prussian patriotism and enrich the High German vocabulary. Disappointed in his hopes of an academic post, he had to earn a living as tutor to a landowner's family. When war broke out between Prussia and France, he tried to join the Prussian army but he was too late. The collapse of Prussia and the subjugation of all Germany to Napoleon moved him deeply and he now bent all his energies to the task of liberation. He first wrote a book on German Nationhood which contained his fundamental views.[1] After the Peace of Tilsit he completed his preparation for teaching at a training college and taught first at the Kollnisches Gymnasium in Berlin and then at the Plamann School, which was run on Pestalozzi's principles. Although Jahn was only a junior teacher with no title or rank, he had such an impressive personality that he established a reputation among wide circles. In particular, he was quick to win the admiration and affection of his own pupils and of young people generally, and this was especially apparent in the sphere of physical training, for which he coined the term Turnen. In 1811 the first gymnasium in Berlin was opened. The exercises themselves came from the curriculum of the schools of the Philanthropes where others had already been using them, but to Jahn must go the credit for developing them. He promoted not only apparatus work but also running, jumping, riding, swimming, fencing, competitions and games. Long walks were organised, which aimed not only at developing physical fitness but also at bringing together people from different parts of Germany and different social classes. Jahn demanded of his pupils frugality, comradeship and morality. The main aim was to prepare young people in mind and body for the struggle for liberation and to pave the way for German unity.

Just like Klopstock before him, Jahn was enthusiastic about the Germani as described by Tacitus. Like Rousseau he had a preference for the lower classes, which in his opinion had preserved the traditional German virtues better than the beau monde, who had adopted the French language and French customs. This was why he rejected good manners and was rough and uncouth in his bearing. Gentlemen in those days were clean-shaven and wore their hair short after the French fashion, so it was only natural that Jahn and his disciples should let theirs grow down to their shoulders and sport a full beard, for this was felt to be Germanic. Incidentally, the French Romantics later adopted the same fashion, and in 1848 German democrats and socialists (and Karl Marx, too) were distinguished by long hair and beards, at which the English mocked. Jahn also devised a Germanic costume, made of cheap material and worn with an open neck and without a cravat; this also served as a kind of identifying mark. When at the Congress of Vienna the Prussian Chancellor, Prince Hardenberg, invited him to a diplomatic banquet, Jahn appeared in this costume and wearing dirty shoes to show that he was a man of the people. Since Jahn possessed both originality and humour, he made an impression even upon cultivated men - Ranke, for instance - though others found his personality repellent. Stein called him a grotesque fool, and insisted that, in any case, Jahn's ideas were not as Germanic as he believed, for he owed many of them to Rousseau and the French Revolution. When national movements arose among the Slav peoples, Jahn's methods of inflaming patriotism - gymnastics, public festivals, distinctive costumes and the like - were adopted.

In 1812, at the insistence of a colleague, Friedrich Friesen, Jahn proposed the foundation of a students' union to inculcate in the younger generation a true Germanism, to remove any friction among them and to induce them to devote their energies to the fatherland and the nation. They were to give up issuing the fashionable challenge to duels, but all the same they would be expected to defend their honour with weapons if the need arose. Fichte, as rector of the University of Berlin, vetoed Jahn's proposals. He declared that Jahn was confusing medieval ideas with Germanism: the manifestation of a chivalrous spirit and a standpoint of honour was, he said, completely un-German. Fichte campaigned energetically against the abuses of student life, particularly duelling. Germanism seemed to him inseparable from a moral task which could in no way be discharged by the sabre. He was, in fact, historically justified, for duelling was something which had grown up among the French nobility and become a kind of sport. Only later did it spread inside Germany.

In his book <u>Deutsches Volkstum</u>, which appeared in 1810, Jahn sums up his ideas. His native Prussia was still completely subject to Napoleon and Jahn could not write as freely as he wished, and whenever he criticised Napoleon or the French he did not name them specifically. The word <u>Volkstum</u> was coined by Jahn to denote both the amalgam of language, kinship, customs and traditions which makes a people into a distinct entity and fills it like one family with reciprocal love and a sense of solidarity, as well as the intellectual aims and forces which spring from such a community. In both French and German usage at that time it was customary to make a distinction between 'nation' (Nation) and 'people' (Volk). The nation denoted the educated and well-to-do classes; the people, the lower strata. <u>Volkstum</u>, therefore, was to form the democratic counterpart to the aristocratic 'nationality' as well as to express a natural organic individuality, whereas nationality in Western usage was more of an artificial legalistic concept. The Germans who were annexed by France acquired French nationality but not French <u>Volkstum</u>. Jahn held the conviction that the people were above the State just as the soul was above the body, and that the natural frontiers of a people did not necessarily coincide with the artificial ones.

Jahn also held that the individuality or the interests of a people did not constitute the highest values. Humanity was above nationality, and morality above interests: humanity could only be bodied forth by peoples; even Christianity could only develop on such soil and was shaped by the mind of the peoples. The Reformation, for example, arose in Germany because there the mind of the people had remained closer to that of early Christianity than elsewhere. The German character was marked by energy, loyalty, openness, piety and honesty. Every people serves humanity best by developing its own individuality, but it must not equate itself with humanity and attack other peoples or try to destroy their national character. The extinction of any <u>Volkstum</u> always impoverishes humanity. All peoples form one large family and are capable only in the aggregate of expressing the full nobility of human nature. Any intermingling of peoples should, however, be avoided.

The Germans, Jahn continued, like the ancient Greeks, are a people who cherish the spirit of humanity; they do not despise other peoples but are just in their dealings with them, perhaps too just, as Klopstock said in one of his odes. It redounds to their credit that they prefer the ploughshare to the sword. Jahn firmly rejects any policy which aims at the subjugation of others; political frontiers should follow those of the peoples, which on the whole coincide with the great natural frontiers. Germany's most natural western frontier was the one which preceded the conquests of Louis XIV. Jahn deplores the dismemberment of Germany and wishes for the <u>Reich</u> national unification under an emperor and a great, though not over-great, position in the councils of the leading European nations. In order to reach this goal, Germany will have to pass through a series of revolutions. The individual German states should not be suppressed. He obviously expects the unification of Germany to come from Prussia and wants Austria to give up several provinces, especially Bohemia - presumably to Prussia. Furthermore, Germany must make her Italian and Polish possessions independent states under Habsburg rulers, in order to expand in her turn east and south-east. Belgrade, not Vienna, should be the Austrian capital. The Habsburg Empire, said Jahn, would never be able to Germanise its numerous nation-alities; it should rather recognise their national rights and form a great con-federation as far as the Balkans but withdraw from Germany. The German confederation should include Switzerland, the Netherlands and Denmark and be given a capital to be founded on the Elbe under the name of Teutona.[2]

Germany was to receive a monarchical constitution, but with a central popular assembly and provincial diets. The franchise should be democratic – graduated according to the natural class structure – and no mere yes-men should be elected, nor should any one people be privileged. Titles should be bestowed only for special services and be non-hereditary. It was the State's task, he said, to promote the unity of the people, its education and the pres-ervation of its traditions. There were to be common German civil rights and one common language (although the local dialects were not to be sup-pressed), as well as a code of common law, standard weights and measures, schools and so forth. The state should also work towards social unity and break down class barriers. At the time, Jahn argued, Germany was a pa-riah among nations because her social divisions approached the caste system of India. He went on to propose that the state should introduce insurance against all natural disasters and war damage, as well as pensions for offi-cials and soldiers, welfare for the widows and orphans of former civil ser-vants and for 'friends of the fatherland who were without means'.

Jahn's great love was education and he put forward a full programme of proposals on this subject which are not restricted to the young. The state appears to him primarily an institution for educating the whole people to be good citisens of the world, the fatherland and the national community as well as for stimulating all the creative powers of the people. First and foremost the mother-tongue must be fostered, and not a foreign language. Education for citizenship of the state was also highly important, and at every stage of education. The history of the fatherland claimed special attention. The British, who in the development of their popular institutions and traditions were far ahead of all other peoples, also possessed the greatest historians, who far surpassed those of Germany. But Jahn condemned those historians who revelled in the representation of wars as 'sabre-rattlers' who had al-ready been 'executed' by Schlözer. School-children must receive instruc-tion in craftwork; physical training was likewise very important for building both the body and the character. Since the Peace of Westphalia what the Germans had lacked most was self-respect. Education was to make the peo-ple one large family which no enemy could possibly subjugate.

Any war not fought in defence of the fatherland appeared to Jahn un-natural, inhuman and foolish; he hated wars of conquest and the regular armies which served this end. Admittedly, he thought, small armies, as well as fortresses and the like, were necessary for warding off a sudden at-tack, but the brunt of the defence was to be borne by the people, who were to be concentrated in a militia and trained in the use of weapons. Every rifle-man should own his weapon and some ammunition and, even when trained, take part in occasional target practice. Those without means would be given their weapons by the state. Officers up to the rank of colonel were to be chosen by the men and paid only while on active service. Corporal punishment was un-German and should be abolished.

Special emphasis was laid on the development of a national sentiment. The predilection for foreign customs, which had merely inculcated a servile spirit in the Germans, would have to go. In particular Jahn attacked slavish adherence to fashion - usually French - as wasteful, in bad taste and injurious to health. Besides, he said, fashion was responsible for the barriers which divided one class from another. Jahn hoped to see the introduction of a simple and cheap German costume, adapted to suit the sex, age and occupation of the wearer and one which only citizens should be entitled to wear. In certain legal proceedings this costume was to be obligatory. As further aids to promoting a sense of community, Jahn recommended festivals, entertainments, theatrical performances, writings and monuments. All these were to be aimed especially at celebrating great historical events and national heroes. Citizens who had performed acts of signal merit should, by popular consent, be honoured at special festivals.

To prefer a foreign language to one's own was particularly harmful to national consciousness. In every province the government and courts should use only the mother tongue and the ruler would have to be able to speak to every subject in his own language. Jahn deplores the fact that Joseph II wanted to replace the Magyar language in Hungary by German, and asserts that in Great Britain many risings would have been prevented if the King had spoken Irish or Gaelic. He regrets that Frederick the Great was not allowed to marry an English princess, for in that case English liberty and civilisation would have prevented him from imitating French models. The mother tongue should also be purged of unnecessary foreign words[3] and German literature would have to produce works which could vie in popularity with those of Homer, Dante or Shakespeare. Hitherto Germany had possessed only the beginnings of such a literature. A German Plutarch should emerge and celebrate national heroes in epic verse. But in the whole history of Germany there were only two great feats: the freeing of the country from Roman domination by Arminius (Hermann) and Henry I's defence of Germany against the Hungarian cavalry in the tenth century and his supposed founding of cities as bulwarks against them. To Jahn, the campaigns of the medieval emperors, for all their romantic glamour, did not seem to be glorious pages in German history, but he did regard as praiseworthy great achievements for the benefit of humanity, such as the better treatment of women, the purer conception of Christianity, freedom of thought, tolerance, development towards world citizenship and the struggle against any power which strove for world domination, whether Romans, Huns, Mongols, Charles V or Louis XIV. For obvious reasons Napoleon was not mentioned in this context.

Jahn was convinced that the moral well-being of a people was closely linked with sound family life. The index of a people's humanity was the extent of its respect for women, and the Germans had done most to give them a fitting place, as Tacitus had already noted. Any lax divorce laws, loose living, the marriage of princes for purely political reasons and the like Jahn therefore found reprehensible. Although he was decidedly against preference for foreign languages and customs, he did not advocate isolationism and even saw in the Germans' penchant for travelling abroad an excellent quality which deserved encouragement. The state should make this possible for young people and thus widen their intellectual horizons. No one who had not travelled and seen the world should be eligible for election as member of a national assembly or as a mayor.

As long as Prussia was still occupied by Napoleon's troops, these national ideas could not be proclaimed openly, but they were fostered in secret societies, to which Jahn and his circle belonged. After Napoleon's defeat in Russia, Jahn and his friends launched into highly diversified activity. His gymnasts volunteered for service and he himself, who was in close contact with Hardenberg, the Chancellor, worked for the formation of volunteer corps. Jahn and Friesen were the first to join the Lützow Volunteers who, incidentally, did not prove a military success.

As already mentioned, Jahn's personality displayed some features which attracted and others which repelled. However, he knew how to handle and inspire young people; many, indeed, idolised him. Older, sober men of high intellectual standing were for the most part very critical of him. Many of the things he taught and did were in themselves sound and are today commonplaces in educational theory; but there was also much about him which aroused serious misgivings and his behaviour and mode of expression often appeared unpleasant or foolish. Jahn, who had an earthy sense of humour, delighted in disregarding conventional turns of phrase and tactful euphemisms and in calling things by the coarsest terms he could think of. This understandably delighted his younger followers. A grammar-school boy compiled an anthology of his sayings in a small volume entitled Grains of Gold from the Lips of Father Jahn. When in 1819 Jahn was suspected of revolutionary tendencies, the police found this book and put a criminal interpretation on many of the sayings in it. One of his ideas was that Germany should be separated from France by an artificially created wilderness, stocked with wild animals and other obstacles to intercourse between the two states, though this plan was certainly intended only as a joke.

Jahn gave such blunt and coarse expression to his Francophobia that after the wars of liberation he began to get on most people's nerves. Thus, for example, he delivered lectures in Berlin in the course of which he said that anyone who allowed his daughter to learn French was making it possible for her to become a whore. A Prussian captain in the audience, who was having his own daughter taught French, complained to Prince Hardenberg. The Chancellor disapproved of the remark and called on Jahn for an explanation. After this Jahn could no longer lecture in public but only in his own home. His book Deutsches Volkstum was translated into French in Lyons in 1825 by a doctor, P. Lortet, and another French doctor named Gilibert read a paper to the Académie in which he called Jahn 'the sage of Germany' and compared his system with that of Rousseau. Lortet repeatedly visited Jahn in Germany and formed a close friendship with him; indeed, he collected money for him when he fell on hard times. Finally they met in 1848, when they were both deputies.

In recent years Jahn has sometimes been represented as a forerunner of Hitler, although the ideas set out in his main work are utterly at variance with Hitler's. The idea that miscegenation should be avoided because it would damage the national character is admittedly non-sensical, but it is far from subscribing to the modern racial illusion, which did not exist at the time. Jews were not excluded from the ranks of Jahn's gymnasts. Wolfgang Menzel, one of Jahn's most thorough-going disciples, tells in his memoirs that on one of the gymnastic tours a Jew who was not over-strong fell out exhausted and earned a violent tirade from Jahn, who was very quick-tempered. Menzel thereupon spoke up for his friend, and after Jahn had cooled down he congratulated Menzel on his intervention.

Certainly modern German nationalism can be traced back in part to Jahn. Like Arndt and others, he attempted to square it with cosmopolitanism by declaring that humanity was above nationality. Both the gymnastic movement founded by Jahn and the student corps, which was influenced by him, made an unusually large contribution to the development of modern nationalism. It is obvious that its seeds were present in Jahn's activities, but history can show many examples of an ideology which has finished up in a form of which its authors never dreamt.

Footnotes

[1] See p. 37. ff. (original text)

[2] Parts of the Netherlands and Denmark later became members of the German confederation. Jahn was, of course, thinking of voluntary association.

[3] Jahn later tried to enrich the German language with new formations from German roots, and this makes many of his sentences almost unintelligible. He understood too little about Germanic philology to do this, as his mistaken derivation of the word Bursche from Bur (neighbour, companion) shows.

Modern Survivals Of Prowess

Thorstein Veblen

The leisure class lives by the industrial community rather than in it. Its relations to industry are of a pecuniary rather than an industrial kind. Admission to the class is gained by exercise of the pecuniary aptitudes-- aptitudes for acquisition rather than for serviceability. There is, therefore, a continued selective sifting of the human material that makes up the leisure class, and this selection proceeds on the ground of fitness for pecuniary pursuits. But the scheme of life of the class is in large part a heritage from the past, and embodies much of the habits and ideals of the earlier barbarian period. This archaic, barbarian scheme of life imposes itself also on the lower orders, with more or less mitigation. In its turn the scheme of life, of conventions, acts selectively and by education to shape the human material, and its action runs chiefly in the direction of conserving traits, habits, and ideals that belong to the early barbarian age,--the age of prowess and predatory life.

The most immediate and unequivocal expression of that archaic human nature which characterises man in the predatory stage is the fighting propensity proper. In cases where the predatory activity is a collective one, this propensity is frequently called the martial spirit, or, latterly, patriotism. It needs no insistence to find assent to the proposition that in the countries of civilised Europe the hereditary leisure class is endowed with this martial spirit in a higher degree than the middle classes. Indeed, the leisure class claims the distinction as a matter of pride, and no doubt with some grounds. War is honourable, and warlike prowess is eminently honorific in the eyes of the generality of men; and this admiration of warlike prowess is itself the best voucher of a predatory temperament in the admirer of war. The enthusiasm for war, and the predatory temper of which it is the index, prevail in the largest measure among the upper classes, especially among the hereditary leisure class. Moreover, the ostensible serious occupation of the upper class is that of government, which, in point of origin and developmental content, is also a predatory occupation.

The only class which could at all dispute with the hereditary leisure class the honour of an habitual bellicose frame of mind is that of the lower-class delinquents. In ordinary times, the large body of the industrial classes is relatively apathetic touching warlike interests. When unexcited, this body of the common people, which makes up the effective force of the industrial community, is rather averse to any other than a defensive fight; indeed,

---

Originally published as Chapter X in The Theory of the Leisure Class, Boston: Houghton-Mifflin Company.

it responds a little tardily even to a provocation which makes for an attitude of defence. In the more civilised communities, or rather in the communities which have reached an advanced industrial development, the spirit of warlike aggression may be said to be obsolescent among the common people. This does not say that there is not an appreciable number of individuals among the industrial classes in whom the martial spirit asserts itself obtrusively. Nor does it say that the body of the people may not be fired with martial ardour for a time under the stimulus of some special provocation, such as is seen in operation today in more than one of the countries of Europe, and for the time in America. But except for such seasons of temporary exaltation, and except for those individuals who are endowed with an archaic temperament of the predatory type, together with the similarly endowed body of individuals among the higher and the lowest classes, the inertness of the mass of any modern civilised community in this respect is probably so great as would make war impracticable, except against actual invasion. The habits and aptitudes of the common run of men make for an unfolding of activity in other, less picturesque directions than that of war.

This class difference in temperament may be due in part to a difference in the inheritance of acquired traits in the several classes, but it seems also, in some measure, to correspond with a difference in ethnic derivation. The class difference is in this respect visibly less in those countries whose population is relatively homogeneous, ethnically, than in the countries where there is a broader divergence between the ethnic elements that make up the several classes of the community. In the same connection it may be noted that the later accessions to the leisure class in the latter countries, in a general way, show less of the martial spirit than contemporary representatives of the aristocracy of the ancient line. These nouveaux arrivés have recently emerged from the commonplace body of the population and owe their emergence into the leisure class to the exercise of traits and propensities which are not to be classed as prowess in the ancient sense.

Apart from warlike activity proper, the institution of the duel is also an expression of the same superior readiness for combat; and the duel is a leisure-class institution. The duel is in substance a more or less deliberate resort to a fight as a final settlement of a difference of opinion. In civilised communities it prevails as a normal phenomenon only where there is an hereditary leisure class, and almost exclusively among that class. The exceptions are (1) military and naval officers--who are ordinarily members of the leisure class, and who are at the same time specially trained to predatory habits of mind--and (2) the lower-class delinquents--who are by inheritance, or training, or both, of a similarly predatory disposition and habit. It is only the high-bred gentleman and the rowdy that normally resort to blows as the universal solvent of differences of opinion. The plain man will ordinarily fight only when excessive momentary irritation or alcoholic exaltation act to inhibit the more complex habits of response to the stimuli that make for provocation. He is then thrown back upon the simpler, less differential forms of the instinct of self-assertion; that is to say, he reverts temporarily and without reflection to an archaic habit of mind.

This institution of the duel as a mode of finally settling disputes and serious questions of precedence shades off into the obligatory, unprovoked private fight, as a social obligation due to one's good repute. As a leisure-class usage of this kind we have, particularly, that bizarre survival of belli-cose chivalry, the German student duel. In the lower or spurious leisure class of the delinquents there is in all countries a similar, though less for-mal, social obligation incumbent on the rowdy to assert his manhood in un-provoked combat with his fellows. And spreading through all grades of soci-ety, a similar usage prevails among the boys of the community. The boy usually knows to a nicety, from day to day, how he and his associates grade in respect of relative fighting capacity; and in the community of boys there is ordinarily no secure basis of reputability for any one who, by exception, will not or can not fight on invitation.

All this applies especially to boys above a certain somewhat vague limit of maturity. The child's temperament does not commonly answer to this description during infancy and the years of close tutelage, when the child still habitually seeks contact with its mother at every turn of its daily life. During this earlier period there is little aggression and little propen-sity for antagonism. The transition from this peaceable temper to the pre-daceous, and in extreme cases malignant, mischievousness of the boy is a gradual one, and it is accomplished with more completeness, covering a larger range of the individual's aptitudes, in some cases than in others. In the earlier stage of his growth, the child, whether boy or girl, shows less of initiative and aggressive self-assertion and less of an inclination to iso-late himself and his interests from the domestic group in which he lives, and he shows more of sensitiveness to rebuke, bashfulness, timidity, and the need of friendly human contact. In the common run of cases this early temperament passes, by a gradual but somewhat rapid obsolescence of the infantile features, into the temperament of the boy proper; though there are also cases where the predaceous features of boy life do not emerge at all, or at the most emerge in but a slight and obscure degree.

In girls the transition to the predaceous stage is seldom accomplished with the same degree of completeness as in boys; and in a relatively large proportion of cases it is scarcely undergone at all. In such cases the tran-sition from infancy to adolescence and maturity is a gradual and unbroken process of the shifting of interest from infantile purposes and aptitudes to the purposes, functions, and relations of adult life. In the girls there is a less general prevalence of a predaceous interval in the development; and in the cases where it occurs, the predaceous and isolating attitude during the interval is commonly less accentuated.

In the male child the predaceous interval is ordinarily fairly well marked and lasts for some time, but it is commonly terminated (if at all) with the attainment of maturity. This last statement may need very mater-ial qualification. The cases are by no means rare in which the transition from the boyish to the adult temperament is not made, or is made only par-tially--understanding by the "adult" temperament the average temperament of those adult individuals in modern industrial life who have some service-ability for the purposes of the collective life process, and who may, there-fore, be said to make up the effective average of the industrial community.

The ethnic composition of the European populations varies. In some cases even the lower classes are in large measure made up of the peace-disturbing dolichoblond; while in others this ethnic element is found chiefly among the hereditary leisure class. The fighting habit seems to prevail to a less extent among the working-class boys in the latter class of populations than among the boys of the upper classes or among those of the populations first named.

If this generalisation as the the temperament of the boy among the working classes should be found true on a fuller and closer scrutiny of the field, it would add force to the view that the bellicose temperament is in some appreciable degree a race characteristic; it appears to enter more largely into the make-up of the dominant, upper-class ethnic type--the dolichoblond--of the European countries than into the subservient, lower-class types of man which are conceived to constitute the body of the population of the same communities.

The case of the boy may seem not to bear seriously on the question of the relative endowment of prowess with which the several classes of society are gifted; but it is at least of some value as going to show that this fighting impulse belongs to a more archaic temperament than that possessed by the average adult man of the industrious classes. In this, as in many other features of child life, the child reproduces, temporarily and in miniature, some of the earlier phases of the development of adult man. Under this interpretation, the boy's predilection for exploit and for isolation of his own interest is to be taken as a transient reversion to the human nature that is normal to the early barbarian culture--the predatory culture proper. In this respect, as in much else, the leisure-class and the delinquent-class character shows a persistence into adult life of traits that are normal to childhood and youth, and that are likewise normal or habitual to the earlier stages of culture. Unless the difference is traceable entirely to a fundamental difference between persistent ethnic types, the traits that distinguish the swaggering delinquent and the punctilious gentleman of leisure from the common crowd are, in some measure, marks of an arrested spiritual development. They mark an immature phase, as compared with the stage of development attained by the average of the adults in the modern industrial community. And it will appear presently that the puerile spiritual make-up of these representatives of the upper and the lowest social strata shows itself also in the presence of other archaic traits than this proclivity to ferocious exploit and isolation.

As if to leave no doubt about the essential immaturity of the fighting temperament, we have, bridging the interval between legitimate boyhood and adult manhood, the aimless and playful, but more or less systematic and elaborate, disturbances of the peace in vogue among schoolboys of a slightly higher age. In the common run of cases, these disturbances are confined to the period of adolescence. They recur with decreasing frequency and acuteness as youth merges into adult life, and so they reproduce, in a general way, in the life of the individual, the sequence by which the group has passed from the predatory to a more settled habit of life. In an appreciable number of cases the spiritual growth of the individual comes to a close before he emerges from this puerile phase; in these cases the fighting temper persists through life. Those individuals who in spiritual development eventually reach man's estate, therefore, ordinarily pass through a temporary archaic phase corresponding to the permanent spiritual level of the fighting and sporting men. Different individuals will, of course, achieve spiritual maturity and sobriety in this respect in different degrees; and those who fail of the average remain as an undissolved residue of crude humanity in the modern industrial community and as a foil for that selective process of adaptation which makes for a heightened industrial efficiency and the fulness of life of the collectivity.

This arrested spiritual development may express itself not only in a direct participation by adults in youthful exploits of ferocity, but also indirectly in aiding and abetting disturbances of this kind on the part of younger persons. It thereby furthers the formation of habits of ferocity which may persist in the later life of the growing generation, and so retard any movement in the direction of a more peaceable effective temperament on the part of the community. If a person so endowed with a proclivity for exploits is in a position to guide the development of habits in the adolescent members of the community, the influence which he exerts in the direction of conservation and reversion to prowess may be very considerable. This is the significance, for instance, of the fostering care latterly bestowed by many clergymen and other pillars of society upon "boys' brigades" and similar pseudo-military organisations. The same is true of the encouragement given to the growth of "college spirit," college athletics, and the like, in the higher institutions of learning.

These manifestations of the predatory temperament are all to be classed under the head of exploit. They are partly simple and unreflected expressions of an attitude of emulative ferocity, partly activities deliberately entered upon with a view to gaining repute for prowess. Sports of all kinds are of the same general character, including prizefights, bullfights, athletics, shooting, angling, yachting, and games of skill, even where the element of destructive physical efficiency is not an obtrusive feature. Sports shade off from the basis of hostile combat, through skill, to cunning and chicanery, without its being possible to draw a line at any point. The ground of an addiction to sports is an archaic spiritual constitution--the possession of the predatory emulative propensity in a relatively high potency. A strong proclivity to adventuresome exploit and to the infliction of damage is especially pronounced in those employments which are in colloquial usage specifically called sportsmanship.

It is perhaps truer, or at least more evident, as regards sports than as regards the other expressions of predatory emulation already spoken of, that the temperament which inclines men to them is essentially a boyish temperament. The addiction to sports, therefore, in a peculiar degree marks an arrested development of the man's moral nature. This peculiar boyishness of temperament in sporting men immediately becomes apparent when attention is directed to the large element of make-believe that is present in all sporting activity. Sports share this character of make-believe with the games and esploits to which children, especially boys, are habitually inclined. Make-believe does not enter in the same proportion into all sports, but it is present in a very appreciable degree in all. It is apparently present in a larger measure in sportsmanship proper and in athletic contests than in set games of skill of a more sedentary character; although this rule may not be found to apply with any great uniformity. It is noticeable, for instance, that even very mild-mannered and matter-of-fact men who go out shooting are apt to carry an excess of arms and accoutrements in order to impress upon their own imagination the seriousness of their undertaking. These huntsmen are also prone to a histrionic, prancing gait and to an elaborate exaggeration of the motions, whether of stealth or of onslaught, involved in their deeds of exploit. Similarly in athletic sports there is almost invariably present a good share of rant and swagger and ostensible mystification--features which mark the histrionic nature of these employments. In all this, of course, the reminder of boyish make-believe is plain enough. The slang of athletics, by the way, is in great part made up of extremely sanguinary locutions borrowed from the terminology of warfare. Except where it is adopted as a necessary means of secret communication, the use of a special slang in any employment is probably to be accepted as evidence that the occupation in question is substantially make-believe.

A further feature in which sports differ from the duel and similar disturbances of the peace is the peculiarity that they admit of other motives being assigned for them besides the impulses of exploit and ferocity. There is probably little if any other motive present in any given case, but the fact that other reasons for indulging in sports are frequently assigned goes to say that other grounds are sometimes present in a subsidiary way. Sportsmen-- hunters and anglers--are more or less in the habit of assigning a love of nature, the need of recreation, and the like, as the incentives to their favourite pastime. These motives are no doubt frequently present and make up a part of the attractiveness of the sportsman's life; but these can not be the chief incentives. These ostensible needs could be more readily and fully satisfied without the accompaniment of a systematic effort to take the life of those creatures that make up an essential feature of that "nature" that is beloved by the sportsman. It is, indeed, the most noticeable effect of the sportsman's activity to keep nature in a state of chronic desolation by killing off all living things whose destructions he can compass.

Still, there is ground for the sportsman's claim that under the existing conventionalities his need of recreation and of contact with nature can best be satisfied by the course which he takes. Certain canons of good breeding have been imposed by the prescriptive example of a predatory leisure class in the past and have been somewhat painstakingly conserved by the usage of the latter-day representatives of that class; and these canons will not permit him, without blame, to seek contact with nature on other terms. From being an honourable employment handed down from the predatory culture as the highest form of everyday leisure, sports have come to be the only form of outdoor activity that has the full sanction of decorum. Among the proximate incentives to shooting and angling, then, may be the need of recreation and outdoor life. The remoter cause which imposes the necessity of seeking these objects under the cover of systematic slaughter is a prescription that can not be violated except at the risk of disrepute and consequent lesion to one's self-respect.

The case of other kinds of sport is somewhat similar. Of these, athletic games are the best example. Prescriptive usage with respect to what forms of activity, exercise, and recreation are permissible under the code of reputable living is of course present here also. Those who are addicted to athletic sports, or who admire them, set up the claim that these afford the best available means of recreation and of "physical culture." And prescriptive usage gives countenance to the claim. The canons of reputable living exclude from the scheme of life of the leisure class all activity that can not be classed as conspicuous leisure. And consequently they tend by prescription to exclude it also from the scheme of life of the community generally. At the same time purposeless physical exertion is tedious and distasteful beyond tolerance. As has been noticed in another connection, recourse is in such a case had to some form of activity which shall at least afford a colourable pretence of purpose, even if the object assigned by only a make-believe. Sports satisfy these requirements of substantial futility together with a colourable make-believe of purpose. In addition to this they afford scope for emulation, and are attractive also on that account. In order to be decorous, an employment must conform to the leisure-class canon of reputable waste; at the same time all activity, in order to be persisted in as an habitual, even if only partial, expression of life, must conform to the generically human canon of efficiency for some serviceable objective end. The leisure-class canon demands strict and comprehensive futility; the instinct of workmanship demands purposeful action. The leisure-class canon of decorum acts slowly and pervasively, by a selective elimination of all substantially useful or purposeful modes of action from the accredited scheme of life; the instinct of workmanship acts impulsively and may be satisfied, provisionally, with a proximate purpose. It is only as the apprehended ulterior futility of a given line of action enters the reflective complex of consciousness as an element essentially alien to the normally purposeful trend of the life process that its disquieting and deterrent effect on the consciousness of the agent is wrought.

The individual's habits of thought make an organic complex, the trend of which is necessarily in the direction of serviceability to the life process. When it is attempted to assimilate systematic waste or futility, as an end in life, into this organic complex, there presently supervenes a revulsion. But this revulsion of the organism may be avoided if the attention can be confined to the proximate, unreflected purpose of dexterous or emulative exertion. Sports--hunting, angling, athletic games, and the like--afford an exercise for dexterity and for the emulative ferocity and astuteness characteristic of predatory life. So long as the individual is but slightly gifted with reflection or with a sense of the ulterior trend of his actions,--so long as his life is substantially a life of naire impulsive action,--so long the immediate and unreflected purposefulness of sports, in the way of an expression of dominance, will measurably satisfy his instinct of workmanship. This is especially true if his dominant impulses are the unreflecting emulative propensities of the predaceous temperament. At the same time the canons of decorum will commend sports to him as expressions of a pecuniarily blameless life. It is by meeting these two requirements, of ulterior wastefulness and proximate purposefulness, that any given employment holds its place as a traditional and habitual mode of decorous recreation. In the sense that other forms of recreation and exercise are morally impossible to persons of good breeding

and delicate sensibilities, then, sports are the best available means of recreation under existing circumstances.

But those members of respectable society who advocate athletic games
commonly justify their attitude on this head to themselves and to their neighbours on the ground that these games serve as an invaluable means of development. They not only improve the contestant's physique, but it is commonly added that they also foster a manly spirit, both in the participants and
in the spectators. Football is the particular game which will probably first
occur to any one in this community when the question of the serviceability of
athletic games is raised, as this form of athletic contest is at present upper-
most in the mind of those who plead for or against games as a means of
physical or moral salvation. This typical athletic sport may, therefore,
serve to illustrate the bearing of athletics upon the development of the contestant's character and physique. It has been said, not inaptly, that the relation of football to physical culture is much the same as that of the bullfight
to agriculture. Serviceability for these lusory institutions requires sedulous
training or breeding. The material used, whether brute or human, is subjected to careful selection and discipline, in order to secure and accentuate
certain aptitudes and propensities which are characteristic of the ferine
state, and which tend to obsolescence under domestication. This does not
mean that the result in either case is an all-around and consistent rehabilitation of the ferine or barbarian habit of mind and body. The result is rather a one-sided return to barbarism or to the _feræ natura_--a rehabilitation
and accentuation of those ferine traits which make for damage and desolation, without a corresponding development of the traits which would serve
the individual's self-preservation and fulness of life in a ferine environment.
The culture bestowed in football gives a product of exotic ferocity and cunning. It is a rehabilitation of the early barbarian temperament, together
with a suppression of those details of temperament which, as seen from the
standpoint of the social and economic exigencies, are the redeeming features
of the savage character.

The physical vigour acquired in the training for athletic games--so far
as the training may be said to have this effect--is of advantage both to the
individual and to the collectivity, in that, other things being equal, it con-
duced to economic serviceability. The spiritual traits which go with athletic
sports are likewise economically advantageous to the individual, as contra-
distinguished from the interests of the collectivity. This holds true in any
community where these traits are present in some degree in the population.
Modern competition is in large part a process of self-assertion on the basis
of these traits of predatory human nature. In the sophisticated form in
which they enter into the modern, peaceable emulation, the possession of
these traits in some measure is almost a necessary of life to the civilised
man. But while they are indispensable to the competitive individual, they
are not directly serviceable to the community. So far as regards the serviceability of the individual for the purposes of the collective life, emulative
efficiency is of use only indirectly if at all. Ferocity and cunning are of no
use to the community except in its hostile dealings with other communities;
and they are useful to the individual only because there is so large a proportion of the same traits actively present in the human environment to which he
is exposed. Any individual who enters the competitive struggle without the

due endowment of these traits is at a disadvantage, somewhat as a hornless steer would find himself at a disadvantage in a drove of horned cattle.

The possession and the cultivation of the predatory traits of character may, of course, be desirable on other then economic grounds. There is a prevalent aesthetic or ethical predilection for the barbarian aptitudes, and the traits in question minister so effectively to this predilection that their serviceability in the aesthetic or ethical respect probably offsets any economic unserviceability which they may give. But for the present purpose that is beside the point. Therefore nothing is said here as to the desirability or advisability of sports on the whole, or as to their value on other than economic grounds.

In popular apprehension there is much that is admirable in the type of manhood which the life of sport fosters. There is self-reliance and good-fellowship, so termed in the somewhat loose colloquial use of the words. From a different point of view the qualities currently so chrracterised might be described as truculence and clannishness. The reason for the current approval and admiration of these manly qualities, as well as for their being called manly, is the same as the reason for their usefulness to the individual. The members of the community, and especially that class of the community which sets the pace in canons of taste, are endowed with this range of propensities in sufficient measure to make their absence in others felt as a shortcoming, and to make their possession in an exceptional degree appreciated as an attribute of superior merit. The traits of predatory man are by no means obsolete in the common run of modern populations. They are present and can be called out in bold relief at any time by any appeal to the sentiments in which they express themselves,--unless this appeal should clash with the specific activities that make up our habitual occupations and comprise the general range of our everyday interests. The common run of the population of any industrial community is emancipated from these, economically considered, untoward propensities only in the sense that, through partial and temporary disuse, they have lapsed into the background of subconscious motives. With varying degrees of potency in different individuals, they remain available for the aggressive shaping of men's actions and sentiments whenever a stimulus of more than everyday intensity comes in to call them forth. And they assert themselves forcibly in any case where no occupation alien to the predatory culture has usurped the individual's everyday range of interest and sentiment. This is the case among the leisure class and among certain portions of the population which are ancillary to that class. Hence the facility with which any new accessions to the leisure class take to sports; and hence the rapid growth of sports and of the sporting sentiment in any industrial community where wealth has accumulated sufficiently to exempt a considerable part of the population from work.

A homely and familiar fact may serve to show that the predaceous impulse does not prevail in the same degree in all classes. Taken simply as a feature of modern life, the habit of carrying a walking-stick may seem at best a trivial detail; but the usage has a significance for the point in question. The classes among whom the habit most prevails--the classes with whom the walking-stick is associated in popular apprehension--are the men of the leisure class proper, sporting men, and the lower-class delinquents.

To these might perhaps be added the men engaged in the pecuniary employments. The same is not true of the common run of men engaged in industry; and it may be noted by the way that women do not carry a stick except in case of infirmity, where it has a use of a different kind. The practice is of course in great measure a matter of polite usage; but the basis of polite usage is, in turn, the proclivities of the class which sets the pace in polite usage. The walking-stick serves the purpose of an advertisement that the bearer's hands are employed otherwise than in useful effort, and it therefore has utility as an evidence of leisure. But it is also a weapon, and it meets a felt need of barbarian man on that ground. The handling of so tangible and primitive a means of offence is very comforting to any one who is gifted with even a moderate share of ferocity.

The exigencies of the language make it impossible to avoid an apparent implication of disapproval of the aptitudes, propensities, and expressions of life here under discussion. It is, however, not intended to imply anything in the way of deprecation or commendation of any one of these phases of human character or of the life process. The various elements of the prevalent human nature are taken up from the point of view of economic theory, and the traits discussed are gauged and graded with regard to their immediate economic bearing on the facility of the collective life process. That is to say, these phenomena are here apprehended from the economic point of view and are valued with respect to their direct action in furtherance or hindrance of a more perfect adjustment of the human collectivity to the environment and to the institutional structure required by the economic situation of the collectivity for the present and for the immediate future. For these purposes the traits handed down from the predatory culture are less serviceable than might be. Although even in this connection it is not to be overlooked that the energetic aggressiveness and pertinacity of predatory man is a heritage of no mean value. The economic value--with some regard also to the social value in the narrower sense--of these aptitudes and propensities is attempted to be passed upon without reflecting on their value as seen from another point of view. When contrasted with the prosy mediocrity of the latter-day industrial scheme of life, and judged by the accredited standards of morality, and more especially by the standards of aesthetics and of poetry, these survivals from a more primitive type of manhood may have a very different value from that here assigned them. But all this being foreign to the purpose in hand, no expression of opinion on this latter head would be in place here. All that is admissible is to enter the caution that these standards of excellence, which are alien to the present purpose, must not be allowed to influence our economic appreciation of these traits of human character or of the activities which foster their growth. This applies both as regards those persons who actively participate in sports and those whose sporting experience consists in contemplation only. What is here said of the sporting propensity is likewise pertinent to sundry reflections presently to be made in this connection on what would colloquially be known as the religious life.

The last paragraph incidentally touches upon the fact that everyday speech can scarcely be employed in discussing this class of aptitudes and activities without implying deprecation or apology. The fact is significant as showing the habitual attitude of the dispassionate common man toward the propensities which express themselves in sports and in exploit generally.

And this is perhaps as convenient a place as any to discuss that undertone of deprecation which runs through all the voluminous discourse in defence or in laudation of athletic sports, as well as of other activities of a predominantly predatory character. The same apologetic frame of mind is at least beginning to be observable in the spokesmen of most other institutions handed down from the barbarian phase of life. Among these archaic institutions which are felt to need apology are comprised, with others, the entire existing system of the distribution of wealth, together with the resulting class distinctions of status; all or nearly all forms of consumption that come under the head of conspicuous waste; the status of women under the patriarchal system; and many features of the traditional creeds and devout observances, especially the exoteric expressions of the creed and the naïve apprehension of received observances. What is to be said in this connection of the apologetic attitude taken in commending sports and the sporting character will therefore apply, with a suitable change in phraseology, to the apologies offered in behalf of these other, related elements of our social heritage.

There is a feeling--usually vague and not commonly avowed in so many words by the apologist himself, but ordinarily perceptible in the manner of his discourse--that these sports, as well as the general range of predaceous impulses and habits of thought which underlie the sporting character, do not altogether commend themselves to common sense. "As to the majority of murderers, they are very incorrect characters." This aphorism offers a valuation of the predaceous temperament, and of the disciplinary effects of its overt expression and exercise, as seen from the moralist's point of view. As such it affords an indication of what is the deliverance of the sober sense of mature men as to the degree of availability of the predatory habit of mind for the purposes of the collective life. It is felt that the presumption is against any activity which involves habituation to the predatory attitude, and that the burden of proof lies with those who speak for the rehabilitation of the predaceous temper and for the practices which strengthen it. There is a strong body of popular sentiment in favour of diversions and enterprise of the kind in question; but there is at the same time present in the community a pervading sense that this ground of sentiment wants legitimation. The required legitimation is ordinarily sought by showing that although sports are substantially of a predatory, socially disintegrating effect; although their proximate effect runs in the direction of reversion to propensities that are industrially disserviceable; yet indirectly and remotely--by some not readily comprehensible process of polar induction, or counter-irritation perhaps --sports are conceived to foster a habit of mind that is serviceable for the social or industrial purpose. That is to say, although sports are essentially of the nature of invidious exploit, it is presumed that by some remote and obscure effect they result in the growth of a temperament conducive to non-invidious work. It is commonly attempted to show all this empirically; or it is rather assumed that this is the empirical generalisation which must be obvious to any one who cares to see it. In conducting the proof of this thesis the treacherous ground of inference from cause to effect is somewhat shrewdly avoided, except so far as to show that the "manly virtues" spoken of above are fostered by sports. But since it is these manly virtues that are (economically) in need of legitimation, the chain of proof breaks off where it should begin. In the most general economic terms, these apologies are an effort to show that, in spite of the logic of the thing, sports do in fact further what may broadly be called workmanship. So long as he has not succeeded in persuading himself or others that this is their effect the thoughtful apologist for sports will not rest content; and commonly, it is to be admitted, he does not rest content. His discontent with his own vindication of the practices in question is ordinarily shown by his truculent tone and by the eagerness with which he heaps up asseverations in support of his position.

But why are apologies needed? If there prevails a body of popular sentiment in favour of sports, why is not that fact a sufficient legitimation? The protracted discipline of prowess to which the race has been subjected under the predatory and quasi-peaceable culture has transmitted to the men of today a temperament that finds gratification in these expressions of ferocity and cunning. So, why not accept these sports as legitimate expressions of a normal and wholesome human nature? What other norm is there that is to be lived up to than that given in the aggregate range of propensities that express themselves in the sentiments of this generation, including the hereditary strain of prowess? The ulterior norm to which appeal is taken is the instinct of workmanship, which is an instinct more fundamental, of more ancient prescription, than the propensity to predatory emulation. The latter is but a special development of the instinct of workmanship, a variant, relatively late and ephemeral in spite of its great absolute antiquity. The emulative predatory impulse--or the instinct of sportsmanship, as it might well be called--is essentially unstable in comparison with the primordial instinct of workmanship out of which it has been developed and differentiated. Tested by this ulterior norm of life, predatory emulation, and therefore the life of sport, falls short.

The manner and the measure in which the institution of a leisure class conduces to the conservation of sports and invidious exploit can of course not be succinctly stated. From the evidence already recited it appears that, in sentiment and inclinations, the leisure class is more favourable to a warlike attitude and animus than the industrial classes. Something similar seems to be true as regards sports. But it is chiefly in its indirect effects, through the canons of decorous living, that the institution has its influence on the prevalent sentiment with respect to the sporting life. This indirect effect goes almost unequivocally in the direction of furthering a survival of the predatory temperament and habits; and this is true even with respect to those variants of the sporting life which the higher leisure-class code of proprieties proscribes; as, e.g., prizefighting, cockfighting, and other like vulgar expressions of the sporting temper. Whatever the latest authenticated schedule of detail proprieties may say, the accredited canons of decency sanctioned by the institution say without equivocation that emulation and waste are good and their opposites are disreputable. In the crepuscular light of the social nether spaces the details of the code are not apprehended with all the facility that might be desired, and these broad underlying canons of decency are therefore applied somewhat unreflectingly, with little question as to the scope of their competence or the exceptions that have been sanctioned in detail.

Addiction to athletic sports, not only in the way of direct participation, but also in the way of sentiment and moral support, is, in a more or less pronounced degree, a characteristic of the leisure class; and it is a trait which that class shares with the lower-class delinquents, and with such atavistic elements throughout the body of the community as are endowed with a dominant predaceous trend. Few individuals among the populations of Western civilised countries aer so far devoid of the predaceous instinct as to find no diversion in contemplating athletic sports and games, but with the common run of individuals among the industrial classes the inclination to sports does not assert itself to the extent of constituting what may fairly be called a sporting habit. With these classes sports are an occasional diversion rather than a serious feature of life. This common body of the people can therefore not be said to cultivate the sporting propensity. Although it is not obsolete in the average of them, or even in any appreciable number of individuals, yet the predilection for sports in the commonplace industrial classes is of the nature of a reminiscence, more or less diverting as an occasional interest, rather than a vital and permanent interest that counts as a dominant factor in shaping the organic complex of habits of thought into which it enters.

As it manifests itself in the sporting life of today, this propensity may not appear to be an economic factor of grave consequence. Taken simply by itself it does not count for a great deal in its direct effects on the industrial efficiency or the consumption of any given individual; but the prevalence and the growth of the type of human nature of which this propensity is a characteristic feature is a matter of some consequence. It affects the economic life of the collectivity both as regards the rate of economic development and as regards the character of the results attained by the development For better or worse, the fact that the popular habits of thought are in any degree dominated by this type of character can not but greatly affect the scope, direction, standards, and ideals of the collective economic life, as well as the degree of adjustment of the collective life to the environment.

Something to a like effect is to be said of other traits that go to make up the barbarian character. For the purposes of economic theory, these further barbarian traits may be taken as concomitant variations of that predaceous temper of which prowess is an expression. In great measure they are not primarily of an economic character, nor do they have much direct economic bearing. They serve to indicate the stage of economic evolution to which the individual possessed of them is adapted. They are of importance, therefore, as extraneous tests of the degree of adaptation of the character in which they are comprised to the economic exigencies of today; but they are also to some extent important as being aptitudes which themselves go to increase or diminish the economic serviceability of the individual.

As it finds expression in the life of the barbarian, prowess manifests itself in two main directions,--force and fraud. In varying degrees these two forms of expression are similarly present in modern warfare, in the pecuniary occupations, and in sports and games. Both lines of aptitudes are cultivated and strengthened by the life of sport as well as by the more serious forms of emulative life. Strategy or cunning is an element invariably present in games, as also in warlike pursuits and in the chase. In all of these employments strategy tends to develop into finesse and chicane. Chicane, falsehood, brow-beating, hold a well-secured place in the method of procedure of any athletic contest and in games generally. The habitual employment of an umpire, and the minute technical regulations governing the limits and details of permissible fraud and strategic advantage, sufficiently attest the fact that fraudulent practices and attempts to overreach one's opponents are not adventitious features of the game. In the nature of the case habituation to sports should conduce to a fuller development of the aptitude for fraud; and the prevalence in the community of that predatory temperament which inclines men to sports connotes a prevalence of sharp practice and callous disregard of the interests of others, individually and collectively. Resort to fraud, in any guise and under any legitimation of law or custom, is an expression of a narrowly self-regarding habit of mind. It is needless to dwell at any length on the economic value of this feature of the sporting character.

In this connection it is to be noted that the most obvious characteristic of the physiognomy affected by athletic and other sporting men is that of an extreme astuteness. The gifts and exploits of Ulysses are scarcely second to those of Achilles, either in their substantial furtherance of the game or in the eclat which they give the astute sporting man among his associates. The pantomime of astuteness is commonly the first step in that assimilation to the professional sporting man which a youth undergoes after matriculation in any reputable school, of the secondary or the higher education, as the case may be. And the physiognomy of astuteness, as a decorative feature, never ceases to receive the thoughtful attention of men whose serious interest lies in athletic games, races, or other contests of a similar emulative nature. As a further indication of their spiritual kinship, it may be pointed out that the members of the lower delinquent class usually show this physiognomy of astuteness in a marked degree, and that they very commonly show the same histrionic exaggeration of it that is often seen in the young candidate for athletic honours. This, by the way, is the most legible mark of what is vulgarly called "toughness" in youthful aspirants for a bad name.

The astute man, it may be remarked, is of no economic value to the community--unless it be for the purpose of sharp practice in dealings with other communities. His functioning is not a furtherance of the generic life process. At its best, in its direct economic bearing, it is a conversion of the economic substance of the collectivity to a growth alien to the collective life process--very much after the analogy of what in medicine would be called a benign tumor, with some tendency to transgress the uncertain line that divides the benign from the malign growths.

The two barbarian traits, ferocity and astuteness, go to make up the predaceous temper or spiritual attitude. They are the expressions of a narrowly self-regarding habit of mind. Both are highly serviceable for individual expediency in a life looking to invidious success. Both also have a high aesthetic value. Both are fostered by the pecuniary culture. But both alike are of no use for the purposes of the collective life.

The Sokol Movement

In Czechoslovakia

L. Jandacek

The Sokols represent the largest voluntary organisation of the Czecho-slovak people; they are banded together into units, that is local companies, the total of which, including branches, is 3,130. In accordance with their statutes these units "aim at improving the physical and moral strength of the Czechoslovak people in the spirit of Tyrš and Fügner," and they seek to at-tain that aim by encouraging regular physical exercises on the part of men, women and young people; by arranging lectures, meetings, discussions, concerts, exhibitions, amusements, theatrical performances, festivals and other recreations. They also encourage community singing and music; they organise and support institutions such as libraries, reading-rooms and book stores which promote the common Sokol welfare. In addition to these more private activities they endeavour to make the Sokol idea widely known and attractive to the general public by tours excursions competitions and public displays. The units are grouped in 52 "clans," together forming the Com-munity of Czechoslovak Sokols (ČOS). This supreme body supports and con-trols the activity of the units, thus ensuring harmony of purpose and continu-ity in the aims laid down.

It is obvious that the Sokols are chiefly educational in intention, orig-nating as they did with Tyrš, whose ideal was the harmonious development of every individual's capacities, both physical and mental, in accordance with the models of classical perfection and harmony. But it would be erro-neous to argue from the name of "Sokol Gymnastic Unit" that they are mere-ly gymnastic in character. The means laid down for acquiring this ideal sufficiently show the breadth and scope of the Sokol intentions. The variety of education afforded is so great that a separation into physical and mental training is inadmissible, and it is an education submitted to by adults (those of 18 years and over), children of school age (6 to 14) and adolescents (14 to 18). Every member is required to be of Czechoslovak or other Slavonic na-tionality (exceptions to be authorised by the Sokol central body only), to be of irreproachable morality and to carry out the duties and tasks imposed on him or her by the authorities, in heart and mind no less than in the letter. The chief obligations undertaken in matters of personal opinion, are not to belong, while a member of the Sokol movement, to any political party whose programme is opposed to Sokol principles (this means in practice the cleri-cal and communist parties), and not consciously or voluntarily to assist

Originally published in Slavonic Review, XI:65-80, July, 1932.

clerical aims in any way. At the beginning of 1930 the total of adult members enrolled in the Sokol units was 352,888, of whom 252,681 were men and 100,201 women; of this total, 91,205 (56,576 men and 34,829 women), or some 25 per cent, participate in physical training. The number includes some men of an advanced age, even septuagenarians. All young people are obliged to engage in physical training. Those between 14 and 18 number 76,305, while the number of children under 14 is 199,943 (94,788 being boys and 105,155 girls). Male and female instructors in charge of the physical training from a total of 22,118 (13,008 men and 9,110 women). The mental and moral education of each unit is in the hands of teaching corps, each with its appointed functions, such, for example, as theatrical and puppet plays, singing and temperance. The total of those engaged in Sokol work in Czechoslovakia is, therefore, almost 630,000.

Work analogous to that of the Sokol but with a political or denominational trend is performed by three other organisations: the Association of Workers' Gymnastic Units, which combines physical training on Sokol lines with Social Democratic party principles; the Communist Federation of Proletarian Gymnastics, a title which explains itself; and the Orel (Eagle), a gymnastic organisation with a Catholic political basis. None of these bodies can compare in numbers with the Sokols. The first named contained, at the end of 1930, 1,220 units with 64,221 members (51,857 men and 12,364 women), 13,144 adolescents and 51,632 children, or close upon 137,000 in all. In numbers and also in importance the Orel falls behind, having only 112,629 adherents (72,037 adults, 15,755 adolescents and 30,358 children). The Communist Federation does not publish any statistics and its activities are closely associated with those of the communist party. All these gymnastic bodies together are therefore far from approaching the Sokols either in numbers or in national importance; they were all originally Sokol offshoots, the party or denominational upbringing of whose members prevented them from association with a non-party and non-denominational body like the Sokols. Their connection with the parent institution is obvious not only in such things as their uniform, public displays and congresses, but also in their organisation, structure, gymnastic and educational methods.

The Sokol clans in Czechoslovakia number 50, of which 27 are in Bohemia, containing 1,772 units and 131 branches, with over 200,000 adult members, 45,000 adolescents and 122,000 children. There are 14 units in Vienna, with a membership of 2,000 adults, forming the independent clan of Austria, and the other foreign units, in Bulgaria, France, Germany and South America, and also in London, are grouped in a special clan of 1,817 members.

In Moravia and Silesia there are 889 units and 142 branches with over 102,000 adult members, almost 26,000 adolescents and over 65,000 children. The Sokol movement has been organised in Slovakia only since the political revolution, having been forbidden under the old Hungarian regime; there are now 129 units and 16 branches, making 6 clans in all, with a membership of 15,000 adults, over 4,000 adolescents and 10,000 children. The movement has spread also to Carpathian Ruthenia, where there is one clan with 14 units and 2 branches, having a membership of over 3,000. In the eastern districts development is handicapped by the great distances between the units and the remoteness from headquarters.

The 52 clans together form the Community of Czechoslovak Sokols, which was not founded till 1904, and then only after long and fruitless attempts. Tyrš realised the great value of an united organisation of all the Sokols, and as early as 1867 he tried to join the score of units then existing into a "central association"; but the Asutrian officials, suspecting political tendencies, vetoed the project then and again in 1872. Tyrš had been dead only a few weeks when efforts were made in 1884 to found the first Sokol clans in Bohemia: the first, that of Kolín, still bears his name. In 1889 the ČOS was founded and contained 11 Czech clans with 152 units and 18,000 adult members; in 1892 the Moravian Sokols united to form the Moravian-Silesian Sokol Community--both of these uniting in 1896 with that of Lower Austria in the "Czechoslav Sokol Association," a title which was changed to "Czech Sokol Community" in 1902. On 29 November, 1915, the community was officially disbanded, but after the political revolution, when the movement had gained ground in Slovakia, it was restored and in 1920 was re-named the Community of Czechoslovak Sokols. It embraces in a single organised entity all the Sokols at home and abroad--except those in America, which have their own administration. The premises of the central body are in "Tyrš House," Prague, which was erected at a cost of 24,000,000 Czech crowns by the Sokols themselves without any external assistance. The Sokol Home was enlarged by the conversion in 1925 of the old Michna Palace in Malá Strana, which was equipped with a model gymnasium, baths and training grounds. All the meetings of the central committees take place there, and there is a regular training school which spends more than half a million crowns annually in training instructors and professionals in the various physical training methods.

Eight hundred and forty-three of the 3,130 units and branches have their own training premises; the others train in schools or local halls, only 124 being still without any premises. There is a great development in summer training and playing grounds; the number of bathing resorts and camping sites is also growing, for training work is being increasingly supplemented, especially in recent years, by national gymnastics, games and the various forms of physical training which were formerly the prerogative of purely sporting organisations. The Sokol statutes have accordingly included, in addition to their regular training, games, touring, camping, riding, water sports, skating, ski-ing, fencing and shooting. Long and high jumping, running and the other athletic exercises also form part of the regular training, especially in the summer months. Increasing emphasis is being laid in recent years on physical training in the open air. Playing and summer grounds were until recently the exception, but now there are only 840 units without them, while 94 units have their own bathing place. Mountain hostels have also been erected in suitable places by some of the clans or societies.

All financial expenditure incurred by the Sokols in their educational and training work is covered by the members themselves. The funds obtained as a result of State assistance are quite negligible, and the bulk of the income is derived from subscriptions, amusements, theatres, films, etc. There are no paid Sokol officials. In accordance with one of the first of the Sokol principles, many thousands of teachers, instructors and officials give their services entirely free, without thought of profit or glory, to the common cause. Only the central body authorises an expenditure of 2 million crowns for annual current needs. If the holdings of the clans and units are reckoned in, and the movable and especially the immovable property of all kinds, we have a good idea of the great importance and standing of the Sokols both economically and socially. The volunteer principle, the ideals of self-sacrifice on behalf of others are applied in practice, each individual serving and helping his neighbour and the body corporate, giving effective assistance to the needy, the unfortunate and all who are less advantageously placed. Very many of the units, almost all the clans, and of course the central body, have special funds which enable assistance to be given to members who are old, unemployed, injured or ill. For example, the Sokol Health Fund for recuperation at the seaside and in the mountains; but most important of all is the independent Accident Insurance Society which spends over a million crowns yearly in rendering assistance. The financial independence of the Sokols is made possible only by voluntary sacrifice. As, however, the growing claims on the Sokol are frequently beyond the means of the members, who are for the most part drawn from the poorer classes, attempts have recently been made to supplement the resources obtained by various ambitious schemes.

Physical and Mental Education

In the firm conviction that physical and mental strength are complementary in every human organism, Tyrš determined to give practical application to the doctrine mens sana in corpore sano in his training system and methods. The Sokol education is of the widest possible scope: it encourages the systematic development of the muscles, the correct functioning of the physical organs and the cultivation of the entire nervous systems. The training is so constituted as to develop all mental qualities at the same time. Habits of self-confidence, resolution and presence of mind are formed; willpower and perseverance are strengthened, quickness of mind and appreciation of beauty are encouraged, discipline and the spirit of sacrifice are inculcated. The idea that all individuals shall make their personal interests and feelings subservient to the common good builds up a corporate body strongly endowed with a sense of brotherhood. This distinguishes Tyrš's method from all other educational and gymnastic systems, for it puts a check on every kind of individualism hurtful to the community. It aims, in a Czech and Slovak spirit, at uniting the "brothers" and "sisters" of the same nation into a great band, ready to perform great achievements for the common welfare. There is therefore a fine harmony of individual and corporate spirit; in team training and exercises the individual is merged in the whole, and his personal efforts or skill contribute to the general success. The Sokol method is not restricted to specially apt or gifted individuals, but endeavours to adapt itself to all by advancing from easy exercises "to the highest goal"; the competitive spirit, which can so easily degenerate into unfriendliness and jealously, is repressed by Tyrš's command of "rivalry in harmony," the insistence on pleasure in a comrade's success. His method and, consequently, the Sokol method of physical training aims at raising the general standard of bodily fitness of the whole nation; this explains the choice of simple, attractive and varied appliances graded according to the physiological needs and capacities of different ages and sexes. The Sokol training is therefore in no sense one-sided; in addition to gymnastic exercises, which were chiefly in vogue before the war, attention is paid to athletics and games. The variety of training methods is evident also from the system of organisation in the central body, where there are two controlling sets of officials for men and for women (on the technical side the women are entirely autonomous). There are a series of special commissions, for Defence, for Sokol Riding, for Medical Examination and scientific investigation, and again Commissions for winter sports, for swimming, canoeing and rowing, and finally for games and competitions, and for fencing. The specialised schools of instruction turn out over 560 instructors annually. Thus every season of the year is utilised for Sokol physical training; but the foundation of everything is the practice lesson, methodically organised and divided so as to afford the whole body harmonious and varied exercise, and to cultivate certain desirable mental and moral qualities.

The Sokol educational activity only developed at a later stage, but its beginnings must be sought in the time of Tyrš, who proclaimed and fostered Sokol thought by word of mouth and in print. The same lines are followed today when each unit has an educational corps with an instructor at the head. It does not aim at providing technical education, but moulds the character according to Sokol principles: it appeals to young people and adults and begins by giving each new member basic instructions on the movement, partly orally in special classes, and partly by printed matter. It then offers instruction in accordance with various educational methods, for which there are special committees. The variety and scope of this work is shown by the fact that in the year 1931 alone there were more than 88,000 addresses, 12,600 lectures, 7,200 excursions, over 9,000 theatrical representations, 7,000 puppet shows, 900 concerts and 135 exhibitions and gymnastic performances.

The central educational body pays special attention to every branch of this work; all activities are followed, the principles of physical health and the tasks connected with social activity are made known to the public; singing competitions are organised at the summer festivals, and many units have musical societies and choirs of their own. General educational questions, artistic and aesthetic education, and, lastly, questions of public life, are not neglected. There are also special commissions for education through the theatre and puppet plays, a competition in this field being included this year for the first time in the programme of the All-Sokol Congress. A special fortnightly course for instructors is, arranged annually at headquarters, and in addition each clan is bound to provide a similar course at least once in two years.

There is great press activity. Every Sokol library is obliged to have a technical section dealing with the movement, and instructive and recreational readings are given there. In 1931 there were 3,090 unit libraries with 643,000 volumes. The Sokol Publishing Company issues some special readers, technical works, popular books and pamphlets. Particular mention may here be made of the Jubilee edition of the collected works of Tyrš.

The Sokols also issue numerous periodicals. The monthly Sokol, founded by Tyrš in 1871, deals with the movement, its theory and practice;

while the weekly Věstník sokolský (Sokol Herald), with a weekly circulation of 40,000, deals with administration. There are also four other monthlies: Vzkříšení (Regeneration), Sokolské Besedy (Sokol Talks) with 25,000 readers, Cvičitel (The Instructor) and Cvičitelka (The Instructress), and the Sokolský Vzdělavatel (Sokol Educator). Besides this, every clan issues a monthly, and even some of the bigger units have recently begun to issue their own bulletins.

The Influence of the Sokols in the National Revival

The present state of the Sokols, their organisation and educational activity on the physical and mental side is founded on the Sokol idea as formulated by Tyrš and his fellow workers at the beginning of the 'sixties of last century. Special merit is due to Jindřich Fügner, the Grégr brothers, both of them leading Czech politicians, and Professor Tonner for having made Tyrš's ideal intelligible to the people and capable of realisation in the Sokol organisation. The classical ideal, which Tyrš cherished throughout life, home traditions and contemporary philosophy, applied to the needs of a nation awakening from long mental lethargy, were welded into an ideal which was to complete the patriotic efforts of previous generations.

When political and religious persecution, following the battle of the White Mountain (1620), deprived the Czechs of all sources of cultural life and of their existence as an independent people, when the country was laid waste by the Thirty Years' War and estranged from the peasantry, material poverty and mental darkness seemed to herald a gloomy future for a nation in whose history many glorious pages had been written. The tenacity with which the remnant clung to its native language and religious traditions, despite the Counter-Reformation and the pressure of Germanisation, enabled the national consciousness and a knowledge of Czech to linger on at least in the thatched cottages of the villagers. These miserable remnants of the one-time glorious nation of Charles IV, George Poděbrad, John Hus, Chelčický, Žižka and Comenius had to suffice for the efforts of the first national awakeners. Spurred on by the glory of the past and the new spirit of liberty, equality and fraternity, they set themselves to revive the dulled national consciousness, they searched for a mental pabulum suitable to the level of an oppressed nation, they endeavoured to foster and purify a forgotten and neglected language. That is the first period of our regeneration.

The next generation followed in their footsteps, and its tasks increased with the growing consciousness of the different classes. Real poets appear, drawing their inspiration partly from the rich store of native poetry and partly from world movements in philosophy and poetry. Science begins to be studied not only in the domains of philology and history, but also in politics. And when the mighty flame of the French Revolution broke out for the third time in 1848, our nation no longer looked on, cowed with terror, but, intoxicated with the breath of freedom, was filled with the hope of securing its own freedom and that of its Slav brothers. It might perhaps have rushed headlong into the uncertainty of revolution, had it not been kept in the steady path of development by sober political leaders, and harkened to the wise counsel of

Havlíček and Palacký, who were convinced that complete national regeneration and political independence were in store only for a coming generation which should be materially, mentally and morally prepared for it.

A flood of new and fruitful ideas now arose in Czech hearts and lasted for some decades. The old national tradition was revived, the old books reprinted and a new literature interpreted to the nation its glorious past. The national consciousness which had fallen so low was further stimulated by the idea of Slav reciprocity, and practical efforts were made to promote the cultural, linguistic and religious rapprochement of all the Slavs. When these dreams of unification proved to be in the main Utopian, efforts were concentrated upon reviving the traditions broken by the White Mountain. The Sokol movement has an important place in this great work, uniting in itself all the pent-up strength of the previous periods. It taught the now awakened nation true patriotism, tireless and unselfish perseverence to that end, even as Havlicek had taught it before Tyrš and as Masaryk is now teaching it. It proclaimed the need of work all the more vigorous and persistent in view of the smallness of our nation in the great European family. The idea of Slav reciprocity was taken over by the Sokols into their programme--not as a slogan, but as a step towards effective, organised work of the Slav nations for a common aim. Moreover it introduced into our national programme the idea of defence, which is only a result of a broader, more general idea, namely, that spiritual must be supplemented by physical regeneration. For if Tyrš's predecessor, Karel Havlíček, regognised that his own generation must die in order to make way for a better generation that should enter the promised land, he was directly calling for someone to continue his work and prepare new generations for the decisive struggle. Six years after his death this work was begun by Dr. Miroslav Tyrš and his great Sokol project, which aimed at creating "a new race, stouter than its predecessors, which, in a strong body preserving a strong will, would once more unite with the dovelike meekness of the Slav the falcon-like boldness of more glorious times; a race which would recognise rights of others, while holding fast to its own, and in days of tempest and storm would weld itself as of old into an impregnable barrier, on which all attacks of our enemies would be shattered."

Such was Tyrš's programme of the new race and the new man. And this programme of renaissance, the ultimate goal of the Sokol efforts, still remains unchanged. The requirements of every period demand its elastic adaptation; methods change and new goals are set up, that Sokoldom--and through it the whole nation--may ever go forward. Hence Tyrš's demand for continual advance, and hence his watchword: "He who is Czech is a Sokol," for a new race cannot be created except by the education of the greatest number of the members of a nation.

This twofold tendency--internal, leading to the intensification of the nation's education by Sokoldom, and external, the spreading of the Sokol idea throughout the broad masses of the nation--fills the history of seventy years, with their temporary failures but also their notable successes.

The Importance of the Sokol Movement

Ever since 1862, when the first germ of the future Sokol was founded, almost till his death, Tyrš was the welding spirit of the whole movement, partly by his activity in the Prague School and partly, since 1871, through his periodical Sokol. Then, under inspiration from Prague, special units began to form, not only in Bohemia and Moravia, but also in the other Slav countries, among the Slovenes, Croats, Poles, and Serbs and also among the various Slavs of America. But for him the movement would have wilted away or perhaps become incorporated with other societies, and disappeared without having any influence on the nation which was to be its raison d'être. For twenty years--with small breaks--he expounded, explained, conducted propaganda, but also defended the Sokol idea against its enemies, and, above all, against the misunderstandings which were even more dangerous--the mistaken conception that it was mere empty parade, a useless waste of time. The many articles in which Tyrš sought to explain the fundamental principles and correct interpretation of the Sokol idea, are a proof of how much effort was needed. He laid down the duty of unity of aim among all Sokol units, leaving the possibility of a difference of opinion only in so far as the means are concerned; and for that reason he rejected, as showing a lack of comprehension of the Sokol idea, such efforts as to transform the units into fire brigade companies. The danger that the Sokol idea would come to grief through being misunderstood or would degenerate into empty, formal patriotism, was especially great because the movement spread with unnatural rapidity, being almost from the outset a mass demonstration. The public displays and festivals, the flags and uniform, were also a danger, in that they caused the enrollment of some members who did not realise the final goal.

In one direction at least there was never any danger of misunderstanding, namely, the need for preparing a politically enslaved people for complete national and political freedom. Tyrš expressed this goal in the quotation from Lucian on the subject of the Olympic training exercises in ancient Greece: "For we reap from them a greater advantage both for the competitors and the whole State: to-wit, the conflict in common. It is a reward of another kind which awaits all the citizens of the State, and the wreath here is not of laurel, nor of ivy, nor of olive, but is another wreath, which includes within it everything that intoxicates a man--the freedom of every individual in particular and of a common fatherland in general, its prosperity and glory, the perservation of the family and of the magnificence of patriotic festivals, in short, all the fairest things that any one might wish to be granted him by the gods." Work and education for political independence was the most pressing and also the most popular task confronting the movement before the outbreak of war. Opposition of the national, political and cultural aims of a foreign dynasty and government was cultivated in the units, while the idea of Slavonic reciprocity was encouraged by excursions to other Slav countries and by participation of other Slav nations in the All-Sokol congresses. National harmony and the consciousness of a common goal were thus fostered on practical lines.

A nation which was gathering all its strength for the final struggle of liberation needed, above all, physical strength and capacity, discipline and harmony, and enthusiasm for the common cause. Consequently the new current, which arose in the spiritual life of the nation not long after Tyrš's death, that "Realism" of which Masaryk was the exponent, remained for a certain time foreign to the Sokol movement, for it was felt to be all too critical, and even to serve as a damper on enthusiasm through its cautious outlook and surety of conviction. But the last phase of regeneration has shown that our national struggle needed both currents. The realist leader Masaryk became also the leader of our movement abroad during the world war; those trained as Sokols, the true disciples of Tyrš, rallied to the standard, full of enthusiasm and ready to sacrifice even their lives for freedom. Then it became evident that Sokoldom had made its preparations successfully and surely. Schools, literature and home training had of course led the way, but there was many a fighter in our ranks for whom the Sokols had meant everything and had imparted the courage and enthusiasm needed for the great sacrifice. The leader of our legions himself, Masaryk, bore witness that in the war "the ideals of Fügner and Tyrš had proved themselves." An extract from a letter written to his parents by one of the leading organisers of our Russian legions, explaining why he had enlisted as a volunteer, will show what the Sokol movement meant. Josef J. Švec writes as follows: "I expect you will find it easy to guess why I am acting in this way. I might have stayed comfortably in the warmth of the Caucasus and been as safe as other people, but I am drawn not, I think, by a desire for adventure or glory (on the contrary I feel I shall not get out alive), but there is something else which forces me to take this step. It is honour, the Sokol honour, and that must remain unsullied; I see that this is a fight for the freedom of us Czechs, and it would be a shame if I were to stay at home and did not help, even if it cost me my life, in the fight for a holy cause." So, too, did Jan Čapek, the founder of the Italian legions, issue the summons to the Czech prisoners at Padua: "Brother Sokols! Turn words into deeds! In these great days let us show that we have felt and understood what our watchword at home means: 'He who is a Czech is a Sokol.' The call of your country is, 'He who is Czech is a Volunteer,' and the call is to you who have followed in the steps of Tyrš and have made yourself ready to defend it . . ." The Paris Sokols to a man enrolled as volunteers as soon as the war broke out and enlisted in the French army: of the 600 who joined up 200 fell and another third were wounded. The English Sokols formed a Czech detachment in the British army, and the same happened in America. The Sokol spirit of brotherhood and democracy found an echo in all our troops abroad: without distinction of military rank all the soldiers used the familiar address of ty (tutoiement) and addressed each other as "brother." The military organisation of our legions was modelled on that of the Sokols, with their qualities of voluntary but strict discipline, courage and readiness to place the general above the particular interest--qualities which in the decisive hour of conflict gave our arms that inner strength without which there can be no victory.

On 28 October, 1918, the first and most urgent task was achieved; the movement now had to find a new goal. It therefore returned to Tyrš and out of his national programme formed new lines of action, in harmony with the changed conditions of a liberated country. It was determined, however, to remain faithful to the aims which Tyrš had laid down once for all and at the same time to obey his behest of continual motion and progress. The movement which in the early days of our new-found liberty had been disorganised, now settled down to the work of consolidating the new State. The establishment of the Sokol forces in Slovakia when it was attacked by the Magyars and the response to the emergencies of the republic, the ready assistance against the Communist attempt at revolution, these tasks followed naturally from the pre-war Sokol programme.

But it was not enough to be the guardian of independence at home and abroad in times of danger. By its ideals and the personalities it produced the movement had helped to create our new State, and its duty was now to help in internal construction, in the spirit of the ideas which had governed it from the beginnings. It was, above all, the national programme, created by a long succession of the best Czech brains, which was to come into its own in the inner life of our republic. Democracy, which demands close co-operation in State affairs for the general well-being--this is the actual outcome of the popular, democratic spirit infused into the movement by Fugner, Tyrš and their fellow workers. Brotherhood, to which Sokoldom had educated its adherents in the spirit of our past history, was to come into its own in our new State as zeal for social justice. And lastly, the movement was also to take its part in making of Czechoslovakia one of the progressive countries, because progress was one of Tyrš's well-known precepts for every sphere of Sokol activity. Into its new post-war programme the Sokol movement also introduced the cultivation of religious honour and progress, based upon Tyrš's "religion of enlightenment and love," and also on the religious activities of its great member, President Masaryk. In 1924 the VIIth Sokol congress expressly laid down, in accordance with Masaryk's principles, that "Every loyal, truly conscious Sokol shall be a defender of our Republic and our democracy, and as such a political and social worker in it."

These resolutions, binding on every member, are to become the groundwork of a new citizen education in the Sokol units.

The VIIth congress also laid down new guiding principles, aimed at the elimination of all thorny questions between the different Slav nations, the promotion of better understanding of each other in a democratic spirit, and a perception of the great mission to which all Slavs are called. Here, too, a great and important work awaits the Czechoslovak movement.

Sokol History

Not only the present position of the Sokol idea, but also its organisation and educational methods are the result of considered reflection during several generations. Tyrš's work culminated outwardly in the first All-Sokol congress, which he arranged in Prague in 1882, on the twentieth anniversary of the foundation of the first Sokol unit. This festival was attended also by the Poles, Slovenes and Croats, and so set an example to posterity. Ever since then the connections with other Slav Sokols have remained and been strengthened by mutual intercourse. The first excursion outside our own territory was the visit to Cracow in 1884, followed by that to Ljubljana in 1888. In 1889 the newly-formed "Czech Sokol Association" in Bohemia took the important step of organising a visit to Paris. This was the first appearance of the Sokols in the international arena, and their model teams secured three first prizes in the competitions open to strangers. Other tours and competitions followed, at Nancy, Lyon, Périgueux, Nice, Arras, Brussels, Zürich, etc. And many were the tours to Poland and to Jugoslav countries, the more important being that to Zagreb and Montenegro in 1906. In 1907 (at the 5th All-Sokol Congress) international gymnastic competitions were arranged in Prague, resulting in a victory for the Sokols, who ever since then have held almost continually the pride of place. In 1909 the Sokol team gained the second prize at the international competitions in Luxemburg, the first going to the French; but the defeat was wiped out in the following year in London, when the Sokols won the silver shield contest; and again at Turin and Paris in 1913 the Sokols won the first prize. Our tours to America in 1909 and to Belgrade and Sofia in 1910 must also be included in our victorious challenge against international teams.

Foreign interest in the movement was also shown by the presence of representatives of foreign gymnastic bodies at the six congresses which took place before the war, and served to make the movement known not only as physical training but also as a national idea. They were our "Olympic Games," and were conceived in accordance with Tyrš's desire, as the manifestation of a great common goal and the preparation thereto: the liberation of the nation. The mass exercises, the fine endurance and the symbolic representations of athletic effort made the meaning of Sokoldom clear even to foreigners; no wonder that this was expressed in the flattering words: "They are not gymnasts, but an army." The All-Sokol congresses also served as an index of the spread of the Sokol idea. The first, in 1882, was attended by 1,600 Sokols (720 performers); the second in 1891 by 7,000 (2,310 performers); the third in 1895 by 10,000 (4,270 performers); the fourth in 1901 by 22,000 (7,000 performers); the fifth in 1907 by 45,000 (11,000 performers), and the last of the pre-war series in 1912, which was also the first congress of the Slav Sokol Union, by 80,000 adult members (21,400 performers).

These congresses had immense importance for the idea of Slavonic reciprocity. Tyrš knew that "the Sokol idea is acquiring an undreamt-of importance for all the Slavs with whom we live in the same state, and is becoming a new and mightly link, more effective, sure and lasting than all others." Greater importance attached to the movement by the presence of representatives of the Slavonic nations at the joint festivals--in the sight of foreigners, chiefly our friends. The second congress in 1891 was attended for the first time by Frenchmen and similarly at the third congress in 1895, not only Slovenes and Croats, but also 212 Poles took part. At subsequent congresses there was an increasing number of visitors, that of 1907 being attended by no less than 450 Slovenes, 800 Croats, 121 Servs, 116 Bulgars and 51 Russians, while the Poles were represented unofficially. The greatest manifestation of Slavonic reciprocity, on the eve of the world war, was the "Slav Congress" of 1912, when 1,100 Serbs, 900 Croats, 500 Slovenes, 300 Bulgars, 800 Russians and 80 Ruthenes were present, together with official representatives of the Russian, Serbian and Montenegrin Governments. Non-Slav foreigners also had an opportunity of seeing how this Slavonic brotherhood was winning more and more ground, for the fourth congress was visited by representatives of the Paris municipality, and the fifth by visitors from Belgium, France, England, Scotland, Greece, Spain and Hungary. At the congress of 1912, 1,000 American Sokols were welcomed in the old country; there were more foreign delegates than ever, and there were important demonstrations of solidarity with the Jugoslavs, and against Austrian foreign policy.

The world war brought severe persecution upon the Sokols at home; but the work was simply transferred abroad, where the Sokol spirit in our legions became a living inspiration to our troops in their fight for the liberation of the nation. After the war the movement assumed undreamt-of proportions. In 1862, when the first units were formed, there were only 9 units with 265 adult members, by the 'nineties there were more than 40,000 adherents, and by the outbreak of war this number had grown to 1,100 units with 130,000 adult members. But after the war this total again increased more than threefold, till in 1920 there were 2,630 units with 557,000 adherents, and since then there has been a steady increase. Despite great difficulties of transport and communication the seventh congress of 1920 proved successful beyond all expectations: exercises were performed by 24,000 men, 15,000 women, about 20,000 adolescents, and 11,000 children, while over 300,000 took part in the triumphant procession through the streets of Prague.

After the war our Sokols began to take part in the international Olympic games and won successes at Antwerp in 1920, at Ljubljana in 1922, at the Olympic Games of Paris in 1924, at Lyons in 1926, at Amsterdam in 1928 and at Luxemburg in 1930. They are not taking part in this year's games at Los Angeles, but are getting ready for the ninth All-Sokol Congress at home, when the Slav Sokol Union will take part, including the Sokols of Czechoslovakia, Poland, Jugoslavia and the Russian emigres; negotiations are on foot for the participation also of the Wends and Bulgarians. This congress will be in honour of the 100th anniversary of the birth of Miroslav Tyrs, the founder of the movement, and also of the first congress which took place half a century ago. The stadium at Strahov will hold 15,000 performers and 150,000 spectators; in the smaller stadium there will be competitions in running, games and athletics together with joint gymnastic displays begun with the winter ski-ing competitions; but the chief days of the congress are in June when on the 12th the schoolchildren of the units from Prague and the immediate neighbourhood will perform; the 16th to 20th will be given up to the children of the secondary schools; the 26th is the day of the Sokol adolescents. The main programme is from 4 to 6 July, and on the latter day an imposing march past of the Sokols will give the salute to the representative of our glorious national history, John Hus of pious memory, and will also honour its greatest "brother," President Masaryk. These celebrations, like those which have gone before, will serve as an impulse for the fresh endeavour in the national cause, by tightening the bonds that unite the Slav nations, and strengthening the solidarity between Czechoslovakia and all other countries which pursue the ideals of perfection, health, strength, beauty and peaceful intercourse.

Gymnastics And Sport In Fin-De-Siecle France: Opium Of The Classes?

Eugen Weber

Despite Huizinga's classic essay, the distance between homo sapiens and homo ludens seems to grow no smaller. The strange suspicion, or even antipathy, that men of pen and study still show for research in the more vulgar manifestations of physical activity deserves a study in itself. While we await a dissertation on such a promising topic, this disinclination leaves us ill-informed on activities that have always taken up a good deal of public attention--not least in the past century.

Grandfather clocks, balloons, and potatoes have benefitted from historical studies that games and sports still lack. Journalists, psychologists, sociologists, and sportsmen themselves have written about sport; historians have paid it only incidental attention. To be specific, no professional historian seems to have traced the cat's cradle of athletic activities rising and spreading in France in the last quarter of the nineteenth century. Significantly, Antoine Prost's excellent Enseignement en France, 1800-1967 (Paris, 1968) ignores the topic, while the 268 pages of Paul Gerbod's Vie Quotidienne dans les lycées et collèges au XIXᵉ siècle (Paris, 1968) devote nine lines to gymnastics and none to other exercises.

Yet physical exercise and the role that men attribute to it, that society envisages for it, can document times and mentalities as suggestively as can their industrial enterprises; and physical training always begs the questions training for what? The question is unanswerable, even if the answer remains tentative. After Prussia's defeat at Jena, Friedrich Ludwig Jahn's Turnkunst trained to withstand the French and, in due course, forge German unity. German gymnasts--Turner--were to rediscover the heroic qualities of their race and help create their still virtual nation. In England there was no defeat to avenge, no nation to forge for the future, but there were schoolboys to tame and civilize. Their physical development presented no great problem, but their wild, sometimes brutal play had to be disciplined. After the 1830s this was done by enlisting high spirits in regulated games and by turning poachers into gamekeepers.

Thus, where physical education on the German model appears as a device to create national or civic sense and to revivify the young, games on the English model first emerged to serve specific ends. The one model addressed itself to the whole nation, the other to a limited educational system. The ideals behind the two approaches sound similar. For Jahn, physical exercise imparted a taste for effort and adventure, taught that the most effective discipline was self-imposed, and developed the moral character of the Turner along with his body. For Thomas Hughes, half a century later, games spurred patriotism, a sense of self-reliance, and a tempering of character and body. Both stressed the importance of freedom, of voluntary emulation, and of the pleasure offered by exercise. Both saw their enterprises as harnessing young energies and instincts to social ends. But where the Jahn tradition deliberately turned to service of the nation (and the state), that of English games, stressing character over discipline, team or individual over abstract collectivities, was elitist. Gymnastics lent themselves better to routine and to mass applications, while their social uses appeared more evident. Games were a kind of conspicuous consumption: they evolved in exclusive schools; they were costly in terms of space, time, and facilities and aristocratic in inspiration and implication.

This very rough distinction was recognized in most of nineteenth century Europe. For example, as the century ended, the Swedish labor movement "would not at first accept the sports movement, which was characterized as 'an invention of the Anglo-Saxon upper class.'"[1] In some countries the distinction remained academic, with one or the other of the two approaches clearly predominant. The Anglo-Saxons paid little heed to physical training, regarded as a poor substitute for livelier organized play.[2] Germans, on the other hand, remained faithful to gymnastics both in and out of school, communicating their enthusiasm for them to neighbors like the Czechs, whose Sokols borrowed both the mass exercises and the patriotic mystique of the Turner. And when, at the century's end, young Germans rebelled against the constraints and corruption of society, their thirst for purity and action was stilled less by team sports than by return to nature and to romantically "primitive" sources of regeneration.[3]

The interesting aspect of the history of sports in France is that the competitive presence of physical education and play both stressed and clarified the difference between them and between their advocates. First to appear, physical education was adopted by the state to serve national purposes. Games--here also recognized as Anglo-Saxon upper-class inventions--appeared and remained for a long time the preserve of the privileged few. They provided training, indeed, whether to bear the burdens of privilege or to face the challenge of the unprivileged many; but they also provided play for the game's sake and for the player's satisfaction--gratuitous, self-sufficing, without ulterior purpose.[4] The possibilities of the topic are clearly vaster than the limited area of sporting history. The following pages attempt to furnish some preliminary information on how sports came to France and whom they were meant to serve. These pages are meant to open the subject rather than to cover a vast, unexplored territory. But they may suggest that far from standing apart, sports were integrated and integrating activities, part of the contemporary scene, reflecting social and ideological preoccupations, and very likely affecting them in turn.[5]

Organized physical activities, which England and Germany had known through the nineteenth century, came to France only late and quite sui generis. They came first of all to serve a patriotic purpose that consisted partly in slamming the stable door after the horse had been stolen. And they approached the self-imposed task of national revivification from several directions. Thus, born in 1874, its founders still "under the impact of their patriotic grief," the Club Alpin Français sought to provide "a school of physical energy and moral vigor," training French youth to be "more virile, more apt to bear military life, more prepared to face a long conflict without discouragement...."[6]

Despite relatively high dues that restricted membership to the upper and middle classes, the Club Alpin counted some seven thousand members by the end of the century. But less exalted and less expensive local walking, climbing, and touring clubs subscribed to the same cause. Witness the Société des Marcheurs touristes de France, set up in Bordeaux in 1885. Its end, proclaimed its statutes, was "both patriotic and scientific, since it favors the study of our country and since, at the opportune moment, excellent guides for our armies might be recruited in its ranks."[7]

Most specific of all these enterprises, and most clearly directed to premilitary training, were the gymnastic societies founded in great numbers "pour rendre aux français des muscles." Physical training would, and should, contribute to national preparedness. Shooting clubs and gymnastic societies, declared a pamphlet of 1886, were the seedbeds where the young soldiers of the future could be nurtured and trained. "Your societies," Octave Gréard, vice-rector of the Académie de Paris reminded the Association of Gymnastic Societies of the Seine in 1898, "were born, nearly all, under the impact of our disasters...all imbued with the same duty."[8]

Everyone knew that Prussian schoolmasters had been the real winners at Sedan and, somehow, Father Jahn's gymnastics seemed easier to imitate than the playing fields of Eton. So, after 1871, rifle clubs, gymnastic societies, and enterprises devoted to premilitary training spread to fulfill their patriotic mission. In Besancon they sported names like La Française, La Patriote, La Vaillante. In 1887 Bordeaux counted ten of them with titles like Patriotes bordelais and Jeunesse patriote de la Gironde, the earliest founded in 1872, the total active membership nearly eighteen hundred.

The great idea inspiring all such clubs, at least in their inception, was that of national unity and revanche. Most, however, soon degenerated into semisocial societies open to those who could afford not only their moderate dues, but also the costly costumes they adopted, which consisted as a rule of body-length tights, special trousers and jacket in blue or white, sports shoes, and a yachting cap or some other suitably martial headgear. By the 1880s many who joined such gymnastic societies did so in the hope of losing weight or, more simply, because they provided convenient occasions for members to to meet, wives to chat, and children to admire their fathers' prowess. Workingmen might occasionally be offered a separate society of their own, like La Fraternité in Bordeaux; but men who worked, when they worked, eleven or more hours a day for six or seven days a week had little time (or strength) left over for self-imposed exercise.

The champions of national revival soon realized that the campaign for physical eevelopment had to begin elsewhere, notably in the schools, where gymnastics could be taught to large numbers of the country's youth. Gymnastics had been talked about well before that time. On August 13, 1793, the Convention had approved a motion of Lepeletier de Saint-Fargeau, supported by Robespierre: "During the course of National Education, the children's time shall be divided between study, manual labor, and gymnastic exercises. If the week belongs to labor, it is good and proper that youth should rediscover corporal exercises during the days of rest." One hears of no practical implementation of such unimpeachable sentiments.

The 1830s and 1840s had seen some desultory official gestures toward introducing physical training into the curriculum, and the Second Republic actually passed a law on March 14, 1850, placing gymnastics among the optional subjects of primary schools. But these schools lacked the resources, let alone the room, for such activities. Other optional subjects, like drawing and singing, could be taught in the classroom. But games and gymnastics required space and equipment, and most schools had only narrow playgrounds. In the 1880s, as in the 1960s, a good urban primary school in Orléans boasted a yard thirty yards long and twenty-seven yards wide.

In 1853 physical training became a compulsory part of the secondary curriculum, but the new requirement was respected largely in the breach. Of seventy-seven lycées, thirteen had no premises available for gymnastics; thirty had some kind of gymnasium, but half of these were useless. Pursuing the principle of la fruite en avant, Victor Duruy's decree of February 3, 1869, made gymnastics a required subject in primary schools. But the sunset years of the Second Empire did not see the new measures progress very far. "The urgency and even the utility of gymnastic instruction," noted one local authority, "do not yet seem evident." In the provinces many reacted as skeptically as the Conseil général of the Nièvre, which alleged the diminished respect that children would bear teachers who "engaged in exercises where the dignity of the man associated to the child can suffer cruel failures." Teachers should not be asked to step off their podium onto a playing field where they could be outrun by their charges or splashed with mud.[9]

This spirit began to change after the war. The ministries of war and of public instruction discussed ways and means of avoiding a break in continuity between gymnastic training at school and in the army. A law of January 27, 1880, made gymnastic training compulsory in all public boys' schools: four half-hours of physical training and military exercises every week. "C'est une oeuvre patriotique que nous poursuivons," stressed Jules Ferry's Circular No. 400, March 29, 1881. Despite enduring reserves--as in Bordeaux, where municipal councilors preferred to equip a local school with a workshop rather than a gymnasium[10]--the approval of the conseils généraux and a swarm of newborn gymnastic societies seemed to endorse Ferry's assertion.

On July 6, 1882, a presidential decree set up bataillons scolaires for military and gymnastic training in all teaching establishments. The civic and patriotic instruction the schools dispensed was to be furthered in premilitary training units that would be its concrete expression. Such bataillons

- 71 -

would also suit the prevailing taste for military music and display. "C'était l'époque douce où, au dimanches soirs,/La grand'ville éclatait de légères fanfares...," recalled Francis Jammes of that time when, in the 1880s, he had been a student of the Lycée de Bordeaux. But, while Sunday tattoos met with appreciation, the attempt to provide premilitary training was destined to only partial success.

Approved by patriotic Republicans, the initiative identified with the secular and revanchard politics of men like Gambetta evoked little enthusiasm in conservative circles. Not only did teachers no longer lead the children to Mass, the Catholics complained, but "thanks to the bataillons, to gymnastics, etc., they prevent them from attending Catechism." Besides, argued the ultramontane Univers, even if the government taught all Frenchmen arms drill and somersaults, such methods could not forge a military force, let alone a nation. "Corporal-instructors and perfect acrobats" did not an army make.[11]

The sartorial expense involved when the bataillons sought to outfit themselves with uniforms,[12] the cost of equipping the little corps with approved rifles, and the difficulty of finding retired soldiers capable of training them discouraged goodwill. The ragged results were often more evident in the provinces. On May 15, 1883, Senator Jules Steeg wrote the prefect of the Gironde to ask why Bordeaux was so slow in setting up its bataillons: "A Paris, c'est une fête lorsque tous les jeudi matins notre jeunesse parcourt les boulevards avec ses clairons et ses tambours: tous se précipitent pour les voir et acclamer." A decade later, in the wake of the Boulanger crisis, the bataillons were quietly faded out: "une erreur patriotique," as a sporting enthusiast would describe them in retrospect.[13]

Whether for bataillons or for straightforward gymnastic instruction, moniteurs and professeurs were recruited in haphazard fashion and hired at cut-rate salaries: from 300 to 700 francs a year in collèges and 1,200 to 1,800 francs a year in lycées. Economically, such men were less off than contemporary miners (1,300 to 1,500 francs a year) or village postmen (1,100 francs a year); they did not even benefit from the local prestige of village schoolteachers, whose annual salaries after 1905 ran between 1,100 and 2,200 francs. Their meager wages had to be supplemented by some other job. Fireman, janitor, shopman, or petty artisan, the professeur de gymnastique was obviously the social inferior of his charges. Whether he took this out on them or dazzled them with acrobatic exhibitions, the few hours spent in his company left little impression. Contemporary evidence suggests that most physical training instructors were retired noncommissioned officers, some of whom had attended a three-month course at the army physical training school at Joinville. Almost all lacked any real teaching method, and their dim figures pass unrecorded but for the boredom or the pranks they aroused.[14]

Avarice could mitigate enthusiasm and affect achievement on other fronts as well. One aspect of the physical exertions involved in gymnastics as in sports was the unusual need for washing they created. This raised difficulties in a France where "at least until 1914 people wash practically not at all, they are not in the habit of washing."[15]

At Sceaux, near Paris, Lakanal, which had been designed as the model lycée of the Third Republic, could pride itself on facilities that permitted its boarders to enjoy a footbath every week and a shower every month. But this was exceptional, and most lycées marched their boarders to a public establishment: once a term at Orleans, once a month at Louis-le-Grand in Paris. Most externes, especially outside the capital, were no better provided, since few private homes were equipped with bathrooms. The soiled and sweaty heroes of playing field or gymnasium could present perplexing problems.

Sporting clubs tried to provide showers on the premises for a membership who often lacked such facilities at home. One reason why, in 1889, the Bordeaux Université Club agreed to merge with the Stade Bordelais was that the latter had showers and proper changing rooms. But such luxuries called for means beyond those of most societies and beyond the credits that municipal councils or the ministry of education would make available to the schools. The fact that gymnasiums had to be endowed with showers, therefore, made for greater cleanliness: it also restricted the number of gymnasiums and playgrounds undertaken by public and local authorities. The public health law of February 5, 1902, led to the appearance by about 1908 of departmental public health services concerning themselves with setting up public washplaces and showers. But as late as 1916 the inspector of health services in the Nièvre complained that "no playgrounds exist, no sporting institutions for adolescents, no one thinks of sports. . ."--certainly not for long, once they became aware of the costs involved. Nevertheless, it is worth remembering that, especially in backward regions like the Nièvre, the patriotic efforts of the 1880s and 1890s produced the first and for a long time the only opportunities for physical activity and hygiene.

Such ends were subordinate to that of national revival. The great Republican educational reformers were also great patriots. In 1881 Paul Bert, the minister of public instruction in Gambetta's short-lived cabinet, appointed Paul Déroulède to preside over the commission of military education of the ministry of public instruction. Its mission was to teach young Frenchmen the cult of the flag, a taste for arms, respect for discipline, and pride in being French.[16] It was Déroulède who organized the national shooting competitions out of which in 1886 there arose the Union des Sociétés de Tir de France. In 1885 Jean Macé, another prominent progressive figure who had begun his teaching career at Beblenheim, in lost Alsace, wrote the preface to a Manuel de tir à l'usage des écoles primaires. Like his ally Fernand Buisson, the founder of the Ligue de l'enseignement had abandoned his pacifism to encourage the bataillons scolaires that drilled in schoolyards with their condemned rifles.

This aspect of physical education went on riding the preparedness wave up to the eve of 1914, when we can find a man like Jaures' friend, Charles Andler, socialist and patriot, referring to the rivalry between Greek cities and their athletic and artistic jousts: "The need to be constantly ready for the final and vital struggle, tempers a humanity of rare physical integrity, sober, well-trained, nervous, muscular, all made for action." In Andler's mind, as in the pages of an anonymous pamphlet of 1898, Ludus pro patria, the need to be prepared provided the ulterior justification of activities that-- ideally--are their own needs.

There was little of play and less of ludic exuberance about such officially sponsored enterprises. French sport did not grow out of the bataillons
scolaires. It grew out of a rival impetus championed by men with very different ideas, like Pierre de Coubertin, whose name remains linked to the
Olympic Games he was responsible for reviving in 1896. Coubertin and his
friends saw athletics as a means of freeing French youth from deadening disciplines, including physical training or physical education. The divergence
between official initiatives and the new wave that Coubertin represented is
what concerns us here.

The first gymnastic society had been founded at Guebwiller, in Alsace,
before the end of the Second Empire. Sports, on the other hand, entered
France via England. For the fin de siècle, the very term "sport" carried an
equivocal sound. Littré had described it as an English word and warned:
"In France one often confuses sport and turf; but turf (racing) is only one
kind of sport." Nevertheless, to most people, the two terms remained in-
terconnected with the "vulgar and unpleasant" overtones of horse racing,
race courses, and betting.[17] Le Sport, "Journal des gens du monde," first
published in 1854, had been chiefly devoted to racing and hunting. The fashionable Société sportive de Bordeaux concerned itself solely with horse
racing. Until the turn of the century, a sportsman was usually a man who
owned, rode, or betted on horses. Thus, when Léon Blum joined Tristan
Bernard to launch a regular "Critique de Sport" in the Revue Blanche of 1894,
their very first article largely equated "sport" and horse racing. And the
same confusion was to reappear (though slightly mitigated) in an 1897 passage of Blum's Nouvelles Conversations de Goethe avec Eckermann.[18]

On a less literary or esthetic plane, contemporary publications mirror
this prejudice. Louis Baume's Moeurs sportives (1895) deals with racing,
betting, and the race course public. Jacques Lozère's Sport et Sportsmen
(1896) consists of racing chronicles. That same year the only reference to
sport in Henri Rochefort's Aventures de ma vie was a comparison between
the "turf" of 1865 and that of his old age, ruined by the introduction of pari
mutuel. When in 1899–1900 Baron de Vaux published two large, magnifi-
cently illustrated volumes on Le Sport en France et à l'étranger, the first
volume (334 pages) was devoted to shooting, fencing, and the sporting activities of crowned heads; the second volume (442 pages) to riding, hunting, fal-
conry, and "athletics." This last section, seventy-three pages long, mixed
pell-mell boxing and wrestling, golf, tennis, skating, running, discus throwing, and football.

There were other sports, recognized leisure activities more or less
athletic according to mood and circumstance, whose names proclaimed their
English origins. The Rowing Club de Paris had been set up in 1853. The
Bordeaux Athletic Club would be founded in 1877 by fourteen British residents of the port. There were also le yachting and le footing.[19] These activities were not taken very seriously. "It was the fashion in those days to
scoff at sports," writes Guillaume Apollinaire revealingly in 1907 about the
mood of the 1880s.[20] At least rowing, riding, and yachting were familiar,
while the new games continued to seem strange. In his memoirs Pierre de
Coubertin remembers how, in the 1890s, le Gaulois referred to "the long,
flat mallets" with which one played football. For the Bonapartist l'Autorité,

football was played with racquets and small, hard balls. And Francisque Sarcey in l'Echo de Paris praised holidays spent at jeu de paume: "journées pleines de charme même quand on les décore du nom anglais de football."[21] By that time, as we shall shortly see, football of one sort or another had been played in France for twenty years. It would remain a quasi-confidential enterprise as long as most people continued to ignore games or regard them as fit only for children.

If press and public gradually became more knowledgeable about different sports, it was probably because of one particular pastime that would become particularly French, a sport that, though partly inspired by English ventures, may well be counted a French creation: "Cours, vélo, cours dans ta lumière/Le Progrès chevauche sur toi!" sand Deckert's "Ode au Véloce." The tone had hardly changed since the first modern sporting publications had sprouted in Paris and in the provinces around 1868-69, all devoted to cycling, symbol of "moral and material progress," means of regenerating man by physical exercise. Edouard Seidler has briefly traced the rise of a French sporting press from uncertain beginnings to 1894, when the weekly Bicyclette printed twenty thousand copies and the daily Vélo, founded three years earlier, boasted sales of eighty thousand.[22] By that time France boasted 132,000 velocipedes of one kind or another. The sporting press that catered to their owners had discovered and would reveal the close relationship between a certain kind of sporting activity, publicity, and circulation.

The first long-distance cycle race, from Paris to Rouen, was held in 1869. The 1870s and 1880s saw a great number of competitions, with the same race involving tricycles, penny-farthings, and other models then in existence. Almost all were amateur competitions, and all were dominated by English cyclists. Thus when the oldest of the great road races still in existence, Bordeaux-Paris, was first run in May 1891, four Englishmen led the winners.[23] It soon became apparent that, properly handled, such enterprises helped to sell newspapers and also cycles. It was le Petit Journal that promoted the great Paris-Brest-Paris race in 1891, and the second great sporting daily, l'Auto, launched the Tour de France in 1903 to promote its sales.

For a long time cycling remained an expensive pastime. The bicycle itself was likely to cost five hundred francs or more, equivalent to two months of a lieutenant's pay or three of an instituteur's. Regarded as a luxury, it was first subjected to direct tax; after 1900 the bicycle was taxed indirectly through the requirement of a license plate. Characteristically, the first prophets, champions, and practitioners of the new sport were fils de famille: the racer and future trainer, Paul Ruinart, was the son of a wholesale wine merchant; Tristan Bernard, who undertook the management of the Vélodrome Buffalo in 1892, was the son of a builder and real estate man. A few years later Henri Desgranges, who took over the new velodrome at the Parc des Princes in 1897 and launched l'Auto--destined to become France's major sporting daily--was a notary's clerk, representing another social group. His humbler origins reflect the relegation of the bicycle from luxury object--one with which an arch-esthete like Robert de Montesquiou did not disdain being photographed--to solid investment accessible to middle- and lower-middle-class budgets. The change had been swift.

Between 1889 and 1891 John Boyd Dunlop's pneumatic tires had begun to replace solid rubber ones, inner tubes permitted André and Edouard Michelin to develop detachable tires, cycle prices began to fall,[24] and cycle racing to attract more popular attention. After 1891, cherished and publicized by the press, cycling became the most popular of sports. The winner of the Paris-Brest race, national champion Charles Terront, had a place of honor reserved for him at the Opera at the gala performance honoring the visiting Russian sailors in 1893. By 1897 H. de Graffigny's Manuel pratique du constructeur et du conducteur de cycles et d'automobiles estimated the number of cyclists in France at three hundred thousand. Graffigny exaggerated, but what a Paris paper had once sneered at as imbéciles à roulettes had become part of the landscape.

A young schoolteacher starting out in the Normandy countryside remembers seeing his first cyclist in 1890 and yearning for the machine that would put the surrounding world within easier reach than walking, which was all he could afford. But "in 1895 bicycles were still very rare, in 1897 their price was still inaccessible for me." Finally, in 1898 help from his farmer father, a loan from an uncle who was a village mason, and fifty francs in savings enabled him to buy a second-hand bicycle. It took five years to repay the loan, but it was worth it. "Henceforth I was king of the road, since I was faster than a horse." But he was one of the privileged few: "perhaps the only one of my class to own an iron steed."[25]

The concrete economics of a major purchase indicate why bicycles remained thin on the ground, but also how--and why--they ceased to count as objects of conspicuous consumption. It is interesting to compare the original membership of the Club vélocipédique de Bordeaux, founded in 1892, an obviously upper-middle-class group, with that of the Cyclistes girondins, founded in 1897, several notches below the middle of the middle class.[26] It was scarcely a coincidence that the first auto club in Bordeaux appeared in 1897, the very year when cycling publicists like Baudry de Saunier abandoned velocipedes for automobiles. Those who could afford it were turning to more exclusive activities. Where in 1891 the first sporting daily had squarely entitled itself Vélo, its rival ten years later hedged by setting out as Auto-Vélo and had shed the second term by 1903.

The cycle was no longer in the forefront of progress. The late 1890s saw it become a sport for shop assistants, whose kind accounted for fifteen out of twenty-seven founder-members of the Cycle Club de Bordeaux and nine out of twenty-one Cyclistes girondins. We witness the appearance of clubs like the Société des cyclistes coiffeurs-parfumeurs (1896) or the Union cycliste des postes et des télégraphes (1897).[27] Figures given by Jean Fourastié suggest a vertiginous fall in prices. The cheapest bicycle of 1893 cost the equivalent of 1,655 hours' wages of a factory hand in the provinces. By 1911, with hourly wages up and bicycle prices down, a cheap model cost only the equivalent of 357 hours--almost half the price of a sewing machine, and hence accessible for bachelors of the working class. The evidence suggests that, for the masses, cycling remained a spectator sport.[28] Yet, even so, its influence upon the fate of other amateur sports was great. It first suggested the pursuit of sport for pleasure in social circles where this was not normally envisaged; numerically important clubs not appealing exclusively to middle and upper classes were formed around it; last but not least, especially in the provinces, cycling enthusiasts contributed some of the first officers and experienced members to the foundation of more broadly oriented clubs.[29]

Though touching smaller numbers, the great sporting revolution of the eighties and nineties was less concerned with cycling or with traditional sports than with organized open-air games of the kind associated with English public school education, particularly running and ball games. And, once again, the English influence is apparent from the start.

The first Club des coureurs, founded in 1875 by two young Parisians (one of them English), died within only a few months. In 1877 André Berthelot (1862-1938), then at the Lycée Saint-Louis, gathered a few friends eager to race each other and play football in the Bois de Boulogne. Apparently passers-by assumed that they were French-speaking Englishmen. This group also did not last very long. In 1880 the future arctic explorer, Jean Charcot, son of the great neurologist, then a fourteen-year-old pupil at the École Alsacienne, started organized games at his school. But the École Alsacienne was exceptional. Most secondary schools had neither room nor sympathy for such goings-on. Hence, in the course of 1881-82, a number of students from Right-Bank institutions--Condorcet, Rollin, Carnot (then the École Monge)--got into the habit of running impromptu races after school in the entrance hall of the nearby Gare St. Lazare. Joined by some veterans of Berthelot's old group, they soon founded the grandiloquently titled Racing Club de France and began to organize regular Sunday races in the more tranquil atmosphere of the Bois de Boulogne.

First of French sporting associations, authorized by a decree of November 23, 1882, the Racing did not belie its name. Its terminology and style were borrowed from the turf. Runners were divided into stables, wore jockey costumes with colored sashes and caps, sometimes carried horsewhips to complete the pretense, idled in the "pesage," ran under assumed horse names in races whose titles were borrowed from Longchamps and Auteuil and whose results were bet on by the assembled sportsmen and their fashionable friends. For Rodolphe Salis in the Chat Noir (Spring 1882), here was "the latest creation of invading anglomania."[30] Soon Ferdinand de Lesseps himself accepted the honorary presidency. On July 6, 1884, he presented the winner of the Prix de Panama with a handsome horsewhip. Very shortly such influential connections secured the Racing a permanent home in the Bois, where running tracks were later joined by football grounds.

Meanwhile, in 1883, students of the Lycée Saint-Louis, who had been informally running and training in the Luxembourg gardens, moved first into the Tuileries, then, with prefectorial consent, to the Orangerie terrace. There they founded the Stade Français, which became the Racing's great Left-Bank rival. It was after a cross-country race in 1887 that the two clubs joined in the Union des Sociétés francaises de courses à pied, followed in 1889 by the more comprehensive Union des Sociétés françaises de sports athlétiques (USFSA), which incorporated tennis, cycling, football, rowing, and similar activities. Some federal organization was needed to facilitate the international encounters that began to take place in the mid-1880s and to encourage sporting activities and spread the sporting gospel, organizing national competitions and keeping people in touch. Les Sports athlétiques, USFSA's weekly bulletin, provides a mirror of their activity, in which ball games played an increasingly important role.

Football, at least, came to France two or three years before it reached Germany.[31] A list of provincial teams in the Almanach des Sports of 1899 confirms the English game's predictable lines of penetration: the ports, the north (and Lyon) with their textile connections, the highway from Normandy to Paris, Paris itself with its large Anglo-Saxon colony. Across the Channel in England, the Football Association had been set up in 1863, but it took some years to make up its mind how the game should be played. By 1871, however, Association football and Rugby football had become clearly separate and autonomous in England; about the same time, the game entered France through Le Havre, where the Havre Athletic Club (HAC) was born in 1872. Founded by Oxford and Cambridge men, its colors combined the blues of the two universities. It is not very clear what game the HAC played, but its first teams do not seem to have known--or cared about--the rules finally set up in England. They played a "combination" game probably close to rugger until 1891, when the Club finally set up two distinct rugger and soccer sections--one of the first French clubs to do so.

For a long time French football was dominated by the HAC, or, if not by the club itself, then by the English sailors, clerks, and students who colonized both soccer and rugger until about 1914. When HAC won the French championship in 1899, six of its players were English. All the earliest Paris soccer clubs were also started by Englishmen. The Paris Football Club (1879-84) lapsed for lack of rivals. It was succeeded in 1890 by the Football Association Club, founded by the personnel of two English firms. Then, in 1891, the White Rovers (inspired by the Cup Final victory of the Blackburn Rovers) was founded at Bécon-les-Bruyères, and soccer clubs multiplied thereafter.

The USFSA--addicted to rugby, which was "more highly regarded in the upper classes of [English] society"--reluctantly admitted the existence of Association football. After soccer clubs had threatened to secede, the USFSA organized a national soccer championship, won in 1894 by the Standard Athletic Club team, comprising one Frenchman and ten Englishmen. In 1895 James Gordon Bennett, editor of the New York Herald, donated the silver cup that would henceforth reward the winners of the Association football championship. By 1899 Association football boasted some three-score clubs in the Paris area alone, and Frantz Reichel, one of the city's great rugby players, noted that soccer--less violent, brutal, and dangerous than rugby-- had spread considerably in France: "Which is a pity, for it is not worth as much as rugby from the educational point of view."[32]

By the turn of the century, French teams began to participate in international competitions, and these, especially against the English, tended to end in catastrophic scores: 15-0 in 1906, 12-0 in 1908, 11-0 in 1909, 10-1 in 1910. In 1911, with a loss of only 3-0, the wind began to turn and, by 1921, French soccer could mark up its first victory against England: 2-1.

The trend probably reflected the gradual acclimatization of the game and the growing number of native clubs from which a truly national team could select its players. We shall see that the slow progress of soccer with its narrow, foreign base contrasts with the swifter adoption of rugby, introduced less by foreign residents than by French schoolboys. It was only after 1919, with athletic sports no longer a preserve of upper-class teenagers, that the spread of ball games at the popular level meant the spread of soccer, which is not only easier to play and demanding of less effort, but easier to play informally and without getting as dirty as one necessarily does in a rugger game.

But this was still in the future. For a long time the men involved in football (or other sports) were very few in number and considered themselves an elite. "The Grand Prix at Longchamps," notes a sporting lycée professor in Les Sports athlétiques, December 12, 1891, "attracts over fifty thousand, a football match hardly five hundred." This remained true for ten or fifteen years. The concomitant elitism may have been a compensation, at least in part; a spurning of grapes less green than out of reach. But elitism, whatever the motives behind it, was a crucial element of contemporary sporting effort. The Racing accepted only amateurs, as defined in 1866 by the English Amateur Athletic Club in a formula that banned professionalism or the possibility of gain, stressed the fact that the amateur is a "gentleman," and excluded "mechanics, laborers and artisans." When the first article of the USFSA's rules barred all but amateurs from membership, it eliminated not only any athlete who had ever competed in an open race, or for money, or for pay, or for a share of the gate receipts, or against professionals, but also specifically, anyone "who has ever been, at any time in his life, a paid teacher or monitor of physical exercises." The latter were professionals, hence barred from activities that gentlemen not only pursued but regulated. The true sporting spirit, as the general secretary of the USFSA explained to a provincial prefect, consisted in opposing "professionalism, money prizes, betting, in a word all that paralyzes the beneficent effects of sport."[33]

No man could devote much time, let alone his life, to sport without a private income and not be somehow a professional. But the pioneers of pure sport addressed themselves to an audience who did not need to face this problem. Their determined stand against professionalism would play its part in the rival fortunes of Rugby and Association football.

Article 51 of the USFSA rules, concerning football competitions, declared that the national championship will be played out "in two series of matchs [sic] played according to the rules adopted by the Rugby Union." The first number of Les Sports athlétiques (April 5, 1890) devoted two pages out of six to "Football." Closer examination shows this to have meant rugby until December 1893 when, soccer having been admitted into the USFSA, the football rubric begins to appear with two separate subheadings: "Rugby" and "Association"--the latter only hardly and very briefly mentioned for several years more. Revealingly, the bulletin of the Club nivernais d'amateurs, founded in 1895, was entitled Le Rugby and continued under that title until the eve of the First World War. When in 1894 a leading figure of the USFSA, Georges de Saint-Clair, published Football (Rugby), it is clear that the subtitle was there only as an afterthought and that, for his friends of the

Racing and the Stade Français, football was rugby. Soccer, tainted by English professionalism, carried too many vulgar associations. Rugby, even when played by the lower classes as in England, allowed for distinctions.[34] Indeed, explains Saint-Clair, referring to possible dangers of the game likely to arouse parental concern, most accidents (in England) occur in those "northern mining districts where the population--very rough and brutal-- does not bring to the game the desirable distinction and courtesy. When played by young, well-bred men, football is not dangerous."[35]

The favorite game of English public schools, rugby was the form of football that most students adopted, especially in Paris. It is striking to find Charles Péguy, who in the early 1890s had introduced Association football in his lycée at Orleans, moving to the cagne at Lakanal and there taking up rugby because it was the game that Paris lyceens played.[36]

Thus rugby spread, carried by the hazards of student life, to university towns and sometimes to other areas--like Nantes, where Parisian influences inspired the Stade Nantais as early as 1886, or Perpignan where, in 1889, a boy who had played the game at the Lycée Michelet in Paris founded the Union athlétique du College perpignanais, seed of the great Catalan rugby school.[37]

The strongest impetus for sport in the southwest came from Bordeaux. The chance presence of a dynamic personality had made the city the first center of athletic activities in the provinces, through the Ligue girondine de l'éducation physique, founded in 1888 by Philippe Tissié. Author of numerous articles and pamphlets on gymnastics and hygiene, Dr. Tissié was one of the many medical men whose patriotic and sanitary concerns turned them into militant missionaries of sport. His energy, his influence, and that of the Ligue he founded, gained the support of the regional rectorate. As a result, the directives of the ministry of education, largely ignored in other areas, were applied in Aquitaine, where most secondary and a great many elementary schools made sports and games part of the regular curriculum. Offspring of modest homes, familiarized with running and games in primary school, could be found practicing sports in associations of their own or in the Stade Bordelais, whose foundation in 1889 was a direct result of the enthusiasm generated by the Ligue.

Thanks to this groundwork, the first USFSA regional committee had been set up in Bordeaux in 1893. Regional committees followed in Toulouse and Lyon four years later. Meanwhile, Bordeaux became the first provincial city to play an important role in the national rugby championship, the Stade Bordelais winning it in 1899, playing in the finals for the next three years, and retaining the cup from 1902 to 1907. Altogether, after 1899, all but six of the national pennants were won by clubs from south of the Loire. The south, above all the southwest, remained rugby country, partly because of the USFSA's prejudices, partly because of the English influences radiating from Bordeaux, Bayonne, Biarritz, and Pau.

Soccer appeared as a kind of Cinderella: "Latecomer, faced with a cold reception.... The wealthy clubs showing no interest, there was no publicity for its matches. . . . School clubs, that is the bourgeoisie, keep away for ten years. Rugby alone seems noble, fascinating."[38] When, in 1909, the Douanier Rousseau painted his _Joueurs de football_, the players were obviously rugby players, and so were those of later painters who depicted ball games, like André Lhôte, Albert Gleizes, and Robert Delaunay. Equally revealing, the illustrated cover of the _Revue des jeux scolaires_ showed two young men in sports costume, one wearing cycling knickers, the other football shorts and carrying a rugby ball under his arm. "It seems as if Association football is essentially popular, and rugby the preserve of an elite," muses an observer, adding that rugby's future depends wholly on how it does _parmi les milieux scolaires_.[39] Remarks such as these suggest a partial explanation of the intriguing hold of rugby on southern and most especially southwestern France.

By 1900, when Association football appeared south of the Loire, established clubs were controlled by rugby players, and a local tradition had grown up. Soccer teams and clubs were set up and, in the bigger centers, flourished. Association football became the great spectator sport of industrial urban centers, drifting to professionalism as a direct result of the role it played, the masses to which it catered, and the resources it commanded. But the small towns and small urban centers of Midi and Languedoc, which lacked both the industrial concentrations that furnished the public of professional soccer and the resources for a variety of sports, remained faithful to the amateur game with which they identified. Cities almost without industry, without an industrial proletariat, an urban network whose evolution in the 1960s can be compared to the stage reached by the industrial regions of the north and east at the end of the nineteenth century, go far to explain the provincial conservatism of a region where the glories of amateur rugby go hand in hand with economic stagnation. The greatest teams of the twentieth century appear in centers like Narbonne, Lourdes, Pau, Bayonne, Dax, and Perpignan. A lawyer from Agen, a town of forty thousand whose team was three times French rugby champion in the 1960s, recently declared: "Agen must grow, prunes and rugby are not enough."[40] Yet it would seem that Agen's rugby flourishes best while its economy rests on prunes. "Sport d'amateurs . . . école de volonté, d'energie," rugby, once favorite of the better off, endures as the game of more backward regions, of communities that, unable to subsidize professionals, continue to play it themselves.

Rugby remained true to the ideals that the first sporting clubs embodied: elitism, amateurism, the educational value of sporting activities were what its followers stood for and what we can find in the writings of men like Pierre de Coubertin. Coubertin, whose efforts played a major role in the spread and acceptance of sporting activities in the late 1880s and 1890s, had seen athletics and games as key educational activities, apt to produce all-round men and to free French youth from moral and physical inertia. What Coubertin had not bargained for was that the athletic revival that he did so much to bring about made a great contribution to the nationalist revival of the pre-1914 years.

Before the turn of the century the _Almanach des Sports_ already celebrated the martial virtues of team games. "Le football," for instance, "is a veritable little war, with its necessary discipline, and its way of getting participants used to danger and to blows." Then, in 1913, Agathon's well-known inquiry into the mood of middle-class youth noted the effect of sports on "the patriotic optimism of youth" and praised "the moral benefit of collective sports, like football, so widespread in our lycées," which "develop and maintain a warlike atmosphere among young people."

Coubertin himself had little use for such conclusions. But he quoted with approval an article in which the journalist Pierre Mille described what his young contemporaries had learned from sport: "They quite often consider a possible war as a match that must be played as well as possible, after having trained for it scientifically. One holds on, keeping one's composure and one's breath to the end. And if you win, you win; if you lose, you lose. It is no dishonor. A game is a game, and that is all."[42]

Going beyond the advantages of preparedness, sport, as Hippolyte Taine had perceived in his Notes sur l'Angleterre (1872), may also be considered as an excellent "outlet ... for the strong and over-ample vigor of youth...." From society's point of view, competitive games offered a means of channeling and regulating violence, especially the savage violence of adolescence. To individuals too ready to follow some subversive drummer, games offered opportunities for self-assertion and sometimes also for indulging in competitive violence in any number of ways that society condemns outside the battlefield. Theodore Roosevelt, a great supporter of Coubertin, always preached the value of sport as a source of energy, but also as a way of channeling excess energy into socially approved directions.[43] If, for children, play is often a work substitute, for adolescents its regulated form may provide a unique occasion for self-expression and immediate success. The kind of adjustment this facilitates may be looked on either with approval or with disfavor. Echoing the denunciations of sport's contribution to the "puerilism of contemporary life" found in Huizinga's Homo ludens, a French psychologist has found that sport provides "an extraordinarily effective appeasement for the insatiable unconscious," and hence "a very powerful means of infantilization." The best statement of this point of view appears in the work of Georges Magnane, for whom the discipline of sports offers "une liberté sous bonne garde." The opportunities opened for social control appear more powerful than those making for self-liberation or self-expression: "Sport is the chief pole of attraction toward approved activities: licit, consciously social and, in the broadest sense of the term, docile."[44]

We know that when problems vital to wild animals are solved by human intervention, surplus energy that may well be employed in play becomes available. Thus, adult domestic animals show tendencies to play that are normally found only in the young. For captive animals, too, play fulfills a hygienic role, providing an opportunity for activity without which animals nourished without effort and protected against natural enemies tend to lapse into aberrant behavior. Captives, all zoologists tell us, need special opportunities for distraction and for the expenditure of surplus energy. Writing about play in animals, Jacques Lecomte treats their games as substitutes designed to protect them against neuroses that may develop when their impulses cannot express themselves either in normal or in substitute activities. Referring to the tendency of animals liberated from tasks related to survival to express their freedom in play, he discerns ludic behavior "among young animals whose childhood is particularly prolonged and whose primary needs are satisfied by their parents."[45]

Even without remembering that Rousseau always insisted that "to educate is to retard," we cannot help recognizing the counterpart of these young animals in the young members of the middle and upper classes then being educated in the schools of France. That the concrete possibilities of this function of sport were soon noticed, and generally approved, can be seen from an essay printed as an appendix to Agathon's inquiry, in which a sporting journalist praised l'éducation sportive for preparing its subjects to be "the right and contented man in the right place."[46] Another contributor described how the practice of football and cross-country running had taught him and his friends the competitive nature of life, persuaded them that men were unequal, and turned them away from socialism with its false ideas of equality, fraternity, and pacifism. "Sport enlightened me on myself and on my real feelings."[47] This brings to mind remarks of a later date, like Lucien Romier's assurance that a football team for every thousand inhabitants would solve the social problem. And it is true that, the hierarchy of players and athletes coinciding only very approximately with the general social hierarchy, games can provide temporary substitutes, artificial detours around irritating real-life barriers. They also provide a temporary opportunity for individuals to communicate--to commune--and to establish personal and social bonds that are otherwise lacking. A few years before the First World War, a rather obscure pamphlet actually pleaded this particular value of sport-- the true equality established on the playing field--as a social educator. But we have seen already that this was not very likely to occur in the circumstances of the 1880s and 1890s, when class distinctions were affirmed rather than threatened by the new athletic clubs.

Romier's words were uttered between the wars, when men of goodwill sometimes sought "a substitute for national union in a football team."[48] In the 1800s the very idea of sporting activities for the common people evoked laughter when raised in a municipal council. Conversely, when the Fédération Sportive Athlétique Socialiste was founded in 1908, it catered only to members of the Socialist party (SFIO). Though this exclusivism was abandoned in 1911, sporting activities for class-conscious workers remained at the mercy of political fluctuations and counted for little until the 1930s. The Swiss Socialists did much better in this respect with their SATUS (Workers' Federation of Gymnastics and Sport), founded in 1874.

There were, of course, the patronages, well-intentioned enterprises designed to improve the character and body of the deserving poor. The name reflects a paternalistic and, finally, patronizing inspiration. Not that, seen in contemporary perspective, there was much wrong in this, but for the fact that the patronages themselves served ulterior ends, while their activities, far from bringing sporting enthusiasts closer together, emphasized their divisions. Since the 1870s many English clubs founded in churches, chapels, or Sunday schools had grown to national prominence. But whereas in England such enterprises were "an innocent source of pleasure and satisfaction for the masses," in France they were too often mere rods to beat a foe. Thus, and especially in those western regions where political divisions were most fierce, many small towns enjoyed two sports clubs where one would have been ample--one Catholic, the other Republican, one for the Right, another for the Left, centers of their party's activities and focus for the hostility of the other side.[49] In the first decade of the century and especially after the separation law of December 1905, the Catholics made very serious efforts to expand and organize the scattered activities of their parish groups and thus regain some of the influence forfeited with the loss of so many teaching establishments. An increasing number of parish patronages, deliberately oriented toward physical activities appealing to the young (Les Jeunes de St. Bruno, de St. Genès, de St. Roch) were grouped in regional gymnastic and sporting unions, and these in turn affiliated to the Fédération Gymnasttique et Sportive des Patronages de France, founded in 1898.

The Union Régionale Gymnastique et Sportive des Patronages du Sud-Ouest was officially registered in 1907. Its directors naturally insisted that it had no political aims, but their political opinions were well known, and these contradicted their professions of neutrality. The authorities were skeptical. "There can be no doubt," noted a police report, "that their true purpose is to gather together the greatest possible number of young Catholics, in order to maintain their confessional hold upon them."[50] Such Catholic zeal spurred the foundation or re-animation of secular competitors: patronages laïques, some founded by private enterprise, others (patronages scolaires) extracurricular enterprises rather half-heartedly undertaken by primary schoolteachers at the urging of the Inspectorat de l'Éducation primaire. In 1909 the southwest counted ninety-nine such patronages scolaires, mostly devoted to gymnastics, shooting, or premilitary training. But the Inspecteur d'Académie still bewailed the incapacity of such "Republican and secular" patronages to meet the challenge of Catholics and "enemies of the secular spirit." "Religious or reactionary patronages," he reported, "open and operate on all sides, seizing our pupils when they step out of school and seeking to destroy that which we have sought to raise in their minds."[51]

Lay and religious patronages sometimes clashed over the use of playgrounds, the latter better served, as a rule, by the generosity of private sympathizers, the former clamoring for the support of the Republican authorities. Neither side lost sight of its ultimate purpose, which the Inspecteur d'Académie quoted above recalled in his report: these children were the electors of tomorrow.

This rivalry probably deserves further study. Meanwhile, whatever their inspiration, it is clear that patronages must have provided some of the first--and few--playgrounds and sporting activities available to the young of the poorer classes, left out of account by regular sporting clubs.

Not that the leaders of the USFSA wished it so. Coubertin, for one, was always keen to bring sports to the workers. But his hostility to professionalism, his indifference to the cost of athletic pastimes--small to the rich, but prohibitive to the poor--were as good as barriers. When in due course the stadiums were opened to the masses it would be less down in the arena than up on the tiers. Indeed, those sporting associations that catered first to the petty bourgeoisie and later, in the 1920s and 1930s, to the working classes, showed less interest in participation and disinterested competition than they did in prizes; professionalism, and spectator sports. Explicit or implicit, elitism ensured that "athletic sports" would remain the privilege of a minority. Social exclusivism could manifest itself in the clubhouse and on the playing field. The elitist aspirations of athletic enthusiasts could be enlisted to meaner ends. "C'est une élite seule qui peut être admise a cette culture intensive du muscle," declared an Aquitainian enthusiast.[52] And student clubs in particular tended to exclusivism. Thus, when the Bordeaux Université Club, founded in 1897, encountered the financial difficulties usual to its kind, it decided to merge with the powerful Stade Bordelais. In the debates that preceded the merger, a speaker warned that the Université Club was a society "of young men with a similar education, stemming from the same milieu, sharing common tastes," and hence more likely to get on together than with the mixed crew they would encounter in the larger club. It is true that the membership of the Stade Bordelais, though generally described in police reports as "de condition aisée" and benefiting from a "bonne éducation primaire," did include a fair number of clerks, shopkeepers, shop assistants, commercial travelers--even a waiter and a shoemaker. Such were no fit company for well-born youths. No wonder the merger soon dissolved, the students taking their leave in 1903 to found the Bordeaux Étudiants Club, explaining that "students who wish to engage in sports are tired of turning to clubs where they must mix with young persons of diverse professions and ages...."[53]

Such attitudes elicited the tacit or overt support of the first sportsmen themselves, whose views may be found in the authoritative Les Sports athlétiques. Concluding a series of articles on the popularization of physical exercises, the organ of the USFSA opposed the ideas of clubs where workers and members "of the ruling classes" would mix: "Nous repoussons avec énergie les associations mixtes." Such contact between rich and poor would be bound to create frictions that were best avoided. Besides, it explained, many young people would never consent to mix with workers, sharing the games of a class they did not know and from whom they were separated by prejudices of birth, wealth, and upbringing. The article quoted "one of our finest runners" waxing indignant at the thought of measuring himself against opponents "sortis des rangs du peuple." That, it affirmed, was how three-quarters of the membership of all athletic societies felt. Evidently, "the hour of popular sports was not yet."[54]

It is hard to say how much of this passed through the minds of the USFSA leaders. Like other pursuits (including war), sport can suggest that its rules are applicable to the rest of existence, that the sense of fair play developed on the playing field may appropriately be indulged elsewhere. This would favor ideas of social justice. Sport can equally well offer evasion from lives too far removed from the clear-cut situations of the playing field, an excuse for not trying to resolve the complexities of the outside world, and a refuge in the simpler, more limited world of club and game. Besides, we have seen that the conclusions men drew from sporting experience differed. Only one thing is sure: the decades before the First World War offered little occasion to use or regard sport as opium for the masses. Its possibilities as an opiate, if any, would apply to higher reaches of society. Despite the fact that Georges Bourdon, historian and veteran of the Racing, writing in 1906, rejoiced that "athletic education, having transformed the youth of the lycées, begins to affect the sons of the people,"[55] the negative evidence of his remark is more convincing than the wishful thinking.

The distance between "the people" and the apologists of sport also appears in Paul Adam's Nietzschean Morale des Sports (1907), when the author argues that "the constant use of the brake is for the driver an incomparable moral exercise." But the term "driver" (chauffeur) refers to the hired hand who drives and cares for the automobile, as in another remark, this time by Coubertin himself, that the automobile makes for social equality by bringing nearer its rich owner and his chauffeur.[56]

A simple list of dates should be enough to tell how far sporting activities could affect the people or their sons. The ten-hour working day was introduced in 1900; a law of July 13, 1906, established one day of rest per week; another of April 23, 1919, cut the working day from ten to eight hours; finally, the official forty-hour week for both sexes was introduced in 1936. Obviously, there was not much free time for games before 1919. Cycling apart, the early history of organized sport in France had narrow scope: schoolboys, foreigners, young men of good family. Most of its protagonists were lycéens and collegians. And there were, in the 1880s and 1890s, only about 52,000 lycéens and 160,000 young people in all secondary establishments, both clerical and lay. These students represented something like five per cent of their age group.[57] Few of them took an interest in organized games. But, then, there were not really that many who enlisted in nationalism, or syndicalism, or in the more passionate pursuit of the arts, and it is always the active minorities that attract our attention, because they affect--or in some way reflect--the rest.

If it is not too rash to draw conclusions from such a cursory survey, I should like to suggest that the appearance of athletics and sports in France at this particular time was no coincidence. The growing interest in sports was connected with patriotism only in an incidental way. The reasons for the relative success of organized sport--and for the particular social location of this success--were more general than sporadic revanchisme alone would account for and more specific than the derivative--or counterirritant --potential of physical exercise.

Sports appeared in France as a leisure activity characteristic of a particular moment when the economic slump, or stagnation, of the 1880s and 1890s liberated the time and energies of the upper and middle classes, or at least of their young. Lower prices; higher relative incomes, especially for the rentier class, members of the liberal professions, and persons on fixed salaries; and a combination of medical advances and economic retrenchment that kept old men alive longer, slowing or blocking possibilities of advancement--all this meant fewer opportunities or temptations in the traditional directions to which young men who did not need to work to eat could turn for a career. A higher proportion of the leisured young could wait, or chose to wait, a relatively long time before turning to money-earning activities. Many sought a career in less traditional directions: literature, the arts, politics, and overseas ventures.

The rash of little reviews that marks the fin de siècle, the rising interest in colonial adventure, the spread of sports where they had not been heeded before, were all reactions against a society often condemned as sclerotic, but also against its products, symptoms of a hardening and aging of social tissues. The growing favor and significance of activities not of a strictly utilitarian nature in social circles that had scorned them not long before was the evidence of a pathological condition, but perhaps also a token of its cure.

Advocates and observers had always remembered the connection between sports and national enterprise. From Thomas Hughes' Tom Brown's School Days, which asserted that rugger captains make capital officers, to Rudyard Kipling's Stalky & Co., there seems little doubt that--even more than the battle of Waterloo--the British Empire was won on the playing fields of Eton. Mid-Victorian reformers urged public schoolboys to athletic sports to make them not only manly but also "handy rifle skirmishers." Sporting enthusiasts like Eton's headmaster Edmund Warre sponsored Volunteer battalions as warmly as they did games. Such men apparently succeeded in turning their schools into "splendid institution(s) for the Nation and for the Empire," dedicated to "turn out a hardy and dashing breed of young officers."[58] And Kipling's view that "India's full of Stalkies--Cheltenham and Haileybury and Marlborough chaps" was shared by many French, among them Father Didon, principal of the Dominican College at Arcueil, one of the first among French schools to introduce games for its students. When Father Didon visited Eton in the late 1890s, he remarked that the boys who learned to command in games were learning to command in the Indies.[59]

Why should a society in search of revival not adopt the recipes that had worked elsewhere? There was some irony about the France of the 1890s turning to observations made in the 1860s about innovations of the 1830s. But there was reason, too. Here were challenges that could be proposed to young men in search of a petite secousse, not yet confronted by a grande secousse. One is struck by the similar language used by advocates of sports and those of colonial life. "Ce ne sont pas les beaux esprits qui partiron pour coloniser Madagascar," wrote a well-known chronicler, "il nous faut du muscle." It is in the colonies, wrote E. M. de Vogué to Colonel Louis Lyautey, that men can find a real field of action, "reforge their head, their heart, their muscles." It is in the sporting clubs, declared Georges de Saint-Clair, that men of action will be trained, "who know how to will, to dare, to venture, organize, govern and be governed." And when we read of "a school for energy and will," it might as well be a rugby enthusiast as a colonialist who used the phrase.[60] So, after 1933, Louis Hémon, the sports enthusiast, left France first for the wilds of Stepney--whence he brought back the quintessential boxing novel, Battling Malone--then for Canada, where he wrote Maria Chapdelaine and was crushed by a train while following the rails through Ontario. And Paul Blanchet, the boy who started the first games at the Lycée Louis-le-Grand in 1889-90, became an explorer and died on an African expedition.

Yet, by the turn of the century, games trained young men less for enterprise than for conformism. It was on this score that Kipling railed at his countrymen who "contented [their] souls/With the flanneled fools at the wicket or the muddied oafs at the goals." And it may be precisely for their power of contenting some souls that anachronistic English recipes appeared exciting. Action, liberation, adventure, and the heroic life were what the colonies seemed to promise. So did sports. Both proposed a way of escape from the drudgery, stultification, and repression of everyday life. Both held out the opportunity to assert oneself, to expend energies little needed or rewarded in the stagnant situation at home. Both reflected a reaction, evident in the little reviews or in the new artistic ventures of the fin de siècle, against an aging, listless way of life, but largely in terms of a fat boy's revolt rather than of a rebellion of the downtrodden.[61] For what the hint is worth, the suicide rate for young people nineteen and under rose faster in the years before 1914 than did that of any other age group and higher than it would do in the next three decades.

A facet of contemporary conditions, then, a footnote for the social history of its time? Yes, but with a difference: "The Greeks trained to adapt themselves to their civilization," wrote Jean Prévost in 1925, praising Les Plaisirs des Sports. "We train to withstand ours."

Footnotes

[1] C. G. Andrae, "Popular Movements in Sweden," Social Science Information, 8, pt. 1 (1969): 75.

[2] In an article in the February 1884 Journal of Education, the author could not understand "that men who know and have tasted the powers and pleasures of play should yet in cold blood drive children into this dead and barren routine." Quoted in P. C. McIntosh, Physical Education in England since 1800 (London, 1968), 58. In the United States, John Dewey omitted gymnastics from his curriculum for the excellent reason that "children do not like it."

[3] Interestingly enough, the major exception that confirms the rule appeared in workers' sporting clubs sponsored after the 1880s by the banned Social-Democrats as front organizations that held the faithful together and helped to collect funds.

[4] And thus evocations--wistful or purposive--of passing or menaced values. Thus, Charles Peguy, speaking of work well done and the sense of workmanship for its own sake among the workers of his youth in the 1880s, compares it to the sporting spirit: "Ce que nous nommons aujourd'hui l'honneur du sport, mais en ce temps-la repandu partout. Non seulement a qui ferait le mieux, mais a qui en ferait le plus, c'etait un beau sport continual, qui etait de toutes les heures, dont la vie meme etait penetree." "L'Argent," in Oeuvres en Prose, 1909-1914 (Paris, 1957), 1051-52.

5 For more detailed discussion of these social and ideological aspects see E. Weber, "Pierre de Coubertin and the Introduction of Sport in France," Journal of Contemporary History, 5 (1970):3-26.

6 Club Alpin Français, presidential address, Apr. 3, 1879, in Annuaire (Paris, 1880), not paginated.

7 Archives départementales (Gironde), Sociétés sportives, unclassified. (Hereafter AD, followed by the name of the French department and the collection.) The name of another walking club, l'Éclair russe, founded at Bordeaux in 1892, commemorated the Franco-Russian Convention that revanchards found so encouraging.

8 Lermusiaux and Tavernier, Pour la Patrie (Paris, 1886). Octave Gréard was vice-rector of the Académie de Paris from 1879 to 1902. Antoine Prost called him the "grey eminence" of all successive ministers of public instruction during this period. L'Enseignement en France, 1800-1967 (Paris, 1968), 224.

9 Paul Gerbod, La Vie quotidienne dans les lycées et les colleges au XIXe siècle (Paris, 1968), 18; AD (Nièvre), Conséil général, Aug. 28, 1869. Compare this with an entry of 1862 in the diary of Edward Thring, the famous headmaster of Uppingham: "I could not help thinking with some pride what headmaster of a great school had ever played a match at football before. Would either dignity or shin suffer for it? I think not." Quoted in David Newsome, Godliness and Good Learning (London, 1961), 220.

10 See Albert Saubeste, L'École Pélégrin (Bordeaux, 1912), 215. The governors of the school felt that "[A workshop] would go much farther than any gymnastics course in satisfying the children's need for movement and physical exercise." Besides, "and above all," such a policy would avoid the risks of training "future mechanics, carpenters and masons" for positions above their station. L'École Pélégrin was an école primare supérieure de garçons.

11 Bulletin de la Société d'Education et d'Enseignement, Dec. 15, 1883; L'Univers, Jan. 27, 1882.

12 The Manuel général de pinstruction primaire, July 22, 1882, described the "ensemble commode et élégant" of Paris detachments participating in July 14 festivities that year as dark blue tunic and trousers and a sailor's cap with a red pompom. It was in this uniform that the apprentice soldiers could be admired by readers of illustrated magazines (see Le Monde Illustré, May 6, 1882), and in a number of paintings exhibited at the salon of 1885. See also Mona Ozouf, L'École, l'Église et la République (Paris, 1963), 126-28.

[13] AD (Gironde), Bataillons scolaires 1881-92; Philippe Tissié, L'Education physique (Paris, 1901), 6. In a less convincing version, a witness told the Royal Commission on Physical Training (1903) that the bataillons had been abandoned because children learned not only drill "but also habits of spitting and swearing in true battack-square manner." P. C. McIntosh, Physical Education in England since 1800 (London, 1968), 151.

[14] For salaries, see Revue des jeux scolaires et d'hygiène sociale, Oct. 1908, pp. 142, 144. Raoul Blanchard (Ma Jeunesse sous Paile de Péguy [Paris, 1961], 147) recalls the occasion in 1896 when Charles Muller, the future author of A la Manière de . . . , presented the ritual good wishes of the cagne of Louis-le-Grand to their gym instructor in a speech ending: "SURSUM CORDA! Tout le monde en haut des cordages," and the instructor's delighted rejoinder: "Bravo, I didn't know that's what it meant." Si non e vero....

[15] Guy Thuillier, "Pour une histoire de l'hygiène corporelle," Revue d'histoire économique et sociale, 46 (1968):233, passim.

[16] See Paul Deroulede, De l'éducation militaire (Paris, 1882). Shortly thereafter, Déroulède himself placed his greatest hopes in the "jeunesse des écoles, gymnastes français, fils d'ouvriers ou de bourgeois, toute la France adolescente et déjà virile. . ." (Le Drapeau, July 14, 1883). Gymnastic societies provided some of the strongest supporters of the Ligue des patriotes, which had been founded in a Paris gymnasium whose owner, Jules Sansboeuf, vice-president of the Association of French Gymnastic Clubs, was one of Déroulède's leading lieutenants in the Ligue.

[17] "Les 'sports athlétiques,' mots nouveaux, mots hostiles et barbares contre lesquels se hérissèrent les préjugés d'un Comité mal informé, enclin a ne retenir de ce terme de 'sport' que son acception vulgaire et déplaisante." Georges Bourdon, La Renaissance athlétique et le Racing Club de France (Paris, 1906), 126. Written by a founder-member of the Racing, Bourdon's book is one of the few authoritative sources for the events of these years.

[18] Revue Blanche, Jan. 1894; Oeuvres de Leon Blum (Paris, 1954), 1:204-06. I am indebted for the indication to Professor Annie Kriegel.

[19] "La Marche, qui se contente de ce substantif quand les personnages qui la cultivent sont de condition moyenne ou inferieure, prend le nom de footing quand ceux qui la pratiquent appartiennent au high-life." Crafty [pesud.], Paris sportif (Paris, 1896), 23. The word rowing was also steadfastly preferred over native terms like aviron or canotage. See categories of that name in Les Sports athlétiques, or even provincial publications like Midi-Football (Toulouse, 1908). The Cyclist Club Lillois, founded in 1803, also bears the mark of English influence.

[20] "Maupassant athlète," La Culture physique, no. 52, Mar. 1907.

21 Pierre de Coubertin, Une Campagne de 21 Ans, 1887-1908 (Paris, 1909), 85; M.-Th. Eyquem, Pierre de Coubertin (Paris, 1966), 59.

22 Le Sport et la Presse (Paris, 1964), 14-35.

23 Incidentally, the Véloce Sport of Bordeaux, organizers of the race, convinced that no man could pedal 572 kilometers at one go, organized a dormitory at Angoulême, 132 kilometers from the state. None of the twenty-eight runners stopped. By September 1891, 211 competitors faced twice the distance: the 1,200-kilometer stretch from Paris to Brest and back. That race was won by Frenchmen.

24 Baudry de Saunier shows an advertisement for a cheap model selling at 375 francs. A good quality model cost fifty francs more. L'Art de bien monter en bicyclette (Paris, 1894), 21.

25 Autobiographical sketch quoted in Jacques Ozouf, Nous les maitres d'école (Paris, 1967), 122-23. A sound social historian, Pierre Pierrard, finds workingmen beginning to use bicycles in 1914. Lille et les Lillois (Paris, 1967), 249.

26 AD (Gironde), Societes sportives, Bordeaux. The Club vélocipédique counted five wholesale merchants, three university professors, a doctor, a dentist, a chief engineer, a builder, and a shopkeeper; Les Cyclistes girondins, presided over by the owner of a bicycle store, listed a printer, six shop assistants, three coiffeurs, and a student, but also a cafetier, a nickeleur, a baker, an ironmonger, a stationer, a sergeant-major, and an armorer-corporal.

27 One may note that in Bordeaux, at any rate, the postmen's union was set up in 1905, eight years after the founding of the cycling club.

28 Relative prices based on figures in Jean Fourastié, Le Grand Espoir du XXe siècle (Paris, 1963), 171. For club memberships, see AD (Gironde), Sociétés sportives, passim. See also the evidence of Henri Desgranges's preface to Marcel Violette, Le Cyclisme (Paris, 1912), x, still clearly addressed to middle-class readers.

29 In 1896 Henri de Toulouse-Lautrec, handy indicator of fashionable trends, produced a lithograph of a driver (his cousin, Tapié de Céleyran, muffled and goggled at the wheel of his automobile) and a sketch of the English champion, Michael, whirling around the track of the Vélodrome Buffalo under the eyes of Frantz Reichel, the athlete. The driver is engaged in a private adventure; the cyclist trains for a public show. But Reichel's presence marks the link between cycling turned into a popular and profitable display and more exclusive sports destined in their turn to provide a public show.

[30] For details of all this, see Bourdon, Renaissance athlétique, 42, passim.

[31] English boys attending private schools in Geneva, Lausanne, and St. Gallen, as well as Swiss graduates of Oxford and Cambridge, established the game in Switzerland before it appeared elsewhere on the Continent: La Chatelaine of Geneva was founded in 1869; the St. Gallen Football Club in 1879; and the Grasshoppers of Zurich in 1886.

[32] See Almanach des Sports, 1899 (Paris, 1899), 420; Almanach des Sports, 1900 (Paris, 1900), 387.

[33] Eyquem, Coubertin, 63; letter of Pierre de Coubertin, Nov. 7, 1892, AD (Gironde), Sociétès sportives (Stade Bordelais).

[34] It was in 1895 that the Rugby Football League broke off from the English Rugby Union on the issue of paying players. Dominant in the Midlands and the north of England, League rugby, with thirteen players, catered to a more working-class public than it did in the southern counties, where the public schools held sway.

[35] Georges de Saint-Clair, Football (Rugby) (Paris, 1894), 20; see also Bourdon, Renaissance athlétique, 248, passim.

[36] See Blanchard, Ma Jeunesse, 112; Jules Isaac, Expériences de ma vie (Paris, 1959), 46, passim. Péguy who had led the Orleans lycée team to victory against its rivals of Chartres in 1891, captained the Lakanal team the following year, playing at fullback.

[37] Albert Bausil and Jean Vidal, Le Rugby Catalan (Perpignan, 1924), 8.

[38] Raoul Fabens, Les Sports pour tous (Paris, 1906), 127.

[39] Edouard Pontie, Le Football Rugby (Paris, 1905), 20. The title suggests that, by this date, the second variant of football had affirmed itself sufficiently to call for clearer definition.

[40] See Pierre Laroque, "Agen ou le modèle d'une équipe," Le Monde, Nov. 25, 1969, p. 17.

[41] See Ernest Seillière, Un Artisan d'énergie française (Paris, 1917); Louis d'Hurcourt, "La Guerre et les Sports," Almanach des Sports, 1899, 35; H. Massis and J. de Tarde [Agathon], Les jeunes gens d'aujourd'hui (Paris, 1913), 35; see also Paul Souchon and Jacques May, La Littérature Sportive contemporaine (Paris, 1924), 10, passim, for other aspects of this mood. The young men whom Massis and de Tarde praised were probably the same we meet in chapter 12 of R. M. du Gard's Jean Barois

(Paris, 1913). They would be exact contemporaries of the École Normale's 1913 "équipe des intellectuels," a xv among whose players were to be found Jean Giraudoux, Alain Fournier, Claude Casimir-Périer, Charles Tardieu, and Alexandre Guinle.

[42] Coubertin, Essais de psychologie sportive (Paris, 1913), 262. Compare in Agathon the young men who declare that sport had given them "the taste of blood" and made them realize that "war was not stupid, cruel and hateful. It was quite simply sport for real." Les jeunes gens, 140-44.

[43] Similarly, Thorstein Veblen, for whom sport helped to preserve "the two most barbarous traits of primitive man: ferocity and cunning," also regarded it as a means of spending excess energy and letting off steam, comparable to war. Theory of the Leisure Class (Boston, 1917), 275, passim.

[44] Etienne de Greeff, Les Instincts de défence et de sympathie (Paris, 1947), 166; Magnane, Sociologie du Sport (Paris, 1964), 43.

[45] Jacques Lecomte, "Jeux des animaux," in Roger Caillois, ed., Jeux et sports (Paris, 1967), 46.

[46] "Dès maintenant, il me semble que l'éducation sportive a préparé notre Emile moderne à être bientôt (en allongeant légèrement la formula anglaise) l'homme convenable et satisfait dans le place qui lui convient.' Ce serait un joli resultat." Georges Rozet, "La Jeunesse et le Sport," in Agathon, Les jeunes gens, 139.

[47] Ibid., 140-44.

[48] Charles de Saint-Cyr, Le Sport, Educateur Social (Paris, 1908), 15-16; J. Dumazedier, Regards neufs sur le sport (Paris, 1950), 29, 161; M. Berger, Pourquoi je suis sportif (Paris, 1939).

[49] For England, see P. C. McIntosh, Sport in Society (London, 1968), 72; for illustrations of the French situation, see J. Ozouf, Nous les maitres, 29, 136.

[50] Report of the Commissaire de Police, Bordeaux, in AD (Gironde), Sociétés sportives (Union régionale gymnastique et sportive).

[51] Bulletin de l'Instruction Primaire (Gironde), Oct. 1910, p. 88. The Union française des Oeuvres laïques d'éducation physique was not formed until 1928.

[52] Maurice Martin, "Un grand sport," Revue philomatique de Bordeaux et du Sud-Ouest, 8 (1905):6.

[53] F. Sauvaire-Jourdan, "Les Sports et les Universités françaises," Revue Internationale de l'Enseignement, Dec. 15, 1913, pp. 3-15; AD (Gironde), Sociétés sportives, unclassified. The seceders never regretted their action. Compare Le BEC, Dec. 23, 1911: "You will not deny that the BEC, being made up of the intellectual élite, is certainly one of the French sports clubs where one finds the fewest cretins."

[54] Les Sports athlétiques, Jan, 10, 1891; Coubertin, Une Campagne, 87.

[55] Bourdon, Renaissance athlétique, 26.

[56] Coubertin, Essais de psychologie sportive, 229. Yet Coubertin was an untiring champion of higher education for workingmen. In 1890 he was proposing the examples of English university extension courses. In the early 1920s he preached universités ouvrières. See, for example, his Entre deux batailles (Paris, 1922).

[57] Compare F. Lagrange: "If our schoolboys get exercise, our students no longer do, any more than our young office employees or shop assistants." L'Exercise chez les adultes (Paris, 1897), 3. Class recruitment appears even more clearly in the beginnings of women's athletics and sports. See M.-Th. Eyquem, La Femme et le Sport (Paris, 1944). The first sportives were titled amazons like General Boulanger's early sponsor, the Duchesse d'Uzès, or Madame Camille du Gast. Their activities were of a costly and exclusive sort: car and boat races, tennis, fencing (in a special ladies' gymnasium, chez Madame Gabrielle), mountain climbing like Andrée Berthelot, or flying like Marie Marvingt.

[58] Newsome, Godliness and Good Learning, 198, 201.

[59] Royal Commission on Physical Training for Scotland (London, 1903), Minute 9628.

[60] Aurelien Scholl, in Almanach des Sports, 1899, ii; Louis Lyautey, Lettres de Tonkin et de Madagascar (Paris, 1921), 621 (Oct. 2, 1898); see also the revealing quotations in W. B. Cohen, "The Lure of Empire: Why Frenchmen Entered the Colonial Service," Journal of Contemporary History, 4, pt. 1 (1969):103-16; Bourdon, Renaissance athlétique, 119; and Martin, "Grand Sport," 7.

[61] For the same story as reflected in the literary activities of the time, see E. Weber, "The Secret World of Jean Barois," in John Weiss, ed., The Origins of Modern Consciousness (Detroit, 1965).

Sport And Cultural Hegemony

Phillip K. Shinnick

The current literature on sport and culture raises the following questions: What is culture? Is there high culture? Is sport culture? What is the difference between work and leisure/play/sport? What is the difference between primitive sport and industrialized sport?[1] Is sport art?[2] Is sport reflective or representative of culture?

I see certain methodological problems with the traditional structural/functionalist approach which looks into the bowels of a society to determine the integration, maintenance, adaptation, and goal attainment of a particular function. A critical analysis starts with the fundamental awareness of the organic lives of people who live and work in a particular society or culture. This departure is necessary not only for the development of a humanistic approach to the questions, but, also, without this fundamental starting point people may well be left out as well as any historical understanding. People have always had their culture but certain classes of people have had more culture in the traditional definition of access to leisure than others, at the expense and exploitation of others.

The amount of culture that was physical--or simply physical culture--has changed with the historical relationships between classes and the dominant form of economic survival. A form of football can be traced to the third and fourth century B.C. in China. Records exist through several dynasties, and at the late part of the Sung dynasty (960 - 1279 A.D.) an aristocrat's mirror depicted football playing. A painting shows Emperor Taitsu (Sung) playing football with his ministers.[3] René Maheu stated that "in modern civilization, the artists and the intellectuals have not managed to master sport and incorporate it in their work."[4] Although Maheu does acknowledge that his discussion of sport and culture is ahistorical and aimed at contemporary sport, nevertheless historically sport has been a subject of art and enjoyed as a part of physical culture and is so today.[5]

A critical analysis of physical culture and sport will provide a framework which does not have the pitfalls of the structuralist-functionalist approach. Functionalism becomes an analysis of the status quo and sports function within that given structure. Theoretically this: a) leaves people outside the main thrust of the analysis, and b) doesn't illuminate the possibility of creating a new culture based upon a critical and class analysis of what exists. A critical analysis is dialectical, historical, and material.

A critical analysis of physical culture and sport cannot separate theory from practice because within a critical analysis are the seeds for practice. A critical analysis:

a) does not leave out the organic link between work and play. [People take their bodies with them, the organic self absorbs tension, is shaped by, gets energy from or has energy taken from both work and play. There is a dialectic between a person and the world--a direct organic line.]

b) cannot separate the instruments of class rule during a particular period of history from sport and culture. [Primitive, feudal, pre-industrial, industrial and post-industrial periods all determine the role of sport and physical culture in people's lives and changes according to historical class relationships.]

and

c) understands that universal values hide contradictions within a social system and the universal values in sport hide class exploitation and domination.

In praxis the questions become: Do we have a right to change our culture?[6] How have cultural revolutions changed the relationship between sport and certain social classes?[7] Answers to questions of practice come from, a) ideals of justice and equality and the distribution of culture and products of production; b) human physical needs to remain alive and creative and the negation of a death culture; c) an understanding of the material conditions (mode of production, relations in production) of a society and international capital and monopolies. Implicit in critical analysis is a recognition of the pleasure of sport, the desire for quality social relations, and a physical understanding of one's organic self. The right to make judgements and act is the realization of knowledge in its organic manifestation.

Theory

A)   Sport, culture or peoples' lives cannot be separated from the material base of existence organically, economically, or politically. Specifically the types of relationships within work and the amount of energy expended at work, all determine the time available for physical culture. For example, if an individual is in a social situation on a continual basis that is controlled not by that individual but by forces beyond that individual's control, and this activity consumes the majority of the day, then this social situation will condition the individual for physical passivity. And if an individual expends all of his or her energy on social labor, there will be little opportunity for physical culture.

Idealists will categorize work and play as two separate intellectual categories and make generalizations as if some people did not have more time available for leisure than others. Football in the Sung dynasty is a good example. Landowners had time for culture, a time afforded by the energy of peasants/chattels. City aristocrats may have played tennis during leisure two thousand years ago at the expense of working people. In South Africa today elites have time to play tennis and one hundred and twenty times more resources are put into elite (White) sportspeople than workers' (Black) sport.

The appreciation of art or culture is very much dependent upon the development of the human organic senses. Discussion of high culture or low culture should not separate the human subjective capacity because "the sense of an object...goes only so far as my senses go."[8] This goes hand in hand with the development of aesthetic education and without this aesthetic education the consumption of the object will be of a commercial type and lack the recreation in the activity of art consumption. Sports with no mass base for organic sense development will narrow the range of enjoyment of objects and the intensity of that richness.

The relations a person has with other people at work is not unlike social relations at play or in sport. The social relations in post-industrial societies become more rational and bureaucratic and these values and behavior permeate the social relations within sport.[9] Football in the United States, with its specialization and division of labor and authority centered control in team situations, is a good example. Marx clarifies these relations as follows:

"The totality of these relations of production constitute the economic structure of society--the real foundation in which legal and political suprastructure arise and to which definite forms of social consciousness correspond. The mode of production of material life determine the general character of the social, political and spiritual processes of life. It is not the consciousness of men that determine their being, but, on the contrary, their social being determine their consciousness."[10]

The first principle in discussing culture is the physical, living human individual and the ways in which humans produce their subsistence and the existing social situation inherited from the historical mode of production and the relations of production. Along with this material heritage is the suprastructure which reinforces these material forces into art, sport, music, religion, education, the judicial system, the civil service in general. The question should be asked: Who owns the production process and to whose best interest does it serve? In examining these relations, sport becomes clearer and assumes the material relations which form the production process.

The ideology of sport serving the interest of commodity production in the cultural process can best be seen from a class analysis.

B)   The dominant values and ideas of the aristocrats in history were honor, loyalty, etc. Because of their class ruling position, these values permeated the culture and suprastructure. As the bourgeois became dominant, concepts of individualism, consumption, competition came into prominence because of the class position of the bourgeois. The expansion of these values in sport will be explored under universal values below but the key to the understanding of class rule is the private ownership of the products of production and of the distribution of those goods among the people. Sport had a particular importance here because culture and sport historically have been very much a part of class rule. The peasant in China had a different sport experience than the aristocrats, as does the black in South Africa in relation to the whites.

It may be argued that cultural values are autonomous from the dominant means of production and to some extent this is true. Working people have always attempted to maintain their own cultural games and heritage but the dominant class has concomitantly attempted to co-op this culture. Sport was a part of voluntary associations in England within the working class in the nineteenth century. Sport had a cultural dimension to it at that time, largely controlled by local voluntary associations but these games were expropriated by privately owned professional sport teams.[11] This could also be said about the lower Eastside of Manhattan during the turn of the century and the development of Jewish street games. Within the consciousness of socialist labor activity in the street, street games went on. These games were expropriated by the parks and recreation department of the city which colonized sport with Christian values and organized playgrounds to discipline the recent immigrants for labor.[12]

Commodity production through reification of the individual as an object, does not provide ideological encouragement for physical culture but in fact promotes mass passivity because labor is recruited as a consumer. The commercialization of sport not only encourages such commodity fetish, by buying and selling (exchanges) athletes as objects by private individuals, but recruits these same general workers as passive consumers to extract surplus income from the accumulation of capital. This capital, instead of being used for the health of the workers in public facilities for physical culture, is turned against the worker in the form of ideological propaganda for the pleasure ideal of consumption and for performance standards needed in the exploitation of capitalism.[13]

Particularly hidden beneath the functionalist or nonmaterialist-idealist approach to sport and culture are: a) the relationship between classes of people, b) the exploitive relationship between individual people, and c) the individual disregard for the physical body, as an idealized object or thing to be used to gain wages. Critical theory is important to expose the private ownership of social processes and how culture is affected by this relationship. I have already discussed the unequal distribution of sport and culture among classes and the exploitation of sport for commodity production and now it is necessary to develop the concept of the state and show how it maintains domination for the distribution of rights to cultural activities and the enjoyment of production objects. The state and civil society are extensions of bourgeois hegemony for the protection of private property and reflect the class in which it is based.[14] John Hargreaves puts this relationship as follows:

> It is important to bring out the central issue which the approaches so far reviewed tend to obfuscate, namely, the question of whether sporting institutions and sports consciousness under capitalism tend to foster social relations and ideological influences conducive to, or inimical

to, or simply irrelevant to the development of working class organization and consciousness. On the available evidence, such as it is, there is a case for concluding that sport has a conservatizing influence on the working class.[15]

At times sport has been a conservatizing influence for bourgeois rule and other times there has been direct manipulation to discipline labor as happened in the turn of the century. The spirit of early bourgeois society was deeply antithetical to play.[16] Popular amusement and sport were suppressed in the name of sobriety and for blocking businesses and also to discipline labor. The Wigs and then the Republican party tried to block these activities through first, ideological scolding and then when the working people fought back, political action. In the mid-nineteenth century, the bourgeois also crusaded against gambling and for strict observance of the sabbath.[17] This took on the overtones of both class and ethnic conflict.

In amateur sport the operation and administration has been controlled by the middle-class because of the material necessity to have excess income in order to administer sport. In the Amateur Athletic Union of the United States people volunteer their time. By the relationship of sport administration to sport, the value of the bourgeois become commonplace. The military in the United States is also a big supporter of sports as are police leagues in large cities. The U. S. President's Commission on Olympic Sports wants athletes to be objects for advertisers in exchange for Olympic support from business.[18]

It is through the sports structure, the structure of the authoritarian family and other cultural social relations, the dominant social order is cemented into the consciousness of the working people in commodity production. Commodity production type of mass culture promotes social relations to take on the character of relations between things. This of course hides the true nature of the social relationships and the contradictions within the process. For example, as mass sport becomes more of an opiate, concomitantly, the nature of people's relationship with their bodies is being subordinated to the reification process of commercialized sport. It absorbs like a social regulator, tensions arising out of everyday life and deflects "frustrations which might otherwise actualize themselves in opposition to the system into channels which serve the system."[19]

Ruling class ideas are "nothing more than the ideal expression of the dominant material relationships, the dominant material relationships grasped as ideas: ...the ideas of its dominance."[20] Since the ruling class has dominance over the material products or production they also have a dominance over the intellectual ideas. There is also a regulation and distribution of ideas and the analysis of sport and culture no less has this class bias. The separation of mental from material labor is such an example and the analysis of sport and physical culture ignores the material aspects of a person's life and instead projects intellectual categories which are abstract to the organic consideration of people. This can be seen in the functionalist or the metaphysical approach to sport.[21] But what are these universal values which the ruling class perpetuates through control of the state apparatus and civil society which cover up the conflicting interests between labor and capital?

C)   In the marketplace, according to bourgeois ideology, market competition functions within the context of a set of rules, like all competitions, otherwise buyers and sellers would not know what was permitted and what was not.[22] It is a rule before bourgeois democracy that all are equal before the law and the rules are objective, thereby ignoring the high price of legal justice and the international market's influence which determine prices as much as supply or demand. The rules are fair and a good sportsperson plays according to the rules. This is a universal value in sport. A good sport doesn't question the rules just as a good citizen doesn't question the rules of the economic or political system--this you must do to be responsible. Loyalty to the leader (and group) within a given context of an authoritarian relationship is a universal value. It is by identifying with the greater whole that the individual discovers his personal worth. The cult of hero worship and the personality of the leader is a bourgeois value which has clear implications in sport. The maintenance of self-esteem through the identification to cultural symbols is exploited by the bourgeois for class domination.[24] This identification covers up personal achievement possible under the limitations of capitalism, the unequal distribution of wealth, and the struggle against and understanding of historical relationships inherited.

Commodity satisfaction as a general value hides the problems of distribution but is pushed by the elites. Hidden is the true organic relationship to sport that most people have as passive consumers and the ailments associated with physical passivity. Leisure activity is permeated by this consumption ethics in sport and is used as a means to expand capitalist production through leisure time products to be consumed by workers. Recreational equipment should be available to working people for their consumption enjoyment, but again the question should be asked: Who gets this equipment and who has access to recreational facilities?

"Not until the late stages of industrial civilization, when the growth of production threatens to overflow the limits set by repressive domination, has the technique of mass manipulation developed an entertainment industry which directly controls leisure time, or has the state directly taken over the enforcement of such controls."[25] These manipulations are more obtuse than early capitalist manipulation. With the rise of the mass media manipulation becomes a consciousness industry.[26] Bourgeois rule stopped with abstract freedom because concretely the distribution problem underpinned abstract freedom. The mass media also hides this contradiction and instead pushes another abstract version of freedom which is individual based. The real gratification of people cannot be realized through such a hidden facade, a new culture must put forth as a demand the transformation of the material conditions of life, "for a new form of labor and of enjoyment."[27] Culture to the bourgeois "means not so much a better world as a nobler one, a world to be brought about not through the overthrow of the material order of life but through events in the individual's soul."[28]

A critical analysis of culture and sport within the framework of commodity production can only be realized through critical theory and the practice of that theory. To be subjects of history rather than objects of domination it is encumbent upon people to regenerate themselves beyond their historical bonds. Regeneration in sport has to be organic or it becomes an abstraction of bourgeois freedom with no material base.

Practice

Physical culture is a difficult concept to comprehend if the physical conditions are such that the very existence of physical culture is an unknown and sport is part of visual display with no organic base in the physical activities of an individual.[29] But the dialectical relationship that exists between people's experiences and utopian idealism (or socialism) are what makes praxis a synthesis for those who try to understand the contradictions which exist between one's own experiences and the hope for something different. Utopian idealism is a tradition of critical theory and becomes revolutionary when people see what exists in less abstract ways and use critical theory to negate what exists and create new relationships. Or, put another way, bourgeois thought does not account for the daily contradictions that are experienced. Critical theory is a weapon to create physical culture by recognizing the contradictions which exist between different classes of people, within a person's life and between nations in colonial or imperialistic relationships.

A)   Local sport can be autonomously controlled, and in many ways continues as long as that activity does not threaten hegemonous rule or there are no plans for expropriation into the dominant cultural form. Cultural monopolies and the mass media have made it hard for subaltern pockets to exist. Professional sport, the cultural equivalent to commodity production, has influenced the society to such an extent that cities are spending millions to bring professional sport to the masses to hide the contradiction of urban life.

No better example exists than the 1976 renovation of Yankee Stadium in the South Bronx of the United States (New York) for an estimated cost of 120 million dollars while the Park Department of the City of New York budget was cut by 14 million dollars, from 66 to 52 million dollars. The South Bronx looks like a city laid in waste by a war. The stadium is a monument to behold in a sea of capitalist carnage of urban plight. The city high school programs in physical culture and sport and the public school Athletic League was cut from the school program at the time of the Yankee renovation. In New Jersey, which has had one of the highest unemployment figures of any state in the United States, millions of dollars have been spent on a sports complex for professional football and horse racing while social services and education were cut. New Jersey needed an image.

Sport and culture cannot be separated from social decisions which determine the roles different workers are to assume during their leisure activity. The question remains: How are cultural services distributed and who do they ultimately service? The answer to this is painfully clear, sport is a part of commodity production and the entertainment industry. Struggles are being waged within that process to buffer some of the more flagrant abuses of human beings in the process. There is a two line struggle going on within professional sport and players are winning rights in the process and federal regulation has changed some of the more blatant tax loopholes for professional teams, but the new television contract for 1978 means revenue for each team of over 5 million dollars in the National Football League.

The South African situation is a problem of distribution of cultural rights and access to that culture. This becomes a similar problem for working people in all capitalist countries and sport should be seen as a people's right.

B)   Radical cultural critics have pointed out the problems of distribution of cultural facilities and some other critics of culture, such as Christopher Lasch, have in turn criticized the radical position as attempting to do away with excellence.[30] Access to the "higher things" of culture implies a development of a sensibility for appreciation and without a mass base for sport the process of spectator/superathletes takes on a demented dimension. The superstar becomes the surrogate body of the fan who projects on the player the performance principles of hegemony and consumes the person as an object, fitting into categories of percentage decimals or the win-loss column. The narrowing of the appreciation of sport as an art into hero worship is not only deadly for the person in relationship to his own body, but a false consciousness develops that athletes are really heroes and not the people who through their human energy make the system work.

A radical critic of sport does not mean that excellence shouldn't be pursued, it does mean that the contradiction of who gets access to sport has to be overcome as a material value of equality. Equality does not mean just equal access to ticket rights to a mass spectacle.[31] Do people have a right to sport? The Cuban constitution spells out this right, the Chinese sport system promotes sport among the workers, and other socialist countries likewise promote equal rights among working people to actively participate in sport of physical culture to improve the quality of life.

It is the reduction of sport and culture to economics and politics that bring it from high abstraction and culture to the "level of those which adhere more closely to the structure itself--in other words, the possibility and necessity of creating a new culture."[32]

The development of a new culture has in it the real possibility of enjoyment without guilt or rationalization, and the body is at the center of that feeling because the body is where the feelings of pleasure originate. "True theory recognizes the misery and lack of happiness prevailing in the established order."[33] The consciousness industry (mass media, etc.) manipulates the leisure of working people for total mobilization toward ideal pleasure and beauty isolated within a given time. The setting apart from the material lives of people and making a separate cultural "beautification time" acknowledges a perpetuation of the historical conditions. Culture should be promoted among all people, art, sport, and games, and put at the disposal of all people.

C)   International hegemony is a thing which brings the South African situation into focus. International capital has international class interests between nations. Investments in South Africa by both the United States and England spread to mutual interests to promote South Africa in the international culture of sports competition.[34] International hegemony works to include, as in South Africa, or to exclude as is the case of the People's Republic of China in the Olympic Games. The International Olympic Committee has class ties to the bourgeois--and to some extent the old aristocrats. China poses a threat to this hegemony and through a series of political moves China was excluded from the Olympic games. Avery Brundage, through manipulations of the executive board of the International Olympic Committee and the general assembly of the I.O.C., was able to exclude China from the Olympics. Within the United States, U. S. Congressman Melvin Laird, through threats to withdraw military engineering support for the 1960 Olympic Games in Squaw Valley, put pressure on the I.O.C. to stop China's participation in the Olympic Games; a conflict between bourgeois politics and socialist politics. Anti-communism has been a pervasive theme of international and national politics within the United States for forty years.[35]

In England a Sports Council has been formed to subsidize sport associations to promote sport. On the one hand there is the move to control or "help to avert social...ills"[36] and on the other, internationally to promote sport for hegemonous international events. A recent President's Commission on Olympic Sport (1977) is concerned about the failure of the United States athletes to win medals in the Olympic Games and the threat of the socialist countries in international competition. Nationalism plays hand in glove with the entrepreneurs of sport.

Footnotes

[1] Lüschen, G., "The Interdependence of Sport and Culture," _International Review of Sport Sociology_, 2:127-142, 1967. The methodological problem with the structuralist and/or functionalist approach is that theory is not united with practice and the analysis becomes idealistically descriptive. Nothing changes except the interworkings of the ongoing status quo system.

[2] Maheu, René, "Sport and Culture," _International Journal of Adult and Youth Education_, 14:129-178, 1962. Formal expression sometimes hides the true nature of things. For example, such concepts as eternal value, inherent nature of things, style, abstract act, nobility, universality, ethics, moral value, brotherhood obfuscate class conflict and bourgeois hegemony. These idealistic categories hide the organic process which exists in the working lives of people. Maheu attempts to unfold the body in relationship to art but not to the production process.

[3] K. K. "Football Game on a Bronze Mirror of Sung," in _Eastern Horizon_, Vol. XVI, No. 11, November, 1977, p. 48. "Football also becomes a theme for decoration on articles of art, like the mirror quoted above and pottery."

[4] Maheu, p. 174.

[5] Lowe, Benjamin, _The Beauty of Sport: A Cross-disciplinary Inquiry_. Englewood Cliffs, New Jersey: Prentice-Hall, Inc., 1977, pp. 138-168.

6 Lasch, Christopher, "The Corruption of Sports," in: New York Review, April 28, 1977. Lasch calls – "emphasize the value of sports as health giving exercise, and promote a more 'cooperative' conception of athletics" – personal and social therapy. Why is a bodily activity categorized as therapy when therapy has traditionally been associated with the mind? The mind/body split has plagued academics since the bourgeois control of the distribution of ideas. Some of the activities of physical culture have philosophical roots to Taoism and the concept of Chi. Chi is energy flow. One aspect of the philosophy, the dialectic of Yin/Yang, is much better analytically than the idealist separation of mind/body. Left radicals call for more physical culture and sport not just sport. Physical culture is not opposed to competition because physical culture is of a different kind than sport. They are different philosophically but not physically. Wu Shu has hand to hand mock combat in dance form. There is movement, expression, intensity, and form. Intensity (energy flow) to physical culture is similar to excellence in sport.

7 Shinnick, Phillip, "The Chinese Sport System" in: Sport Sociology Bulletin, Fall, 1976 and "Are Superstars Really Necessary?" in New China, Spring, 1977. Since the peasants were the revolutionary force in the 1948 Chinese Revolution and came to class power, the private ownership of the means of production changed. The cultural revolution established workers' culture since the material relations in production had changed and culture did not have to serve narrow class interests. Social relations in production and culture change dialectically in both directions. In China's case, the YMCA, YWCA influenced the type of games now enjoyed by workers. Through this semi-colonial relationship, cultural China is in a position to play other nations in volleyball, basketball, swimming, track and field, soccer, etc. because of mass sport, but the international hegemony of the oligarchy of the International Olympics Committee will not permit China in the Olympics. One of the reasons given is that the state should not be involved in sport. The other socialist countries in the Olympics are exceptions to their own rule. The right-wing National Olympic Committee fled Peking for Taiwan in post-liberation days and is now recognized by the I.O.C. A United States citizen, Avery Brundage, lobbied to keep Communist China out of the Olympics because of class interest and hegemony.

8 Mescaros, Istvan, Marx's Theory of Alienation. New York: Harper and Row, 1970. (Marx on the Jewish Question), p. 210.

9 Ingham, Alan, "The Rationalization of Sport" (coauthored by Guroeep Singh) in: Donald Ball and John Loy, Sport and Social Order: Contributions to the Sociology of Sport. Reading, Massachusetts: Addison-Wesley, 1975.

10 Bottomore, T. B. and Maximilien Rubel, Karl Marx Selected Writings in Sociology and Social Philosophy. Middlesex, England: Penguin Harmondworth, 1961, pp. 67-68.

[11] Yeo, Stephen, English Associations of Working Men in the Nineteenth and Twentieth Century. Davis Center Seminar, Princeton University, May 31, 1975. Unpublished. This control fluctuated from 1840 until recently with the establishment of a Sports Council in England.

[12] Goodman, Gary, Choosing Sides: Labor, Capital and Organized Play. Doctoral Dissertation, Union Graduate School. Unpublished 1977.

[13] Hoch, Paul, Rip Off the Big Game: The Exploitation of Sport by the Power Elite. New York: Anchor Books, 1972. Performance standards are also vehicles for excellence in sport but when these standards become pervasive and narrow the multi-dimensioned ideals of cultural richness give way to fetishness.

[14] Gramsci, Antonio, Prison Notebooks. New York: International Publishers, 1973, pp. 216, 269. "Negatively, middle class means nonpopular, i.e. those not workers or peasants; positively, it means the intellectual strata, the professional strata, the public employees." p. 216. "at all events, the fact that the State/government, conceived as an autonomous force, should reflect back its prestige upon the class upon which it is based, is of the greatest practical and theoretical importance, ... it can, it seems, be incorporated into the function of elites or vanguards, i.e. of parties, in relation to the class which they represent. This class, often, as an economic fact (which is what every class is essentially) might not enjoy an intellectual or moral prestige, i.e. might be incapable of establishing its hegemony, hence of founding a State."

[15] Hargreaves, John, "Mass Sport and Ideological Hegemony," Revision of a paper in S. Parker, et al, eds., Sport and Leisure in Contemporary Society, BSA Studies in Sociology, 13 Endsleigh Street, London WCI, p. 4.

[16] Lasch, p. 27.

[17] Ibid., p. 26.

[18] The Final Report of the President's Commission on Olympic Sports, Vol. I and Vol. II, 1 U. S. Government Printing Office, Washington, D.C. "Corporate avtivity in this area is good for the company and its employees. At a time when business and labor are under increasing scrutiny and our private sector institutions are attempting to make the public understand their raison d'etre, what is a more unifying force than activity in amateur sport? Instead of spending millions of dollars to explain our economic system to the public, companies could financially adopt national governing bodies, fund developmental programs, or hire athletes as bona fide employees but give them some time off to train with pay. The labor force would certainly be proud of 'their' athlete, providing any potential labor problems are worked out beforehand." p. 80, Vol. I.

"Many of the markets can be penetrated if the sports goals are matched with the marketing goals of the corporation." p. 81, Vol. I.

"If amateur sports wish to generate significant funds from the private sector, it will be effected only by demonstrating the potential return on investment to business, industry and labor. Private enterprise is not in business for philanthropic reasons." p. 82, Vol. I.

[19] Oronowitz, Stanley, The Shaping of Working Class Consciousness. New York: McGraw-Hill, 1973, p. 54.

[20] Marx, Karl and Frederick Engels. The German Ideology edited by C. J. Arthur. New York: International Publishers, 1974, p. 65.

[21] Weiss, Paul, Sport: A Philosophic Inquiry. Carbondale, Illinois: Southern Illinois University Press, 1969.

[22] Hargreaves, p. 13.

[23] Ibid., p. 15.

[24] Becker, Ernest, The Structure of Evil: An Essay On the Unification of the Science of Man. New York: Brazeller, 1968, pp. 332-333.

[25] Marcuse, Herbert, Eros and Civilization. New York: Vantage Books, 1962, p. 43.

[26] Gouldner, Alvin, The Dialectic of Ideology and Technology. New York: Seaburgy Press, 1976. See chapter seven on "Ideology, the Cultural Apparatus, and the New Consciousness Industry." See also Jurgen Habermas, Theory and Practice. Boston: Beacon Press, 1973, p. 195. Mas Tse-Tung, "On Practice" in Four Essays on Philosophy, Foreign Language Press, 1968. "If you want to know a certain thing or certain class of things directly, you must personally participate in the practical struggle to change reality, to change that thing or class of things, for only thus can you come into contact with them as phenomena..." p. 8.

[27] Marcuse, Negations. Boston: Beacon Press, 1969, p. 100.

[28] Ibid., p. 103.

[29] Shinnick, Phillip, "A Critical Analysis of Capitalist Physical Culture and Sport." An unpublished paper prepared for a Sports for the People "Sportsfest," 1977, p. 22.

[30] Lasch.

[31] An organization has formed with the help of seed money from Ralph Nader to investigate purchase of tickets and prices, food distribution and other consumer rights. F.A.N.S. attempts to democratize the production/consumption process away from private decisions.

[32] Gramsci, p. 276.

[33] Marcus, Negations. p. 118.

[34] Lapchick, Richard, The Politics of Race and International Sport: The Case of South Africa. Westport, Connecticut: Greenwood Press, 1975. See also Joan Brickhill, "Race Against Race: South Africa's 'Multinational' Sport Fraud," International Defense and Aide Fund, London, England, 1976.

[35] The issue has historical roots in the move of certain Olympic Committee officials from Peking to Taiwan after the Chinese revolution in 1948 and the separate recognition of Taiwan by the I.O.C. after their move and Avery Brundage's special friendships with these officials.

[36] Hargreaves, p. 24.

Section 2

OLYMPISM

Introduction

The Games of the XXI Olympiad of the modern era were held in Montreal in 1976, some eighty years after the first of the modern Olympic Games took place in Athens. There were twenty-one sports listed on the official Montreal programs. However, the most popular sports event was not to be found on any of the entry lists. Almost every nation entered in the Games participated in varying degrees in this particular event before the Games in Montreal ended. No medals were awarded and no national anthems were played for the winners; there were no formal rules and regulations to govern play. Yet this special sport commanded more attention around the world and in the media than any other sporting event. The name of this game, which assumed a variety of forms? Politics, of course. Politics have always been a part of the Olympic Movement, even from its inception, something which many have chosen to ignore.

The Montreal Games opened with the Taiwan issue. Canada, the host country, became the first host nation ever to bar another member of the Olympic Movement from entering the Games. The Canadian government refused to grant visas to 43 athletes from the Republic of China (ROC), unless they agreed to forsake the name and flag of the ROC and to compete under the designation Taiwan. Canadian Prime Minister Elliot Trudeau and External Affairs Minister Allan MacEachen refused to yield to pressures by Lord Killanin, President of the International Olympic Committee (IOC). Official Canadian foreign policy since 1970 had been to discourage all official contact with the ROC and to cultivate better relations with the Peoples Republic of China. Canada had recognized the PRC in 1970 and at the same time served ties with Taipei. The IOC accused the Canadian government of breach of faith, since one of the preconditions for hosting the Games is the promise by the host organizing committee to the supreme sports body in the Olympic Movement, the IOC, that all members of the IOC will be admitted. Despite several attempts at negotiation, the Nationalist Chinese ultimately rejected a compromise solution offered by the IOC which would have permitted them to march under the IOC banner. Instead, they departed for home.

What began as a Chinese-Canadian dispute became more complicated with the entrance of the United States into the fray on the side of Taiwan. President Ford urged American Olympic officials to attempt to influence the IOC decision. Philip Krumm, President of the United States Olympic Committee threatened to withdraw the American delegation, a move which would have seriously weakened the Games and have resulted in the departure of ABC television. The latter's payments for broadcasting rights were the sole source of income for the IOC, and a major source for the organizing committee in Montreal. The United States did not carry out its threat of a walkout, but the affair seriously strained U.S.-Canadian diplomatic relations.

Meanwhile, the Peoples Republic of China, a spectator on the sidelines due to its own refusal to compete as long as the ROC was admitted to the Games and remained a member of the IOC, accused the Soviet Union of supporting the ROC bid and of working in collusion with Taiwan.

This episode was just a warmup. The next few days brought a walkout by 28 African countries along with Guyana and Iraq to protest the continuance of sports contacts between New Zealand and the Republic of South Africa. The immediate catalyst was the tour of South Africa by a rugby team from New Zealand. Led by Tanzania, the Africans argued that not only commercial and political, but also sports links helped strengthen the apartheid regime of South Africa and give it respectability. Ever since the Supreme Council for Sport in Africa had been formed in 1962, the African countries had been fighting to ban the white racist regimes of southern Africa from competing in the Games. South Africa did not compete in 1964, and threats of a boycott in Mexico in 1968 and in Munich in 1972 kept South Africa and then Rhodesia out of the Games. (Cheffers, 1972). New Zealand refused to withdraw from the Games in Montreal or to make any public statements indicating a change in policy. Rather, it was emphasized that rugby was a non-Olympic sport and that sports organizations in New Zealand were autonomous. Tanzania therefore withdrew. Mauritius followed. Nigeria, Uganda and Zambia joined in, and one by one the other African nations withdrew their delegations from Montreal. The absences were evident in the opening ceremonies on July 17th. Never before had so many countries walked out of the Games.

With this brief opening commentary on events associated with the most recent of the Olympic Games, it is salutory to recall a few words by Baron Pierre de Coubertin:

> The aims of the Olympic Movement are to promote the development of those fine physical and moral qualities which are the basis of amateur sport and to bring together the athletes of the world in a great quadrennial festival of sports thereby creating international respect and goodwill and thus helping to construct a better and more peaceful world. (Cited in Olympism, Lausanne; International Olympic Committee, n.d.) p. 1.

Modern sport is a process formed as a result of the political and technological factors covered in Sections 1 and 2 of this anthology. The ideology of sport, however, has been dominated by "Olympism." Olympism is a curious combination of Greek mythology and nineteenth century English public (private) school philosophy which extrapolates societal goals from perceived benefits of athletic contest. Baron Pierre de Coubertin, a French educator, served as catalyst in a process which created transnational organization dedicated to "sportsmanship" and human development.

There are three issues to be kept in mind concerning Olympism:

(1) the contrast between ideology and history in the origins of the Olympic Movement.

(2)   the distinction between Olympic mythology and Olympic organization in relation to the political content of sport,
(3)   the relative importance of individuals and of institutions they created in the evolution of political sport.

How is it that Olympians have been successful in creating the impression that transnational sport is somehow outside the "politics" of the international system? Much of the answer lies in the <u>claim</u> to remain outside politics--on the part of athletes, Olympic officials, and many spectators as well. It is easy to ignore the foundations of political sport in favor of the excitement of athletic celebration. When such events as the Olympic Games draw attention to obvious connections between political foundations and political action, apologists simply dismiss such events as aberrations, or look with nostalgia upon the legend that there once were international sports events unfettered by politics.

This "head-in-sand" attitude is ironic, considering the political importance accorded the ancient Games. Wars may have been stopped during Olympic celebration, but only to allow the Games to carry out politics by other means. Olympic victors provided not only prestige for their cities, but also a way to rally public support for community policies. Aegina, for example, may have perceived the growing threat from Athens, but it had enough athletic victors in order for Pindar to write odes comforting to the declining political spirit.

While modern Olympicans deny any cultural bias or national favoritism, the ancient Games were fervently religious and ethnically exclusive. Coubertin may have appealed to all the states of the "World" (meaning Europe, its dependencies, and North America), but the ancients had no inclination to allow barbarians to compete, at least while the Games--and Greece--were at their height.

There were those, such as J. Ashley Cooper, who drew from the lesson of Greece and sought to limit the participants of transnational sport on an ethnic basis. In 1892 Cooper ("An Anglo-Saxon Olympiad," <u>The Nineteenth Century</u>, XXXII, #187, September, 1892:380-388) suggested that an "Olympiad" should be limited to the Anglo-Saxon peoples. In place of religion, Cooper would have substituted periodic business and trade fairs to complement sports celebration.

In an international sense, sports were basically apolitical as long as they were conducted by the English upper class on a club basis. As soon as the International Olympic Committee came into being on June 23, 1894, sport changed its character radically. The IOC, with its claims to internationalism, independence and moralism, injected itself into the realm of politics. Indeed, the IOC was born in political intrigue surrounding the personal machinations of de Coubertin, and so could hardly avoid political involvement.

To the initial meeting in 1894, Coubertin invited only those who were in agreement with his ideas and were sure to vote with him. In addition, he' added a number of people to his Committee who were not even present in Paris, but whose international status was useful to the newly founded Olympic

Movement. The politics of participation, of designation of delegations and of flags to be flown, was part of the Olympics from that day on.

No German was named to the original Committee, perhaps a result of ongoing Franco-German hostility. Needing more support for his project in Central Europe, however, Coubertin nominated Willibald Gebhart to the IOC in 1895.

Even though Coubertin has selected his group with considerable care, all did not go smoothly at the founding IOC meeting. Coubertin wanted to begin the modern Olympic calendar in Paris in 1900. The majority of the IOC, however, resisted this motion in favor of Greece. The ancient Olympic country received the honor of the First Olympiad, scheduled for Athens in 1896. A Greek, Demetrius Bikelas was named to serve as IOC President until 1896, when Coubertin would assume the post. In the meantime he became general secretary, which in his own words was a position "more interesting than that of the President, since it meant control of the level of administration." (Scherer, 1974, p. 101.)

As Coubertin relates, there was significant opposition in Greece to the award. The Prime Minister, Chariaos Trikoupes, felt that the country simply could not afford the show. He was supported by members of the Zappaion Commission, the organization responsible for the administration of the ancient Hellenic stadium. The President of the Commission, Etienne Dragoumis, advised Coubertin to stay home, as he was not welcome in Athens.

Coubertin, however, did go to Greece, where he used his considerable political skill in alliance with the Crown Prince Constantine to secure domestic approval of the Games. By the time King George returned from his Russian trip, he was faced with accepting the decision of his son to tie the dynasty's prestige of the Olympic Games. Olympic opponents, including Trikoupes, were ousted from their positions. The royal family used the Olympics in order to connect themselves to the ancient glories of their adopted country (the Greek dynasty was actually a Danish house). In addition, the spectator of Olympid gold was used as a diplomatic tool in the ongoing Greek dispute with Turkey over the islands between them (at this time the argument was centered on Crete).

The institutions of sport followed Western politics. From the time of the first Olympic Games, the units of sport corresponded in name and territorial jurisdiction to states. While the ideology of sport put forth a program calling for peaceful gatherings of the youth of the world, the organization of sport made the states represented more important than the athletes themselves. Contemporary pleas for a return to sport, for consideration of the athlete's feelings before removing him/her from sport on political grounds, are quite irrelevant. State representation has created state interest. Athletes have become political extensions of states which increasingly have taken responsibility for their development, training, and expenses.

Professor Sloane's article demonstrates another facet of this process. The early Olympic Games adopted existing judging processes. Host sport federations were put in charge of judging as well as Olympic management.

But political organization led to political dispute. Anglo-American squabbles over the 1908 Olympics were so severe (resulting in propaganda broadsides from each side after the Games were over) that Sloane (an IOC member) came to the conclusion that the systems had to be changed. His call for a more active role by international sport federations resulted in those bodies gaining crucial responsibility over their events - even when celebrated in the Olympic Games. As federation jurisdiction increased, IOC power decreased. The necessities of political sport organization resulted in decreased importance for the system's central body.

Organizational politics thus proved stronger than even the will of Coubertin. Indeed, his political skill as well as his idealistic vision created the Olympic Games. He had to go beyond appeals to elite sportsmanship. It was not enough to borrow Thomas Arnold's philosophy and show how physical competition could help bring the adult world into miniature for the adolescent. Coubertin also had to appeal to states whose existing physical education programs were designed to serve national strength, not individual altruism. The German and Bohemian models provided sport organization with a much broader appeal than could have been developed through classical nostalgia.

Coubertin's own national background led to a national adaptation of Olympic ideals to political reality. His appeal to his own countrymen was based on an understanding of the national malaise which followed the debacle of 1870. It is incorrect to assert that Coubertin himself was simply a nationalist without any sense of vision, but the politics of France contributed to the politics of his Olympic creation. France needed strong physical specimens to deal with her more numerous neighbors across the Rhine, and Coubertin offered his country a means of obtaining them.

Thus, while Coubertin could retain personal influence in the IOC, he was constrained by the reflections of the international system inherent in his Olympic organization. His IOC could only present itself as above politics in terms of mythology contending that it was above politics. As the IOC lost force, it tended to push ever harder on the subject of Olympic ideals. States did not object to this, as it permitted them expressions of national pride without exposing them to retaliation by the states whose sport representatives were defeated.

At one point, Coubertin did try to graft his system onto international politics. This happened when "internationalism" became a popular philosophy. World War I seemed to prove the bankruptcy of old diplomacy, and Wilsonian (neo-Kantian) Internationalism seemed to offer hope for the future. In the 1920's, rather than claiming to be aloof from "politics," Coubertin altered the meaning of "Olympism" in order to make it seem as if the IOC all all along had been a preeminent international organization. The decline of the League of Nations, of course, meant the end of this ideological tie to politics. The period of the decline of the League of Nations coincided broadly with the rise to power of Adolt Hitler and the birth of the Third Reich in Germany.

The 1936 Olympics were awarded to the Weimar Republic, not the Nazis. Theodor Lewald was elected to the IOC in 1924 as an opening to the gradual process of allowing Germany back into international sports. Once more sport aped politics, this process could not be completed until the culmination of Locarno diplomacy and the admission of Germany to the League of Nations.

At the 28th meeting of the IOC in 1930 in Berlin, Lewald, with lobbying help from the Austrian member, Dr. Schmidt, secured the Games of the XIth Olympiad for Berlin by a vote of 43-16 over Barcelona. The Winter Games were awarded to Garmisch-Partenkirchen.

Hitler thus simply fell heir to the Games. He was originally opposed to them, but soon perceived the propaganda potential inherent in political sport. Here was a chance to show the world how modern and progressive Germany was, how far she had come since the days of Versailles, and how happy and prosperous Germans were under the Nazi system. As Krueger (1972) states:

> The world cannot believe its eyes: the same Germany
> which withdrew from the League of Nations, and is de-
> scribed everywhere as wanting to isolate itself not only
> politically but also culturally, and whose protestations
> of her desire for peace are constantly labeled as nothing
> but lies--this same Germany has made herself suddenly
> one of the driving forces in the movement for peace. It
> is something that everyone can test for himself by com-
> ing and experiencing the Olympic Games first hand.
> That is what is so special about this all. (p. 12)

Mandell shows how the Germans were able to counter boycott and transfer movements, all the while intensifying their propaganda efforts through the Olympic Games News Service of Carl Diem. In short, the Games were a political success for the Nazis even before the opening ceremony.

The spectrum of readings in this Section devoted to inquiry concerning Olympism includes philosophis extremes of "idealism" and "pragmatism." The idealism of Olympism comes closer to representing the mythology of precise social behavior through sport (the model for all social behavior), than through any other representative repertoire of behaviors (the arts, commerce, military, etc.). Values and virtues for the "youth of today," the society of tomorrow, stem from interpretations of Classical systems of behavior, unilaterally believed to be sound by reason of their tested antiquity. Those values found new expression in nineteenth century European philosophy, and remain popular today in view of the basic principles of human rights that they supposedly address.

In the opening reading in Section 2, the founder of the modern Olympic movement exults in the success of the First Olympiad, and hopes that it will be followed by celebrations of sport in other Western states. Emphasis is laid on the spirit of festival accompanying the cultural rebirth of one of man's most ancient and honored customs, most appropriately founded in Athens.

Historical documentation of events lends authenticity to the festival. Coubertin notes the importance of the Games to Greek politics, and hopes that future political effects from the Olympics will be as positive.

The "Olympic Idea" is supposed to involve friendship and friendly competition, but, in the wake of friction at recent Olympiads, Sloane calls on the sport federations to take an active role in "standardizing" the Games. The author stresses the global reach of the "Olympic Idea," from America to Young Turkey, Japan, and China. He states: "Primarily sport must be the medium of international conciliation." (p. 409) This article offsets omissions of the Veblen contribution in Section 1.

Weber analyzes the founder of the modern Olympic Games in terms of his political ideology and in the context of French social and political life. The influence of Coubertin's class background and of English elite sport education are examined along with that of Coubertin's French contemporaries. Sport interest is shown to be associated with a "leftist" persuasion of political ideology, endorsed by young intellectuals seeking to create a better world to live in through a Nietschean formulation of developing superior human beings. Concordant with comments above, Mandell illustrates how a resurgent Germany became an attractive model of national development and progress in a world recovering from the effects of war and economic collapse. Supremacist thinking carried over into Germany's policy regarding sport, to the attempted disbarrment of Jews from competition. Eleventh-hour realizations by other countries prompted threats of boycott, and reports of social activism by Americans against American participation in the XI Olympiad spelled the mood in which the Olympic spirit was to be viewed and upheld.

Thirer provides a brief encapsulation of the various forms of political protest and activism occurring in conjunction with the Olympic Games over the past eighty years. Most significantly, he points to the 1968 Mexico City demonstrations by Smith and Carlos as being symbolic of a greater civil rights movement becoming enflamed in the U.S.A., and to the effects this had on professional sport franchises. The actions of Matthews and Collett at Munich in 1972 echoed the earlier protest, but now had wider significance for a world faced with an awakening attention focused on apartheid and international black oppression. In contrast with Thirer, Nafziger presents historical commentary on the role and function of the Olympic Movement as the IOC has developed its "Olympic Rules and Regulations." The institutionalization of the IOC is shown to be well developed. On this basis, a model for "shared goals of transnational sport" is assumed to exist. The subversion of the institution is indicated by such stress factors as "creeping professionalism." The model is further tested by questions of public order, "ping-pong diplomacy," and the protection of human rights.

In the last contribution, Hatfield brings into sharp focus the effects of technological developments in application to sports performance and discusses how these effects challenge the model of the IOC as an institution. Formerly "politically naive," the Olympic Movement has now become like all social movements in history, both (i) active/volatile and (ii) subject to stresses from outside pressures and groups. State and commercial (private sector) subsidization provide further stresses to IOC ideology.

In the broadest sense, political conditions today are causing people to take the Olympic Movement to task. Some want the Olympics discontinued, or at least reshaped and reorganized. The Olympian athlete with purely expressive athletic motives and intentions may foster an idealistic Olympian spirit; the athlete seeking prestige or pecuniary reward certainly subscribes to an instrumental or utilitarian value system couched in a fundamental realism. _Citius_, _altius_ and _fortius_ in sport, pursued in a world of sociopolitical and economic priorities, engender the stresses taking place in the transference from idealistic to pragmatic bases of dependency. Thus, the permeability of Olympism, the substance of an idea--a ground concept subjugated by the realization of its own absolute dicta--becomes evident from the selection of readings in this section.

The Olympic Games Of 1896

Baron Pierre de Coubertin

The Olympic games which recently took place at Athens were modern in character, not alone because of their programs, which substituted bicycle for chariot races, and fencing for the brutalities of pugilism, but because in their origin and regulations they were international and universal, and consequently adapted to the conditions in which athletics have developed at the present day. The ancient games had an exclusively Hellenic character; they were always held in the same place, and Greek blood was a necessary condition of admission to them. It is true that strangers were in time tolerated; but their presence at Olympia was rather a tribute paid to the superiority of Greek civilization than a right exercised in the name of racial equality. With the modern games it is quite otherwise. Their creation is the work of "barbarians." It is due to the delegates of the athletic associations of all countries assembled in congress at Paris in 1894. It was there agreed that every country should celebrate the Olympic games in turn. The first place belonged by right to Greece; it was accorded by unanimous vote; and in order to emphasize the permanence of the institution, its wide bearings, and its essentially cosmopolitan character, an international committee was appointed, the members of which were to represent the various nations, European and American, with whom athletics are held in honor. The presidency of this committee falls to the country in which the next games are to be held. A Greek, M. Bikelas, has presided for the last two years. A Frenchman now presides, and will continue to do so until 1900, since the next games are to take place at Paris during the Exposition. Where will those of 1904 take place? Perhaps at New York, perhaps at Berlin, or at Stockholm. The question is soon to be decided.

It was in virtue of these resolutions passed during the Paris Congress that the recent festivals were organized. Their successful issue is largely owing to the active and energetic cooperation of the Greek crown prince Constantine. When they realized all that was expected of them, the Athenians lost courage. They felt that the city's resources were not equal to the demands that would be made upon them; nor would the government (M. Tricoupis being then prime minister) consent to increase facilities. M. Tricoupis did not believe in the success of the games. He argued that the Athenians knew nothing about athletics; that they had neither the adequate grounds for the contests, nor athletes of their own to bring into line; and that, moreover, the financial situation of Greece forbade her inviting the world to an event preparations for which would entail such large expenditures. There was reason in these objections; but on the one hand, the prime minister greatly exaggerated the importance of the expenditures, and on the other, it was not

Originally published in The Century Magazine, LIII, #1 (November, 1896).

necessary that the government should bear the burden of them directly. Modern Athens, which recalls in so many ways the Athens of ancient days, has inherited from her the privilege of being beautified and enriched by her children. The public treasury was not always very well filled in those times any more than in the present, but wealthy citizens who had made fortunes at a distance liked to crown their commercial career by some act of liberality to the mother-country. They endowed the land with superb edifices of general utility--theaters, gymnasia, temples. The modern city is likewise full of monuments which she owes to such generosity. It was easy to obtain from private individuals what the state could not give. The Olympic games had burned with so bright a luster in the past of the Greeks that they could not but have their revival at heart. And furthermore, the moral benefits would compensate largely for all pecuniary sacrifice.

This the crown prince apprehended at once, and it decided him to lend his authority to the organizing of the first Olympic games. He appointed a commission, with headquarters in his own palace; made M. Philemon, ex-mayor of Athens and a man of much zeal and enthusiasm, secretary-general; and appealed to the nation to subscribe the necessary funds. Subscriptions began to come in from Greece, but particularly from London, Marseilles, and Constantinople, where there are wealthy and influential Greek colonies. The chief gift came from Alexandria. It was this gift which made it possible to restore the Stadion to its condition in the time of Atticus Herodes. The intention had been from the first to hold the contests in this justly celebrated spot. No one, however, had dreamed that it might be possible to restore to their former splendor the marble seats which, it is said, could accommodate forty thousand persons. The great enclosure would have been utilized, and provisional wooden seats placed on the grassy slopes which surround it. Thanks to the generosity of M. Averoff, Greece is now the richer by a monument unique of its kind, and its visitors have seen a spectacle which they can never forget.

Two years ago the Stadion resembled a deep gash, made by some fabled giant, in the side of the hill which rises abruptly by the Ilissus, and opposite Lycabettus and the Acropolis, in a retired, picturesque quarter of Athens. All that was visible of it then were the two high earth embankments which faced each other on opposite sides of the long, narrow race-course. They met at the end in an imposing hemicycle. Grass grew between the cobblestones. For centuries the spectators of ancient days had sat on the ground on these embankments. Then, one day, an army of workmen, taking possession of the Stadion, had covered it with stone and marble. This is the work that has now been repeated. The first covering served as a quarry during the Turkish domination; not a trace of it was left. With its innumerable rows of seats, and the flights of steps which divide it into sections and lead to the upper tiers, the Stadion no longer has the look of being cut out of the hill. It is the hill which seems to have been placed there by the hand of man to support this enormous pile of masonry. One detail only is modern. One does not notice it at first. The dusty track is now a cinder-path, prepared according to the latest rules of modern athletics by an expert brought over from London for the purpose. In the center a sort of esplanade has been erected for the gymnastic exhibitions. At the end, on each side of the turning, antiquity is represented by two large boundary-stones, forming two human figures, and excavated while the foundations were being dug. These were the only finds; they add but little to archaeological data. Work on the Stadion is far from being completed, eighteen months having been quite insufficient for the undertaking. Where marble could not be placed, painted wood was hastily made to do duty. That clever architect M. Metaxas cherishes the hope, however, of seeing all the antique decorations restored—statues, columns, bronze quadrigae, and, at the entrance, majestic propylaea.

When this shall be done, Athens will in truth possess the temple of athletic sports. Yet it is doubtful whether such a sanctuary be the one best suited to the worship of human vigor and beauty in these modern days. The Anglo-Saxons, to whom we owe the revival of athletics, frame their contests delightfully in grass and verdure. Nothing could differ more than the Athenian Stadion than Travers Island, the summer home of the New York Athletic Club, where the championship games are decided. In this green enclosure, where nature is left to have her way, the spectators sit under the trees on the sloping declivities, a few feet away from the Sound, which murmurs against the rocks. One finds something of the same idea at Paris, and at San Francisco, under those Californian skies which so recall the skies of Greece, at the foot of those mountains which have the pure outlines and the iridescent reflections of Hymettus. If the ancient amphitheater was more grandiose and more solemn, the modern picture is more *intime* and pleasing. The music floating under the trees makes a softer accompaniment to the exercises; the spectators move about at friendly ease, whereas the ancients, packed together in rigid lines on their marble benches, sat broiling in the sun or chilled in the shade.

The Stadion is not the only enduring token that will remain to Athens of her inauguration of the new Olympiads: she has also a velodrome and a shooting-stand. The former is in the plain of the modern Phalerum, along the railway which connects Athens with the Piraeus. It is copied after the model of that at Copenhagen, where the crown prince of Greece and his brothers had an opportunity of appreciating its advantages during a visit to the King of Denmark, their grandfather. The bicyclists, it is true, have complained that the track is not long enough, and that the turnings are too abrupt; but when were bicyclists ever content? The tennis courts are in the center of the velodrome. The shooting-stand makes a goodly appearance, with its manor-like medieval crenelations. The contestants are comfortably situated under monumental arches. Then there are large pavilions for the rowers, built of wood, but prettily decorated, with boat-houses and dressing-rooms.

While the Hellenic Committee thus labored over the scenic requirements, the international committee and the national committees were occupied in recruiting competitors. The matter was not as easy as one might think. Not only had indifference and distrust to be overcome, but the revival of the Olympic games had aroused a certain hostility. Although the Paris Congress had been careful to decree that every form of physical exercise practised in the world should have its place on the program, the gymnasts took offense. They considered that they had not been given sufficient prominence. The greater part of the gymnastic associations of Germany, France, and Belgium are animated by a rigorously exclusive spirit; they are not inclined to tolerate the presence of those forms of athletics which they themselves do not practise; what they disdainfully designate as "English sports" have become, because of their popularity, especially odious to them. These associations were not satisfied with declining the invitation sent them to repair to Athens. The Belgian federation wrote to the other federations, suggesting a concerted stand against the work of the Paris Congress. These incidents confirmed the opinions of the pessimists who had been foretelling the failure of the fêtes, or their probably postponement. Athens is far away, the journey is expensive, and the Easter vacations are short. The contestants were not willing to undertake the voyage unless they could be sure that the occasion would be worth the effort. The different associations were not willing to send representatives unless they could be informed of the amount of interest which the contests would create. An unfortunate occurrence took place almost at the last moment. The German press, commenting on an article which had appeared in a Paris newspaper, declared that it was an exclusively Franco-Greek affair; that attempts were being made to shut out other nations; and furthermore, that the German associations had been intentionally kept aloof from the Paris Congress of 1894. The assertion was acknowledged to be incorrect, and was powerless to check the efforts of the German committee under Dr. Gebhardt. M. Kémény in Hungary, Major Balck in Sweden, General de Boutonski in Russia, Professor W. M. Sloane in the United States, Lord Ampthill in England, Dr. Jiri Guth in Bohemia, were, meantime, doing their best to awaken interest in the event, and to reassure the doubting. They did not always succeed. Many people took a sarcastic view, and the newspapers indulged in much pleasantry on the subject of the Olympic games.

EASTER MONDAY, April 6, the streets of Athens wore a look of extraordinary animation. All the public buildings were draped in bunting; multicolored streamers floated in the wind; green wreaths decked the house-fronts. Everywhere were the two letters "O. A.," the Greek initials of the Olympic games, and the two dates, B.C. 776, A.D. 1896, indicating their ancient past and their present renaisience. At two o'clock in the afternoon the crowd began to throng the Stadion and to take possession of the seats. It was a joyous and motley concourse. The skirts and braided jackets of the palikars contrasted with the somber and ugly European habiliments. The women used large paper fans to shield them from the sun, parasols, which would have obstructed the view, being prohibited. The king and the queen drove up a little before three o'clock, followed by Princess Marie, their daughter, and her fiancé, Grand Duke George of Russia. They were received by the crown prince and his brothers, by M. Delyannis, president of the Council of Ministers, and by the members of the Hellenic Committee and the international committee. Flowers were presented to the queen and princess, and the cortege made its way into the hemicycle to the strains of the Greek national hymn and the cheers of the crowd. Within, the court ladies and functionaries, the diplomatic corps, and the deputies awaited the sovereigns, for whom two marble armchairs were in readiness. The crown prince, taking his stand in the arena, facing the king, then made a short speech, in which he touched upon the origin of the enterprise, and the obstacles surmounted in bringing it to fruition. Addressing the king, he asked him to proclaim the opening of the Olympic games, and the king, rising, declared them opened.

It was a thrilling moment. Fifteen hundred and two years before, the Emperor Theodosius had suppressed the Olympic games, thinking, no doubt, that in abolishing this hated survival of paganism he was furthering the cause of progress; and here was a Christian monarch, amid the applause of an assemblage composed almost exclusively of Christians, announcing the formal annulment of the imperial decree; while a few feet away stood the archbishop of Athens, and Père Didon, the celebrated Dominican preacher, who, in his Easter sermon in the Catholic cathedral the day before, had paid an eloquent tribute to pagan Greece. When the king had resumed his seat, the Olympic ode, written for the occasion by the Greek composer Samara, was sung by a chorus of one hundred and fifty voices. Once before music had been associated with the revival of the Olympic games. The first session of the Paris Congress had been held June 16, 1894, in the great amphitheater of the Sorbonne, decorated by Puvis de Chavannes; and after the address of the president of the congress, Baron de Coubertin, the large audience had listened to that fragment of the music of antiquity, the hymn to Apollo, discovered in the ruins of Delphi. But this time the connection between art and athletics was more direct. The games began with the sounding of the last chords of the Olympic ode. That first day established the success of the games beyond a doubt. The ensuing days confirmed the fact in spite of the bad weather. The royal family was assiduous in its attendance. In the shooting-contest the queen fired the first shot with a flower-wreathed rifle. The fencing-matches were held in the marble rotunda of the Exposition Palace, given by the Messrs, Zappas, and known as the Zappeion. Then the crowd made its way back to the Stadion for the foot-faces, weight-putting, discus-throwing, high and long jumps, pole-vaulting, and gymnastic exhibitions. A Princeton student, Robert Garrett, scored highest in throwing the discus. His victory was unexpected. He had asked me the day before if I did not think that it would be ridiculous should he enter for an event for which he had trained so little! The stars and stripes seemed destined to carry off all the laurels. When they ran up the "victor's mast," the sailors of the San Francisco, who stood in a group at the top of the Stadion, waved their caps, and the members of the Boston Athletic Association below broke out frantically, "B.A.A.! rah! rah! rah!" These cries greatly amused the Greeks. They applauded the triumph of the Americans, between whom and themselves there is a warm feeling of goodwill.

The Greeks are novices in the matter of athletic sports, and had not looked for much scucess for their own country. One event only seemed likely to be theirs from its very nature—the long-distance run from Marathon, a prize for which has been newly founded by M. Michel Bréal, a member of the French Institute, in commemoration of that soldier of antiquity who ran all the way to Athens to tell his fellow-citizens of the happy issue of the battle. The distance from Marathon to Athens is 42 kilometers. The road is rough and stony. The Greeks had trained for this run for a year past. Even in the remote districts of Thessaly young peasants prepared to enter as contestants. In three cases it is said that the enthusiasm and the inexperience of these young fellows cost them their lives, so exaggerated were their preparatory efforts. As the great day approached, women offered up prayers and votive tapers in the churches, that the victor might be a Greek!

The wish was fulfilled. A young peasant named Louës, from the village of Marousi, was the winner in two hours and fifty-five minutes. He reached the goal fresh and in fine form. He was followed by two other Greeks. The excellent Australian sprinter Flack, and the Frenchman Lermusiaux, who had been in the lead the first 35 kilometers, had fallen out by the way. When Louës came into the Stadion, the crowd, which numbered sixty thousand persons, rose to its feet like one man, swayed by extraordinary excitement. The King of Servia, who was present, will probably not forget the sight he saw that day. A flight of white pigeons was let loose, women waved fans and handkerchiefs, and some of the spectators who were nearest to Louës left their seats, and tried to reach him and carry him in triumph. He would have been suffocated if the crown prince and Prince George had not bodily led him away. A lady who stood next to me unfastened her watch, a gold one set with pearls, and sent it to him; an innkeeper presented him with an order good for three hundred and sixty-five free meals; and a wealthy citizen had to be dissuaded from signing a check for ten thousand francs to his credit. Louës himself, however, when he was told of this generous offer, refused it. The sense of honor, which is very strong in the Greek peasant, thus saved the non-professional spirit from a very great danger.

Needless to say that the various contests were held under amateur regulations. An exception was made for the fencing-matches, since in several countries professors of military fencing hold the rank of officers. For them a special contest was arranged. To all other branches of the athletic sports only amateurs were admitted. It is impossible to conceive the Olympic games with money prizes. But these rules, which seem simple enough, are a good deal complicated in their practical application by the fact that definitions of what constitutes an amateur differ from one country to another, sometimes even from one club to another. Several definitions are current in England; the Italians and the Dutch admit one which appears too rigid at one point, too loose at another. How conciliate these divergent or contradictory utterances? The Paris Congress made an attempt in that direction, but its decisions are not accepted everywhere as law, nor is its definition of amateurship everywhere adopted as the best. The rules and regulations, properly so-called, are not any more uniform. This and that are forbidden in one country, authorized in another. All that one can do, until there shall be an Olympic code formulated in accordance with the ideas and the usages of the majority of athletes, is to choose among the codes now existing. It was decided, therefore, that the foot-races should be under the rules of the Union Française des Sports Athletiques; jumping, putting the shot, etc., under those of the Amateur Athletic Association of England; the bicycle-races under those of the International Cyclists' Association, etc. This had appeared to us the best way out of the difficulty; but we should have had many disputes if the judges (to whom had been given the Greek name of ephors) had not been headed by Prince George, who acted as final referee. His presence gave weight and authority to the decisions of the ephors, among whom there were, naturally, representatives of different countries. The prince took his duties seriously, and fulfilled them conscientiously. He was always on the track, personally supervising every detail, an easily recognizable figure, owing to his height and athletic build. It will be remembered that Prince

George, while traveling in Japan with his cousin, the czarevitch (now Emperor Nicholas II), felled with his fist the ruffian who had tried to assassinate the latter. During the weight lifting in the Stadion, Prince George lifted with ease an enormous dumbbell, and tossed it out of the way. The audience broke into applause, as if it would have liked to make him the victor in the event.

Every night while the games were in progress the streets of Athens were illuminated. There were torchlight processions, bands played the different national hymns, and the students of the university got up ovations under the windows of the foreign athletic crews, and harangued them in the noble tongue of Demosthenes. Perhaps this tongue was somewhat abused. That Americans might not be compelled to understand French, nor Hungarians forced to speak German, the daily programs of the games, and even invitations to luncheon, were written in Greek. On receipt of these cards, covered with mysterious formulae, where even the date was not clear (the Greek calendar is twelve days behind ours), every man carried them to his hotel porter for elucidation.

Many banquets were given. The mayor of Athens gave one at Cephissia, a little shaded village at the foot of Pentelicus. M. Bikelas, the retiring president of the international committee, gave another at Phalerum. The king himself entertained all the competitors, and the members of the committees, three hundred guests in all, at luncheon in the ballroom of the palace. The outside of this edifice, which was built by King Otho, is heavy and graceless; but the center of the interior is occupied by a suite of large rooms with very high ceilings, opening one into another through colonnades. The decorations are simple and imposing. The tables were set in the largest of these rooms. At the table of honor sat the king, the princes, and the ministers, and here also were the members of the committees. The competitors were seated at the other tables according to their nationality. The king, at dessert, thanked and congratulated his guests, first in French, afterward in Greek. The Americans cried "Hurrah!" the Germans, "Hoch!" the Hungarians, "Eljen!" the Greeks, "Zito!" the French, "Vive le Roi!" After the repast the king and his sons chatted long and amicably with the athletes. It was a really charming scene, the republican simplicity of which was a matter of wonderment particularly to the Austrians and the Russians, little used as they are to the spectacle of monarchy thus meeting democracy on an equal footing.

Then there were nocturnal festivities on the Acropolis, where the Parthenon was illuminated with colored lights, and at the Piraeus, where the vessels were hung with Japanese lanterns. Unluckily, the weather changed, and the sea was so high on the day appointed for the boat-races, which were to have taken place in the roadstead of Phalerum, that the project was abandoned. The distribution of prizes was likewise postponed for twenty-four hours. It came off with much solemnity, on the morning of April 15, in the Stadion. The sun shone again, and sparkled on the officers' uniforms. When the roll of the victors was called, it became evident, after all, that the international character of the institution was well guarded by the results of the contests. America had won nine prizes for athletic sports alone (flat races for 100 and 400 meters; 110-meter hurdle-race; high jump; broad jump; pole-vault; hop, step, and jump; putting the shot; throwing the discus), and two prizes for shooting (revolver, 25 and 30 meters); but France had the prizes for foil-fencing and for four bicycle-races; England scored highest in the one-handed weight lifting contest, and in single lawn-tennis; Greece won the run from Marathon, two gymnastic contests (rings, climbing the smooth rope), three prizes for shooting (carbine, 200 and 300 meters; pistol, 25 meters), a prize for fencing with sabers, and a bicycle-race; Germany won in wrestling, in gymnastics (parallel bars, fixed bar, horse-leaping), and in double lawn-tennis; Australia, the 800-meter and 1500-meter foot-races on the flat; Hungary, swimming-matches of 100 and 1200 meters; Austria, the 500-meter swimming-match and the 12-hour bicycle-race; Switzerland, a gymnastic prize; Denmark, the two-handed weight lifting contest.

The prizes were an olive-branch from the very spot, at Olympia, where stood the ancient Altis, a diploma drawn by a Greek artist, and a silver medal chiseled by the celebrated French engraver Chaplain. On one side of the medal is the Acropolis, with the Parthenon and the Propylaea; on the other a colossal head of the Olympian Zeus, after the type created by Phidias. The head of the god is blurred, as if by distance and the lapse of centuries, while in the foreground, in clear relief, is the Victory which Zeus holds on his hand. It is a striking and original conception. After the distribution of the prizes, the athletes formed for the traditional procession around the Stadion. Louës, the victor of Marathon, came first, bearing the Greek flag; then the Americans, the Hungarians, the French, the Germans. The ceremony, moreover, was made more memorable by a charming incident. One of the contestants, Mr. Robertson, an Oxford student, recited an ode which he had composed, in ancient Greek and in the Pindaric mode, in honor of the games. Music had opened them, and Poetry was present at their close; and thus was the bond once more renewed which in the past united the Muses with feats of physical strength, the mind with the well-trained body. The king announced that the first Olympiad was at an end, and left the Stadion, the band playing the Greek national hymn, and the crowd cheering. A few days later Athens was emptied of its guests. Torn wreaths littered the public squares; the banners which had floated merrily in the streets disappeared; the sun and the wind held sole possession of the marble sidewalks of Stadion street.

It is interesting to ask oneself what are likely to be the results of the Olympic games of 1896, as regards both Greece and the rest of the world. In the case of Greece, the games will be found to have had a double effect, one athletic, the other political. It is a well-known fact that the Greeks had lost completely, during their centuries of oppression, the taste for physical sports. There were good walkers among the mountaineers, and good swimmers in the scattered villages along the coast. It was a matter of pride with the young palikar to wrestle and to dance well, but that was because bravery and a gallant bearing were admired by those about him. Greek dances are far from athletic, and the wrestling-matches of peasants have none of the characteristics of true sports. The men of the towns had come to know no diversion beyond reading the newspapers, and violently discussing politics about the tables of the cafés. The Greek race, however, is free from the natural indolence of the Oriental, and it was manifest that the athletic habit would, if the opportunity offered, easily take root again among its men.

Indeed, several gymnastic associations had been formed in recent years at Athens and Patras, and a rowing-club at Piraeus, and the public was showing a growing interest in their feats. It was therefore a favorable moment to speak the words, "Olympic games." No sooner had it been made clear that Athens was to aid in the revival of the Olympiads than a perfect fever of muscular activity broke out all over the kingdom. And this was nothing to what followed the games. I have seen, in little villages far from the capital, small boys, scarcely out of long clothes, throwing big stones, or jumping improvised hurdles, and two urchins never met in the streets of Athens with without running races. Nothing could exceed the enthusiasm with which the victors in the contests were received, on their return to their native towns, by their fellow-citizens. They were met by the mayor and municipal authorities, and cheered by a crowd bearing branches of wild olive and laurel. In ancient times the victor entered the city through a breach made expressly in its walls. The Greek cities are no longer walled in, but one may say that athletics have made a breach in the heart of the nation. When one realizes the influence that the practice of physical exercises may have on the future of a country, and on the force of a whole race, one is tempted to wonder whether Greece is not likely to date a new era from the year 1896. It would be curious indeed if athletics were to become one of the factors in the Eastern question! Who can tell whether, by bringing a notable increase of vigor to the inhabitants of the country, it may not hasten the solution of this thorny problem? These are hypotheses, and circumstances make light of such calculations at long range. But a local and immediate consequence of the games may already be found in the internal politics of Greece. I have spoken of the active part taken by the crown prince and his brothers, Prince George and Prince Nicholas, in the labors of the organizing committee. It was the first time that the heir apparent had had an opportunity of thus coming into contact with his future subjects. They knew him to be patriotic and high-minded, but they did not know his other admirable and solid qualities. Prince Constantine inherits his fine blue eyes and fair coloring from his Danish ancestors, and his frank, open manner, his self-poise, and his mental lucidity come from the same source; but Greece has given him enthusiasm and ardor, and this happy combination of prudence and high spirit makes him especially adapted to govern the Hellenes. The authority, mingled with perfect liberality with which he managed the committee, his exactitude in detail, and more particularly his quiet perseverance when those about him were inclined to hesitate and to lose courage, make it clear that his reign will be one of fruitful labor, which can only strengthen and enrich his country. The Greek people have now a better idea of the worth of their future sovereign: they have seen him at work, and have gained respect for and confidence in him.

So much for Greece. On the world at large the Olympic games have, of course, exerted no influence as yet; but I am profoundly convinced that they will do so. May I be permitted to say that this was my reason for founding them? Modern athletics need to be unified and purified. Those who have followed the renaissance of physical sports in this century know that discord reigns supreme from one end of them to the other. Every country has its own rules; it is not possible even to come to an agreement as to who is an amateur, and who is not. All over the world there is one perpetual dispute, which is further fed by innumerable weekly, and even daily, newspapers. In this deplorable state of things professionalism tends to grow apace. Men give up their whole existence to one particular sport, grow rich by practising it, and thus deprive it of all nobility, and destroy the just equilibrium of man by making the muscles preponderate over the mind. It is my belief that no education, particularly in democratic times, can be good and complete without the aid of athletics; but athletics, in order to play their proper educational rôle, must be based on perfect disinterestedness and the sentiment of honor.

If we are to guard them against these threatening evils, we must put an end to the quarrels of amateurs, that they may be united among themselves, and willing to measure their skill in frequent international encounters. But what country is to impose its rules and its habits on the others? The Swedes will not yield to the Germans, nor the French to the English. Nothing better than the international Olympic games could therefore be devised. Each country will take its turn in organizing them. When they come to meet every four years in these contests, further ennobled by the memories of the past, athletes all over the world will learn to know one another better, to make mutual concessions, and to seek no other reward in the competition than the honor of the victory. One may be filled with desire to see the colors of one's club or college triumph in a national meeting; but how much stronger is the feeling when the colors of one's country are at stake! I am well assured that the victors in the Stadion at Athens wished for no other recompense when they heard the people cheer the flag of their country in honor of their achievement.

It was with these thoughts in mind that I sought to revive the Olympic games. I have succeeded after many efforts. Should the institution prosper, --as I am persuaded, all civilized nations aiding, that it will,--it may be a potent, if indirect, factor in securing universal peace. Wars break out because nations misunderstand each other. We shall not have peace until the prejudices which now separate the different races shall have been outlived. To attain this end, what better means than to bring the youth of all countries periodically together for amicable trials of muscular strength and agility? The Olympic games, with the ancients, controlled athletics and promoted peace. It is not visionary to look to them for similar benefactions in the future.

The Olympic Idea--Its Origin,

Foundation, And Progress

William Milligan Sloane

There are probably forty thousand practising amateur athletes in the United States today. They are a splendid body of youths, and the hundreds of thousands of spectators who throng to witness their sports offer convincing testimony of the far-reaching influence of athleticism in America. These numbers are even larger in Great Britain. Once more the "god of the open air" has risen to Olympian rank, and the devotees of other than athletic sports can be counted by millions. Organization for the purpose of intelligent, regulated emulation is instinctive in us. Associations have been formed, definitions established, and rules promulgated, for nearly all forms of legitimate sport in Anglo-Saxon countries, and this example has not passed unnoticed on the Continent.

Some thirty years ago, M. Pierre de Coubertin, a young Frenchman whose heartstrings had been wrung by the humiliation of his country in 1870, began to study outdoor life in England and America. He traveled extensively, published several books on the subject, and in his own land was the organizer of clubs for cultivating the more strenuous, inspiriting, and daring sports which had hitherto been neglected.

Almost simultaneously there was a revival of the vigorous old French games, and a movement to study and introduce the German methods of physical training. All three of these agitations met with success, and they attracted attention to such an extent that even those countries which had been formerly most indifferent to such matters felt the lure of sports and athletics to an amazing degree, though chiefly as adjuncts to the means of physical training already in use.

The motto of M. de Coubertin was "Ludus pro Patria." Its spirit took possession of all continental Europe (especially where patriotism was strongest), either because of its comparative novelty or because the particular country was menaced by internal or external danger. Within a few years there sprang up a natural desire among these neophytes to measure their progress in international contests with those long accustomed to the various

Originally published in The Century Magazine, LXXXIV, 2:408-414, June, 1912.

sports, and especially to test their prowess with that of Great Britain. Kindly acquaintance is the best solvent of international jealously and enmity. Putting this and that together, the idea occurred almost simultaneously to several men--professors, soldiers, writers, and publicists--that here was a neglected means of international conciliation. Correspondence followed, and a few personal conferences were held as to the feasibility of extending and intensifying the common interest for such a purpose. France is the alluvism of ages and peoples, the fertile seed-plot of generous ideas, and in this enterprise M. de Coubertin again took the lead, summoning to the Sorbonne representative delegates, selected chiefly from his wide personal acquaintance in different countries, for the combined purpose of deliberation and action.

The meeting, which assembled on June 23, 1894, was not imposing either in numbers or in the personal distinction of those who attended it; but it was impressive from the place of its session, from the associations aroused by the great hall of the Sorbonne, oldest of Western universities, from the interest it awakened in the enlightened public, and, above all, from the earnestness of the delegates. And there was faith, that mighty mustard-seed. The result of the conference was the adoption of the Olympic Idea, and the formation of an International Olympic Committee, the object of which was, first and above all else, to define and promulgate a purpose, until then rather vague; secondly, in the fullness of time to revive Olympic contests.

Of this committee the writer has been a member from the beginning, until now, by priority of interest and anticipation, he is almost, if not quite, the dean of its regular floor members. The president, ever premier in council and prime mover in action, is Baron Pierre de Coubertin. The com committee's foremost task--that with which it began its labors--was to arrive at some general definition of the Olympic Idea by the study of the merits and demerits of the spirit shown at ancient Olympia in Greece; to select those concepts which were still vital and useful, and to adapt them to modern conditions; in short, to get an outline of policy, and try it out by experiment and practice.

For this purpose the president, a man of classical training and spirit, consulted not only men of similar caliber in his own land, but those in other countries as well, making extended journeys for the purpose. In America he was greeted enthusiastically, winning many valiant hearts to his cause. Here, as elsewhere among the select few, the Olympic Idea became almost an obsession; the many of course could not find time to bother with an idealist and his strange doctrines. But the little handful in each country was undismayed. There was lively corresponding, comparing, and suggesting; finally came the appointment of a small volunteer executive committee in Paris, whose modest expenses were borne in part by slender contributions from those in the International Committee, but mainly however by themselves. So by fairly rapid stages the idea took form and grew.

Primarily sport must be the medium of international conciliation. There can be no rivalry without some friction, but rivalry in sport should, and must, be the most generous of all rivalries--a contest in magnanimity. The contestants and their friends at any given Olympiad might not number more than a few hundred; but suppose there were only a hundred from each of the contesting nations and that forty nations were represented! This assembling together is no unimportant agency for reciprocal acquaintance. That several thousand strangers are temporarily the guests at any national capital makes for present fellowship and future friendship. The common interest in the competitions and daily intercourse at other times, the appreciation of representative delegations, tend naturally to sweep away the cobwebs of international suspicion and distrust.

That the nucleus of the Olympic meetings must be field- and track-athletics is inevitable, because these have become the common possession of vigorous, enterprising youth the world over. The various events can, moreover, be standardized with greater ease; that is, the details of rules, judges, and possible styles are not difficult to arrange with equal justice to all. In regard to field- and track-athletics there is likely to be less particularism, less national jealousy, than in other forms of contests. From the very outset, in the first Olympic gathering at Athens, common ground for friendly emulation was easily established. Besides, there was the perennial question of the amateur and the professional, the most knotty, elusive, and exasperating of all questions connected with sport. Even this was so handled as to give general contentment, the basic principle being that no matter how perfect the performance, the performer was an amateur if his practice were an avocation and not a vocation, if he had performed in public neither for money nor for money's worth.

From this position it was inevitable that further discussion would ensue, and for twenty years it has gone on in the public forum of all countries, until opinion has become alert, conceptions have been clarified, and the earnest desire for definition applicable to the widest field has become poignant. Clear, stable, and definite legislation will be possible if, as proposed, a congress of delegates from all the great federations of sports can meet at Paris in 1914 in order to establish the standard Olympiad and thereby to celebrate the twenty-fifth anniversary of the first meeting at the Sorbonne. Lack of space forbids the history of Olympic evolution or even the recapitulation of the events which have furnished its environment. There have been thirteen plenary sessions of the International Committee, in Paris (1894, 1901, 1902); Athens (1896, 1906); Havre (1897); London (1904, 1908); Brussels (1905); The Hague (1907); Berlin (1909); Luxemburg (1910); and Budapest (1911). Four general congresses have been summoned by the committee, and held under its auspices, for the discussion of vital questions, and a fifth should be held in 1914 to create the type Olympiad. Throughout this period "The Olympic Review," now in its seventy-fourth number, has appeared regularly; and most important of all, under the auspices of the committee, four great international contests have been held: the first at Athens, as was seemly (1896); the second in Paris (1900); the third in St. Louis (1904); the fourth in London (1908). The fifth is to be held in Stockholm, in July of the present year. The committee has forty-four members, from thirty-one countries; each of these has a National Olympic Committee, larger or smaller, and for the Stockholm games there are entries from forty nations.

These few facts and figures are given to show the acceleration alike of interest and of practical results. It is probable that Germany will be the host of the next contest in 1916, though three other European lands desire the honor. The International Committee is thus embarrassed by the rich harvest of its planting rather than discouraged by indifference. This zeal might easily devour the ideal. It is useless to ignore human nature, personal or collective, least of all that patriotism which is self-seeking, or the passions within national limits which breed disruption of control and dissensions of varied interests. In the past a certain form of such discontent has been eager to make the International Committee a court of appeal, to demand from it definitions and decisions, to force upon it a representative character, and exact from it final legislation.

This role of law-giver and dictator it has wisely and persistently refused, being a purely voluntary association of disinterested men, who consider themselves the keepers of the Olympic Idea, nothing more, but nothing else. Precisely for this reason the national belegations in it, in most cases, but not as yet in all, enjoy the complete confidence of the athletic associations in their respective countries. Under stress of work its meetings have become annual, and they have an average attendance of more than half of the members in sessions prolonged from day to day for a week. As a self-perpetuating body, selecting its own members and filling its own vacancies, the cost in time, money, and interest is borne by the members themselves purely for the love of the enterprise. Its members regard themselves as plenipotentiaries of the international at the seats of the respective national Olympic committees. These have uncontrolled and full power in organizing national representation at the successive Olympiads.

How far the Olympic Idea may go is not yet determined. Its definition for present uses is sufficiently fixed on the lines of its first appearance: first, to create and strengthen bonds of friendship, such as ought to exist among all civilized nations, by frequent, peaceful intercourse; secondly, to purify sport, abolish selfish and underhand methods in the struggle for athletic supremacy, secure fair play for all, even the weakest, and, as far as possible, make the contest and not the victory the joy of the young. Incidentally the Olympic Idea in this form is steadily and beneficently permeating the physical training of most nations today. That is an enormous gain; but there is more to be hoped for. To realize these hopes, athletic habits must be common to all. Thus far, whichever nation has been our host for the four-year period has naturally exercised a high measure of control in preparing the program, fixing the rules, and selecting the judges. The system has worked fairly well, and it would be rather utopian to suppose that a people taxing itself to the extent of half a million dollars for building a stadium, creating an administration, entertaining its guests, and for all incidentals besides, should forego any advantage for its own contestants by the complete surrender of itself and its athletic ways into the hands of such an international body as has been described. Yet such a surrender to a competent athletic senate would be a superb tribute on the altar of international friendship, and there is a way to secure it, a method already suggested earlier in this article, a plan still inchoate, but in process of careful study; namely, the summoning of a representative, federal, athletic congress of all nations, composed of delegates formally elected by the different national federations of sports, and granted full power to legislate.

It would be the duty of this congress, probably meeting at long intervals, first, to fix a type program; secondly, to promulgate rules; and thirdly, to create a body of impartial, international judges and juries, possibly even a final court of appeal for the adjustment of unforeseen difficulties--a body which would be continuous and easily summoned at short notice. It is almost certain that such a congress will meet in Paris during 1914. All depends on how widely it is desired. Its success would mean the fixing of the Olympic Idea and its perpetuation. All nations proposing to hold the Olympic games would thus be cognizant of the conditions beforehand, and graceful acquiescence in them would be as far-reaching an influence as that of The Hague Tribunal, and an example of priceless value to the rising generations.

Another extension of the Olympic Idea is already in progress; that is the inclusion of other sports in the period of the Olympiad. The Stockholm program includes tennis, horsemanship, yachting, cycling, shooting, swimming, gymnastics, and a modern pentathlon, to test the ability of those who do several things well, and are not expert in one to the exclusion of everything else.

The state of mind known as democracy tends to exclude from participation in modern life all who have hitherto been assigned to the "upper class," the opulent, the patrician, the official, and the military classes. According to this creed, wisdom is to be found only in the plain folk of the world, the peasant, the artisan, the tradesman, the ignorant, and the contentedly inefficient. The Olympic Idea does full justice to all men, for national generosity has made it possible for any athlete who proves his fitness to compete without cost to himself except his time. True democracy finds place for all who are true men, and the coming Olympiad will see those in competition who cultivate as true sportsmen the various sports which are costly. Moreover, although mechanical vehicles have taken the place of the horse in many of his former spheres of activity, they cannot displace him from warfare or supplant him in the affections of those who since Biblical times have rejoiced in his strength and beauty. All exhibitions of his supreme animal intelligence in connection with his rider must properly have a place in international contests, and these in time will promote the acquaintance, intercourse, and goodwill in those classes which are at least as influential in forming national policies as are the people at large. Indeed, in the present day what are known as the upper classes in Europe vie in democratic spirit with any others. Seamanship and horsemanship have always been powerful levelers of social rank, and they always will be.

The third expansion of the Olympic Idea is still inchoate and embryonic, but its nature seems likely to find the necessary nurture; namely, the recurrence of artistic competition in various forms of both the fine and applied arts. In this age we are almost literally dancing and singing through life. We bask in esthetic joys of the slumberous, sensuous, and Oriental variety. All Western nations are more or less under this spell, and as the correspondence of intellectual movement in all of these has been noteworthy for nearly two centuries, increasing with the advance in swift and cheap transportation, so the return of the Western peoples to their real nature, which is before them inevitably, will be hastened by competition. The difficulties are of course enormous, but they are not insuperable. In proportion as these difficulties are overcome, so will there be a peaceful, harmonious forgathering among those who both interpret and guide the mind of the nations and of civilization everywhere, that creative class, the writers and the artists, the makers as well as the doers.

At present the interest of the hour is centered in the successful exploration of earth and air, mountain-climbing and adventure generally. The rudimentary form which it has taken is the "entering" of the achievements of the most worthy contestants by the various national societies. An international jury awards the palms. A similar movement has been undertaken in every form of literature and art. Competition between nations along these lines has already been instituted by the offering of the Nobel prizes; but this jury is a national one, and its decisions might naturally be biased. Moreover, the prizes are tremendous, and are paid in ringing coin, a thing which is not contemplated in the Olympic Idea, which places honor above material reward. Such a concept alone can arouse and stimulate the inborn fire, energy, and sturdy ambition of the Western spirit, and thereby redeem it from the bondage of an elusive, overpowering, and stealthy Orient. For this reason the congress of 1906 at Paris resolved that five competitions ought to be and should be added: to wit, in architecture, painting, music, sculpture, and literature.

In ancient Greece there was only one Olympia to which at first all the little nationalities, and eventually the greater ones, repaired without question, and during the contests there was a general truce in order that all might be safe in their going and coming. The modern Olympiads so far have been favored by peace, but should there be war between the nations, the idea of rotation in meeting-places would have of necessity to be abandoned, at least temporarily. What then? The struggle for balance of power between the free and the slave State systems of America, between the Northern and Southern countries of Europe, has wrought havoc in the past by setting one nation against another, fanning ambition into selfish rivalry and rivalry into bloodshed, conquest, and expansion, the end of which has been empire. But it has had one beneficent result—the neutralizing of the small states of Europe—states which are models to the world in showing what peace and security can enable men to accomplish for the general welfare. Of these states the most central is Switzerland, which has been called the railway turntable of Europe. Wherever and whenever war-dogs may be unchained, it is at peace.

Sentimentally, of course, Athens would be the natural refuge for a peace movement based on international competition under the Olympic Idea. Its superb stadium, restored by the generosity of Averof, further emphasizes its fitness. The Greeks were so impressed with this conviction that after the first successful meeting they and their friends set on foot a movement to secure all future Olympic meetings for their city. Other nations, through their representatives, protested, with the very sound argument that general interest must be secured and intensified by a long period of rotation. Then was evolved the plan of interim meetings, alternating every two years with the others. But a single trial sufficed to show plainly that there could be only one series to Olympiads, and the interim meetings were abandoned.

Athens is as remote from European centers as America, and, notwithstanding the luxuries of ocean greayhounds, ten days of travel is still a troublesome barrier. Perhaps in the future the main Olympia will be in Switzerland, with a subsidiary one in America. Of course these are only visions. Meanwhile other visions have become realities, and these realities have brought about other international contests for which the name Olympic is earnestly desired. This cannot be fairly or honestly granted, although to all such contests the International Committee is friendly. It has pledged its hearty cooperation with the Panama games at San Francisco in 1915, and has offered an Olympic medal for excellence in the modern pentathlon. But one must protest and cry aloud, appealing to the general sense of fairness, against calling even such an important international contest "Olympic." That designation should be reserved primarily for the quadrennial contests of athletes, but likewise for those contests of other generous rivals in sport and the arts which occur in rotation at the great capitals of the world under the auspices not of one nation, but of all.

Other possible extensions of the Olympic Idea will occur to every reader of this sketch, but confusion must be avoided in a momentous enterprise which is still in its infancy. With the suggestions here given there is plenty of work for the International Committee for years to come. Its membership will change, but not the remembrance of its initial work, which has profoundly impressed both lovers of sport and of mankind. The Olympic Idea has proved a living germ from which already a vast organization has sprung and which has enthusiastic workers and recruits in every civilized country today. It has members in the new Japan and in the still newer Turkey, and it is confidently expected that before long the movement will have a representative from the new China.

The record of American athletics at the four Olympiads is brilliant in two ways: first, that interested friends have been so liberal in raising funds sufficient to send on long journeys the many selected to represent the country, and, second, in the success of the contestants. Our victors have taken as many first prizes, twice over, as those of all other lands combined; and of three Marathon races they have won two. It has been largely due to American enthusiasm and interest that other lands have come to exhibit the same qualities. Four of the original founders remain at their posts beside the president and the writer: Colonel Balck of Sweden, M. Collot of France, and the famous Bohemian novelist, Dr. Jiri Guth. These, with many who are dead, and more who are still alive, have maintained the cause against many discouragements, until now it is triumphant. But the lifelong devotion of M. de Coubertin, his tact, his ingenuity, his self-sacrifice in time and money, in short, the qualities of faith and merit, have been the chief reason for the solid establishment of the enterprise.

Sportsmanship And Nazi Olympism

R. D. Mandell

Preparations for the eleventh modern Olympiad took place, both in Germany and abroad, in an international political climate that was turbulent and grimly portentous. The Games of 1932 in Los Angeles four years earlier had provided festive diversion for many disillusioned Americans. The Los Angeles Games, however, had been prepared when it was far from evident that the economic crisis would be as severe or as disruptive as it turned out to be. In the years 1930 and 1931 few nations had made radical attempts to halt the deepening crisis.

The international economic and political expectations were very much different in 1934 and 1935 when not only Germany but the whole world was preparing for the Games in Berlin. Though we now know that the worst of the slump has passed, at the time the statistical basis for optimism was inconclusive and correctly appraised by only a few experts. It is important to note that the various national recoveries were to a large extent attributable (and even then widely recognized as such) to the interference of the national state into domestic affairs. The state, often reluctantly, began to direct labor, banking, and international commerce--activities that the conventional wisdom had barred from heavy-handed civil interference. The conventional wisdom (and by this I mean a view of politics and economics based on philosophical assumptions that became current in the eighteenth and nineteenth centuries) had decreed that these forces should be freely determined by the world's millions of voters, buyers, sellers, and producers. However, nations recovered from the pervading economic and consequent psychological corrosion most dramatically to the extent that they did not respect the conventional liberal assumptions, those abstract ideas about the necessary course of political action that had been the guides for Europe's elites since the French Revolution.

The Germans were not the only people who submitted to radical experiments in the face of peril. In the United States the steel industry was operating, for a while, at one-tenth of its capacity and primary producers such as miners and farmers were suffering keenly from a halving of world commodity prices. The Americans finally submitted, in late 1932, to the New Deal which was pledged to economic leadership far more vigorous than the role heretofore assigned to the federal government. The traditionally stable British political system was maintained by granting emergency powers to the

Reprinted by kind permission of the author and the publisher, this chapter first appeared as Chapter 3 in The Nazi Olympics, Macmillan Company Incorporated, 1972.

national government which frequently bypassed parliamentary procedure. Even France, which had a balanced industrial and agricultural economy that partially isolated her from the worst of the international economic crisis, was torn by internal political dissension--dissension that paralyzed her and prevented French action against the international political swashbucklers unleashed in the middle 1930's. Even the sealed-off, supposedly autonomous Soviet Union (which will remain outside the narrative scope of this book since she did not participate in the Olympics) was badly damaged by the decline in commodity prices, since she had to export twice as much wheat and other raw materials in order to obtain machinery for her second five-year plan. The Soviet purges of the late 1930's were the Russian variety of a world-wide epidemic of convulsive political experimentation and consequent adjustments.

In Germany the economic and political confusions due to the depression moved to a climax early in 1933 and then were roughly eliminated or at least masked after the National Socialist revolution. Super-politics--totalitarian politics--were the antidote. The tales of the refugees from Germany and articles quoted from the Nazi newspapers such as Der Angriff and Der Volkische Beobachter revealed to the world that the German solution to the crisis was planned and put into effect by aggressively disregarding many traditional concepts of justice and, indeed, by contemptuously flouting firmly held, abstract ideas produced in the Western tradition--ideas about the nature of man and society. Liberals were horrified. Many romantic intellectuals and many disillusioned or frightened political figures, however, were enchanted with the tales of economic and political success coming out of energized Germany and were not opposed to ending the confusion and agony in their own lands in a similar fashion. In several nations that were traditional supporters of the modern Olympic Games, Nazism and indeed a certain enthusiastic, though slovenly, kind of Nietzschean, anti-philosophical, political philosophy became chic. Here and there one heard pragmatical praise for Adolf Hitler. After all, crazy as his program might have sounded in the 1920's, it was working in the 1930's. So, in spite of the fact that, in their preparations for their Olympics as well as in other aspects of life, the National Socialists were violating established rules of domestic and international behavior, protests from outside Germany were unusual.

In Great Britain, traditionally a refuge for political persecutees and the place where such German-Jewish athletes as Daniel Prenn and Alex Natan fled shortly after the revolution of 1933, totalitarian projects as antidotes to the inactivity of the traditional politicians were having a vogue. In his newspaper articles Winston Churchill praised Benito Mussolini and Adolf Hitler as preferable to the specter of Communism--then considered the likely ideological haven of the desperate masses of unemployed. Walter MacLennon (also Baron Citrine, a Trades Union official and consulting member of the Government) write a pamphlet, "Under the Heel of Hitler: The Dictatorship over Sport In Nazi Germany." MacLennon's trumpeting for a campaign of formal protests against the Nazification of German sport made little impression on the English. The British Olympic Committee, itself composed principally of the titled aristocrats whose moral assistance Baron Pierre de Coubertin had always preferred, was frightened by the prospects of a Red revolution and was inclined to reject any political calls to action by

an avowed leftist. The British Olympic Committee devoted itself to the task
of locating funds for a large team for 1936.

The turmoil in French political affairs was felt by the French Olympic
Committee which was traditionally dependent upon a government subsidy.
Financing was not granted until the very last moment and the boon was based
upon a cold calculation. When the Popular Front of Premier Léon Blum
voted for credits to support a large French Olympic team, the expense was
justified as a gesture for reciprocal participation in France's own grandiose
adventure in internationalism about the same time. France would spread a
feast for the world at her ambitious Universal Exposition of 1937 in Paris.
The fact that Blum was himself a socialist and a Jew besides indicated a
certain lack of alarm in the Third Republic over the implications of Nazi
racial doctrines as evidenced in Germany's policy regarding sport. Expressions of disgust and tentative movements for the formation of a boycott
of the 1936 Olympics were voiced in Sweden, the Netherlands, and Czechoslovakia. The Spanish Republic refused to grant credits to their Olympic
Committee and Spain, like the Soviet Union, had no team in Berlin in 1936.
In view of the fact that small countries such as Finland and Hungary had long
used their performances at the Olympiads as means of increasing their international renown, one could hardly expect that their politicians would express official protests, much less threaten non-participation. Still, the
only really enthusiastic greetings of the preparations for the 1936 Games
came from Japan and Italy. Indeed, Italy and Finland were the first to accept Dr. Carl Diem's invitations to the Berlin Olympics.

Japan had long since embarked on a national sports program the results of which were demonstrated at Los Angeles in 1932. Japanese eagerness to make a mark at Berlin was intense, since the nation was in the control of military adventurers who viewed sport as a paramilitary activity.
Like Hitler and his lieutenants, the Japanese leaders were keen to use the
sporting fields as stages for advancing the prestige of the nation. The
Japanese were also determined to demonstrate sporting sophistication in
order to obtain the Olympiad for Tokyo in 1940. Mussolini's Fascists also
favored a patriotically oriented sports program and saw in National Socialist
Germany a sort of sister regime. Italian preparations for the eleventh modern Olympiad were costly and characteristically enthusiastic.

The American reaction to the Gleichschaltung or forced coordination
of German sport was quite another matter. The Americans actually produced a serious and frightening (for the Nazis at least) protest movement.
Since the protest movement tells us much about American intellectual life at
the time and since the protests influenced the 1936 Games, the American objections to Nazi sport deserve some description and analysis. It should be
emphasized here that the passionate devotion to Olympism--or more specifically, the view that despite the political obstacles, the Olympic Games had
to go on--had been deeply impressed upon all the high-minded followers of
Baron Pierre de Coubertin. For the elderly bureaucrats of international
sport, the progress of the Olympics was somehow linked with the orderly
spinning of the globe. Olympic officials, American and otherwise, had tended to think like the ancient Greeks: that chronology itself may have depended upon the orderly progress of the quadrennial agonistic displays of the
world's best.

American newspaper readers in 1933 were able to read on their sports pages of the imposition of the Nazi racial laws. For high-minded American sports bureaucrats a shocking incident had been the removal of Dr. Theodor Lewald from his post as president of the German Olympic Committee because of his Mischling or partly Jewish ancestry. The International Olympic Committee met in Vienna on June 6, 1933. American Olympic officials were stalwarts in a campaign to remove the Games from Germany if she did not cease to discriminate against her Jewish athletes. They demanded the firm reinstatement of Dr. Lewald. On June 7, 1933, Lewald, who had been given the post of "adviser" to the German Organizing Committee for the Olympiad, himself announced from Berlin that his government had authorized him to promise that Germany would observe all the Olympic resolutions and that "as a principle" Jews would not be excluded from German teams. Brigadier General Charles E. Sherrill, a crisp looking, bristle-mustached, American member of the I.O.C. and a former outstanding sprinter (he was credited with being in 1888 the first to use the crouching start for the dashes) demanded proper manners from the Germans. Sherrill later wrote to Rabbi Stephen S. Wise in New York:

> It was a trying fight. We were six on the Executive Committee, and even my English colleagues thought we ought not to interfere in the internal arrangements of the German team. The Germans yielded slowly--very slowly. First they conceded that other nations could bring Jews. Then, after the fight was over, telephones [sic] came from Berlin that no publication [sic] should be given to their Government's back-down on Jews, but only the vague statement that they agreed to follow our rules.... Then I went at them hard, insisting that as they had expressly excluded Jews, now they must expressly declare that Jews would not even be excluded from German teams. All sorts of influence was exerted to change my American stand. Finally they yielded because they found that I had lined up the necessary votes.

Sherrill, in order to have concrete proof of the Germans' compliance, requested that Helene Mayer, the championship fencer from Offenbach then living in Los Angeles, be invited to join the German Olympic team. Five days after the concession by officials in Berlin, Hans von Tschammer und Osten, Hitler's alte Kämpfer and now Reichssportführer who had just replaced Lewald as president of the German Olympic Committee, declared to a meeting of German sports officials: "You are probably astonished by the decision in Vienna, but we had to consider the foreign political situation." Tschammer und Osten also declared his satisfaction with the on-going racial cleansing of the German sporting clubs. At that moment, since Jews were being barred from practice and from the sporting clubs whose members alone had access to the Olympic trials, Jews were, of course, being barred from the trial for the German team.

At a meeting in the United States of the Amateur Athletic Union (A.A.U.) on November 21, 1933, the delegates, with but one exception, voted for a boycott of the 1936 Games unless the position of Germany vis-à-vis her Jewish athletes be "changed in fact as well as in theory." Gustavus T. Kirby of the American Olympic Committee had proposed the resolution and was vigorously supported by Avery Brundage, then president of the American Olympic Committee.

Brundage had long been a figure of some importance in American sport and in American business. Avery Brundage had competed in the 1912 Olympics in Stockholm when he was twenty-five years old and was sixth in the decathlon which was taken by the great American Indian, Jim Thorpe. Thorpe, one of the greatest athletes of all time, was far superior to anyone else. At the same Olympiad Jim Thorpe also won the pentathlon (old style--it then consisted, like the decathlon, only of track and field events) taking first in four of the five events. Thorpe's record in the decathlon stood for fifteen years, though when it was learned that he had played bush-league professional baseball in 1909 and 1910, his medals were taken from him and his name wiped from the official record books.

Significantly, in the long and sincere campaign of American sports writers to restore the medals to Thorpe, who eventually became a broken drunk, Brundage was an influential judge adamant for the strict upholding of the principles of amateurism. In 1914, 1916, and 1918, years when there were no Olympic competitions, Brundage was voted the Amateur all-around Champion of America. In 1915 in Chicago he had founded the Avery Brundage Company, a construction and real estate firm which became the foundation of his growing financial interests. Brundage's energy, affability, devotion to sport, and rigid code of personal behavior were apparent when he began to campaign to centralize the bureaucracy of American amateur sport in the 1920's. He was in close touch with aging Pierre de Coubertin who throughout his life had made eloquent pronouncements in favor of purity in athletics. Like almost all the bureaucrats of international amateur sport, Brundage was convinced that the founder was a genius and a saint. Perhaps Brundage's touchiness over the issues of lucre or sharp practices in the world of athletics was moral compensation for his survival in the shark-infested waters of American big business. Avery Brundage became and remained a very rich self-made man.

Brundage was first elected president of the American Olympic Committee and of the American Olympic Association in 1930. For years he had had the backing of the National Collegiate Athletic Association (N.C.A.A.) and the Amateur Athletic Union (A.A.U.). Bickering withint the Balkanized world of American amateur sport declined under his leadership and the conscious moral separation of American amateur athletics from professional sport became greater than similar gaps in any other sporting nation. American sports journalists have long included in their number a few very clever writers and many cynics. The organizational isolation of amateur sport from professional sport has seemed to them artificial and, in many cases, hypocritical. Brundage personified much of the frigidity and false cleanliness of American amateurism and obliged the sportswriters by occasional rudeness and pious pronouncements that were both nettlesome and newsworthy.

It was only during the preparations for the 1936 Games that Avery Brundage first assumed major controversial prominence. After the anti-Nazi resolution of the A.A.U. of November 1933, the American Olympic

Committee continued to postpone acceptance of the German invitation. As the facilities for the Games in Berlin became another prime public works project of the National Socialists and as Germany as well as other countries selected and trained their teams, well-publicized suggestions appeared here and there that the United States ought to boycott the Nazi Olympics. Nervously and with a fanfare of international publicity, the German Olympic Committee finally announced in June 1934 that twenty-one Jewish athletes had been nominated for the German training camps. Understandably suspicious, the American Olympic Committee dispatched Brundage himself to Germany to make an on-the-spot investigation.

Upon his return, Brundage revealed himself to be one more important personage dazzled by the order, relative prosperity, and joy that most travelers observed in Germany in those years. On the basis of his interviews with Jewish leaders (who, one hostile journalist noted, were always met in cafés and were always chaperoned by Nazi officials) Brundage concluded that the Germans were observing the letter and the spirit of Olympism. And on the basis of his recommendations the American Olympic Committee voted to participate in the XIth Olympiad. This particular decision did not, however, dispose of American suspicions of the Nazis. The body that supervised the Olympic trials, the A.A.U., was still on record as opposing American participation. Furthermore, its president, former Judge Jeremiah T. Mahoney, a Catholic deeply troubled by the aggressive paganism of the Nazis, was forming a "Committee on Fair Play in Sports" to channel and make more effective the growing domestic alarm over the news about Nazi atrocities. For, despite Brundage's claims to the contrary, trustworthy stories of religious and racial persecutions continued to leak out of Germany. For example, it was learned that, though twenty-one Jews were "nominated" for the Olympic training camps, noen were "invited" to attend.

By the summer of 1935, American hesitation had dragged on for two years. A modern Olympiad was an extremely complex affair to organize. It was far too late to arrange for elaborate or even acceptable staging of the Olympiad anywhere except in Berlin where everyone knew that grandiose preparations had been underway for some time. Most American Olympic officials had accepted Coubertin's commandment that, whatever the obstacles, the regular march of the modern Olympiads must somehow take place. Brundage and those loyal to him therefore took the position that: (a) the Germans were keeping their promises to behave and (b) Olympism was so important a movement that its modern opponents, however high-minded they claimed to be, had to be silenced, since they were placing in peril an institution that was far more important than their petty egos. One consequence of such determination was that Commodore Ernest Lee Jahncke, who was of German ancestry, an upholder of a less pragmatic Olympic ideal, and one of the three American members of the International Olympic Committee, was squeezed from his position on that body. As an emergency measure, Brundage was also making tentative preparations to form a rump organization, parallel with the A.A.U., that could hold the tryouts for the 1936 American Olympic team.

In 1935 several other matters tended to produce a crisis atmosphere around preparations for the Olympic Games scheduled for the next summer.

At Nuremberg in 1935, Hitler strayed from his usual policy of staging the party rallies as merely ceremonial cult rituals. At a great meeting at Nuremberg's _Kulturvereinhaus_ on Sunday evening, September 15, 1935, Hitler brazenly proclaimed the "Nuremberg Laws" which deprived German Jews of their citizenship and the protection of the laws of the Reich and which established social policies (e.g., forbidding intermarriage and making it illegal for German girls to work as servants for Jews) designed to preserve "the purity of Aryan blood." Naturally these extraordinary pronouncements attracted journalistic attention and were generally viewed with horror in the United States.

As this rally was taking place in Nuremberg, General Sherrill, a member of both the American and International Olympic Committees, was on _his_ tour of Germany. He sailed from Europe on the _Normandie_ and landed in New York on October 22, 1935--a day after Jeremiah T. Mahoney released a long public letter to Theodor Lewald, charging the National Socialists with a list of abuses against Mahoney's view of what was a sacred Olympic ideal. As he was interviewed for his reactions to Mahoney's letter Sherrill stated:

> I went to Germany for the purpose of getting at least one Jew on the German Olympic team and I feel that my job is finished. As for obstacles placed in the way of Jewish athletes or any others in trying to reach Olympic ability, I would have no more business discussing that in Germany than if the Germans attempted to discuss the Negro situation in the American South or the treatment of the Japanese in California.

Sherrill also ominously hinted that the imprudent level of Yankee concern with the internal policies of Nazi Germany could very well lead to a wave of anti-Semitism in the United States. The General condemned the boycott leaders and claimed he knew many American Jews who themselves opposed any boycott and feared "that it would be overplaying the Jewish hand in America as it was overplayed in Germany before the present suppression and expulsion of the Jews were undertaken." The next day, Frederick W. Rubien, secretary of the American Olympic Committee, presented his position. He announced:

> Germans are not discriminating against Jews in their Olympic tryouts. The Jews are eliminated because they are not good enough as athletes. Why there are not a dozen Jews in the world of Olympic calibre.

Other American Olympic officials were competing with Brundage for the attention of the sportswriters. Sherrill was more emphatic when he claimed that "there was never a prominent Jewish athlete in history." He hinted that the power center of the agitation against the Olympic Games was close to President Roosevelt, namely, two Jews, one of whom was the Secretary of the Treasury, Henry Morgenthau, and another he would not specify, only claiming that his family had long since Anglicized its surname. By this time Sherrill was the most flamboyant polemicist against the agitators. It did not help his reputation for wisdom when he spoke (and was widely quoted) before the Italian Chamber of Commerce in New York and praised Mussolini as "a man of courage in a world of pussyfooters" and declared, "I wish to God he'd come over here and have a chance to do that same thing."

The American protests frightened the Nazis. Just before Sherrill left for his tour of Germany, an American correspondent predicted "concessions" at the last moment.

> In such a case they will be found in categories in which Germany stands slight chances of success because a German-Jewish victory would raise serious problems. Croquet and chess have been suggested as suitable categories.

One actual concession was the case of Rudi Ball who was invited back from his exile in France which he had entered as a refugee in 1933. He rejoined the German ice hockey team. In addition, Sherrill had, as he claimed, succeeded in getting another Jew on the German team. The candidature that he had been particularly exercised about was that of Helene Mayer, the half-Jewish fencer, who lived in Los Angeles. While in Germany in the summer of 1935, Sherrill had, in fact, hounded the Nazi sporting officials, since they had not yet invited Miss Mayer despite their promises of two years before. The blonde fencer had already issued a statement that she would be pleased to represent Germany, since she had done so in two previous Olympiads and because she was eager to visit her mother and two brothers. Finally Tschammer und Osten invited the girl and attempted to side-step some embarrassment by declaring Miss Mayer to be "Aryan" (indeed, she looked like an advertisement for one) despite her mixed parentage. Rumors immediately became current that Helene Mayer was being forced to compete for Germany out of fear for her family. Many American Jews tried to dissuade her from competing. Once she accepted the invitation, however, she eschewed politics and called Rabbi Wise "a meddler." Two other German Jews who were known to be of Olympic caliber, the high jumper Gretl Bergmann and the sprinter Werner Schattmann, were indirectly refused a chance at Olympic berths by being denied the opportunity to participate in the tryouts for the German Field Sports Championships, which were really pre-Olympic qualifying trials.

In the United States the pressure to boycott the Olympics gathered strength from sectors of public opinion that were neither Jewish nor notoriously pro-Semitic. The Gleichschaltung had also required the merging of all Catholic and Protestant sporting organizations into the Nazi system. The Berlin Olympics became an issue upon which aroused Christians and militant liberals could meet for the expression of their fears and disgust. The liberal Catholic magazine Commonweal felt that the "Nazi youth organizations are flagrantly and purely pagan" and took the position that to support the 1936 Games would be to "set the seal of approval on the radically anti-Christian, Nazi doctrine of youth." The National Council of the Methodist Church passed a resolution against holding the 1936 Games in Germany. The American Federation of Labor declared itself against American participation in the German Games because the Nazis were anti-labor and because there was "nothing noble" in the persecution by sixty million Germans of 600,000 Jews --100 to one was not fair odds. Many city councils, trade unions, and civic organizations passed resolutions against honoring the Nazi festival with an

American presence. The American National Society of Mural Painters voted that no member of their organization would take part in an exhibit of painting that the Nazis were giving in connection with the XIth Olympiad. Many American newspapers including all the New York dailies opposed the continued preparations for choosing a Yankee team. New York's governor, Al Smith, telegraphed his objections to Brundage. The sportswriter Damon Runyon wrote that "Germany's pagan putsch makes its acceptance of the real Olympic oath either an impossibility or a hypocrisy." Many other sportswriters including John Kieran of The New York Times were shocked at Germany's "poor sportsmanship." Ed Sullivan of the New York Daily News noted with astonishment, "I read in the papers yesterday that Germany now proposes to wipe from the war records the names of Jewish war veterans who were killed or maimed in her defense." As the A.A.U. prepared for its meeting in December 1935 it had before its executive board resolutions from organizations representing memberships of 1,500,000 and petitions containing the signatures of 500,000 persons who opposed the staging of the 1936 Games in Germany. There was a mass meeting against American participation in Madison Square Garden on December 3.

It should be noted once more than those favoring (indeed, at the same time forming) a strong American team also assumed a high moral stance. Like their boycotting opponents, they too could decry the decline in international trustworthiness and, while doing so, defend the Olympics as being superior to the maneuvers of local politicians--German, American, or whatever. Unlike the half-cocked and passionately vocal organizers of the boycott movement, the defenders of international Olympism claimed they were supporting a movement that encouraged tolerance and peaceful understanding. Brundage and his supporters posed as being far above petty chauvinism--a position that did not prevent them from occasionally praising the visible accomplishments of the Nazis and from slurring the adherents of Mahoney's Committee on Fair Play as being "Reds" or even "Communists."

Both sides gathered rhetorical ammunition for a great rebate at the national convention of the Amateur Athletic Union which opened in New York in early December. The proponents of a boycott were armed with resolutions to that effect from regional associations of the A.A.U. The delegates met tensely, but the expected battle was never really joined. The executive committee of the A.A.U. met at the Hotel Commodore on Sunday, December 8, to listen to five hours of speeches for and against participation. The moguls of American amateur sport were hungry and tired when time for a vote came. The executives (who had weighted voting rights) defeated the proposed resolution against sending an American team by 2 1/2 votes. The narrow majority then succeeded in passing a motion in favor of participation, adding the specific rider that their affirmative action was not to be "construed to imply endorsement of the Nazi government."

The expected debate, then, was never presented to the membership of the A.A.U. and the inspired defenders of a less Olympically disposed sporting ideal were not permitted oratorically to clarify their position. Brundage and his lieutenants were immovable in the face of accusations of parliamentary double-crossing and unscrupulous floor maneuvers. Then, in rapid succession, the press learned that Jeremiah Mahoney, the most prominent publicist favoring an American boycott and president of the A.A.U., had resigned from his position, that Brundage had been nominated for that post and almost unanimously elected and that, having combined in himself the offices of the American Olympic Committee and the Amateur Athletic Union, Brundage at once urged the voluntary resignation from their posts of all the officers of these organizations who were "anti-Olympic." It should be emphasized here that, at the time, the question among the delegates and the membership was not whether racial persecutions should be approved of, but who should be believed: Brundage who denied their existence or Mahoney who said they were rampant in the world of German sport. Naturally, the wreckage due to clashing reputations left a great deal of bitterness among amateur sportsmen in the United States.

The boycott movement did not just end there. The president of the Maccabi World Union, an international organization of Jewish sporting clubs, wrote a public letter to Count Henri Baillet-Latour, president of the International Olympic Committee, saying that, while he could not question the decision of the I.O.C. to keep the Games in Berlin and while he sympathized with a desire not to mix politics with sport,

> We cannot as Jews accept lightly the situation created by the Olympic Games being held in Berlin. I, in common with all other Jews and many non-Jews, look upon the state of affairs in Germany from the point of view of general humanity and social decency. We certainly do urge all Jewish sportsmen, for their own self-respect, to refrain from competing in a country where they are discriminated against as a race and our Jewish brethren are treated with unexampled brutality.

This plea led to no wholesale boycott by Jews of the Olympics. As we have seen Rudi Ball and Helene Mayer rushed to join the German team. Many Polish, Czechoslovakian, and Hungarian Jews were on their homelands' Olympic teams. In fact, one Hungarian, Ilona Schacherer-Elek, was Helene Mayer's nearest competitor in fencing. A few famous Jewish athletes avoided Berlin. Judith Deutsch, an Austrian swimmer of world record caliber, boycotted the 1936 Olympics. French Jews who eschewed Berlin were bobsled champions Philippe de Rothschild and Jean Rheims and a famous fencer, Albert Wolff. However, in Great Britain Harold M. Abrahams, of a prominent family of Jewish civil servants and noted athletes, most vociferously headed off any movement for a boycott. Abrahams had won (and established an Olympic record) in the 100-meter dash at the 1924 Olympics in Paris.

At the time, Americans appeared to possess a near monopoly on moral outrage, even though the movement to boycott the Olympics was in the end ineffective. An anti-Nazi campaign to urge the withdrawal of Negro athletes scarcely got off the ground, but at least the indignation was expressed. On August 23, 1935, the Amsterdam News (published in Harlem) urged Negro athletes, "to display that spirit of sacrifice which is the true mark of all greatness." No doubt some American athletes ignored the Olympic trials out of strong feelings about certain trends in Germany; many were doubtless conscience-stricken as they struggled to do their best in the trials that would produce the eventual Yankee team. The campaign for a boycott also surely provided meritricious explanations for some athletes who failed to make the American team in 1936. There were, in fact, several Jews on the American team: Sam Stoller and Marty Glickman, who were sprinters and members of the 400-meter relay team, David Mayer, a weight lifter, Sam Balter, a basketball player, Max Bly, a bobsledder, and Hyman Goldberg, who was on the team for an exhibition of baseball in Berlin. While most of the world's sports fans were distracted by the preparations and the actual unfolding of the German Olympics of 1936, Judge Mahoney and many other morally offended Americans and Europeans were arranging to hold some "People's Olympics" or "Workers' Games" in Barcelona (which, we remember, had been Berlin's rival to host the XIth Olympiad) as a protest against the Nazification of international sport.

For those who were eager for a splendid American presence in Germany in 1936 the debate over whether or not the United States should participate was not without helpful results. Avery Brundage who, besides his several other posts, was also chairman of the American Finance Committee for the Olympic Games, observed that "the active boycott by Jews and Communists" was in some ways "beneficial." The pressure for chastisement of the Nazis

> aroused the resentment of the athletic leaders, the sportsmen, and patriotic citizens of America and induced them to work harder, and to contribute more. It destroyed much of the ignorance and apathy present in prior years.

In any case, despite the fact that the depression was by no means past and the sum asked for, $350,000, was a record for an American team, all the bills were paid and Brundage was able, in the end, to give a surplus of $50,000 to the American Olympic Association.

Pre-Olympic trials had begun before the A.A.U. finally voted to consent to authorizing an American team for Germany's Olympics. The finals of the ice hockey tryouts were, in fact, taking place in New Haven, New York City, and Rye, New York, just as the Brundage steamroller squashed the boycott movement at the A.A.U. meeting in early December 1935. Final trials to select the teams for the winter Games then proceeded in several locations in the United States. The speed skating finals were in Minneapolis in January 1936. Lake Placid hosted most of the skiing events except for the jumping trials which were held in Salt Lake City and the combined downhill slalom eliminations which were in Mount Rainier National Park, Washington.

Trials for the varied program of the summer Olympics were similarly dispersed all over the United States. The yachting candidates were determined in SandPedro, California. The finals of the equestrian competitions were at the army's cavalry base at Fort Riley, Kansas. The swimmers and divers met in Providence, Rhode Island, Chicago, and in Astoria, New York, for the women's events. Most of the final track and field tryouts were in New York City early in July of 1936, but there were two final trials for the marathon (which by that time had attained the status as possibly the most prestigious event of the Olympic program) in Boston and in Washington, D.C. Decathlon finalists met in Milwaukee. Women track and field candidates learned whether they would go overseas in Providence, Rhode Island, on July 4, 1936. The dispersion of these well-publicized trials of course provided a wide geographical base for the local committees raising funds for what eventually became the largest American Olympic team yet assembled. Since Negroes were accepted for the American team, no trials could take place in or even near the deep South. A sports fan from Georgia or Alabama eager to move the minimum distance to see some Olympic candidates would have to travel to Baltimore or Cincinnati to see the pre-Olympic finals for, respectively, baseball and the 50-kilometer walk--sports which at the time attracted no Negro entries. The American Olympic Committee awarded some 3,000 certificates to contestants placing in the preliminary, sectional, semifinal, and final tryouts. The American team for the winter Olympics eventually consisted of 76 athletes and 14 officials. Of the 384 athletes and 87 officials selected for the summer Olympics, 383 were on board the <u>Manhattan</u> ("the Largest Steamer Ever Built in America") on Wednesday, July 15, 1936, when tugs pulled the confettied and streamered great ship out of New York Harbor.

As the <u>Manhattan</u> steamed east almost all of her 800 passengers who were not athletes or trainers were reporters or sports fans also on their way to the sporting festival in Germany. An exception was the young American diplomat George F. Kennan who "dodged the motions of the gum-chewing supermen, and a variety of hefty Amazons." Certain decks had been set aside for workouts and those present felt they were traveling on a floating gym.

Harold Smallwood, a sprinter, had a shipboard attack of appendicitis. Winds and cold rain produced dozens of colds, but still the huge American team arrived cheerful and eager the morning of July 24 at Hamburg where they happily submitted to well-rehearsed welcoming ceremonies by the city authorities there. They then took trains for Berlin where there were more elaborate ceremonies in the afternoon. Further genial speeches, band music, and even a corridor of torch-bearing German youths greeted the American team when they arrived, tired, at the Olympic Village fifteen miles west of the center of Berlin and about ten miles from the sporting complex.

The lavish production at Los Angeles had been for some 1,500 athletes. Berlin was preparing for 3,500. After the Germans, the Americans had the largest team. Despite the continuing economic slump and the uncertainty of international politics (or, on the other hand, perhaps as psychological antidotes to them) other nations also sent large teams. Like the citizens of the ancient Greek city-states, all the world's patriots were eager to grasp at the prestige to be gathered by their Olympic victors. The Germans had overconscientiously prepared welcomes to impress, even overwhelm their visitors. For example, when their own misscheduling forced the French team to appear at the Olympic Village at 1:30 A.M. they were still greeted by corridors of Hitler youths holding torches high and playing waltzes.

The man most responsible for all these preparations was Dr. Carl Diem. He was born in Würzburg on June 24, 1882. As a teenager in the

1890's he was a middle- and long-distance runner at a time when track events as practiced among the Anglo-Saxons were almost unknown among his countrymen who were quite devoted to gymnastics. Diem founded his first sporting club, Macromannia, in Berlin when he was seventeen. He was a burly, short man and a perfect miracle of channeled energy. After 1900 his special track event was competition army field pack marching. He led the German expeditions to the Athens Games of 1906 and to the Olympics of 1912 in Stockholm, 1928 in Amdterdam, and 1932 in Los Angeles. For twenty years after 1913, Dr. Diem was the secretary of the German government's Commission for Sport and Recreation (Generalsekretar des Deutschen Reichanschusses fur Leibesubungen) and during this time he founded and built the principal German school for recreation teachers, Die deutsche Hochschule fur Leibesubungen, in Cologne. Diem traveled a lot and knew many languages. The Turkish government consulted him regularly concerning its recreation programs. He designed athletic architecture and athletic festivals in Germany. All the while Diem was engaged in his promotional work he was producing a stream of scholarly and theoretical writings of the highest quality. Only a fanatically uncritical admirer of Pierre de Coubertin would dispute the claim that Carl Diem is the greatest sports historian and most profound theorist of sport education of this century. He was expertly knowledgeable about the ball games of the pre-Columbian Indians, field hockey in ancient Egypt, Mongolian polo, and the starting lines for the sprinters in ancient Greek stadiums.

Like most prominent bureaucrats in the amateur athletics movement, Diem was an almost slavish admirer of Coubertin. Perhaps this reverential attitude toward the founder was without-which-nothing prerequisite for admission to international sport's inner councils. Diem had even investigated the Italian origins of the Fredy-Coubertin family and solemnly collected and edited the baron's frequently derivative and often fatuous utterances about the philosophical bases of sport. Like Coubertin, Carl Diem cheerfully and paradoxically believed that pure sport was really for the world's elite though it should also enliven and inspire the masses to higher accomplishments. Like Coubertin, Brundage, and most other directors of the many national Olympic committees, Diem doubted not that sport could both inspire the most passionate patriotism and soothe aggressive tempers and was therefore a contributor to the harmony of nations.

A calamity for young Carl Diem had been the canceling, due to the Great War, of the VIth Olympiad, intended for Berlin in 1916. The war wiped out years of his architectural planning and detailed scheduling of the events and festivities. Through the 1920's, Diem and Lewald (who resembled one another--and both were near doubles of Count Henri Baillet-Latour, president of the International Olympic Committee) succeeded first in getting German teams readmitted to Olympic competition in 1928 and then repeatedly presented the case for an Olympiad in Berlin. After all, the facilities intended for 1916 were ready for use. The two men were delighted when Baillet-Latour on May 13, 1932, announced the award of the 1936 Games to Berlin rather than Barcelona. During the summer of 1932 Diem became a perfect demon of released energy running about Los Angeles collecting data about the American experience so he could learn from the Yankees and surpass them. Late in 1932 Diem returned to troubled Germany to get ready for the climax of his life.

The extreme complexity of the planning required to stage adequately an international festival heralded long in advance as the most lavish and biggest ever, was not so great as to daunt Carl Diem. Diem issued the invitations, scheduled the many parts of the program, and acquired the land and appointed the architect for the German Olympic Village. The facilities left over from 1916 were quickly shown to be generally meager in view of the Hollywoodian architecture and landscaping provided in 1932 by the Californians--who, of course, had to be surpassed. Diem got the Fuhrer to lease until 1943 the Berlin Racing Association's very extensive land holdings which adjoined the twenty-year-old Olympic stadium.

To tout the coming festival, the Ministry of Propaganda was in charge of more general kinds of international and domestic advertising. Diem himself established an "Olympic Games News Serviee" which issued its first press notices on February 17, 1933. In January 1934 the News Service began issuing a monthly newspaper which "was sent to every administrative and sporting center in Germany and abroad that was in any way connected with the Olympic Games as well as to the international press." At first the bulletins were published in five languages, but, as the circulation reached its peak of 25,000 the languages were increased to fourteen. Another monthly, Olympic Games 1936: Official Organ of the XI Olympic Games, began its run of fifteen issues in four languages in June 1935. A daily Olympia Zeitung appeared in thirty numbers between July 21 and August 19, 1936. Diem edited them all and fretted about technical details:

> How many telephones should be provided for the Reichs Sports
> Field; which should be local and which connected with a central of-
> fice; where a light system; where a microphone and where a loud-
> speaker? How high should the flag poles be; how high the steps;
> how should the seats be covered and how should the galleries be
> floored? How should the temperature of the swimming pools be
> regulated; how can it be kept clear and transparent? Should the
> box for the referees and judges be connected with the entrance for
> athletes? Where are elevators for transporting food? Which
> countries for hot and which for cold food? What about garages,
> work shops, the surface of the running tracks....

Dr. Diem assigned artists the tasks of designating the medals, the award certificates, a new gold chain of office for members of the International Olympic Committee, special postage stamps, advertising posters, press passes, and entrance tickets. Half the tickets for any particular competition were reserved for Germans; half for foreigners. For tourists from abroad he obtained reductions of 60 per cent in rail fares and a 20 per cent reduction in air and steamship fares on German carriers. One of his committees was charged with arranging a world festival of youth consisting of thirty "future exponents of the Olympic ideals" from each nation in the world. The hosts for this particular rally that eventually assembled 11,148 participants were devoted cadres of the Hitler Youth who together with their guests led a "simple camp life" in tent villages in the Grunewald as they all attended the Games.

Diem also introduced some technological innovations into the projected sports meeting. Since the new stadium would hold more than 100,000 people, there was an urgent need for a strong loudspeaker that would not produce interior echoes. The German electrical industry complied, improving the loudspeaker devised for the Nuremberg rallies. The Physikalisch-technische Reichsanstalt produced three new scoring devices. One was a much improved photographic apparatus to determine the placings at close finishes of the track and swimming events. Another was a combined scoring board and primitive computer for showing the decisions of the judges of springboard and platform diving. A third invention was designed to minimize the effect of dramatic action in the fencing matches. A fencing judge had to combine a minute knowledge of the refinements of the contest, perfect concentration, and the keenest eyesight with a deep, incorruptible cynicism. In international competition a jury had often been swayed by "a fast thrust, executed with a triumphant shout and followed by a confident attitude usually indicated by an immediate dropping of the guard or removal of the mask"-- this, even though the exultant competitor may have been hit by a counter movement. Brio was almost wiped out of the 1936 fencing competitions by the introduction of an impartial electrical touch-recording device.

A new showplace in Berlin and a sort of tour de force that combined German hospitality with German method was the Olympic Village in Berlin. In 1932 the Californians had provided isolated, simple housing for the athletes who had come to America to compete. Diem established a new standard. The army engineers were in charge of erecting the German Olympic Village. Its builder and organizer, Captain Wolfgang Fuerstner, had been in charge of the Wehrmacht's sporting program. Like so many other functionaries who at this time directed programs intenedd to impress the foreigners, Fuerstner was given almost a free hand relative to the financial and other resources he could draw on. The village itself was situated in a birch forest and near some small lakes beyond the western suburbs of Berlin. Besides the meeting halls and commons, there were 160 houses of brick, stone, and concrete. A house held 24 to 26 men in double rooms each of which had a wash basin, a shower, and a toilet. Two stewards speaking the athletes' language were quartered in every house. Just before the athletes arrived the whole area had been landscaped and the peaceful lake provided with coveys of snow-white ducks. All this was intended to obliterate the signs of rapid construction.

Like the participants in the Nuremberg rallies, each of the thousands of athletes, coaches, and officials at the village had long before been given a series of colored slips that plainly cited the house, room, and bed he was to occupy. He also had color-coded books of meal tickets indicating for him and for the staff of the village the food he would get and details of his special care. The athletes were told of the precise kinds of transportation they would use from the village to the sites of the various events. The British official report afterward recalled the terrific melee on the first morning of the Games when 3,000 men tried all at once to board the buses for the Reichssportfield, the central athletic complex. There would have been no confusion "provided the competitors carried out the instructions issued by the German authorities with regard to departure."

The international camaraderie that the Nazis were eager to demonstrate to the photographers and journalists who were directed to the Olympic
Village was, in fact, achieved. Planning, painstaking care, and the alert
sensitivity of the domestic staffs had, among the male athletes at least,
made for an atmosphere of easy sociability. Shotputters met to compare
notes of technique; weight lifters publicly flexed. Tourists gathered to observe the seriousness, strenuousness, and amazing agility of the Japanese
swimmers as they limbered up. No one publicly objected to the incessant
noise making and ebullient horseplay of the Italian soccer players. In the
evening athletes from all over the world gathered in the common rooms for
reading, card games, or to watch movies of events that had taken place that
day. The gymnasts were especially grateful for the daily films that permitted them to see what the judges had seen shortly before. Fuerstner had provided barbers, medical care, and even dentists. The Ministry of Propaganda offered for free distribution a picture of a Chinese athlete suffering
some complicated dental work that would have been terribly dear at home.
Tasteful bulletin boards had indexes of masseurs including special ones for
the cyclists. The Americans had American mattresses; the Swiss and Austrians had their familiar feather comforters; the Japanese had mats on the
floor. Around the quiet, idyllic lake at the village was a tree-shaded jogging
track. On the lake, for the use of the Finns, was a faultless, torrid sauna
the benefits of which they eagerly extended to others.

The care and feeding of the almost four thousand men from fifty nations at the Olympic Village was entrusted to the stewards' department of
the North German Lloyd combine whose network of passenger ship lines
covered the whole word. There was no common menu. Each national cui-
sine was reproduced for the guests of new Germany. Following are some
observations made afterward by the head of the stewards' department of the
Olympic Village:

France: The French sportsman is also an epicure, paying less
attention to practical nourishment than to tasty and varied dishes. English steaks prepared Chateaubriand fashion with white
bread and red wine preferred for weight lifters; all kinds of meat
requested, this being prepared in the form of steaks, filets, cutlets, roasts, and ragouts; delicacies such as mushrooms, an-
chovies, corn on the cob, green peppers, etc. popular; stewed
fruit with every meal; vegetables steamed in butter but without
sauces; cheese, fruit, and coffee after the principal meals.

Germany: The weight lifters received beefsteak Tartar, chopped
raw liver, cream cheese with oil and considerable quantities of
eggs, often four per meal. Light refreshment before training
and more substantial food afterward. The athletes required normal meals, steaks, cutlets, pork chops, roast beef, and fowl
being principally requested. Large quantities of fruit; vegetables being prepared with flour; potatoes but practically no rice;
tomatoes and salads popular; milk with grape-sugar and fruit
juices preferred as drinks; various kinds of bread with large
quantities of butter....

Great Britain: Moderate eaters; grilled meat "medium" done, especially popular; three to four eggs, oatmeal, tea, milk, fruit, and toast for breakfast, Horlick's malted milk; plainly cooked vegetables.

U.S.A.: Beefsteaks as well as lamb and veal daily for lunch and dinner; no form of fried meat except fowl; underdone steaks before competition; for breakfast, eggs with ham, bacon, oatmeal or hominy, and orange juice; large quantities of fresh or stewed fruit; no kippered herrings; vegetables and baked potatoes with principal meals; sweet dishes including custards and ice cream.

The steward's department also noted that the Chileans loved "large quantities of marmalade," the Czechs preferred pork fat in the preparation of all meat dishes, the Finns, besides their rye bread, were especially appreciative of the blueberries, the Hungarians asked for macaroni and sour cream for an "extra." Several East Indians were vegetarians. The Japanese wanted soy with everything and brought with them some of their more exotic condiments and preserves. The Peruvian weight lifters ate as many as ten eggs a day. The athletes from the Philippines refused spinach and cauliflower, but demanded one lemon per day per person. Many athletes were devoted to the quaffing of great quantities of orange juice. The American consensus afterward was, "The best place to eat in Berlin was the Olympic Village."

Of course, the housing for the male athletes in Berlin was devised not only for their benefit, but for purposes of putting the new regime in a good light. The women who competed were much less observed and much less comfortable. The forty-nine American female athletes and officials were taken to the women's dormitory, Friedrich Friesen Haus, a utilitarian dormitory near the Reichssportfield that was surrounded by a high, wrought-iron fence. Once there, the women of all nations were isolated and put under the strict supervision of the Baroness von Wangenheim, a humorless Prussian with tiny eyes and great jowls below which she wore a thin string of very fine pearls. For some time there was no heat in the rooms and the food was inadequate both as regards quality and quantity. The Baroness was unresponsive to frequent requests for improvement in living conditions.

Another center for the athletes was at the old castle of Köpenick which housed the rowers. The horses and men who were to compete in the equestrian events had arrived earlier in Berlin and had quarters far outside the sprawling capital. The sailing events took place near Kiel, 200 miles to the north, and the participants there just arranged for local housing on their own.

There is a strange postscript to add about the devoted administrator who oversaw the planning and construction of the Olympic Village. As was mentioned earlier, Captain Fuerstner was director of the German army's athletic program. It happened that he was also one of the few non-Aryan "blind spots" that the Wehrmacht was permitted by the Nazis. A few weeks before the foreign athletes arrived, Fuerstner was suddenly and inexplicably replaced at the Olympic Village by a certain Lieutenant Colonel Werner von und zu Gilsa. Then he was dismissed from the army--a personal calamity the loyal officer had never considered possible because of the frequent testimonials he had received for his good work. Though he, like the <u>Mischling</u> Dr. Theodor Lewald, was grossly demoted to being a piece of smiling window dressing, Fuerstner publicly voiced no displeasure and continued to serve nominally as second in command at the village until after the Games were over. Then, after a banquet honoring von und zu Gilsa for his services to the Reich in making the 1936 Olympics a success, Fuerstner killed himself with a single shot when he returned to his army barracks. The German press was at once instructed to explain that the officer had died after an automobile accident, but the truth leaked to foreign journalists. This unforeseen vignette required some sort of cover-up and retribution. General Werner von Blomberg, the Minister of Defense, arranged for a well-publicized funeral with full military honors. For some weeks afterward the walls of the deserted Olympic Village were a favorite place for the Nazi zealots to scrawl obscene slogans against "the Jew Fuerstner" and against the Jews in general.

High-ranking Nazis were, of course, keenly aware that Germany was being watched by travelers for corroborating incidents of racial atrocities. There was, in fact, a confrontation between Hitler and Count Baillet-Latour, the Belgian grand seigneur who was president of the International Olympic Committee and who, publicly at least, made strong pronouncements that the Nazis were keeping their promises not to offend the sensibilities of their foreign guests. While motoring to Garmisch-Partenkirchen to open the winter Games, Baillet-Latour was astonished to see many vicious anti-Semetic posters along the German highways. As soon as he arrived at Garmisch he demanded and obtained an immediate audience with the Fuhrer and through Paul Schmidt, the interpreter, they argued. Such ornaments were impossible preludes for a festival for all races and nations, shouted the great aristocrat. Hitler declared he could not alter "a question of the highest importance within Germany . . . for a small point of Olympic protocol." Baillet-Latour asserted that it was "a question of the most elementary courtesy," assumed an air of intransigency and threatened a cancellation of the winter and summer Games.

> Though stymied a bit at first, Hitler began to talk glibly, exciting himself more and more while staring at a corner of the ceiling. Soon he seemed oblivious to the presence of his companion and it was almost as though he was in a sort of trance. Schmidt ceased translating and waited for "the crisis" to pass--being familiar with this kind of scene.

Then the chancellor fell silent for several tense minutes. The Belgian was silent too. Suddenly Hitler blurted, "You will be satisfied; the orders shall be given," and brusquely ended the interview by leaving the room. When Baillet-Latour returned to Brussels by car, he saw no signs. The offensive placards were taken from the roads until the Games were over.

Politics And Protest

At The Olympic Games

Joel Thirer

When international sport competition was reintroduced in the form of
the modern Olympic Games in 1896, no one could have imagined how quickly they would grow in popularity and notoriety. The intent of Baron Pierre
de Coubertin was to institute athletic competition among the great amateur
athletes of the world in a similar fashion to the original Greek Olympic
Games. It is most unlikely that de Coubertin could have foresaw the dramatic shift from the individual to the country he represents.

The focus of the ancient Olympic Games was on individual athletic excellence. Little attention was placed on the city/state, or country that the
athlete was from. By contrast, if we view the more recent Olympiads, with
a few notable exceptions all that the press and public tend to remember is
how many Gold, Silver, and Bronze medals each country accumulated.

The change in emphasis from the individual athlete to the "team" or
country that the athlete is from was initiated from the very first Olympiad
by de Coubertin himself. Due to an intense, personal dislike of the Germans, de Coubertin banned them from participating in the games. The ban
was lifted at the last moment but at this late time the Germans were able to
only send a token team.

The sense of national affiliation was also furthered during the first
modern Olympiad by the inclusion of raising the flag of the victors country at
the conclusion of each event. This act in itself diminished that attention toward the individual winner, and instead focused it on the country he represented.

The United States made its entrance into the Olympics in a political
sense in 1908. At the 1908 Olympiad in London, the British neglected to display both the American and Swedish flags in the stadium during the opening
ceremonies. Responding to what they deemed to be an insult, the Americans
refused to dip their flag to the King and Queen during the parade of athletes.
This action on the part of the American athletes popularized the phrase,
"this flag dips to no earthly king."

The Swedes, who were distressed at the absence of their flag took no action during the opening ceremonies. However, after a protest involving a decision in a wrestling match, the Swedish team officially withdrew from the games and returned home.

The flag dipping scenario, although the most memorable was not the only dispute the Americans were involved in during the 1908 Olympics. During the finals of the 400-meter race British favorite Wyndham Halswelle was blocked from winning. Instead of just disqualifying the American who had run out of his lane, British officials stopped the race and insisted it be rerun.

From an American viewpoint, the highlight of the 1912 Olympiad was the heroic efforts of an American Indian, Jim Thorpe. Thorpe accomplished the unheard of feat of winning both the Pentathalon and Decathalon competitions, and was hailed as the world's greatest athlete. Shortly after the games ended, it became known that Thorpe had played semi-professional baseball one summer, for nothing more than expense money. He was summarily stripped of his medals and his name removed from the record books. There was much contention at the time that had Thorpe not been an American, or more precisely, an Indian, that the issue of his professionalism would not have created the turmoil that it did.

Sporadic incidents of nationalistic, or political behaviors continued ot permeate the Olympic Games as they steadily grew in both size and popularity. For the sake of simplification only occurrences dircctly or indirectly involving the United States will be examined.

The 1928 Olympiad in Amsterdam occasioned the first appearance of women competitors in track and field events. Despite the fact that overall, the United States won only a single individual gold medal in track and field, we were quick to point out that the United States finished first in total team points.

In 1932, President Herbert Hoover became the first head of government of a nation hosting the Olympics to not show up for the games. He sent the Vice President in his stead. This was quite a departure from the pomp and pagentry associated with recent past Olympiads, and this formality was destined to return to form in the 1936 games. In fact the 1936 Olympiad held in Berlin on the dawn of World War II remains unmatched in its blatant exhibition of international politics.

Adolph Hitler cranked his Nazi propaganda machine into full gear when Berlin became the sight of the 1936 games. In order to present a positive picture of "Aryan supremacy" to the rest of the world, efforts were taken to temporarily ease the persecution of Jews and other minorities that the "master race" deemed as subhuman. The events of this era are excellently described in Richard Mandell's (1971) the Nazi Olympics.

There was a large movement afoot in the United States to withhold the American team from competing in the hate-filled hostile environment of Nazi Germany. As dissension mounted at home, Avery Brundage, then the head of the United States Olympic Committee "took an almost fanatical approach toward going. As more opponents of the Olympic Committee began rising all over the country, the statements from the USOC transcended all morality" (Johnson, 1972; p. 176).

Despite the home opposition, the United States did indeed go the the 1936 Olympics Games. Brundage's statements commending the great "Olympic spirit" of Hitler and the Germans apparently had effect on at least some of the people associated with the United States Olympic contingent. Two American Jewish sprinters, Marty Glickman and Sam Stoller were mysteriously withheld from their events by their American Coaches, despite their both having qualified for the finals.

The United States was not without its political heroes in 1936. Who will ever forget the tremendous efforts of Jesse Owens in winning gold medals and breaking Olympic records despite the pressure of being a black man in a white, racist, hostile country? The United States press was quick to adopt Owens' heroics as a counterattack to the Nazi "master race" propaganda.

Due to the outbreak of World War II, the Olympic Games were not reconvened until 1948, in a shell shocked London. Not uncharacteristically, Germany, Japan, and Italy, were banned from participating by the victorious allies.

The first appearance of a team representing the Soviet Union was marked in 1952. The cold war was well underway at this point, and a great deal of tension was present for all the athletes concerned. This tension was carried over to the 1956 games in Melbourne, Australia. When the Hungarian Olympic team arrived at Melbourne airport, thousands of Hungarian refugees were there to meet them. In response to the emotional crowd that was openly crying and shouting phrases such as "Long live free Hungary", the Hungarian athletes responded with revolutionary slogans and statements.

A relative calm pervaded for the next 12 years. The Soviet Union and other Eastern European teams steadily improved in their performance and in the number of medals won. Organized funding for Eastern European teams became the rule and athletes were able to dedicate all of their time to training for international competition in government subsidized programs. The United States still maintained strict regulation providing against "professionalism", and the Soviets used their Olympic successes to its fullest political advantage.

No one would have predicted that the blossoming of the civil rights movement in the United States would ultimately have such a great impact of the Olympic Games. The 1968 Olympiad was characterized by demonstrtions by individuals, a unique development when compared with the organized grandstanding previously conducted by teams or Olympic Committees.

If it were possible to lay credit to one man for the demonstrations in Mexico City in 1968 it would have to be to a man who was not even among the participants, Harry Edwards. Edwards, then a professor of Sociology at

San Jose State University, is the man who successfully organized a good number of the black participants in the games into a militant, political activist group. His efforts, which started years before the 1968 Olympiad, succeeded in the boycotting of the Olympic trials by such notable athletes as Lew Alcindor (now known as Kareem Abdul-Jabbar) and his then UCLA teammates Lucius Allen and Mike Warren. Numerous black athletes refused to even participate in the Olympic trials, thus eliminating many of the top United States performers in their respective sports from trying out for positions on the team. A great many more athletes, although deciding against staging a boycott, went into the games as a mobile, politically oriented force. The demonstration by Smith and Carlos early in the games set off many additional demonstrations, some resulting directly from the subsequent banishment of the two track stars from the games. Edwards goes into a great deal of the background of how he became involved and actually one of the leading figures and inspirers of the movement in his book The Revolt of the Black Athlete.

American athletes of all races were clearly growing discontent with the American amateur and professional sports scene in the mid-1960's. This activist sentiment was a typical offshoot of the general activism that was prevalent on college campuses all over the country. Black athletes were by no means the only ones to protest against discriminatory or unfair practices by coaches, owners, and administrators. Simultaneously, battles by white athletes were being waged against dehumanization and denial of civil liberties.

Harry Edwards, one of the major leaders of black activism in sports, adopted the dark glasses and beret that were symbolic of the Black Panther uniform as part of his regular wardrobe. Tommy Smith appeared on the cover of Newsweek magazine, sprinting, while wearing dark glasses, characteristic of the black militants, under a title story about black militants in sports.

The amateur and professional athletic scene in the United States had and still has many inadequacies as far as racial equality and the existence of prejudice is concerned. The mood of activism that swept America in the mid-1960's was bound to carry over into the sports scene which has been, for the most part, years behind the rest of the nation in terms of enlightenment. Anarchy, totalitarianism, racism, segregation, sexism, and monopoly were characteristics of both the American and international sports scene. To a large extent these conditions still exist in many aspects of sport. But certainly the activist sentiment that was aroused in the 1960's and that still pervades today has tremendously aided in eliminating or weakening many of those barriers.

What the medium of the Olympic Games has done is to have provided America and the world with a center stage in which to voice protests against injustices, real and imagined. Perhaps a disproportionate amount of attention is given to the sports world in the United States. To ignore this fact would be ridiculous. All one has to do is turn on the television set Saturday or Sunday afternoon or see what percentage of the daily newspaper is occupied by sports. What better area is there to draw attention to a protest movement than the Olympic Games. Where else is so much attention by so many people focused?

Olsen (1968) wrote a series of five articles for Sports Illustrated just prior to the 1968 Olympics. Each article ranged from the personal problems individual athletes have encountered in their climb from poverty and the ghettos to national fame, to a disturbing expose of the blatant racism that existed in the National Football League's St. Louis Cardinals as well as in other professional teams. Olsen's articles were perfectly timed because while the last one was fresh on the newsstands the Olympic troubles were coming to the boiling point. The complete text of Olsen's book was published soon afterward under the title of The Black Athlete: A Shameful Story.

Following the 1968 Olympics, Scott and Cochran (1968) examined the immediate ramifications of the suspension of Carlos and Smith. What they basically point out is the fact that by suspending and verbally chastising the pair, the Olympic Committee succeeded in making martyrs of the two of them. People all over the world avidly followed this, and the reactions were very mixed.

Edwards (1968 a) was and still is trying to convince young blacks not to move into the world of sports despite the advances that have and are continuing to be made in that area concerning the black man. It is his contention that the way of advancement for black people is not on the athletic field, but rather through advanced education and by movement into professional fields. He resents the whole image of the great black athlete, and states that although this is very nice, the future of the black man is dependent on his escaping this particular stereotyping and establishing his new identity as a lawyer, doctor, teacher, businessman, etc. Many young black athletes have taken a lead from Edwards, and view former black Olympians such as Jesse Owens as "establishment men."

The summer Olympic Games of 1972, which were marked by the tragedy of the brutal murder of eight Israeli athletes, were also noted by individual protests similar to the type staged at the 1968 games. Formal verbal protests were issued by both blacks and whites against the allowing of South Africa and Rhodesia to participate in the games. One demonstration was staged by two track stars, Vince Matthews and Wayne Collett. Theirs was not taken so much as a protest as an exhibition of lack of manners and propriety. They appeared on the victory stand casually dressed, moving about uncomfortably, and not facing the flag. Collett later explained that his and Matthews' demeanor on the victory stand during the playing of the U.S. national anthem was meant to reflect the casual attitude of white America toward black Americans. Matthews had felt guilty about not taking a stronger stance in 1968. His explanation was that he wanted to get some self-satisfaction by getting on peoples' nerves. He regarded the response of the crowd to his actions as "vicious."

It is a reasonable assumption that neither Matthews nor Collett foresaw the ramifications of their actions. The following letter was sent to the President of the U.S. Olympic Committee:

TO: Clifford Buck, President USOC

Dear Mr. Buck:

The whole world saw the disgusting display of your two athletes when they received their gold and silver medals for the 400 m. event yesterday.

This is the second time the USOC has permitted such occurrences on the athletic field. It is the Executive Board's opinion that these two athletes have broken Rule 26, Paragraph 1, in respect of the traditional Olympic spirit and ethic, and are, therefore, eliminated from taking part in any future Olympic competition.

If such a performance should happen in the future, please be advised that the medals will be withheld from the athletes in question.

Yours sincerely,

Avery Brundage, President
International Olympic Committee

It is interesting to note that this was not the only demonstration after winning a medal at the 1972 Olympic Games. One little heard of incident was that of George Foreman waving a small American flag in the ring after winning the heavyweight boxing gold medal. This was regarded as a patriotic gesture, and needless to say Foreman was not the subject of a letter from Avery Brundage.

Interestingly, Bruce Jenner also waved a flag after winning the decathalon at the 1976 Olympiad. His symbolic demonstration resulted in his immortalization on the box cover of a breakfast cereal.

What is the prognosis for change regarding the politicising of the Olympic Games? Unfortunately, it is very unlikely that athletes will compete simply as athletes in the foreseeable future. The trend is definitely going in the direction of governmental subsidies for athletes of national calibre. Along with these subsidies there will be an inherent dependency on the national "team." While individual incidents of protest may diminish (at least temporarily), there is still likely to be overt demonstration of a political nature.

The role of the media cannot be overlooked in this respect. Every four years, millions of Americans tune in to watch events bring performed by athletes whom most have never heard of. What better opportunity for patriotism and pride in this country than during the Olympic spectacle?

Even the officiating is likely to be affected by political bias, with the judges' decisions often being influenced by the nationality of an athlete. How frustrating it must be for an athlete to lose a competition because of the obvious bias of a judge.

In conclusion, it is most unfortunate to say that at this point in time the presence of politics is very strongly felt in Olympic competition both at the national and international levels. Without a total restructuring of the concept of the Olympic Games, it will continue to be an arena for political and social protest.

References

Axthelm, P. The Angry Black Athlete, Newsweek Magazine, July 15, 1968.

Edwards, H. The Revolt of the Black Athlete. New York: Time-Life Books, 1968a.

Edwards, H. Why Negroes Should Boycott Whitey's Olympics, Saturday Evening Post Magazine, March 9, 1968.

Johnson, W. O. All that Glitters is not Gold. New York: Pitman, 1972.

Mandell, R. D. The Nazi Olympics. New York: The Macmillan Co. 1971.

Matthews, V. and Amdur, N. My Race Be Won. New York: Charterhouse. 1974.

Olsen, J. The Black Athlete - A Shameful Story. New York: Time-Life Books, Inc. 1968.

"Olympic Jolt: Hell No, Don't Go-," Life Magazine, April 15, 1969.

"Olympics - Black Complaint," Time Magazine, October 25, 1968.

Scott, J. The Athletic Revolution. New York: The Free Press. 1971.

Scott, J. The White Olympics, Sports Illustrated, 6:9-10, May, 1968.

Scott, J. and Edwards, H. After the Olympics: Buying off Protest, Ramparts Magazine, November, 1960.

Thirer, J. The Olympic Games as a Medium for Black Activism and Protest. Review of Sport and Leisure, 1:15-31, 1976.

The Regulation Of Transnational

Sports Competition: Down

From Mount Olympus

James A. R. Nafziger

The continuing reverberations from the "ping-pong diplomacy" of the Peoples' Republic of China, political pulsations from the 1969 "soccer war" between Honduras and El Salvador, and the emerging influence of world sports standards in combatting <u>apartheid</u> policies in southern Africa have stimulated fresh interest in the interplay between transnational sports and politics. The growing importance of this interaction is underscored by the increasing frequency of such sports-related items in international coverage by the mass media.

Despite the apparent importance of such athletic diplomacy within the world community, the informed scholarly response has been negligible. To be sure, the role of transnational competition as either an agent or a catalyst of world order has been the focus of considerable intuitive and theoretical commentary. Only rarely, however, have the resulting theories and hypotheses been submitted to empirical examination and anslysis.[1] Consequently, it is not surprising that there has been little systematic study of the world-order implications of the rules and norms that govern the administration of transnational sports competition. This deficiency may reflect that lesser importance is attached to the underlying scope-value of skill than to such values as power, wealth and well-being.

This article seeks first to identify the behavioral and organizational characteristics, and to clarify the shared goals of transnational sports competition. Against this background, the article will examine the formal characteristics of decision-making within the Olympic Movement,[2] whose quadrennial Games provide the most highly developed fora for these events. Finally, four case studies are used to evaluate the Olympic organization's performance--that is, the efficacy of relevant policies, rules and procedures that are available to decision-makers to achieve the shared goals of the organization. Several modest proposals are advanced. Aside from these, however, a comprehensive prescription of alternative policies, rules and procedures must await subsequent research.

Reproduced by kind permission of the author and the <u>Vanderbilt Journal of Transnational Law</u>, 5(1):180-212, 1971.

I. Characteristics and Goals of Sports Competition

A. General Characteristics of Athletic Activity

Sports competition is conflict for its own sake involving rewards which
are typically intrinsic: individual pleasure, satisfaction and accolades.
Such conflict generally constitutes a zero-sum game--what one side wins,
the other loses.[3] This characterization may not apply, however, to the individual activities of the Olympic Games, such as track and field events and
swimming, where the multiplicity of both national allegiance and rewards in
the form of gold, silver and bronze medals suggest a more than zero-sum
game. This diffusion of gain and loss may reduce the threat of international
tension in the Olympics. Notwithstanding this qualification, sports contests
seem to function characteristically as a ritual of conflict or pseudo-event in
which action is influenced, not by shared tasks which might generate cooperation, but rather by shared ritual and rules,[4] which both engender and control conflict. Whether that conflict leads to international tension is of major
concern to all participants in transnational sports competition.

In all team endeavors, two relevant concepts of social interaction may
be distinguished: cooperation among members of the same team, and association among members of opposing teams. Cooperation, with its elements
of liking and mutual dependency, emerges when rewards are shared within a
group. Association, on the other hand, is merely a degree of toleration by
which groups accommodate their respective self-interests, but not so much
as to preclude conflicts of interests and continuing competition.[5] The
strength of the association among members of opposing teams relates to such
external influences as sports organizations; spectators; symbolic identification with schools, communities and nations; and the social-cultural milieu.
In regulated sports competition, these influences operate within a competitive
atmosphere characterized by an artificially generated and controlled tension.
Other characteristics include the non-representative nature of the conflict,
the observation of ritual, and a systemic response fundamentally to a rule-
premised equilibrium. The external influences operating within this context
may serve to expose sports competition to disassociation and unprescribed
conflict as contrasted with the characteristic task-sharing patterns of cooperation present among members of the same team.

Although it is widely believed that sport functions cathartically to eliminate conflict among groups, available data suggest that this is an overstate-
ment. Actually, since genuine cooperation would be self-defeating in athletic
competition, the social relationship between athletic opponents indicates only
a limited integrative function.[6] There is no established correlation between
transnational athletic activity and the development of social order.

A better case can be made, however, for the argument that sport is a
microcosm of society. This contention is supported by the close correlation
between individual motivation and capacity,[7] the presence of increased specialization[8] among athletes as in society as a whole and by the demise of the
myth that sport operates as a privileged sanctuary from real life. One need
only be reminded that although the Greek Olympic tradition was inspired by
the ideal of educating harmonious human types, and was self-enforced for
1200 years, it nonetheless degenerated into commercialism, violence and

eventual dissolution in 394 A.D.[9] Further proof that sport is a microcosm of society is found in the recent incidents involving drugs in sport, racism among athletes and an obvious indication that the sports establishment is quite capable of defying the public interest.[10]

B. Clarification of Shared Goals

While the introduction of a common enemy, or the creation in vacuo of organizational goals, may stimulate efforts to overcome intergroup conflicts, these conflicts are most readily surmounted by a concurrence among the participants regarding superordinate problems and goals. The perceived necessity of attaining these goals and of overcoming these problems will encourage the growth of communication, leader contacts and, ultimately, attitude changes.

One recent study[11] of socializing behavior in a summer sports camp, frighteningly suggestive of Golding's classic, Lord of the Flies, is illustrative of this sharing effect. The camp was first fragmented into mutually hostile groups by the artificial kindling of interpersonal conflict. To resolve this conflict, several conventional techniques were initially employed, including mutual information gathering, intergroup leadership conferences and negotiation, the introduction of a common enemy (which proved temporarily productive) and limited mutual contacts and communication. Having achieved little success thereby, the experimenters then created conditions for the emergence of superordinate goals; these staged conditions included an imminent campwide water shortage and the stalling of a truck en route to a vital food distribution point. The resulting forced cooperation among previously hostile groups developed intergroup ties and interpersonal attitude changes. Once this harmony was achieved, it continued even without the presence of shared problems.[12]

The results of this experiment appear to support the hypotheses of scholars concerning functional cooperation on an international plane: that transnational cooperation in resolving superordinate problems leads to persistent patterns of cooperation among participating nations.[13] The integration or convergence of policies and values among decision-makers within the International Labor Organization is an excellent example. This organization advantageously harnesses the competition and frequent political conflict between divergent interests. Through a dynamic process of interaction, "certain kinds of organizational tasks most intimately related to groups and national aspirations can be expected to result in integration even though the actors responsible for this development may not deliberately work toward such an end."[14]

What, then, are the implications for this article of the importance to social integration of superordinate group goals? The earlier discussion about the fundamentally associational, as opposed to cooperative, nature of intergroup athletic activity raises a serious question about the relevance of such goals. The response by an association of opposing participants to what is essentially an equilibrium, is not extrinsically rewarding or materially productive, but rather is conditioned upon intrinsic, individual satisfactions. Rewards within the Olympic context are often unshared. They are either intangible or, when tangible, they are individualized; for example, winners receive special medals, and all participants receive commendation medals. Therefore, if the intergroup association carries with it little potential for the emergence of mutual rewards and the resolution of common problems, then the chance is small that superordinate goals can simply emerge, as in the summer camp experiment.

It is similarly unlikely that articulated goals that are designed to provide a fundamental symbolic reference, as with the standards set by the International Labor Organization, will produce cooperation among competing athletes and athletic organizations. Sports competition is not only a form of conflict unrelated to the performance of productive tasks, but also a highly artificial and regulated form with prescribed limits of outcome and a fixed order. Only if the system itself were to be jeopardized would mutual, superordinate goals become important. Occasionally, relations between nations with teams engaged in athletic competition are, indeed, strained to the breaking point and existing patterns of athletic competition are thereby jeopardized, such as in the Central American soccer war. As the Olympic experience instructs us, however, systemic breakdown generally is not likely in pseudo-events that are rooted in configurations of artificially induced and rationally controlled encounters. Hence, decision-making within the Olympic model is usually concerned not with the achievement of goals that transcend the system and potentially encourage cooperation, but rather with more modest shared goals for the maintenance of an equilibrium in which association may occur. And yet, four principal Olympic goals, expressed in rule 3 of the Olympic Rules and Regulations, indicate higher, superordinate purposes while relating primarily to this maintenance of equilibrium:

The aims of the Olympic Movement are [1] to promote the development of those fine physical and moral qualities which are the basis of amateur sport and [2] to bring together the athletes of the world in a great quadrennial festival of sports thereby creating international respect and goodwill and [3] thus helping to construct a better and [4] more peaceful world.[15]

In considering the role of established norms and law in the process of achieving these goals, it is useful to note three bases which have been used to justify a permanent, authoritative, domestic intervention into sports competition. These are, first, amelioration of the physical condition of the population; second, the safeguarding of the public order; and third, the affirmation of national prestige.[16] On the international plane, similarly, there are arrangements which address these same aims. These arrangements include, respectively, international controls over the conduct of boxing matches and the use of stimulants and drugs;[17] the encouragement of transnational track and field contests which, in turn, have generated mass physical training programs; and bilateral agreements, often based upon FNC treaties, to stimulate joint international sports rivalry with third states.[18]

In promoting the goals expressed in rule 3, the Olympic model assumes the first two of these three bases for legal implementation and explicitly rejects the third in favor of a denationalization of competition. In addition, a fourth basis for legal implementation, which might be seen to encompass the first three, is introduced: the promotion of more comprehensive, external goals, such as the protection of human rights through the interaction of competitive sports. This basis for legal implementation can be related to the goal of "helping to construct a better ... world."[19]

After briefly examining the structure and characteristics of the Olympic model, this article will consider its performance in response to four current situations, each of which relates to one of the four basic goals of the Olympic movement articulated in rule 3 and each of which affords a study of one or more of the corresponding bases for legal implementation. The situations to be considered ase "creeping professionalism"; the politicization of competition by nations; the "ping-pong diplomacy" of China especially as it bears on the conduct of the Olympic Games; and the conflict between the apartheid practices of South Africa and the Olympic rules, as officially interpreted.

II. Structure and Characteristics of Olympic Decision-Making

A. The Institutional Structure

The 1894 Congress of Paris launched the modern Olympic Games and established a permanent International Olympic Committee (I.O.C.) which is "the final authority on all questions concerning the Olympic Games and the Olympic Movement."[20] Specifically, it is responsible principally for creating rules and regulations applicable to Olympic decision-making, electing its own efficers and chairmen of certain committees, determining the qualifications of Olympic participants and selecting a site for each Olympiad.[21] According to one classification of non-governmental organizations, the I.O.C. is a "cosmopolitan" organization—that is, one composed of individuals rather than nation-states or organizational representatives.[22] The I.O.C., together with several other bodies, forms an Olympic organization which includes individual, national and international members.

The I.O.C. is unique in coopting its membership not on the basis of their representation from, but rather to, other organizations—namely, to officially recognized national federations and committees.[23] Before elaborating further on the characteristics of the I.O.C.'s membership, let us look briefly at the remaining institutional structure of the Olympic organization.

An Executive Board, composed of the President, three Vice-Presidents, and five additional members, performs ministerial duties assigned to it by the I.O.C.[24] Administrative support is provided by an efficient secretariat, located in Lausanne, Switzerland.[25] Income is derived from the annual subscriptions of the I.O.C. itself. Technical control over the conduct of sports competition is given to the 26 authorized international federations, each of which employs technical rules to govern a particular official sport.[26] For example, the International Amateur Athletic Federation, the body with responsibility for rule-making, supervision, control and development in respect to track and field competitions, announced in early 1971 its own new qualifying standards for the 1972 Games in order to reflect "the bettering of world standards in both track and field events."[27] The international federations also regulate the number of entrants in each sport within limits set by the I.O.C., the equipment standards and controls, the selection of judges and the exercise of what could be described as limited appellate jurisdiction. Municipal components of the international federations are called national federations. Five of these components constitute a national Olumpic committee.[28] The authority and role of the national Olympic committees in Olympic decision-making[29] are comparable to those of the National Red Cross Societies in relation to the International Committee of the Red Cross. All I.O.C. rules and regulations must be adopted and enforced by the national committees through their own rules and regulations.[30] Two delegates from each of the international federations and national committees are invited from time to time to confer on a consultative basis with the Executive Board of the I.O.C.[31] Occasionally, an Olympic Congress is convened, which for discussion and planning purposes brings together the I.O.C., and representatives from the international federations and the national committees.

B. The Participants and Their Perspectives

Participants in the Olympic process include the individual competitors, whose average age in the 1968 Olympics ranged from 17.6 (women swimmers) to 32.5 (men rifle shooters);[32] nations; and the officially designated decision-making institutions and individuals within the Olympic institutional apparatus. The individual competitors are selected during try-outs by the national Olympic committees. These athletes play only a minor role in formal decision-making but are instrumental in shaping, sharing and promoting the goals of the system.

Recruitment of the primary decision-makers, the I.O.C. members, is conducted by that body itself according to several criteria: facility in French or English, citizenship and residency in a country with a national Olympic committee, and independence from binding instructions from any individual, organization, or sovereign government.[33] It is provided that "there shall be only one member in any country except in the largest and most active in the Olympic Movement, and in the countries where the Olympic Games have been held, where there may be two."[34] The President of the I.O.C. is elected for an eight-year term by absolute majority, by a secret ballot, and is eligible for reelection for successive four-year terms.[35] The remaining members of an Executive Board are elected for four-year terms.

The I.O.C. has been criticized frequently because its membership appears to be based upon wealth, elitism, age and geographical non-representation.[36] The I.O.C. for long has been identified with Western Europe; it has had, for example, only three members from sub-Saharan Africa, one of whome was an aristocratic Englishman from Kenya. In addition, the amount of power and prerogative formally accorded the office of the President has been especially criticized.[37] Without evaluating such criticism, it should be noted that the three newest members of the I.O.C. are from Ethiopia, Thailand, and the U.S.S.R.,[38] and that the President's discretion is increasingly subject to the application of the organizational rules.

Several rules and regulations would seem to encourage the traditional pattern of membership on the I.O.C.: members are coopted and must be free of governmental and private influence, and who but the rich, it is argued, can be free of such influence; they are elected for life, although rule 12(2) now requires retirement at age 72 of members elected after 1965; one of the three Vice-Presidents mube be a European; past host countries are entitled to double membership; and the size of the I.O.C. is restricted, despite the growth in the number of national committees.[39]

The I.O.C., its Executive Board, and particularly its President, have been given great discretionary powers in the administration of the Olympic Games by the international federations, national committees, and responsible individuals. For example, the President may take action or make a decision subject to later ratification by the I.O.C. when "circumstances" do not permit such action to be taken by the I.O.C. or its Executive Board.[40] Moreover, the continuing practice of the Olympic organization to keep its deliberations secret and unpublished, except in summary form, serves to protect the freedom of discretion in decision-making. However, the trend in recent years seems to have been away from discretionary administration by a narrowly representative "clique" of gentlemen toward a rule-oriented administration by a more widely representative I.O.C. Only the pace of this transformation is controversial.

C. Legal Tools of Regulation

Legal tools available to the Olympic organization include the technical rules governing competition within each sport, to which reference has been made and about which this article is not primarily concerned; and the organizational rules, about which this article is primarily concerned. The Charter of the Olympic Games and various ministerial and protocol provisions form a document entitled Olympic Rules and Regulations,[41] which includes the organizational rules, together with an Eligibility Code and "decisions" made under it. The document is a curious composite of "basic law" provisions, rules, norms and a few admonitions. In style, it is rather loosely written and presents several conflicts of language between the English and French versions. In addition, it contains several spelling and grammatical errors.[42] Proposals for changes in the rules are referred to a Legislation Commission which drafts revisions for submission to and adoption by the I.O.C.

Under the rules, technical disputes, such as disqualifications, timekeeping and the like, are settled by a jury for each sport. The jury is appointed by the appropriate international federation. The jury's decisions are final.[43] All controversies of a non-technical nature must be submitted to the I.O.C. Executive Board by a national committee, an international federation or the organizing committee of the city where the games are being held.[44] Violations under rule 26, which governs eligibility, until recently were handled under the provisions of the Eligibility Code and referred to a special committee of the Executive Board "for investigation and report with a view to action."[45] It is unclear what action could properly be taken. The single sanction seems to be disqualification, either of an individual or a team, depending upon the circumstances.[46] As will be noted later,[47] the enforcement machinery was changed in 1971, but the question of available or contemplated sanctions persists.

Rule-creation and rule-supervision with the Olympic arena are shared by the international federations, which also deal with technical matters; the national committees; and the I.O.C. The nature of the legal tools available to both recognized and non-recognized international athletic federations varies; but in general, the devices are better defined and more penetrating than those available in the I.O.C. For example, the International Federation of Motor Cyclists, a non-recognized federation, proceeds according to a code containing a defined hierarchy of sanctions for rule infractions, e.g., reprimand, apology, suspension and exclusion. Similarly, the code of the International Association of Recognized Automobile Clubs imposes standards on automobile manufacturers of racing vehicles in international competition; this feature is reputedly "one of the principal causes of automobile progress."[48]

III. Case Studies

A. Creeping Professionalism

"to promote the development of those fine physical and moral qualities which are the basis of amateur sport"[49]

The Olympic Games subordinate universal participation to the above expressed goal.[50] Thus, all participants must be "amateur,"[51] as interpreted by rule 26 of the Olympic Rules, which governs eligibility. Until April, 1971, rule 26 read:

> To be eligible for the Olympic Games a competitor must always have participated in sport as an avocation without material gain of any kind. He can avail himself of this qualification: a) if he has a basic occupation designed to ensure his present and future livelihood; b) if he does not receive or has never received any remuneration for participation in sport; c) if he complies with the rules of the International Federation concerned, and the official interpretations of this rule (see Eligibility Code).

As indicated, an Eligibility Code was adopted as a means of interpreting these provisions. In general, it barred eligible amateurs from accepting any compensation, other than limited expense money, which might be attributable to their athletic activity or status.[52] This prohibition extended to receiving compensation for playing, teaching or coaching competitive sports and making promotional endorsements or appearances. The athlete could neither use his fame to obtain a job nor interrupt his job or studies for more than four weeks of training in a camp per year. Eligibility "decisions" by the I.O.C. interpreted these rules strictly. For instance, individuals subsidized because of their athletic ability by governments, institutions or business concerns were held not to be amateurs.[53]

The Eligibility Code was useful up to a point. But by 1971, fed by demands for greater precision in response to individual cases, the Code had become a rather baroque and disorganized framework for decision making. Moreover, it was an interpretative device, not a set of binding rules. Ranging from overly detailed provisions to "ball-park" size injunctions, the Code's provisions offered little legal support to the principle of amateur participation.

In April, 1971, the I.O.C. adopted a new rule 25.[54] It provides a clarified, streamlined and better focused restatement of the pre-1971 Eligibility Code. Moreover, it is binding on the participants. The Code itself was reduced to four matters: the use of dope; the participation of women, a matter to be revised later and incorporated into rule 27; penalties in the case of fraud; and non-amateurs and semi-professionals. The incorporation of most of the Code into rule 26 represents another step in the gradual transformation of the I.O.C. into a rule-creating and rule-enforcing organization.

More important than the rephrasing and editing of the bulk of the Eligibility Code, as incorporated into rule 26, were the several substantive modifications. The subjective "intent to become a professional" provision and the even more subjective "neglect of usual employment" provisions were eliminated; physical education teachers or beginners became eligible without qualification as to the extent of the teaching or the existence of another occupation; the definition of acceptable assistance was broadened to include prizes without dollar limit, insurance related to training, medical care, and sports equipment; scholarships to athletes became acceptable when awarded on the basis of "academic and technical" standards; and the recognized period for full-time training was extended from 30 to 60 days in one calendar year. In general, the new rule 26, though strict, is responsive to changing conditions.

Most important were three new "directives." One of these appears to limit the advertising prohibition to those cases where an athlete permits his name, photograph, or sports performance to be used "individually" for advertising purposes. A second directive permits athletes to associate themselves or their names with the mass media during the Olympic Games, subject to the approval of their <u>chefs de mission</u>. The third directive provides that, subject to certain controls, advertising is permitted that results from equipment contracts entered into by the national federations.

Finally, a flexible enforcement mechanism is provided in the form of a commission which was established to "consult and cooperate" with the international federations and the national Olympic committees.[55] The old provision had provided for a more formal investigatory committee that proved weak because it did not involve the federations and committees in the enforcement process.

To understand the reasons for these modifications of rule 26, we must examine the background and recent history of the "amateur" requirement. Fundamentally, it is the product of the times and personal philosophy of the founder of the modern Olympic Games, Baron de Coubertin. The amateur requirement marked a sharp departure from the practice of the ancient Greek Olympics, whose participants were state-supported and had official status. Arising when organized sports were thought of principally as activities of "gentlemen," the protection of the amateur character of the Olympics has continued to appeal not only to those genuinely concerned about the encouragement of mass participation in athletics, but also to those who favor a perpetuation of elitism. To them, professionalism is "entertainment"--only amateurism is "sport." Recent developments, however, have tended to undermine the concept of amateurism: there has been an emerging pattern of correspondence between athletic status and closely related professional endeavor, such as physical education teaching; temptation in the form of increasing advertising money has grown in proportion to the expansion of the sports equipment industry; and finally, an increased interest by the spectator public in, and its demand for, higher levels of performance has required amateurs to devote increased amounts of time to training and dry-runs.[56] Nevertheless, unlike other sports organizations, such as the British Lawn Tennis Association, which have removed the distinction between "professional" and "amateur," the Olympic rule has not only remained on the books but the pre-1971 Eligibility Code had become more and more elaborate in response to specific claims that it was flagrantly breached. For this reason, the rule was becoming not only hypocritical, but probably dysfunctional. For example, in Africa a good "amateur" athlete is often a police inspector or an army lieutenant who may spend 90 per cent of his time in training. In Scandinavia, an Olympic bound cross-country skier is often a customs official who can devote much of his time to training. In the Soviet Union, athletes are state supported; and in the United States, top "amateur" college athletes typically receive compensation in the form of all-inclusive scholarships.

The ineffectiveness of the old rule 26 and Code provisions was seen in the dispute over the wisdom and legality of permitting Olympic participants to receive money for releasing their image or name for advertising purposes. Rule 34 provides that "no commercial advertising is permitted on equipment used in the Games nor on the uniforms or numbers worn by contestants or officials." Enforcement is provided by rule 54:

> The display of any clothing or equipment such as shoes, skis [,] handbags, hats, etc. marked conspicuously for advertising purposes in any Olympic venue (training grounds, Olympic Village, or fields of competition), by participants [,] either competitors, coaches trainers, or anyone else associated with an Olympic team in [an] official capacity, will normally result in immediate disqualifications or withdrawal of credentials.

Rules 34 and 54 cover the athletes during the Games only. Rule 26 and the Eligibility Code had to be inboked to determine initial eligibility of competitors for the Olympic competition. Apparently ignoring the limited enforcement machinery available to him under the Eligibility Code, the President of the I.O.C. took the highly unusual step in 1971 of proposing the elimination of alpine skiing from the 1972 Winter Olympics because of numerous incidents involving the remuneration of alpine skiers by ski equipment manufacturers. Acting primarily in response to the President's threat, the I.O.C. Executive Board, meeting March 13-14, 1971, unanimously approved the text of the revised rule 26, which was subsequently adopted by the I.O.C. As we have seen, the new rule considerably relaxes restraints on monetary inducements, while at the same time retaining a dichotomy between amateurs and professionals. The rule is, of course, applicable to the eligibility of all athletes, but was intended immediately to resolve the alpine skiing crisis by means of the directive that bars any athlete who has "directly or indirectly allowed his name, his photograph or his sports performance to be used individually for advertising purposes."[57] Because of the lack of enforcement machinery within the Olympic apparatus, aside from the consultative commission; the importance to the Winter Olympics of alpine skiing, which represents about 50 per cent of all events; and the Japanese investment of an estimated $20 million in preparation of the 1972 site, the authority of rule 26 was put to a severe early test.

Despite the customary precedence of Olympic rules over conflicting decisions by the international federations, the real efficacy of the new rule depended on its acceptance by the international ski federation, Federation Internationale de Ski (F.I.S.), whose first response was to threaten a boycott of the 1972 Winter Games.[58] The conflict between the F.I.S. and the I.O.C. is noteworthy because it arose out of a direct clash between the new Olympic rule and a recently revised and far more liberal rule of the F.I.S.[59] Ironically, the F.I.S. rule might be given some force by a provision in the new rule 26 that "[a] competitor must observe and abide by the Rules of the International Federation that controls the sport in which he participates, even if these Rules should be stricter than those imposed by the International Olympic Committee." Although the intent of the provision was no doubt to further fortify resistance to creeping professionalism, a literal reading would seem to upset the customary precedence of the Olympic rules. A subsequent provision, however, may rescue the presumption favoring Olympic regulation whenever a rule of an international federation, such as the F.I.S., is weaker than rule 26: "[the competitor] must comply with his Federation's directives and those issued by the International Olympic Committee." Thus, it would seem that, to comply with the latter provision, a prospective competitor would have to observe the stricter of two conflicting provisions, in this case the I.O.C. directives.

The new enforcement machinery, which is established by rule and emphasizes consultation and conciliation, rather than formal quasi-adjudication, offers hope for a resolution of this conflict despite the initial reaction of of the F.I.S. Such dilemmas could, of course, be avoided if the I.O.C. interpreted its rules as prohibiting the commercialization of only the actual sports competition, not the non-competitive aspects of sport.[60] This would not, however, eliminate fundamental differences in philosophy such as that between the I.O.C. and the F.I.S.

Although rule 26 appears to be resolving a major crisis, it is unequivocally clear that the Olympic rules regarding amateur standing have been honored more in their breach than in practice. Moreover, the increasing complexity of the pre-1971 Code further weakened their authority. Hopefully, the new rule will restore this authority. It is apparent, however, that no evidence exists to support the notion that the amateur requirement serves to encourage truly amateur athletic participation. Thus, faced with growing professionalism among the ranks of participants, the blurring of the dichotomy between "amateur" and "professional" status, and the deteriorating authority of the entire legal regime, the I.O.C. proved itself both sensitive and sensible in revising rule 26. But further relaxation of its strictures may be indicated. Aside from the establishments of a costly monitoring system, the only alternative to the process of reshaping rule 26 to meet changing conditions would appear to be either the creation of two levels of competition, one for professionals and one for amateurs in the modern sense, or the more direct and effective remedy of complete elimination of the amateur requirement.

B. Sports and Minimum Public Order: The Nation-State Politicization of Competition

"to bring together the athletes of the world ... thereby creating international respect and goodwill"[61]

The symbolic importance of Olympic participation and success to national prestige, which may serve to inject international politics into the Olympic arena, suggests the need for responsive rules to safeguard the public order by denationalizing the Games.[62] Mutual hostility between nations is often channeled into the pseudo-event of sports competition, where, ironically, it may serve to create or exacerbate political conflict.

> The thousands of spectators, and sometime the players as well, seem to behold a mighty contest between their 'country' and the 'enemy.' The national prestige is at stake; a victory is no longer the success of the team that could play better but becomes a national victory and is an occasion for national rejoicings, out of all proportion with reality. Such an attitude is not favorable to international understanding.[63]

Resulting tension may range from unfavorable propaganda and diplomatic strain, as in the aftermath of the Swedish victory over Germany in the 1962 World Soccer Championships, to the open warfare of the 1969 "soccer war."[64] Available data suggest that a strong "reference group" relationship between two competing countries greatly enhances the possibility of such tension. Thus, rival countries that habitually turn to each other for power cues are very apt to experience the most serious mutual tension from sports competition between their nationals.

The group dynamics of tension between "in-groups" and "out-groups" serve to establish patterns of identification which resist otherwise transcending values. These group identifications, fed by stereotyped national perceptions, are quickly exaggerated into ethnocentrism. Two other situational determinants, publicity and professionalism, also tend to produce an arousal of inter-group conflict, and as victory becomes paramount, lead to a lessening of loyalty to prescribed rules.[65] Only full adherence to the technical rules of fair play and the internalization by participants of the organization goals of respect and goodwill can overcome these situational determinants.[66]

The competition itself may serve to create a measure of respect and goodwill. Various sociological data and commentaries support the theoretical notion,[67] implicit in the "Objects and Powers" provision of rule 10(4),[68] that well-organized athletic competition can generate mutual contacts and confidences and decrease social distance among participants.[69] It has also been contended that athletes with record-breaking aspirations lay more stress on personal and fellowship relations than on more objective, competitive values.[70] There are heroic instances of goodwill overcoming the compulsions of national prestige in Olympic competition, as, for example, the crucial assistance that was given to Jesse Owens by his chief competitor in the broad jump in the politically-charged 1936 Olympics. In addition, the rule-based nature of sports activity prevents individual and group tensions from developing into more dangerous forms of power conflict. Moreover, the individual nature of most events minimizes the potentiality of conflict in the Olympic Games as compared with the more volatile team-oriented contests, notwithstanding the tension generated by any transnational competition, including the Olympics.[71] Thus, within the Games, conflict can be controlled in such a way as to encourage a degree of associational comraderie during the contests. Yet, on the whole, it is probable that beyond the contests themselves transnational sports competition supports world social integration no more than disintegration.[72]

Although the Olympic Games are expressly "between individuals and not between countries or areas,"[73] the disintegrating influence of nation-states cannot be avoided.[74] The mere presence of an element as innocuous as a national flag has prompted controversy and complaints over the creation of unnecessary international rivalry. There is a danger of increased political pressure resulting from subtle diplomatic ploys designed to pollute the non-political atmosphere of Olympic competition. To the extent that such pressure is successful, the world-ordering potential of the Games is correspondingly inhibited.

The interplay of nation-state politics and Olympic competition is, of course, often not so much a result of the sports competition, itself, as it is of external factors. It is obvious, first, that established patterns of political rivalry and conflict can enhance the possibility of unprescribed conflict in the sports arena. An example is the outbreak centering on the Honduras-El Salvador soccer match. Sometimes exclusionary manucipal law stimulates controversy and poses conflicts between Olympic decisions and municipal law. One such conflict concerns the policy of state recognition pursued by participating countries. Rule 7 provides for recognition by a national Olympic committee when a "country or area [has] had a stable government for a reasonable period." Disparities between applications of this criterion and the application by nation-states of other recognition policies have proved troublesome. Thus, although Australia did not recognize the Soviet Union of 1956, it was obliged, against its initial objection, to permit the participation of Soviet athletes in the Melbourne Games that year. Similarly, France permitted East Germans to participate in the 1968 Winter Olympics, although the issuance of visas to them ordinarily would have violated NATO regulations. Finally, contrary to a U.N. resolution, the West German Government, not a U.N. member, has drawn upon these Olympic precedents to clear the way for the participation of Rhodesian athletes in the 1972 Games. In each of these cases, a conflict of laws was settled by the waiver of municipal visa requirements and the issuance of special clearance papers.

Thus, we can readily see the problems in merely "bring[ing] together the athletes of the world," much less in "thereby creating international respect and goodwill." But the Olympic regime nevertheless had proven effective in resisting a preponderance of diplomatic machinations within the Olympic arena[75] and in assuring a continuing measure of universality to the Games. In doing so, the Olympic model depends not on the efforts of the I.O.C. alone, but, perhaps more importantly, on a close working association between the I.O.C. and the international federations, and on the national committees which are charged "not to associate themselves with affairs of a political or commercial nature"[76] but to "be completely independent and autonomous and [to] resist all political ... pressure."[77]

Beyond the success of the Olympic rules in promoting stability in transnational sports competition, the potential impact of the Olympic model in harmonizing nation-state interaction is apt to be limited. Indeed, the wisest course for the I.O.C. would seem to be that of maintaining a delicate balance between a tolerance for national identity, with its presumed importance in generating mass public interest in sports, and the individual-oriented spirit of the Olympic model, with its importance in dampening potentially disruptive factionalism. Such a balance is encouraged by existing rules, which permit the display of national symbols at appropriate times, while at the same time advancing the overarching Olympic ideal by means of such well known symbols as the torch runner and the Olympic emblem, with its interlocking rings; and by denying official recognition to national standings based on the composite scores of individual participants.

C. Ping-Pong Diplomacy

"and thus helping to construct a ... more peaceful world"[78]

In April, 1971, during the 31st World Table Tennis Championships in Nagoya, Japan, the government of the Peoples' Republic of China invited the United States table tennis team to visit mainland China. The invitation was the first one officially extended to a group of United States citizens since the establishment of the Peking Government and it was quickly accepted by the team members. During the visit, media accounts consistently emphasized the warmth of both the reception and the interaction of hosts and guests.[79] As the United States press noted, ping-pong, with its onomatopoetic symbolism of initiative and response, was an especially appropriate metaphor for the process or rapprochement between the two countries. Later, the United States Government officially proposed a reciprocal visit by Chinese players. Fresh diplomatic overtures, including the President's acceptance of an invitation to visit China, followed. For their part, the Chinese succeeded in generating an immense amount of favorable global opinion in a manner that saved face for both countries involved. Rarely has athletic competition been employed so effectively as a tool of international diplomacy.

The timing and location of the Chinese invitation was propitious. It occurred in the year of China's return to world table tennis competition after a six year absence. The United States appeared to be committed to a gradual renewal of amicable ties with China,[80] and had in fact already implemented unilateral offers of cultural exchange and limited trade. It was also signifi-cant that the United States had begun its military withdrawal from Viet Nam.

The Chinese seem to have taken pains to de-emphasize any political underpinnings of their hospitality, ostensibly inviting the Americans so that each side could learn athletic skills from the other and thereby elevate their standards of performance.[81] This represented a significant change from the stridently political International Table Tennis Tournament hosted in 1966 by Peking, at which almost all participants were from countries friendly with China. But there are games that nations as well as people play, and no doubt the Chinese felt that the prevailing political atmosphere was most conducive to this move. The demise of the Cultural Revolution and perhaps the inclin-ation of some United States citizens to engage in interpersonal diplomacy in pursuit of peace in Indochina encouraged rapprochement with the United States.

The Chinese wisely selected a posture which stressed the merits of conducting "people's diplomacy" in preference to nation-state dealings. Two incidental aspects of this approach are noteworthy: first, the hosts chose a sport in which any competitive tension would be minimized, and the visitor's national prestige least tied to athletic success; second, the almost simultan-eous withdrawal of the Chinese from the International Lawn Tennis Federa-tion in protest over the admission of Taiwan to membership indicates that ping-pong diplomacy operates only within an organizational context free of the "two China" threat or any other possible undermining of the fundamental tenets of Communist Chinese sovereignty and diplomacy.[82]

The relevance of ping-pong diplomacy to the present discussion is to illustrate the continuing interplay of politics and the pseudo-events of sports competition. The role of an athletic contest seems to be, first, to provide an orderly, ritualized, but politically harmless setting for initiating a pro-cess of interaction among former adversaries; second, to prepare for diplo-matic contacts by means of interpersonal contacts that are consonant with conceptions of "people's diplomacy"; third, through public opinion to stimu-late popular approval of forthcoming diplomatic initiatives; and, fourth, to permit the host some assurance of victory without significant loss-of-face to guest nationals.

It is unlikely that ping-pong diplomacy would be as effective within the Olympic arena. There, the lack of bilateral confrontation and the diffusion of actors and types of encounter renders directed, bilateral diplomacy al-most impossible. Participation in the Olympics, however, may serve either intentionally or inadvertently as a less dramatic process of encounter among political adversaries in which political stakes are minimal and the highly ritualized nature of the interaction is predetermined and therefore depend-able. With this potential, the pertinent rules should continue to be designed and exercised to permit maximum participation without regard to national affiliation.

In any event, the minimal impact that the Olympic model may have for the promotion of friendly relations among nation-states should not diminish expectations that other forums of sports competition, particularly bilateral ones, will continue to serve as relatively low risk, face-saving vehicles of rapprochement. Thus in August, 1971, the government of Syria opened its doors to American citizens for the first time in several years by inviting a United States team to participate in an international basketball tournament. This invitation arrived and reports of a growing interest of the Syrian Government to improve its relations with the United States. Once again, sports competition represented a calculated first step.

D. The Protection of Human Rights

"and thus helping to construct a better ... world."[83]

Rule 1 of the Olympic Rules and Regulations prohibits discrimination in the Games against any country or person on grounds of race, religion or politics. Moreover, rule 34 requires that "National Olympic Committees must ... make sure that no one has been left out for racial, religious, or political reasons." These provisions have served as legal references for a growing controversy within the I.OlC. concerning the relationship between the I.O.C. and participants from nation-states whose governments pursue racist domestic policies. To be sure, rule 1 appears simply to bar the I.O.C. from three types of discrimination against participants and their parent countries and, indeed, might at first be interpreted to bar the I.O.C. from "discriminating" against countries which pursue politically racist policies. But the I.O.C. is charged also with supervision of the obligations of the national committees, which, as noted above, are responsible under rule 34 for assuring that "no one has been left out for racial ... reasons." The I.O.C. has, therefore, invoked rule 1 to bar participation of nationals of several countries, reasoning that admission of persons from countries whose governments engage in racial discrimination would put the I.O.C. in the position of sanctioning de facto segregation against the victims of the discriminatory policies. In adopting this principle, the prime targets of the I.O.C. have been the governments of Rhodesia and South Africa. Each presents an illuminating case history.

1. South Africa.--All South African athletes were prevented from participating in the 1964 Olympics because of opposition to a strict apartheid policy that restricted South African Olympic candidates to whites. Between the 1964 and 1968 Olympics, the South African Government agreed to adopt a non-discriminatory policy of training, selecting[84] and lodging its Olympic participants, but continued to enforce its policy against the holding of multiracial competition within the country by insisting on segregated trials. Despite this latter manifestation of a continued adherence to apartheid policies, the I.O.C. decided by majority vote on February 15, 1968, that South Africa was in fact meeting the standards demanded by the Olympic rules and could therefore participate in the Mexico City Games. Thirty-two nations, however, were incensed by South Africa's apartheid restrictions on tryouts for membership on teams, and threatened a boycott of the Games by their nationals unless the I.O.C. excluded South African nationals. The I.O.C. President, apparently adhering to a strict interpretation of rule 1, maintained that South Africa had satisfied the literal requirements of rule 1 and that an exclusion would harm South Africa's black athletes more than anyone else.

Throughout the controversy his basic premise was that "[w]e can't change the politics of any country--that's not our business." Furthermore, he maintained that "if participation in sport is to be stopped every time the laws of humanity are violated, there will never be any international contests."[85] The goals of promoting world athletic participation and the implementation of global standards of human rights were in seeming conflict.

Pressure quickly mounted in favor of rescinding the invitation to the South Africans. The Olympic host, Mexico, was justifiably nervous about the probable effect of a massive boycott of the games, and an incipient black-power movement threatening the composition and quality of the U. S. team. On the request of the Supreme Council for Sports in Africa, representing 33 African nations, and supported by a South African black pressure group, the I.O.C. President under the "urgency" provision of rule 20 agreed to submit a resolution by mail to the I.O.C. members that would bar South African participation in the 1968 games.[86]

The I.O.C. voted to rescind the invitation. Its decision was supported and amplified after the games by the U.N. General Assembly,[87] which requested all states and organizations to suspend domestic sports competition with South Africa and any organizations and institutions in that country which continued to practice apartheid. The U. N. Committee on the Elimination of Racial Discrimination, established in January, 1970, called for strict implementation of the resolution. The Committee publicized the identity of both violators and adherents of the resolution.[88] On May 15, 1970, the I.O.C. voted to exclude not only South African competitors from the 1972 games, but also their national committee from the Olympic Movement.

Pressures exerted through sports competition to protect human rights in South Africa are apt to be surprisingly effective because of the importance traditionally given to athletics in South Africa, which even has a Minister of Sports. Consequently, it is not surprising that the application of legal sanctions by the I.O.C. and affiliated international sports federations has in every instance resulted in more liberal policies and practices in South African sports competition.

In addition to these actions by the U.N. and the I.O.C., pressure from various other sources has been leveled against the South African Government to modify its racial restrictions in sports competition. Objections and threats were voiced by the otherwise conservative South African Cricket Association when the Pretoria Government refused to allow two non-white cricketers to accompany a domestic team on a tour of Australia. The International Amateur Athletics Federation and the International Lawn Tennis Association have both taken stands against the South African policy. Nationally and internationally prominent athletes have demanded reform.[89] In response-sponse, the South African Government has further eased its rules in several selected sports--principally lawn tennis and Olympic competition.[90] Despite this undoubted improvement, much unpalatable racism remains. For example, multi-racial teams of South Africans are still prohibited; thus, South African participation in international sporting events would be by teams or groups of racially segregated athletes. White and non-white South African teams cannot compete against each other except in "international" events.[91]

Furthermore, whites are prohibited from watching matches between white and non-white teams.

The impact of the Olympic sanctions on the easing of <u>apartheid</u> in South Africa is demonstrated not only by the announcement of the policy with its special provisions for integration of participation in Olympic sports, but in the decision of the South African Amateur Athletic Union in taking a first step to get back into the Olympic Games by organizing a completely integrated invitational meet to be held there in 1972.[92]

The world community may well continue to be dissatisfied with the slow pace of incursions into the policy of <u>apartheid</u> and will not doubt wish to continue to press for further change.[93] But even a brief study of the Olympics regime verifies its efficacy in setting in motion a gradual transformation in an external system, a transformation attributable both to a combination of Olympic influences and to special cultural factors in the target country.

A global consensus to exclude individuals of target nation-states from such an important stage of non-political interaction as the Olympics, if judiciously employed, may well provide one of the sharpest tools for implementing such broad human objectives as racial equality. The conversion of the Olympic model from a politically free to a politically involved instrument of human rights is consonant with the injunction of rule 3, and may eventually prove to be one of the most significant contributions to world order of organized, transnational sports competition.

2. <u>Rhodesia</u>.--The <u>apartheid</u> policies of the Rhodesian Government[94] have had only limited recent application to sports competition. Multi-racial competition of foreign teams is permitted in the country, and multi-racial teams representing Rhodesia have competed outside the country since July, 1971. An investigatory mission dispatched by the I.O.C. reported favorably on conditions in Rhodesia, and recommended that country's continued involvement in the Games. Accordingly, the Rhodesian Olympic Committee, which was not invited to participate in the 1968 Olympics, has been invited for 1972. In response to this invitation, 20 of the 24 members of the U.N. Special Committee on Decolonization adopted a resolution which urged the I.O.C. to take urgent steps to "suspend the so-called 'National Olympic Committee of Rhodesia' from its membership and to ask the Organizing Committee of the 20th Olympic Games to annul forthwith its invitation for the Olympic Games in Munich."[95]

The response of the I.O.C. to the resolution of the U.N. Special Committee struck a sensible compromise that served to accommodate the relatively favorable situation for black athletes in Rhodesia, to distinguish Rhodesia from South Africa in this respect, and permit Rhodesian nationals to compete in 1972, and yet to suspend official recognition of an independent, white-supremist government in Salisbury. On September 10, 1971, during a joint meeting between the I.O.C. Executive Board and representatives of he National Olympic Committees, the President of the I.O.C., referring to his recent meetings with African delegates to the joint meetings, proposed on behalf of the committees that a Rhodesian team compete with the same flag and anthem, namely the Union Jack and British anthem, under which they had competed in the "pre-independence" 1964 Games while still a member of the British Commonwealth, and that the matter be reviewed after the 1972 Games.[96] The proposal, which had been drafted by a special commission consisting of an Australian, a Nigerian, and a Swiss national, already had been accepted by both the Rhodesian delegation, participating as an observer, and their adversaries from black Africa. It had also been endorsed by the Permanent General Assembly of the National Olympic Committees (70 affirmative votes to 6 abstentions). The I.O.C. Executive Board concurred.

The Rhodesian compromise is especially interesting because it is explicitly premised in the "uncertain international position" of Rhodesia. Accordingly, although the Rhodesian team will be identified by colonial symbols it has rejected, and may therefore decline to compete in the 1972 Games, no official political significance is to be attributed to these symbols. At the same time, no recognition will be given to the "post-independence" regime, since its trappings will be barred from the Games. Thus, the Olympic system was able to meet the threat of politicization, and at the same time to apply basic standards of participation in a highly political context in order to encourage the involvement of a national entity in one of the only spheres of human interaction in which that national entity has, for whatever reason, committed itself to global standards of racial non-discrimination. Unlike the South African context, that of Rhodesia may not admit of any further impact on internal development from Olympic participatory standards; nevertheless, it is significant that the Olympic system has proven capable of positively encouraging sovereign adherence to basic human rights. In doing so, an acceptable resolution of an essentially political issue was achieved without further politicizing the system.

IV. Conclusion

These four studies confirm the continuing vitality of sports competition as a setting for transnational interaction involving both political and non-political participants. In examining the Olympic organization as a paradigm, we have seen that this vitality is nourished not only by such technical rules as qualifying standards, but by organizational rules as well. These organizational rules, particularly rules 1 and 26, are playing an increasingly important role in internal dispute settlement and pattern maintenance within the Olympic Movement. In the process of creating, invoking and applying them, the Olympic organization has come to rely less on administrative discretion and more on formal decision-making.

As we have seen, the Olympic organization has performed satisfactorily in meeting the perceived threats to its internal operation of professionalism and politicization, despite external pressures to yield to these threats. Whether the success of the Olympic organization in maintaining internal order and stability bodes well for the accomplishment of the lofty goals expressed in rule 3 is of great interest. Available historical and sociological data do not indicate any inherent capacity of sports competition to create world order and integration. Nevertheless, the growth of Olympic decision-making as a rule-oriented process offers much promise. We have seen that in insisting upon an adherence to a minimum global standard of racial equality, the I.O.C. has employed legal tools as much as elitist discretion to convert the Olympics into a potentially effective agent of human aspirations. Moreover, recent experience outside the Olympic context with "ping-pong diplomacy" teaches us that transnational sports competition may serve as a setting for international rapprochement.

The regulation of transnational sports competition has been concerned primarily with the enhancement of association among competitors, rather than with the inducement of cooperation among them sufficient to spill over into the global environment.[97] What sustained contributions the Olympic organization has made to world order seem to have been more the unintended consequences of pluralistic decision-making than the result of a conscientious promotion of its organizational goals. In this respect, the I.O.C. has performed in a manner similar to the I.L.O. Nevertheless, as the Olympic Movement becomes legitimatized through the growing authority of its rules, its decision-making structure may be expected to become more goal-oriented. As the techniques of the I.O.C. develop to implement the values and goals that transcend its internal system, the Olympic organization may well assume importance as an agent of world order.

Footnotes

[1] But see J. Meynaud, Sport Et Politique (1966).

[2] The organization of the modern Olympic Games has been chosen as a paradigm for this study because of several factors: first, the propinquity of the 1972 Olympics and the length of the pertinent historical experience; second, the importance from the public viewpoint of the Games as a theater of interaction within the athletic sphere; third, the availability of related data; fourth, the significance to international law of the continuing transformation within the Olympic organization from a reliance upon discretionary decision-making to a quasi-legal process of rule-creation and supervision; and finally, the organizational feature of interaction among individual, non-governmental and governmental components.

[3] See, e.g., Lüschen, Cooperation, Association, and Contest, 14 J. Conflict Resolution 21 (1970). This article contains a very useful theoretical and empirical study of certain sociological components of athletic competition.

[4] See Nieburg, Agonistics--Rituals of Conflict, 391 Annals 56 (1970). The philosopher Paul Weiss has defined sport as a "rule-governed bodily adventure."

[5] Lüschen, supra note 3, at 25, 26. Lüschen acknowledges his debt to Max Weber for the distinction between vergemeinschaftung and vergesellschaftung.

[6] Lüschen, supra note 3; Heinilä, Notes on the Inter-Group Conflicts in International Sport, 1 Int'l. Rev. of Sport Sociology 31 (1966). This study which is premised on an analytical distinction between "in-group" and "out-group" attitudes is noteworthy to the international lawyer particularly because of its rule-oriented plea for an "identification and clarification of the very concept of fair play," about which there is a surprising lack of consensus, and thereafter for a "common recognition of and a commitment to the clarified principles and norms by international authorities." Id. at 37.

[7] Janeau, Sport et Psychologie, 3 Sport: Revue Belge de L'Education Physique, des Sports et de la Vie en Plein Air 194 (1970).

[8] Noting a trend toward greater specialization, quantification and reliance on equipment, one writer comments that "play is changing everywhere from a complex, multi-dimensional activity which earlier helped man to relate to his social and cultural environment, to a simple but extremely specialized activity which affords him greater and greater control over a small and, in itself insignificant, area of experience." Csikszentmihalyi, The Rigors of Play, 208 The Nation 210, 212 (1969).

[9] See Paleologis, Causes of the Decadence of the Ancient Games, 48 Olympic Rev. 475 (1971).

[10] Rather than being a romantically inspired panacea for the world's ills or an escape from them, the "plain truth is that sport is reflection of the society, that it is human life in microcosm, that it has within it the maladies of the society, that some athletes do drink, that some athletes do take drugs, that there is racism in sport, that the sports establishment is quite capable of defying the public interest, and that in this contemporary civilization sport does invade sociology, economics, law and politics." Cosell, Sports and Good-by to All That, N. Y. Times, April 5, 1971, at 33, col. 1.

[11] M. Sherif, In Common Predicament: Social Psychology of Intergroup Conflict and Cooperation (1966).

[12] Focusing on a much higher and more complex level of social interaction, recent legal scholarship has reflected an interest in problem-oriented premises of global integration that transcend available nation-state machinery. See, e.g., R. A. Falk, This Endangered Planet: Prospects and Proposals for Human Survival (1971); Lasswell, International Lawyers and Scientists as Agents and Counter Agents of World Public Order, 65 Am. J. Int'l. L. 366 (Proceedings) (1971) (address delivered at the American Society of International Law Annual Dinner, April 30, 1971).

[13] D. Mitrany, A Working Peace System (Quadrangle ed. 1966); Mitrany, The Functional Approach in Historical Perspective, 47 Int'l. Affairs 532

(1971). The assumption that international cooperation in non-political activities leads to cooperation in political activities was recommended for reexamination by the 1965 White House Conference on International Cooperation. Report of the Committee on Peaceful Settlement of Disputes, Dec. 1, 1965.

[14] E. Haas, Beyond the Nation State: Functionalism and International Organization 35 (1964).

[15] Rule 3, Olympic Rules and Regulations 11 (1971) [hereinafter Rules are cited as Rule with reference to enumerated rule or regulation, not page; for citation to Eligibility Code see infra note 17].

[16] J. Meynaud, supra note 1, at 126-27.

[17] See, e.g., Eligibility Code, Olympic Rules and Regulations 47 (1971) (prohibition against the use of drugs) [hereinafter the Eligibility Code is cided as Olympic Eligibility Code with reference to page]; Constant, Belgian Legislation Against the Use of Drugs in Sport, 19 N. Ir. L.Q. 160 (1968).

[18] See, e.g., Agreement between the German Association for Gymnastics and Sports (DTSB) of East Germany and the Main Committee for Physical Culture and Sports of Poland, based on a 1967 FNC treaty between the two countries and directed against West Germany. Treaty on Friendship, Cooperation and Mutual Assistance between the German Democratic Republic and the People's Republic of Poland, 6 Int'l. Legal Materials 514 (1967), ratification noted 6 Int'l. Legal Materials 862 (1967). Article 2 of the agreement reads: "In this spirit, both sides will come out for a strict observation of the principles of mutual respect, recognition, and equal rights; they will oppose all forms of discrimination in international sports and fight for the adherence to the statutes and rules of the international sports organizations." For recent examples of the importance of Olympic sports participation to national prestige see, Moscow's Olympic Dialogue, Sport in the U.S.S.R., No. 4 (1970); Olympic Ideas Put into Practice, 10 Foreign Affairs Bull. 219 (1970) (published by the Press and Information Department of the Ministry of Foreign Affairs of the German Democratic Republic).

[19] Rule 3, supra note 15.

[20] Rule 23, supra note 15.

[21] Rule 4, 13, 14 & 34, supra note 15.

[22] L. C. White, The Structure of Private International Organizations 34 (1933). See generally id. at 244–48; L. C. White, International Non–Governmental Organizations: Their Purposes, Methods, and Accomplishments 199–200 (1951).

[23] Rule 11, supra note 15.

[24] The Executive Board is assigned the responsibility for observation of the Rules and Regulations, the preparation of an agenda for meetings of the I.O.C., the nomination of members of the I.O.C., the management of the I.O.C.'s finances, the preparation of its annual report, the appointment of its Director, the ultimate responsibility for its administration and the maintenance of its records. Rule 15, supra note 15.

[25] Rule 22, supra note 15.

[26] Rule 46, supra note 15.

[27] See Announcement of the International Amateur Athletic Federation (IAAF), April 4, 1971 (published in London). The IAAF's decision, inter alia, raised the pole vault minimum to 16 feet 8 3/4 inches and the mens' high jump to 7 feet.

[28] Rule 24, supra note 15.

[29] Rule 24, 25 supra note 15.

[30] Rule 24, supra note 15.

[31] Rule 17, supra note 15.

[32] 38, 39 Olympic Rev. (1979).

[33] Rule 11, supra note 15.

[34] Rule 13, supra note 15.

[35] Rule 13, supra note 15.

[36] On the perspectives of the incumbent president, see Brundage, The Olympic Movement: Objectives and Achievements, 3 Gymnasion 3 (1966).

[37] See, e.g., J. Meynaud, supra note 1, at 105.

[38] I.O.C., Report on the 71st Session (Sept. 15-17, 1971) and Meeting of Executive Board (Sept. 10-11, 1971), at 8, Oct. 4, 1971 [hereinafter cited as I.O.C., Report].

[39] See Rule 11, supra note 15.

[40] Rule 16, supra note 15. The President is authorized to name the time and place of I.O.C. meetings, although he must convoke a meeting upon the request of one-third of the membership. He settles all "procedural" questions and exercises independent discretion at I.O.C. sessions in deciding whether or not to entertain new action not indicated by the agenda. Rule 17, 18 & 19, supra note 15.

[41] See note 15 supra.

[42] E.g., "[The] Olympiad and Games are numbered consecutively from [1896], even though it has been impossible to hold the Games in any [sic] Olympiad." Rule 2, supra note 15 (emphasis added). See generally Rule 15, at line 12 & Rule 54, supra note 15; Olympic Eligibility Code, supra note 17. The punctuation and wording of rule 45 was improved during the September, 1971 meeting of the I.O.C. In case of discrepancy between the French and English text, the French text prevails. Rule 19, supra note 15.

[43] Rule 40, supra note 15.

[44] Rule 41, supra note 15.

[45] Olympic Eligibility Code, supra note 17, at 44.

[46] Rule 42, supra note 15.

[47] See Part III. A. of this article infra.

[48] L. C. White, International Non-Governmental Organizations: Their Purposes, Methods, and Accomplishments 199 (1951).

[49] Rule 3, supra note 15.

[50] One writer has summarized the several leading theoretical commentaries on the developmental value of athletics as follows: "(Barnes and Ruedi) Spencer held that play was needed to get rid of surplus energy. Tarde pointed out the role of imitation in play. Lazarus felt play was 'recreative' and a means of recovering from fatigue. Groos held that play was preparation for adult life. Appleton assigned to play a physical basis and associated it with bodily changes occurring during growth. Hall developed

the 'Recapitulation Theory' in which play was viewed as a reliving of our savage ancestral activities. Shand saw play as expressing joy. McDougall felt play was motivated by the instinct of rivalry. Adler held play was used to overcome inferiority complexes." Daniels, The Study of Sport as an Element of the Culture, 1 Int'l. Rev. of Sport Sociology 153, 157 (1966).

[51] Rule 1 & 25, supra note 15.

[52] Any athlete was disqualified who, without permission of the appropriate national federation, accepted any prize worth $50 or more; had capitalized on or secured employment promotion on the basis of athletic form or success; became a professional in any sport or had decided to become one or played in a professional team with a view to become a professional; had been paid for teaching or coaching others for competition in sport; had been awarded a scholarship mainly for his athletic ability; had demanded payment or expense money for a manager, coach, relative or friend; had received payment of expenses in excess of the actual outlay, although he might receive clothing and equipment in addition to reimbursement of expenses or "pocket money to cover petty daily expenses during the Games;" interrupted his occupation, studies or employment for special training in a camp for more than four weeks in any one calendar year; had received expense money for more than 30 days exclusive of the time spent in travelling in any one calendar year; had neglected his usual vocation or employment for competitive sport whether at home or abroad; or was paid for the use of his name or picture or for a radio or television appearance. Olympic Eligibility Code, supra note 17, at 44-46.

[53] "Business and industrial concerns sometimes employ athletes for their advertising value. The athletes are given paid employment with little work to do and are free to practice and compete at all times. For national aggrandizement, governments occasionally adopt the same methods and give athletes positions in the Army, on the police force or in a government office. They also operate training camps for extended periods. Some colleges and universities offer outstanding athletes scholarships and inducements of various kinds. Recipients of these special favors which are granted only because of athletic ability are not eligible to compete in the Olympic Games." Olympic Eligibility Code, supra note 17, at 48. However, "An athlete paid for teaching elementary sport (beginners or schoolchildren) on a temporary basis without abandoning his usual occupation remains eligible. An athlete may be a full time professional journalist, radio or television reporter or a full time manager of or worker in an athletic facility without forfeiting his amateur status." Olympic Eligibility Code, supra note 17, at 47.

[54] See 43 Olympic Rev. 202 (1971).

[55] The Commission was appointed on November 23, 1971, to serve primarily as a watchdog over the national Olympic committees. N. Y. Times, Nov. 24, 1971, § C, at 42, col. 2.

[56] See generally J. Meynaud, supra note 1, at 144-49.

[57] Washington Post, March 27, 1971, § E, at 3, col. 3.

[58] As this article was going to press in February, 1972, the author was able
to summarize the resolution of this conflict as of the beginning of the 1972
Winter Olympic Games. Briefly, the boycott was never undertaken and to
a limited extent rule 26 prevailed. One important national committee implemented rule 26 be expelling several top skiers although the general reaction to rule 26 remained mixed and the threat of a boycott persisted.
Washington Post, Nov. 30, 1971, § D, at 5, col. 3. The I.O.C. warned
the national committees that they risked the disqualification of entire
teams if they should nominate individual entries who were later found to
have violated rule 26. Washington Post, Jan. 1, 1972, § C, at 3, col. 4.
Shortly before the 1972 Winter Olympics, the F.I.S., ostensibly out of
deference to the Japanese Organizing Committee, dropped its plans to
boycott the Games with the qualification that if the I.O.C. did not accept
its "good faith" interpretation of the rules it would not recognize the
Olympics as the world championships. Also on the eve of the Games, a
four man eligibility commission, established under the new rule and
chaired by Hugh Weir of Australia, reviewed evidence of individual rule
26 violations that had been submitted to it from several quarters, primarily from the I.O.C. President. Washington Post, Jan. 28, 1972, § F, at 4,
col. 5. The I.O.C. President remained firm in asserting his conviction
that many skiers were "trained seals," captive of the ski equipment industry. Washington Post, Jan. 30, 1972, § K, at 8, col. 1.

   The evidence presented to the Weir Commission included the testimony of several athletes, including an East German refugee who charged
the East German Government with encouraging "state amateurism" in
violation of rule 26 by providing successful athletes with handsome cash
bonuses, higher salaries, priority in military promotions and special
housing and automobile allocations. Washington Post, Jan. 28, 1972, § F,
at 4, col. 6. Aside from such testimony, the evidence was limited apparently to scattered clippings of advertisements from newspapers and periodicals. This evidence, however, was found to be unacceptable by both
the eligibility commission and the Executive Board. Moreover, the commission refused to apply rule 26 retroactively prior to April 2, 1971,
when it went into force and before which many of the alleged violations had
occurred. In doing so, the commission clearly distinguished the ineffectiveness of the old code provisions from the effectiveness of the new rule
26. N. Y. Times, Jan. 29, 1972, at 22, col. 5; Washington Post, Jan.
29, 1972, § E, at 1, col. 4. After deciding these procedural questions,
the Weir Commission reported its somewhat surprising recommendation
to the I.O.C. that only one athlete, Karl Schranz of Austria, be disqualified for violations of rule 26. The commission's report was adopted by
the I.O.C. after a two hour debate. Mr. Schranz was excluded from the
1972 Olympics and all threats of boycott by several national committees
fizzled upon the decision of the Austrian National Committee to participate
in the Games. The feeling remained in the Austrian Committee, however,

that Mr. Schranz was "singled-out" and excluded because of his candidness and militancy in opposing both the I.O.C. President and the application of rule 26 by the President and the I.O.C. N. Y. Times, Feb. 1, 1972, at 43, col. 6.

The resolution of the amateur standing crisis on the eve of the 1972 Winter Games was accomplished politically by the last minute cooperation of the F.I.S., and legally by the application of the new rule 26, together with a skillful treatment of evidence that had been submitted to the Weir Commission. In predicting the continuing vitality of rule 26, it is important to recognize that its application may have been restricted in context of the skiing crisis to a single, notorious violation of rule 26 as a sort of expedient that may preserve it for a time but cannot often be repeated without disparaging the due process, objectivity and equal protection afforded by Olympic decision-making, and thereby damaging the organization's legitimacy. With an eye to the future, a few final observations may be cogent: in resolving the dispute, which had clearly challenged the integrity of the entire Olympic organization, the I.O.C. and its eligibility commission, though acting reasonably, proceeded without granting a hearing to either Mr. Schranz or to any of the others accused of violating rule 26; nor was its decision adequately subjected to the appellate process. On the other hand, the prosecutorial process seems to have been handicapped by the I.O.C.'s lack of policing authority and capability in gathering evidence, a lack of cooperation from the national committees and a consensus that a lawsuit for perjury in sports is inappropriate. Washington Post, Jan. 30, 1972, § K, at 8, col. 1, These are the types of problems that characterize most transnational organizations; they are nevertheless problems that deserve serious and sustained attention. Perhaps the 1973 Olympic Congress in Sofia would provide one appropriate forum for discussion of such matters. See note 97 infra.

59 This rule allows compensation for the loss of income during training, open competition between amateurs and professionals, more liberal compensation for travel accommodations and insurance coverage. Washington Post, June 12, 1971, § D, at 6, col. 2.

60 A decision of the I.O.C. under rule 26 permits the I.O.C. to make an exception, so long as the "basic principles" are not infringed, that an athlete does not "make a profit or livelihood out of his sport." Arguably the words "his sport" might be construed to refer to a particular act of competition, rather than to his image as an athlete; thus, profit related not to a specific sports event might be considered beyond the reach of the provision. But the line is fine.

61 Rule 3, supra note 15.

62 "Participation" of nation-states in the Olympic Games as a political technique, with its concomitant regimentation and exploitation of the athlete and insistence upon winning, dates back generally to the Berlin Olympics

of 1936. J. Holmes, Olympiad 1936 (1971); R. D. Mandell, The Nazi
Olympics (1971).

[63] Jones, Sport and International Understanding, Report of the UNESCO--
Congress "Sport--Work--Culture" in Helsinki 1959, at 163 (1959), quoted
in Heinilä, supra note 6, at 33 & n. 6.

[64] See generally Documents Concerning Conflict Between El Salvador and
Honduras, 8 Int'l. Legal Materials 1079 (1969). These documents relate
to the serious ensuing crisis between El Salvador and Honduras and include material relating to the action taken by the O.A.S.

[65] Heinilä, supra note 6, at 36.

[66] Heinilä, supra note 6, at 36-37.

[67] See, e.g., Nieburg, supra note 4, at 66.

[68] "[The I.O.C. is responsible for] inspiring, and leading sport within the
Olympic ideal, thereby promoting and strengthening friendship between
the sportsmen of all countries." Rule 10 (4), supra note 15.

[69] See Bouet, The Function of Sport in Human Relations, 1 Int'l. Rev. of
Sport Sociology 137, 139 (1966).

[70] See G. Lüschen, 2 Die Freizeit der Arbeiterschaft und ihre Beziehung
zum Sport (1962), noted in Hammerich, Critical Remarks Regarding the
State of Sociological Research in the German Federal Republic, 1 Int'l.
Rev. of Sport Sociology 229, 236 n. 51 (1966).

[71] See, e.g., Heinilä, supra note 6, at 33.

[72] See Wohl, Conception and Range of Sport Sociology, 1 Int'l. Rev. of Sport
Sociology 5 (1966). The author of a history of the politically charged 1936
Games in Berlin concludes that they "seem to have contributed more to
international misunderstanding than to the peace of the world and the furtherance of international sportsmanship." J. Holmes, supra note 62, at
159. Two fiction writers have echoed the notion that sports competition
helps relieve interjurisdictional tensions. Albert Camus wrote, "And unable to lay seige to each other, Oran and Algiers meet, compete and insult each other on the field of sports...." A. Camus, "Sports" from
The Minotaur in The Myth of Sisyphus and Other Essays 123 (Vintage
Books ed. 1955). Agatha Christie, too, wrote, "You know, I don't like
the sound of Vietnam at all. It's all very confusing, North Vietnam and
South Vietnam and the Viet-Cong and the Viet--whatever the other thing is
and all wanting each other and nobody wanting to stop. They won't go to
Paris or wherever it is and sit round tables and talk sensible....I've

been thinking it over and I thought it would be a very nice solution--
couldn't you make a lot of football fields and then they could all go and
fight each other there, but with less lethal weapons. Not that nasty pain
burning stuff. You know. Just hit each other and punch each other and all
that. They'd enjoy it, everyone would enjoy it and you could charge admission for people to go and see them do it. I do think really that we
don't understand giving people the things they really want." A. Christie,
Passenger to Frankfurt 50-51 (1970).

[73] Rule 8, supra note 15. "Governments cannot designate members of National Olympic Committees." Rule 24, supra note 15. "[The] Olympics
are not contests between nations and no scoring by countries is recognized." Rule 44, supra note 15. Further, a decision of the I.O.C. considered it "dangerous to the Olympic ideals, that, besides the proper development of sports in accordance with the principles of amateurism,
certain tendencies which aim primarily at a national exaltation of the results gained instead of the realization that the sharing of friendly effort
and rivalry is the essential aim of the Olympic Games." Olympic Eligibility Code, supra note 17, at 48. The President reiterated the importance of the Olympic Movement's independence from governments at the
I.O.C. September, 1971 meetings. I.O.C., Report, supra note 38, at 13.

[74] The use of national anthems and flags at appropriate ceremonial times
during the Games, authorized by rules 56, 57, 58 and 59, has proven to
be controversial. According to one viewpoint, the use of national symbols, unlike the use of the Olympic torch, flag and other symbols designed to promote association, unnecessarily promotes international rivalry
and derogates from the individualized spirit of the competition. An opposing viewpoint identified especially with the developing countries and
those of the socialist bloc, maintains that their use serves to stimulate
all three classes of Olympic participants, as well as the public. This
seems to have been the view of the national Olympic committees during
their 1969 Dubrovnik meeting when they approved the practice of raising
national flags and playing national anthems. 3 Sport, Nos. 5 & 6 (Prague
1969).

[75] At times, the I.O.C. has taken positive action to discourage politics from
entering the sports arena. For example, it suspended Indonesia in 1962
for refusing to permit Israeli and Taiwanese athletes to come to Djakarta
for that year's Asian Games, See also J. Meynaud, supra note 1.

[76] Rule 24, supra note 15.

[77] Rule 25, supra note 15.

[78] Rule 3, supra note 15.

[79] It should, of course, be remembered that similar invitations were extended to other co-participants from the United Kingdom, Canada, Colombia

and Nigeria. The circumstances of the invitation nevertheless indicate strongly that bilateral considerations centered on Chinese-American relations were paramount in the Chinese initiatives.

[80] For example, the notation on United States passports of their invalidity for travel to China had been scrapped only three weeks prior to the invitation.

[81] See 14 Peking Rev. 10-12 (1971).

[82] See N. Y. Times, Apr. 23, 1971, at 7, col. 1 (city ed.).

[83] Rule 3, supra note 15.

[84] The selection was to be performed by an eight-man committee consisting of four whites and four non-whites.

[85] Furlong, A Bad Week for Mr. B., Sports Illus., March 11, 1968, at 18.

[86] Lobbying for the banishment of South African nationals was skillfully led by a Congolese, Jean Claude Ganga. In addition to what was reported to be a well argued brief in legal support of his position, Mr. Ganga was substantially aided by current fears of a retaliatory boycott by United States black athletes. Moreover, the Congolese Government had created a receptive atmosphere by presenting the President of the I.O.C. with the Insignia of the Commander of the Republic of the Congo.

[87] The General Assembly obviously assumed that its intervention did not contravene article 2 of the U. N. Charter, which provides: "Nothing contained in the present Charter shall authorize the United Nations to intervene in matters which are essentially within the domestic jurisdiction of any state or shall require the Members to submit such matters to settlement under the present Charter ...." U. N. Charter art. 2. para. 7.

[88] G. A. Res. 2396, 23 U. N. GAOR Supp. 18, at 19, U. N. Doc. A/7348 (1968).

[89] See, e.g., Statements by Gary Player, Arthur Ashe and Dennis Brutus in Racism and International Sports, 2 Objective: Justice, No. 3, at 4 (U.N. Office of Public Information, July, 1970). The latter two individuals appeared before the U.N. Special Committee on Apartheid.

[90] See Washington Post, April 20, 1971, § D, at 3, col. 3; id., April 23, 1971, § D at 4, col. 2. The Davis Cup organization has responded by lifting a controversial two year ban on South African participation, while at the same time maintaining a ban on Rhodesian participation in view of

U.N. sanctions against Rhodesia, Washington Post, Jan. 15, 1972, § C, at 3, col. 4.

[91] See Washington Post, June 20, 1971, § C, at 6, col. 5. This is an account of the first competition between white and non-white South African athletes, which took place in Salisbury, Rhodesia. Because of the participation of athletes from Malawi and Rhodesia, the competition was "international" under the new South African definition.

[92] Announcement of the South African Amateur Athletic Union, May 16, 1971.

[93] For an interesting commentary on the efficacy of another non-governmental initiative in combatting apartheid, see generally Reisman, Polaroid Power: Taxing Business for Human Rights, 4 Foreign Policy 101 (1971). The U.N. General Assembly recently adopted a resolution that expressed its concern and "affirmed that merit should be the sole criterion for participation in sports activities." U.N. Press Release WS/531, at 3, Dec. 3, 1971 (publicizing adoption of G.A. Res. 2775 D).

[94] Separative practices are encouraged by the laws and policies of Rhodesia. See, e.g., Zimmerli, Human Rights and the Rule of Law in Southern Rhodesia, 20 Int'l. & Comp. L.Q. 239 (1971).

[95] Decolonization Committee Deplores Olympic Invitation to Rhodesian Team, U.N. Press Release WS/501, at 4, May 7, 1971.

[96] I.O.C., Report, supra note 38, at 9.

[97] The 1973 Olympic Congress to be held in Sofia, Bulgaria will bring together all components of the Olympic organization and will address three themes: the promotion of the Olympic Movement and amateur sport: the definition of jurisdictions among the I.O.C., the international federations and the national committees; and a consideration of the pattern and resulting consequences of future Olympic Games. I.O.C., Report, supra note 38, at 10.

Ethnocentrism And Conflict In Olympic Competition: Parallels And Trends

Frederick C. Hatfield

The Moor

Men stick staffs in spongy ground,
And sniff to see what they have found,
Was there a tragedy out on the moor?
Knowing some of the silent thrills of man,
I'm not so sure.

Introduction

The past century has seen more wars and mass devastation of a global nature than ever before in the history of man. While one shudders to refer to this fact as a trend, it is explicable in light of exponentially increasing advances in technology and an attendant increase in world intradependence.

The rise in prominence of international sport has paralleled this trend and is inextricably related to it. It seems appropriate that the Olympic Movement was originally conceived as a measure to restore moral and physical vitality to France after Her defeat in the 1870 Franco-Prussian War (Lipsyte, 1972). Coubertin's vision that sport should serve as a vehicle for fostering world brotherhood and international goodwill has, through the Olympiads, been the rallying cry of the International Olympic Committee. This creed presupposes--indeed, invites--political involvement in the Games. Yet, in the countless examples where sport between nations has attenuated, or in fact created, ethnocentric boundaries, rival nations have blamed each other for allowing politics to impinge on the sanctity of the Olympic arena.

Pointedly, Olympic sport has evolved from a politically naive vision into a politically volatile reality, and from a socially innocuous phenomenon into an event capable of eliciting such ethnocentric behavior as to plunge nations into all-out warfare. It is this evolutionary process that this paper is concerned with, and some striking parallels presented between it and the technocratic advances of the world's societies.

Reprinted from the Review of Sport and Leisure 1, 1976.

Such an excursion necessarily falls short of offering precise remedies for the extent of ethnocentrism and conflict noted throughout the history of the Olympics, and well it should. Time has shown that, in spite of the I.O.C.'s stated ideal that the site of the Olympics be neutral and autonomous, competing athletes, and especially their coaches and officials, bring with them their ideologies, their nationalistic pride, their prejudices, their social learning, and very often their instructions regarding required conduct. Sport is viewed differently by many societies, and pointing out trends applicable to disparate lifestyles and political persuasions must be regarded as only a step towards full understanding of such complex problems.

Technological Innovations

The first and perhaps the most obvious of these parallels is the trend of societies during the past century advancing from relatively unmechanized and unscientific to highly mechanized and scientifically advanced. With this trend came commensurate changes in sport. Advances in architecture enabled the construction of greater indoor arenas, free of pillars, in which sports previously relegated to summer or outdoor participation could be conducted. Also, stadia capacities are increasing because of the same architectural advancements. The age of plastics gave rise to springier vaulting poles, lightweight materials for equipment and uniforms, and a host of other sport-related innovations. Scientific and medical advances have supplied athletes with highly sophisticated training techniques which involve not only a profound knowledge of exercise physiology, but sociopsychological considerations as well.

At first glance, these changes appear unrelated to the problem of hostilities or conflict occurring in sport. However, they are underscored and supported by other related trends which, when viewed together, are apparently catalytic in this regard. Consider first that the biological and psychological natures of man have not appreciably changed over the last century. Technological advances have obliged man, a relatively stable biological unit, to continually advance toward his ceiling of human tolerance. As this advance continues, and tolerance ceilings of athletes are realized,[1] new mechanisms, techniques, and strategies must, in the interest of victory, be devised. Many of them are known to significantly diminish the competing life of the athlete, or, in fact, to be related to premature death. Many others are suspected of doing so. These techniques, including violent checking strategies in hockey, increasingly riskier and more spectacular stunts in gymnastics, the low squat position in weight lifting, blood doping, glycogen loading, steroid and amphetamine usage, local or general anesthetics to mask pain, hypnotism, electrical stimulation of muscle tissue--the list is too long to briefly mention--are examples of the compensatory devices resorted to in order that the athlete may mitigate for his or her inherent biological or psychological limitations.

As already alluded to, the avenue taken by athletes which involves taking advantage of better facilities, more efficient equipment, and the like, appears to have become of limited benefit in their struggle for record performances. Only limited change or progress in performance levels can be attributed to such advances nowadays, since rules are explicit with regard to equipment usage and specifications, and bigger buildings cannot be regarded as necessary. This trend has served to increase the need for riskier mechanisms and strategies of the type mentioned above.

Augmented Frustration

For reasons not unlike those which increase the risk of physical harm, psychological risk has increased also. Athletes operating at, or near, their optimum performance level are, for example, extremely susceptible to severe frustration over their incapacity to improve sufficiently to beat their rivals. Commonly, such frustration is vented in several ways, often involving lashing out at the perceived source of their frustration. Quitting the sport, working harder (often to the point of overtraining), or fighting with their coach, their competition, or even the system under which they live and train are such examples. This type of frustration appears to be more common today than ever before. Athletes of past decades did not have the ceiling of human tolerance so close to their heads, and consequently sought other, less risky, avenues to improve by. Better equipment and facilities is the standing example.

Social Movements

Many investigators (e.g., Edwards, 1969, 1973; Scott, 1971) have observed that the youth movements of the past decade have had their effect on sport. For example, the civil rights movement is seen to have been the source of the "revolt of the black athlete" which Scott wrote about. This trend can be clearly demonstrated by comparing past athletes' points of view with those of today's black athletes. Jesse Owens was quoted recently as observing, "We went there (the 1936 Olympic Games) to run against 55 other nations of the world." On the other hand, Tom Smith observed, "I'm very proud to be a black man...you finally have a release to prove yourself in the eyes of the world."

The apparently heightened social consciousness of the youth of the late 1960's was seen to have been the cause of the striking changes in athlete-coach relationships. No longer would athletes yield to the dogmatic, outdated ethics and impositions of their coaches, a situation which appears to have fostered both beneficial as well as detrimental effects in sport in general. For example, the athlete now thinks for himself, accepting or rejecting coaches' advice on the basis of personal preference. Arguable here is the notion that the years of experience behind the coach are questioned to the point that athletes are not producing maximally. Many coaches point to the tremendous increases Soviet bloc athletes have made in recent years over those which the Western countries have been able to muster to substantiate their viewpoint that coaching must be a matter of blind acceptance on the part of the athlete.

The advent of the womens' liberation movement appears to have had its effect in the sport world as well. Women athletes are now being given many of the same advantages in training, facilities and equipment that men have had. Whether this trend will result in better performance in competition remains to be seen. Some argue that the effect will be generally harmful to the Olympic effort, since many sport pursuits heretofore closed to women are now available, thus siphoning many top women athletes away from Olympic sports. Western countries, particularly the United States, have seen this happen in mens' sports. Many of the finest athletes are socialized into pursuit of professional sports, leaving the amateur ranks comprised largely of athletes who, for various reasons, couldn't make it professionally.

Howard Cosell (1976) stated that the Olympics have become "a forum for international protest." He described the 1968 Olympics as giving seed to the 1972 Black September Massacre. It was during and around the 1968 Olympic Games that much of the youth-oriented protests were occurring throughout the world, and much was carried into the Olympic arena. While politically motivated actions were certainly not new to the Olympic scene, the extent of protestation and sociopolitically oriented conflict appears to be on the rise, a trend seen to be related to the increasing appeal and consumption of the Olympic competition. This increased spectator appeal has greatly increased the utility of the Olympic arena in giving international coverage to protesters' and terrorists' particular causes. Of course, underlying the increased spectator appeal and consumption is the fact that satellite communications and supersonic travel are now a reality.

State Subsidization

Perhaps the most discussed issue among athletes involved in Olympic competition is the practice of some countries of the world to subsidize their athletes. Such subsidy often involves military induction as a means of circumventing the amateur code. However, coaching, medical care including highly specialized dietary advice, drug administration, bonuses for exceptional performances, choice jobs, and, along different lines, selective breeding for future athletic "stock" are not unknown examples of the State supporting the sport effort in Olympic competition, and seem to be increasing.

The question, then, becomes one involving the social risk of losing. Countries of the world have, from the beginning of the modern Olympics, recognized the political and ideological advantages of having their athletes win in the Olympics. They have, correspondingly, recognized the social disadvantage in being represented by losers. Much international animosity has been directly attributed to this belief. In fact, as vested interests of the State become greater through subsidization practices, the greater is their implication in subsequent victories or defeats. This vicious cycle perpetuates and attenuates chauvinism more than perhaps any other single factor.

Commercial Subsidization

Other examples in which risk appears on an upward trend are seen in the increased subsidization of athletes by athletic equipment companies and other commercial enterprises. As is the case in State subsidization, as the stakes get higher, so too does the risk. Similarly, greater chances for pecuniary or positional advancement following competitive years are present now more than ever before. Again, only the gifted few will be able to compete for these _ex post facto_ rewards, rendering the expenditures in time and effort of the majority of athletes relatively wasted except for the intrinsic rewards gleaned. Therein lies the trend—whereas once sport was intrinsically rewarding, it has become financially and socially rewarding as well, apparently as much the latter as the former.

Augmented Spectator Appeal

The increasing risk component in sport is related to yet another change taking place in many countries of the world. Sport appears to be progressing from an athlete-oriented endeavor to a spectator-oriented one. Notwithstanding the increasing financial importance of sport for reasons already discussed, not the least of which is the advances in communicating sport to the masses, either through the media or through greater stadia capacities, this trend appears to be related to the increasing risk component in sport. Mumford (1934), commenting on the increasing regimentation or routinization in the world's societies and the attendant decrease in the role of chance, claimed that sport contests are one of the last places (along with circuses and similar spectacles) in which modern man could identify with life. He writes, "Since the principal aim of mechanical routine in industry is to reduce the domain of chance, it is in the glorification of chance and the unexpected, which sport provides, that the element extruded by the machine returns, with an accumulated emotional charge, to life in general" (p. 304). Mumford believed that this over-glorification by the general public of mass sport was indicative of a decadent society, analogous to the fall of the Greek and Roman empires, a view not totally shared by most modern sociologists. His remarks concerning sport becoming mass spectacle, however, were prophetic, particularly with regard to professional and Olympic sport. Yet, sport is losing even this quality—that of chance—for, with decreased variance in athletic performance resulting from athletes approaching their physical limitations, chance is also decreased. Spectacle viewers must derive their vicarious need for the unexpected from other sources, most of which appear to involve an augmenting of the risk factor.[2] The increasing demand for more violent and aggressive tactics, the "win at all costs" syndrome, the heightening of ethnocentrism all seem to have become alternative avenues for the pleasure-seeking fan to derive satisfaction for their thwarted sensibilities. In the event that the applicability of the introductory poem escaped the reader, it should be somewhat more clear at this point.

Another focal point, however, should be used to view the increasing spectator appeal of the Olympic Games. The trend noted previously that communications advances have greatly increased the consumption of Olympic and other sport has had an unexpected side effect. Lord Killanin (1974) denounced critics of the Olympics as seeing only the headlines of the newspapers, and hearing only the Cosells of broadcasting, both of which tend to accentuate the negative aspects of the Olympics. These are the exceptions, Killanin declared, and most of what goes on is "sports getting people together." However, true as this may be, it does not alleviate the problem that the great masses of people around the world leave their newspapers, radios and televisions believing that the Olympic movement is, or is becoming, harmful to international understanding and world brotherhood.

The Media, Shrinking World, and Social Complexity

The parallel evolution of efficient international travel and communication, with the attendant increase in international sport competition and world awareness of it through the media, and the increasing conflict and chauvinism in sport is, perhaps, the single-most important trend confronting the Olympic Movement today. The 19th century big world has become the 20th century small world in many regards. Greater freedom and speed of travel, greater world awareness by the public, more money invested in sport, more free time to engage in sport, greater numbers of sport events in international competition, and correspondingly greater numbers of athletes all have had the net effect of increasing the social complexity of sport.

As societies' machines become more complex, so also do the maintenance requirements and skill requirements of the operator. Correspondingly, the increased monetary expenditures of developing, operating, and maintaining the machine as well as its increased output capacity must be reckoned with. So also must its impact on the marketplace. So it is with sport in society. The Olympic Games, in particular, are a product of this industrialized era, and have been subjected to proselytism and change to the point of nonrecognition--much as the airplane has.

Such complexity increases the risk of problems, misunderstandings, ambiguity and, to extend the analogy of the machine, breakdown. It appears that proper training of personal, proper marketing and management all could have an effective role in making Olympic competition less rife with conflict and ethnocentrism. For this to happen, however, a major overhaul or perhaps a completely new blueprint for sport organizations throughout the world would be required, an extremely complex understanding in itself.

Many sport historians, sport philosophers, sport leaders, athletes, and especially sport columnists, have offered their formulae for such change. These offerings are believed to point to the inevitability of change. Many of the formulae are meritous of consideration, but by whom? The athletes? Sport organization officials? The State? The sport investers or equipment manufacturers? The sport consumers? Perhaps the sport sociologist? In the meantime, we of the sport world ride the wing of our airplane machine and suffer the risk of falling off.

Footnotes

[1] For example, Miller (1976) has shown that there may be a ceiling effect in max VO_2 uptake, beyond which little or no advantage is gained by long distance runners.

[2] Note that "chance" and "risk" are spoken of differentially. Within the context of this paper, chance refers to apparent lack of cause or design (luck), while risk is used to infer danger of injury, either physical, psychological or social in nature.

References

Cosell, Howard. Triumph and Tragedy: The Olympic Experience. ABC Special Broadcast, January 5, 1976.

Edwards, Harry. Revolt of the Black Athlete. New York: The Free Press, 1969.

_____. Sociology of Sport. Homewood, Illinois: Dorsey Press, 1973.

Killanin, Lord. Reprint of Lord Killanin's address to the Olympic Solidarity Symposium at Teheran, New York Times, Dec. 15, 1974, V, 2(1).

Lipsyte, R. New York Times (Editorial), Sept. 10, 1972, IV, 1.

Miller, R. Unpublished document, Bowie State College, 1976.

Mumford, L. Sport and the Bitch-Goddess, Technics and Civilization. New York: Harcourt, Brace & World, 1934, pp. 303-07.

Owens, Jesse. Triumph and Tragedy: The Olympic Experience. ABC Special Report, Jan. 5, 1976.

Scott, J. The Athletic Revolution. New York: The Free Press, 1971.

Smith, Tom. Triumph and Tragedy: The Olympic Experience. ABC Special Report, Jan. 5, 1976.

Section 3

IDEOLOGY

Introduction

Current debate in 1978 speculates on the amount of Soviet propaganda that will be piped into the homes of Americans as a result of the $90 million contract to broadcast the 1980 Olympics signed between the National Broadcasting Corporation and the Russians. Part of the agreement, it seems, entails options to televise cultural events and other "specials" from Russia. Social commentators, such as William F. Buckley, drawing attention to this fact during the same week that Rostropovich was stripped of his Soviet citizenship, severaly doubt that the type of broadcast censored for release by the Russians will be truly culturally representative. In effect, then, it is suggested that the Russians will be attempting "to persuade persons to accept a certain point of view"--by definition, propaganda. (Palmer and Perkins, 1969).

Propaganda is the communications process by which ideology is disseminated, and a technique of communications usch as television is the perfect medium for mass propagandizing. The Olympic Games have been proclaimed by many authors as the spectacle par excellence for exploiting the full potential of the medium of television. But just as the potential of mass communications can be reflected in bringing the Olympic Games to millions, so too, the Games can be employed as the instrument for bringing mass attention to ideological principles.

In 1936, the Nazis hosted the Olympic Games in Berlin, employing the situation to increase their prestige in the world by showing how modern, progressive and well organized Nazi Germany had become. Some twelve years later, those Germans who had repudiated Hitler were not allowed to compete in the Olympiad of 1948. Two German states were formed out of the allied occupation zones in 1949--the German Federal Republic and the German Democratic Republic. Their diplomatic, ideological and propaganda "cold war" carried over into the sports world. In 1952, 1956, 1960 and 1964 they competed as one German team in the Olympic Games, but the years in between were filled with unending political and ideological battles over every minute point. By 1965, the I.O.C., tiring of the endless quarrels, finally granted East Berlin's request for a separate team. Two German teams started in Mexico under the same banner and same insignia.

Political considerations urged a counter to the defeat of 1965, so the West German sport chief Willi Daume decided to acquire the Olympic Games for Munich. West German Chancellor Willi Brandt saw in the 1972 Games a chance too good to miss in acquainting world opinion with the new modern Germany, and in scoring a propaganda triumph over the GDR. Foreign Minister Walter Scheel noted:

A once in a lifetime opportunity has been offered to us to use the worldwide interest in sports to present a picture of our development and our political system abroad, and to transmit the image of a modern Germany in all its political economic, social and cultural aspects... (cited in Die Auswaetige Politik der Bundersrepublik Deutschland, p. 749).

In Munich, the GDR was allowed to start under its own flag, as was the GFR, and the Beethoven hymn was replaced by the respective German anthems. The Olympics were seen as a way of bringing the divided condition of the German people to the world's attention. Both East and West Germany regarded their athletes as political emissaries who could and would recommend their way of life to those who had not decided which Germany to support in other international disagreements.

The organs of international sport not only ensure a continued political role for this most popular form of transnational interchange, they also permit the adoption of sport activity for ideological and national purposes by each state unit. There is no limit to the use of sport for propaganda, prestige, and political development. Anyone can interpret sports triumph for the celebration of any national purpose. Edwards (1973) has called this the "liquid quality" of sport.

Olympic politics are structured to favor the status quo, with certain exceptions. The only sub-state actors in the Olympics come from Puerto Rico (a situation with much political potential). When football teams from Wales and Scotland compete in "international" matches, burgeoning "devolutionary" pride is given a mass political focus. By and large, however, a state must achieve political recognition before its athletes can be celebrated in the transnational sport system. Groups opposed to certain states must demonstrate from the outside, as they do not usually gain admittance to mainstream sport politics.

In addition, states opposed to the recognition of other states through sport have a problem. While sport politics turn athletic participation into diplomatic legitimacy, Olympic ideology proclaims that "politics" have no place in sport. The fact of political reinforcement continues to further the political claims and national morale of those participating in sport - without making waves. In order to challenge the political status quo, however, a state must make a public demonstration of opposition to continued sport legitimacy for the opponent in question. Such a challenge interrupts athletic events through boycott, demonstration, and diplomatic retaliation. The impression is made that the "sports process" has been intruded upon, when in fact the political status quo has merely been put into question. Whether Indonesian President Sukarno's Games of the New Emerging Forces or the Third World boycott of the 1976 Olympic Games provided clumsy cases of misapplication of sport, or legitimate uses of the political processes of transnational sport organization is a matter for debate.

The relative merits of the social-political system are expressed in the ideology of a nation. Political and social leaders of a given society have their lives and identities symbolically transmitted to provide evidence for the strength and superiority of the system that they serve. It is no surprise, then, given the recent history of the People's Republic of China, for Goodhart and Chattaway (1968) to state: "Ideologically, Mao's swim must rank as the most important sporting event of 1966." (p. 106). An historical analysis of the official Chinese newspapers reporting the swims of Mao over the previous ten years reveals the ideological metaphor of parable and slogan substantiating the efforts of the great leader in behalf of his people. The sport metaphor took an ironic turn, for the report that Chairman Mao had swum a distance of nine miles in 65 minutes appeared to be a new world record, until it was realized that the swiftness of the current of the Yangtze had had some influence. Invocations to the little Red Book (the Thoughts of Chairman Mao) by Chinese athletes in their athletic endeavors are widely reported and serve as example to reinforce a sentiment expressing political faith in success.

In like manner, Fidel Castro participates in sport for the value it serves to show his people that political leadership and education through sport go hand in glove. Similarly, the major use of sport for ideological socialization or for political development comes through exploitation of national sport heroes. National propaganda is served by the top performance of Olympic athletes and teams. In the smaller and lesser developed nations of the world, superlative athletes who make their marks in international competition are exalted and even canonized (deified) upon their death, thereby serving yet a grander ideological purpose of the state. An example in which the appreciation of athletic excellence will cross ideological boundaries is the 1972 Fischer-Spassky chess match.

The Soviets had vilified Bobby Fischer as an example of the worst in bourgeois sport. He loved money, had quit high school, and was highly anti-Communist. His specialization in chess showed that he was a mere craftsman, that he failed to recognize the value of chees as one manifestation of human creativity. But his victory over Boris Spassky was accomplished with a skill that even such Soviet commentators as former World Champion Mikhail Tal had to admire. The quality of his play brought him respect from an audience more concerned with the nuances of his plan than with the reactionary nature of his existence.

Spassky, on the other hand, appealed to an American sense of "fair play." Where Fischer seemed rude and cantankerous, Spassky appeared friendly, understanding, and the perfect image of a "good sport." Some Americans (including editorial writers for certain newspapers) expressed respect for Spassky, whose dignity in defeat put him in the role of the perfect "underdog."

It is interesting to note that Soviet ideology did not put Spassky in the same light. His defeat resulted in significant restrictions on his foreign travel and public appearances. Part of this, no doubt, was due to personal depression, but the memory of his defeat--and the scandal of a Western romance--did him no good. After several years of seclusion, Spassky moved to France.

Athletes, if they are to be a useful collection of ideological specimens, must be useful social models. Since the political content of sport triumph is as important as the victory itself, "correct" behavior is crucial to the state in question. In this context it can be seen how serious the question of sport defection is taken by the deserted society. Research into rates of defection by athletes still awaits the efforts of scholars and others, but occasional commentary appears in the press and in texts on sport in society. A case in point is cited by Goodhart and Chattaway (1968):

> After the 1956 Melbourne Olympics, held in the shadow of the Hungarian uprising, no less than 48 Hungarian athletes and officials defected, along with seven Romanians and a Czech. Most of the Hungarians were flown to America, where they were welcomed by the Governor of California with the words 'God has brought you here'. Meanwhile a Hungarian Minister of State greeted the remnants of the Hungarian squad (it had originally numbered 175) on its return to Budapest and attacked the men who had arranged political asylum for the defecting athletes as 'traders in human beings' who went to Melbourne to 'buy victims for political purposes'.
>
> Of the Olympic defectors, Laszlo Tabori, the great middle-distance runner, went on to complete a distinguished athletic career in America, but an even more lasting impact on world opinion was made by the Hungarian football team Honved, which defied orders to return to their occupied homeland after they had left to play a club match in Brazil. (pp. 131-132).

In many states, athletes are granted privileges which place them near the top of the social ladder (such privileges are relative--in determining the level of athletic pampering it is relevant to compare the standard of living of the athlete to that of his fellow citizens, not to that of the athletes of other states). When these most favored of citizens choose to desert their homeland, it is highly embarrassing to the state which has subsidized them and publicized their exploits. At the 1962 Caribbean Games in Jamaica, the Cuban Premier Fidel Castro sent his Cuban team on their way with the message that their mission was to win and thereby demonstrate that socialism was superior to capitalism. Some 142 plain-clothesmen accompanied the team. Once there, the ideological struggle became intense, as the Cuban exile Frank Diaz led a free-lance defection unit intent on helping Cubans defect, providing getaway cars and special hiding places for those defecting. The second in command of the Cuban delegation, Jose Raul Grande, the basketball coach, Jose Sarasa, a basketball player, four weightlifters and a photographer were among those defecting with the aid of Diaz's unit.

The social model provided by an athlete defecting from a country is a blow to the internal credibility--and sometimes legitimacy--of that regime. States are even more vulnerable to the effects of sport defection than to most other forms of political escape. Athletic heroes are mass heroes. The same publicity which makes a well behaved athlete a valuable asset also makes a defector a national embarrassment.

There are times when a regime can use athletes from other states in the cause of political development (sometimes mislabeled the "nation-building" process). McIntosh (1963) states: "The best performers anywhere want to test their skill against the best from elsewhere, but because at international level the best performer merges some of his identity in the nation itself, whether he wants to do so or not, success in sport has political importance." (p. 197) Mass media communications and information networks allow a relatively unknown country to inject itself into the consciousness of milions of television viewers and newspaper readers by scoring triumphs in international sports competitions.

Success on an international scale in sports brings with it a certain amount of respectability, prestige and status, especially among newly emerging, undeveloped, ex-colonial powers. Such was the victory of Akii Bua from Uganda in the 400-meter hurdles race in Munich. Kenya scored important triumphs in Mexico to emerge as a track and field power when Kip Keino won the 1500 meters distance race, Naftali Temu the 10,000 meters and Amos Biwott the 3000 meters. Mohammed Gammoudi brought recognition to Tunisia with a victory in the 5000 meters in Mexico, in 1968. The victories of Abele Bikila and Mamo Wolde in the marathons of Rome, Tokyo and Mexico were enormous triumphs for not only the two runners, but for Ethiopia as well. Victory on the track brought with it instant recognition, as millions of television screens flashed the results in the homes of people around the world

Kenya had its Keino, Tanzania its Filbert Bayi, but President Mobutu of Zaire did not have an athletic tool to use in his campaign to mold the two hundred ethnic groups of his country into "One Great Zaire."

He did however, discover Muhammad Ali. The 1974 Ali-George Foreman fight was used by Mobutu as an arena for his own prestige. A cabinet position was created to handle the fight. For months before it the two boxers toured the country with Mobutu. Signs were erected complete with the slogans of an ideology known as "Mobutism." Village leaders from all over the former Belgian Congo had their pictures taken with the President and the fighters. On the night of the event, televisions were put in thousands of villages so that people could watch a dance festival (containing their entries, of course). Leaders were flown in from all over Zaire to sit at ringside, and the entire evening was supervised by a huge portrait of President Mobutu.

It should be noted that such attempts are not always successful. Sport victory is fine, but it cannot forever gloss over basic political, economic, or ethnic problems. No amount of identification with Muhammad Ali could prevent the Zairois province of Shaba (once called Katanga) from being invaded by people opposed to its connection with the rest of the country. Sport is a useful ideological tool, but in the long run it can make poor political cement.

The section of readings under "Ideology" (Section 3) present the student with a wide interpretation of the meaning of ideology. The opening classical piece by Pleket draws upon anthropological and historical evidence to discuss the social symbolism of agonistic encounter among groups. The paper focuses on the material effects of sport in culture, linking with Section 1 (Foundations in Culture: Antecedents to Political Sport), in the culture/politics context of ideology.

In a more contemporary context, "Sport and Political Ideology," by John Hoberman, draws together the broader philosophical orientations of Huizinga (Homo Ludens; In the Shadow of Tomorrow), Caillois (Lex Jeux et les Hommes) and de Coubertin. The classic literature of sports--Hessen, Der Sport; Adam, La Morale des Sports, and others--is reviewed from the standpoint of ideology. He discusses sport as an "organic image" of the state, and as a force "embodying a chivalric ideal stressing elitism, asceticism, and notion of the enemy as a purely formal opponent."

While most authors represented here concentrate on specific countries or regions, Pleket and Hoberman attempt to construct a more general conceptual framework for understanding the interaction of sport and society. Their attempts are as important as detailed analyses of each state, since through them the reader can consider the interaction of diverse political cultures within a common network of transnational sport institutions.

Entering another thematic interpretation of the meaning of ideology, Murray discusses the emergence of the Australian Collective Identity as a function of developing statehood and suggests that sport is one of the dominant forms of symbolic dialogue for the collectivity. Sport takes a historical place as being a "natural" force in the development of Australian "Social Health." Murray presents two models: (i) System Idolatry, and (ii) Sport Ideology. The former model sets the scene for a discussion of the latter. In the Kanin contribution, "Superpower Sport in Cold War and Detente," sport is seen as a tool in an on-going adversary relationship which can not be settled in the usual fashion (to date) because of nuclear weapons. Ideological warfare is mixed with "peaceful coexistence" as sport is used to alter or reinforce mass perceptions of the temper of inter-superpower relations.

The next reading by Kanin, "Ideology and Diplomacy: The International Dimensions of Chinese Political Sport," illustrates how Western sport was adopted in China at the same time as other aspects of Western culture and political ideology (including Marxism). Mao's thought on sport is combined with the political uses of international sport organization to create policy toward Taiwan, the superpowers, and the Third World.

Finally, a distinction can be drawn between states of Western origin and those of independent foundation. It was mentioned in the introduction of Section I, that the institutions of sport are constructed within a framework corresponding to Western political culture. The Western perspective has been useful, however, when viewed from a traditional Eastern frame of reference, as Sie illustrates. Briefly, his paper on the case of the Asian Games and the Games of the New Emerging Forces shows that the separation of politics and sport (a crucial principle of the International Olympic Committee) has not been shared by many newly independent nations of the world who have traditionally seen sports as a valuable tool in the forging of political and economic alliances. When the exclusion of Israel and Taiwan from the IVth Asian Games provoked the wrath of the I.O.C., the I.O.C. was left accused of practicing the same type of political discrimination it sought to condemn. Countries frustrated by the policies and actions of the I.O.C. and the Western power bloc dreamed of a "New World Order." The triumphant staging of the Games of the Newly Emerging Forces became the first step in an attempt to unite the Third World and alter the world balance of power.

The Ideology Of Athleticism

H. W. Pleket

From Pindar's time until Roman Imperial times members of the upper class were never absent in sport (neither in the running events nor in the body-contact sports) and the prevailing ideology of Greek sport always was a product of that same class. Let us first take the <u>problem of the partici-pants</u>. There is no prosopography of ancient athletes, but there is a decent substitute, L. Moretti's list of Olympic victors (<u>Olympionikai</u>).[1]

All these <u>Olympionikai</u> are either known to have participated in many other games or may be assumed to have done so. A statistical approach is unwise. First--the record provides only a very small percentage of the total of actual winners; second--it is only in relatively few cases that the social background of the athlete is more or less clear. General consider-ations, a few specific pieces of evidence, and a number of solid examples of upper-class athletes enable us to determine the main trends. For reasons of space I refer the reader to my article <u>Zur Soziologie des antiken Sports</u> for a short list of those upper-class athletes who are known to have per-formed successfully in a great many contests and who, because of the parti-cipation of highly specialized, "professional", lower-class athletes, must have been equally specialized and "professional".[2] The general consider-ations are as follows:

1) It is improbable that before the rise of the gymnasion, which occurred after 650 B.C., non-nobles participated at Olympia or in the other, still rare, athletic contests;

2) It is also improbable that immediately after the rise of the gymna-sion non-nobles penetrated into the Olympic realm. Training requirements, travel costs, the obligation to stay a month in Olympia before the beginning of the games and the resulting loss of income were decisive obstacles for the poor. Subsidization would have been indispensable, but the earliest evidence for that is much later: an inscription from Ephesus (ca 300 B.C.), which tells us that the trainer of an obviously promising but not wealthy young ath-lete asked the city to subsidize his client's "training and travelling abroad".[3] A well-known passage from Isocrates' Περὶ ζεύγους says that, according to the well-to-do Athenian politician Alcibiades, ca 400 B.C. <u>some</u> (ἐνίους) of the athletes who performed at Olympia were of low birth and mean education. Obviously <u>most</u> participants still belonged to the upper-class; it looks as if

---

Adapted from "Games, Prizes, Athletes, and Ideology". <u>Stadion I</u> (1):49-89, 1975.

the recruitment of lower-class Olympic athletes was a relatively recent phenomenon on the basis of which Alcibiades began to disdain the gymnastic contests and turned to the breeding of racehorses and to the equestrian contests "possible only for those most blest by Fortune and not to be pursued by one of low estate". Alcibiades would have been happier in Pindar's time when the true kaloikagathoi still predominated at Olympia.

3) It is probably in the local contests, which increased rapidly from the 6th century onwards, that the hoplite middle class got its first chance to participate, but we cannot substantiate this probability because of the usual lack of evidence.

What deserves to be emphasized is that after 400 B.C. there is no question of lower class athletes monopolizing the athletic scene and of upper-class athletes withdrawing from athletics and restricting themselves to the equestrian games. In the Hellenistic-Roman material it is often impossible to determine the social background of an athlete: sometimes we have only name; in other cases we happen to know that an athlete received honorary citizenship or a political function in his own city but we can rarely decide whether the man was a product of social mobility or belonged to a municipal elite family ab origine.

Fortunately we do have a number of certain and a number of very probable examples of members of the city bourgeoisie who after 400 B.C. and before 300 A.D. continued to practice high sport on a high level. In my article "Zur Soziologie des antiken Sports" (p. 72-73) I emphasized the importance of the ephebeia, i.e., the urban youth-organization of the scions of the municipal upper-ten who in their gymnasia devoted considerable time to physical education and games and on the basis of the ephebic training ventured to go in for the very specialized and (at least from our point of view) professionalized sport of the public contests, sacred and thematic alike. The ephebic training was basically a physical and para-military training, to which in the Hellenistic-Roman period some cultural activities (lectures by itinerant rhetoricians and philosophers) were added.[4] This ephebeia functioned as a bridge for members of the urban elite between gymnasium sport and the world of the public contests. How many crossed that bridge we do not know; but we may be certain that a number did. At present it is much harder to give a list of athletes who were lower class certainly than one of those from the upper-class. For the former we have to rely on the following evidence:

1) the above-mentioned Isocrates passage; 2) some passages in the 2nd century A.D. physician Galen (born in Pergamum and practicing as a doctor in Rome) in which he criticizes the lack of education of trainers (and since trainers were generally ex-athletes, his statement may be taken to be valid for athletes as well);[5] 3) the fact that in the so-called Herminus papyrus-- the membership certificate of an Egyptian boxer Herminus issued by the oecumenical association of professional athletes[6]--some officials and athletes happen to be a-grammatos (illiterate), which, at least for Asia Minor and Greece, would seem to imply that they did not belong to the jeunesse dorée of the city elite.[7]

It cannot be doubted that from Pindar's time onwards there was one very important constant in Greek athletics: the participantion of members of the urban elite. There is another constant and that is that these aristocrats did not restrict themselves to the running events (200 metres, 400 metres and the long-distance race (4800 metres)); among the certain instances of upper-class athletes there are boxers, wrestlers and pankratiasts, from Pindar's time until Roman imperial times.[8]

I. The Ideology of the Athletes

A third constant leads us straight into our third main question: the ideology of athletics. There is a clear ideological constant from the time of Pindar's athletes onwards. A full analysis would require a detailed discussion of Pindar's odes, of Dio of Prusa's two essays on the Carian boxer Melancomas who died during the Sebasta in Naples in the 1st century A.D.,[9] of Lucian's dialogue Anacharsis (2nd century A.D., containing a fictitious discussion between Solon and the Stythian prince Anacharsis about the use and value of athletics both in the gymnasium and in the public games), of Philostratus' manual On Gymnastics (early 3rd century A.D.)[10] and of the various honorary decrees and epigrams for successful athletes.[11] This would clearly take us too far and moreover would entail an accumulation of rather monotonous ideological language. I shall restrict myself to a few essentials. Firstly, relatively trivial values like physical beauty and strength receive due and constant attention. Pindar describes an Olympic wrestler as καλὸς ἐσορᾶν ("comely he was to look upon"); elsewhere he describes an athlete as εὔχειρ, δεξιόγυιος and ὁρῶν τα ἀλκάν ("with deftness of hands and litheness of limbs and with valour in his glance").[12] If reality happened to be different, he tactfully called an aristocratic boxer πελώριος ("a giant giant").[13] Melancomas is praised for being the most handsome boxer;[14] and in Lucian's Anacharsis the beauty of the athletes' bodies is duly emphasized by Solon.[15] In the world of the practicing athletes themselves the pankratiast Kallikrates is praised by his colleagues for the natural qualities of his body which were admired all over the world.[16] A colleague, M. Alfidius, a promising champion in one of the body-contact sports, is said to have had εὐφυεία (beauty and talent) and to have died in his καλλίσπη ἀ̓κμή ("the finest prime of his life").[17]

There were at least two official interpretations of beauty. Philostratos preached the message of the beautiful young ephebe, idealized product of the gymnasium, "mit leichten schlanken Körperbau und frei und hoch gehobenen Hals". The Heracles-statues from the ephebic gymnasium exemplified this type: it is the ἐλευθέριον ἄγαλμα (the statue which befits a gentleman).[18] The association of professional athletes also chose Heracles as its patron but that Heracles showed "kolossale Fleischfülle, ein mächtiger Nacken bei verhältnismässig kleinem Kopf und kurzem Hals", i.e., Heracles with a bull's neck.[19] Significantly the Milesian boxer and Olympic victor Nichophon, high-priest and magistrate in his city (Miletus) and probably a member of the urban elite, is explicitly praised in an epigram for having the heavy neck of a bull, the iron shoulders of Atlas, the beard and hair of Heracles and the eyes of a lion.[20] This emphasis on physical beauty is the more remarkable if we realize that in reality sports like boxing and pankration

were notorious for the blood and the injuries of the contestants. To win
$\overset{\text{'}}{\alpha}\tau\rho\alpha\upsilon\mu\overset{\text{'}}{\alpha}\tau\iota\sigma\tau\text{o}\varsigma$ (unwounded) was exceptional.[21]

Much more interesting is the strong and continuous emphasis on the
manly and military values of sport. In Homer Nestor's son is both the fast-
est runner and a warrior.[22] Pindar frequently compares athletes with old
heroes and identifies the athlete's aretē (courage) with that of the warrior.[23]
Dion of Prusa and Lucian regard athletics as an ideal preparation for war.
Dion argues that an athlete is even superior to a warrior.[24] Keywords in
this respect are $\overset{\text{'}}{\alpha}\nu\delta\rho\epsilon\iota\alpha$ (courage), $\pi\acute{o}\nu\text{o}\varsigma$ (toil) and $\eta\alpha\rho\tau\epsilon\rho\acute{\iota}\alpha$ (endurance).
These words have been studied in detail by L. Robert who has showed that
they are to be found both in the authors and the documents from the 5th cen-
tury B.C. onwards.[25] A special feature of the $\eta\alpha\rho\tau\epsilon\rho\acute{\iota}\alpha$ (endurance) is that
the athlete who 'endures' wants either to win or to die. This "philosophy" is
on record from the 6th century B.C. onwards, when the renowned pankratiast
Arrichion was exhorted by his trainer with the memorable words: "What a
beautiful funeral it is not to give up at Olympia". In the 1st century A.D.
another pankratiast is said to have continued fighting in the final at Olympia,
until it became dark because he "thought that it was better to sacrifice one's
life than to give up hope of winning the wreath." A 2nd century A.D. Olympic boxer prayed to Zeus for "either the wreath or death". We know from
his epitaph that the poor unfortunate died. L. Robert has pointed out that
precisely the same ideology is on record in an epitaph for a citizen soldier
from Thyrreion in Acarnania.[26] The epitaph of the Olympic boxer has a
splendid parallel in a funerary epigram on a warrior from Elis (i.e., the
area round Olympia). The first two lines run as follows, in Beckby's German translation: "Unter den ersten im Kampf, Chaironides, standest du
betend: 'Zeus, gib mir jetzt den Sieg oder den Tod in der Schlacht' ."[27]
Robert's words deserve quotation: "L'idéal des athlètes, c'est la gloire de
la couronne. On parle avec mépris de athlètes 'professionels' de l'epoque
impériale. Il faut reconnaître qu'ils ont adopté l'idéal des 'amateurs' et des
citoyens grecs" (italics are mine, H.W.P.).[28]

The continuity in the value systems of Pindaric kaloikagathoi and of
Hellenistic-Roman athletes is, I think, to be explained by the simple fact
that aristocrats continued to function in athletics after the breakdown of the
monopoly of the nobles. The ephebes of the Hellenistic-Roman gymnasium
provided the channel through which the old values could be transported to
later periods.[29] The ideology and mentality of the urban elites of the
Hellenistic-Roman polis, i.e., of the leisure class of the cities, reminds
one of the value system of the modern leisure class, as described by
Th. Veblen in his famous The Theory of the Leisure Class. The leisure
class is a group of wealthy citizens who know how to accumulate wealth but
do not actually work themselves in the physical sense of the word.
R. MacMullen's characteristisation of the Roman upper-class seems applicable both to the elites of the Greco-Roman cities and to Veblen's modern
American "leisure class": "At one end lay the very best thing of all, wealth
without a person's having to get it himself, that is, inherited. The active
pursuit of it aroused certain misgivings, at least among the topmost nobility.
They simply had money. Next along the spectrum lay wealth enjoyed in retirement; and verging towards the unrespectable, wealth still in the process
of accumulation."[30] The Hellenistic-Roman city elite had hardly anything

to do with war in the period of the Pax Augusta and in an empire where Roman legions had ousted the old citizen militiae. This leisure class could afford to spend their lives in comfortable idleness: "...the scheme of life of the class is in large part a heritage from the past, and embodies much of the habits and ideals of the earlier barbarian period".[31] In the para-military atmosphere of the gymnasium and in the athletic contests, which were adorned with the old warrior's ideology, the leisure class reenacted the civilization of the archaic warriors who did not bother about production but lived as gentlemen of leisure, i.e. as warriors on the battlefield and as athletes between battles: "From being an honourable employment handed down from the predatory culture as the highest form of everyday leisure, sports have come to be the only form of outdoor activity[32] that has the full sanction of decorum".[33] Veblen's remark about modern athletics ("The slang of athletics...is in great part made up of extremely sanguinary locutions borrowed from the terminology of warfare")[34] can be applied with a good deal of justification to the world of sport of the ancient leisure class.

An overriding value was the everlasting glory of the victorious athlete. "To participate is more important than to win"--the slogan of the Coubertinians in 1896 and of their successors at the present day--is probably the most un-Greek statement that can be made, as I. Weiler has recently emphasized once again with a wealth of details.[35] It would be boring to quote passages from Pindar to Philostratus about the profound importance of κλέος, κῦδος and εὐηλεια (fame, reputation). The epigraphic documents reflect the monotony of the literary sources in this respect. Victory in itself was not enough. There is a tendency to add, so to speak, a "surplus-value" to that of the victory in itself. I shall not give a long list of these "surplus-values" here; I have in mind athletes who won ἀκονιτί[36] (i.e. without having to fight, because all opponents withdrew before the beginning of the games out of fear of the superstar) and ἀπτῶτος[37] (without having fallen on one's knee; a surplus-value for wrestlers, who had won when they had thrown their opponents on the floor three times) or who achieved a series of victories on one day or for the first time; in the latter case he could be first of all human beings or first of his fellow-citizens or first of his fellow-provincials. It would be wrong to think that such statements were a product of lying, arrogant athletes. There is no reason "de prendre pour des mensonges ou des exagerations les mentions de victoires πρῶτος Μιλησίων, πρωτος Ἰώνων, πρῶτος πάντων, et de les traiter dans un esprit de plaisanterie suppconneuse et sarcastique".[38]

Incidentally, the continuous emphasis on these surplus-values shows how wrong it is to think that Greek athletes were only interested in harmony and beauty or that Greek sport was "zweckfrei". What matters above all is that this tendency not to be satisfied with the victory as such but to amplify it is already on record in Pindar's poems (see Ol. 13, 37-38, II, 92). In later sources it may have become stronger, sometimes even exuberant but basically the development is one from the vanity of a small group of archaic aristocratic winners to the more-loudly-proclaimed vanity of a larger number of athletes, aristocrats and non-aristocrats alike.[39] When in Roman imperial times the anonymous author of a Protreptikos for athletes writes that the winner will be praised and "pointed at with the finger in the whole world",[40] the words may be new and the vocabulary certainly has become more verbose but the attitude reflected in the words is the same as that behind Pindar's poetry.

Let us finally turn to the most important ideological problem of our time: that of "professionalism" versus "amateurism". These are modern, almost anachronistic concepts, but this does not imply that they cannot be useful heuristic tools in the hands of the historian who must anyway always try to manoeuvre between the Scylla of the reconstruction of a completely anachronistic past and the Charybdis of the servile re-telling of the stories of the past themselves.

Nowadays by professionals we mean sportsmen who make money out of their sport. Full professionals are those who devote all their time to their sport and make a living out of it;[41] semi-professionals devote a certain percentage of their time to sport and derive only part of their daily bread from it. In antiquity as far as I know there was never disapproval of the fact that successful athletes received material rewards for their victories. Olympionikai (Olympic victors) were not debarred from participation in thematic games and we know (cf. above p. 62) that from the 6th century onwards they received official rewards from their mother cities for their Olympic wreaths. A recent inscription from Sybaris (in Southern Italy) implies that Olympiionikai received a substantial amount of money from their home city.[42] Eight centuries later the above-mentioned Anonymus writes, without the slightest trace of criticism, that successful athletes (Olympic and otherwise) could count, after their retirement, "on a life of affluence and on the fruits of their victories".[43]

Does this mean that all ancient athletes were basically professionals? By no means: firstly, it would be unwarranted to assume that all recorded athletes devoted all their time and their entire youth to training and games. A recent text from Hellenistic (1st century B.C.) Colophon in Asia Minor tells us about a certain Polemaios who as an ephebe trained in the gymnasium and won prizes in many sacred contests abroad but soon afterwards gave up athletics and decided to devote himself to the study of rhetoric and philosophy in Rhodes. During a short span of time he must have devoted all his energy to sport because he would otherwise have been unable to win in hieroi agones at a time when competition was very strong and full-time professionals active.[44] The same may be true of some of Pindar's clients. Others went further. In the 5th century B. C. Theogenes of Thasos practised boxing and pankration during 22 years and gained 1300 victories: 1300 may be a suspiciously round figure but I do not see why this should lead us to reject the fact that we have here an athlete who for 22 years won on an average a victory a week.[45] This need not be exceptional. In Pindar's poems we have (admittedly poetical) parallels: some of his heroes are said to have won "innumerable" victories, or "victories as numerous as the grains of sand on the beach" (cf. also above p. 56).

It is undoubtedly among late archaic aristocrats like Theogenes of Thasos that the first professionals are to be found.[46] They would have accepted the title of professional if one defines it as a man who does nothing but athletics during a longer of shorter period of time; they would have rejected this label, if we had given the following definition: a professional is a man who derives his income from his sport. They would have objected because they did not earn or did not have to earn their daily bread; they were wealthy; they did not have a profession. They embody "the truth that in antiquity land ownership on a sufficient scale marks "the absence of any occupation" ".[47] What they in fact did was to accumulate wealth in a honourable way. That was such a normal part of their way of life that they neither talked about it nor expected Pindar to mention it. They took it for granted.

Sometime in the Hellenistic period, at any rate before 50 B.C., an association of ecumenical athletes came into existence. It is customary, and from our point of view correct, to speak about the association of professional athletes;[48] however, there is not a single document in which it is said that the members exercised a profession (τέχνη, ἐπιτήδευμα) and made a living out of it. The documents mostly contain monotonous lists of victories, first those in the hieroi agones (and among them the periodos on the first place) and at the end as a single total the thematic victories, as if apologizing to the reader that they participated in such pedestrian, material events. It is a variant on the above-mentioned (cf. p. 70) attitude of the Athenian gentleman T. Domitius who tried to make the thematic games less thematic by calling them hieroi. The anonymous Roman author talks about περιουσία ἄφθονος and καρποί <οἱ> ἀπὸ τῆς νίκης, i.e. about "affluence" and "fruits of the victories", not about professional moneymaking.

It is the critics who apply the word technē or epitēdeuma (with the meaning of 'profession') to athletics. Galen used it for contemporary athletics and he also writes that "the profession of the athletes" (τὸ τῶν ἀθλητῶν ἐπιτήδευμα) came into existence in the early 4th century B.C. In a Pseudo-Platonic text athletics are compared with other banausic crafts.[49] We do find the word techne in a few agonistic documents but it there pertains to a boxer or wrestler who relies on his technical skill rather than on brute strength: techne denotes a specific skill or style in boxing, not boxing as such, let alone athletics in general.[50] Galen does not criticize athletics because it is a technē but rather because it is an example of kakotechnia ("base art").[51] Galen was himself a technitēs but he called his technē a manifestation of well-doing; his technē was a "logikē technē" (intellectual art) and a "semnē technē" (honourable art) and as such superior to a banausic technē, but in Galen's view even the latter can be useful to society and to the person who exercises it.[52] Professional athletics is neither a semnē nor a banausic techne: it is kakotechnia, not so much because this profession enables people to collect large sums of money but because these people fail to achieve a honourable way of life with their wealth: it is a φαῦλον ἐπιτήδευμα (a "mean, base profession"); it destroys body and soul.[53] It does not produce beautiful bodies; on the contrary, over-specialization and one-sided diets bring about ugly πολυσαρκία ("fleshiness", "plumpness").[54] Galen admits (and apparently accepts it) that athletic achievements provide the athletes with glory among the masses and with money, but he argues that they are unable to administer their wealth correctly: during and after their career the athletes are in debt and just as poor as an οἰκονόμος (steward, manager) of a wealthy gentleman's estate picked at random.[55]

Galen joins in with and explicitly quotes Euripides who in a fragment of his Autolykos set the tone for later critics of athletics: "For when there are ten thousand ills in Greece, there's none that's worse than the whole race of athletes. For, first of all, they learn not to live well, nor could they do so; for could any man being a slave to his own jaws and appetite acquire more prosperity than that of this father?"[56] There is a distinct undertone of class-prejudice in both authors. Euripides points out that the athletes of his time never manage to acquire more prosperity than their fathers had. This is perhaps another way of saying that they end their life in poverty which in turn implies that their fathers were poor as well. When lower class athletes begin to perform successfully in athletics, both on the local and the international level, misery starts. Euripides was contemporary with Alcibiades (cf. above p. 73) who noticed and sharply criticised the presence of lower class athletes at Olympia. Euripides is known to have celebrated Alcibiades' equestrian victories ca 416/415 B.C. (though I must add that after the Sicilian expedition, launched on the initiative of Alcibiades, Euripides' sympathy for Alcibiades seems to have cooled).[57] Galen's comparison of an ex-athlete with the manager of a rich man's estate suggests that athletes were despicable: "management throughout the classical period, Greek as well as Roman, urban as well as rural, was the preserve of slaves and freedman, at least in those larger undertakings in which the owner himself did not normally take an active part".[58] Galen does not condemn people who exercise a <u>techne</u> in order to earn their living; he condemns people who exercise a dishonorable <u>techne</u>. He distinguishes between good and had <u>technai</u> because as a doctor he is also considered a <u>technites</u> and because he wants to raise the status of his <u>techne</u> (epitedeuma).

In the athlete's counter-ideology--a combined product of Pindaric <u>kaloikagathoi</u> and the Hellenistic-Roman aristocracy (the εὐγενεῖς[59] = well-born, noble)--athletics is never called a <u>techne</u>. It is significant that <u>techne</u> (profession, 'métier') was however used of the profession of <u>trainer</u>. In an inscription from Bouthrôtos (in ancient Epirus, now in Albania) we hear of a certain Chaireas, son of Dioskourides, who was employed as <u>epistates</u> by a young member of the urban elite, Antipatros, son of Archias. As L. Robert has brilliantly shown, Chaireas was not a magistrate (as the editor of the inscription supposed) but a trainer, a teacher of gymnastics. Ἐπιστάτης is the <u>terminus technicus</u> for this profession. Chaireas is praised because "τὰν πᾶσαν ἐπιμέλειαν μετ' εὐνοίας ἔν τε τᾶι τέχναι ηαὶ τᾶι ἄλλαι ἀναστροφαι εἰς Ἀντίπατρον ποιεῖται" ("in his 'métier' and in his behaviour in general he shows all good care and goodwill towards Antipatros"). In Robert's paraphrase: "Il a fourni avec zèle au jeune notable Antipatros les sécours de son métier, de son art, de sa technique,--le pédotribe, le γυμναστής, l'épistate est un τεχνίτης--pour l'entraînement et la formation physique et athlétique de son élève, cependant qu'il était, plus généralement, un maître et instructeur de compaigne agréable (ἡ ἄλλη ἀναστροφή)".[60]

A trainer had a profession, just like a sculptor, an architect, a doctor or an actor. They are contracted, hired by an individual or a community for a specific job at a specific salary (μισός: wage). Wage-labour had a low social status in Greco-Roman antiquity: "illiberal and mean are the employments of all who work for wages, whom we pay for their labour and not

- 214 -

for their art; for in their case their very wages are the warrant of their slavery". That is the view of Cicero who in the same paragraph condemns all craftsmen who work in their workshops for clients.[61] Though the category of those who "worked for clients (private or public) has a higher status than the man who worked for wages",[62] in the last resort both categories are held by the upper-class to be of inferior status. In the 2nd century A. D. Lucian vehemently attacked literary men who accepted salaried positions in the homes of wealthy Romans: "their slavery is manifest and they differ little from purchased or bred slaves".[63]

By avoiding the word technē and epitēdeuma the athletes avoided giving the impression that obtaining money through their sport was tantamount to professional work for one's daily bread. In its origin the world of athletics was dominated by aristocrats who introduced their value-system; members of the urban aristocracies continued to dominate, if not the sports, at any rate the ideology of sport. Technē was inferior; as a successful athlete one did not receive a misthos--that was reserved for trainers--but prizes or gifts. Galen actually writes that in his days athletes were daily honoured with gifts of money;[64] prize games were even called ἀγῶνεc δωρῖται (gift games).[65] "Greeks of high station and hereditary wealth" did not wish to obtain "an income overtly from professional earnings".[66] Even what we nowadays call the intellectual professions--medicine, architecture, teaching --are admittedly called "occupations in which either a higher degree of in telligence is required or from which society derives no small benefit" but they are "respectable for those whose status they befit".[67] The latter were of a "evidently inferios social status",[68] not only for Cicero but for the entire Greco-Roman upper class. Significantly those intellectuals who are known to have charged fees for their teaching or services show a "tendency to treat fees as gifts"[69] (my italics, H.W.P.). The prevailing ideology was against fees, wages, salaries: these words smacked too much of "professional earnings": a gentleman "had no occupation"; nor had those gentlemen who specialized in athletics.

From the above it appears that our definition of professionalism would have appalled the ancient athlete, precisely because it starts from a positive attitude to people having a paid job. The ancient aristocrats simply had money, "the active pursuit of it aroused certain misgivings";[70] "work was no disgrace to a Greek of high status, provided that he was not compelled to resort to it to earn his daily bread".[71] The athletes had their own πόνος ("toil", "hard work"); but that was honourable πόνος, not to be confused with the πόνος of the πενῆτες, i.e. of those who had to work for their daily bread.[72] The question will be asked whether and to what extent lower class athletes complied with this ideology; there is no way of knowing whether a successful lower class Egyptian athlete talked openly with his colleagues in terms of misthos about the fees he received as a result of being "contracted" by a wealthy local politician to take part in one of the municipal contests. In fact Dion of Prusa uses the verb μισθοῦσθαι (to hire for misthos) in the above-mentioned (see p. 65) story to denote nothing more nor less than the agreement made by a local benefactor and a renowned Olympic victor. However, what matters is that in the official ideology, as shown by the documents left by the athletes themselves, there is no question at all of money, wages, rewards or anything similar. On the contrary, in all extant catalogues of victories the victors list their victories in sacred games in detail whereas the prize games are mentioned almost casually at the end of the text, and then merely as a total, not by name. The "closed" ideology of the athletic world is in accord with what P. A. Brunt has suggested about the relation between aristocratic values and the views of the lower classes in general: "Aristocratic conceptions may have been pervasive and dominant because the lower classes were not sufficiently reflective or articulate to criticize them or to substitute something different. Nor must we underrate the inherent attractiveness of the aristocratic ideal of independence and leisure".[73] Sociologists call this attitude imitatio domini.[74]

One final point: why is it that, in contrast with the conceptions of de Coubertin and others, there was never a movement in antiquity to ban monetary rewards and prizes completely from sport. It would be too simple to argue that throughout antiquity wealth as such as unequivocally good and always respectable. Admittedly, to borrow a few significant words from the emperor Claudius in a speech to the Roman senate,[75] all the "good men" (boni) were "wealthy" (locupletes) but the converse would not necessarily be true. The concept of nouveaux riches is a Greek invention ($\nu\epsilon\acute{o}\pi\lambda o\nu\tau o\varsigma$; $\mathring{\alpha}\rho\tau\acute{\iota}\pi\lambda o\nu o\varsigma$). Aristotle criticizes contemporary Athenian nouveaux riches as follows: "and since that which is old seems closely to resemble that which is natural, it follows that, if two parties have the same good, men are more indignant with the one who has recently acquired it and owes his prosperity to it".[76] The term has especially been applied to people who have seen fit to acquire wealth in trade, commerce and "industry". The same phenomenon and the same prejudice is on record in 1st century B.C. Rome, as T. P. Wiseman has shown in his New Man in the Roman Senate, 139 B.C. -A.D. 14.[77] In short, there was good wealth and bad wealth; consequently one cannot say that wealth as such was beyond criticism and that therefore there was no reason to separate sport and money.

In a recent article the Dutch sociologist R. Stokvis pointed out that in 17th and 18th century England the old landowning aristocracy had no objection to participating in contests with "professionals", or to competing for money-prizes.[78] It was not until the 19th century—he argues—that it became aristocratic to separate sport and money: why? His answer is that in that same 19th century new social groups, whose wealth was movable, based on cash, commerce, and operations on the markets, threatened the position of the landowning nobility: new-rich, entrepreneurs as opposed to the old nobility. The latter formerly combined honour and status with wealth;[79] from the very moment that people who "had nothing but money", rose to prominence, the old nobility focussed on its code of honour, as being its exclusive preserve, and refused to participate in contests for money prizes. Let us assume that this hypothesis is acceptable; we can perhaps then understand why the old public school code and that of de Coubertin who, incidentally, was strongly impressed by Thomas Arnold's system, had no predecessor in antiquity.

Admittedly, as pointed out above, the phenomenon of "nouveau riches" was not unknown in Greco-Roman antiquity but I doubt very much whether they ever seriously threatened the predominance of the landowning elite.[80] In this respect the recent books by M. I. Finley and R. MacMullen mentioned above leave no doubt about the fundamental predominance of the landowning elite in the ancient world.[81] In other words: in antiquity the aristocracy never ceased to accept monetary rewards for their sporting achievements, because their position was never threatened by a commercial business oligarchy, whose only merit, in the eyes of their adversaries, was wealth, and new wealth at that. It is clear that only a comparative analysis of the economic roles and attitudes of ancient and early-modern European aristocracies can corroborate or refute this hypothesis, which has been advanced here mainly to encourage further research. It is of course obvious that the history of sport cannot be separated from the history of society at large.

Footnotes

[1] L. Moretti, "Olympionikai, I vincitori negli antichi agoni olimpici", in: Memorie Accad. Lincei, Sc. Mor., serie VIII, vol. VIII, fasc. 2, 1957, 53-198 (with J.-L. Robert, "Bulletin Épigraphique", in: Revue des Études Grecques 71 (1958), nr. 160, 221-223); cf. also L. Moretti, "Supplemento al catalogo degli Olympionikai", in: Klio 52 (1970), 295-303.

[2] Cf. above note 18; in this article one also finds the necessary references for what follows.

[3] L. Robert, "Décrets d'Éphese pour des athlètes", in: Revue de Philologie 1967, 14-32; cf. id. in: Comptes Rendus Académie des Inscriptions et Belles Lettres, 1974, 524.

[4] Cf. my article: "Collegium Iuvenum Nemesiorum. A Note on Ancient Youth-Organizations", in: Mnemosyne 1969, 281-298, esp. 286.

[5] Cf. J. Jüthner, Philostratos über Gymnastik, Leipzig-Berlin 1909 (reprint Amsterdam 1969), 7 and 236.

[6] For these cf. my article: "Some Aspects of the History of the Athletic Guilds", in: Zeitschrift für Papyrologie und Epigraphik 10 (1973), 197-227.

[7] See "Zur Soziologie ...", 76/77.

[8] See above p. 53, with note 18.

[9] Dion, Or. 28 and 29, with L. Robert, Hellenica XI/XII, 338, note 4; id.: L'Antiquité Classique 37 (1968), 409 f.

[10] To be consulted in J. Jüthner's magnificent edition (see above note 91).

[11] See the list in L. Robert, OMS, I, 614-617; id.: Hellenica XIII, 134-154; add the decree for M. Alfidius published by G. E. Bean in: Belleten, Türk Tarih Kurumu 29 (1965), 588-593 and commented upon by L. Robert, in: L'Antiquite Classique 37 (1968), 406-417.

[12] Pindar, Olympian Odes 8, v. 19; 9, v. 94, 111; 10, v. 100-105.

[13] Ol., 7, 15; cf. C. M. Bowra, Pindar (Oxford, 1964), 167 f.

[14] Dion, Or. 28, § 2-3 (on Melancomas' opponent); 5; 12; Or. 29, §3.

[15] Lucian, Anacharsis (Loeb-edition vol. IV) § 12.

[16] L. Robert, Hellenica XIII, 134 ff., l. 15-17.

[17] Cf. above note 97.

[18] Cf. J. Jüthner, Philostratos über Gymnastik, 253 and ch. 35 of Philostratus' text.

[19] J. Jüthner, ibidem.

[20] Cf. L. Robert, "Les Épigrammes satiriques ..." (cf. note 17), 268-273.

[21] L. Robert, art. cit. (cf. note 106), 234-236; 204.

[22] Homer, Odysseia 3, 111-112.

[23] C. M. Bowra, Pindar (Oxford, 1964), 164 f. and 177; D. C. Young, Pindar Isthmian 7, Myth and Exempla (Leiden, 1971), 18-19.

[24] Dion, Or. 29, 9 and 15; Lucian, Anacharsis (cf. above note 101), § 24; cf. also J. Ebert, Griechische Epigramme (cf. above note 33), 21.

[25] "Les Épigrammes satiriques ..." (cf. note 17), 235, note 2; id., in: L'Antiquité Classique 35 (1966), 429 ($\dot{\alpha}\nu\delta\rho\epsilon\iota\alpha$); for πόνος cf. L. Robert, Hellenica XI-XII, 344-349; XIII, 140 f.; Kl. Kramer. op. cit. (cf. note 28), 135 (πόνος); L. Robert, "Les Épigrammes ...", 288, with note 4; in Lucian's Anacharsis (§ 24) μαρτερία)is recommended as a boxer's virtue; cf. also L. Moretti, op. cit. (cf. note 8), nr. 21 (4th century B.C.), l. 3; cf. also R. Merkelbach, "Der griechische Wortschatz und die Christen", in: Zeitschrift für Papyrologie und Epigraphik 18 (1975), 101-148, esp. 116, 123 (μαρτερία), 118/9 ($\dot{\alpha}\nu\delta\rho\epsilon\iota\alpha$), 100/1, 116 (πόνος).

[26] L. Robert, "Les Épigrammes ...", 198-199, 288; cf. Merkelbach, art. cit., 122/3.

[27] H. Beckby, Anthologia Graeca, Munchen 1957, vol. II, 320/1 (+ Bk VII, 541 = W. Peek; Griechische Versinschriften (Berlin 1955), nr. 1503).

[28] "Les Épigrammes ...", 288.

[29] Cf. above p. 73 f.

[30] R. MacMullen, Roman Social Relations, 50 B.C. to A.D. 284, New Haven and London 1974, 117.

[31] Th. Veblen, The Theory of the Leisure Class. An economic study of Institutions (London 1924), 246.

[32] The last five words do not seem to be applicable to the ancient city-elites. They acted as local politicians and benefactors and as ambassadors to the Roman authorities; as heads of the local city police (eirenarchos, paraphylax) they also came into touch with para-military activities. In general it may be said that violence was much more endemic in the ancient socieites: cf. N. Elias, "The Genesis of Sport as a Sociological Problem", in: E. Dunning (ed.), The Sociology of Sport. A Selection of Readings, Longon 1971, 88 ff.; cf. also my "Zur Soziologie ...", 85, note 148a.

[33] Veblen, op. cit., 258.

[34] Veblen, op. cit., cf. note 107 above.

[35] Cf. also p. 52, with note 16.

[36] L. Robert, "Deux Inscriptions agonistiques de Rhodes", in: 'Αρχ. 'Εφημερίϛ 1966, 110; cf. id.: "Les Épigrammes ...", 247.

[37] L. Robert, "Les Épigrammes ...", 249-251.

[38] L. Robert, "Les Épigrammes ...", 183, note 2; id.: 'Αϝχ. 'Εφημερίϛ 1966, 112-118; id.: Monnaies Grecques, Paris 1967, 114/5.

[39] See e.g. L. Moretti, op. cit. (cf. note 8), nr. 79, l. 10-17.

[40] Dion, Halic. vol. VI (Teubner), Opuscula vol. II, 1, p. 283-292, esp. 288, ch. 4, l. 9 (εὐφημεῖσθαι ϰαὶ δαϰτυλοδειϰτεῖσθαι); cf. also R. Merkelbach, in: ZPE 18 (1975), 125.

[41] Cf. W. Rudolph, art. cit. (cf. note 27 above).

[42] J. Ebert, Griechische Epigramme (cf. above note 33), 251-255.

[43] Op. cit. (cf. note 126), p. 288, ch. 4, l. 19-20 (οἱ καρποὶ <οἱ> ἀπο τῆς νίκης, τὴν περιουσίαν τοῦ βίου ἄφθονον).

[44] L. Robert, in: Revue de Philologie 1967, 17; id., "Les Juges étrangers dans la cité grecque", in: Festschr. P. J. Zépos (Athens 1971), 778/9.

[45] J. Ebert, Griechische Epigramme (cf. above note 33), nr. 27, p. 118-126.

[46] Cf. my "Zur Soziologie ..." (cf. note 18 above), 63-67.

[47] M. I. Finley, The Ancient Economy (London, 1973), 44.

[48] Cf. note 92 above.

[49] Cf. Zeitschrift für Papyrologie und Epigraphik 10 (1973), 197; for ἐπιτήδευμα cf. Fl. Josephus, AJ, XV, 269: συνελεγησάν τε οἱ κορυφαιότατοι τῶν ἐν τοῖς ἐπιτηδεύμασιν. See Lämmer, Jerusalem (cf. note 5), 188.

[50] Cf. J. Ebert, Griechische Epigramme, Index, 278, s.v. τέχνη.

[51] Galen, Προτρεπτικὸς ἐπὶ τέχνας (Teubner; ed. I. Marquardt, Scripta Minora I), cap. 9, § 20.

[52] Galen, ibidem, cap. 14, § 38-39; for an analysis of Galen's view on τέχναι cf. J. Christes, Bildung und Gesellschaft (Darmstadt 1975), 77-78, 123-125.

[53] Galen, ibidem, cap. 10, § 25.

[54] Galen, ibidem, cap. 12, § 32.

[55] Galen, ibidem, cap. 14, § 37.

[56] Euripides, fr. 282 (ed. Nauck); cf. my "Zur Soziologie ...", 68; 80, note 3; 83, note 105.

[57] C. M. Bowra, "Euripides' Epinician for Alcibiades", in: Historia 9 (1960), 68-79.

[58] M. I. Finley, op. cit. (cf. note 133), 76.

[59] For eugeneia cf. my "Zur Soziologie ...", 87, note 193. Aristotle, Politica 1294a, 22-23 writes that 'nobility' (εὐγενεία) means ancient wealth (ἀρχαίος πλοῦτος) and virtue; cf. also G. E. M. de StéCroix, The origins of the Peloponnesian War (London 1973), 373 ff. and D. Loenen, Eugeneia. Adel en Adeldom binnen de Atheense Demokratie (Amsterdam 1965), passim.

[60] L. Robert, "Un citoyen de Téos à Bouthrôtos d'Épire", in: Comptes Rendus Académie des Inscriptions et Belles Lettres 1974, 508-529, esp. 517, 519/20, 528/9.

[61] Cicero, De officiis I, 150-1; M. I. Finley, op. cit., 41/2.

[62] M. I. Finley, op. cit., 75.

[63] M. I. Finley, op. cit., 76; P. A. Brunt, "Aspects of the social thought of Dio Chrysostom and of the Stoics", in: Proceedings Cambridge Philological Society 199 (1973), 9-34, esp. 32.

[64] Galen, Προτρεπτικός ... (cf. note 137), cap. 9, § 21 (δημοσία παρὰ τοῖς πατράσι τετιμημένον ἀργυρίου δόσεσιν).

[65] J. H. Krause, Olympia (Vienna, 1838), 6, note 3 (on p. 7).

[66] P. A. Brunt, art. cit., 33.

[67] Cicero, De officiis I, 150/1; M. I. Finley, op. cit., 42.

[68] P. A. Brunt, art. cit., 30; in inscriptions physicians, teachers and city-councillors sometimes receive the same gifts from a local benefactor; nevertheless the doctors and teachers are carefully distinguished from the councillors, who constituted the city elite; see my Epigraphica, II, Leiden 1969, nr. 21 (with further references).

[69] P. A. Brunt, art. cit., 33. It is worthy of note that in Homer, Iliad X, 303-4 μισθός is used as an equivalent of δῶρον (gift). The gift, promised by the Trojan prince Hector to the man who was prepared to spy in the Greek camp is called a misthos in the next line. The meaning is "celui d'un don, d'un prix, d'une récompense rémunérant un exploit" (Ed. Will, Notes sur ΜΙΣΘΟΣ in: Hommages à Cl. Préaux, Brussels 1975, 426-438). Nevertheless, Achilles does not call the prizes offered by him to the winners in the funeral games for Patroclus μισθοί but ἄεθλα. The aristocratic, elitist interpreation of misthos, on record in Iliad X, 303-4, can also be found in Plato's Politeia (613e-614a: the righteous receive the ἆθλα, μισθοί and the δῶρα from the gods; 345e-347d: magistrates

should receive a <u>misthos</u> consisting either of money or of τιμή (honour))
and in Aristotle's Nicomachean Ethics (1134^b 1. 6 ff.: magistrates should
receive <u>misthos</u>, consisting of τιμή and γέρας (gift of honour, prerogative; all these examples apud Will)). Due to a long process of democrati-
sation and increasing societal differentiation the word <u>misthos</u> had acquired such a pejorative meaning for aristocrats in the Hellenistic-Roman
period that it could no longer be used as an innocent equivalent of ἆθλα
(prizes) or δῶρα (gifts). The tendency to interpret 'wages' and prizes
(cf. note 150 and 151) as "gifts", of course, betrays an age-old aristocratic mentality.

70 Cf. above p. 78, with note 116.

71 P. A. Brunt, <u>art. cit.</u>, 12.

72 M. I. Finley, <u>op. cit.</u>, 41.

73 <u>Art. cit.</u>, 14.

74 J. S. Wigboldus, "Ontwikkelingen van de stratificatietheorie in geschied-
sociologisch perspectief", in: <u>Tijdschrift voor Geschiedenis</u> 84 (1971),
179-215, esp. 190; cf. also in the same periodical p. 245.

75 M. P. Charlesworth, <u>Documents illustrating the reigns of Claudius and</u>
<u>Nero</u> (Cambridge, 1939), 10, col. 2, 1. 3.

76 Cf. W. R. Connor, <u>The local Politicians of Fifth Century Athens</u>, Princeton 1971, 155. In Athenian commedy the νεόπλουτοι are characterized
as νεοπλουτοπόνηροι, "nouveaux riches die hun welstand aan de uitbreid-
ing en consolidatie van het Atheens imperium te danken hadden" (J. Th.
M. F. Pieters, "Pericles en het Toneel", in: <u>Hermeneus</u> 46 (1975), 242)
cf. also note 145 (nobility-ancient wealth) and Ed. Will, "Fonctions de la
monnaie dans les cités grecques de l'époque classique", in: <u>Numisma-</u>
<u>tique Antique</u>. Problèmes et Méthodes (Études d'Archéologie Classique,
IV, Annales de l'Est, Univ. de Nancy, II, 1975), 233-246, esp. 238/9,
note 18 on the <u>archaioploutoi</u> and the positive picture of these given by
Cratinus in his comedy <u>Ploutoi</u>.

77 Oxford 1971, 70-94.

78 R. Stokvis, "Traditionalisme in de Sportwereld", in: <u>Mens en Maat-</u>
<u>schappij</u> 49 (1974), 185-207, esp. 191.

79 Just as their ancient predecessors did, both in agonistic life and in society at large. They combined the glory (δόξα) of the wreath with the "prof
"profit" (κέρδος) of the prize games (cf. J. H. Krause, op. cit. (cf. note
151), 6, note 3; κέρδος is the word used by a late scholiast on Pindar; it

is, of course, not to be found in athletes' language). They even combined wreaths with 'value prizes', but in their ideology they emphasized the δοξα of the wreath: they could do so, because they could afford to compete for wreaths from time to time and because participation in thematic games could produce 'profit' (κερδοc) anyway.

[80] I doubt whether R. Seager is right when he writes: "The old association between birth and wealth had first been seriously underlined (italics are mine, H.W.P.) at about the time of the outbreak of the Peloponnesian War, when a new type of politician began to appear: the son of a wealthy factory-owner ..." ("Elitism and Democracy in Classical Athens", in: F. Cople Jaher, The Rich, The Well Born and the Powerful. Elites and Upper Classes in History, Urbana 1973, 7-26, esp. 11). New politicians admittedly appeared but they were hardly numerous enough to transform the urban elite into an industrial-commercial group. For a vigorous and sound attack on theories about the existence or rise of 'commercial aristocracies' and 'industrial and merchant classes' both in the Greek city-states and in Rome see G. E. M. de SteCroix, "Karl Marx and the History of Classical Antiquity", in: Arethusa 8 (1975), 7-41, esp. 17-18.

[81] Cf. my review article: "Afscheid van Rostovtzeff", in: Lampas 8 (1975), 267-284; see also my forthcoming review of Finley's book in Mnemosyne 1976 or 1977. J. Andreau, "Le tremblement de terre de Pompee", in: Annales. Economies, Societes, Civilisations 28 (1973), 369-395, esp. 370-371 draws attention to the weakness of Rostovtzeff's thesis about the rise of an industrial and commercial bourgeoisie in the Roman Empire, which is supposed to have threatened the dominant position of the landowning aristocracy.

Sport And Political Ideology

John M. Hoberman

Relating Sport and Ideology

That sport is related to political ideology is an historical fact which i constantly in evidence and virtually never subjected to convincing proof. Though this formulation may seem paradoxical, it can be accounted for by distinguishing two ways in which sport and ideology can coexist in history. On the one hand, as recent history shows, sport can serve as an innocuous pretext for initiating formal contact between hostile ideologies. For sport, as Michel Bouet has pointed out, "is in itself alien to conflicts of ideas and words, which are properly the domain of conflict for those ideologies on which politics feeds."[1] On this level of contact, the sporting and political worlds commingle easily so long as Bouet's thesis, which certainly antedates him, is accepted as valid. Sport, it is assumed, constitutes an ideological terra nullius which defuses political conflict by virtue of its power t symbolize the very antithesis of thought itself.

There is no question but that the notion of sport's ideological innocence, what may be called its innocuous character, has exerted a powerful appeal upon twentieth century students of sport. Johan Huizinga himself wrote of "the segregation of play from the domain of the great categorial antitheses." "Play," he insists, "lies outside the antithesis of wisdom and folly, and equally outside those of truth and falsehood, good and evil." And what is more: "The play-concept must always remain distinct from all the other forms of thought in which we express the structure of mental and social life."[2] Lest one suspect that these citations exploit an unmentioned dichotomy between "play" and "sport" in Huizinga's idiom, we may cite the following statements from the final chapter of Homo Ludens: "In modern so cial life," the historian writes, "sport occupies a place alongside and apart from the cultural process"; "sport has become profane, 'unholy' in every way and has no organic connection whatever with the structure of society, least of all when prescribed by the government."[3] This is not to say that sport had ever been, in Huizinga's view, a politically determined activity; i had, however, been a cultural one,[4] and his lament is that sport has now been vulgarized down to a sub-cultural level. What remains intact is sport extra-political character, and that is our point here.

Reprinted from the Journal of Sport and Social Issues by kind permission of the publisher, ARENA.

So far we have dealt only with the first conception of the coexistence of sport and ideology: being seen as antithetical to each other, neither obtrudes upon the other and ideological tensions are made to seem irrelevant. The second case, however, is more complex and constitutes the subject of this essay. In addition, it should be noted that these hypotheses positing a deeper structural relationship between sport and political ideology necessarily call into question the idea of sport's non-ideological character. It will rather be argued that an inductive approach, brought to bear on historical evidence, suggests that sport is not a neutral entity with respect to the ideological spectrum.

Crucial to the thesis outlined above is what I shall call the appropriation of sport by ideologically oriented observers of all kinds: political figures, novelists, sociologists, and others. Sport, according to this view, is indeed innocuous if viewed as a mere physical act. The point may be illustrated by an anecdote related by Hegel in his essay "On Art," where he compares the sterility of merely copying another's original work to "the feat of the man who had taught himself to throw lentils through a small opening with without missing. He displayed this skill of his before Alexander, and Alexander presented him with a bushel of lentils as a reward for his frivolous and meaningless art."[5] The lentil-thrower may be taken as a representative of the athlete prior to his interpretation by others, or by himself. For the crucial fact regarding the humiliated lentil-thrower is the absence of self-reflection and the sense of meaning and proportion it confers. From here we may argue that sport gives birth to meaning, including ideological "appropriation," only when it is reflected on in some way by an observer. As Yukio Mishima, the body-builder and novelist put it: "it [is] a special property of muscles that they [feed] the imagination of others while remaining totally devoid of imagination themselves..."[6] Thus the utilitarian goals of sport activity are determined by its sheerly physical nature. All societies, irrespective of ideology, use sport, if they use it at all, to improve the health of soldiers, production workers, and the citizenry, whereas even something as apparently innocuous as the use of sport for recreation is open to political interpretation: some regimes inflict sport on their societies as a means of neutralizing ideological interests. In this case, sport has been first interpreted and then made an instrument of policy and thus a part of the political culture as a whole. It has been appropriated by observers with ideological interests and thereby been integrated into a political Weltanschauung, the mental world of the ideologist.

We are now in a position to describe more fully what I have called the second way in which sport and political ideology relate to each other. On this second, or deeper, level, an interest in sport is assumed to coincide with certain ideological interests, to reinforce or even to amplify them. What is more, it will be argued below that there is a specific ideological orientation which shows a special affinity for sport, and that this orientation is right-wing or conservative in character. Conversely, it will be suggested, though only briefly in this essay, that, however great the international sporting successes of the Socialist states, Marxist ideology does not integrate sport into its theories of man and society in as deep a psychological level as the conservative or fascist. It should be pointed out that the analysis which follows is based primarily on the writings of a variety of political intellectuals who have commented on sport. This is, after all, an analysis of ideology, and the history we are concerned with is intellectual history rather than the history of sport per se.

Sport and Cultural Conservatism

It must be admitted at the outset that to claim in an overall sense that the politically nuanced literature of sport is predominantly a right-wing phenomenon, and that the enormous Marxist literature which has been accumulating for a century contains relatively less and reveals in addition a basic lack of affinity for the subject itself, is of necessity a somewhat impressionistic judgement rather than one subject to quantitative verification. Nevertheless, I believe this claim is valid, and that factors inhering in the respective ideologies of Right and Left can be shown to account for the perceived difference. When the French sport sociologist Georges Magnane writes that: "In itself, sport can be neither 'progressive' nor 'regressive',"[7] he is just begging the question from an historical, or empiricist, standpoint. And it is the historical evidence which sport scholarship has conspicuously failed to deal with.

Sport, it is maintained, shows an affinity for conservative instincts, which are defined here to include the apolitical disposition, the thinker who conceives the world for the most part outside of or beyond political categories, an orientation whose historical position has been situated consistently on the political Right in Europe. In this sense, it is interesting to note that the two classic works on the world of the ludique, Huizinga's Homo Ludens and Roger Caillois' Les jeux et les hommes (1958), both derive from basically apolitical sensibilities. Homo Ludens, I might add, should be read in conjunction with the same author's eloquent polemic titled In the Shadow of Tomorrow (1935), a humane and affecting diagnosis of a modern age which Huizinga frankly calls "demented," and which contains pointed remarks on the vulgarization of sport in the twentieth century. It is furthermore of interest to us that Huizinga's tract is only one of a number of conservative critiques of modern civilization which appeared during the interwar period in which the role of sport is seen as a matter of concern.

In the Shadow of Tomorrow reveals Huizinga to be a cultural pessimist who welcomed Spengler as a shock to complacency[8] even while judging him (elsewhere) a seducer and, in part, a fraud.[9] In his concern for the "publicity-crazed modernities of our century" that "the delimitations between the logical, the aesthetic and the emotive functions are purposely ignored," and in his call for "the recognition or retrieval of eternal truths, truths that are above the stream of evolution and change,"[10] Huizinga enunciates a cultural conservatism similar to that of Søren Kierkegaard, a philosopher whose influence can be demonstrated to be present in the work of two other thinkers whose comments on sport in the modern world also appeared during the 1930's, namely Karl Jaspers and Ortega y Gasset. "Even in the field of sport," Huizinga writes, "that vastly important part of modern culture, there is a growing tendency for the masses to have others play for them." He points to "the fact that modern puerilism has also found its way into sport It is present wherever athletic rivalry assumes proportions tending to push intellectual interests into the background, as is the case at some American universities. It threatens to creep in with over-organization of sport and with the disproportionate place which the sporting page and the sporting magazines have come to occupy in the mental diet of untold numbers."[11] "More and more individuals," Kierkegaard wrote in 1846, "owing to their bloodless indolence, will aspire to be nothing at all--in order to become the public: that abstract whole formed in the most ludicrous way, by all participants becoming a third party (an on-looker)." (It is interesting to note that one of Kierkegaard's examples of an age without passion is a crowd which experiences risk vicariously by watching a daring skater.)[12] Had Huizinga read the Danish philosopher's social critique titled The Present Age, he would have recognized a spiritual predecessor who had already begun the analysis of mass society which sport-minded European intellectuals of the interwar period would eventually revive. Marx and Kierkegaard, as Karl Löwith puts it, "comprehend 'what is' as a world determined by merchandise and money, and as an existence shot through with irony and the 'drudgery' of boredom."[13] It is of interest for us to note that the numerous conservative intellectuals who wrote on sport during the 1920's and 1930's saw sport as an antithesis to, and sometimes a therapeutic for, problems associated by Löwith with Kierkegaard and Marx: the commercialization of culture and the boredom-ridden existence which goes along with it.

In the Shadow of Tomorrow was reviewed unenthusiastically in 1936 by a young Frankfurt Marxist named Herbert Marcuse. "He wants to be on the right side," Marcuse observes; "he wants to oppose reaction; but he opposes it with weapons which are more likely to wound its opponents. Again and again he works with concepts which belong to the rigid character of Weltanschauung of the totalitarian state and whose present function can only be a psychic and intellectual subordination to that state."[14] Less radical and more appreciative readers of Huizinga have frankly acknowledged his inability, even unwillingness, to deal with political reality. "He was sixty-eight years old," one sympathetic scholar has written, "when he learned that even if a man can ignore politics, politics does not ignore him." And she adds: "The democratic political theory, such as it is, is by definition activist; to some extent or another, the democrat has to assume political responsibility. 'Culture' is less demanding, for the student of culture need not expect of himself active immixture in contemporary affairs."[15] It is at this point that we do well to recall the immunity from reality Huizinga confers upon the ludique, and the ease with which sportsmen move across all but the most impenetrable ideological boundaries. Huizinga's anti-Freudianism, too, can be seen to co-relate with his passion for the play-element in culture. Psychoanalysis, R. L. Colie has correctly pointed out, "violated a basic law of his civilization, the right to privacy within the recesses of one's being."[16] Huizinga, like many cultural conservatives of his time, experienced Freudianism as an invasive and degrading misrepresentation of human motivation, much as certain Englishmen, ten years later, would combine fascist sympathies and an outraged sense of sportsmanship to question the propriety of prosecuting idealistic Nazis. It is striking that, even in 1935, Huizinga understood, and condemned, the notion that one could "proceed from this recognized impeccability of the soldier to the vindication of the impeccability of political hostility in general or, in other words, of the good right of the State to wage war for its own interests."[17] In this sense, Huizinga, who pitied Nietzsche his inheritors, might well have pitied himself some of his own.

Selections From the Literature of Sport: 1908-1944

It is not overstating the case to say that sport, viewed as a form of culture, has scarcely existed for intellectual history. Defining the cultural, as opposed to the sub-cultural, literature of sport requires sifting the contents of established humanistic disciplines (fiction being excluded here) and assigning to what turns up an order of one's own. The next section of this essay is an account of what I have found on the cultural level, and in connection with this material I propose two theses: (1) its ideological range is from the extreme right to the center in terms of political orientation, since Marxist interest in sport has largely been confined to sociological analyses, often polemical in tone, rather than meditations on sport as a phenomenon having other than socially practical implications; and (2) a disproportionate amount of this writing appears during the interwar period, and apparent concentration of interest which may be accounted for in at least two ways. First, sport did not become a mass cultural phenomenon in Europe until the turn-of-the-century period, so a rise in interest during this period is understandable. But this does not account for what I am identifying as the diminishing of interest by prominent cultural figures after about 1940. The proposed second factor is, then, actually two: (a) the fact that this period saw the rise of a mass society which, in Karl Mannheim's words, "tends to encourage its citizens to return to nature by means of systematic physical culture, sport, and fresh air,"[18] at the same time, however, offering unprecedented threats to human individuality against which sport may be invoked as a countermeasure; and (b) the fact that the experience of fascism discredited the culture of the European Right which had produced so much of what little sport literature had existed between the wars. It is only suggested here that, however scantly from the historian's standpoint, its ideologi-homogeneity tells us something significant about the relationship between sport and political ideology.

The ease with which sport has been able to charm most of the (non-Marxist) intellectuals who have confronted it--thereby de-intellectualizing its own reception--is all too apparent in the first of the documents to be examined below. Robert Hessen's Der Sport (1908), which somehow appeared in a social psychology series edited by Martin Buber, represents less the work of a sociologist than of a precursor to the interwar theorists, such as Huizinga, for whom sport functioned as a cultural stimulant. The author's main purpose is to persuade his fellow Germans that sport practiced along English lines would have an invigorating effect on the nation as a whole and thereby serve the national interest. In addition to articulating the conjunction of sport and nationalism, Hessen advances several arguments which are of interest here, most of them signifying a culturally conservative bent. Hessen clucks his tongue over the notorious homosexual English aesthete Oscar Wilde, who he says, would have better resisted falling into a blithe effeminacy had he been a practicing sportsman. There is no better preventive measure against such degeneration, he insists, than open-air sport. Hessen also maintains that physical and intellectual culture are easily combined, given the requisite good will. (This, it should be added, is the only idea in Hessen's book which points ahead to the French literary sport aestheticism of the 1920's.) And it is interesting to see him regretting the cultivation of technical perfection in fencing at the expense of a lustier match. The emphasis on style reminds the author of a higher stoicism recalling, he says, the Japanese <u>harakiri</u>. The monograph ends with a passage which, in retrospect, may be seen to contain the seed of things to come. "Our race," he declares, "has attained too high a stature in world history to end up as a menagerie of coughing, stunted weaklings with withered arms and potbellies."[19] However suggestive such a passage may read today, it in fact contains less parlor Nietzscheanism than the frank ebullience of a nationalism which had not yet lost its innocence. In Hessen, sport is still viewed as a stimulant and not as a therapeutic for social malaise.

Pierre de Coubertin's <u>Essais de psychologie sportive</u>, a collection by the founder of the modern Olympics which he composed during the period 1906-1912, represent a turning point in the literature of sport in that they demonstrate the appropriation of sport--now a growing mass cultural phenomenon--by a cultural ideology bent on assigning new meanings to a range of new experiences, or to old experiences which had not yet been subjected to interpretation. Of Coubertin's conservatism there can be no doubt. As Eugen Weber has written: "Coubertin <u>was</u> a reactionary figure, albeit an enlightened one...He suspected what he regarded as the dehumanizing forces of State, and Science, and Press. He recruited his committees by co-option, and ran them at his own expense with an iron will and a velvet voice."[20] To political opponents, Weber notes: "The social background of the first sportsmen and of their supporters seemed to justify suspicion, and their ideology confirmed it. <u>Political neutrality was already associated with conservatism</u>"[21] [emphasis added]. It is this correlation of sport and political "neutrality" which was to be perpetuated by more intellectually distinguished observers like Huizinga and Caillois.

Coubertin's goal in the <u>Essais</u> is nothing less than "a philosophy of physical culture" which is in effect a program for culture itself. By establishing "the correlation between psychology and physical movement," the reformer develops a concept of sport as the social therapeutic required by modern life, which has given rise to what he calls "the universal neurosis." Two chapters of the <u>Essais</u> are in fact titled "Can Sport Stem the Universal Neurosis?" and "Sporting Remedies for Neurasthenics." "Sport," Coubertin writes, "is an incomparable psychic instrument and, we may note in passing, a dynamic to which one can profitably appeal in the treatment of many psychoneuroses. For, very often, the psychoneuroses are distinguished by a kind of disappearance of the virile sensibility [<u>sentiment</u>], and there is nothing like sport to revive and maintain it."[22]

The concern with virility--Coubertin talks of "the art of virilizing bodies and souls" and calls sport "the very symbol of virility"--is one aspect of a general theory of cultural health and of the forces which may subvert it. Most important is what Coubertin calls "the intensive character of this civilization": "Man is in a position to fear everything and to hope for everything at the same time. This state of affairs has given rise to an agitation which is encouraged and amplified by transformations occurring outside the self. Inside and out, the brain is kept in a kind of constant state of boiling. Points of view, the various aspects of things, combinations, possibilities, as much for individuals as for collectivities, succeed each other so quickly that, in order to make allowance for them and put them to use, one must keep oneself alert, as if in a state of permanent mobilization."

The crisis of modern civilization is occurring within the human nervous system itself, and here sport can offer a physical means of restoring health. "Given the considerable expenditure of nervous and mental energy required by modern civilization [of most people], an equivalent measure of muscular force is required of them; for, these days, it is the individual in equilibrium for whom fortune reserves her favors." What Coubertin calls an "excess of civilization" has destroyed an equilibrium which must, as he puts it, be reestablished "artificially." The ideological message borne by this argument is, of course, a literary reactionary one: anti-modernity itself. And, good conservative that he is, Coubertin's nostalgic look backwards is not to anything envisioned by the disciples of Rousseau, a group he rejects, but to the classical harmony of the Greeks. "Our existence," he writes, "is contrary to good health [hygiene] to such a degree that we will almost never be able to enjoy ourselves as the Greeks could..." in his concern for preserving the capacity for sensation itself, Coubertin voices another theme, in addition to that of degeneration, which recalls the intense aesthete such as the perverse Oscar Wilde may have scorned sport, Coubertin rehabilitates the relationship by making of sport a kind of sedative for jangled--and, therefore, unrefined--nerves, and by associating sport with "aesthetic perfections." And he emphasizes that sport's curative powers are dependent on a state of calm for their successful application; otherwise, the effect will simply be to impose additional stress on an already overburdened nervous system.[23]

Coubertin's interest in promoting sport as a sedative does not, however, go so far as to discourage striving for world records, and he identifies the three sources of these surpassing efforts, namely: adaptation to new types of equipment or movements, a general perfecting of the race, and specialization pursued by the individual. Though schoolmasters, he says, may favor the pursuit of collective records by his charges: "The true sportsman will always love to try to conquer himself or his neighbor by surpassing the previously attained result. And it is good that it should be so."[24]

It is an index of their ideological nature--though not necessarily of their value--that certain of Coubertin's ideas appear quite intact in an essay by the French neo-fascist Maurice Bardèche, published in his periodical Défense de L'Occident shortly after the Olympic massacre in Munich in 1972. Aside from using the occasion to bitterly criticize the Israelis, Bardèche denounces the modern form of the Olympic Games in an idiom Coubertin-- who had revived the Games in 1896--would have appreciated: "The Olympic Games, as they display themselves in their democratic disguise, have lost all meaning. The admiration of the Greeks for their athletes was not directed at the cult of muscle and a gaping astonishment at the performances. The Olympic Games of antiquity paid hommage to the virile qualities, to the discipline which the athlete imposed on himself, to the courage he showed, to the energy expended in his effort...In those days, the Olympic Games had a meaning. And they still had one in Hitler's Germany." Why is this the case? Because, Bardèche says, the Nazi Olympics were a salute to "the force, the health, and the fullness of the 'hero' that the new civilization of energy presented as its human ideal." Nor does Bardèche admire the unnatural character of the modern athlete: "The champions who are admired [today] represent," as he puts it, "a variation on the human cannonball. They are products of the forcing technique, like calves stuffed with hormones or chickens with pills embedded in their necks."25 Worst of all, the Olympics have become a vehicle for ideological merchandizers--including, one might note, the merchants of internationalism and good will who are an important part of Coubertin's legacy. But Bardèche, too, it seems, has a stake in the setting of records, conceding (elsewhere) that "les recordmen"26 are among those whose exploits demonstrate that virility has not disappeared from the face of the earth.

Bardèche's interpretation of the Nazi athletic ideal--and, for that matter, his own notion of virility--have a distinctly Nietzschean ring. Coubertin, on the other hand, never partial to excess, argues that introducing le culte du moi into the sphere of physical culture would result in the Nietzschean superman, a creature he does not welcome: "Adoring his own body like an idol, one would see him gradually subordinate everything to its development and the preservation of its perfection. One shudders to think of the reserves of refined ferocity and, consequently, an eventual barbarity which would affect human nature thus influenced. For it would require only a small number of such types surging out of the crowd to have a strong impact on those around them and to leave a terrible mark on the society of their time."27

Coubertin's ostensibly Nietzschean contemporary in France is Paul Adam, author of La Morale des Sports (1907), and a writer who, fortunately, is far more interested in pursuing his own fantasies than in quoting from the German master. Adam's (shallow) Nietzscheanism views sport as a "daily stimulant" to the Will of Power, and he predicts for "the coming era" a hegemony of "Americanism and Nietzscheanism" for which sports constitutes the best preparation.28 All in all, his doctrines do not differ much from those of Coubertin. Adam's real role is that of a fantast whose ideas about the role of sport in stimulating mental life reappear during the twenties in the essays of French authors of much greater literary stature. "In the course of watching Alcibiades throw the discus," Adam writes, "Socrates pronounced sentences for eternity. Plato listened and wrote." If the casual sequence here is not exactly compelling, the point is clear: mental and physical life are to be married to each other. Physical and intellectual effort constitute together the "two faces of the aesthetic," and Adam assures his readers that the collegiate neurasthenic who learns how to connect "the desire for action to the pleasures of meditation" will thereby "exteriorize his unconscious and occult process [oeuvre], thereby acquiring the habit of enforcing a correspondence between a coordinated series of sport movements and the variations of his thought." One of Adam's more important ideas is that of "mental sports" analogous to physical ones, both serving to promote the formation of character. "The finest among the mental sports," he says, "are polite civility and deportment."29

From the standpoint of ideology, it may be remarked that all of this is unthinkable as Marxist doctrine. Adam invokes the symbolist Verlaine on "the cult of the Nuance," speaks of a "mental gymnastic," and flatly states: "We are in search of sensations..." For the logic of these fantasies points in one direction only, and that is toward the isolation of the aesthete and away from the public for whose "infirmity," according to Adam, sport is to provide a remedy.[30] Adam's concern with the public, however, is superficial compared to that of Coubertin, who eschews vulgar Nietzscheanism, the cult of speed, and indulgence in aestheticism in favor of more practical reflections about the public uses of sport.

Adams's aestheticism anticipates by fifteen or twenty years what must be termed, on a comparative historical scale, a burst of non-fictional sport prose by a very distinguished group of French literati whose ideological center of gravity lies, once again, to the extreme right. Essays by Pierre Drieu la Rochelle, Henry de Montherlant, Jean Prévost, Jean Giraudoux, and a novel by Paul Morand cover the period 1921-1930 and emphasize sport as a salvation discipline of the spirit. Having dealt with this literature elsewhere at some length,[31] I offer only one quotation from Giraudoux. "Sport," he writes, "is the art by which man liberates himself from himself."[32] This idea, which may be taken as generally representative of the genre as a whole, is revived in a paean to body-building titled Sun and Steel by the deceased Japanese novelist and right-wing political fanatic Yukio Mishima, whose literary tastes, be it noted, prominently included French aestheticism.

It is during the 1930's that references to sport appear with some frequency in critiques of mass culture. While Huizinga is the best known of these critics, the conservative Spanish philosopher José Ortega y Gasset antedates him in print. Ortega y Gasset's famous manifesto The Revolt of the Masses (1930), which expressed what the author calls "a radically aristocratic interpretation of history," includes several themes familiar from the earlier French writing, as well as a new and discordant note: "the mania for physical sports" must now be distinguished from sport itself; and the football "fan" has sacrificed the "faculty of wonder" made possible by high culture. Elsewhere, the author endorses the pursuit of records as a worthwhile goal because it convinces us "that the human organism possesses in our days capacities superior to any it had previously had." But, like Coubertin, he simultaneously condemns "that worship of mere speed which is at present being indulged in by our contemporaries." The author sounds a particularly Adamesque note when he calls transmigration of souls "the supreme form of sport."[33] His essay titled "The Sportive Origin of the State" will be discussed at the conclusion of this essay.

Like Huizinga, who called sport "a positive cultural factor of the greatest value," the German existential psychiatrist and philosopher Karl Jaspers finds sport a basically healthy form of culture for mass man. In Man and the Modern Age (1930), Jaspers makes three points: first, sport takes the form of the "self-preservative impulse as a form of vitality," it is "a soaring and a refreshment"; second, "Sport as a mass phenomenon...provides an outlet for impulses which would otherwise endanger the [social] apparatus. By occupying their leisure, it keeps the masses quiet"--a function to which Jaspers does not appear to object; his third observation, however, contains the hint of a misgiving: sport, though a source of relief, "lacks transcendent substantiality." For "even though sport imposes one of the limits upon the rationalized life-order, through sport alone man cannot win to freedom."[34] This important idea recurs in a stronger form in an essay by the German novelist Hermann Broch, himself the author of a Massenpsychologie. In his Essays Broch writes: "The role of play and games in metropolitan life is highly significant. Technology, sport and the tendency toward records are additional proofs of such solely structural behavior [emphasis added]. Their mental basis is akin to the nihilistic trend of fascism as exhibited by the latter's striving for victory for victory's sake."[35] It is apparent that this sort of extrapolation from an alleged characteristic of sport to political meaning, which goes beyond the idea that sport is reactionary because it depoliticizes the masses, represents a theoretical innovation on the mass culture theories of sport which appear during the thirties.

In the same year that Huizinga referred to him as "the politically Left-thinking sociologist," Karl Mannheim, author of the classic Ideology and Utopia, offered some thoughts on sport which echo Jasper's notion of sport as a kind of sociological absorbent. In his book Man and Society in an Age of Reconstruction (1935), Mannheim describes sport as a socially valuable example of an irrational manifestation, "an outlet for an abreaction of impulses since the matter-of-factness of everyday life which is due to widespread rationalization means a constant repression of impulses." For while Mannheim may have appeared a leftist in Huizinga's eyes--that, after all, was not so difficult--it is nevertheless the French conservatives one thinks of when one reads of the "psychological processes of degeneration which are common in mass society" with respect to which sport can play a therapeutic role. For both Coubertin, the anti-modern activist, and Mannheim, the democratic social planner, sport is conceived, paradoxically, as both a stimulant and a soporific, a defense against modernity both in its internal (psychological) and external (social) manifestations. When Mannheim writes in 1935 that "we all are sitting on a volcano,"[36] he is speaking the thoughts of his predecessor, as well, who had experienced the same sensation for different historical reasons. Small wonder that the cultural conservative Freud, in his 1930 book, Civilization and its Discontents, had shown an avuncular tolerance for minor feuds, or what he termed "the narcissims of minor differences"--such as, we might suggest, interterritorial sports rivalries--on account of their capacity to absorb aggression and promote communal cohesion.[37] That sport could function as a sexual soporific was an idea Freud recorded as early as 1905 in his Three Contributions to the Theory of Sex. "As everybody knows," he writes, "modern cultural education utilizes sports to a great extent in order to turn youth away from sexual activity..."[38]

As a concluding bit of specimen writing from the interwar period I include excerpts from two essays by the brilliant, right-wing German nihilist Guttfried Benn, which, although dating from 1944, clearly look back to the peacetime conditions of the thirties. It is typical of Benn to offer us a spectacle of degeneration for which no therapeutic is in sight.

"As for the present-day phenotype," Benn writes with a perhaps excessive naturalism," its moral factor has largely been shed and replaced by the legislative factor and hygiene; the moral factor as genuine feeling, such as was obviously still present in Kant, is no longer there. Nor has <u>Nature</u> for him any longer the lyrical quality and tension that it had, to judge by the testimonies, for the representative men of the eighteenth and nineteenth centuries; it has been dissolved by the sporting, therapeutic medium: toughening of the body, ski slopes, ultraviolet rays on mountain-peaks..." For Benn, the cultivation of sport is not only untherapeutic, it is actually a part of the cultural disease. And, echoing Jaspers, Benn points out that "the vast existential emptiness of today's German man" will not be filled by "a vacuum of historic twaddle, crushed education, bumptious political forgeries by the regime, and cheap sports."[39] Here, of course, he is referring to the Hitlerian sport culture Bardèche still admires to this day. But for Benn, Nazi sport (perhaps all sport) had become both anti-nature and one part of a lame and vulgar attempt to heal an enormous spiritual wound.

The Conservative Appropriation of Sport

The conservative appropriation of sport for ideological ends may be summarized as follows:

(1) Sport furnishes an organic image of the state. The statesman, and the fascist leader in particular, is conceived as an athlete, while the state is conceived as an athlete team or even as a kind of human organism. It was the British fascist Oswald Mosley, a man almost obsessed with the idea of the athletic, who dreamed of "a State organized like the human body."[40] while it was the fascist novelist Robert Brasillach who wrote that "a nation is <u>one</u>, exactly as a sports team is <u>one</u>."[41] I have never seen the body-state or team-state analogies employed by a spokesman of the Left.

(2) Sport is seen as embodying a chivalric ideal stressing elitism, asceticism, and a notion of the enemy as a purely formly opponent whose ideological proclivities are irrelevant in light of his courage and sense of "fairness." Thus it was the fascist fellow-traveller Montgomery Belgion, author of a bitter <u>Epitaph on Nuremberg</u>, who found that particular war crimes tribunal unsportsmanlike. "I was brought up in a tradition of English sportsmanship and fair play," he declares. "I was taught that an Englishman never hits another when he is down..."

(3) Politics and war are viewed as forms of sport. It was the French reactionary Maurice Barrès who called politics an excellent "gymnastic,"[42] while conservative interpretations of was as sport occur frequently.

(4) The figure of the athlete is expanded to characterize non-athletic roles traditionally associated with inspiration; the notion of the athletic is thereby given a transcendental significance. Profoundly conservative poets like W. B. Yeats and Stefan George idealize athleticism in verse,[43] and it is not simply fortuitous that it is Nietzsche who refers to ascetics as "<u>sportsmen</u> of 'sanctity'," and who maintains that: "it is not chastity when an athlete or jockey abstains from women: it is rather the will of their dominating instinct, at least during their periods of great pregnancy."[44] "The actor," Antonin Artaud wrote, "is an athlete of the heart."[45]

(5) Sport is associated with the idea of a revolution of the body, which is viewed as the sphere of cultural and spiritual progress. Virility is equated with cultivation of the spirit, whereas physical degeneration is equated with cultural or spiritual decline. "For the cult of the hero," Mishima wrote, "is, ultimately, the basic principle of the body."[46] And it is the right-wing German author Ernst von Salomon who declares that "gymnastics are an attitude toward the world, the racial metaphysics of the body."[47]

Sport and the Marxists

When R. Palme Dutt, a founder and for many years the leading theoretician of the British Communist Party, was asked by the International Who's Who to list his leisure interests, his reply was: "anything except sports."[48] While Dutt's remark cannot, of course, be considered as definitive for the Marxist position, it nevertheless illustrates a point. For it is a fact that the sort of "appropriation" of sport achieved by conservative ideology in Europe has not been duplicated by the Left in its own terms. Aside from expediting mass recreation, mobilization, and gaining international prestige--interests which are hardly peculiar to Socialist societies--sport has not been integrated into the Marxist <u>Weltanschauung</u>, and to examine the nature of the conservative affinity to sport is to understand why.[49] For, discounting the mass conditioning and depoliticizing uses which it may serve, sport does not offer the space required for ideological overlapping. There is no devotional literature of sport inflected into a Marxist mode. For so long as sport fundamentally--that is to say, transideologically--represents organicism, chivalry, the disinterested exercise, the primacy of the individual spirit, and the cult of the body--and for Western culture sport has represented and still does represent these ideas--it will remain an essentially foreign element in the Marxist world-view, no matter how strenuous the efforts to integrate it.

An examination of an essay by the Marxist sport sociologist A. Wohl, titled "Fifty Years of Physical Culture in the U.S.S.R.," demonstrates the <u>reactive</u> character of the standard Marxist position. By Wohl's account, the role of sport in the Soviet Union following the 1917 Revolution was largely determined by a group he calls the "hygienists," who "intended to eliminate all the other functions of sport, with the exception of its prophylactic functions and those that were important for the health." The allies of the "hygienists" were a group who called themselves adherents of "proletarian physical culture," who "demanded rejection of competitive sport and sports events as remnants of the past and signs of the degeneration of bourgeois culture. They rejected all the achievements of world sport, thinking that one can be completely detached from the past and <u>begin to create physical culture from scratch</u>" [emphasis added]. Wohl is very impatient with these ideological purists, and he is relieved to be able to tell us that on July 13, 1925, the Party, in addition to adopting a resolution supporting the "hygienist" and other practical roles for sport, "also expressed itself in favour of top-level performances in sport, provided there is the necessary medical and pedagogical control and also in favor of competitive sport as a means to reveal collective achievements as well as individual ones." Wohl's impatience with the purists, and his eagerness to see "top-level performances," is a reflection of his realism, which recognizes--but refuses to declare outright--the bourgeois, i.e. conservative, origins of sport culture. The key to his opposition to the purists is his observation that they were people "who had no understanding whatsoever for the emotions of the athlete, for the fight in sports, to put it in a nutshell: for the culture-creating functions of sport."[50] But there is a problem here: If athletic emotion creates a culture which, let us hope, transcends the wholesome fellowship of the gymnasium or the rowing club, where is it in Socialist society? That such a culture, and a pervasive one at that, has grown up elsewhere along conservative lines is a matter of record which is documented above. But what is a Marxist appropriation of athletic emotion which can be called something other than re-labelled strength through joy? Wohl's silence on what he calls "the emotions of the athlete," aside from labelling them a "culture-creating function," indicates that he knows perfectly well where such emotions are likely to lead if given a chance to create "culture." And this direction is not, I think, in harmony with Marxist ideals.

The idea that a form of culture may be inherently conservative is hardly unknown on the Left. Trotsky, for example, claimed that both art and human psychology itself are conservative by nature.[51] And it is worth noting that in the same author's collection titled Problems of Everyday Life--a volume which had room for essays like "The Struggle for Cultured Speech" and "Leninism and Library Work"--sport is referred to exactly twice, and both times only in passing.[52] Trotsky is simply not interested, and if, at the end of Literature and Revolution (1924), he dreams of a time when man's "body will become more harmonized, his movements more rhythmic," this is representative of a revolutionary aestheticism which Soviet sport has never really embraced. That Trotsky had not thought out this issue is evident in his confident prediction that the society of the future would feature constructive arguments about, among other things, "a best system of sports."[53] Poor Lenin, a man who was genuinely interested in athletics, had only his friend Valentinov to discuss sport with. "To Lenin's other companions," the former writes, "the subject made no more sense than embroidery or knitting."[54]

What Trotsky recognized about art and human psychology, the French ultraleftist Pierre Laguillaumie recognizes about sport. "The Olympic ideology," he writes, "is an ideology universally accepted as the common property of all humanity...The Olympic ideal of Coubertin has thus become the transcendental ideal of all sporting peoples"[55] [emphasis added]. There is a high irony in the manner in which the sport theory of the group to which Laguillaumie belongs, the Partisans, has been denounced by the Central Committee of the French Communist Party: "One finds the old reactionary idea of a culture of the body, of free, spontaneous, natural enjoyment, a kind of cult of the élan vital and of the instinct once glorified by Bergson ..."[56] In the world of sport, it would seem, the ultraleft is ultimately the ultraright, and they meet within the body's capacity for physical (and mental) joy.

In conclusion, I wish to point out a fundamental theoretical disagreement between Marxist and anti-Marxist writers which serves to distinguish the two ideological positions with respect to sport. In his essay "The Sportive Origins of the State," Ortèga y Gasset[57] writes: "Sportive activity seems to us the foremost and creative, the most exalted, serious, and important part of life, while labor ranks second as its derivative and precipitate." What Ortèga proposes is the "sportive" or "irrational historical origin" of the state. "Again we see that in the beginning there is vigor and not utility."

It is not surprising that the philosophies of sport of Ortega (and Huizinga) are denounced in an essay by the East German sport theorist Willi Nitschke,[58] because the notion of the primary role of the play-element in culture is subversive to Marxist theory. In his essay "Labor, Play, and Art," the Marxist theorist Georgi Plekhanov even goes so far as to say: "If play is indeed older than labour and if art is indeed older than the production of useful objects, then the materialist explanation of history, at any rate as expounded by the author of <u>Capital, will not stand up to the cricitism of the facts</u> and all my reasoning must be turned upside down..." It, therefore, becomes necessary to demonstrate "that utilitarian activity <u>precedes play, that the former</u> is 'older' than the latter," and Plekhanov, needless to say, is as good as his word.[59] But whomever one chooses to agree with, this debate is useful if only because of its necessarily inconclusive nature. For ideological dispositions to sport, we realize, are grounded in political psychology, which in turn finds its own sources in questions of philosophy. In this sense, sport can function as a powerful instrument in the search for the origins of ideology itself.

References

1. Michel Bouet, <u>Signification du sport</u>. (Paris: Ed. univ., 1968), p. 576.

2. Johan Huizinga, <u>Homo Ludens</u>. (Boston: Beacon Press, 1955), pp. 6, 7.

3. <u>Ibid</u>., pp. 197, 198.

4. Johan Huizinga, <u>In the Shadow of Tomorrow</u>. (New York: Norton, 1964), p. 174.

5. G. W. F. Hegel, "On Art," in <u>On Art, Religion, Philosophy</u>. (New York: Harper Torchbooks, 1970), p. 73.

6. Yukio Mishima, <u>Sun and Steel</u>. (New York: Grove Press, 1970), p. 45.

7. Georges Magnane, <u>Sociologie du sport</u>. (Paris: Gallimard, 1964), p. 81.

8. <u>In the Shadow of Tomorrow</u>, p. 19.

9. R. L. Colie, "Johan Huizinga and the Task of Cultural History," <u>American Historical Review</u>, Vol. LXIX, No. 3 (April 1964), p. 627.

10. <u>In the Shadow of Tomorrow</u>, pp. 33, 82, 238.

11. Ibid., pp. 75, 174-175.

12. Søren Kierkegaard, The Present Age. (New York: Harper Torchbooks, 1962), p. 64.

13. Karl Löwith, From Hegel to Nietzsche. (New York: Anchor Books, 1967), p. 160.

14. Herbert Marcuse, Review of Johan Huizinga, Im Schatten von Morgen. Zeitschrift für Sozialforschung, Vol. 5 (1936), p. 23.

15. "Johan Huizinga and the Task of Cultural History," pp. 620, 626, 629.

16. Ibid., p. 626.

17. In the Shadow of Tomorrow, p. 118.

18. Karl Mannheim, Man and Society in an Age of Reconstruction. (New York: Harvest Books, 1975), p. 313.

19. Robert Hessen, Der Sport. (Frankfurt am Main: Literarische Anstalt, 1908), pp. 34, 69, 78, 83.

20. Eugen Weber, "Pierre de Coubertin and the introduction of organised Sport in France," Journal of Contemporary History, Vol. 5, No. 2 (1970), p. 15.

21. Ibid., p. 25.

22. Pierre de Coubertin, Essais de psychologie sportive. (Lausanne et Paris: Librairie Payot & Cie, 1913), pp. 79, 154 ff., 159, 166, 242 242 ff.

23. Ibid., 27, 55, 70, 105, 117, 155-156, 166-167, 197.

24. Ibid., pp. 124, 128.

25. Maurice Bardèche, "Jeux Olympiques, Maquisards et nantis," Défense de l'Occident (Aug.-Sept. 1972), pp. 3-4, 4.

26. Maurice Bardèche, Sparte et les sudistes. (Paris: Les Sept Couleurs, 1969), p. 19.

27. Essais de psychologie sportive, pp. 133-134.

28. Paul Adam, La morale des Sports. (Paris: Librairie Mondiale, 1907), pp. 12-13, 17.

29. Ibid., pp. 5, 22-23, 25-26, 206.

30. Ibid., pp. 12, 143, 149, 274.

31. John M. Hoberman, "Per Olov Enquist and the Literature of Sport." Presented at the 65th Annual Meeting of the Society for the Advancement of Scandinavian Study, University of Wisconsin, Madison, Wisconsin, May 2, 1975.

32. Jean Giraudoux, "Le Sport" [1928], in De pleins pouvoirs à sans pouvoirs. (Paris: Gallimard, 1950), p. 236; see also: Pierre Drieu la Rochelle, "A props d'une saison de football" [1921], in Mesure de la France (Paris: Editions Grasset, 1964); Henry de Montherlant, Les Olympiques [1924] (Paris: Gallimard, 1954); Jean Prévost, Plaisirs des sports (Paris: Gallimard, 1925); Paul Morand, Champions du monde (Paris: Bernard Grasset, 1930).

33. José Ortèga y Gasset, The Revolt of the Masses. (New York: Norton, 1960), pp. 4, 12, 39, 42, 69, 182.

34. Karl Jaspers, Man in the Modern Age. (New York: Anchor Books, 1957), pp. 68-71.

35. Herman Broch, Essays. (Zürich: Rhein-Verlag, 1955), pp. 259-260.

36. Man and Society in an Age of Reconstruction, pp. 5, 63, 313n.

37. Sigmund Freud, Civilization and its Discontents. (New York: Norton, 1961), p. 61.

38. Sigmund Freud, Three Contributions to the Theory of Sex. (New York: Dutton, 1962), p. 62n.

39. Gottfried Benn, Primal Vision. (London: The Bodley Head, 1961), pp. 120, 140.

40. Oswald Mosley, Fascism in Britain, quoted in R. Osborn, The Psychology of Reaction. (London: Victor Gollancz, 1938), p. 60.

41. Robert Brasillach, Notre avant-guerre. (Paris: Livre de Poche, 1973), pp. 361-362.

42. Robert Soucy, Fascism in France: The Case of Maurice Barrès, p. 65.

43. See Frank Kermode, Romantic Image. (New York: Vintage Books, 1957), p. 32; C. M. Bowra, The Heritage of Symbolism (New York: Schocken Books, 1961), p. 108.

44. Friedrich Nietzsche, On the Genealogy of Morals. (New York: Vintage Books, 1969), pp. 111, 132.

45. Antonin Artaud, Oeuvres complètes, IV. (Paris: Gallimard, 1964), p. 154.

46. Sun and Steel, p. 41.

47. Ernst von Salomon, _Fragebogen_ [The Questionnaire]. (Garden City, N. Y.: Doubleday & Company, Inc., 1955), p. 94.

48. "R. Palme Dutt, 79, British Marxist," _New York Times_, December 21, 1974, p. 30.

49. See John M. Hoberman, "Sport and the Marxists," ARENA _Newsletter_, Vol. 1, No. 2 (February 1977).

50. A. Wohl, "Fifty Years of Physical Culture in the U.S.S.R.: Reflections and Conclusions," _International Review of Sport Sociology_, Vol. 3 (1968), pp. 173-195.

51. Leon Trotsky, _Problems of Everyday Life_. (New York: Monad Press, 1973), pp. 26, 54.

52. _Ibid._, pp. 80, 223.

53. Leon Trotsky, _Literature and Revolution_. (Ann Arbor: University of Michigan Press, 1966), pp. 231, 256.

54. Nikolay Valentinov, _Encounters with Lenin_. (New York: Oxford University Press, 1968), pp. 79, 81.

55. Pierre Laguillaumie, "Pour une critique fondamentale du sport," in _Sport, culture et répression_. (Paris: François Maspero, 1972), p. 48.

56. Quoted in _Sport, culture et répression_, p. 7.

57. José Ortega y Gasset, "The Sportive Origin of the State," in _History as a System_. (New York: Norton, 1961), pp. 18, 31.

58. Willi Nitschke, _Kann der Sport Neutral Sein?_ (Berlin: Sportverlag, 1961), p. 10.

59. Georgi Plekhanov, "Labor, Play, and Art," in Maynard Solomon ed., _Marxism and Art_. (New York: Vintage Books, 1974), pp. 142, 143.

Some Ideological Qualities Of Australian Sport

Louis Murray

The Ideological Antecedents of Sport in Australia

Many writers concerned with Australian popular culture seem to attach some major social significance to the phenomenon of sport. While covertly hinting at a value orientation of the Nation towards sport, the emphasis is seldom other than journalistic and remains content with a description of leisure behaviours rather than attempting to construe meaning from such behaviours. Keith Dunstan (1973) has been rather more rigorous in developing an interesting and wide-ranging study of Australian sports. In adopting a largely historical perspective it is his suggestion that the 'obsession' is essentially attributable to such criteria as:

a. An interest derived from a sport-conscious parent nation, i.e. Britain.

b. An attempt to ameliorate "cultural poverty" by using sport as a social substitute.

c. A 'natural' extension of the 'bush ethos' and 'bronzed Aussie' images given some credence in the works of Lawson, Paterson and others.

d. A suitable expression of "masculinity" in a climate which is ideal and yet set in an environment demanding 'ruggedness' and 'mastery'.

The meticulous observer of society will probably find Dunstan's argument persuasive but oversimplified. Hancock (1944), in his now classic 'Australia,' presents a stronger case in suggesting that physical expressions of value in Australia are related to the centrality of 'achievement' which has been synthesized into a prevailing mystique--a movement with its roots deep in the early struggles for independence.

For Hancock, the dominant theme in Australian political and social history has been the 'lament of an unsatisfied land hunger.' Such a theme was said to have 'swelled angrily' in the decades which followed the Gold

Reprinted by kind permission of the author and the <u>Australian Journal of Health, Physical Education and Recreation</u>, 73:7-10, 1976.

Rushes when men who had been their own masters on the "diggings" had to re-orient their beliefs, motivations and relations in order to fight for new independence as farmers. Most were driven back, partly by vested interests and inadequate laws, chiefly by forces of economics and geography. One consequence of this social upheaval was the emergence of what might be termed the <u>Australian Collective Identity</u>—defined by the unifying of the population masses into a coherent and relatively homogeneous body. This collectivity, if deprived of land and material wealth, at least possessed themselves of the "State", the organized expression of group misfortune. Thus for Hancock (and many subsequent writers) the much vaunted Australian notions of egalitarianism and democracy derive from a focus originating in the Chartist style movements largely following the Gold Rushes. The 'State,' however, developed few doctrinaire advocates but more generally came to be regarded as a public utility which in Platolian terms was expected to provide the greatest good for the greatest number. Here we have Le Socialisme Sans Doctrine emerging as Hancock puts it, "from the levelling tendencies of migrations which have destroyed old ranks and relationships and scattered over wide lands a confused aggregate of individuals bound together by nothing save their powerful collectivity."

Sport has been regarded, and still is, as one form of symbolic dialogue for this collectivity. Its appeal has long been acknowledged as universal and its power to communicate as significant. Being synonymous cross-nationally with achievement, old insecurities could be ameliorated by way of international competition (in cricket matches for example), utilitarian ideals could be appropriately sub-sumed, and the collective commitment gradually reinforced. The fraternal aspiration (mateship) of the average Australian could, however, be too easily expressed in the criticism and destruction of those social isolates who were unable to fraternize. It was necessary for sport to become available in many forms and to the greatest number in order to meet the criteria of the emerging Australian ideology. This was defined so lucidly by Hancock as, 'the sentiment of justice, the claim of the right, the conception of equality, and the appeal to government as the instrument of self-realization.'

Hancock's brilliant discourse on the origins of Australian social democracy seems to have influenced many writers who have shown a concern for the perceived, if not the actual value structure in Australia. Sport is viewed by these writers as a 'natural' product of the kinds of interactions talked about by Hancock. Sport is regarded as somehow contributing to 'Social Health' and is given legitimate status as a means of sound achievement both utilitarian and expressive. A selection of contemporary viewpoints includes:

John Hallows (1973:83)
> Australians play a greater variety of sports than any other nation, a reflection of their varied origins and the multifarious influences they feel.

Ian Moffitt (1972:144)
> Australians love sport and gambling—and they demand only relentless competence from their heroes; not wit, courtesy, or the art of public speaking, but a continuing ability to earn big money.

Ronald Conway (1972:52)

By the Second World War, attitudes to sport had become a yardstick by which most men and women were judged. It was assumed that to be a good sportsman was to incarnate the most desirable human qualities. To be indifferent to sports was somehow to be un-Australian.

Craig McGregor (1966:134)

Life in Australia is __par excellence__, the creation of ordinary people. Because classical culture has had such a brief history it is the popular culture which has come to count most, which provides the best guide to Australians and the way they live.

These generally astute but untested observations are given important empirical support in the wide-ranging studies of W. F. Connell et al (1975: 189).

Sports interests are spread widely among teenagers and are associated with all social classes and all levels of intelligence...He has a well-developed sense of self-esteem which helps him to compete with determination and to work hard to improve his performance. As a spectator, he may transfer this to his chosen team, and become the phenomenon familiar to all sports groups--the one-eyed barracker.

Sequentially we may say with some degree of certainty that tradition has merged with the relatively high standards of living that create extra dimensions to leisure time in Australia. The climate remains constant, open space is available, and the media of public communication has elevated sport to such a prominent position that the social effects have multiplied. Sport has attained a position of centrality in popular culture and it has become commonplace for people to be involved either actively or vicariously. To divorce oneself from sport means to isolate oneself from a whole area of communal interest.

Chronologically, the antecedent influences to sport in Australia are depicted in Figure 1.

Sport as Contemporary Australian Ideology

Although sport as a chief means of social expression in Australia, is remaining constant, certain emphases seem to be recurring. Conway (1971) argues convincingly for a recognition of Jeremy Bentham's psychology of pleasure versus pain as the new spiritual ideology of most contemporary Australians. Juxtaposing some traditional elements of Australian motivation against modern trends, the quest for 'territory' is subsumed under 'home ownership' and 'self status' in many cases by 'material goods.' The concern with material advantage and domestic comfort is a strikingly visual facet of Australian social life in the 70's. This modern form of mass expression is a latter day equivalent to Hancock's "claim of the right."

It seems more than possible that the newer, hedonistic inclinations of Australian people, their relentless pursuit of pleasure, may well defuse or ameliorate the competitive ethic for so long pervasive throughout the formal,

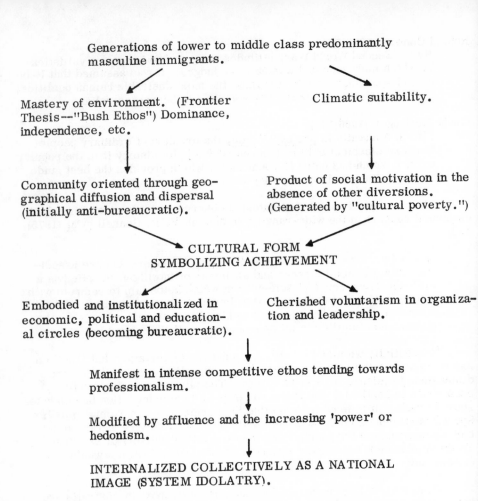

Figure 1. The Ideological Antecedents of Sport in Australia.

overt sporting structures in Australia. Indeed, it is possible to notice such effects (partial at least) in the relative decline in Australian successes in recent Olympic games. Something akin to monastic dedication has often been needed to excel in some sports, particularly those with international outlets, such as tennis, squash and swimming. It is publicly acknowledged that most sporting activities, especially team games, are essentially utilitarian or instrumental in their conduct or process. This means that the performer must adapt himself to austere training regimen, to repeated practice of difficult skills, to highly idiosyncratic coaching patterns and so forth, if he is to achieve a measure of competence or 'success'. In short, he must WORK at improving prowess and performance. The reward for such endeavours is essentially non-utilitarian in the sense that the performer is not able to privatize the outcomes. Certainly each athlete gains incrementally in such things as skill and fitness but his active involvement becomes more and more part of a public domain. Widespread public concern tends to focus upon the high quality components of performances of individuals, teams and groups. Such concern is evident among the mass of SECONDARY vicarious followers of sports; it is equally evident in the form of social comparison among the participants, or those in face to face PRIMARY playing and coaching situations. This ever more discriminant focus on high quality performance, the very exceptional and intensive/expressive physical demands involved, and the mutual value-orientation of both participant and larger society, combine in Australia (as they have similarly and most notably done so in Britain and the U.S.A.) to attract widespread public interest and commitment to a competitive ethos. As physical abilities and traits of a competitive kind have traditionally been supraordinate in the contest with environment, economy and misfortune in Australia, it is not surprising that the competitive edge in sports remains sharp and persistent.

However, OBJECTIVE CONDITIONS in Australia have changed and are changing. Real income, for example, has increased despite the ravages of inflation. In 1978 the average Australian worker earned $212 per week, not inconsiderable sum by world standards. Consequently, his choices and potentials in regard to leisure are broadened in scope and character. At the national level such changes mean that tightly enshrined values must in response, be affected, and that modified or differing value - orientations can be expected to arise.

By definition an institution manifests some stability or continuity over time. The rather unique institutional features of sport - clearly defined rules and procedures for equalizing competition, stratified levels of power and authority external to the playing arena, bureaucratic hierarchies of administration at national coaching level, etc. have been preeminent in regulating the degree to which behavioural values within the sphere of sport could legitimately vary from strongly emphasized social ideals. Generally such features have provided the institution of sport with stability in times of incipient change. Arguably, they also contribute to an inflexibility to alter internal structures to accommodate newer, external social realities. In 1977, the game of cricket, with an almost religious-like following in Australia, has been turned upside down by the departure of a dozen or so of the country's top players from the more or less 'gentleman amateur' national side in order to join a fully professional 'traveling circus' organized by media magnates. Such a move is a major blow to the cricket establishment in Australia. Their spokesman argued that the passionate (if unwritten) precept that cricket has nobler qualities than mere physical encounter, and that selection to the national team is the most worthy of privileges, are being defiled on the altar of rampant professionalism. Large sections of the general public and the media have responded in the opposite manner by their enthusiastic support for many of the recently organized games. Clearly this affair points to the fragility of the perceived ideology with which most Australians have traditionally viewed the game of cricket. Many sports followers are welcoming such indicators of structural change. In other realms of sport (most notably Australian Rules Football and Athletics) frequent charges of 'parochialism' and 'bureaucracy' have been directed at the attendant administrative hierarchies. Such charges may be an indication of either a reemphasis of the values originally prescribed in the culture for sport (and which have been lost in the process of institutionalization); or a plea for a more individualized conception of competition. That sports must somehow return to the 'social' dimensions of life.

Ideology is defined in the International Encyclopedia of the Social Sciences as consisting of "selected or distorted ideas about a social system when these ideas purport to be factual, and also carries a more or less explicit evaluation of the facts." The argument reported here suggests that sport is an ideology in Australia in which an exaggeration of the extent to which social values can be institutionalized in the social system has been made.

Hancock's treatise suggests the reasons for this exaggeration as essentially historic. Elias and Dunning (1970) have developed an additional perspective. It is their contention 'that in a society where the propensities for the serious and threatening excitement have diminished, the compensating function of play-excitement has increased.' Presumably Hancock's 'unfortunate collectivity' handed down a strong excitatory potential which has been manifested in the pursuit of intrinsically rewarding activity.

Certainly it is one of Caldwell's (1974:21) beliefs that excitement satisfaction is at the basis of Australian involvement in sport. Without isolating specific structural characteristics which might support the notion (though these are surely to be located through the types of interactions depicted in Figure 1), the presumption is that lack of "involvement" with persons and issues automatically leads to alternative searches for excitement. Such searches culminate in intensive interest in sport, gambling and other leisure pursuits. Ellis (1969), however, defines the ideological qualities of sport, and increasingly leisure, in simpler and more pragmatic terms. Increased post-war affluence and the meteoric rise to prominence of the motorcar provided the freedom and mobility that the pre-war generation essentially lacked. The youth of Australia appear to have readily accepted the affluence bestowed on them by their parents, even though this could have been interpreted as an attempt to "buy" affection from a generation whose behaviours were becoming increasingly difficult to understand. Acceptance of the values of security, career competence, etc., clearly espoused by parents, has apparently been forsaken for what Ellis describes as a 'vague kind of hedonistic liberalism.' The expansion of surfing in recent years may be indicative of this "new" direction of Australian youth. However, the symbolic and traditional aspects of sport are not necessarily lost in these hedonistic pursuits. Ellis describes the sub-cultural characteristics of surfing as representing "a life-style with a vernacular all its own, yet which still offers an ideal vehicle for living out the Australian image of the bronzed, all-male Spartan."

Participation in hedonistic pursuits is apparently on the increase in Australia. Skin-diving, orienteering, hang-gliding, and sky-diving are all basically individual activities which demonstrate some potential for self-expression and detachment from the exigencies of urban routines and mass-participation sports. Hedonism may be regarded as a more intensive if not new symbolism in the Australian way of life. Miller (1966:278) explains hedonism as a form of consciousness resulting from the pleasure derived from acute sensory stimulation. Behaviours are the outcome of "choices" or "tendencies" which men analyse in relation to their potential for maximizing pleasure or minimizing discomfort. Everyone is dependent upon the symbolic interpretation of social "realities" in order to both comprehend 'meaning' and to initiate appropriate responsory behaviours.

People can always behave idiosyncratically or on the basis of private interpretation of symbols. The cultural definitions of sport and leisure appear to have institutionalized "autonomy." As such, the pursuit of pleasure in Australia is a recognizably individual process and yet quite clearly a collective right.

In contemporary terms the ideological qualities ascribed to sport in Australia are the outcomes of a dynamic relationship between the following primary factors. (Figure 2).

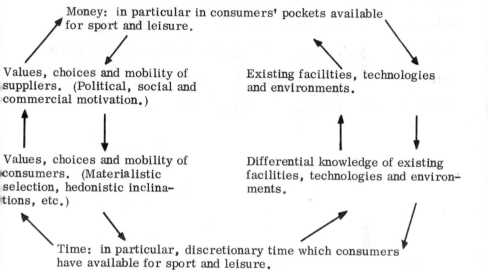

Derived from ideas in:
I. Griffiths 'Gentlemen suppliers and with it consumers,'
International Review of Sport Sociology. 5:59-68 1970.

Figure 2. Sport as a Contemporary Australian Ideology.

References

Caldwell, G. T. 1974. 'The gambling Australian,' in D. Edgar (ed.), Social Change in Australia. Melbourne, Cheshire.

Connell, W. F., et al. 1975. 12-20--Studies in City Youth. Sydney, Hicks Smith & Sons.

Conway, R. 1971. The Great Australian Stupor. Melbourne, Sun Books.

Elias, E. and Dunning, E. 1970. 'The quest for excitement in unexciting societies,' in G. Luschen (ed.), Cross-Cultural Analysis of Sports and Games. Stipes Publishing, Champaign, Ill.

Ellis, R. 1969. 'Are we playing the game?' Walkabout. 35(12).

Hallows, J. 1970. The Dreamtime Society. Sydney, Collins.

Hancock, W. K. 1944. Australia. Sydney, Ernest Benn.

McGregor, C. 1966. Profile of Australia. Ringwood, Vic. Penguin.

Miller, G. A. 1966. Psychology. London, Penguin.

Moffitt, I. 1972. The U Jack Society. Sydney, Ure Smith.

Superpower Sport In Cold War
And "Detente"

David B. Kanin

The Cold War has been fought with a massive commitment of re-sources by the two most powerful states in the world. Yet, the questions of ideology and power which divide them have not been tested in the usual manner; there has been no convulsive contest of arms to determine the stronger, the smarter, the society with History on its side.

If these states have not gone to war, neither have they settled their differences. The fact that both have placed restraints on their use of strategic power has not meant that the intense struggle between them has come to an end. They have competed in any non-strategic way available to them, and sporting "combat" has been one of these.

Both the United States and the Soviet Union have perceived for sport a significant role in the creation of popular perceptions as to relative national strength and as to the temper of international affairs. Each has influenced the sporting system through the athletic expression of national goals and values. As the leading political powers of the contemporary era, the United States and Soviet Union have each helped to make sport a leading medium by which global relations are brought into focus for the understanding of millions of people.

The American use of sport was the prototype for other national athletic efforts. The United States was the first country to advertise itself through its victories in the modern political sport system. American teams dominated most early Olympic contests. At the Paris Olympics of 1900, for example, the Amateur Athletic Union (AAU) had the idea of building a huge athletic club in order to demonstrate to Europeans the advantages of the American training system.[1] The <u>New York Times</u> referred to those Games as the "World Amateur Championships," and announced that the United States had won them.[2] By 1906 the American press had begun to score the Olympics on a national basis, a practice which has become universal, despite being banned by the International Olympic Committee.

In the American use of sport abroad, athletic activity was touted as a democratizing agent as well as a route for individual social mobility. Until the recent explosion of "professional" sport, the "sportsman" was thought of as an upper-class amateur. He was often a gentleman of leisure with enough free time to indulge in athletic recreation. If one played with the rich, one was perceived to have grasped at least a precarious hold on the next rung of the social ladder.

Americans thus perceived sport to be the primary occupation of an elite caste of Europeans whose main purpose in life was the organization of their own leisure. It was with pride that these aristocratic athletes were defeated by strapping republican youths who took time away from their useful occupations in order to compete. Such superiority of human resources demonstrated that America was the society of the future.

Americans were the first to institute rigorous training programs which forced athletes to spend as much time on their sports as on their jobs. While Europe's Gentleman Sportsmen relegated their training to leisure time and recreation, Americans worked out under the guidance of stern coaches.

America's role in international sport has been to set a standard for aggressive competition. To win was to show evidence of a superior social system. General Douglas MacArthur, the leader of the 1928 United States Olympic team, presented the American position:

> Athletic America is a telling phrase. It is talismanic. It suggests health and happiness. It arouses national pride. It enkindles the national spirit....Nothing is more characteristic of the genius of the American people than is their genius for athletics.*

In 1974 Gerald Ford, then Vice-President, suggested a rationale for such an attitude:

> Do we realize how important it is to compete successfully with other nations? Not just the Russians, but many nations that are growing and challenging. Being a leader, the U. S. has an obligation to set high standards.... The broader the achievement, the greater the impact. There is much to be said for Ping Pong Diplomacy.
>
> With communications what they are, a sports triumph can be as uplifting to a nation's spirit as, well, a battlefield victory.[3]

Americans were proud of their sport heroes and took it upon themselves to lend athletes out for the enrichment of others. Such "roving ambassadors" were used in the belief that they would improve the American image abroad. The Chicago White Sox went on a prototype world tour in 1888-1889. Later trips of the New York Yankees were applauded by President Harding for their contributions to the American image.[4] More recently, the State Department has taken it upon itself to arrange such public diplomacy through its "People-to-People" program.

The United States thus had a history of political sport diplomacy before the Soviet Union even existed. Once created, however, the U.S.S.R. demonstrated that it, too, understood the diplomatic potential of sport. Sporting

---

* This statement is immortalized in bronze on a wall in the "MacArthur Room" at United States Olympic Committee headquarters in New York.

relations in the Cold War have been extensive because both sides have had a clear understanding of their political function.

Soviet attitudes toward sport have been shaped by the perceived place of physical culture and athletic competition in a society dominated by the tenets of Marxism-Leninism. The Marxian nature of Soviet sport has been stressed in Soviet athletic policy. Class consciousness could be developed under Socialism along with physical prowess. Stalin, therefore, supported Pavlov's work on conditioned reflexes as evidence of the unity of the spiritual and physical.[5]

The Soviets credit the Proletariat and the ideology of Marxism-Levinism for the popularity of physical culture in the U.S.S.R. Only the Proletariat can understand the true nature of sport because only the working class has the consciousness to learn and appreciate teamwork, patience, and the will to win. This results from the workers' understanding that these virtues apply to all aspects of life, not just to the playing fields.

To a Marxist, sport reflects the ideas of the class dominant in each society. Proletarians win not only because of superior training, but also because of the superior relationship between the New Soviet Man and the means of production. Since bourgeois athletes must serve the purposes of the Capitalist ruling class, international sport competition is another form of class warfare.[6] The bourgeois athlete, because of his relationship to his Capitalist masters, is a much different sort of person than his Socialist counterpart:

(He is a) savage man... (the society's influences) degrade him morally, develop low criminal instincts, and are utilized for criminal purposes by the warmongers.[7]

The Soviets thus take a strictly class orientation as to the nature of sport in society, and the place of sport in international relations. The "scientific" focus of their ideology is reflected in the enthusiasm with which Soviet coaches and trainers adopt the most modern methods and technological gadgetry in their preparations for sport competition.

Soviet social science uses the most contemporary methods of data collection to demonstrate the differences between sport in rival social systems. Novikov and Maximenko, for example, used quantitative research methods to demonstrate that Socialist sport programs were more effective than their Capitalist counterparts.[8] Other Socialist articles concentrated on the social origins of athletes. Their conclusions often stressed the contention that Socialist athletes came from working class backgrounds more often than their Capitalist counterparts.[9]

These working class sports performers are expected to behave in a manner befitting their class origins. It has been noted, however, that even Soviet sport is not free from some bourgeois diseases, such as greed, arrogance, and individualism.[10] Such sickness is blamed on foreign contamination, rather than on anything endemic to Soviet society. Since the social body is viewed as healthier than these individual athletes, the society's disciplinary organs often attempt to root out and destroy anti-Socialist abberations.

Problems relating to contact between Soviet athletes and their bourgeois opponents only became important after World War II, when the U.S.S.R. entered the international sport system. Before this Soviet athletes were as outcast from sport as their state was from international politics.

After 1945, however, the Soviet Union could no longer be ignored; it occupied half of Europe and pressed policies around the world. In the organs of sport as in the rest of international politics Soviet representatives began to challenge American supremacy and to look for a following in the international community.

The first Socialist representatives to participate in an Olympic celebration were those East European athletes who went to the 1948 London Olympic Games. Their countries had been members of the Olympic system before the War, and change of government did not mean disbandment of national Olympic committees. The Socialist governments thus had little to worry from those in exile claiming to represent ousted national elements. The Olympic authorities always accepted participation by any government in power.

The Soviet Union first celebrated an Olympiad in Helsinki in 1952. Those Games were used as a demonstration of the depths of the Cold War. Soviet bloc athletes remained apart and aloof from the others. The United States was accused of being a vast military camp, and Americans were charged with trying to take over in international sport as they had in international politics.[11] This was embellished by the concept that "Olympic" meant "business."[12] The Games were described as a vast profit-making circus in which Capitalists squeezed money from a public bombarded with phony Olympic ideology.

The Americans were not at a loss for words either. Stalin was said to have established athletic factories in which he trained unfeeling mechanical athletes to be unleashed upon Helsinki.[13]

In 1952, the Soviet Union copied the American Olympic model in order to compete with the United States. The U.S.S.R. was not content to allow the American scoring system to go unchallenged.[14] It invented its own scoring system, which did not put as much of a premium on first place, and which emphasized the importance of team depth.

Using the two scoring systems, each side could claim victory.[15] Each declared its athletes' superiority over the other's, while the International Olympic Committee insisted that no scoring system was allowed. Later, the U.S.S.R. relented somewhat; a book on Soviet sport listed the 1952 Olympic Games as a tie (and then proceeded to show how Soviet athletes outstripped the U. S. over the next three Olympiads).[16]

If the 1952 Games provided a demonstration of Soviet-American hatred those of 1956 seemed to indicate a thaw in that attitude. While propaganda on both sides continued to treat each other's athletes as rivals to be measured against, Soviet and American athletes displayed a suddenly friendly attitude toward each other once the Melbourne Games opened.

This reversal was all the more striking since the 1956 Olympics open-ed almost at the same moment as the twin crises of Suez and Budapest con-vulsed world politics. The latter was represented in Olympic affairs by the mass defection of the majority of the Hungarian Olympic team to the West. The prevailing atmosphere in Melbourne, however, was more an accurate reflection of the cooperation between the superpowers over the Suez problem, where Soviet and American policies had in common the desire to secure British, French, and Israeli withdrawal.

In a deeper sense, "friendship" at the 1956 Olympics represented the onset of "Peaceful Coexistence" as the general line of the Soviet Communist Party. This policy, articulated by Khrushchev a few months earlier, did not mean an end to the struggle against Capitalism. It involved a way to structure the fight against Capitalism in an era when nuclear weapons could destroy both sides, and when the Prime Adversary was still too strong to be confronted in a direct fashion. Competition was to be carried on using all means short of nuclear war.

Sport was a perfect medium for such conflict. It was peripheral to the international system, therefore American athletes could be defeated without fear of military reprisal. Sport was among the most publicized of interna-tional political transactions, therefore Soviet victories would become known around the world. The Cold War did not end, its atmosphere was merely altered in line with Soviet policy.

Organs of the Olympic Movement could only serve a secondary role in future athletic relations between the superpowers. The United States was not a member of regional European athletic federations and, therefore, could not use regional contests to gain contact with the U.S.S.R. Those federations that did hold world championships did not (with the exception of association football) attract the public attention necessary for full utilization of political sport as a tool in public diplomacy. The Olympic Games them-selves were points of contact, but they took place only once in four years, and therefore could not serve as a channel for regular sport relations.

So the major medium of Cold War athletic diplomacy became direct bi-lateral exchanges between the two sides. These were arranged on a case by case basis, and therefore remained quite susceptible to the effects of chang-ing political moods.

There had been limited examples of such relations before 1956. American chess players had gone to Moscow in 1946, following by one year a radio match between the two sides.[17] Chess was the first sport in which the Soviet Union demonstrated superiority to the United States, and the In-ternational Chess Federation (F.I.D.E.) was the first organ of international sport which the Soviets joined. In December, 1949 the U.S.S.R. hosted its first international sporting event attended by Capitalist representatives, a women's chess tournament.[18]

Chess, however, could not serve as the basis for systematic Soviet-American sport relations. It was not popular enough in the United States, and pre-1956 Cold War problems retarded the development of relations.

While the Soviet leadership after the death of Stalin proved willing to widen sport exchanges, even inviting an American weightlifting team to compete in Moscow,[19] the American proved slow to react. The State Department blocked continued chess exchanges.[20]

The American government proved to be so hard to deal with that the U.S.S.R. began to concentrate on private American sport organizations. The Amateur Athletic Union became the focus for such approaches, since it controlled most American participation in international sport. The A.A.U. was also the largest American amateur athletic organization, and the one set up most closely to the European pattern. It had the most experience with the international sport federations that the Soviet Union was becoming a part of.

A.A.U. officials, in their capacity as representatives of the United States Olympic Committee, dealt with the suddenly friendly Soviets in Melbourne during the 1956 Olympic Games. While events in Budapest and Suez absorbed the attention of the world, Soviet and American sport officials arranged the basis for future sport exchanges.[21]

In late 1957, the A.A.U. came to terms with Soviet officials on financial and athletic arrangements for sport exchanges. Once the State Department relaxed its demand that Soviet athletes be subjected to a finger-printing process, relations in several sports could commence.

In January, 1958, the adversaries signed the first of a series of agreements authorizing cultural, technical, and educational exchanges.[22] The two sides had already come to terms on most procedural issues,* and in April Soviet wrestlers became the first Soviet athletes to put the new agreement into practice.[23]

The first U.S.-U.S.S.R. track and field meet was held that same year. As with the Melbourne Olympics, it opened despite the deterioration of the international political situation. The Offshore Islands and Lebanon problems elevated levels of tension, and the incipient stage of the second Berlin crisis was in progress. Sport could provide nothing in the way of a solution to these problems, but it could coat them with a gloss of superpower cooperation.

Soviet-American track and field exchanges were the most important sporting events of the Cold War. Track was popular in both countries; the 1958 meet was the first exchange to draw an audience large enough to give political sport atmospheric significance. The great meets of the period 1958-1966 always draw many fans, commercial sponsors, and a great deal of television coverage.

---

* The scoring system for track meets was still a problem. Each side had a system under which it felt national victory would be most likely. The desire for better relations did not preclude the importance of winning for the major adversaries of representative political sport.

These track and field meets became a regular and systematic form of Soviet-American public diplomacy. They were annual affairs, hosted alternatively by each side. They served to reduce the stereotyped fear of the "Enemy" as presented to both publics by their respective national presses. Already by 1959, in contrast to the virulent propaganda of the early and middle parts of the decade, American sportswriting allowed the Soviets to be portrayed as "ordinary human beings."[24] The ground breaking nature of the first track and field meets was such that they helped prepare the American public for the visit of Soviet Premier Khrushchev to the United States in the autumn of 1959.*

This atmosphere was extended by the 1960 Winter Olympics in Squaw Valley, California. The Soviet team put on a friendly face, and was given credit for it in the American press.[25] The coach of the Soviet ice hockey team even went to the American team's locker room during its final match to encourage its victory. This was done despite the fact that the Americans had previously defeated the Soviet team, and was playing against another Socialist side, that from Czechoslovakia.

The U-2 incident dampened the atmosphere of the 1960 Rome summer Olympics, but track and field meets went on without interruption. The meets flourished throughout the second Berlin crisis, and represented the feeling of relief felt when war was averted over the question of Soviet missile installations in Cuba.

In 1966, however, the Soviet Union abruptly cancelled the track and field meet which was to have been held in Los Angeles that summer. A State Department spokesman offered one possible reason for that move - "They saw a bad licking staring them in the face."[26]

There is no evidence showing that the U.S.S.R. was ashamed of its 1966 track and field team. The Soviets had scored their most impressive triumph in 1965, winning both the male and female track and field contests; it was the first time they had accomplished this. Even if defeat was expected, it is less than likely that the Soviet Union would have taken such an abrupt approach. The U.S.S.R. had already demonstrated an ability to take defeat in such events as its first test in Davis Cup competition in 1962. The impact of defeat was less of a problem when it was not witnessed on Soviet soil (the tennis match was played outside the U.S.S.R. at Soviet request). As mentioned above, the 1966 meet was scheduled for Los Angeles.

A more plausible explanation was the one the Soviets themselves offered. The meet was cancelled because of the Vietnam War. The Soviet Union was greatly embarrassed by its inability to halt the American air offensive against North Vietnam. The Soviet leadership was put on the defensive by the harsh Chinese reaction to the lack of aggressive Soviet action in the area. The termination of the major sport institution of the Cold War was the most

---

* Sports Illustrated reported that Khrushchev's doctors had advised him to take up golf for his health. Of all forms of exercise, it is interesting that Khrushchev's doctors had suggested the sport most closely identified with President Eisenhower.[27]

public way in which the Soviet Union could demonstrate its annoyance with the American air war without risking the kind of political tension both super-powers were trying to avoid. This negative application of athletic diplomacy, the only action the Soviets could take under the circumstances, demonstrated the impotence of the U.S.S.R. in Southeast Asia. It underscored the limits of a superpower's influence in the contemporary era (something the other superpower was learning at the same time in the same place).

There were other manifestations of this Soviet use of sport. The World University Games of 1966 were a forum for an apparently sullen and uncommunicative Soviet team, one which reverted to the "Cold War" style of the 1952 Olympic Games.[28] In that same year, the U.S.S.R. cancelled a basketball match that was to have been played between Soviet and American sides in Moscow. Foy Kohler, the American ambassador to the U.S.S.R., delivered an official protest of the action to the Soviet Foreign Ministry. The Soviet Union responded that this cancellation was caused by a spontane-ous demonstration against American policy on the part of Soviet athletes. The Americans alleged that the Soviet government had stopped all ticket sales to the event a week before this "spontaneous" demonstration took place.[29]

The most blatant use of sport to represent opposition to American pol-icy in Asia came in 1968 at the initiation of the Bulgarian government. Dur-ing the arrangements for a track and field meet to be held in Sofia, it was announced that the medals to be awarded would be made out of metal taken from American warplanes shot down over North Vietnam.[30]

Meanwhile, the Soviet Union itself had troubles which led it to con-sider an improvement in relations with the United States. The Sino-Soviet split continued to be a serious difficulty for the Kremlin, as did signs of un-rest in Eastern Europe. Rivalry in ice hockey caused a sharpening of intra-Soviet bloc disputes in 1969. In August of the previous year, Soviet and War-saw Pact troops had invaded Czechoslovakia, putting an end to the "Prague Spring." The next confrontation between Soviet and Czechoslovakian sides came at the 1969 World Ice Hockey Championships. Czechoslovakia won the title, beating the Soviets in this competition for the first time in nearly a decade. The result was something between a riot and a revolution. The streets of Prague filled with rioters, rocks, bottles, and anti-Soviet pla-cards. It was a classic example of a sporting victory making up for a mili-tary defeat in the minds of the people. The riot was used as the excuse the Soviets needed to rid themselves once and for all of Alexander Dubcek.[31]

Pravda reacted by the blaming the violence on reactionaries bent on whipping up national passion.[32] In an unusual action, the Soviet press carri-ed quotes from Czech newspapers expressing exultation in anti-Soviet feel-ing.[33] The intensity of hatred in the pieces was, in fact, the reason for their reprinting; one of the reasons given for the 1968 invasion had been the inabil-ity of the Czechoslovakian Communist Party to discipline its own press.

The problems faced by the U.S.S.R. in Eastern Europe were magnifi-ed by their juxtaposition to Soviet clashes with the Chinese along their huge border. With so much trouble from fellow Socialists, the Soviets sought to minimize difficulties with the Americans. They found that the United States was in a similar mood, in the wake of its disasterous and unpopular war in Vietnam. "Detente" was born as much out of mutual frustration as out of any hope for world peace.

This process has not involved any diminution of the tension between the two sides. It has merely been a cosmetic arrangement designed to define certain parameters of conflict, and to create an atmosphere of hope regarding, to use Nixon's term, a "generation of peace." Sport was used to create such perceptions. Since it involved exchanges peripheral to the issues dividing the two states, it could be used as a public demonstration of good will without involving any substantive negotiation of any of the thorny problems still to be settled.

Track and field exchanges, for example, were resumed. These proved to be popular, but not as politically significant as their ancestors in the "Peaceful Coexistence" years. Even though they received significant publicity, they could not recreate previous political atmosphere, because they were no longer groundbreaking. The public was used to such Soviet-American exchanges. The public of sport concentrated on scores and records, rather than on the protestations of friendship they had heard so many times before. The resumption of track and field meets proved not to be nearly as significant as the "Ping Pong Diplomacy" of the same period. The latter was groundbreaking, altering public perception in much the same fashion as the original Soviet-American track meets.

With the cooperative purpose of sport exchange thus compromised, the competitive nature of sport activity became more important in inter-superpower relations. Soviet and American athletes have always considered each other to be the prime adversary. Both sides have used sport in a conscious attempt to demonstrate societal superiority. The shaky assumption that friendly contact can overcome the sting of defeat was made even more shaky by the sporting process of the 1970's. The "Detente" era, in fact, became one where friction over sport gained as much notice as "friendship."

Defeat or victory in certain sports has always been more significant than in others, because each society has built up pride in different sport activities. The Soviet Union proved adept in learning another country's national sport and then defeating it at it. Soviet sides succeeded in surpassing Canada in amateur ice hockey; Soviet sights were then set on American basketball. The United States, through the singular personality of Bobby Fischer, returned the favor in chess.

Basketball is the only sport played at the global level which was invented in the United States (Baseball is played in relatively few places, despite many American attempts to export it). Americans were proud of their traditional supremacy in track and field because it was the most prestigious part of the Olympic program. The mania for basketball, however, stemmed from the genuine national feeling that this was "our game." Basketball players were among the first Americans to go to the U.S.S.R. in the wake of the 1958 cultural agreement.[34]

"First Sputnik, Now This!" screamed <u>Sports Illustrated</u> after a Soviet basketball team defeated an American squad at a tournament in 1959.[35] This dismay reflected both the status of the sport in the U. S., and the remnants of "Sputnik-Shock" still evident two years after the fact.

Basketball competition continued throughout the 1960's, with the Americans winning all the Olympic contests. The two countries exchanged national teams in a recurring test of each other's skills. Then came Munich, and the very disputed basketball finals of the 1972 Olympics. For the first time the United States lost the basketball gold medal, losing both it and its first Olympic basketball game to the Soviet Union.

A rematch of some sort was inevitable, and a Soviet tour of the United States was arranged in 1973. When the old A.A.U. feud with the National Collegiate Athletic Association came up during the American team selection process, several congressmen threatened legislation to force both organizations to allow participation by the best American players.[36]

American pride was salvaged when its team won four out of six games played between the two national sides. It was a series marked by rough play and erratic officiating. Further problems were created by the fact that American players still were not used to playing under international rules (since it was "our game," Americans resisted conforming to rules common to the rest of the world). It is difficult to have a successful sport exchange if each side is used to different standards of play. Conflict in such a situation becomes politically focused when matches are played between two representative national sides.

Soviet basketball fortunes turned downward after 1973. The U.S.S.R. team lost the European basketball championship, began a string of losses to Yugoslavia's national team, and fared poorly in the 1976 Olympics. Some Soviet athletes were accused of having a <u>prima donna</u> attitude, and of profiteering on the black market. Since Soviet athletes are supposed to have certain spiritual advantages over their bourgeois rivals, defeat in sport was taken to represent pollution of certain individuals by too much contact with the bourgeois world.[37]

The difference between Socialist and bourgeois values is important to the Soviets when it comes to reasons for their superiority in chess. The Soviets like to think of their country as "the classical land of chess."[38] Chess was not only the first sport exchanged with the West by the Soviet Union, it was also a primary propaganda tool of the U.S.S.R. from the earliest days of the Cold War. In December, 1948, at the height of the first Berlin Crisis, World Chess Champion Mikhail Botvinnik compared the development of chess in rival social systems:

The bourgeois school of chess tends to reduce the game to an idle pastime and develops players as mere idle craftsmen...(the Socialist School)...regards chess as one of the remarkable manifestations of man's reason.[39]

In the 1960's the U.S.S.R. faced the challenge of Bobby Fischer. He symbolized everything the Soviets detested: he was individualistic, interested in money, and highly anti-Communist. He was also a player of consummate skill. In the early part of the decade he charged that Soviet players, using the round-robin system of play, rigged the World Championships. According to Fischer, Soviet players would play draws against each other in order to save their strength for foreign challengers such as himself. Fischer's charges were never officially accepted, but the International Chess Federation did change the rules of championship play.

In 1972, after a series of squabbles over money, television rights, lighting, and the location of spectator seats, Fischer contested for the championship against Boris Spassky. Spassky, the reigning champion, was defeated by Fischer, often denounced by the Soviet Union as representative of the worst in bourgeois sport. Soviet officials, distressed by the defeat, charged Fischer with such tactics as using chemicals and electricity to weaken Spassky's play.[40]

The chess match was another example demonstrating that an atmosphere of political competition is often intrinsic to a sporting event which is so highly valued by at least one of the sides. The question of victory is more than a sporting one when prime adversaries are involved. Each sporting contestant is viewed as directly representative of his state and social order.

In the case of the Fischer-Spassky match, some spectators began to find fault with their own champion. The U.S.S.R. was, of course, disappointed by Spassky's performance. Losing this match posed a serious threat to the position he had gained in Soviet society as a result of his skills. The material incentives offered to Soviet athletic role models involve significant disincentives to lose. The New Soviet Man defeats his bourgeois opponent because of advantages gained from his social order. If the athlete loses to a bourgeois rival, it is due either to raw luck or to a flaw in the way of life of the individual. If such a flaw is perceived, the athlete can face severe criticism or loss of status. Spassky was criticized by such players as former champion Mikhail Tal, and remained out of the public eye for months after his defeat. He now lives in semi-exile in France.

As with the Americans and Olympic basketball, the Soviet Union has regained its chess championship. Fischer gave up his crown in another dispute with chess officials over rules. One of the best Soviet players, however, provided another embarrassment by defecting to the West.[41] Should Viktor Korchnoi ever take the title from a Soviet champion, his example might serve to underscore problems inherent in the process of giving great publicity to sport heroes.

The two superpowers are now more used to defeats by the other. Indeed, their publics are quite accustomed to the process of sport exchange; sport is now both more accepted and less politically dramatic. The fact of sport exchanges has not enhanced the process of "detente" so much as the competition of sport has reminded people of the continuing rivalry between the two sides. In 1976, for example, the Soviet Union boycotted the World Chess Olympics because it was played in Israel,[42] and American and Soviet officials took opposite sides in the dispute over Taiwan's admittance to the Montreal Olympics.[43]

The Soviet Olympics of 1980 may be a showcase for "detente," a forum for renewed Soviet-American rivalry, or both. The United States fought Moscow for these Games; the Soviets had already charged the Americans with aiding Canada in its successful competition with the U.S.S.R. for the 1976 Olympics.[44] Whether or not the two sides intend to put on a display of friendship may be less important than the fact that they will be competing for victory and prestige in front of one side's national spectators. With the groundbreaking diplomacy of sport long finished, what is left to the superpowers is the natural rivalry of competition between representative national teams.

References

[1] Bill Henry, An Approved History of the Olympic Games. (New York: G. P. Putnam's Sons, 1948), p. 60.

[2] The New York Times, July 23, 1900.

[3] Sports Illustrated, XLI, #2 (July 8, 1974), p. 16.

[4] Donald P. Zingale, "A History of the Involvement of the American Presidency in School and College Physical Education and Sports during the Twentieth Century". (Ph.D. dissertation, Ohio State University, 1973), p. 42.

[5] I. P. Pavlov, Selected Works. (Moscow: Foreign Languages Printing House, 1955), introduction.

[6] Henry Morton, "Sport in Soviet Russia," in John Talamini and Charles H. Page, ed., Sport and Society, An Anthology. (New York: Little Brown, 1973), p. 112.

[7] Ibid., p. 113.

[8] A. D. Novikov and A. M. Maximenko, "The Influence of Selected Socio-Economic Factors on the Level of Sports Achievement in Various Countries," International Review of Sport Sociology, VII (1972), pp. 27-44.

[9] E. g., W. Starosta, "Some Data Concerning Social Characteristics of Figure Skaters," International Review of Sport Sociology, II (1967), pp. 165-175.

[10] Current Digest of the Soviet Press, XV, #7, p. 31, Trud, February 7, 1963.

[11] The New York Times, January 27, 1952.

[12] The New York Times, February 20, 1952.

[13] The New York Times, April 20, 1952.

[14] Current Digest of the Soviet Press, IV, #31, pp. 25-27, Pravda, July 31, 1952.

[15] The New York Times, August 3, 1952; August 5, 1952.

[16] Nikolai Tarasov, Soviet Sport Today. (Moscow: Novosti, 1964), p. 45.

[17] D. J. Richards, Soviet Chess. (Oxford: Clarendon Press, 1965), pp. 79-80.

[18] Current Digest of the Soviet Press, I, #31, p. 6, Pravda, June 30, 1949.

[19] Current Digest of the Soviet Press, VII, #24, pp. 17-18, Pravda, June 12, 1955.

[20] The Times. (London), July 10, 1953.

[21] Author Interview with Mr. Daniel Ferris, Executive-Secretary Emeritus of the A.A.U., November 30, 1973.

[22] Current Digest of the Soviet Press, X, #4, pp. 33-34, Sovietskaya Esthonia, January 30, 1958.

[23] Sports Illustrated, VIII, #16 (April 21, 1958), pp. 14-16.

[24] Sports Illustrated, XI, #5 (August 3, 1959), p. 31.

[25] Sports Illustrated, XII, #10 (March 7, 1960), p. 14.

[26] Sports Illustrated, XXV, #3 (July 18, 1966), p. 12.

[27] Sports Illustrated, X, #16 (April 20, 1959), p. 31.

[28] Sports Illustrated, XXIV, #9 (February 28, 1966), p. 44.

29 The New York Times, July 12, 1966; July 13, 1966.

30 Sports Illustrated, XXVIII, #15 (April 15, 1968), p. 29.

31 Edward Taborsky, "Czechoslovakia: The Return to Normalcy," Problems of Communism, XIX, #6 (November/December, 1970), p. 32.

32 Current Digest of the Soviet Press, XXI, #13, p. 18, Pravda, March 31, 1969.

33 See Current Digest of the Soviet Press, XXI, #14, p. 6, Komsomolskaya Pravda, April 1, 1969.

34 Sports Illustrated, VIII, #18 (May 6, 1958), pp. 24-25.

35 Sports Illustrated, X, #6 (February 9, 1959), p. 10.

36 The New York Times, March 6, 1973; March 27, 1973.

37 The New York Times, October 25, 1973.

38 D. J. Richards, Soviet Chess, p. 60.

39 The Times. (London), December 31, 1948.

40 The New York Times, August 23, 1972.

41 The New York Times, July 28, 1976.

42 Current Digest of the Soviet Press, XXVIII, #21, p. 18, Pravda, May 22, 1976.

43 The New York Times, July 15, 1976.

44 Alexander Dobrov, Moscow is Ready to Host the 1980 Olympic Games. (Moscow: Novosti, 1974), p. 5.

Ideology And Diplomacy:

The Dimension Of Chinese

Political Sport

David B. Kanin

Although China is a society with a deep cultural and political heritage independent of Western concepts of political development, in the contemporary era it has embraced Western forms of government and political ideology. Chinese experiments with capitalism, militarism, and Marxism-Leninism have led it to assimilate forms of Western culture as well.

Modern international sport is a Western phenomenon. The ideology of sport traces its origins to Olympic mythology and British educational sociology. The organization of sport is a system owing legitimacy to its use as a tool in European nationalism. The growth of Chinese activity in transnational sport mirrored its absorption of Western ideology and political institutions.

China was introduced to some forms of Western sport around the turn of the century, especially through the efforts of the YMCA.[1] The latter spread Western ideas on physical culture much as missionaries spread Christianity to segments of the Chinese population. By the 1920's, Western sport influence had reached a point where it equalled that of Japan in Chinese society.[2]

Chiang Kai-shek and the Kuomintang took an active part in the spread of Western-style sport once maximum Nationalist control was established. In 1929, the National Physical Education Law was passed for the purpose of strengthening human resources in the drive to develop China's capacity for national defense.[3] The next year the Government recognized the China Amateur Athletic Federation as having the primary responsibility for getting this done. As it turned out, the Japanese invasion came before national sport could prepare national defense; the Kuomintang never could complete its plan to use sport to advance national unity.

By creating a national Federation, however, the government enabled China to take part in organized transnational sport. China was a pillar of the Far Eastern Games from 1913 until 1934. These Games were grafted on to the Olympic Movement through the adoption of the metric system,[4] and because the IOC found itself without anywhere to celebrate during World War I. While the 1916 Olympics were cancelled, the Far Eastern Games of 1915 provided an international event which the IOC could claim as its own. The Olympic Movement needed such an event to tide it over until 1919.

The Japanese wars of hegemony in Asia brought the Far Eastern Games to an end. The last of these events died in Manila in 1934, when Japan tried to enter athletes from "Manchukuo" as a separate team. China would not permit such a challenge to its integrity. Manchuria was an integral part of China, and Chinese sport policy toward it was much the same as a later regime's would be toward Taiwan.

The Kuomintang joined the Olympic Movement in 1923, but did not attend a meeting of an Olympic body until 1928. The first Chinese athlete to attend an Olympic Game went to Los Angeles in 1932, but only as a diplomatic afterthought. Chiang had no intention of sending a team until Japan tried to get "Manchukuo" into the Olympics. The United States saw to it that the Stimson Doctrine of non-recognition of conquests by aggression was enforced - Japan failed in this use of political sport. [5]

While Japan could scuttle the Far Eastern Games, it could not end the Olympics, and China sent its athlete. After this incident, Chiang recognized that the Olympics were a political forum, and imported a German coach to train his team.* The Chinese delegation to the 1936 Berlin Olympics totaled 107 people; this was the height of Kuomintang presence in international sport. [6] In 1948, China sent only seven athletes to London.

The Chinese Communists have also used sport to provide human resources with the strength for national defense, but have had a clearer ideological purpose behind their physical culture. Sport has served as a tool in the process of changing a way of life older than any in the world. Even before 1949, "Lenin Clubs" encouraged the use of table tennis in the training of the Chinese revolutionary soldier. [7] Sports such as basketball, swimming, volleyball, and skating, were popular among Communist troops.

The use of sport as a tool in ideological education has ensured its popularity in the People's Republic of China (PRC). So has its personal ties to Mao Tse-tung. Mao was active in writing about physical education before he became a Communist. In 1917 he wrote "A Study of Physical Education," urging the use of sport for national rejuvination. [8] His approach to physical culture was the same as that of Father Jahn or the Sokols; the national spirit was to be awakened by means of strenuous physical activity.

This early article showed that Mao hoped to strengthen China by taking Western forms and giving them Chinese content. His references were nearly always traditional; his ideology would continue to be molded with the Chinese context in mind. When Mao incorporated his continuing interest in physical culture into his system of Marxist thought, the specific considerations of Chinese demography and culture he had developed remained important.

---

* There was a great deal of German influence in China at the time. Hans von Seeckt and other German officers planned out some of Chiang's most successful attacks against Communist rural bases before World War II.

His sport had to be mass sport, both for the sake of national defense and for the reeducation of the largest population on earth. Sport was used to create the self-confidence needed in people who were expected to be ready to fight an enemy that was better armed and more technologically advanced. Since China had a lot of people, and most of these were peasants, Mao's "Thought" stressed the importance of the peasantry as a revolutionary class, and insisted that the weapons of war were not as important as the human combatants.

The preoccupation with the human factor in revolution and war continues to define a difference between Soviet and Chinese sport. The Chinese have the same respect for scientific training methods as have the Soviets. They try to learn the most modern methods in each sport from whomever is the best at it. While the Soviets place their major emphasis on scientific training and on the Pavlovian repetition of skills, however, the Chinese care more about the human will. The successful athlete will be the one with the correct ideological position in all aspects of life, not the one devoted to athletic training. The Soviets expect their athletes to be well-rounded physically and intellectually, but the Chinese place special emphasis on constant positive ideological reaffirmation on the part of the athlete wishing to demonstrate his or her loyalty.

The athlete is expected to be effusive in gratitude to Chairman Mao for the correct thought which allowed for the development of physical skills. Credit for triumph and achievement is supposed to go to the creators of the atmosphere in which they could flourish. As in many societies, the athlete is expected to be a social model. In China, this means that he or she must be the most public in expressions of gratitude and rapture over the genius of Chairman Mao. High jumper Ni Chih-chin, said to have high-jumped seven feet, six and one-half inches (which would have been a world record when it was done), knew where to place credit for his feat: "When I read the thoughts of Chairman Mao, I feel I could jump higher than a fireman's ladder."[9] The spectators are expected to react accordingly. When Ni accomplished this jump, spectators were reported to have screamed ecstatically, "Long Live Chairman Mao! Long live the victory of Chairman Mao's revolutionary line!"[10] It is hard to tell what effect the death of Mao and of the Great Proletarian Cultural Revolution will have on such exclamations.

The development of Communist sport was a mirror of the development of Socialist society in China, since the former was a tool of the latter. Total state control of this tool developed in stages. Nearly a month after the victory of October, 1949, a preparatory commission was set up to investigate the possible establishment of an umbrella organization for Chinese sport. Its result, the All-China Athletic Federation (ACAF), was finally created in June, 1952.[11] In November, the People's Culture and Sport Committee (PCSC) was formed, and associations were created in each sport. While the ACAF was created as a "mass organization," the PCSC was overtly a part of the government.[12]

Physical culture was put into the 1954 constitution, and became a tool in the sweeping social changes of the late 1950's. A sport program accompanied the institution of the "Great Leap Forward."

The physical expansion of China into Tibet was also a focus for the use of political sport in this period. Tibetans were paraded in athletic uniforms before huge crowds and pointed out as proof of the benefits of Chinese Communism. An article in China Sport (an official Chinese organ) was entitled, "Former Slave Girl Now Good Basketballer," and contained testimony of how Tibetan girls had been rescued from Feudalism and retrained for that sport.[13] Tibetan athletes were shown on the road to full social equality. Another article, in 1965, showed how Tibetan serfs had become crack archers.[14] After being saved from slavery, these people had been taught a sport which could contribute to the national defense.

Shortly after the Tibetan conquest in 1959, pictures were distributed showing Tibetan athletes in a huge, new stadium wearing shirts with inscriptions in both Chinese and their native language.[15] The sport propaganda of the next years reflected the political gyrations through which that leadership was going. Sport, as a tool in political propaganda, proved to be a useful signal in an unclear political situation.

Those 1959 photographs reflected the partial eclipse of Mao in favor of Liu Shao-chi. Liu sat at the direct left of Mao. Later propaganda catapulted Liu into even more prominence. In 1964, it was both Liu and Mao who went for a two hour swim, together urging the rest of China to do the same.[16] The next year, 8000 people were reported to have swum the 900 meters across the Yangtse at Chungking.[17]

The Great Proletarian Cultural Revolution (GPCR) had begun, but it was far from clear who was going to emerge from it in control of China. In 1965 both Mao and Liu were reported to have swum in the Ming Tombs Reservoir.[18] Again they encouraged everyone to swim everywhere. It was Liu who greeted the Guinean basketball team by himself later that year.[19] The November, 1965 issue of China Sport carried an article headlined "Chairman Mao has arrived!" which began, "Chairman Mao has arrived! Chairman Liu has arrived!" Then it went on to tell who else in the Chinese leadership had arrived.[20]

In 1966 there was another swim, but this time it was by Mao alone. Liu was being eclipsed, and Mao used swimming to demonstrate that he was physically and politically strong enough to seize control of the Party and stay at the helm of his country.[21] In 1968 he was in the water again, urging the Cantonese on to greater physical and ideological feats.[22]*

The use of sport in China has thus been similar to that in most other states. National defense, internal propaganda, the increase of the prestige of the leadership, and signals concerning the relative status of its members have all been accomplished through sport. Where the Chinese have made an original contribution to the use of sport has been in their attitude toward athletic diplomacy.

---

* Some got a little too inspired. It appears that police patrols were sent to prevent over-zealous swimmers from losing their way and swimming over to Hong Kong.

The Chinese have a different attitude than do the superpowers concerning the use of sport as a diplomatic tool. Since the GPCR, the slogan "Friendship First, Competition Second," has been the guiding concept of Chinese sport diplomacy. Winning sporting events has not been the primary focus of Chinese sport. Unlike the superpowers, the Chinese recognize that their opponents do not react with awe and admiration every time they are defeated.

For the Chinese, the athlete is a different sort of class ambassador. He or she reaches out to raise the consciousness of others throughout the world who have the common framework of the athletic field, but who lack the common knowledge of Marxism-Leninism-Maoism. Winning is not as important as is the process which brings Chinese athletes together with their opponents. In the political world of international sport, it is the sport person's class consciousness which causes victory both on the field and off. It is the duty of the political athlete to spread this Truth to his or her competitors through personal example. Radio Peking expressed this policy at an important juncture in 1971, a few months after the advent of "Ping Pong Diplomacy."

Whether or not a team or an individual is victorious and gains honor depends on whether or not he gives prominence to proletarian politics during the competition, whether or not he wins in the realm of ideology, whether or not he can lose without losing the spirit of sportsmanship, and whether or not he puts proletarian politics in command of the tournament and participates for the sake of proletarian politics.[23]

The Chinese expressed nothing but contempt for the Soviet ("Bourgeois Revisionist") concentration on winning, a policy which they referred to as "championship mentality." They called it:

a hideous trick devised by bourgeois revisionism to corrupt people's souls...a disease which poisons the minds of people so that they fight for individual fame and profit...a monster which tempts people to serve the ruling class.[24]

For all of this, the Chinese did not use the Olympic Movement any differently than other states. As all countries, China recognized that the Olympic Games involve questions of political recognition and prestige. The Olympics were the focus of the Chinese drive for the expulsion of Taiwan from transnational relations.

A PRC team entered the 1952 Olympics, but the International Olympic Committee refused to accept the credentials of either "China." As it was, the PRC was not a member of the five Olympic sport federations required in order that a country might qualify for the Olympic Games.[25]

In 1954, the IOC voted 23-21 in favor of admitting the PRC, but the Chinese did not attend the Melbourne Games of 1956. They expressed a desire to participate,[26] but refused to accept IOC insistence on a "Two China" policy. Such a policy was impossible in the Olympic Movement as in the rest of the international system. Both "Chinas" were agreed on two things:

there was only one China and Taiwan was part of it. The issue was always simple; it all depended on which government one recognized.

Each superpower campaigned for its own "China." The United States counted on keeping the PRC out of individual federations, so that Olympic rules themselves would work against PRC participation.[27] The Soviet Union's representative at the 1954 meeting of the IOC called the KMT "political leftovers," and pushed for PRC representation on the IOC.[28]

In 1960, the IOC ended up with no "China" at all. In protest of the Olympic acceptance of "two Chinas," the PRC withdrew its claims from the Olympic Movement in 1958.[29] Taiwan pressed for participation, but ran into problems stemming from the IOC's own political criteria for membership. Since the Kuomintang no longer controlled China, it could no longer compete as "China" in Olympic competitions. This was based on the profoundly political argument that a national Olympic committee could only represent the territory and people controlled by its sponsoring regime.

Taiwan was forced to march its team in Rome behind a sign reading "Formosa."[30] The Kuomintang considered withdrawal, but the political legitimacy of athletic competition was one of the last political forums left to Taiwan, along with its position on the United Nations Security Council. One of the athletes marching behind the sign "Formosa" held his own sign reading "Under Protest."

By 1964, the IOC edged back toward recognition of Taiwan. The PRC remained outside the Olympic Movement, concentrating on the idea of a "Third World" sport organization, and then retreating into itself during the convulsive GPCR. Lacking two Chinas, the IOC leaned toward the one which recognized its authority, and Kuomintang participation was not seriously challenged until the 1970's.

Although the Chinese had established some sporting contacts with France and Britain, the main focus of Chinese sport had been on relations with other Communist states. This changed with the Sino-Soviet split. The Chinese gradually became as afraid of their Socialist neighbor as of the class enemy. While the United States was far away, the Soviet Union shared with China the longest common border in the world, a border which was soon ringed by the largest concentration of peacetime armament in history.

Relations with the Soviet Union were never completely cordial. When Mao traveled to Moscow after his victory over the Kuomintang, he was greeted by Stalin as just another representative of a foreign country, rather than as a victorious Socialist brother. The Sino-Soviet "Friendship" Treaty of 1950 left Soviet troops in occupation zones in China, and included a loan which China was expected to repay with interest. Stalin's cool attitude toward his huge neighbor was reflected athletically in 1951. A Soviet basketball team traveled to China and became the cause of a series of complaints from Peking to Moscow. The Soviet team insisted on bringing its own ball (which the Chinese considered too heavy), its own referee, and on changing the rules of play.[31]

---

* The Games of the Newly Emerging Forces (GANEFO).

Despite this, most Soviet-Chinese athletic exchanges of the 1950's were held in a friendly atmosphere. The Chinese would often picture themselves as "learning" from their Soviet comrades. Slowly, however, this image began to change. A 1962 description of a "friendly" volleyball match pictured the Soviet athletes as aggressive attackers, and the Chinese as skillful defenders.[32] The action was described as "fierce fighting over the net."

By 1964, the PRC was using sport to underscore differences in the Communist camp. A military sport meet was held, with the flags of thirteen Communist states on display. Those singled out for attention at the meet included Albania, Poland, Rumania, Mongolia, North Korea, and North Vietnam.[33] Each of these states was either allied with China, neutral in the dispute, or under the impression that it could mediate between the Communist giants. In 1965 the split was openly advertised at a table tennis match between Soviet and Chinese teams. The match was held up for forty minutes over a vehement Soviet protest against a type of service used by their opponents.[34]

At first China sought to offset its loss of Soviet "friendship" with general international ties. While withdrawing from the Asian Athletic Federation, which recognized Taiwan, the PRC remained a member of those international federations in sports at which they could compete respectably (winning did matter a little, even to the Chinese).[35] China began hosting international events in 1958, with the First Friendly Shooting Competition.[36] In 1961, Peking was the site of the World Table Tennis Championships, at which such Capitalist states as Denmark and West Germany were represented.[37]

In the period before the GPCR, however, the Chinese concentrated upon neutral "Third World" countries which had been the object of Soviet diplomacy since articulation of the general line of "Peaceful Coexistence." The most favored state during this period was Sukarno's Indonesia. Sukarno, at the 1962 Forth Asian Games in Djakarta, made it clear that he was looking for Chinese sport by responding to the following Chinese declaration:

> On order of U.S. imperialism, the Chiang Kai-shek clique has rigged up a number of so-called representative sportsmen to prepare for competition at the Fourth Asian Games. This shows once again that U.S. imperialism is bent on creating a structure of "two Chinas" in international sports, so as to provide a pretext for its perpetual occupation of the Chinese territory of Taiwan.[38]

Sukarno took the hint; Kuomintang athletes were barred from the Fourth Asian Games. The IOC disciplined Sukarno for his exclusion of IOC members from IOC-sanctioned events (Israel had also been excluded); Sukarno reacted by leaving the Olympic Movement and by pushing the Games of the Newly Emerging Forces (GANEFO). In this action he was strenuously supported by the Chinese, themselves outside the Olympic Movement. The Soviet Union also tried to be friendly to Indonesia, but found itself at a distant disadvantage. The Soviets were members of the Olympic Movement and intended to remain so. Sukarno's friendship in the struggle against Peking

was not worth threatening the Soviet position in a movement so perfectly organized for the demonstration of Soviet athletic prowess. While the U.S.S.R.
financed many of GANEFO facilities, the Chinese team was clearly the most
favored by Sukarno at the First GANEFO in Djakarta in 1963.[39]

In 1965, China stressed ties with the Third World, and considered itself a part of it. In the period before the GPCR, China looked forward to a
Third World alternative to international organization, and GANEFO was
exulted over as an ongoing Third World sport organization.

But 1965 was also the year of the abortive coup of the Indonesian Communist Party. This Putsch resulted in the fall of Sukarno in favor of an
anti-Communist military regime. The latter reestablished ties with the
United Nations and the Olympic Movement (Sukarno had withdrawn from both).
The Chinese themselves entered the GPCR, and from approximately 1966-
1970 had very few international relations at all. When Egypt was shattered
in the 1967 Middle East War, GANEFO was left without anyone to cultivate it.

The approach to the Third World remains a cornerstone of Chinese
policy. But, since the end of GANEFO and of the GPCR, the Chinese have
waged their battles for proletarian politics and against Taiwan within regular channels of transnational sport. The Chinese have also entered into a
more open relationship with the class enemy, the United States.

Despite the Vietnam War, the Soviet Union, not the United States, has
emerged as the Prime Adversary (for this period, at least). China, no longer expecting a Third World alternative to the United Nations or the Olympic
Movement, has come to an accommodation with both.

To make this work, Americans had to be shown that China, despite the
the virulent, ongoing anti-American propaganda campaign, was sincerely
interested in better relations with the United States. Sport exchange was to
be an instrument in this process.

The Chinese had to break down many barriers in order to make this
policy work. In the early days of the Cold War, "Red China" was even more
mysterious to many Americans than was the U.S.S.R. There were many
warnings, such as the following from Sports Illustrated, of the Chinese drive
to sporting supremacy:

> Its avowed purpose is to improve the health – and the ability to work –
> of every Chinese citizen. Obviously, should the occasion arise, it
> would also make better soldiers of them....Woe to the world's best
> athletes when the Chinese sports colossus gets into real stride.[40]

This rhetoric implied an interesting facet of the American attitude toward China. There was the rebirth (if it had ever died) of the old fear of
the "Yellow Peril." The spector was raised of 700,000,000 Chinese mobilized against America in the form of athletic competition. It was clear that
China, as well as the superpowers, was interested in physical culture as a
method of maximizing the strength, stamina, and effectiveness of human resources. The Chinese had more of these than anyone else.

Such attitudes (plus the fear of Communism) had to be softened before diplomatic contacts could begin. Sport was one of the tools in a process which involved the growth of American self-doubt during the Vietnam War, and the decline of the good/evil view that Americans held of themselves and of the "Communist menace."

As with Soviet-American sport relations, the Chinese conducted much of their athletic diplomacy through private organizations in the United States. This was even more necessary in the Chinese case since they and the Americans had no diplomatic relations. When the time did come for athletic exchange, it came in the form of a favorite Chinese sport, table tennis.

This was a sport in which certain American officials could be considered cooperative. Rufford Harrison, of the U. S. Table Tennis Federation (USTTF) had voted at an International Table Tennis Federation (ITTF) meeting in favor of the motion which brought the world championships to Peking. He had further expressed the hope that someday his country would allow him to attend such an event.[41] No member of an official American government delegation could have made such a statement in the early '60's, or could have voted to hold a diplomatic event on the Chinese mainland under Maoist jurisdiction. Harrison told the author that, at a later ITTF meeting, he was greeted with a bear hug from the leader of the Chinese delegation.[42]

The chances for "Ping Pong Diplomacy" were interrupted by the GPCR, during which Chinese athletes dropped from the transnational scene. In 1965, Chinese players won the World Table Tennis Championships in Japan. Two years later, the Chinese team withdrew from the tournament, and Chuang Tse-tung, the men's world champion, disappeared from view.

His reappearance in 1970 (and eventual elevation to Sport Minister) signaled the early stages of Chinese reemergence into world affairs.[43] The next year China sent its team to the World Table Tennis Championships in Nagoya, Japan. The Chinese team in this meet invited the British to send a team to visit China. It was during the same competition that Harrison was approached with a similar offer from Sung Chung, the head of the Chinese delegation.[44] Within a week the Americans were on their way to Peking. The trip was a highly publicized success which included a series of exhibitions and a meeting with Chou En-lai. It was followed by more journeys between the two countries, and finally by the 1972 Chinese visit of President Nixon.

"Ping Pong Diplomacy" was similar in importance to earlier U.S.-Soviet track and field meets, and the U.S.S.R. gave significant attention to the table tennis exchange in their press.[45] It was a warning signal to the Soviet Union regarding a new factor in its strange relationship with the P.R.C.

As with Soviet-American meets, repeating the event merely made the process more commonplace and, therefore, less politically dramatic. Still, "Ping Pong Diplomacy," and subsequent tours of gymnasts, basketballers, and others, prepared the public to accept the idea of normal relations with what had been the archenemy. With the lack of tangible political progress since the fall of Nixon, sport was used to demonstrate that the process of normalization was still going on. The Chinese, now involved in a drive to enter the Olympic Movement, this time used track and field, the most prestigious Olympic sport.

In May, 1975 an American track and field team went to China (the Chinese invitation had been extended in March). Once more, the Amateur Athletic Union, Committee on U.S.-China Relations, and other organizations served as diplomatic conduits. China expressed a desire to put "Friendship First, Competition Second," and even hoped to learn a few lessons from the Americans.[46] The A.A.U. made public its own desire to invite the Chinese to return the visit.[47]

The meet was conducted in a style different from that of the Olympic Games. There were no national flags, anthems, or point totals (except by the American press, which recounted how the Americans were winning most of the events). The crowd reportedly cheered both sides, and the athletes were all smiles. According to John Underwood, the only protest came when the Chinese objected to the American practice of exhorting their comrades, yelling out times, and insisting on displaying commercial brand names on athletic uniforms and baggage.[48] In the diplomatic box at the stadium, U.S. diplomatic liaison George Bush was joined by Chuang Tse-tung, an appropriate, if low level, government representative.[49] The event was marred by the somewhat raucous behavior of several American athletes at the farewell banquet,[50] but otherwise went very well.

Such sport exchanges were useful in altering public perceptions, but could not themselves arrange diplomatic relations. Sport, being peripheral to international politics, was of no use when it came to the settlement of such issues as Taiwan and differehces in attitudes toward Soviet-American "Detente." China disappointed in American policy on both matters, showed that sport could open up relations with other countries as well.

China arranged track meets with Italy, Rumania, and Spain in 1975. As early as 1971, "Ping Pong Diplomacy" was extended to Yugoslavia.[51] Two Communist states with histories of independence from the Soviet demonstrated that the latter would not be able to count on the end of their deviant policies. Albania, as well as the U.S.S.R., was treated to the possibility of better Sino-Yugoslav relations, and Sino-Albanian relations subsequently deteriorated.

China also held a great eighty-state table tennis meet in Peking. Harrison pointed out that China could boast of having hosted a more globally representative event than any ITTF-sponsored championship.[52] It was a Third World meet; the states represented were from Asia, Africa, and Latin America. If sport was used to relate to the class enemy, it was also a tool in the process whereby China advanced itself as a leader of the Third World, and as an ally in the struggle against superpower aggression.

The same attitude was at the basis of an approach of the Chinese to India, a power which had had friendly relations with the Soviet Union since the Sino-Indian border war of 1962. China had supported Pakistan against India in their 1971 clash, but after this war used sport to soften relations with a neighbor beginning to feel like a world power.

In the early 1970's, Indian sport reporting often noted the decline of American and Pakistani sportsmanship in the same sentence.[53] The Chinese were apparently not in the same class; in 1971 and 1973 Indian table tennis teams went to China.

In January, 1975, China sent a team to the World Table Tennis Championships in Calcutta. This team was the first organized Chinese group to go to India since the 1962 war. They were greeted with shouts of "Indians and Chinese are brothers," a slogan from the pre-1962 era.[54] The head of the Chinese delegation, Hsu Yin-sheng, told the Indians of his team's political purpose:

> We have come to promote friendship and good will between our nations. Please extend our best wishes - on behalf of the People of China - to the people of your country.[55]

This rapprochement was short-lived. China was annoyed at the Indian take-over of Sikkim, as it involved the kind of Indian border advance which had led to the 1962 war.[56] Mrs. Ghandi's seizure of total power was greeted by much Chinese criticism, and the government which replaced her has tended to be more pro-Western than its predecessors.

This Chinese sport offensive of the 1970's had one unexpected facet. In June, 1973 it was announced that a Taiwan table tennis team would be invited to Peking.[57] No answer from the Kuomintang was ever recorded. The main Chinese drive against Taiwan has actually heated up. Renewed Chinese interest in the transnational sport system has been accompanied by demands for Taiwan's ouster. China has increased its membership in the federations, and has always insisted that each of these expel the Kuomintang from its ranks. By 1974 China was a member of fencing, volleyball, swimming, and ice hockey. The latter sport was the medium by which the PRC made an abortive approach to Canada, the next Olympic host.[58] In April, 1975 China applied for membership in the International Lawn Tennis Federation, and expressed interest in Davis Cup competition.[59] In September, the PRC was admitted to the World University Games Federation.[60]

The Chinese have had more trouble in other sports. After Taiwan was ousted from, and the PRC was admitted to, the Asian Games Federation, China became eligible for the 1974 Asian Games in Teheran. The International Association Football (soccer) Federation, however, refused to oust Taiwan, and the PRC refused to allow it a "two China" policy.[61] China was barred from the International Amateur Athletic Federation for the same reason. So China could go to Teheran, but could only compete in those sports in which it had federation membership. The Chinese decided that their presence in Teheran was important enough to try to appear in as many sports as possible, so they did make some accommodations with specific federations. The International Swimming Federation (FINA), for example, allowed Chinese athletes to compete while China allowed FINA to table the question of Taiwan.[62]

China sent a 270 member delegation to Teheran, and won more medals than any country besides Japan. Chinese athletes demonstrated, however, that "Friendship First, Competition Second," was a doctrine dependent on the political situation. The PRC refused to play tennis or fence against Israel.[63] Chinese medal winners refused to shake the hands of any Israelis sharing medal winner pedestals with them. China claimed that this was done in order not to offend Iraq. In fact, China merely extended its political policy into a forum where it could be publicly demonstrated. The natural connection between sport and politics was used by a state which was in the process of reentering the international system in both activities.

The Olympic Games, being a primary form of political sport, appears to be the next target of Chinese sport diplomacy. In April, 1975, it was reported that the IOC would treat a PRC membership application with favor.[64] China took the hint and, being a member of more than the five federations required for Olympic participation, applied for admission to the Olympics.[65] The issue of Taiwan remained a problem. China seemed content to oust Taiwan in federation after federation, hoping to present the IOC with a situation where Taiwan was no longer a member of enough transnational sport bodies to allow Olympic representation.

This policy was aided by the fact that the next two Olympic hosts were states which had no diplomatic relations with Taiwan. Canada extended this diplomatic fact to its sport policy when it refused to allow Taiwan athletes to enter the country under passports reading "Republic of China."[66] In addition, Taiwan was barred from flying its flag in the Olympic display. American threats to boycott the Games, and IOC motions to transfer them were irrelevant; Canada merely made an appropriate (in terms of previous Olympic politics and diplomatic conduct) demonstration of its foreign policy. The IOC eventually gave in and offered Kuomintang athletes the chance to march behind the Olympic banner. Taiwan refused to accept this, as it would have involved diminution of their legitimacy, and of their own foreign policy.[67]

The issue of China presents the Soviet Union with a dilemma as it prepares for the 1980 Olympic Games. To admit Taiwan would not only be a breach of its foreign policy, but would cause great embarrassment to the Soviets throughout the Communist world. Peking has already insulted the Soviets by insisting that it is certain Taiwan will be invited to Moscow.[68]

If Peking is admitted, on the other hand, it will mean that Soviet promises to admit all Olympic member states would have been broken (assuming, of course, that Peking does not replace Taipei as an Olympic member before 1980). More importantly, the presence of Chinese athletes in Moscow would be the most public juxtaposition of the two adversaries in some time. Friction between the two sides could mar what the Soviet Union hopes will be a celebration of the First Socialist State.

There need not be such friction, of course. Chinese athletes might put on a show of "Friendship First, Competition Second." Indeed, there is the possibility that Sino-Soviet relations might improve by the time of the Moscow Olympics. Chinese disappointment with the United States, as well as the death of Chairman Mao, might make such a detente possible. There would be no need for better Party-to-Party relations; sport could be used to demonstrate merely correct State-to-State contacts. Friendly contact between the two Communist giants at the Olympics could prepare the publics in both countries for normal relations, without necessitating discussion of the main issues dividing them.

The death of Mao, and the defeat of the "Gang of Four," makes this a real possibility. In July, 1976 the tenth anniversary of one of Mao's swims was celebrated throughout China.[69] Bathers were reported to have called for the Chairman to live for 10,000 years.[70] Mao himself was too feeble to swim, a fact which may have served as a signal to the public to the extent of his weakness. His passing brings all Chinese policies into question, including "Friendship First, Competition Second." How future Chinese sport attitudes and slogans will unfold will depend on the perceived relationship between the policies of the new leaders and required public support. In any case, Chinese sport ideology will depend, for form and content, on its perceived role in future Chinese politics.

References

[1] Jonathon Kolatch, Sport, Politics, and Ideology in China. (Middle Village, New York: Jonathon David, 1972), pp. 7-9.

[2] Ibid., pp. 32-3.

[3] Ibid.

[4] Ibid., p. 62.

[5] The New York Times, May 26, 1932.

[6] Kolatch, Sport, Politics, and Ideology in China. pp. 45-45.

[7] Ibid., p. 83.

[8] Mao Tse-tung, "A Study of Physical Education," in S. Schramm, ed., The Political Thought of Mao Tse-tung. (New York: Praeger, 1969), pp. 152-160.

[9] Sports Illustrated, XXXIII, #22 (November 30, 1970), p. 12.

[10] Sports Illustrated, XXXIII, #24 (December 14, 1970), p. 14.

[11] Kolatch, p. 98.

[12] Ibid.

[13] China Sport, January, 1962, p. 22.

[14] China Sport, November, 1965, p. 41.

[15] Sports Illustrated, XI, #14 (October 5, 1959), p. 35.

[16] Kolatch, p. 160.

[17] Ibid.

[18] China Sport, August, 1965, p. 1.

[19] China Sport, September, 1965, p. 1.

[20] China Sport, November, 1965, p. 14.

[21] Kolatch, p. 162.

[22] Sports Illustrated, XXIX, #7 (August 12, 1968), p. 8.

[23] Radio Peking, July 27, 1971, quoted in China Notes, #421 (August 16, 1971).

[24] Ibid.

[25] Kolatch, p. 170.

[26] China Sport, April, 1963, p. 12.

[27] The New York Times, July 29, 1952.

[28] The New York Times, May 11, 1954.

[29] See Olympic Review, #66-67, May-June, 1973, pp. 171-174.

[30] Ibid.

[31] Philip Goodhart and Christopher Chataway, War Without Weapons. (London: W. H. Allen, 1968), p. 128.

[32] China Sport, April, 1962, p. 2.

[33] China Sport, June, 1962, p. 1.

[34] Goodhart and Chataway, War Without Weapons, p. 129.

[35] Kolatch, p. 169.

[36] Ibid.

[37] Ibid.

[38] China Sport, March, 1962, p. 1.

[39] See Ewa T. Pauker, GANEFO I: Sports and Politics in Djakarta. (Santa Monica, Calif.: RAND, July, 1964).

[40] Sports Illustrated, XIV, #23 (June 12, 1961), pp. 26-27.

[41] Author interview with Dr. Harrison, December 13, 1973.

[42] Ibid.

[43] Sports Illustrated, XXXII, #7 (February 16, 1970), p. 7.

[44] Rufford Harrison in Chemical Technology, May, 1972, pp. 276-279.

[45] Current Digest of the Soviet Press, XXIII, #16, pp. 20-21, Literaturnaya Gazeta, April 21, 1971.

[46] The New York Times, May 11, 1975.

[47] The New York Times, May 22, 1975.

[48] Sports Illustrated, XLII, #22 (June 2, 1975), p. 26.

[49] The New York Times, May 28, 1975.

[50] The New York Times, May 31, 1975.

[51] Foreign Broadcast Information Service (FBIS), October 22, 1971 (People's Republic of China), p. A10, New China News Agency, October 21, 1971.

[52] Letter from Dr. Harrison to the author, October 1, 1973.

[53] E.g., The Times of India, September 13, 1972.

[54] The New York Times, January 12, 1975.

[55] Ibid.

[56] The New York Times, May 4, 1975.

[57] The New York Times, June 30, 1973.

[58] The New York Times, November 27, 1973.

[59] The New York Times, April 11, 1975.

[60] The New York Times, September 17, 1975.

[61] The New York Times, November 20, 1973.

[62] The New York Times, September 22, 1973.

[63] Sports Illustrated, XLI, #12 (September 23, 1974), pp. 61-63.

[64] The New York Times, April 14, 1975.

[65] The New York Times, April 18, 1975.

[66] The New York Times, July 2, 1976.

[67] The New York Times, July 12, 1976.

[68] Far Eastern Economic Review, XCIII, #34 (August 20, 1976), p. 27.

[69] The New York Times, July 17, 1976.

[70] Ibid.

Sports And Politics: The Case Of

The Asian Games And The GANEFO

Swanpo Sie

Although the Olympic Movement has traditionally maintained that political intervention in sports must be avoided, history raises the question of whether this is a practical ideal. It could be charged that the International Olympic Committee itself sanctions political overtones in sports since the modern Olympic Games, from its conception by Pierre de Coubertin, has recognized the political color of the Games by honouring the flags of nations and by playing national anthems in victory ceremonies. Even the Olympic Oath of the modern games places politics before sports: "...for the honour of our country and the glory of sport."*

The focus of this paper is to trace briefly the historical evidence of the interplay between sports movements and the political struggles of nations emerging from colonial rule towards the end of World War II, with emphasis on the Asian Games and the Games of the New Emerging Forces.

The Asian Games

At the end of World War II when the Western colonial powers were at their weakest point, the nations of Asia and Africa took advantage of the situation to press for liberation from colonial control. With a common goal of independence which would be enhanced by Asian solidarity against common enemies--i.e., European and American colonial rulers--representatives of several major Asian nations met at an Asian Relations Conference held in New Delhi, India on March 23, 1947. When representatives discussed cultural and sports affairs the Indian delegation proposed the establishment of an Asian sports movement. This idea was accepted by the other representatives because they agreed that Asian relations through sports would encourage Asian unity. Such unity was aimed at strengthening the independence

---

* Full text of the Olympic Oath is as follows: "We swear that we will take part in the Olympic Games in loyal competition, respecting the regulations which govern them and desirous of participating in them in the true spirit of sportsmanship, for the honour of our country and the glory of sport." Quoted in: British Olympic Association Official Report of the London Olympic Games, July 29-August 14, 1948, a "World Sports" publication, London, 1948, p. 9.

movements of those Asian countries which were still struggling for independence against colonial rulers. It was agreed that a more elaborate meeting among Asian representatives in the field of sports would be called during the Olympic Games in London in 1948.

In London a meeting of representatives of Asian countries who participated in the Olympic Games was held. A proposal forwarded by the Indian representative, G. D. Sondhi, concerning the establishment of a sports federation among Asian nations was accepted and agreement was reached to draft the constitution of the federation.

On January 20, 1949, on the initiative of the late Indian Prime Minister Jawaharlal Nehru, an Asian Conference was held in New Delhi. The main purposes of the Conference were to promote Asian unity against Western colonialism and to support the Indonesian independence movement by proposing to the United Nations Security Council that Dutch military forces be withdrawn from Indonesia.

Within the spirit of this Asian Conference, an attempt was made to institute a regional Olympic Games in Asia in order to improve friendship, relations and cooperation among Asians. This idea was supported by most of the Asian countries, and a provisional title of Asiatic Games was suggested. Prime Minister Nehru later proposed the name of Asian Games, which was accepted by the Asian representatives.

On February 12, 1949 representatives of eight Asian countries—Afghanistan, Burma, Ceylon, India, Indonesia, Pakistan, the Philippines and Thailand—met in New Delhi for the Asian Games Conference. At this conference the Constitution of the Asian Amateur Athletic Federation, which had been drafted at the London meeting in 1948, was adopted. The name was later changed to the Constitution of the Asian Games Federation. The First Asian Games, originally planned to be held in 1950, was postponed and held in March of 1951 in New Delhi. Subsequently, under the supervision of the Asian Games Federation, the Asian Games were held at four year intervals. The Second Asian Games was held in Manila in 1954 and the Third in Tokyo in 1958 without major political implications.

Political Aspects Related to the Fourth Asian Games

By a narrow margin of 22 to 20 the Asian Games Federation, meeting in Tokyo on May 23, 1958, chose Indonesia as the site of the Fourth Asian Games. This decision was criticized by many of the Asian nations. Comments from the press in Tokyo at that time were very pessimistic since Indonesia was considered too underdeveloped, and too politically and economically unstable, to effectively organize an international competition of such magnitude. Members of the International Olympic Committee frequently asked Indonesian sports authorities how Indonesia would be able to organize an adequate international sports competition with no previous experience and with no suitable sports facilities or stadium. The press in Singapore announced that the Fourth Asian Games in Jakarta would fail and guaranteed that the death knell of the Asian Games would be heard from Jakarta.

The Asian Games Federation decision was accepted with enthusiasm by the Indonesian sports organizations and sports authorities. Government authorities and politicians, however, were worried about the financial situation of the country and the political consequences of the Games, especially the admission of athletes from countries which did not have diplomatic relations with Indonesia--at that time Israel, the Republic of China (Taiwan) and South Korea.

The pessimistic tone of international opinion concerning the Indonesian ability to host an international sports event goaded the Indonesian government into swinging full support behind the staging of the Games in Jakarta. Indonesian President Soekarno granted his full support and stated on behalf of the Indonesian government that Indonesia was prepared to make an all-out effort to ensure the success of the Fourth Asian Games. In his message to the Indonesian Olympic Committee, Soekarno maintained that the Fourth Asian Games in Jakarta had to be bigger and better organized than the Third Asian Games in Tokyo. In a meeting with representatives of the Indonesian Olympic Committee at Merdeka Palace on June 9, 1958, he stated:

> The celebration of the Fourth Asian Games in Jakarta has to be organized in such a way that it will become a source of national prestige for the Indonesian nation, and that it will build the foundations for future improvements in the nation's development in the broadest sense of the word--materially, physically and morally. In addition, it must strengthen relations between Indonesia and the other Asian nations, based on the understanding and sympathies of those nations with respect to the struggle and ideals for survival of the Indonesian nation.*

Since almost all of the facilities for the sports competitions--including hotels and roads--had to be built, technical assistance from abroad was a necessity. The first target for technical assistance was the United States of America, and in September of 1958 the Indonesian Olympic Committee submitted to the U. S. government a request for assistance. Despite repeated inquiries, no response was forthcoming. This lack of response may have been because no provision for technical assistance in the area of sports existed in the programs of the U. S. Department of State and the U. S. Agency for International Development. At any rate, Indonesian leaders became increasingly worried. December of 1958 arrived with no U. S. commitment,

---

* The original Indonesian text is as follows: Perayaan Asian Games IV di Jakarta harus dilaksanakan demikian rupa, sehingga menjadi kebanggaan nasional bangsa Indonesia, serta dapat menanamkan dasar-dasar yang akan membawa kemajuan-kemajuan dikemudian hari kepada pembangunan negara dalam arti yang seluas-luasnya, baik dari segi materiel, maupun dari segi fisik, moril dan mental, serta pula mempererat hubungan baik Indonesia dengan negara-negara Asia, berdasarkan pengertian dan simpati negara-negara tsb. terhadap perjoangan dan cita-cita kehidupan bangsa I Indonesia. Quoted in: Maladi, "Hubungan Gelora Senayan dengan Hari Depan Keolahragaan Indonesia," Unpublished document, Directorate General of Sports and Youth, Department of Education and Culture, Republic of Indonesia, Jakarta, 1972.

and fear arose that the extensive facilities needed would not be ready in time for the Games. The Indonesian government decided to seek out other avenues of foreign assistance.

President Soekarno informally approached the Embassy of the U.S.S.R. in Jakarta to explore possibilities for Soviet assistance to build the necessary sports facilities. The unexpected response was immediate and favourable. Official approval from Moscow for the assistance was submitted to the Indonesian government on December 27, 1958. An agreement was reached between the governments of Indonesia and the Soviet Union for a credit loan in the amount of 50 million rubles to build the sports facilities for the Fourth Asian Games. The facilities were to consist of a main stadium of 100,000 seats, a swimming stadium of 10,000 seats, a sports palace of 8,000 seats, a track and field stadium, a basketball hall, a volleyball hall, a tennis stadium and a number of open air tennis courts, volleyball fields and basketball fields.

Following confirmation of technical assistance from the Soviet Union, the Japanese government granted Indonesia a credit loan for the construction of a modern international hotel, now known as Hotel Indonesia, in Jakarta.

The U. S. finally approved developmental aid to Indonesia for construction of a highway connecting Tanjung Priok, the harbour of Jakarta, with the sports complex. The highway became known as the Jakarta By-pass and was constructed as part of the AID program for Indonesia. Although this highway was not planned to serve the purposes of the Fourth Asian Games, AID agreed to complete that part of the highway needed for the Games in time for the celebrations. The U. S. government never considered this aid to be a contribution to the Games; however, the Indonesian government recognized the highway as a major American contribution to the Asian Games facilities development project. This was mentioned in a documentary report dated June 8, 1972 submitted by the Indonesian Minister of Sports at that time, Maladi, at the request of the Director General of Sports and Youth of the Department of Education and Culture of Indonesia.

The political effects of all this technical assistance were rather unique. While the U.S. contributed the only direct financial aid to the Fourth Asian Games project, via the Jakarta By-Pass, this contribution remained unofficial because the U. S. would not and/or could not link it directly to the Games. The Soviet Union and Japan, in contrast, merely granted loans to the Indonesian government; Indonesia is still making payments to the U.S.S.R. for the stadium facilities in Jakarta. The moral support of the Soviet Union in granting its loan without hesitation at a crucial time and the direct technical assistance of Soviet experts in building the sports facilities undoubtedly accounts for the widespread impression that the Soviets paid for the Fourth Asian games facilities. There is some evidence also that Soviet propaganda concerning the facilities may have failed to mention the loan aspect of the financial assistance. In any case, the Soviet Union made use of its position to promote its foreign relations policies by sending Anastas Mikoyan, then Vice Prime Minister of the U.S.S.R., to Indonesia to attend the celebrations of the Opening Dedication of the Sports Complex by Soekarno.

An understanding of Indonesia's volatile domestic and international situations at this time is essential if subsequent developments are to be seen in context. As a very young country Indonesia was still politically and economically unstable. Because of its vast natural resources, its large land mass and population, and its strategic importance in the South East Asian area, Indonesia was the subject of intense interest on the part of both Western-bloc and socialist-bloc countries. Soekarno's vision was of an independent, self-sufficient nation; Indonesians had borne the yoke of Dutch colonial rule too long to become second-class citizens in a Western or socialist puppet country. Thus it became Indonesian policy to encourage the major world powers to "compete" for Indonesia via technical assistance, foreign aid programs and the like. By pitting the U.S. and the U.S.S.R. against each other in this way, Indonesia could maintain a precarious independence and neutrality while reaping developmental aid from each.

The U.S. and the U.S.S.R., both established world powers, were viewed as potential threats to Indonesian independence. The People's Republic of China, however, was seen as a powerful friend. Like Indonesia it was a new nation, rich in natural resources and with a large land mass and population. Many of its problems were similar to Indonesia's, and it had similar concerns regarding economic development and the safeguarding of territory and independence. Furthermore, the People's Republic of China was not in a position to actively subvert--by political and economic means--the Indonesian goals of political independence and economic self-sufficiency. The People's Republic of China was also sufficiently at odds with both the U.S. and the U.S.S.R. to lend weight to Indonesia's struggle to maintain a politically and economically independent national government. For these reasons and others, it was extremely important for Indonesia to maintain good relations with the People's Republic of China.

It was also important for Indonesia to maintain friendly relations with its Arab allies. Aside from the international strength gained by such ties, there were crucial factors on the domestic front which determined Indonesian policy. The overwhelmingly Moslem population and the powerful Moslem political parties of Indonesia meant that a serious rift with the Arab countries would result in a political explosion at home, with conceivably disastrous consequences for the Indonesian government.

Taking into consideration the various forces which were molding the Indonesian nation, it is not surprising that the Indonesian government decided it would be political suicide to publicly recognize the existence of the Republic of China (Taiwan) and Israel by granting permission to nationals from these countries to enter Indonesia.

The refusal of the Indonesian Department of Foreign Affairs to issue visas to nationals from Taiwan and Israel forced the Organizing Committee for the Fourth Asian Games to delay sending invitations to the member countries of the Asian Games Federation. This created curiosity among several member countries. In order to show that the Games would be held on time and that the Organizing Committee intended to invite all member countries of the Asian Games Federation, an extraordinary meeting of the Asian Games Federation Executive Committee was called in Jakarta in April of 1962. In order to convince the Executive Committee members that the Organizing Committee was planning to issue invitations to Taiwan and Israel, an inspection was made of the "international village" where the athletes would be boarded. During the open house inspection, the name boards and national flags of Taiwan and Israel were displayed along with those of the other countries. The Executive Committee members were satisfied with the preparations, and representatives from Taiwan and Israel who attended the meeting had their suspicions somewhat allayed. However, even this mild show elicited concerned enquiries from Indonesian politicians and the foreign diplomatic authorities from the Arab countries and the People's Republic of China. They became even more upset when they learned that the national anthems of Taiwan and Israel were being practiced by the Fourth Asian Games music corps.

In July of 1962, a month before the Games, the Indonesian ambassador to the People's Republic of China in Peking suddenly appeared in Jakarta with a message and an official letter from Chinese Prime Minister Chou En-Lai to President Soekarno, indicating that the government of the People's Republic of China would submit a strong protest to the government of the Republic of Indonesia if Taiwan were allowed to take part in the Fourth Asian Games as a representative of China. At the same time the National Olympic Committee of the Republic of China (Taiwan) was making an appeal to the member countries of the Asian Games Federation and to the International Olympic Committee to boycott the Fourth Asian Games in Jakarta if Taiwan was not included in the Games.

On August 21, 1962 when all contingents from member countries, including South Korea--but with the exception of Taiwan and Israel--had arrived in Jakarta, the Indonesian government was still refusing to grant visas to the athletes from Taiwan and Israel. An attempt was made by the representative of Taiwan, Dr. Gun-Sun Hoh, to enter Indonesia without a visa. He arrived on August 21, 1962 at Kemayoran Airport in Jakarta by Cathay Airways from Bangkok, but the Indonesian Immigration Officer denied him entry into the country and sent him back to Bangkok.

At this point the Indian representative, G. D. Sondhi, initiated a campaign to cancel the Fourth Asian Games. He proposed that the sports competitions be held not under the name of the Fourth Asian Games, but under the title of the Jakarta Games. A plenary meeting of the Asian Games Federation was called on August 22 but failed to reach a consensus. The meeting was extended to August 23 and lasted into the morning of August 24 without any agreement being reached. The Indonesian government stood firmly on its denial of visas to the Taiwanese and Israelis while Sondhi remained adamant that the Fourth Asian Games could not take place unless permission were granted to the teams from Taiwan and Israel to enter Indonesia. Since the opening of the Games was scheduled for the afternoon of August 24, a temporary agreement was reached to extend the meeting once again so the Organizing Committee could proceed with the Opening Ceremony according to schedule. At 4:00 p.m. on Friday, August 24, 1962, President Soekarno officially opened the Fourth Asian Games.

Sondhi then proposed to the President of the Asian Games Federation, the Indonesian Sultan Hamengku Buwono IX, that the continuation of the plenary meeting of August 22, 23/24 be held on August 26. Since the decision to extend the plenary meeting had not specified the date of the next extension, this proposal was rejected on the grounds that most of the delegates who were supposed to attend the meeting were busy with their competing teams. Frustrated by the decision of the President of the Asian Games Federation, Sondhi called a meeting of the Executive Committee of the Asian Games Federation. Since this meeting was called without the knowledge of the President of the Asian Games Federation, the Indonesian Olympic Committee considered Sondhi's action a violation of the Asian Games Federation Constitution and illegal. Sondhi, however, may have looked upon his action as a kind of coup d'etat. Obviously considering the meeting legal, he issued a statement to the press stating that the Executive Committee of the Asian Games Federation in its meeting of August 26, 1962 had decided not to recognize the games in Jakarta as the Fourth Asian Games, but called the games the Jakarta Games. This press release caused the International Weight Lifting Federation and the International Basketball Federation to withdraw their recognition, resulting in the cancellation of the weight lifting and basketball competitions.

To forestall further action on the part of Sondhi, a plenary meeting of the Asian Games Federation was called again on August 28, 1962. Participants at this meeting decided not to change the agreements reached on August 23/24, i.e., that the Fourth Asian Games was to be opened on August 24 and that a Fact Finding Committee consisting of three member representatives from Thailand, Burma and South Korea should gather information concerning the case of Taiwan and Israel.

On September 3, the day before the closing of the Games, an anti-Sondhi demonstration was organized by political parties and youth organizations consisting mostly of left-wing and anti-Israeli groups. This demonstration was secretly blessed by the Indonesian government and the Organizing Committee. Understanding that Sondhi had heart trouble, the Organizing Committee for the Fourth Asian Games persuaded Sondhi to move from Hotel Indonesia to one of the homes of the Organizing Committee members. When demonstrators arrived at Hotel Indonesia and could not find Sondhi in his room, they became frustrated and destroyed some of the hotel's property. Assuming that Sondhi would be at the Indian Embassy for protection, the demonstrators marched to the Office of the Indian Embassy. When they found Sondhi was not there either, the demonstration turned into a riot. Taking advantage of the political situation and the "hot" anti-Sondhi demonstrations, the Organizing Committee advised Sondhi to leave Jakarta the afternoon of September 3. Although Sondhi resisted the idea at first, the Organizing Committee finally succeeded in persuading him to leave Jakarta for New Delhi the afternoon of September 3. The Fourth Asian Games was closed September 4 without further political incidents.

Meanwhile, Sondhi's determination to condemn Indonesia's political manipulations against Taiwan and Israel spurred him to use his position as a member of the Executive Board of the International Olympic Committee to involve the IOC in the Fourth Asian Games controversy. His appeal to the

IOC accused the Indonesian Olympic Committee of violating the Olympic Charter and bringing politics into sports via the refusal of the Indonesian government to grant visas to the teams from Taiwan and Israel. The subsequent decision of the IOC Executive Board sent shock waves through the Indonesian community and hardened Indonesian resolves to challenge Western "imperialism."

The Indonesian View of the IOC Decision*

An AP report from Lausanne dated February 9, 1963 stated that IOC President Avery Brundage, emerging from a February 7 meeting of the IOC Executive Board, announced that the membership of the Indonesian National Olympic Committee had been suspended indefinitely. The reason cited for the suspension was "the scandalous occurrence at last year's Fourth Asian Games in Jakarta," referring to the refusal of Indonesian government authorities to grant visas to the athletes from Taiwan and Israel. Brundage stated that the decision of the IOC Executive Board was final and did not require approval of the IOC Congress scheduled to meet in Nairobi later that year. Brundage went on to state that the suspension would be rescinded only if the Indonesian National Olympic Committee came up with guarantees that there would be no further political discrimination in the country. One IOC member who refused to be quoted said he expected Indonesian representatives to show up in Nairobi with the guarantees. The Indonesian reaction could not have been more misjudged.

There were a number of reasons why Indonesia rejected the censure of the IOC Executive Board. Common to all the Indonesian charges was the theme of political manipulation on the part of the IOC to support the policies of certain Western-bloc countries. An examination of the Indonesian position gives an idea of the feelings of outrage which prompted Indonesian withdrawal from the IOC.

First of all, Indonesian authorities were caught off-guard by press reports of the February 7 decision. Since the issue of the Fourth Asian Games dispute was on the agenda of a meeting dealing with "Sports and Politics" scheduled for February 8 between the IOC and 26 International sports federations, early news bulletins citing the February 7 suspension were widely discounted in Indonesia as being of doubtful accuracy. It was not until the detailed AP release of February 9 that Indonesian authorities realized how the decision had been reached. The abrupt suspension was doubly unexpected since in November of 1962 IOC Chancellor Otto Mayer had assured the President of the Indonesian Olympic Committee, Prince Paku Alam VIII, that Indonesia would be given an opportunity to present its side of the dispute to the Executive Board of the IOC.

Furthermore, Indonesian leaders were deeply angered by the statements Brundage made to the press before Indonesia was notified of its suspension. The two-sentence letter of Otto Mayer informing the Indonesian Olympic Committee of the suspension "...because of the manner in which

---

* Source: Indonesian Olympic Committee, <u>Indonesia and the International Olympic Committee</u>, Jakarta: Komite Olympiade Indonesia, 1963.

the so-called Fourth Asian Games were conducted and because of occurrences in connection therewith..." was dated February 13 and arrived in Indonesia considerably later.

Of special concern to Indonesian authorities was the statement by Brundage that the decision of the Executive Board was final and did not require approval of the IOC Congress. The suspension of the Indonesian Olympic Committee was a decision unprecedented in the 69-year history of the IOC, yet it was reached during a meeting at which only four of the eight members of the IOC Executive Board were present. Brundage's dictum was viewed as in direct violation of Article 15 of the Rules and Regulations of the International Olympic Committee:

> 15. The Executive Board or the President alone may take action or make a decision where circumstances do not permit it to be taken by the International Olympic Committee. Such action or decision is subject to ratification by the Committee at its next meeting. *

Since the IOC Charter contains no articles specifying sanctions for infringements of the Olympic Games regulations, Indonesia felt singled out for extraordinarily harsh punishment. Speculation arose as to whether the IOC regarded Indonesia as so relatively insignificant it could be used as an experimental guinea pig. For the most part, however, Indonesians saw the suspension as one more arbitrary IOC decision designed to support the political policies of the NATO nations.

The IOC's recognition of two China's was seen to mirror "imperialistic" Western policy. The IOC's paradoxical failure to recognize two Germanies was likewise interpreted as in support of "imperialistic" Western policies. The latter IOC position was seen as enabling the U.S. to refuse visas to athletes from the German Democratic Republic for the winter Olympic Games in 1960 without fear of IOC reprisal. In the case of South Africa it was noted that racial discrimination in the selection of athletes for the Rome Olympics in 1960 elicited a warning but not a suspension from the IOC, another policy in line with that of "imperialistic" Western countries.

Indonesia thus saw the IOC as manipulating its sports policies to serve the political interests of the NATO-bloc countries. In this context the IOC suspension of the Indonesian Olympic Committee represented--not only in the severity of the sanction, but also in the manner in which it was carried out--an extension of "imperialistic" Western policy which was intolerable to a nation which had recently struggled for independence from Western colonial rulers.

On February 14, 1963 the Indonesian Olympic Committee sent a cable to the IOC in Lausanne. The cable announced Indonesia's decision to withdraw from the IOC and accused the IOC Executive Board of violating the IOC Charter in order to serve the political maneuvers of Taiwan and Israel. No

---

* Quoted in: Ibid., p. 9.

reply was forthcoming from the IOC, but sympathy for the Indonesian position was voiced by a number of countries, including the People's Republic of China, Cambodia, Vietnam, the Arab League, and the U.S.S.R. In April, 1963 Iraq officially notified the IOC of its withdrawal from the Tokyo Olympics as a token of solidarity with Indonesia. The IOC decision thus added momentum to the Third World movement towards a political alliance, of which the Games of the New Emerging Forces was to be the first step.

The Games of the New Emerging Forces

Five years after Nehru initiated the Asian Conference to promote Asian unity against Western colonialism, Indonesian Prime Minister Ali Sastroamidjojo elaborated the idea to incorporate Asian-African cooperation. This idea was proposed to and accepted by the Conference of the five Asian Prime Ministers--U Nu of Burma, Sir John Kotelawala of Ceylon, Jawaharlal Nehru of India, Ali Sastroamidjojo of Indonesia and Mohammed Ali of Pakistan--held at Colombo and Kandy in April-May of 1954. The five Asian prime ministers met again in Bogor, Indonesia in December of 1954. At this Bogor meeting the final agreement was reached that an Asian-African Conference would be held in April of 1955 in the city of Bandung, Indonesia for the following purposes:

1. to poomote goodwill and cooperation among the nations of Asia and Africa, to explore and advance their mutual as well as common interests and to establish and further friendliness and neighbourly relations;
2. to consider social, economic and cultural problems and relations of the countries represented;
3. to consider problems of special interest to Asian and African peoples, e.g. problems affecting national sovereignty and of racialism and colonialism;
4. to view the position of Asia and Africa and their peoples in the world of today and the contribution they can make to the promotion of world peace and cooperation.*

This idea of an Asian-African Conference was well accepted by the newly independent nations of Asia and Africa. The Conference was held in Bandung, Indonesia April 18-24, 1955, attended by prime ministers and state representatives and their delegates from twenty-nine Asian and African countries. The Conference issued a statement called the "Final Communique of the Asian-African Conference" which included a general outlined agreement on economic cooperation, cultural cooperation, support of the fundamental principles of human rights as set forth in the Charter of the United Nations, the condemnation of colonialism and the promotion of world peace. The Conference, which was politically aimed at challenging the world balance of power, did not have nearly as much effect as had been desired. This was evident in the political attitudes of the dominant Western

---

* Indonesia, Republic of, Ministry of Foreign Affairs, Asia-Africa Speaks from Bandung, Jakarta, Ministry of Foreign Affairs, Republic of Indonesia, 1955, p. 13.

countries in the world political arena. However, the Conference did facilitate communication between the Asian and African countries, particularly between the People's Republic of China and other countries in Asia and Africa. Four years later Indonesian President Soekarno extended the idea of Asian-African unity and cooperation to include Latin America.

Soekarno's attempt to develop a New World Order which would give a strong voice to the developing nations of Asia, Africa and Latin America was inspired by a number of factors in the Indonesian and world situation at that time. These included Soekarno's frustration over failures to improve Indonesia's economic and industrial development; the termination of negotiations between the Indonesian and Dutch governments concerning the status of New Irian (West New Guinea); the struggle of the People's Republic of China to obtain admission to the United Nations; political tensions in the Middle East, especially between the Arab countries and Israel; unsatisfactory relations between North America and the South American countries; and Soekarno's personal ambition to be recognized as the political leader of the developing nations. By unifying the Asian, African and Latin American countries on a basis of common interests, Soekarno hoped to shake the world balance of power and weaken the economic domination of the world by the industrialized countries. The developing nations, which Soekarno considered as consisting of three-fourths of the world population, were the New Emerging Forces while the industrialized countries were the Old Established Order. These ideas of Soekarno were reflected in several of his national and international speeches.

In his Independence Day Address on August 17, 1959, Soekarno stated that three-fourths of the world's population was still in revolution and that the emerging nations had to help each other, inspire each other, give to and take from each other in the search for new concepts of revolution.

During his Address to the Fifteenth General Assembly of the United Nations on September 30, 1960 Soekarno declared that the voices of the New Emerging Nations in Asia and Africa should be heard. He said that the older established nations should not underestimate the force of nationalism among the peoples of Asia and Africa, who were opposed to imperialism and colonialism. He stated that the fate of humanity could no longer be decided by a few large and powerful nations. Finally, he strongly supported the admission of the People's Republic of China to the United Nations.

In his Address on Indonesia's Heroes Day, which he delivered from Tokyo on November 10, 1962, Soekarno stated that he was taking one more step towards the liberation of all mankind from the slavery and exploitation of imperialism and colonialism. For this reason he announced his intention to extend the Asian-African Solidarity Conference to an Asian-African-Latin American Solidarity Conference. Finding the Asian Games too limited in scope, he was planning to create the "Games of the New Emerging Forces of the World." He defined the GANEFO as the Games of the Asian Peoples, Games of the African Peoples, Games of the Latin American Peoples, and Games of the Peoples of the Socialist Countries. The socialist countries were included primarily because their more advanced technology, industry and experts represented a dimension of strength which could be used to add weight to the Third World movement.

In his Opening Address to the Asian-African Journalists' Conference in Jakarta on April 24, 1963, Soekarno made the following remarks:

> Let us look around us. What do we see? The vast continents of Asia, Africa and Latin America are still involved in upheaval, are still involved in turmoil, are still involved in turbulence. Why is this? This is part of a process of struggle to burst asunder the chains of suppression and exploitation that linger even after we have achieved political independence for our nations, obstructing our growth.

> To release ourselves from the spiritual and mental bondage of the colonial past, and then to explore and exploit our personality, our potentials and those of our nation--these are the essentials of nationhood in the modern age. It is the search for these things as the basis for new nationhood that is the cause of this upheaval in our continents, an upheaval which constitutes a confrontation between the New Emerging Forces and that Old Established Order which throve upon the exploitation of its fellowmen.

> This upheaval, this process of growth is to be seen in the Latin American countries, as we see it in Cuba; it is to be seen in many countries of Africa, as we see it in Ghana, Guinea, and the United Arab Republic; it is to be seen in many countries in Asia, including here in Indonesia.*

The time was becoming ripe for Soekarno to initiate the GANEFO. Situations at the national and international levels which led to and strengthened this move included: political anomalies associated with international sport movements, of which the Fourth Asian Games was the prominent example; Indonesia's break with the IOC; the "two China's" and "one Germany" policies of the IOC, which were perceived by Soekarno as extensions of imperialistic Western domination; racial discrimination in sports, of which South Africa was the leading example; and Indonesia's deteriorating relations with the United Nations, an organization which was viewed by Soekarno as a tool of Western imperialistic policies. The extensive facilities and experience gained from the Fourth Asian Games provided the perfect setting for an organized challenge to the Old Established Order.

The underlying idea behind the GANEFO was to set the stage for the Conference of the New Emerging Forces, which was intended to establish a Third World United Nations style organization composed primarily of Asian, African and Latin American countries. The cooperative aspects of GANEFO

---

* Indonesia, Republic of, Department of Information, Let Us Transform the World, Opening Address by H. E. President Sukarno at the Asian-African Journalists' Conference on April 24, 1963, Jakarta: Department of Information, Republic of Indonesia, 1963, pp. 8-9.

were planned to be a forerunner of a parallel alliance in the political arena. The purpose of such an alliance was to give the resource-rich Third World countries a unified political power base from which to bargain with the technologically advanced countries. The prospect of two United Nations organizations had political ramifications which were designed to shake the world balance of power.

A Preparatory Conference for the GANEFO was held in Jakarta April 27-29, 1963. This Conference was attended by representatives from Cambodia, China (People's Republic), Guinea, Indonesia, Iraq, Mali, Pakistan, Vietnam (Democratic Republic), the United Arab Republic, and the U.S.S.R., with observers from Ceylon and Yugoslavia. The Conference granted full support to Soekarno's proposals and announced to the world the birth of the GANEFO on April 29, 1963. Some of the important decisions of the Conference were stated as follows:

1. the GANEFO are based on the SPIRIT of the ASIAN-AFRICAN CONFERENCE in BANDUNG and the Olympic Ideals and are aimed at:
   a. encouraging the promotion of the independent development of sports and physical culture and of sports movements in all countries of the NEW EMERGING FORCES;
   b. stimulating sport competitions among the youth of the NEW EMERGING FORCES in particular and to promote friendship [sic] and world-peace in general.
2. The GANEFO will be held for the first time in the middle of NOVEMBER 1963 in DJAKARTA.
3. The GANEFO are celebrated every four years among the youth of the NEW EMERGING FORCES in friendly and equal amateur sports-competitions.*

The Conference further decided that:

Invitations to take part in the First G.A.N.E.F.O. in Djakarta will be sent out to all countries of the NEW EMERGING FORCES which are:
(1) Countries, which are faithful to the BANDUNG-PRINCIPLES;
(2) Countries participating in the Preparatory Conference of the G.A.N.E.F.O. in Djakarta, 27-29, April 1963;
(3) Countries which have stated that they support the G.A.N.E.F.O. IDEA;
(4) Socialist countries;
(5) Other countries or communities of the New Emerging Forces in Asia, Africa, Latin America and Europe which apply to take part in the first G.A.N.E.F.O. in Djakarta.**

---

* Games of the New Emerging Forces, Documents on the Preparatory Conference for the GANEFO Held in Djakarta, 27th, 28th and 29th, April 1963. Printed by DITTOP. AD., 1963, pp. 8-9.
** Ibid., Appendix, p. 23.

Sixty-eight countries from Asia, Africa, the Americas and Europe were invited to take part in the First GANEFO. Despite the strong opposition of the International Olympic Committee, which threatened disqualification of GANEFO participants from the 1964 Tokyo Olympic Games, fifty-one of the sixty-eight countries responded favorably to the invitations. Of these, forty-eight countries actually sent sports teams to Jakarta.

Soekarno employed astute political diplomacy with some countries to persuade them to send representatives to the First GANEFO. When relations between Indonesia and the Netherlands were normalized in 1963, the Netherlands and Belgium were suddenly considered by Soekarno as belonging to the New Emerging Forces and were invited to participate in the GANEFO. Malaysia and Singapore, on the other hand, were considered allies of the Old Established Force of Great Britain and were not invited. For both psychological and political reasons, the Dutch and the Belgians accepted Soekarno's invitation and subsequently participated in the GANEFO.

Although the U.S.A. was not on the official list of the sixty-eight invited countries, it was secretly considered a potential New Emerging Force. Soekarno even made an informal approach to the U. S. Ambassador to Indonesia at that time, Jones, to try to persuade the U.S. government to send a team to the GANEFO. Aside from the fact that the U.S. government certainly would not consider such an invitation, the administrative and political systems in the U.S. made it impossible for Washington to form a "Federal Government Sport Team" to represent the U.S. in the GANEFO. Above all, since the U.S. opposed the Conference of the New Emerging Forces and the establishment of the Federation of the New Emerging Forces, U.S. participation in the GANEFO would have weakened the U.S. position.

It was a major triumph for Indonesia when Japan, which would be the site of the 1964 Olympic Games, accepted the invitation to take part in the GANEFO. The Japanese decision was motivated by a desire to improve political and business relations with Indonesia and its supporters. At the same time, the Arab countries were planning to launch a movement to boycott the Olympic Games unless the IOC removed sanctions against GANEFO participants. This combination of developments forced the IOC to back down from its rigid position and, in order to save the 1964 Olympic Games, soften its sanctions against GANEFO participants. Furthermore, in its meeting on June 26, 1964 in Lausanne, the IOC rescinded its suspension of the Indonesian Olympic Committee.*

The U.S.S.R. and the Eastern European countries played somewhat cautious "wait and see" politics. This was due to an awareness that they were being used by Soekarno to strengthen his attempt to establish a major Third World power which would not necessarily have been in the best interests of the U.S.S.R. and its satellite countries. These countries participated in the GANEFO, but sent only small limited teams.

---

* Indonesia did not officially respond to the new IOC decision but did send a team to the Tokyo Olympics. Dissension arose concerning inconsistencies in the application of sanctions against GANEFO participants, and Indonesia withdrew its team from competition in protest.

The largest GANEFO teams were those of Indonesia and the People's Republic of China. Much speculation exists concerning the extent of assistance rendered the GANEFO by the People's Republic of China. Whatever its extent, it remained low key and behind-the-scenes; however, the Chinese did demonstrate their support by publicly congratulating Soekarno and the Indonesians for their success in initiating and realizing the GANEFO. Nothing detracted from the center stage role of Indonesia in the GANEFO movement.

The forty-eight countries which participated in the First GANEFO were: Afghanistan, Albania, Algeria, Argentina, Arab Palestine, Belgium, Bolivia, Brazil, Bulgaria, Burma, Cambodia, Ceylon, Chile, China (People's Republic), Cuba, Czechoslovakia, Dominican Republic, Finland, France, Germany (Democratic Republic), Guinea, Hungary, Indonesia, Iraq, Italy, Japan, Korea (North), Laos, Lebanon, Mali, Morocco, Mexico, Netherlands, Nigeria, Pakistan, Philippines, Poland, Rumania, Saudi Arabia, Somalia, Syria, Thailand, Tunisia, United Arab Republic, U.S.S.R., Uruguay, Vietnam (Democratic Republic), and Yugoslavia. The three countries which were planning to participate but which were unable to attend were Mongolia, Senegal and Venezuela.

The first GANEFO, held in Jakarta November 10-22, 1963, was a triumphant success. Most of the emerging nations were represented, approximately 3,000 participants were reported to have taken part, and several world records were broken.

Immediately following the GANEFO celebrations, the First GANEFO Congress was held in Jakarta, November 24-25, 1963. In a keynote address at the opening of the Congress, Soekarno expanded his definition of the New Emerging Forces to include all those forces--whether in new countries or old--which were fighting against the concept of "exploitation de l'homme par l'homme" and struggling for a new world of friendship among nations and brotherhood among men. The Congress adopted the Charter of the GANEFO and the establishment of the GANEFO Federation,* and awarded Soekarno the title of Founder and Honorary President of the GANEFO. The Indonesian Minister of Sports, Maladi, was elected President of the Executive Board of the GANEFO Federation, and Jakarta was specified as the site of the permanent headquarters of the GANEFO.

Despite the overwhelming success of the First GANEFO, the far-reaching political plan with which it was associated was never realized. Strong opposition from the U.S.A. and Western European countries, political developments in Asia, Africa and Latin America, and the fall of Soekarno after the confused coup attempt of the Indonesian Communist Party in 1965, all conspired to prevent the Conference of the New Emerging Forces from ever being held. The plan for the establishment of a world Federation of the New Emerging Forces was foiled by extensive shifts in the international political scene.

---

* The establishment of the GANEFO Federation was included in the Charter of the GANEFO, Chapter III, Article 4, paragraph (1).

The Second GANEFO, which was scheduled to be held in Cairo with Peking as an alternative site, was never held. Cairo withdrew its bid to host the Second GANEFO due to political developments in Asia and the Middle East and Egypt's internal political and economic problems. Peking, the alternate site, did not take over since China's major political supporters, including Indonesia, were no longer interested in the GANEFO. For the People's Republic of China itself, the GANEFO and the establishment of a new world organization were no longer major political strategies due to changes in the world political situation. The political position of the People's Republic of China had become stronger on the international front; Canada, the U.S. and its allies had become more friendly, and Taiwan was no longer considered a threat. In Southeast Asia the new anti-communist government of Indonesia accused the People's Republic of China of supporting the Indonesian Communist Party, froze diplomatic relations, and opened a business relationship with Taiwan. Indonesia also became more dependent on the U.S. and its allies. Meanwhile, the Philippines, Singapore, Malaysia and Thailand became friendlier to the People's Republic of China. Finally, Peking's effort to replace Taiwan in the United Nations Organization had become stronger, in effect rendering the creation of a new world organization unnecessary to the achievement of Peking's goals on the international scene. Although the member countries of the Federation of the GANEFO never met to officially dissolve the organization, the GANEFO and its dreams of a united Third World power sank into quiet oblivion.

Prior to the deterioration of relations between Indonesia and the Peking government, an Asian Regional GANEFO Committee was formed in September of 1965 in Peking. The Committee decided to hold an Asian GANEFO in Pnom Penh, Cambodia. The First Asian GANEFO, which was held in Pnom Penh from November 25 to December 6, 1966, was attended by fifteen Asian countries, mostly non-members of the Asian Games Federation. These fifteen countries were: Arab Palestine, Cambodia, Ceylon, China (People's Republic), Indonesia, Iraq, Korea (People's Democratic Republic), Laos, Lebanon, Mongolia, Pakistan, Saudi Arabia, Syria, Vietnam (Democratic Republic), and Yemen. Due to political developments in Asia, particularly in Indonesia and Indo-China, the Asian GANEFO became inactive and no subsequent games were held.

The Fifth and Following Asian Games

Three days after the First Asian GANEFO took place, the Fifth Asian Games was held in Bangkok, Thailand, December 9-20, 1966. It was attended by the usual members of the Asian Games Federation, including Indonesia, Israel and Taiwan, without political incident. The Sixth Asian Games was held in Bangkok in December of 1970 with no major political changes. However, at the Seventh Asian Games held in Teheran, Iran in 1974, the People's Republic of China replaced the Republic of China (Taiwan) as the representative of China. A minor political incident occurred when countries sympathizing with the Arabs refused to compete against Israel. The Eighth Asian Games will be held in Bangkok again at the end of 1978, with the provision that Israel be excluded from participation.

Conclusion

The first and only GANEFO is an interesting study of the power of sports in international political and economic struggles. It represented a singular and impressive display symbolizing the economic and political independence sought by nations recently freed from the bonds of colonial rule. Its time came and its time passed but its symbolism remains, a footnote in history.

The Fourth Asian Games and the GANEFO highlight the interplay among politics, power struggles and sports competitions. The principle of separation of politics and sports is a laudable ideal, but failure to recognize the realities which limit achievement of an ideal can only lead to a position of weakness and hypocrisy. In sports, winning is the name of the game; in politics, it is power. To ignore the power of politics in sports is to lose the ability to cope with it.

The history of the modern Olympic Games is riddled with breakdowns in the doctrine of separation of sports and politics--some of them minor, some of them violent. All of them have related directly or indirectly to world politics and international power struggles. Perhaps it is time for proponents of a "pure" Olympic movement to begin making provision for the realities of politics in sports.

Bibliography

Games of the New Emerging Forces, Charter of the Federation of the Games of the New Emerging Forces, the GANEFO, 1963.

_____, Documents of the First GANEFO Congress, Djakarta, 24th-25th, November, 1963. Printed by DITTOP. AD., 62, 1964.

_____, Documents of the GANEFO Preparatory Committee, Djakarta, 23rd-24th-25th, November, 1963. Printed by DITTOP. AD., 67, 1964.

_____, Documents on the Preparatory Conference for the GANEFO Held in Djakarta, 27th, 28th and 29th, April, 1963. Printed by DITTOP. AD., 1963.

Hanna, W. A., "The Politics of Sports," American University Field Staff, Southeast Asia Series, Vol. X:No. 19, October, 1962.

Indonesian Olympic Committee, Indonesia and the International Olympic Committee, Jakarta: Komite Olympiade Indonesia, 1963.

Indonesia, Republic of, Department of Information, Let Us Transform the World, Opening Address by H. E. President Sukarno at the Asian-African Journalists' Conference on April 24, 1963, Jakarta: Department of Information, Republic of Indonesia, 1963.

_____, Department of Information, To Build the World Anew, President Sukarno's Address Before the Fifteenth General Assembly of the United Nations on Friday 30th, September, 1960, Special Issue No. 6 Jakarta: Department of Information, Republic of Indonesia, 1960.

_____, Department of Information, Penemuan Kembali Revolusi Kita, Penerbitan Chusus No. 60, Jakarta: Kementerian Penerangan Republik Indonesia, 1959. (The Rediscovery of Our Revolution, Address of the President of the Republic of Indonesia on August 17, 1959.)

_____, Ministry of Foreign Affairs, Asia-Africa Speaks from Bandung Jakarta: Ministry of Foreign Affairs, Republic of Indonesia, 1955.

Komite Nasional GANEFO, Dokumen-Dokumen Kelahiran GANEFO, Siaran 3 - Komite Nasional GANEFO, Jakarta: Sekretariat Komite Nasional GANEFO, 1963. (Documents of the Birth of GANEFO.)

Maladi, "Hubungan Gelora Senajan dengan Hari Depan Keolahragaan Indonesia." Unpublished Document, Directorate General of Sports and Youth Department of Education and Culture, Republic of Indonesia, Jakarta 1972. ("The Relationship of the Senayan Stadium Complex to the Future of Sports in Indonesia.")

Organizing Committee of the Preparatory Conference for the GANEFO, Preparatory Conference for the GANEFO and the Asian-African Football Tournament, Djakarta, April, 1963, Jakarta: The Organizing Committee of the Preparatory Conference for the GANEFO, 1963.

Sie, Swanpo, "Sports and Politics in Asia." Paper presented to the Scientific Congress held in conjunction with the Olympic Games in Munich August 21-25, 1972.

_____, "The Problem of Sport and Nation Building in Southeast Asia, Zeitschrift für Kulturaustausch, 27: No. 4, 59-65, 1977; ditto in Sport und Kulturwandel, (Redaktion: Ernst J. Tetsch), Band 5, Stuttgart: Institut für Auslandsbeziehungen, 1978, pp. 59-65.

Section 4

POLICY AND INTERNATIONAL SPORT

Introduction

The national sports policies of governments have come into prominence as states have developed international sports relationships. Governments use the identification between athlete and state to demonstrate the temper of relations between the nations involved, and modern communication systems make the general public aware of competitions with various other states. Thus, contests become a form of public diplomacy. Today, when a state holds athletic events with another country, the existence of such a contact has come to symbolize recognition of that country and its government. Conversely, the refusal to have sports exchanges with another state or to allow its athletes to be given visas has generally meant diplomatic non-recognition.

In this Section of the anthology, the domestic organization of sport relational to foreign policy is the focus of inquiry, not international institutions or transnational interchange. Sport is seen either as a tool of a given regime or as a function of social behavior deserving particularized consideration and emphasis. Depending on the government, sport fits well or imprecisely into existing policy; it has a special significance when it interfaces with concerns of foreign policy. Comparative, rather than International Politics, is the subject-matter of this selection of national sports policies. It is important to consider comparative sport policy in order that each state's use of international sport institutions is better understood. Since common organs serve as the arena of political sport, the same methods of policy articulations can be used by states with very different intentions behind them. When transnational sport is considered separately from its political units, as well as apart from its general political content, there is a tendency to misunderstand the purposes of each participant. As in any political process, asymmetry of perceptions can lead to an experience more likely to increase than decrease frustration and hostility.

The number of competitions between states on a bilateral basis has increased dramatically, as has the number of international invitational meets. This increase in sports events has been accompanied by a rise in governmental interest in sports. Any reluctance on the part of states to use sport politics has been dispelled as success in international sport has become an objective in the modern era.

In the foregoing Sections of this anthology, we have dealt with transnational sport as an institutional whole. While keeping in mind the cultural diversity of sport participants, the system of sport has been approached from a point of view consistent with its institutional universality.

This focus is altered in Section 4, Policy and International Sport. Comparative Politics, rather than International Relations, is the discipline represented here. The authors of these readings are concerned with the domestic processes of states interested in the use of sport for political socialization. To be sure, the line between domestic politics and foreign policy is a fine one. There are those, of course, who believe that domestic political considerations are the most important factors in shaping a state's international policy. It is certain that internal constraints and the national political culture have a marked influence on the stance assumed by a regime in international affairs. At times, the strain between "rational" state interest and perceived domestic political pressures causes a hybrid foreign policy corresponding neither to domestic demands nor to international expectations.

National sport programs contribute to a number of state goals. Each individual can be made to feel a part in the shaping of national purpose. An extraordinary symbolic case of this principle occurred in the 1964 Summer Olympiad, when Japan hosted the Games. The last torch runner into the stadium, Yoshenori Sakai, was chosen because he had been born in Hiroshima on the day that the atomic bomb had leveled the city. No other single gesture could have been more dramatic or better demonstrated the difference between the old and the new Japan.

The degree to which an athlete must serve in a socialization process differs from state to state, depending on local conditions and ethnic make-up. In all societies, however, the publicity of sport makes its most successful practitioners logical tools for attempted infusions of patriotism.

The athlete usually realizes this. Sometimes, however, Olympic mythology, in combination with inflated ego, leads some athletes to believe that they are on their own. The state can face a difficult choice when faced with sport heroes who both bring glory to their country and refuse to accept the political structures of its leadership. Can a state afford the fame of an individual who takes full advantage of state favor and yet refuses to pay the state homage?

The answer varies with each regime. In general, it depends on how closely each state seeks to control the social life (as opposed to political life) of its citizens. If every aspect of social existence comes under the institutional scrutiny of the government, serious deviation from state policy cannot be tolerated. In more open societies, however, the regime can be satisfied with the benefits of sport triumph, as limited complaints from athletes need not become direct challenges to the state. If the United States can be considered an open society, then the greatest challenge it faced was under the inspiration of Harry Edwards whose boycott leadership prompted the black gloved fist salutes of Tommie Smith and John Carlos. In this case, however, the government of the U.S. does not appear to have been rattled so much as the sports governing body and the citizenry. More substantively, Edwards could not have published the following in any but an open society; speaking of the Black athlete, he says:

> Whether they boycott this year's Olympics because of Nazi-white South Africa (where millions of Blacks suffer an unspeakable slavery and degradation) or because they want the world to know that not all the gold medals in hell are worth

glorifying America's disguised system of Black genocide,
or whether they simply have too much pride and humanity
to prance around in playful Olympics representing a nation
engaged in destroying millions of innocent Vietnamese in a
war the world recognizes as the most inhuman in history,
they must become, not simply "sports," but heroes of humanity. (The Revolt of the Black Athlete, p. 191).

It might be speculated that The Revolt of the Black Athlete is one of the
26,000 books banned by the Publications Control Board of South Africa.

Thus, we are reminded that it is the state, not the "nation" that we are
dealing with. Western modes of political organization do not always correspond to actual boundaries between ethnic groups (the construction "nation-
state" is an often-used term which has little meaning except for units in
which political loyalty and ethnic identification coincide). As in the case of
Mobutu and the Ali-Foreman fight, state leaders can try to forge patriotic
(as opposed to nationalistic) consciousness through exploitation of national
heroes.

Athletes become important in the search for legitimacy through their
bonds with spectators. In domestic sport, as well as in the Olympic Games
or World Cup, the fan is more important than the athlete. The social model
of patriotic behavior matters more than the simple record of sports achievement.

Once more, however, the athlete must behave. Defection is as great
an embarrassment in the political as in the ideological sense. Short of that,
the image of a drunken or rowdy egotist who uses the privileges of state
honor for purposes of individual dissipation does nothing for the prestige of
the state which pampers the athlete.

In a multi-national state, athletes must maintain a precarious balance
(if they are to "let go," it must be abroad--as with the Soviet ice hockey
players who used trips to the West as a means of acquiring fancy clothes and
entrance to pornographic movies). On one hand, of course, athletes must be
loyal to the state, for the honors and standard of living acquired through
sport must be viewed as a medium of gratitude to the state. On the other
hand, athletes must not lose ties with their own people. Fans who perceive
that an athlete has shed the signs of national origins (language, accent, religion, style of dress, residence, etc.) may lose interest. In conforming too
closely to a dominant "staatsvolk" culture, the athlete might lose value to
the state. The very adoption of the trappings of dominant culture can cause
the sports person to become alienated from the very people whose political
support the athlete is supposed to obtain.

Internal government policy and policy for the prestige of the state in
international relations often overlap when international sports events are the
focus of attention. The proximity of sport and tourism, each often falling
within the aegis of a Department of Cultural Affairs in government, provides
suitable occasion for bringing internal and foreign policy closer together.
Many countries have combined the cabinet posts of tourism and sports into

one office. The staging of large international events results in large press coverage. Athletes, coaches, officials and managers can take back reports which add to the press coverage. The status of a country as a vacation or convention center, as well as a sports mecca, can be raised. Egypt established rowing races at Luxor and sponsored the Arabian Horse Show in attempts to encourage tourism. Austria has benefitted greatly from the two Winter Olympics held in Innsbruck. Grenoble built a new city hall, post office, school, hospital, police station, airport, congress hall, cultural center and many miles of new roads for the 1968 Winter Olympics at a cost of $200 million. Munich constructed a huge new airport and a subway system, in addition to the customary new sports complex, when the city hosted the 1972 Games. Tunisia hoped to stimulate tourism by hosting the 1967 Mediterranean Games. The prestige of becoming an international tourist center was seen by all these countries as outweighing the initial costs, since tourists would bring in foreign currencies and improve the balance of payments.

Since countries often invested so much in planning for such international sport contests and staked their prestige on the successful conclusion of these events, they often tried to conceal various problems such as labor strikes, work stoppages, construction delays, terrorism, the presence of epidemics and domestic unrest from the outside word. A postponement or cancellation could cause a loss of prestige. It would be taken as a sign of weakness and disorganization. The Mexican government took great pains to control and quiet student unrest prior to the 1968 Games. The Brazilians continually promised that everything would be ready on time for the 1975 Pan American Games scheduled for Sao Paulo. Ultimately Mexico City had to step in and take over the Games.

The Olympic velodrome was to be finished in 1974 in Montreal for the 1974 World Championships in cycling. The city council insisted on maintaining the fiction that the facility would be ready on time. Finally six weeks before the meet was to start, the council admitted defeat and spent $400,000 to build a temporary facility. The council was afraid that it might appear that the facilities for the Olympics would not be finished either and the I.O.C. might move the Games elsewhere. The Canadian government actually had little to do with this affair. Still, the Canadian government stood to profit in terms of prestige just as much from a successful Games as did the city of Montreal. As costs for the Games skyrocketed from an original $130 million to $1.5 billion, the city council and the mayor of Montreal, Jean Drapeau, sought to keep this development as secret as possible and continue the fiction that the Games would be simple and cost the taxpayers nothing. Drapeau was afraid that if the true costs became known, the I.O.C. would take the Games elsewhere. While not supporting the Montreal council financially, the federal government did not make much of an attempt to discern what really was occurring. (Auf der Maur, 1976.)

The Montreal episode is interesting because the main support for the Games did not come from the national government, but rather from a national minority which still felt that it was being discriminated against after three centuries of rule by English speaking settlers. The French Canadians saw a chance to gain a world forum for their demands of more control over their own affairs. Mayor Drapeau and his circle of Club Canadian friends saw the chance to host another international event (after the World's Fair of 1967) that would help place French speaking Canada in the limelight, attract investment and tourists, fill the pockets of the local French Canadian élite with fat construction contracts and decrease the unemployment rate among the French Canadian masses. The fact that Montreal did not have the money to pay for such a spectacle, and still lacked a water filtration plant, adequate low cost housing and enough money to pay municipal employees to keep them from striking, was deemed unimportant. As Drapeau viewed it: "The people will support the Olympics. But they will not support public housing. There is no glory in public housing." This attitude was characteristic of many underdeveloped countries that hosted various regional games and constructed magnificent sports stadiums in the midst of squalid hovels. Such an attitude can become critical in a variety of circumstances. For example, in South America, barbed wire fences around villages of athletes, supplemented by squads of machine-gun carrying soldiers in every possible corner, have become necessary to protect foreign sports teams from radical domestic groups critical of their government's social or political programs, and who are willing to protest the lack of social justice or political liberties with terrorism.

In a particularized study of Canadian Federal Government policy towards the Olympics, Richard Baka traces the history of federal government support for sport both by legislation and by the allocation of funds--particularly for high-level performance sport. Levels of governmental interest and involvement are explored to the point where federal support was shown by government representatives appearing in Innsbruck in 1964 at the bidding of the Winter Olympics to be held in Banff in 1968. For the XX Olympiad to be held in Montreal in 1972, Mayor Jean Drapeau conducted a campaign of "politics of grandeur," pursued with undaunted vigor to successfully win the XXI Olympiad for his city in 1976. Many government agencies were involved to ensure their success.

Riordan suggests that success in sport is regarded by many people of the Soviet Union as a measure of national vitality and prestige; it excites nationalist instincts and fosters group identification. Although there are several distinct periods in the history of Soviet participation in international sport, the post-war period (from 1945 to the present) is most significant in light of the U.S.S.R. emerging as a world power. When the U.S.S.R. enters international competition, it is usually with a team of world-class performance, allowing no risk of humiliation through the medium of sport. Athletes are often used as "ambassadors of goodwill" to propagandize the communist state system before the world at large. In conjunction with the contribution by Riordan, Andrew Strenk investigates the ways in which the German Democratic Republic, a small European nation of 17 million people, used sports to further its foreign policy goals of winning international diplomatic recognition and full sovereignty, as well as bolstering its image in the world as a successful Communist state worthy of emulation by Third World nations. The G.D.R. established a well-organized, administered and financed sports program in the 1950's, refused to bow to pressure by the Federal Republic of Germany, NATO, the International Olympic Committee and the international sports federations, and ultimately by the late 1960's and early 1970's had risen to be one of the premier sports nations in the world. There is no better example of the interaction of sports and politics.

The essay by Lapchick discusses how apartheid became an official government policy in South Africa with the election of the National Party in 1948. Sport has been seen by the South Africans as a valuable means of demonstrating to the world the workings of their social system. The efforts of SAN-ROC (the South African Non-Racial Olympic Committee) were condemned by the government, and the Committee outlawed, thereby officially restricting non-white athletes from participation in the Olympic Games. Cricket and tennis are two non-Olympic sports which South Africa has had trouble pursuing in international tournament due to political activism of athletes and others against apartheid.

The essay by the Shaws, "Sport as Transnational Politics: A Preliminary Analysis of Africa," distinguishes "transnational" as unofficial or informal political ties from "international," the formal nature of political interaction between nations. Sport appears to be a neglected subject in transnational analysis, yet it appears also to have sound potential to test such mechanisms of international intercourse. African states place special emphasis on international sport in their search for prestige. National sports bodies and Pan-African Games are reflected in the international recognition given to the Supreme Council for Sports in Africa (SCSA). Sport as antiracist ideology in the fight against apartheid is discussed to test a model of an international sports institution. The boycott of South Africa from international competition is cited as proof of the success of transnational sports politics.

Roy Clumpner developed "Federal Involvement in Sport to Promote American Interests or Foreign Policy Objectives" from his doctoral dissertation. He examines the effects of international athletic successes (notably by the Soviet Union) on the minds and opinions of congressmen. The concern expressed by Congress found support for the President's Council on Physical Fitness, and Senator Humphrey launched his own proposal for federal support for athletics. Besides Congressional proposals, the Department of State sponsored athletic exchanges with a variety of countries. Some athletic teams were used specifically with foreign policy in mind, explicitly for "ice-breaking" purposes with the Chinese, but also more informally in Peace Corps and People-to-People sports programs. (The editors recall U.S. Government policy in refusing to grant visas to East Germans in 1959 to compete in the modern pentathlon world championships in Harrisburg, Penn., and again in February, 1960, to East German journalists and Olympic staff members to attend the Winter Olympic Games in Squaw Valley. Furthermore, the U.S.A. eventually lost the World Weight Lifting Championships in 1962 to Budapest, because the U.S. Government would not permit the East Germans to enter the United States to compete at Columbus, Ohio—the International Weight Lifting Federation moved the Championships to Budapest.)

In the concluding reading, Nafziger explores legal aspects of a United States foreign sports policy. He raises the question: should the United States have a foreign sports policy? Sport is now a popular movement, and governments harness popular support of sport for diplomatic purposes.

Three levels of government involvement are postulated for the U.S.A., with implications for domestic as well as transnational policy making. An Amateur Athletic Act is proposed, and a foreign sports policy is suggested as a means of protecting individual athletes from political injury.

Clearly, a great deal more work is needed from both the standpoint of individual states and from that of general comparative politics. Just as transnational sport is an intrinsically political process, domestic sport is part of a more general political system. The reader, and researcher as well, will have to distinguish between work which contains a view of sport within its political context, and that which serves as an apology for a particular state or ideology.

Canadian Federal Government Policy

And The 1976 Summer Olympics

Richard Baka

These last few months prior to the opening of the XXI Summer Olympics in Montreal may not be the most appropriate time to examine the topic of our federal government's involvement in these games; this is an issue which was supposedly resolved a number of years ago. However, as the preparations for the 1976 Summer Games stumble along from one crisis to the next, Canadians can ponder where our highest governing body has stood with respect to this issue. What has been the official policy guiding federal support of this unique sports festival which is being held for the first time in our country? One might further ask whether this policy reflects a consistent, rational approach.

Prior to examining such a volatile subject, it is necessary to take a brief historical look at the Canadian federal government's involvement with sport as it specifically relates to the Olympics. Such an examination should help to bring the present situation surrounding the Montreal Games into a contemporary perspective.

As far back as the 1920 Olympics, the Canadian parliament allocated funds to enable Canadians to participate in this major sports event: at that time a sum of $15,000 was given to the Canadian Olympic Association (COA) to help defray the cost of sending athletes to the 1920 Antwerp Games. With the precedent set, federal funds totalling $25,000 and $26,000 were also given to the COA for the 1924 and 1928 Olympic Games respectively. Probably for reasons associated with the depression and the economic hardships which it imposed, reduced sums of $10,000 were made available to the COA for the 1932 and 1936 Olympics.[1]

During this early period when federal funds were first being designated for Olympic participation, an interesting development occurred in the form of a proposal in the House of Commons calling for a Ministry of Sports. A Liberal M.P., H. J. Plaxton, put forth a private member's bill on January 20, 1937 proposing such a ministry with control over athletics and physical

"Reprinted by permission of the Canadian Association for Health, Physical Education and Recreation from the CAHPER Journal, Vol. 42, No. 4, March/April, 1976."

and recreational training. One of his reasons for introducing this bill involved Canada's poor showing at the 1936 Olympics, in particular, the loss of the world ice hockey title to Great Britain. In commenting on Canada's Olympic efforts, Mr. Plaxton was of the following opinion:

> "Need I say more, sir, to convince hon. members of this house that the time is long past when any athlete or group of athletes who presume to represent Canada in Canada's name should be permitted to do so in any international contest without proper supervision and control by someone responsible to this government."[2]

Unfortunately, other members of parliament did not share a similar enthusiasm for such legislation and it died quietly in the house. Despite this failure, new developments in this field soon occurred at the federal level.

During the war years large numbers of unfit Canadians were discovered as a consequence of the armed forces' medical examinations. This was a most important factor in the passage of the 1943 National Physical Fitness Act, the object of which was to promote the physical fitness of Canadians through various programs linked to physical education, sports and athletics. It proved to be a novel and bold attempt which brought about certain positive changes, but over the course of some eleven years the realized policies seldom produced overwhelming or effective results.[3,4] One of the act's inadequacies was its failure to provide any additional support to the COA, or for that matter any type of organized sport, beyond the usual Olympic year grant ($35,000 in 1948 and $40,000 in 1952). One note of interest during this period was a comment in 1947 by a Calgary M.P., A. L. Smith, suggesting that the next Winter Olympics take place in Banff, Alberta, the proposal received no support and was not pursued.[5]

Basically due to ill-conceived legislation, ill-defined objectives and a lack of leadership and direction, Bill 475, An Act to Repeal the National Physical Fitness Act was passed on June 26, 1954.[6] Although the federal government was now absolved of its responsibility in the sport domain, financial support was still given to enhance Canadian participation in international sport. For the 1954 British Empire and Commonwealth Games held in Vancouver, $200,000 in federal grants were given to help finance these games. An additional $10,000 was provided to the British Empire and Commonwealth Games Association of Canada to help send Canadian athletes to this sports festival. Customary grants to the COA also continued and two separate payments of $60,000 were given to help subsidize Canadian athletes who were to represent Canada in the 1956 and 1960 Olympics. A portion of these payments was used to help finance Canadian participation in the Olympic-affiliated Pan-American Games which Canada first took part in at the Second Pan-American Games held in Mexico City in 1955.[7]

During the years immediately following the 1954 Repeal, a strong lobby emerged advocating some type of reinvolvement by the federal government in the area of sport and fitness. One important factor which caused the federal sector to reevaluate its position in this regard was the diminishing success of Canadian athletes and teams in international sporting contests such as the Olympics. Of special concern was the loss of world ice hockey supremacy, considered to be the Canadian forte in the world of athletics. Together with other motives, this led to the passage in 1961 of Bill C-131, An Act to Encourage Fitness and Amateur Sport, a piece of legislation which even to the present day serves as the basis of the federal government's involvement in sport. To carry out the designated functions outlined in the bill, the Fitness and Amateur Sport Directorate[8] was established within the Department of National Health and Welfare and during the 1960's sport-related programs, grants, etc., became much more prominent than in previous years.

One area of support concerned federal grants associated with the Olympics. Between 1961 and the present, substantial sums of money were given to the COA. (See Table 1). This money was used to help meet the expenses incurred during Olympic years, at times when the Pan-American Games were held, and for certain administrative costs and special projects. Furthermore, annual grants were made available to numerous sports governing bodies, many of which used the funds to some extent to aid athletic development for the Olympics.

Table 1. Federal Government Grants to the Canadian Olympic Association.[9]

Year	Amount	Year	Amount
1920	$15,000	1963-64	$106,000
1924	$25,000	1964-65	$134,500
1928	$26,000	1965-66	$ 30,000
1932	$10,000	1966-67	$ 30,000
1936	$10,000	1967-68	$ 86,953
1948	$35,000	1968-69	$150,137
1952	$40,000	1969-70	$ 4,650
1956	$60,000	1970-71	$ 30,779
1960	$60,000	1971-72	$333,054
1961-62	$10,000	1972-73	$229,978
1962-63	$80,000	1973-74	$ 12,000

On another level, interest was once again beginning to grow on the subject of Canada hosting the Olympics for the first time in history.[10] In 1958 a committee in Calgary representing Banff began preparations towards hosting the Olympics and approached the federal government by means of an interim submission through a member of parliament.[11] As these preparations continued in the ensuing years, federal grants were given to three different bodies; the Calgary Olympic Development Association, Olympic '72, and the Garibaldi Olympic Development Association were established to attempt to bring the Olympics to Canada for the 1968, 1972 and 1976 Winter Games respectively.

During this period of lobbying for the right to host the Olympics, the Calgary Olympic Development Association was the largest recipient of federal aid and support. To aid its efforts to obtain the 1968 Games, a total of $110,000 from the Fitness and Amateur Sport Program was allocated to this body between 1962 and 1964. This total, incidentally, constituted only a portion of a shared cost program involving the federal level, the Alberta provincial government and the city of Calgary. Also, since Banff was within the confines of national parkland, federal monies were used to upgrade certain facilities in the area as part of the preparations should the bid be successful. In addition, extensive planning and federal assistance were provided through an interdisciplinary committee chaired by the Deputy Minister of Welfare with representatives from the Departments of External Affairs, Finance, National Defence, Northern Affairs and Natural Resources, and the Canadian Government Travel Bureau.[12] The Minister of National Health and Welfare, the Hon. J. W. Monteith, also reported in 1962 that the total federal costs involved in staging the games would be approximately $8,000,000.[13]

When the bidding for the 1968 Olympics was held in Innsbruck in 1964, the Minister of National Health and Welfare, the Hon. Judy LaMarsh, and other federal representatives were on hand to show the Canadian federal government's support for this application.[14] There is no doubt that the federal government was actively supporting the Banff bid for the 1968 Winter Olympics. After Banff lost out in the bidding for the 1968 Games and later for the 1972 Winter Olympics, members of parliament, especially those of the opposition party, did not hesitate to express their disappointment and to claim that perhaps the government was to blame for not doing enough. Regardless of such accusations, the federal level had been very helpful in the efforts to secure the Winter Olympics as evidenced by the many forms of assistance which were provided or which would have been made available if Banff had been the successful bidder. The incidents involving the Banff application merit discussion because they provide a most interesting contrast to the 1976 Summer Olympics awarded to Montreal.

During the 1960's Montreal's Mayor, Jean Drapeau, began implementing his scheme of making Montreal "a city of the world". By pursuing a policy which might be described as the "politics of grandeur", the mayor succeeded in hosting the now famous Expo '67. In the process this brought Montreal into the international limelight. Among other things, an internationally renowned event which Drapeau envisioned for his city was that it be granted the right to host the Olympic Games. With this vision clearly fixed, Montreal made its bid for the 1972 Summer Olympics at the 1966 International Olympic Committee meeting in Rome. Largely because of a lack of preparation and the fact that it was Montreal's first such bid of recent times (Most successful cities require at least two such attempts), the Canadian application lost out to Munich. An unusual feature in this bid was that of the absence of federal government involvement to any significant degree except for an official endorsement given to the bid.

Undaunted by his initial failure, Drapeau began in earnest to make preparations for Montreal's next bid for the Summer Olympics in 1976. His preliminary work, unlike Banff, did not include close cooperation and planning with the federal sector. No advance arrangement relative to a cost-sharing scheme was prepared nor were other such agreements for federal monies entered into by Montreal. The only federal monies expected by Montreal were indirect financial support under either existing legislation or future legislation concerning public housing and urban renewal.[15] Under the circumstances of indirect support, the federal government basically was in favor of the Montreal bid. In fact, as part of its backing Prime Minister Trudeau even sent a letter to the International Olympic Committee on May 21, 1969 inviting athletes of the world to come to Canada and Montreal in 1976.[16]

A key component of this eventually successful application was that while the federal government generally approved of these games, it had minimal direct involvement, a feature purposefully designed by Mayor Drapeau. Above all, they were to be Montreal's Games and a new breed of Olympics at that. As the very persuasive and dynamic mayor stated on May 12, 1970 in Amsterdam during bidding for the games:

> "The Olympics should not come as an astronomical enterprise. We promise that in Canada, in Montreal, we will present the Games in the true spirit of Olympism, very humble, with simplicity and dignity."[17]

Such a proposal convinced the International Olympic Committee that Montreal deserved the games. The Canadian federal government also, was agreeable to this type of approach. Considering that large amounts of federal monies had been used to cover the deficit incurred by Montreal's Expo '67, there was ready-made opposition to the possibility of providing additional direct federal monies if they had been requested by Montreal. With the political climate being such, the federal government gave its tacit approval to the games on the condition that they were to be self-financing, a unique venture unknown to Olympic Games of the modern era.

At this juncture, a useful exercise is to compare the case of the Montreal application for the games with that of the Vancouver-Garibaldi bid for the 1976 Winter Olympics. Interestingly enough, the west coast group followed in line with the policy used by the earlier Banff attempts and officially requested that the federal government participate financially through a federal/provincial/municipal cost-sharing agreement. In 1969 and 1970 a sum totalling $75,000 was advanced to the Garibaldi Olympic Development Association by the Fitness and Amateur Sport Directorate to help cover promotional expenses associated with the bidding for the games. Likewise, the British Columbia provincial government and the city of Vancouver provided additional funds for this purpose. The fiscal arrangements agreed upon were that if the Garibaldi bid was successful a conditional fixed grant of $10,000,000 would be made available by the federal government towards the deficit of a non-profit cooperation to be established for the staging and operation of the games. The grant was conditional provided that the provincial government of British Columbia and the city of Vancouver also allocated funds for the remaining deficit.[18]

In citing the above example, an obvious contradiction in federal policy becomes apparent: two different bids by one country in the same year--two separate federal fiscal arrangements. All things considered, the Montreal Olympics contravened the established convention calling for federal involvement by means of a cost-sharing program. The 1954 British Empire and Commonwealth Games witnessed federal participation in a limited type of governmental cost-sharing scheme. Indeed, a true cost-sharing agreement was in effect for the 1967 Pan-American Games in Winnipeg. At these games the federal share amounted to $2,839,516 or 46 per cent of the total costs with the Government of Manitoba covering 42 per cent, and the city of Winnipeg 12 per cent. Included in the federal subsidy was a grant of $589,516 paid after the games were completed to cover the city's share of the deficit.[19] With respect to Banff and Garibaldi, similar types of cost-sharing arrangements were agreed upon well in advance. Even the 1978 Commonwealth Games slated for Edmonton will utilize this type of fiscal policy with the federal government promising a fixed grant of $12,000,000 covering approximately 33 per cent of the capital costs along with an estimated $8,000,000 in federal goods and services and possibly even federal permission to mint a series of special commemorative coins. With the Alberta Government and the city of Edmonton also providing funds, these games have the support of all levels of the public sector.[20]

These examples have a relationship to the Montreal Games by pointing out that what appeared to be established policy concerning the hosting of international sports festivals was bypassed in the planning of the 1976 Summer Olympics. How such a situation developed is indeed very complex. Suffice to say that, lacking foresight about the game's true costs, caught up by Drapeau's magnetism with his adamant proclamation that the Olympics would be self-financing, and still smarting from the Expo '67 deficit payments, the federal government chose the route of indirect support with no direct financing. Thus occurred a deviation from past policy and a compliance to Montreal's, and more specifically Mayor Drapeau's, wishes to "go to alone" with minimal federal involvement. At the time such an agreement was satisfactory to all concerned parties, including the Canadian public. Events occurring over the next six years revealed that such an approach was not feasible.

The self-financing scheme was, in itself, somewhat of a misnomer, for while no direct federal aid was requested substantial federal assistance and supposed indirect financing were necessary. In the period following Montreal's acceptance as host city for the XXI Summer Olympics, negotiations began, with the federal government, the Quebec Government, the city of Montreal, and the Organizing Committee of the Olympic Games of Montreal (COJO), all participating. The result was an agreement to pass legislation which was required to legalize special self-financing schemes in the form of a national lottery, and the minting of Olympic coins and stamps. This legislation received royal assent in the House of Commons on July 27, 1973, under the title of Bill C-196, The Olympic (1976) Bill and covered five specific items: (1) the minting of special Olympic coins, (2) the production of special Olympic stamps and related products, (3) the right to conduct a national lottery, (4) establishment of an Olympic Account in the accounts of Canada, (5) granting of tax exempt status for gifts made to COJO.[21] In June, 1975 there was an amendment to this bill which provided for the issuance of special $100 gold coins and also granted COJO propiety rights in trademarks and copyrights.[22]

In addition to this support, other federal programs pertaining to the Olympics also came into being. Some of the major ones included:

1. Funds provided by the federally sponsored Central Mortgage and Housing Corporation for the construction costs of the Olympic Village.

2. Security provided by the RCMP and the Department of National Defence.

3. CBC responsibility as the host nation for radio and television facilities.

4. The Fitness and Amateur Sport Branch of the Department of National Health and Welfare participating together with the COA, the Olympic Trust, and the provincial governments in Game Plan, an assistance program for Olympic sports and their athletes.

5. Involvement in various capacities by numerous other departments (e.g., Post Office, the Department of Agriculture, the Department of Industry, Trade and Commerce, etc.).[23]

In June, 1975 the Hon. C. M. Drury on behalf of the Treasury Board reported that"...the support provided to the 1976 Olympic Games by the federal government through normal programs involves some 30 departments and agencies and is expected to amount to approximately $130 million."[24] This estimated total was not a completely accurate representation considering the numerous hidden costs of civil service man-hours, administrative services, etc. borne within existing federal government operations. For what was described as "no direct financing" the federal level was heavily subsidizing the cost of the games.

Despite these heavy financial commitments, the federal government maintained little say in the administration and planning of the games. As one member of parliament accurately summarized, "...neutral participation...that is the extent of the federal government's involvement."[25] The outcome of permitting complete control to be in the hands of Montreal, essentially Mayor Drapeau, became evident too late, with the result of chaos and a resounding failure in the preparatory stages of what were once billed as the modest games. Hit hard by innumerable problems including runaway inflation, strikes by construction workers, faults in structural design, questionable administrative practices such as the failure to put contracts out to tender, possible fraud and corruption (the list could go on at some length), the Montreal Olympics blossomed into a colossal national headache.

Fortunately, on November 20, 1975, the Quebec Government which earlier had promised financial assistance to the games in case of a deficit, took a drastic measure by wrestling control of facility construction away from the city of Montreal; it promptly established a provincially controlled Olympic Installations Board. Through such action Quebec assumed responsibility for not only construction but the financial responsibilities of the

Olympics with their estimated $600,000,000 deficit. Fully aware of the federal policy of no direct financing and no subsidy for a deficit incurred by the games, the Quebec government, nevertheless, sought some form of federal assistance. While there were discreet negotiations for direct federal aid, there were also some other avenues suggested by Quebec to get around the policy of no direct federal financing. These included a straight loan possibly interest free from Ottawa, a federal rebate (estimated at $200,000), to Quebec on the amount of federal taxes paid on the escalating costs of the Olympic facilities, and an extension of the Olympic lottery past the scheduled expiry date of the summer of 1976.[26]

The federal government, through Prime Minister Trudeau, repeatedly and emphatically stated no to any of the appeals for direct aid; at the present time it is still hedging on the indirect measures proposed by Quebec. To change direction in mid-stream would spell political suicide for the federal government. Simply by refusing to subsidize the deficit, the federal level maintains its integrity by adhering to a policy agreed upon previously by all involved parties. In these last few months prior to the opening of the 1976 Summer Olympics, it will be interesting to follow this hot issue. In all likelihood, if the federal government does relent at all it will not be for direct subsidization but rather the safest way out--by allowing an extension of the Olympic lottery or by some other indirect means.

One could very well go on at some length arguing the pros and cons of providing federal aid in a post facto manner to the financially plagued XXI Summer Olympics, but what is not required at this time is a long debate. While blame for the Olympic fiasco should rightfully be spread around among various levels, with Montreal and Mayor Drapeau taking by far the largest share, some important lessons should be there for other involved levels. In the case of the federal government what is clear is the need for a more consistently enforced and all-encompassing sports policy applicable to all areas including such items as the hosting of major international sports events and festivals. How is it possible to rationally explain or justify federal policy towards the 1976 Montreal Olympics in light of federal action and direct support given to the 1954 British Empire and Commonwealth Games, the 1967 Pan-American Games, the Banff and Garibaldi bids for the Winter Olympics, and more recently, the 1978 Commonwealth Games? Furthermore, the 1972 Munich Games held in West Germany should have provided a model for the Montreal Games. Reference here is to the cost-sharing scheme employed, whereby the federal government of the Federal Republic of Germany provided 48 per cent of the 1972 Game's costs. Such substantial federal subsidies, in fact, have been the norm in Olympic Games of the modern era.

It becomes obvious that if the Canadian federal government is to remain involved in the area of sport as indicated by the 1961 Fitness and Amateur Sport Act it cannot continue to support certain select areas while adopting a laissez-faire policy on others. The circumstances surrounding the Montreal Olympics indicate that on this issue, as well as on other occasions, the federal government has treated sport in a trivial, haphazard manner, often paying only token lip-service to the field. A billion dollar plus price tag, regardless of who is actually footing the bill, is no trivial matter! Such an expense, on an event of extreme national and international importance should have warranted not only direct federal aid but extensive federal government planning and assistance from the outset.

In promulgating such views, one should not lose sight of the fact that federal involvement in sport has not been totally lacking; far from it, it has been a gradually expanding process. Part of the reason for the late arrival of the public sector into this realm stems back to the British North America Act. At the time of Confederation the responsibility for the sport/recreation area was not spelled out. Although constitutionally it seemed to be left in the hands of the provinces, over the years it eventually became a concurrent area of responsibility between the federal and provincial levels. In recent years, involvement in this domain has increased tremendously among the federal and provincial governments alike. To some degree, the Montreal Olympics were ill-timed and disrupted this developmental process. On the other hand, they speeded it up greatly. But incongruencies and fuzzy areas still exist with policies not clearly defined. While the 1969 Report of the Task Force on Sports for Canadians was a landmark report which greatly influenced federal sports policies, it was not an all-inclusive document. Furthermore, A Proposed Sports Policy for Canadians issued in 1970 by the Minister of National Health and Welfare, the Hon. John Munro, made no mention of the hosting of international sports festivals such as the Olympics. The same is true of more recent policy papers issued by the federal government. Such oversights in policy-making had a direct bearing on the Montreal Olympics and in a way reflect the low priority accorded to sport in this country.

Perhaps a Ministry of Sports is required as proposed by Mr. Plaxton back in January, 1937, and more recently, by Mr. H. Herbert in March, 1975.[27] Perhaps also, federal funds should be substantially increased in the sport recreation field; the 1975-76 budget of the Fitness and Amateur Sport Program totalling $21,785,000 still amounts to less than a $1 per annum per person expenditure--quite a paltry amount by any standards. If nothing else, let the events and furor surrounding the 1976 Montreal Olympics be a lesson well learned, and hopefully be the catalyst required in the continuing and long overdue development of a rational, philosophically-sound and functioning sports policy for this country.

Footnotes and References

[1] Canada. Hansard. April 26, 1928, p. 2394.

[2] Canada. Hansard. January 20, 1937, p. 115.

[3] Orban, W. A. R. The Fitness Movement in Canada in Physical Education in Canada, ed. by M. L. Van Vliet. Scarborough, Ontario: Prentice-Hall of Canada, Ltd., 1965, p. 239.

[4] Sawula, L. W. The National Physical Fitness Act of Canada 1943-1954. Unpublished doctoral dissertation, University of Alberta, 1976.

[5] Canada. Hansard. March 6, 1947, p. 1104.

[6] Orban, W. A. R. op.cit.

[7] Canada. Public Accounts. 1951, 1952, 1953, 1954, 1956, 1960.

[8] From 1961 the official title remained the Fitness and Amateur Sport Directorate until 1973 at which time it became the Fitness and Amateur Sport Branch.

[9] Information for this table was obtained from Official Reports of the Canadian Olympic Association 1924 to 1972 and from the Annual Reports of the Fitness and Amateur Sport Program 1961-62 to 1973-4. It should be emphasized that despite substantial public sector grants (from federal, provincial and certain larger municipal governments), the COA remains an independent, non-profit corporation charged with the responsibility of raising most of its own finances from the private sector. Since 1970 it has even had an affiliated body--the Olympic Trust--which is responsible for the fund-raising activities of the association. With the advent of the Olympic coin and stamp program, the COA has also received funds from the profits of these schemes; on October 17, 1974 $800,000 was turned over to the COA from this source to help it promote amateur sport in Canada.

[10] In 1924 there was some action taken towards a bid by Montreal to host the 1928 Olympic Games. Also, in 1929, the city made an application to host the 1932 Winter Games and again in 1939 for the 1944 Winter Games.

[11] Canada. Hansard. July 28, 1958, p. 2771.

[12] Canada. Department of National Health and Welfare. Fitness and Amateur Sport Program Annual Report 1963-64, p. 3.

[13] Canada. Hansard. November 1, 1962, p. 1167.

[14] Canada. Hansard. July 24, 1964, p. 6964.

[15] Canada. Hansard. January 22, 1970, p. 2729.

[16] Canada. Hansard. June 28, 1973, p. 5183.

[17] Martin, L. Games Hopes Rise as Board Named (Olympic Mess IV). The Globe and Mail, December 20, 1975, p. 43.

[18] Canada. Hansard. May 11, 1970, p. 6786.

[19] Canada. _Hansard_. March 11, 1970, p. 4699.

[20] Butters, B. '78 Games Organizers Hope Lady Luck Watching Budget. _Edmonton Journal_, January 10, 1976, p. 10.

[21] Canada. _Hansard_. June 28, 1973, p. 5156.

[22] Canada. _Hansard_. June 20, 1975, p. 6961.

[23] _Ibid._, p. 6962.

[24] _Ibid._

[25] Canada. _Hansard_. June 28, 1973, p. 5167.

[26] Editorial. _The Toronto Star_. January 23, 1976, p. B4.

[27] Canada. _Hansard_. March 21, 1975, p. 4392.

Soviet Sport And Soviet Foreign Policy

James Riordan

Sport everywhere, being bound up with the values of communities, has a political aspect and is seldom (if ever) free of politics. The influence of politics on sport is particularly evident in relation to foreign policy, where sporting success is seen by many as a measure of national vitality and prestige; it can therefore serve as an unobtrusive form of propaganda. As a consequence, 'international competitive sport has become an arena for ideologies, mirroring the same tensions as are seen throughout the world on the purely political plane'.[1] UNESCO drew attention in the mid-1950s to the increasing 'politicisation' of international sport, to the extent that 'the Olympic Games are now regarded by many as merely a testing ground for two great political units'.[2]

With the division of much of the world into two camps in the 1950s with the nuclear stalemate and the intensifying 'battle for men's minds', sport became an area of great social significance. It is today employed by statesmen in East and West as a propaganda weapon in world affairs, a relatively modern method of psychological warfare. By its nature, sport is suited to the task: it excites nationalist instincts and encourages group identification; it is superficially apolitical and readily understandable; sporting activity can take place across barriers of race, class, religion and nationality; and, through modern means of communication, sporting spectacles can be transmitted throughout the world.[3] A Soviet writer has noted that 'the deepening and widening influence of socialist sport on the condition of and trends in the world sports movement is one of the best and most comprehensible means of explaining to the masses the advantages which the socialist system has over capitalism'.[4]

It is apparent that, today, the nations of the world rank differently according to the amount of interest their governments take in the organisation and conduct of sport. On the one side are those states whose sports movement is fully integrated into the social and political system and thus becomes an important instrument of government policies. On the other are countries in which sport is largely organised by non-government bodies and tends to be free of state control--except, possibly, when it involves international competition. It is efficiency and command over resources that today count most towards success in international sport--and this is a factor that favours state-socialist systems, the Soviet Union's above all.

Reprinted by permission of the author and the Cambridge University Press.

While sport in the West is by no means free of politics or foreign policy aims, in centrally planned, Soviet-type societies, it occupies a more central position and its functions and interrelationship with the polity (especially the military), the economy and the culture are more manifest than in Western societies. In the U.S.S.R., the dependence of sport on politics has always been explicit--and that includes the area of foreign policy. The following three points from a Soviet sports book make explicit some of the political tasks which Soviet sports organisations are today expected to discharge:

(1) to ensure top performance by Soviet athletes abroad as a means of widely publicising our attainments in building communism and in promoting physical culture and sport and to gain a prominent position internationally in the major sports;

(2) systematically to propagate the aims and tasks of the Soviet sports movement, to explain the attitudes of Soviet sports organisations to the principal problems confronting the international sports movement, vigorously to combat slander and misinformation in regard to Soviet sport, anti-communism and ideological diversions made by imperialist circles in world sport, to expose the real nature of bourgeois sport and the strategy and tactics of bourgeois sports organisations, to thwart actions directed against the sports organisations of the Soviet Union and of other socialist and young independent states;

(3) to unite progressive forces in the international sports movement, to consolidate the united front of sports organisations of the socialist states, of the young independent states and the workers' sports organisations in capitalist states for the purpose of reaching progressive decisions on issues facing the international sports movement and of using sport as a weapon in the campaign for peace and mutual understanding.[5]

These do not, in fact, exhaust the overtly stated aims assigned to Soviet sport as an instrument of Soviet foreign policy. This chapter attempts to examine these and other functions of Soviet sport in relation specifically to Soviet foreign policy since 1945. During this period, four aims seem to have been pursued in Soviet sporting relations with the rest of the world-- some more or less consistently throughout the whole time span and others only in one or other phase of foreign politics. We can consider the pursuit of these state goals as functions assigned to the sports movement and attempt to assess how successfully it has coped with fulfilling them:

Continuously: (1) promoting good-neighbourly relations both with states bordering on the U.S.S.R. and with those in strategically important areas close to the U.S.S.R. (such as the Baltic, Balkans and Middle East)--a policy promoted both for reasons of strategy and, where regional contacts were encouraged with bordering states, for demonstrating the progress made by kindred peoples under socialism;

Post-war: (2) attaining superiority as a nation-state--a policy
aimed at enhancing the status of the U.S.S.R. and Soviet communism
abroad:

(3) maintaining and reinforcing the unity of the socialist bloc and
the Soviet 'vanguard' position within it;

(4) winning support for the U.S.S.R. and its policies among developing states of Africa, Asia and Latin America.

U.S.S.R. as a world power: 1945 Onward

Status as a world power

The Soviet Union emerged from the war a victor, its military power having
penetrated into Central and Eastern Europe, thus altering radically the balance of power in Europe and the world. Within the space of the four immediate post-war years, ten Soviet-aligned states came into existence.[6] In the
circumstances of international friction ('Cold War') which developed after
World War II, the existence of two 'hostile camps' and rival military blocs
confronting one another in a divided Europe, sport became an obvious arena
for international competition, 'defeating' one's ideological opponent. In the
West, it was initially felt by most governments valuable and expedient to
have sporting contacts with the Soviet Union, both as an expression of the
formal victors' unity that survived the war and as a relatively harmless
means of keeping certain options open for a more cooperative future (as in
other cultural exchanges). In the U.S.S.R., domestic sport was now thought
strong enough to take on the world; victories over bourgeois states would
demonstrate the vitality of the Soviet system. In a speech to the Party Central Committee in 1946, the Party spokesman then responsible for ideological and cultural affairs, Andrei Zhdanov, lauded the supremacy of Soviet
culture and urged an offensive against the 'decadent' Western world,[7] in a
mood of nationalistic fervour that accompanied a great military victory.
Soviet sport, too, an 'inalienable part of the overall culture of society',[8]
was therefore to take the offensive and, in the words of a Party resolution or
sport, 'win world supremacy in the major sports in the immediate future'.[9]
To do this would be to advertise the socialist system: 'The increasing number of successes achieved by Soviet sportsmen in sport has particular political significance today. Each new victory is a victory for the Soviet form of
society and the socialist sports system; it provides irrefutable proof of the
superiority of socialist culture over the decaying culture of the capitalist
states.'[10]

Before the war, apart from the sports exchange between the U.S.S.R.
and Nazi Germany and the Baltic states in 1940, few official representatives
of foreign states had visited the Soviet Union for a sporting event, nor had
Soviet athletes competed, except (as we have seen) on rare occasions, with
athletes other than those belonging to workers' sports associations. Nor had
Soviet sports associations joined or been invited to join international federations. Further, since tsarist Russia's participation in the 1912 Games, no
Russian or Soviet team had contested the Olympics.[11] That is not to say
that standards in Soviet sport were necessarily inferior to those in the West.

It is claimed that, by 1939, 44 Soviet records bettered world records, including 23 in weight lifting, 9 in athletics, 9 in pistol shooting, 2 in swimming and 1 in speed skating.[12] They could not be registered because the Soviet Union was not party to international federations.

In the immediate post-war years, Soviet sports associations affiliated to nearly all the major international sports federations (See Table 1) and Soviet athletes were competing regularly at home and abroad against foreign 'bourgeois' opposition (See Table 2).

Table 1. Affiliation to International Federations,
by Sports: 1946-1973.

Year	Sports federations affiliated to in given year	Cumulative total sports affiliated (no.)
1946	Basketball, soccer, skiing, weight lifting	4
1947	Athletics, chess, speed and ice skating, swimming (including diving and water polo), wrestling	9
1948	Gymnastics, volleyball	11
1949	Boxing	12
1951	(Soviet Olympic Committee formed and affiliated to the I.O.C.)	12
1952	Cycling, canoeing, equestrianism, fencing, ice hockey, modern pentathlon and biathlon, pistol shooting, rifle shooting, rowing, yachting	22
1954	Table tennis	23
1955	Bandy	24
1956	Draughts, lawn tennis, motorcycle racing, motor racing	28
1958	Gliding, handball	30
1962	Judo, radio sport	32
1965	Sub-aqua sport	33
1966	Model boatcraft sport	34
1967	Archery, mountaineering, orienteering	37
1969	Motor boat sport	38
1970	Field hockey	39
1971	Toboganning	40
1973	Trampoline, rugby	42

Source: A. O. Romanov, Mezhdunarodnoye sportivnoye dvizhenie (Moscow, 1973), pp. 236-242; A. O. Romanov, Mezhdunarodnye sportivnye ob'yedineniya i turistskie organizatsii (Moscow, 1973), pp. 309-317.

Table 2. Foreign Sports Groups Visiting the U.S.S.R. and Soviet Sports Groups Travelling Abroad: Selected Years, 1948-1973.

Year	Foreign sports groups visiting the U.S.S.R. (no.)	Soviet sports groups travelling abroad (no.)
1948	12	23
1954	131	142
1958	294	330
1959	352	353
1960	407	399
1961	490	455
1965	439	507
1967	699	806
1969	594	533
1971[a]	389	477
1973	617	598

[a] More than two-thirds of the exchange was with other socialist states.
Sources: F. I. Samoukov (ed.), Istoriya fizicheskoi kul'tury (Moscow, 1964) pp. 350, 371; V. V. Stolbov and I. G. Chudinov, Istoriya fizicheskoi kul'tury (Moscow, 1970), p. 219 (for 1965 data); A. O. Romanov, Mezhdunarodnoye sportivnoye dvizhenie (Moscow, 1973), p. 196 (post-1965 data); Sport v SSSR (1974), No. 8, p. 1.

Between 1946 and 1958, the U.S.S.R. joined 30 international federations, and by 1973-1942, thereby embracing nearly all the major world sports. Moreover, some 200 Soviet officials held posts in international sports organisations in 1975.[13]

Spearheading the assault on the 'bourgeois' fortress was the Moscow Dinamo soccer team which, only two months after the war, accepted invitations to visit Sweden, Norway and Britain and played four matches against leading British clubs without defeat (beating Cardiff 10-1, Arsenal 4-3, and drawing with Chelsea 3-3 and Glasgow Rangers 2-2)--and this at a time when British soccer was still considered to be supreme in the world. The tour should be seen as part of the effort to show that, despite the war losses, the U.S.S.R. was still strong and that conditions were reasonably 'normal'. In 1946, Soviet weight lifters came second to the Americans in the world championships. In 1947, Soviet wrestlers competed in the European championships and won three divisions. In 1948, Botvinnik won the world class title and, in 1949, Ludmila Rudenko won the women's world chess title (the men's title was retained until 1972, when it was won by Robert Fisher of the U.S.A [the title reverted to the U.S.S.R. in 1974]; the women's is still [1976] held by the U.S.S.R.). Also in 1949, the Soviet men's volleyball team became world champions and the women's team, European champions. These were, to say the least, extremely auspicious international débuts.

Despite these early successes, Soviet sportsmen moved cautiously into international competition and, before 1952, tended not to enter an event without reasonable expectation of victory. No Soviet team was sent to the Londo

Olympic Games of 1948; in many Olympic events--notably in athletics and swimming (the 'anchor' sports of the Games)--it was felt that Soviet standards were still insufficiently high for the U.S.S.R. to do well. Instead, a number of officials attended the Games as observers. Only in May 1951 was a Soviet Olympic Committee formed and accepted by the International Olympic Committee.

The Soviet authorities came to recognize that competition with Western athletes provided the strongest world opposition, and "defeating" the ideological opponents would boost Soviet prestige: 'Our ties with Western Europe, the U.S.A. and Canada are determined primarily by sporting expediency and the need to meet strong sports-competitors; this is the best way Soviet sportsmen can prepare for European and world championships.'[14]

Alongside national rivalries there developed after the war a number of political rivalries or confrontations--e.g., U.S.S.R. v. U.S.A., the socialist v. capitalist "bloc", East v. West Germany, Cuba v. other American countries. The central arena for these trials of strength has traditionally been the Olympic Games. As A. Ivonin, Vice-Chairman of the Committee for Physical Culture and Sport, has said: 'In evaluating the significance of sport in international tournaments, we must not forget that, while world and European championships are extremely important, victory at the Olympics acquires a political resonance (my italics--JR).'[15] The Olympic Games evidently attract more publicity and prestige for the successful nations.

The U.S.S.R. made its Olympic début at the 15th Olympic Games, held in Helsinki, in 1952. The extent of Soviet preparation was evident from the fact that Soviet athletes were to contest all events in the Olympic programme (with the exception of field hockey). Bearing in mind that nearly all the Soviet sportsmen and sportswomen had never competed previously against world-class opposition from outside the U.S.S.R., the Soviet performance was remarkable. Although, in the unofficial Olympic table (See Table 3), the U.S.S.R. gained fewer gold medals than the Americans (22:40), it gained more silver (30:19) and bronze (19:17) and tied with the U.S.A. in points allotted for the first six places (according to the system used in the Olympic Bulletin).

The U.S.S.R. took no part in the 1952 Winter Olympics and made its winter début only in 1956 at Cortina d'Ampezzo in Italy. There is amassed most medals and points, winning gold medals in speed skating, skiing and ice hockey. The ice hockey success was particularly creditable since the sport had been taken up in the Soviet Union only after the war; even two years before the 1956 Winter Olympics, the Soviet ice hockey team had won the world championships at its first attempt.

At the next Olympics, held in Melbourne in 1956, the U.S.S.R. sent a team of over 300 athletes. Once again, all events except field hockey were contested, and, this time, the scope of the challenge was much wider; besides gaining more medals and points than any other nation, the Soviet Union reaped the first gold medals in track events (both won by Vladimir Kuts), boxing, soccer, sculling, canoeing and the modern pentathlon.

Table 3. Soviet Performance in the Olympic Games: 1952-1976.

	Summer Games						Winter Games					
					Nearest rival						Nearest rival	
Year	Gold medals	Medal total[h]	Points[a]	Position	Medals	Points[a]	Gold medals	Medal total	Points[a]	Position	Medals	Points[a]
1952	22	71	494	1	76	494[c]	—[b]	—[b]	—[b]	—[b]	—[b]	—[b]
1956	37	98	624.5	1	74	498[c]	7	16	103	1	11	66.5[d]
1960	43	103	683	1	71	463.5[c]	7	21	146.5	1	7	62.5[e]
1964	30	96	608.3	1	90	581.8[c]	11	25	183	1	15	89.3[f]
1968	29	91	591.5	2	106	709[c]	5	13	92	2	14	103[f]
1972	50	99	665.5	1	93	636.5[c]	8	16	120	1	14	83[g]
1976	47	125	788.5	1	90	636.5[g]	13	27	201	1	19	138[g]

a The points allocation is that used in the Olympic Bulletin: awarding seven points for first place, five for second and so on down to one point for sixth place.

b U.S.S.R. not participating.

c U.S.A.

d Austria.

e Sweden.

f Norway.

g East Germany.

h The comparative British medal totals for the Summer Olympics were: 1952–11, 1956–24, 1960–20, 1964–18, 1968–13, 1972–18, 1976–13.

Sources: K. A. Andrianov et al. (eds.), Olimpiiskie igry (Moscow, 1970); Sovetsky sport, 16th February 1972; Sport v. SSSR, 1976, No. 3, p. 1; The Times, 2 August 1976, p. 8. Sportsworld, September 1972; p. 4;

There was no mistaking the boost that Olympic success gave at the time to many Soviet people's pride in their sportsmen and, by extension, in the country and even the system that had produced such world beaters. Nor were the leaders slow to appreciate the benefit the U.S.S.R. could reap from its enhanced reputation at home and abroad. By a decree of the Presidium of the Supreme Soviet of the U.S.S.R. of 27 April 1957, a large group of Soviet athletes, coaches and sports officials were rewarded with some of the country's highest honours.[16]

At the 1960 Olympic Games, held in the winter at Squaw Valley in the U.S.A. and in the summer in Rome, the U.S.S.R. provided by far the most successful performance. In the winter, it won three times as many medals as its nearest rival (Sweden). In the summer events, it gained 103 to the 71 medals of its nearest rival (U.S.A.). Victories were recorded in sports comparatively new to the Soviet Union, like cycling, yachting, fencing and show jumping.

In the following Olympic Games, held in the winter at Innsbruck in Austria and in the summer of 1964 in Tokyo, the U.S.S.R. once more emerged triumphant, winning first gold medals in pairs' figure skating (by Belousova and Protopopov) and in the biathlon in the Winter Olympics, and with Soviet contestants first in 7 of the 23 sports in the summer programme: Graeco-Roman wrestling, weight lifting, boxing, gymnastics, fencing, the modern pentathlon and, for the first time, men's volleyball. A gold medal was also won for the first time in swimming.

At the 1968 Olympics, however, the Soviet winter and summer contingents showed they were not invincible by being placed second to Norway in the Winter Olympics, held at Grenoble in France, and second to the U.S.A. in the Summer Olympics, held in Mexico City.

One conclusion to be drawn from the 1968 Olympics was that other nations, too, were reaping rewards from extensive sports planning. At the summer Olympics, for example, six competing East European nations (excluding the U.S.S.R. and the non-participant Albania) aggregated 120 medals, including 40 gold (with a total population of 100 million); the six leading West European states accumulated 81 medals, including 25 gold (with an aggregate population of 230 million). Hungary alone, with a population of only 10 million, gained twice as many medals (32) as Britain (53 million and 15 medals). West Germany (with a population of 57 million) won 25 medals, including 5 gold--the same number as East Germany, whose total included 9 gold (with a population of only 17 million). Spain (with a population of 30 million) obtained no medals at all. Mongolia, on the other hand (with a population of just over a million) gained 4 medals. Despite the Soviet setback in not 'winning' the Olympic Games for the first time in its short history of competition, the team's versatility was some indication of the comprehensive planning of the sports movement in the U.S.S.R. Not only did Soviet athletes contest 22 of the 23 sports at the Mexico Olympics (the exception, as before, was field hockey), but they gathered medals in all sports except cycling--by far the most balanced achievement by any nation in the history of the modern Olympics.

In the winter and summer Olympic Games held during 1972 at Sapporo (Japan) and Munich (West Germany), the Soviet Union reclaimed its leading position. In the summer Olympics, the U.S.S.R. acquired more gold medals and points than any nation had done before--this despite the obvious improvements in worldwide athletic standards, particularly in Eastern Europe and the 'third world'. Soviet success was achieved largely at the expense of the more established sports nations, primarily the U.S.A.

The 'spread' of Soviet performance and success in the Olympics may be seen in Table 4 below which shows the first six team placings in every sport contested at Munich. Field hockey was, once again, the only sport uncontested by the U.S.S.R.

Table 4 confirms that the U.S.S.R. was the best all-round and most successful nation at the Summer Games, winning 9 of the 23 sports in which it competed, coming second in 6 and third in 2; by comparison, the U.S.A. had 4 firsts, 3 seconds and 1 third. Besides being superior overall, the U.S.S.R. also was the most consistently versatile, being placed in the first six nations in 23 of the 24 sports in the Games (the U.S.A.--in 14, East Germany--12, West Germany--9). In terms of population-medal balance, the most outstanding nations were East Germany, Cuba and Hungary. Overall, the 11 socialist countries (Bulgaria, Cuba, Czechoslovakia, East Germany, Hungary, Mongolia, North Korea, Poland, Rumania, U.S.S.R. and Yugoslavia) out of the 121 states represented at the 1972 Summer Olympic Games, accounted for over half the gold medals (100 out of 194) and 47 per cent of the medals. The improvement of the socialist states is noteworthy; when most of them made their Olympic debut in 1952, only 3 featured in the top ten nations in the unofficial points table--the U.S.S.R. (1st), Hungary (3rd) and Czechoslovakia (10th). In 1968, there were 4: U.S.S.R. (2nd), East Germany (3rd), Hungary (4th) and Poland (8th). At the 1952 Summer Olympics, socialist states won 20 per cent of the total points and 29 per cent of the medals, in 1956--33 per cent and 34 per cent, 1960--40 per cent and 40 per cent, 1964--38 per cent and 38.9 per cent, 1968--40.6 per cent and 40.7 per cent and 1972--46.4 per cent and 47 per cent respectively. Commenting on the successes of the U.S.S.R. and the fraternal states in 1972, Pravda left no doubt that it saw them as a victory internationally for the socialist system: 'The grand victories of the U.S.S.R. and the fraternal states convincingly demonstrate that socialism opens up the greatest opportunities for man's physical and spiritual perfection.'[17] In recognition of Soviet success, athletes, coaches and officials who excelled during the 1972 Olympics were rewarded by a decree of the Presidium of the U.S.S.R. Supreme Soviet (5 October 1972):[18] six persons received the Order of Lenin (including Borzov--winner of the 100 m and 200 m sprints, Alexeyev--winner of the super-heavy weight lifting division, and Saneyev--winner of the triple jump for the third Olympics in succession), 20--the Order of the Red Banner of Labour, 105--the Badge of Honour, 48--the medal 'For Outstanding Labour' and 74--the medal 'For Excellent Labour'. Though high, the number of awards was more modest than that after the 1956 Melbourne Olympics, when the Soviet Union first gained most points in the unofficial table.

That is not to say other high-level contests in the full glare of world publicity are seen as unimportant. Several international contests rank high

Sport	First	Second	Third	Fourth	Fifth	Sixth
Archery	U.S.A.	U.S.S.R.	Poland	Sweden	Finland	Belgium
Athletics	U.S.A.	East Germany	U.S.S.R.	West Germany	Kenya	Britain
Basketball	U.S.S.R.	U.S.A.	Cuba	Italy	Yugoslavia	Puerto Rico
Boxing	Cuba	Hungary	Poland	U.S.A.	U.S.S.R.	Bulgaria/ Kenya
Canoeing	U.S.S.R.	2-3 Hungary	/Rumania	4-5 East Germany	/West Germany	Bulgaria
Cycling	U.S.S.R.	Australia	3-5 East Germany	/West Germany	/Poland	France
Diving	U.S.A.	Italy	Sweden	East Germany	U.S.S.R.	Czecho- slovakia
Equestrian	West Germany	England	U.S.S.R.	4-5 Italy	/U.S.A.	Sweden
Fencing	Hungary	U.S.S.R.	France	Italy	Poland	Rumania
Football	Poland	Hungary	3-4 East Germany	/U.S.S.R.	------	------
Gymnastics	U.S.S.R.	Japan	East Germany	Hungary	Poland	U.S.A.
Handball	Yugoslavia	Czecho- slovakia	Rumania	East	U.S.S.R.	West Germany
Hockey[a]	West Germany	Pakistan	India	Nether- lands	Australia	Britain
Judo	Japan	U.S.S.R.	Nether- lands	Britain	France	West Germany
Modern pentathlon	U.S.S.R.	Hungary	Finland	4-6 Britain	/Sweden	/U.S.A.
Rowing	East Germany	U.S.S.R.	West Germany	4-5 Czecho- slovakia	/New Zealand	U.S.A.
Shooting	U.S.S.R.	U.S.A.	East Germany	Czecho- slovakia	5-6 Italy	/Poland
Swimming	U.S.A.	Australia	East Germany	U.S.S.R.	West Germany	Canada
Volleyball	Japan	U.S.S.R.	East Germany	North Korea	5-6 Bulgaria	/South Korea
Water polo	U.S.S.R.	Hungary	U.S.A.	West Germany	Yugoslavia	Italy
Weight lifting	Bulgaria	U.S.S.R.	Hungary	Poland	East Germany	Iran
Wrestling:						
free-style	U.S.S.R.	U.S.A.	Japan	Bulgaria	Hungary	Iran
Graeco- Roman	U.S.S.R.	Bulgaria	Rumania	Hungary	Yugoslavia	Czecho- slovakia
Yachting	Australia	Sweden	3-4 France	/U.S.A.	Britain	U.S.S.R.
Soviet Total 23	9	6	2	2	3	1

Obliques indicated combined award.

[a] U.S.S.R. was a non-participant.

Source: The Times, 12 September 1972, p. 8.

in prestige value to the winners--e.g. the biennial U.S.A. v. U.S.S.R. athletics match, the World Cup in soccer, and the various European and world championships. Outside the Olympics, therefore, the range of Soviet international competition grew steadily after the war. At the beginning of the 1960s, the reaffirmation of the policy of 'peaceful coexistence between countries with different social and political systems' by N. S. Krushchov at the 22nd Party Congress in 1961 found reflection in sport in the shape of rapidly increasing contacts between Soviet and foreign teams in a wide variety of sports. Sportsmen from abroad were invited to many Soviet cities and Soviet people were able, more often than not, to cheer and take pride in successes scored by their own athletes against foreign opposition. In 1961, as many as 490 foreign teams visited the U.S.S.R. (See Table 2), competing in more than 40 Soviet towns; in the same year, Soviet sports organisations were in contact with 77 countries. The foreign visits were all the more significant since this was the first time most ordinary Soviet people outside Moscow and Leningrad had seen foreigners since World War II.

Sport was regarded as a means of merging the individual in the group and identifying him with his country and government and, indirectly, with the regime's policies. It was seen as a cohesive agent--a sort of ludus francus--in a vast multinational country and helped to reconcile the individual to relatively new urban, industrial and Soviet mores. Moreover, the employment of sport as part of foreign policy has been a largely dependable factor in promoting a Soviet nationalism and feelings of national unity: 'To perform in international contests under a single flag encourages the growth of national awareness, the unity and strengthening of a nation.'[19] Following success at the Munich Olympics in 1972 much play was made of the multinational composition of the Soviet Olympic contingent (on the U.S.S.R.'s fiftieth anniversary) which contained: 'Russians and Ukrainians, Belorussians and Georgians, Kazakhs and Uzbeks, representatives of all the Union Republics. In their red vests bearing the Soviet emblem they competed as equal representatives of their Soviet land.'[20] Sport, then, was to play its part in generating nationalist feelings and identifying people with Soviet achievements, with their Soviet team (especially against foreign opposition) and hence with the Soviet system and its leaders. This illustrates a point made by a Finnish sociologist, namely that 'created beliefs in national success and superiority are conducive to strengthening group identification.'[21] In the case of the Soviet Union, however, by virtue of its unique position in the minds of many communists and sympathizers throughout the world as the "standard-bearer" of the communist ideology, its international sports success may be enjoyed by all those who share such a common identity--whether as communists, "fellow-travelers" or plain anti-imperialists in Cuba, Zimbabwe, France or Vietnam. Soviet superiority in sport, particularly over capitalist states, the U.S.A. above all, enables all these people to triumph vicariously through Soviet success.

It seemed that few sports were outside the winning range of Soviet sportsmen once they had made their international début. Even old 'aristocratic' sports like yachting, rowing, fencing, lawn tennis, show jumping and horse racing were not out of reach. Soviet yachtsmen gained their first gold medal in yachting at the 1960 Olympics, Soviet rowers visited the Henley Regatta in 1961, winning two cups (including the top prize--the Grand Challenge

Cup for Eights), Soviet men and women fencers won their first gold medals at the 1960 Olympics, tennis players entered the Davis Cup world tennis tournament in 1962, show jumpers (attired in the top hat and tails which the sport had inherited from the English country gentry) gained their first gold medal at the 1960 Olympics and Soviet horses and jockeys ventured onto the world's leading flat and steeplechase courses in the early 1960s.

As the 1960s progressed and relatively new sports came to be practised in the Soviet Union, Soviet competitors and teams extended their range of international competition and took part--now often without serious hope of immediate success (e.g. in motor rallies, rugby, badminton and field hockey)--in order to acquire experience. They even competed against foreign professionals in soccer, tennis and ice hockey, though in the complex world of amateur/professional distinctions, there is a number of sports in which the best Soviet competitors never meet the best foreign competitors. This is so in boxing, basketball, cycling and figure skating. In other sports, 'amateurs' and 'professionals' may compete together--e.g. in soccer, motor racing and motorcycle racing. In yet others, there is a partial distinction--so that, for example, all tennis players may mix in 'open' tournaments, as at Wimbledon, but no 'professionals' may compete in the Davis Cup.

Soviet soccer teams entered nearly all the major international tournaments, winning the European Nations' Cup in 1962 and the European Cup Winners Cup in 1975, though failing to win successive World Cups. Soviet archers made a winning debut in the European championships in 1969 and 1971; Soviet motorcyclists--on dirt, grass and ice--won world titles at the end of the 1960s, and Soviet cars and crews entered the Monte Carlo Rally (1964), the London-to-Sydney Marathon (1968) and the London-to-Mexico Marathon (1970), and won the golden team trophy in the 1971 Tour of Europe Motor Rally; they also entered a number of Grand Prix. In skin-diving, the U.S.S.R. won the European championships on its international debut in 1967, and, the next year, won 20 of the 25 medals in the European championships. In parachuting, a Soviet man and woman won the absolute world individual titles in 1970 and the U.S.S.R. won the women's team title. Soviet table tennis players won the European League in 1969 and again in 1970. Two Soviet tennis players, Olga Morozova and Alexander Metreveli, collected a major international title in 1971 (the South Australian Open Singles). In draughts, the Soviet team dominated the European championship after 1967. In trampoline sport, Soviet athletes won three of the four titles on their international debut in the 1973 European championships. In the not-so-distant future, it is not unrealistic to forecast, the U.S.S.R. is likely to be a leading power in world badminton, rugby, field hockey and motor racing, at all of which its sportsmen are practising hard. Nor, one may predict, will it be long before Soviet winter athletes enter (and do well in) such sophisticated sports as the slalom, bobsleigh and tobogganning events--just as they have of late come to dominate figure skating and ice dancing and have won the world ski jumping championship. There are signs at the moment of them taking up golf and squash--even bridge, karate, ladies' soccer and body building are all developing an (unofficial) following.

As an example of thorough preparation for a 'new' sport, the U.S.S.R. formed a field hockey federation in 1968 and affiliated to the International

Hockey Federation in 1970--with virtually no popular support for the game at home--with the declared aim of fielding a team in the Munich Olympics in 1972. Almost the entire Soviet world-champion bandy team was drafted into grasshockey in order to form the nucleus of the Olympic squad. It made its international debut at the European championships in 1970, coming third of four teams in its group; it did not, however, qualify for Munich. Nevertheless, the official campaign to promote hockey resulted in eight teams contesting the first Soviet Hockey Championship in Alma Ata in 1971. The importance to the U.S.S.R. of hockey is that it is the only sport for which the country has so far been unable to field a team at the Olympics.

During the 1960s, the U.S.S.R. won over twice as many world titles in a wide range of major sports as the U.S.A., and over three times as many European titles as its nearest rival (West Germany), Moreover, of eleven matches (1958-1973) held between the two world athletics giants, the U.S.A. and U.S.S.R. (also regarded by many as the world representatives of their respective ideologies), the U.S.A. won only twice overall; it is noteworthy that Soviet men won three times only and Soviet women lost once only--that this occurred says much for the part played by women in Soviet sport.

These results and those at the Olympic Games examined earlier suggest that the Soviet Union has gone a considerable way to achieving its aim of world supremacy in sport, but essentially in aggregate terms of points over the whole range of amateur Olympic sports taken together. Until the anomalies that keep some amateurs and professionals apart are removed, it is difficult to gain an overall perspective of Soviet performance in relation to human maxima. The U.S.S.R. appears to be more successful in the amalgam of combat sports (wrestling, weight lifting and judo), artistic expression (gymnastics and figure skating), quasi-military sports (fencing, shooting, archery, biathlon, modern pentathlon, skiing, parachuting and equestrian sports) and cerebral skills (chess and draughts). Harnessed to a purposeful planning system, these skills may have their roots in the physical strength of the Russian peasant and belligerent border peoples like the Cossacks and Transcaucasians (who produce many of the weight lifters, wrestlers and boxers); in the artistic body movements of gymnastics and figure skating by a people keenly appreciative of aesthetic self-expression in ballet and folk music; in the long-established (pre- and post-revolutionary) association between sport and military training; and in the intellectual skill of chess in a society in which intellectual and cultural activities are held in high esteem.[22] It is less successful in swimming and athletics, and 'newer' (for it) sports like field hockey, rugby, badminton and tennis. The failure to dominate world athletics and swimming may be attributed partly to the climate, partly to the late start in sport of most Soviet children (due to the lack of facilities and instructors and to the high priority given to scholastic work) and partly to the paucity of amenities generally--school playing fields, soccer pitches, tennis courts, indoor stadiums and swimming pools being few and far between even in the 1970s.[23] The international success in, and popular following for, team sports in the U.S.S.R. may be due to the vigorous official encouragement given to them for the values they are felt to impart; discipline, reliance on others and the merging of the individual in the group have long been valued by the Soviet authorities. It seems not an unreasonable hypothesis that the reasons behind such popularity of team play and international success in it may be sought in a societal environment that stresses collectivism and cooperation over individualism and self-interest.

As we have seen above, the Soviet Union is keenly aware of the advantages that are thought to accrue from international sporting success and, of course, deliberately prepares its athletes for international events. A recent statement of sports aims makes the point that, 'The main purpose of our international sports ties is to consolidate the authority of the Soviet Union by ensuring that Soviet athletes play a leading rôle internationally, that their sports skill constantly grows, that the successes of the Soviet people in building communism are made widely known and that physical culture and sport are promoted in our country.'[24] Testimony to the attention devoted to participation in international sport comes (wryly) from an unlikely source: the eminent biochemist, dissenter and now exile, Zhores Medvedev (himself denied an exit visa to address the CIBA Foundation on gerontology) wrote of the high priority given by the Party Secretariat to international sports events: 'I knew of a case of a soccer player who was suddenly required for an international match and was summoned and rushed by air from the resort where he was on holiday, approved by all departments, including the visa section, delivered from Moscow to England, driven straight from the airport to the stadium, and all this within twenty-four hours. He was to play for the Rest of the World against an All-England side...But this, of course, was a special case: soccer, sport, the glamour, the prestige! It was not a lecture on gerontology.'[25]

The Soviet Union is not slow to capitalise on international sporting success by using its outstanding sportsmen as 'ambassadors of goodwill', not infrequently as a 'try-out' for political initiatives. For example, in 1972, as part of an intensive campaign for a détente with the U.S.A. and as a prelude to President Nixon's visit to Moscow, the Soviet leaders sent their leading girl gymnasts (including Olga Korbut and Ludmilla Turishcheva) on a gymnastics display tour of America. Two months later, when the USA-USSR Treaty on Contacts, Exchanges and Cooperation was signed in Moscow, it included a clause (Article XIII) on sports exchanges, on which Sovetsky sport commented 'the foreign policy of our Party and government is reflected in international sports relations which must play their part in establishing firm foundations of mutual understanding and friendship between our peoples.'[26] A month after the signing of the new agreement (and at the end of the year's Soviet-American athletics match, in which the U.S.S.R. had soundly beaten its rival), the new entente was symbolically represented on the track by Soviet and American athletes linking arms, doing a lap of honour together and waving to spectators—a far cry from the atmosphere of the relations between the 'bastions of communism and capitalism' over the prewar and most of the postwar years.

Relations with state-socialist countries

Today, the bulk of Soviet foreign sports competition, like that of foreign trade, is with other socialist states—above all with those of Eastern Europe.

During 1969, for example, 825, or some 58 per cent, of the 1,420 international contests in which Soviet athletes were involved were confined to members of the East European bloc; in bilateral and multilateral contests, East Germany and the Soviet Union met 187 times, Bulgaria and the U.S.S.R.--151 times, Poland and the U.S.S.R.--127 times and Czechoslovakia and the U.S.S.R.--74 times.[27] 'Sporting relations with socialist states are central to Soviet foreign sports contacts and every year exceed half the entire Soviet sports exchange. Thus, in 1970, they amounted to 55 per cent and, in 1971, to 67 per cent of the total exchange.'[28]

Insofar as sport is centrally controlled in all these states and fully integrated in the political system, it can be wielded for manifestly functional purposes. 'The overriding principle [of socialist states' international sporting relations] consists in developing relations between fraternal communist and workers' parties which control physical culture and sport and formulate the foreign policy tasks of the national sports organisations.'[29] Sports contacts 'help to strengthen fraternal cooperation and friendship and develop a sense of patriotism and internationalism among young people of the socialist states'.[30] From the Soviet point of view, this can enable Soviet leaders to use sport to integrate the various socialist societies, to bind them to Soviet institutions and policies and to maintain and reinforce the U.S.S.R.'s 'vanguard' position within the bloc.

Relations have tended to reflect the political tenor within the bloc, with the Soviet Union defending (or imposing) its 'special relationship' as the 'most advanced socialist state', and the other socialist states striving for compensatory supremacies that are denied them elsewhere. In the period 1945 to 1956, most of the other socialist states (with Yugoslavia becoming the notable exception) were more or less obliged to learn from the Soviet model, to form Soviet-type administrative organisations and run physical fitness programmes like the GTO--this, despite the long sporting traditions of Hungary, Czechoslovakia (with its Sokol gymnastics) and East Germany, all of which had competed successfully in international sport many years before Soviet participation. Since 1956, however, there has been a gradual loosening of the Soviet grip on sport in other socialist states. Albania has, of course, gone its own way, following China, while other states have resurrected certain national sporting traditions and institutions which were submerged during the last Stalin era. Thus, for example, the Sokol gymnastics movement now plays a major part, once more, in Czechoslovak sport, and East Germany pioneered the use of sports boarding schools in the early 1960s. In place of Soviet-organised exchanges, new bilateral agreements have been drawn up and negotiated separately between the U.S.S.R. and other socialist states--and among the members of the bloc. The U.S.S.R. signed a five-year sports exchange agreement in 1966 with East Germany, in 1969 with Bulgaria, in 1971 with Poland and Hungary, in 1972 with Czechoslovakia and Cuba, and in 1973 with Mongolia, Yugoslavia and Rumania. These last two states pursue the most independent sports policy in Eastern Europe, paralleling their greater autonomy today in other spheres.[31]

Sports contacts between the socialist states embrace a variety of sports and take place at various levels. Their sportsmen come together in such single-sport tournaments as the annual Peace cycling race across Eastern

Europe and the Znamensky[32] Memorial athletics meeting (held in Moscow), in such multi-sport tournaments for specific groups and organisations as the Friendship sports tourneys for junior sportsmen,[33] socialist rural games, twinned-city games, the Baltic Sea Week and annual sports meetings between army and security forces' sports clubs. Few opportunities are lost to associate sporting events with a political occasion or to employ sport to cement loyalties within the bloc. Thus, to celebrate the fiftieth anniversary of the formation of the U.S.S.R., a mass assault was made on its highest mountain, Peak Commission (formerly Peak Stalin - 7,495 m). In all, 87 climbers reached the summit and planted there the flags of the 15 union republics of the U.S.S.R. and of eight other socialist states (Bulgaria, Czechoslovakia, East Germany, Hungary, Mongolia, Poland, Rumania and Yugoslavia) as 'a symbol of unshakable friendship and inspired by the ideal of proletarian internationalism, peace and friendship between peoples'.[34] To mark the same anniversary, one outstanding athlete from each socialist state (with the exceptions of Albania, China and North Vietnam, but including Cuba, Mongolia and North Korea) was made a Merited Master of Sport of the U.S.S.R.[35]

The sporting ties between army and security forces' clubs are particularly illustrative of the Soviet policy of military integration--or, at least, the desire to put a friendly face on some of the possibly less popular aspects of the Warsaw Pact. A Sports Committee of Friendly Armies (SCFA) was formed in Moscow in 1958, three years after the establishment of the Warsaw Pact. It embraced all members of the Pact plus China, North Korea and North Vietnam. Neither the Pact nor the SCFA included Yugoslavia. Cuba joined the SCFA in 1969 and the Somali Democratic Republic in 1973; China, Albania and North Vietnam took no part in it after 1960. The declared aims of the SFCA are 'to strengthen friendship between the armies, improve the quality of physical fitness and sport among servicemen and popularise the attainments of army sport'.[36] Each year, SCFA arranges, on average, 15 army championships in a variety of Olympic and paramilitary sports; by 1972, it was holding some 200 championships in member counries, including two summer multi-sport SCFA spartakiads (held in East Germany and the U.S.S.R.) and three winter spartakiads (held twice in Poland and once in Czechoslovakia). The third summer spartakiad was held in Czechoslovakia in 1973,[37] and the fourth winter games in Bulgaria in late 1973. Apart from these interstate army meetings, army clubs compete regularly against one another: thus, during 1972, army clubs met in Bulgaria for a Friendship Sports Week to contest events in weight lifting, the modern pentathlon, boxing, wrestling and shooting--sports with a distinctively military utility. In the same year, in September, a Dinamo Soccer Tourney was held in Moscow's Dinamo Stadium for junior teams of security forces' clubs from Bulgaria, Czechoslovakia, East Germany, Hungary, North Korea, Poland, Rumania and the U.S.S.R.

The improving sports standards in other countries of the bloc are reflected in the changing pattern of sporting aid. During the 1950s and early 1960s, this was mostly a one-way process, coaches, instructors and officials from the U.S.S.R. going abroad in order to fashion (or refashion) the sports movements in the countries of its allies and to help raise standards in individual sports to world levels. The sporting aid given by the Soviet Union and other socialist countries to Cuba was part of the process whereby that country was drawn into the ambit of state-socialist powers after a period of isolation and hesitation. The immediate aim was to help harness and build up Cuban sporting skill in order that Cuba might put up a good showing in sports confrontations with other states on the American continent. In the years 1969-1972, 'more than 50 Soviet coaches helped train Cuban athletes for the Olympic and Pan-American Games.'[38] The subsequent Cuban successes[39] in both tournaments provided ample material for linking sporting successes with the political system and demonstrating through the popular and readily understandable (particularly so in Latin America) medium of sport the advantages of the 'Cuban road to socialism' for other Latin American states: 'More and more Latin American states realise that Cuban victories in international sport are invariably connected with the successes of the Cuban revolution and the country's progressive system.'[40]

In recent years, however, a number of coaches and instructors from socialist states have been assisting Soviet athletes in sports in which the Soviet standard is below world class. In 1972, East Germany was training a Soviet team in bobsleighing (a sport only recently taken up by the U.S.S.R.); in the same year, the Cuban sprinter Ernesto Figarola was coaching in Odessa and Minsk. Hungarian fencing, swimming and pentathlon coaches have been training Soviet sportsmen in these sports and Czechoslovak ice hockey coaches have been working with Soviet squads. As a number of the U.S.S.R.'s allies build up specialised facilities and sports amenities, they become increasingly in a position to enable other sportsmen from within the bloc to gather together on the eve of important international events for joint training; thus, in recent years, Soviet athletes have attended training camps in East Germany, Poland, Czechoslovakia and Bulgaria. These and other forms of mutual assistance and integration are said to have become an important contributory factor in the sporting successes of socialist states internationally.

The overall advance of the socialist nations is impressive. When most of them made their Olympic debut in 1952, they accounted for 29 per cent of the medals; two decades later, in 1972, they won 47 per cent. And in Montreal, they won 57 per cent of the medals. Individual performances are even more remarkable: socialist Cuba has progressed from 53rd place in the 1960 Olympics to 23rd in 1972, and 8th in Montreal. East Germany, with a population of less than 17 million, won more gold medals in Montreal than the U.S.A., Britain and Canada put together. It may be recalled that the GDR came second to the U.S.S.R. in the 1976 Winter Olympics.

One last important feature of intra-community relations ought not to be overlooked. Sport, it would seem, enables non-Soviet socialist nations to assert a certain degree of autonomy and national dignity by victory over Soviet teams, that are denied them in other spheres. Besides serving thus as a compensatory mechanism, sport may also act as a "safety valve" for the release of pent-up feelings among participants and spectators alike. Contests between the U.S.S.R. and non-Soviet states have not always taken place in a fraternal spirit, as demonstrated in several U.S.S.R. v. Yugoslavia matches-cum-brawls in the 1950's; the Manchester Guardian wrote during the 1956 Olympics that 'the last twenty minutes of the football final between Russia and Yugoslavia resembled a wrestling match in which no holds were barred.'[41] Similar scenes accompanied a number of U.S.S.R. v. Hungary "duels" after 1956 (particularly in Olympic water polo matches) and U.S.S.R. v. Czechoslovakia meetings since 1968; it is reported that the Czechoslovak ice hockey victory in 1969 over the previously undefeated Soviet team evoked celebrations bordering an hysterical national rejoicing, with night-long dancing in the streets of Prague.[42] By providing this relatively harmless outlet for potentially harmful impulses--which may find no satisfactory alternative outlet in non-sporting spheres--sports contests would appear to perform a useful function of social control within the socialist "bloc".

Relations with newly independent countries

Since the early 1960s, especially since the priority given to the policy of peaceful coexistence (mentioned above), the Soviet authorities have paid increasing attention to aid to the 'third world' in the field of sport as well as in the economic and in other cultural spheres. This assistance takes the form of sending coaches and instructors abroad, building sports amenities, training foreign sports administrators in the Soviet Union, arranging tours and displays by Soviet athletes and holding Sports Friendship Weeks that often have an unabashedly political character. Much of this aid, including the provision of sports amenities, is said to be given free of charge.[43] Sometimes the sports contact is used as a prelude to political contacts. After all, 'Sporting ties are one way of establishing contacts between states even when diplomatic relations are absent.'[44]

In the five years up to 1971, over 100 Soviet coaches and instructors had worked in 37 Afro-Asian states (i.e., an average of 3 per country), including Algeria, Egypt, Iraq, Lebanon, Syria and Tunisia in the Middle East, Chad, Congo, Ghana, Guinea, Mali, Senegal and Togo in Africa, and Afghanistan, Burma, Cambodia, India, Indonesia and Malaysia in Asia.[45] In late 1972, there were said to be more than 200 such people working in 28 foreign states (i.e., an average of 7 per country).[46] Sports cooperation treaties were signed with Egypt in 1969, Nigeria and the Sudan in 1970, Algeria, Iraq and Syria in 1972 and the Lebanon in 1973 (in which Soviet volleyball, fencing, gymnastics and athletics coaches had been working).[47] That such cooperation is not entirely motivated by altruistic considerations is apparent in a comment on the Nigerian-Soviet Sport Friendship Week held in Nigeria in the autumn of 1972: 'Sporting attainments today have an immense power of influence. It is not at all surprising, therefore, that Nigeria should arrange a sports week of friendship dedicated to the fiftieth anniversary of the formation of the U.S.S.R.'[48] Nigeria, like Egypt and the Sudan, had held a sports week, with the participation of Soviet athletes, also to mark the Lenin centenary in 1970.

The U.S.S.R. has built sports centres in Afghanistan, Algeria, Cambodia, Congo, Indonesia, Iraq, Senegal and Togo. By 1970, students from 25 Afro-Asian states had received a Soviet coaching diploma and over 100 persons (from Afghanistan, Cambodia, Egypt, Ethiopia, Ghana, Guinea, Iraq, Malaysia, Mali, Sudan, Syria and Tunisia) had graduated from Soviet institues of physical culture. Another 50 had completed dissertations in the field of sport and physical education in Soviet colleges.[49]

Judging by the rapidly mounting scale of operations for promoting sport in developing countries, the Soviet leaders obviously regard sport as an important weapon in the 'battle for men's minds'. It is a serious business: 'the authority of sport in the world has grown enormously; there is no longer any place for dilettantism in the politics of sport.'[50] Given the signal Soviet successes in international sport, such sporting aid is seen as an effective means of demonstrating the possibilities of the 'socialist path of development'. In arranging contacts and assistance, much emphasis is placed on the propaganda value of the successes attained in erstwhile backward areas of the Soviet Union: 'In arranging these ties, we attach special importance to the sports organisations of the various republics, to sportsmen from Kazakhstan, Uzbekistan, Azerbaidzhan, Armenia and Georgia, when they visit Africa and Asia, and when the representatives of those countries meet our republican sportsmen at home.'[51] As a prelude to Brezhnev's visit to India in November 1973, an 'Indo-Soviet Friendship Week' took place with the famous ex-soccer player Lev Yashin and the tennis star Alex Metreveli prominent in the Soviet delegation. The leader of the Soviet group was, significantly, the Secretary of the Tadzhikistan Komsomol.[52] Prior to that, a Kazakh gymnastics team had been the first Soviet sports group to visit India under the Indo-Soviet Cultural Agreement;[53] in the same year, another Kazakh group, the Dorozhnik volleyball team from Alma Ata, became the first Soviet sports delegation to visit the Malagasy Republic. Naturally enough, the sports emissaries 'told them of sport in Kazakhstan, of its rôle in the life of the family of equal fraternal Soviet republics'.[54]

It is remarkable that, apart from individual visiting sportsmen, Western states have tended to dismiss officially sponsored sporting aid to developing countries. In fact, the pattern has generally been one in which promising 'colonial' athletes are attracted away from their homelands to seek fame and fortune in the teams of metropolitan countries. Such a trend is particularly evident in Italian, French, Spanish and Portuguese soccer and in British cricket and boxing.

One final aspect of Soviet 'aid' to Afro-Asian states has been support for third-world campaigns to exclude from international contests countries believed to be operating racial discrimination in sport. The Soviet Olympic Committee instigated moves in 1962 within the International Olympic Committee to exclude South Africa from the Olympic Games; the moves succeeded, and South Africa has subsequently not been able to compete in the Olympics. The U.S.S.R. has lent its considerable authority to moves to have South Africa and Rhodesia banned from all international sports tournaments. It is not unusual for Soviet competitors to forfeit matches (in tennis, for example) rather than play against white South Africans and Rhodesians. There is little doubt that such Soviet action wins much sympathy among wide circles in the 'third world', which see in the U.S.S.R. a champion of their cause.[55] This attitude is reinforced in frequent Soviet references to the multinational nature of Soviet sport: 'The Soviet Olympic delegation of 1972 was a mirror of Soviet multinational sport...Patriotism and collectivism, friendship and mutual assistance have become integral to the outlook of our athletes. They therefore look upon racial discrimination in sport as monstrous and inhuman.'[56] 'The internatlionalist character of socialist sport', the conclusion is drawn, 'has a great effect on the newly liberated ex-colonies.'[57]

Relations with non-state groupings

The U.S.S.R. promotes sports contacts with pro-Soviet and potentially sympathetic groupings in foreign countries, such as the Finnish Labour Union (TUL); it encourages the participation of Soviet and foreign athletes in annual races through Paris and Moscow (sponsored by the French communist newspaper l'Humanité and by Izvestiya respectively) and it sponsors the World Youth Festival, in whose programme sport plays a prominent part. The 10th World Youth Festival, held in East Berlin over 9 days in August 1973 with the participation of 20,000 foreign visitors from more than 120 countries, was described in the Soviet press as 'a festival of unity and solidarity of the international communist and the entire democratic youth and student movement, a vivid demonstration of the solidarity of young people in the fight against imperialism'[58]--and in the British press as 'a massive propaganda effort to demonstrate the virtue, strength and inevitability of Soviet-style communism'.[59]

As a measure of the importance attached by the Soviet Union to sport as a means of demonstrating its vanguard position in the communist youth movement, a 138-strong sports delegation was sent to the 1973 Festival; it included Olympic and world champions Ludmilla Turishcheva (gymnastics), Valery Borzov (sprinting), Faina Mel'nik (discus and shot), Irina Rodnina (figure skating), Mikhail Tahl and Anatoly Karpov (chess). 'The language of sport', it was claimed, 'became the language of friendship.' Ludmilla Turishcheva, after taking part in a symbolic relay through East Berlin ('In Honour of the Peoples of Vietnam, Laos and Cambodia') made the point that 'we took part in this race to demonstrate once again our solidarity with the working people of the whole world, particularly young people'.[60]

The second main type of such contact is with trade and professional associations, such as the International Sports Union of Railwaymen and the International Federation of University Sport.

The International Sports Union of Railwaymen (ISUR) was set up after the war, in 1947; in Austria with the participation of trade unions from Austria, Belgium, Czechoslovakia, Finland, France, Hungary and Italy. Despite the presence of the two East European members, the leadership was predominantly social-democratic until the affiliation of other East European states in 1956 (Bulgaria and Rumania) and 1957 (East Germany, Poland and the U.S.S.R.). The Union has now expanded to cover virtually all European states and many railwaymen's organisations in other parts of the world. That internal relations are not entirely smooth is testified to by the strict delineation of countries during championships into two independently competing groups--socialist and the remainder, so as to ensure opportunities for athletes from non-socialist states to win events. A compromise has been reached on representation on the ISUR governing body giving six places to non-socialist states (currently Belgium, Finland, France, Holland, Italy and West Germany) and six to socialist (Czechoslovakia, East Germany, Poland, Rumania, U.S.S.R. and Yugoslavia). At least four individual sports championships are held annually, each sport (of the 19 cultivated) being contested once every four years.[61]

Soviet sports relations with foreign student sports unions have also had their vicissitudes since the end of the war. International university games had been held before the war at two-yearly intervals since 1923, but without Soviet participation. After the war, a new International Union of Students (IUS) was formed in 1947; its sports section arranged student games in Paris the same year, in which Soviet students made their international début. The domination of the IUS and its sports section by the students' unions of social-ist states and their sympathisers in Western students' unions led to the stu-dent games of 1949 and 1951 being given an explicitly political slant by being combined with communist-sponsored World Youth Festivals. A split occur-red when several Western students' unions tried to bar their members from taking part in the youth festivals and set up a breakaway organisation--the International Federation of University Sport (FISU) in 1949. Between 1949 and 1958, the two student sports organisations held their games separately; they came together again in 1959 when all the sports organisations of Eastern Europe (with the exceptions of East Germany and Albania) were admitted, on application, to FISU. As mutual compromises, the sports council of the In-ternational Union of Students was dissolved and the FISU Games were renam-ed Universiad, or World Student Games. Disagreement again occurred, how-ever, in 1967 when the socialist states boycotted the Universiad as a protest against the presence of the Taiwan students as representatives of China. Nonetheless, the socialist states continue to hold their student and youth games within the bounds of the overtly political World Youth Festival, al-though prime Soviet attention is today concentrated on the Universiad which, in 1973, was held in Moscow.[62]

Since the war, therefore, there has been no serious effort to turn either communist or social-democratic sports organisations into alternatives to the existing sports federations, as happened prior to the war. Nor has 'loyalty' to communist sports organisations abroad been permitted to inter-fere with the Soviet policy of 'peaceful coexistence' and, latterly, détente. A leading Soviet sports journal has editorialised: 'Sport is an essential element in contemporary international relations; it affects their development, their forms of organisation and their content. Sport effectively helps to break down national barriers, create international associations, and strengthen the international sports movement. It is a great social force helping to establish and promote international contacts between national sports-associations of countries with different social systems.'[63]

Relations with adjacent states: 1917-1974

The final aspect under which Soviet foreign sports policy may be considered is that in regard to adjacent or geographically close states.[64] For several years after the 1917 revolution, the U.S.S.R.'s ability to bargain with the Great Powers was severely limited by its weakness as well as by the mis-trust in which it was held. On the other hand, the Soviet Union was less handicapped in its dealings with its immediate neighbours, all of whom, with the exception of Poland, were extremely weak. The Soviet aim was, as Beloff has written, 'to link these (states) to Russia by treaties embodying the three major principles of "non-intervention", "non-aggression" and "neu-trality".'[65] In 1929, the so-called Litvinov Protocol on renunciation of war was signed in Moscow, originally by Estonia, Latvia, Poland and Rumania, then by Danzig, Lithuania, Persia and Turkey. Finland remained the only one of the U.S.S.R's neighbours outside the Soviet security system. Sports contacts reflected these strategic considerations.

Right from the outset, Soviet policy was to encourage sports relations with 'bourgeois' (or even 'feudal') states that were adjacent or geographically close to the U.S.S.R. Contacts took two forms: between All-Union and foreign national teams (e.g. between the U.S.S.R. and Turkey, Finland or Sweden), and between local Soviet and local and national foreign teams from just across the border (e.g. between Baku and Iran, Odessa and Turkey, Leningrad and Finnish town clubs).

Table 5 gives an indication of the pattern of sports contacts on an official level (i.e., not with workers' sports associations) between the U.S.S.R. and countries that border on or are geographically close to it. Of the pre-war neighbours in Europe, official sporting relations were maintained regularly with Finland, Estonia and Latvia. With Germany, they only began in 1940 after the signing of the non-aggression pact with the Nazis. The notable exceptions are Poland and Rumania, both of whose governments refused sporting and other cultural contacts with the Soviet Union before the war. Of the geographically close European states, relations with Norway, Denmark and Sweden were more or less regular before the war, those with Czecho-slovakia spasmodic and sports exchanges were non-existent with Albania, Hungary and Yugoslavia. The first contact with Bulgaria accompanied that with Germany in 1940. In the south, relations with Iran and Turkey were regular, particularly with Turkey, with whom the U.S.S.R. maintained sporting contact during the latter part of the 1930s at a time when sports contacts with the rest of the world virtually came to a halt due to the tense situation in Europe and the mass repression within the U.S.S.R.

Since the end of the last war, the range of contact has corresponded to the international situation and Soviet concepts--first, that of 'two camps' and then, that of 'peaceful coexistence'. Nonetheless, priority in sports relations with non-socialist states has continued to go to the good-neighbourly policy, with particular emphasis on meetings between the U.S.S.R.'s neighbours and adjoining Soviet cross-frontier (often ethnically related) peoples. Thus, a Black Sea regional soccer competition was launched in 1970 which included teams from Odessa, Sevastopol, Novorossiisk and Batumi, on the one hand, and from Turkey, Rumania and Bulgaria, on the other. A similar regional contest has existed for several years in the Baltic basin for Finnish, Swedish, Estonian and Leningrad teams. Similarly, in 1972, a Baltic Cup weight lifting competition was held with participants from Finland, Norway, Sweden, East and West Germany, Poland and the U.S.S.R. The first tourna-ment was held in Riga, capital of Latvia. In the summer of 1973, Baku was the venue of a now traditional 2-day athletics match between Iran and Azer-baidzhan.

Although sports ties with Middle Eastern countries might fall into the category of 'seeking support among developing states' (see 'Relations with newly independent countries' above), the fact that the Soviet Union often promotes contacts between their athletes and Soviet Central Asian nationals indicates also that some priority is being given to these contacts for regional,

Table 5. Official Sports Contacts Between the U.S.S.R. and Nearby States: 1920-1975.

Country	1920-1925	1926-1930	1931-1935	1936-1939	1940-1941	1945-1950	1951-1955	1956-1960	1961-1975
Albania							X	X	
Afghanistan							X	X	X
Bulgaria					X	X	X	X	X
China							X	X	
Czechoslovakia			X			X	X	X	X
Denmark	X	X	X			X	X	X	X
Estonia[a]	X	X	X		X	—	—	—	—
Finland	X	X	X			X	X	X	X
East Germany					X	X	X	X	X
West Germany								X	X
Hungary						X	X	X	X
Iran		X	X			X	X	X	X
Japan							X	X	X
Latvia[a]	X	X	X		X	—	—	—	—
Lithuania[a]		X	X		X	—	—	—	—
Mongolia									X
Norway	X	X	X		X		X	X	X
North Korea									X
Poland						X	X	X	X
Rumania						X	X	X	X
Sweden	X	X	X			X	X	X	X
Turkey	X	X	X	X		X	X	X	X
Yugoslavia						X			X

[a] Contacts with the pre-war Baltic States (Estonia, Latvia and Lithuania) are shown here up to 1940, when these countries were incorporated into the Soviet Union.

Sources: A. O. Romanov, Mezhdunarodnoye sportivnoye dvizhenie (Moscow, 1973); N. Y. Kiseley (ed.), 70 futbol'nykh let (Lenizdat, 1970); F. I. Samoukov and V. V. Stolbov (eds.), Ocherki po istorii fizicheskoi kul'tury (Moscow, 1967).

'strategic' reasons. Bilateral sports meetings with Egyptian, Syrian, Iraqi, Lebanese and Algerian athletes, which have grown since 1969 (in line with heightened Soviet interest in the Middle East), have generally taken place in the Soviet Union within the former Islamic area. Under the terms of the sports cooperation treaty between the U.S.S.R. and Egypt, signed in 1969, it was agreed to hold annual 'Soviet-Arab Sports Weeks' alternately in the two states; the first such 'Sports Week' was held in Egypt in 1970, when a team of Uzbek, Kirgiz and Kazakh sportsmen was sent. The next year, a group of Egyptian athletes, weight lifters, swimmers and wrestlers competed against Soviet Uzbek opponents in Tashkent, Samarkand and Andizhan. A similar agreement was signed with Iraq, Syria and Algeria in 1972, and with the Lebanon in 1973.[66]

Other countries with whom sports relations might be said to be promoted for 'strategic' reasons are Austria and Japan--the only capitalist states (along with Finland) in which Soviet sports coaches and players were working (up to 1975). Soviet ice hockey coaches and players were (in 1973) employed by the Austrian Atletik-Klub, KAS (Klagenfurt), Graz ATSE and the Viennese club WAT-Stadtlau.[67] A long-term sports exchange agreement was signed with Japan in 1971 and an ice hockey tournament was held in April 1973 in Sapporo between Japanese players from Hokkaido and Soviet players from the Soviet Far East and Siberia.

Contacts with other neighbours have depended on certain other factors; for example, with Afghanistan, Mongolia, China and North Korea they were long inhibited by the backwardness of sport in those countries. Sporting contacts were established with Afghanistan in 1955 and exchanges now take place regularly between Uzbek and Afghan athletes. Exchanges with Mongolia and North Korea commenced in the mid-1960s. With China, sports relations have closely followed the course of the Sino-Soviet dispute: bilateral contacts, which began only in 1955, were abruptly halted in 1961. Thus, for example, the Leningrad Zenit soccer team played 11 matches in China in September 1955 (winning ten and drawing one) and the Soviet National soccer team toured China in the spring of 1958. The last recorded Sino-Soviet soccer match was between Peking and Leningrad Zenit in Leningrad (won 3-2 by Zenit) on 29 July 1961.[68] The post-cultural revolution resumption of political contacts between China and the West, said to have been presaged by table tennis matches in 1971, has not yet been paralleled by a similar renewal of sports contacts with the U.S.S.R.

On balance, the Soviet policy of promoting sporting ties with neighbouring states--a quite deliberate attempt to use sport to cement good-neighbourly relations--has been fairly successful. This policy has been pursued in regard to neighbouring states even when general foreign and sports policies towards other 'bourgeois' countries have been radically at variance with this.

It has to be noted that, in most sports, the U.S.S.R.'s neighbours lag, often considerably, behind the world's foremost sporting nations and have generally been inferior to their Soviet opponents. By encouraging regional as often as national contacts, the U.S.S.R. has avoided completely demoralising or publicly shaming opponents; pitting its strongest teams against them might well have had the opposite effect to the one desired. Pursuit of the goal of demonstrating the progress made by kindred peoples under socialism is in no way vitiated by this. The success of, say, Azerbaidzhanian against Turkish athletes is often cited by Soviet publicists as evidence of the progress made by national minorities under socialism.

Summary

To sum up, the pattern of foreign sports competition involving the U.S.S.R. has closely followed the course of Soviet foreign policy and displays clearly differentiated contours in regard to the geopolitical situation of other countries. With the new balance of power after the last war (the creation of a group of socialist buffer-states, the emergence of newly independent Afro-Asian states and a nuclear stalemate), the Soviet leaders have assigned sport such tasks as demonstrating the superiority of and winning support for the communist system, encouraging friendly, commercial and good-neighbourly relations with the U.S.S.R. and, within the socialist bloc, achieving unity on Soviet terms.

With its control of the sports system, the Soviet leadership has been able to mobilise resources to achieve the maximum efficiency of its sport challenge and, hence, to perform what it believes to be salient political functions. It evidently considers that sports emissaries can sometimes do more than diplomats to recommend a political philosophy and way of life to the outside world. It is hardly possible to measure the impact of international success in sport on the behaviour of individuals or states--to discover whether such success can, in fact, ever affect policies. What is certain is that there can no longer be any belief that success is, as it was in the past, primarily a matter of the physical and moral resources of the individual participant.

The Soviet Union has demonstrated that the highest realisation of human potential can be most effectively achieved through the planned application of societal resources towards that desired end. It has done this in sport (and many other fields of human endeavour and excellence--e.g. musicianship) and it has done this for the conscious (political) demonstration-effect which it is supposed, quite plausibly, to have. In general, in the Western world, the whipping-up of popular fervour in sport has, consciously or unconsciously, resulted in the sacrifice of the sporting ideal on the altar of national or ethnic chauvinism. In the U.S.S.R., thanks partly to its multi-national population, this has largely been avoided; it is not some innate ethnic or national superiority which has been seen to triumph, but a political system.

That Soviet international sporting contacts are in general subordinate to the general lines of Soviet foreign policy is indisputable, and this has resulted on occasion in the grossest political opportunism. Yet it is equally true that this has also resulted in giving sport a preeminent rôle in moral leadership in world political terms, as exemplified by the apartheid issue. The increasing political isolation of South Africa in world affairs must be due in no small measure to the catalytic rôle played by the now very extensive boycott of sporting contacts with that country and to which the Soviet Union has made a notable, even leading, contribution.

Footnotes

[1] A. Nathan, 'Sport and Policits', in J. W. Loy and G. S. Kenyon (eds.), Sport, Culture and Society (Macmillan, 1969), p. 206.

[2] The Place of Sport in Education, UNESCO, Paris, 1956, p. 57.

[3] The 1973 U.S.S.R. v. U.S.A. athletics match in Minsk, for example, was attended by over 200 journalists, half of whom were from the West; BBC TV transmitted two half-hour programmes on the two days of the tournament at peak viewing times (6:45 p.m. and 7:30 p.m.)—even though no British athletes were involved.

[4] Y. A. Talayev, 'Sport—oblast' mirnovo sorevnovaniya', Teoriya i praktika fizicheskoi kul'tury, 1973, No. 1, p. 8.

[5] A. O. Romanov, Mezhdunarodnoye sportivnoye dvizhenie (Moscow, 1973), p. 185.

[6] These states were Yugoslavia (1945), Bulgaria (1946), Albania (1946), Hungary (1946), Rumania (1946), Poland (1947), Czechoslovakia (1948), North Korea (1948), the German Democratic Republic (1949) and China (1949).

[7] In an admonition to Soviet writers, Zhdanov had said: 'Is it right for Soviet patriots like us, representatives of progressive Soviet culture, to play the part of admirers of disciples of bourgeois culture? Our literature reflects a society which is on a higher plane than any bourgeois-democratic society, a culture which is obviously superior to bourgeois culture and, therefore, it need hardly be said, has the right to teach others the new, universal morals. Where can one find another people like ours, or a country like ours? Where can one find such wonderful human qualities?' Pravda, 6 June 1946, p. 1.

[8] See Entsiklopedichesky slovar' po fizicheskoi kul'ture i sportu, Vol. III (Moscow, 1963), p. 226.

[9] Kul'tura i zhizn', 1 November 1949, gives the full text of the resolution 'On the Work of the All-Union Committee on Physical Culture and Sports Affairs in Implementing the Directives of the Party and the Government on the Development of the Mass Sports Movement in the Country and on Improving the Skill of Soviet Athletes'.

[10] Y. D. Kotov and I. I. Yudovich, Sovetskaya shakhmatnaya shkola (Moscow, 1951), p. 4.

[11] The International Olympic Committee continued to recognise the old tsarist Russian Olympic Committee for several years after 1917. Such ROC members as General Butovsky, Count Ribopierre, Baron Vilebrandt and Prince Urusov all served on the IOC in the period 1917-1932.

[12] Romanov, Mezhdunarodnoye sportivnoye dvizhenie, p. 193.

[13] S. Pavlov, 'Vklad sporta v ukreplenie mezhdunarodnovo sotrudnichestva', Teoriya i praktika fizicheskoi kul'tury, 1975, No. 7, p. 4.

[14] V. S. Rodichenko (ed.), Rekordy, sobytiya, lyudi, 1969 (Moscow, 1970), p. 109.

[15] K. K. Platonov, S. S. Groshenkov, 'O professional'noi i sportivnoi orientatsii uchashcheisya molodyozhi,' Teoriya: praktika fizicheskoi kul'tury, 1968, No. 5, p. 42.

[16] Pravda, 30 April 1957. Twenty-seven beneficiaries received the supreme accolade, the Order of Lenin, 145--the Order of the Red Banner of Labour, 367--the Badge of Honour, 353--the medal 'For Outstanding Labour' and 75--the medal 'For Excellent Labour'. Never before--or since --have the leaders honoured so highly the efforts of Soviet sportsmen.

[17] Pravda, 17 September 1972, p. 1.

[18] Sovetsky sport, 6 October 1972, pp. 1-2. 'On Awarding U.S.S.R. Orders and Medals to Athletes, Trainers and Physical Culture and Sports Officials in Connection with the Results of the XX Summer Olympic Games.'

[19] Sport v. SSSR, 1972, No. 12, p. 25.

[20] Sport v. SSSR, 1972, No. 11, p. 3.

[21] K. Heinila, 'Notes on Intergroup Conflicts in International Sport,' International Review of Sport Sociology, Vol. I, Warsaw, 1967, p. 34.

[22] In the world chess ranking list issued by the International Chess Federation in 1972, Soviet men occupied 7 of the top 10 places, 15 of the top 20 and 52 of the top 100 places; Soviet women filled the top 7 places and 19 of the first 25 places. Sovetsky sport, 11 November 1972, p. 3.

[23] It provides some measure of the impact in recent years of sports needs on state thinking to recall that until the year of the Soviet Olympic début, 1952, there were only three indoor swimming pools in the whole of the Soviet Union (i.e., one pool per 61 million people). Even in 1970, the

U.S.S.R. had only 1 pool per 100,000 people (1 per 250,000 in the Russian Federation); in the same year, Britain, despite extensive access to the sea, had 1 indoor swimming pool per 37,000 people. See Sport v. SSSR, 1971, No. 7, p. 14; World Sports, June 1970, p. 43.

[24] V. S. Rodichenko (ed.), Rekordy, sobytiya, lyudi, 1969 (Moscow, 1970), p. 105. To emphasize the international impact of success in sport by socialist states, one writer has referred to 'the interesting fact that 8 per cent of West Germans who advocate recognition of the GDR do so because of the successes of the German socialist state in international sport and, especially, the Olympic Games'. See Teoriya i praktika fizicheskoi kul'tury, 1973, No. 8, p. 5.

[25] Z. Medvedev, The Medvedev Papers (Macmillan, London, 1971), pp. 160-161.

[26] Sovetsky sport, 27 June 1973, p. 4.

[27] Rodichenko, Rekordy, sobytiya, lyudy, 1969, p. 106.

[28] Romanov, Mezhdunarodnoye sportivnoye dvizhenie, p. 196.

[29] Ibid., pp. 183-184.

[30] Ibid., p. 177.

[31] Rumania has, for example, permitted some athletes and coaches to travel and work abroad with far greater freedom, particularly in regard to disposing of their foreign income, than athletes from other socialist states (except Yugoslavia). A Rumanian soccer trainer worked (until 1973) for three years with the famous Dutch and European champions Ajax: the unrestrained behaviour of the globe-trotting tennis star Ilia Nastase is certainly something the Soviet authorities would not condone among its players.

[32] The Znamensky brothers were outstanding Soviet athletes before the war.

[33] The 1973 Friendship junior athletics match took place in the Soviet city of Odessa with teams from Bulgaria, Cuba, Czechoslovakia, East Germany, Hungary, Mongolia, Poland, Rumania and the U.S.S.R. competing. By convention, no team score is made during these matches. See Sovetsky sport, 8 August 1973, p. 2.

[34] Sport v. SSSR, 1972, No. 9, p. 2.

[35] Sovetsky sport, 21 December 1972, p. 1.

[36] Romanov, _Mezhdunarodnoye sportivnoye dvizhenie_, p. 90.

[37] For the first time at this _SCFA spartakiad_, a team from outside the bloc participated--Horsed, the army team of the Somali Democratic Republic. Although its members won no medals, one athlete received a special prize awarded by the U.S.S.R. Ministry of Defence. The Republic subsequently became a member of SCFA. See _Sovetsky sport_, 23 February 1974, p. 4.

[38] Romanov, _Mezhdunarodnoye sportivnoye dvizhenie_, p. 178.

[39] Cuba came second, not many points behind the U.S.A., in the 1972 and 1975 Pan-American Games, and won 3 gold, 1 silver and 4 bronze medals in the 1972 Olympic Games. Eight Soviet coaches accompanied the Cuban team to the Olympics and 12 to the 1972 Pan-American Games. _Sovetsky sport_, 22 June 1973, p. 3.

[40] _Sovetsky sport_, 30 January 1974, p. 4.

[41] _Manchester Guardian_, 26 October, 1956.

[42] Reported to me by an Englishman then living in Prague. The two Czechoslovakia-U.S.S.R. matches in the 1973 world ice-hockey championship (won by the U.S.S.R.) played in Moscow (that I witnessed on Moscow TV) where marked by exceedingly rough play, mainly from the Czechoslovaks, that was largely absent in other championship matches.

[43] See D. Prokhorov, 'Nam nuzhyn vashi spetsialisty', _Sport v. SSSR_, 1970, No. 11, p. 14.

[44] Romanov, _Mezhdunarodnoye sportivnoye dvizhenie_, p. 182.

[45] Prokhorov, 'Nam nuzhny vashi spetsialisty', p. 15.

[46] _Sport v. SSSR_, 1972, No. 12, p. 25.

[47] _Sovetsky sport_, 22 April 1973, p. 4.

[48] _Sport v. SSSR_, 1972, No. 12, p. 25.

[49] _Sovetsky sport_, 14 July 1971, p. 4.

[50] _Sport v. SSSR_, 1972, No. 12, p. 24.

[51] Fizkul'tura i sport, 1971, No. 3, p. 1.

[52] Sovetsky sport, 25 November 1973, p. 4.

[53] Sovetsky sport, 2 Ausust 1973, p. 1.

[54] Ibid., p. 4.

[55] The U.S.S.R. refusal in November 1978 to play its World Cup qualifying soccer match in Chile, following the right-wing coup that brought down President Allende, may be seen in a similar light--as a moral decision that meets with the approval of national liberation movements.

[56] Sportivnaya zhizn' Rossii, 1972, No. 11, p. 7; the further point was made that representatives of 26 Soviet nationalities, including some from all 15 union republics, were present at the 1972 Munich Olympics--'eloquent testimony for all the world to see of the triumph of the Leninist national policy in physical culture and sport'.

[57] Sport v. SSSR, 1973, No. 2, p. 19.

[58] Sovetsky sport, 27 July 1973, p. 1.

[59] The Times, 17 August 1973, p. 14.

[60] Sovetsky sport, 31 July 1973, p. 4.

[61] See Romanov, Mezhrunarodnoye sportivnoye dvizhenie, pp. 84-87. The 19 sports are athletics, basketball, bowls, boxing, chess, cross country running, cycling, fishing, soccer, handball, shooting, skiing, swimming, table tennis, tennis, volleyball, water polo, weight lifting and wrestling.

[62] The Moscow Universiad was held on the Olympic model in the following 11 sports: athletics, basketball, diving, fencing, free style and Graeco-Roman wrestling, gymnastics, swimming, tennis, volleyball and water polo.

[63] Teoriya i praktika fizicheskoi kul'tury, 1971, No. 3, p. 5.

[64] Today, immediate neighbours include six states in Europe (Norway, Finland, Poland, Czechoslovakia, Hungary and Rumania) and six in Asia (Turkey, Iran, Afghanistan, Mongolia, China and North Korea). Countries whose geopolitical situation brings them within the category of strategically important 'neighbours' of the Soviet Union are evidently Sweden and Denmark in the Baltic area, Bulgaria, Albania and Yugoslavia in the

Balkans, Egypt, Algeria, Iraq, Syria and the Lebanon in the Middle East, and Japan in the Far East.

[65] Beloff, The Foreign Policy of Soviet Russia, p. 5.

[66] The five-year sports cooperation agreement with Syria covered bilateral and multilateral competitions in both countries, joint training and seminars, exchange of documents and agreements to build sports amenities and manufacture equipment.

[67] Sovetsky sport, 27 January 1973, p. 4. The strategic value of Austria is that it acts as a neutral wedge some 500 miles deep between West Germany and Italy, thus splitting the Western bloc in two.

[68] N. Y. Kiselev (ed.), 70 fulbol'nykh let (Lenizdat, 1970), pp. 210, 222, 242. Sports ties with Albania followed a similar pattern: the Leningrad Labour Reserves soccer team played matches a Tirana in 1954 and Tirana Dinamo played in Moscow and Leningrad in 1956. No matches are recorded after 1960, when Albania withdrew from international competition (except with China). It is noteworthy that, following China's resumption of competition against foreign athletes in 1971, Albania joined the International Weight Lifting Federation (in 1972).

Diplomats In Track Suits: Linkages

Between Sports And Foreign Policy

In The German Democratic Republic

Andrew Strenk

On October 7, 1949, the Provisional Volkskammer was voted into existence by the Volksrat of the Soviet occupied area of Germany. A constitution
was adopted, and the German Democratic Republic thus came into existence,
following by five months the formation of the Federal Republic of Germany in
the three zones occupied by the Americans, British and French. The GDR
was modeled in the system of the Soviet Union in its economic, social and
economic structures and institutions. One of the most immediate problems
of the GDR was the problem of diplomatic recognition, which was to be the
chief thrust of the new state's foreign policy for the next two decades.

The GDR was immediately recognized as a sovereign state by the
U.S.S.R., Bulgaria, Poland, Czechoslovakia, Hungary, Rumania, the Peoples Republic of China, the Korean Peoples Republic, Albania and in 1950,
by the Democratic Republic of Vietnam and the Peoples Republic of Mongolia.
That was all the international recognition on a formal diplomatic level that
the GDR received until 1957, when Yugoslavia opened diplomatic relations
with East Berlin. Cuba followed in 1963. By the beginning of 1969, only
these thirteen nations had formally granted the GDR recognition.[1]

All new states face the problem of obtaining diplomatic recognition,
but the GDR had an extraordinary hard time due to the historical circumstances surrounding its foundation and the fact that there existed another
Germany to the west. The Federal Republic of Germany not only came into
existence earlier, but with its official title (Bundesrepublik Deutschland),
also laid claim to represent the entire German nation and people, although
the FRG was restricted geographically to a fraction of the pre-1945 Germany.
The FRG claimed to be the legal successor to the Reich of Hitler and the
heir to the German tradition and culture. The FRG received support from
the three Western powers at the New York Foreign Ministers Conference in
September, 1950, when the FRG was declared to be the sole legitimate representative of the German people and as such, empowered to speak for all

Germans. This was based on the idea that the FRG possessed the only freely elected government in Germany.[2]

The Federal Republic was rather quickly recognized around the world
and within a few years had over a hundred diplomatic posts abroad.[3] A series of treaties with the Western occupying powers, above all the Americans,
resulted in the FRG becoming a member in various international organizations such as the Organization for European Economic Cooperation (OEEC)
(December 15, 1949) and the Council of Europe (1950). The Declaration of
Sovereignity by the GDR on March 25, 1954 was rejected by the Bonn government. Dr. Walter Hallstein of the FRG Foreign Office proclaimed a doctrine which came to be known as the "Hallstein Doctrine". In essence, this
policy threatened any state with the break-off of diplomatic relations by the
FRG if that state recognized the GDR.[4] The GDR was referred to as the
"Ostzone" (East Zone), "Mitteldeutschland" (Middle Germany) or SBZ (Sow-
jetische Bestazungszone, or Soviet Occupied Zone) by West German policy
makers in the 1950's and 1960's. The GDR was "Inland" ("domestic" not
"Ausland" foreign); relations with the GDR were administered not by the
Foreign Office, but by the Ministerium fuer gesamtdeutsche Fragen (Pan
German Issues), later by the Ministerium fuer Innerdeutsche Beziehungen
(Inner German Relations). Since the FRG had the support of the Western
powers, the GDR was very isolated.[5]

A society in this situation has four basic choices to make: either
change the domestic structures to bring them in line with the demands of the
external environment; or change the environment to meet the demands of the
domestic political structure; or attempt to shape the demands of the domestic situation with those of the foreign environment; or to attempt to live with
the situation and the demands of the internal structures and foreign environment. In each case, however, adaption--the need to explicitly relate the
essential political and socioeconomic structures of a society to the external
surroundings--is required. The four choices have been classified and described as acquiescent, intransigent, promotive and preventive by James
Rosenau.[6] The GDR's foreign policy could be classified as being within the
framework of an intransigent society, since its main goal was to alter the
hostile environment in which it found itself. While certain internal structures were refined and developed further, the salient internal characteristics
of the GDR political structure--a one party state under control of the Sozialistische Einheitspartei (SED)--were not altered. Rather than changing its
basic policies, the GDR political elite set out to bend the environment to the
country's internal attributes. Therefore, the main need in foreign policy
was to be both uncompromising and yet innovative. The GDR leadership saw
itself in a zero-sum game, in which they had to be the winners. The basic
characteristics of the GDR society were too important to these leaders to be
bargained or compromised away.[7]

Changing the environment was not a simple thing for a nation to do,
especially for a small nation the size of the GDR with a population of less
than twenty million. The routine measures of trade, commerce, diplomacy
and negotiation were not available to the GDR for use in influencing the world
beyond the borders of Eastern Europe. Neither was military force a viable
option. Since the normal means were ineffective, the GDR turned to sports

as a medium of cultural diplomacy to obtain its foreign policy goals. Sports exchanges would generate a constant outflow of persons from the GDR to other countries, especially if world class athletes could be developed. Athletes would be utilized to gain support abroad and undermine the political isolation of the GDR. GDR officials told their athletes departing for foreign competition, "You are sports-diplomats in track suits."[8]

The GDR demands for recognition fell into four main categories: (1) the demand for the recognition of the existence as a state; (2) the establishment of formal diplomatic relations; (3) the demand that the GDR be accorded a status equal to the FRG; and (4) that relations be established according to the international laws regarding such matters.[9] According to the GDR legal experts, who followed the interpretation of declaratory legal theory, the GDR already possessed the status of a recognized state, since the GDR existed in fact. However, since the prevailing world opinion followed the conclusive theory, whereby the recognition of other states was necessary for full acceptance into the community of nations, this approval had to be gained too. Sports would be one vehicle for accomplishing this end. East German athletes competing on foreign soil would force a de facto recognition of the GDR and would lead ultimately to a de jure recognition.[10] A second and parallel goal became the acceptance of the GDR sports organizations into the international sports organizations, which while not as effective as the establishment of diplomatic relations or the signing of treaties in the short run, would bring a form of recognition in the longer run. Tied in with the drive to acquire membership in international organizations was the campaign to participate in international conferences.[11]

The sports campaign was nothing short of phenomenal in its results. The GDR sports program brought many benefits to the German Democratic Republic, such as a high standard of military preparedness, ideological education of broad segments of the population, increased productivity on the assembly lines and in the offices due to better health, opportunities for recreation and a chance to work off excess energies for much of the population, as well as aiding in the development of a national consciousness separate from that of West Germany.[12] The main goal was also achieved. (See Figure 1).

Immediately after the formation of the GDR in October of 1949, an East German soccer team, disguised as a Saxony all-star team, played a match against Hungary, which for the sake of international soccer (FIFA) rules, played as a labor union team. The Hungarians won, but the East Germans did not lose; the match was recorded as their first "Laenderspiel". The game demonstrated the existence of the GDR as an independent political entity, and therefore capable of conducting sports relations with other nations. This was the opening move in the East German sports offensive.

The International Olympic Committee recognized the National Olympic Committee for Germany at its 45th Session in Vienna in 1951. The West Germans had reconstituted their Olympic organization under the old Nazi sports leader and IOC member Ritter von Halt, who had returned from several years in a Soviet prisoner of war labor camp. The West German committee, formed September 24, 1951, was granted official Olympic recognition

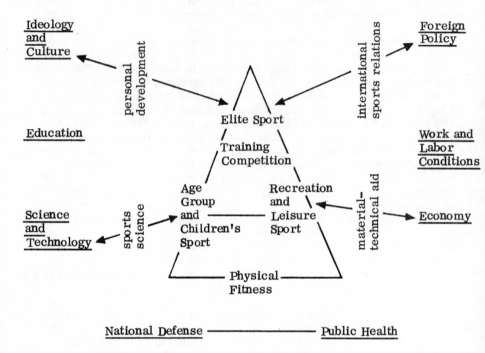

Figure 1. The Role of Physical Culture and Sport in the GDR.

This diagram illustrates the role that sport plays in the East German society and the linkages between the various societal structures and sport. Physical culture and sport were placed in the center of the diagram for clarity, not to imply that sport is the central concern of the GDR political elite, but rather to show the multifaceted uses of sport in the GDR system. From: Guenther Starke, "Gesellschaftliche Stellung und gesellschaftliche Funktionen von Koerperkultur und Sport in der DDR", Theorie und Praxis der Koerperkultur, Vol. 24, No. 10 (October 1975), p. 905.

largely because von Halt and IOC President Sigfrid Edstroem and Vice-President Avery Brundage were old friends. The IOC advised the GDR Olympic delegation to meet together with the West Germans for the purpose of forming a unified team for the 1952 Olympic Games to be held in Helsinki. In Lausanne that summer, the Olympic committees of both Germanies met to work out an agreement, since the IOC permitted only one delegation per country, and the GDR representatives insisted that they were Germans and were interested in reunification. The negotiations led to the signature by Ritter von Halt and GDR delegation head Kurt Edel of a contract pledging them to form a Pan-German team "consisting of the best German athletes without regard for their place of residence." A subsequent declaration on September 2, 1951 by the GDR chief of state Walter Ulbricht declared the agreement to be invalid, since the contract gave the control of the Olympic team to the FRG until the Games in Helsinki. [13]

The National Olympic Committee of the GDR (NOC-GDR) demanded that the IOC first recognize the GDR as a necessary prerequisite to East German participation in the 1952 Olympics. An attempt by Baron von Frenckell of Finland to reopen negotiations failed in 1952 when the GDR delegation arrived late for a meeting with the IOC Executive Board in Copenhagen, and then made no attempt to meet with the IOC and remained instead in their hotel.

As a result, no East Germans participated in the Olympic Games in 1952. However, the GDR was successful on other fronts. Supported by the Soviet Union and other Eastern European allies, the GDR was admitted to the international ski (FIS), volleyball (FIVB) and table tennis (ITTF) federations. One year later, the GDR had acquired membership in the international boxing, basketball, soccer, canoeing, wrestling, swimming and sailing federations.

The GDR did not wait for its athletes to begin winning international championships or for the international federations to award international championships to the GDR. The East Germans organized their own international events to help develop their international profile. The I Deutsches Turn and Sportfest was held in Leipzig in 1954. In addition to the 30,000 East Germans, some 5,000 West Germans were invited to participate. The GDR became in 1952 a co-host of the Friedensfahrt bicycle tour from Prague to Warsaw/Warsaw-Prague. East Berlin was added to the course, with the course being changed accordingly and the start and finish cities rotating yearly. This cycling competiton became one of the most popular in Europe, and most instrumental in the GDR cycling federation being accepted in the international federation (UCI). [14]

In 1955, the GDR Olympic delegation was finally granted "provisional" recognition by the 50th IOC Session meeting in Paris with the condition that such recognition would be erased should it prove impossible to send an all-German team to the Olympics at Melbourne in 1956. An additional sentence added that it was understood by the IOC that following reunification there would be only one German Olympic Committee for the entire country. All-German teams competed at the Olympics in 1956, 1960 and 1964 under a common flag and emblem. Despite the appearances, the team was never an integrated whole but rather two sections. The East Germans had separate quarters, their own medical staff, and limited contact between the GDR athletes and the West German sportsmen to the minimum possible. The GDR brought out their own pressbook and passed out their own pins.[15]

The sports politics of the GDR were not only innovative, but they were uncompromising. In a decision of March 17, 1951, the Central Committee of the SED advised the East German sports organization DSA (Deutsche Sportausschluss) to engage in the so-called "Westarbeit" during sports exchanges. This was a program designed to infiltrate the Western zones of Germany, and undermine the West German state structure. No opportunity was overlooked in the course of sports events to engage in ideological conversations in an attempt to influence public opinion in the Federal Republic. The GDR ideological position was:

> Sports and politics cannot be separated any more than one can separate a gymnast from the bars or vault, a swimmer from the water, or a soccer player from the soccer field. Sports are a social phenomenon. They are connected with the coming together of people and therefore tied together with the political structure. For that reason, sportsmen can and will only understand and consciously conduct their assignments when they understand the basic structures, i.e., the politics of their state.[16]

Erich Honecker, currently general secretary of the SED and chairman of the State Council (Staatsrat) of the GDR, has said, "Sport is not an end in itself, but rather the means to an end."[17] West Germany was bombarded with propaganda.

> The gymnasts and athletes of the German Democratic Republic must recognize that they have the responsibility to support the fight for the liberation of the West German population. It is their patriotic duty to enlighten the West German gymnasts and sportsmen during sports exchanges about the criminal plans of the American and West German imperialists and to mobilize them against these forces.[18]

Besides agitating and holding political speeches at Western sports competitions, starting in 1951, West German athletes were invited to the Oberhofer Sports Talks held in the GDR. Attempts were made to recruit West German athletes to move east by offering them material and financial advantages. Emil Reinicke, Wolfgang Rupe, Horst Tuller and Manfred von Brauntisch were some of the West German athletes who moved east.[19]

As a reply to the agitation and propaganda, the West German sports organization DSB (Deutsche Sportbund) met with the FRG Olympic Committee May 27, 1951 to draw up a list of regulations to cover East-West relations. A prohibition against political influence and reference was included. The sport leadership of the GDR reacted with a series of "open letters" to clubs and individuals in West Germany starting January 25, 1952. The DSA also demanded that West Berliners be excluded from West German national teams

The result was that the DSB decided that due to the discriminatory handling of athletes from West Berlin and the misuse of sports exchanges, to break off all inner-German sports contacts. This decision taken at Oberwesel lasted from September 21 to December 12, 1952. The GDR found itself being boycotted by West German teams. The impasse led to an agreement worked out in West Berlin, whereby the delegates of the DSA and the DSB agreed that political propaganda would be prohibited and that the discrimination against West Berlin athletes would be ended. The DSB agreed to cease opposing the entrance of GDR sport sections into the international federations.[20]

The GDR did not send sports officials to the international congresses who were unpaid amateurs, as was often the case with Western delegates. Instead, professionally trained negotiators armed with the latest directives of the SED were sent out. All athletes and journalists in the GDR teams were under the authority of a special delegate, who received his orders in code direct from East Berlin.[21]

Despite the agreement, the propaganda war did not subside. Various political events served as stimuli for letter writing campaigns by East German athletes in an attempt to incite West German athletes to demonstrate against the "General War Treaty" (January, 1952), the European Defense Community (May, 1954), the Paris Treaties (March, 1955), compulsory military service in the FRG (February, 1957), the Bundestag elections (August, 1957) and the Bundeswehr (December, 1960). Other letters advocated support for various peace proposals of the Communist bloc (December, 1957), the Rapacki Plan (February, 1958), the Confederation idea of two German states (April, 1958), the SED peace treaty proposal (October, 1958), and the creation of West Berlin as a free city (January, 1959).[22]

Chairman of the DSA, Rudi Reichert, stated:

> It is our patriotic and national duty to win the support of all the athletes of West Berlin and West Germany for the Soviet proposals to turn West Berlin into a free, demilitarized city and to sign a peace treaty with all of Germany.[23]

> In the years following the destruction of the fascist Greater Germany there arose two independent states in Germany. The one is the German Democratic Republic which is a state of the workers and farmers, which consequently followed the path of democratic development as laid out for all of Germany in the Potsdam Agreement. The other is the Federal Republic of Germany, which was created with the help of the U.S.A. imperialists in order to prevent the Potsdam Agreement from being carried out in all of Germany...the right to speak for Germany belongs solely to the GDR, the state of freindship, peace and real democracy, the state of socialism, to which the future belongs.[24]

In the fight for peace and freedom, playing and sport
relations must be subordinated to the political objective.
That is why the sport meetings between east and west
must be politically prepared in a suitable way.[25]

Athletes in the West should cooperate in the great protest movements, strikes and demonstrations against the
order existing in the Federal Republic.[26]

Physical culture and sport are, insolubly linked with
the social life of mankind... The history of physical
culture is a history of class struggles... All our measures, both inside our own Republic, and those concerning our sport efforts in West Germany and abroad
must be directed towards this end.[27]

Such pronouncements were not limited to sports officials from the GDR. The
distance runner Friedrich Janke was not untypical of many East German athletes in the 1950's when after establishing a new world indoor mark, said:

I am delighted over my victory in this beautiful facility.
However, we must insure that this facility will continue
to exist and that we will acquire more of its kind... A
nuclear free zone in Central Europe would be the first
step to ending such a terrible threat. We must fight
against it. I do not know exactly, but I would imagine
that for the cost of one atomic weapon, one could construct quite a few such sports arenas.[28]

Tensions continued to run high between the two German sports organizations. Negotiations in 1957 in Dortmund and in Delecke/Moehnesee ended
without any success. The DTSB (German Gymnastics and Sports Federation)
replaced the DSA in the GDR on April 28, 1957 as the government organization responsible for the sports program. The various sports federations became organs of the DTSB, which received its instructions direct from the
Central Committee of the SED and was administered by the State Committee
for Physical Culture and Sport of the Council of Ministers. (See Figure 2).

Relations between the two Germanies were not helped by the steady
leakage of GDR athletes who defected to the West and competed on West German club and national teams. Internationally, the GDR faced continuing
problems with acceptance. The United States refused to grant East Germans
visas to compete in the World Modern Pentathlon Championships in Harrisburg in 1959 and ten members of the German team who came from East Germany for the 1960 Winter Olympics at Squaw Valley were not admitted to the
United States. Typical of the hostile attitudes which faced East German athletes competing was this comment by Los Angeles Times journalist Bill
Henry in 1959:

The suspicion is, however, that this year's East German
entry was more of a diplomatic than an athletic proposition.
Nations whose sovereignty is open to suspicion, have for

POLITBURO

SECRETARIAT

Central Committee/Working Group
for Physical Culture and Sport

PRESIDIUM

COUNCIL OF MINISTERS

STATE SECRETARIAT FOR PHYSICAL CULTURE AND
SPORT (Guenther Erbach)

*Scientific and Methodological Council

Youth Commission

Youth Commission

State Committee for   Office for Youth
Tourism and Hiling   Issues

DHfK (Deutsche Hochschule fuer
Koerperkultur—Leipzig)

National Olympic Committee   *Young   *Free   *Free   *German
(Pres. Heinz Schoebel)   Pioneers   German   Trade   Gymnastic
                                               Youth   Union   and
                                               (FDJ)   Federation   Sports
                                                             (FDGB)   Federation
                                                                             (DTSB)
                                                                             (Pres. Manfred Ewald)

Wismut (bismuth)   BSGs   Aktivist (mining)
Wissenschaft   Lokomotive (transport)   (Factory Sport   Aufbau (construction)
(scientific   Medizin (public health)   Clubs)   Empor (trade)
research)   Motor (metal working)   Einheit (administration)
                    Stahl (steel)   Fortschritt (textiles)
                    Traktor (agricultural)   Chemie (chemicals)
                    Turbine (energy)

Figure 2. The Sports System in the GDR.

these many years, sought any sort of diplomatic recognition like a damsel of ill-repute hoping against hope that she'll be seen somewhere in the vicinity of a legitimate society leader...the valley (Squaw Valley) has achieved the distinction of being the center of an international squabble. This one has to do with the proposed entry of several human avalanches who insist on being regarded as a team representing a country called East Germany, which, as far as the U.S. is concerned, simply doesn't exist... And everybody knows that the only real reason for sending their entry is just that--to gain a certain amount of recognition of East Germany as a separate nation. [29]

That same year, the GDR took another step in the campaign to establish its right to exist by adopting a new national flag and national emblem. The GDR sought out sports competitions with any nation which would hoist the GDR flag and play the GDR national hymn at award ceremonies. The West Germans refused to recognize the right of the East Germans to compete under their national insignia and insisted that the GDR athletes continue to compete under their club emblems. A decree by the DTSB on April 25, 1960 ordered all GDR sportsmen to wear the DDR emblem on a conspicuous part of their uniforms. A threat by the DSB to break off sports relations caused the DTSB to temporarily retreat on the emblem issue. Continued GDR insistence at various international championships that the GDR protocol be accepted along with continued political agitation and the blockade of West German athletes living in West Berlin led the DSB and the West German Olympic Committee (officially, National Olympische Komitee fuer Deutschland) to break off all sports exchanges with the GDR on August 16, 1961. This so-called "Duesseldorfer Beschluss" was also a reaction against the Berlin Wall, which had been erected a few days earlier. [30]

Following that decision, the Allied Travel Office in West Berlin refused to grant any visas to athletes from the GDR who wanted to attend competitions in various North Atlantic Treaty Organization (NATO) states. In the period 1957-1967, the GDR was refused visas on at least 35 different occasions by Italy, the U.S.A., France, Holland, Great Britain, Norway, Belgium, Denmark, Iceland, Portugal, Spain, Switzerland and Japan. This did not include refusals by the FRG. In the same period, some twelve GDR sports teams departed international sports events in France, Great Britain, Holland, Denmark, Portugal, the U.S.A., Norway and Mexico. On other occasions, the award ceremony would be canceled if a GDR athlete won an event. Whether the East Germans packed their bags and departed, or stayed, almost every international competition where they appeared in this period was interrupted by the controversy over the flag, emblem and designation of the GDR delegation. GDR officials demanded that the state flag of the GDR be flown and that the GDR hymn be played during award ceremonies. They were resisted by the West Germans supported by the Americans and other Western officials. In West Germany, police broke up matches where the East Germans wore their state emblems, such as happened at the 1962 BC Bochum Hordel-Lokomotiv Engelsdorf soccer match. [31]

German Gymnastic and Sports Federation

Factory Sports
Clubs

Dynamo
ex: Dynamo Berlin
Dynamo Dresden
Dynamo Hoppegarten
Dynamo Luckenwalde

Vorwaerts
ex: Vorwaerts Potsdam
Vorwaerts Rostock
Vorwaerts Frankfurt/
Oder

*Society for
Sport and
Technology
(GST)

*Ministry of the
Interior
(Minister: Friedrich
Dickel)

*Ministry for
National Defense
(Minister: Heinz
Hoffmann)

POLITBURO

Schools

*Ministry of Education
(Minister: Margot Honecker–
Feist)

Ministry
for
Higher
Learning
(Minister:
Hans Joachim
Boehme)

Universities
Advanced
Technical
Institutes

* = represented in the DTSB

Source: Karl Ihmels, Sport und Spaltung in der Politik der Sed, (Cologne: Verlag Wissenschaft und Politik, 1965), p. 19.

Figure 3. The German Gymnastic and Sports Federation (DTSB).

The GDR did not compromise, East Germans continued to win international titles and East Germany increased its efforts to hold world and European championship events. These were, in turn, celebrated as examples of the ever increasing recognition of the GDR. Such triumphs were proclaimed to demonstrate the superiority of "our system over the capitalistic system" and "the reputation and legitimacy of our workers and farmers state."[32] Every record set and every medal won was demonstrating the existence of the East German state. "Gymnasts and sportsmen strengthen and build up the GDR--achieve good sports results for the honor of our socialistic home", was one of the popular slogans.[33]

The restrictions by the Allied Travel Office were partially lifted in 1964 and completely eliminated in 1965. The revision of the Duesseldorfer Beschluss occurred on October 30, 1965 in Cologne. The IOC decided at its Session in Madrid in the same month to recognize the National Olympic Committee of the GDR with responsibility for the territory of East Germany. East Germany was granted the right to enter a separate Olympic team at the 1968 Olympics in Mexico, but it would have to compete under the same flag, hymn and emblem as the West German team and as the previous all-German teams had done. The constant quarrels between the two German factions finally forced the IOC to recognize two separate teams.

The DTSB notified the DSB in late 1965 that it was ready to resume negotiations on inner-German sports exchanges. Six offers by the DSB to negotiate went unanswered by the DTSB from 1966-1970. Finally in 1970, the two Germanies met at two sports meetings in 1970 to discuss the future. The demand by the GDR that the DSB restrict its area of operations to West Germany and exclude Berlin caused the negotiations to fail. Since the late 1950's, the GDR sports organizations had followed the official state policy on the "three state theory". According to this interpretation, West Berlin was a separate state and could not be represented by the FRG. Meanwhile in 1968, the IOC had granted the GDR the right to compete as a national team with its own emblems at the 1972 Olympics in Munich. A West German news magazine summed up the situation in 1972:

> "From the 26th of August on, the athletes of the German Democratic Republic will appear in the stadiums, sports halls and regatta basins of Munich in front of four million spectators and almost a billion television viewers to gain by competition what the diplomats have constantly failed to do--the recognition of the second German state."[34]

Actually, by 1972, the GDR was well on the way to obtaining international recognition. Six nations recognized the GDR in 1969, followed by seven in 1970, two in 1971 and twenty-four in 1972. Forty six nations followed suit in 1973, including France and Great Britain, while the United States and ten others joined in establishing relations in 1974. The Federal Republic signed the Basic Treaty regulating inner-German relations on December 21, 1972. The long battle for international diplomatic recognition was over. The contribution of the East German athletes was and continues to be impressive. Through 1976, the GDR had won 225 Olympic medals. A total of 950 medals had been won in world championships and 901 in European championships. Seventy nine international sports federations had recognized the GDR. Some 117 East Germans filled positions within these organizations, far outnumbering the number of West Germans in similar situations. The GDR had hosted 39 European and 24 world championship events. [34] Guenther Heinze, currently vice president of the DTSB, has stated: "GDR sport did its part in obtaining recognition internationally for the GDR. Sport led the way in increasing the international prestige of our socialistic republic and led to its diplomatic recognition by a majority of the states of the world."[35]

Although the main foreign policy goal of the GDR was achieved, East German sports did not cease to be of importance in East German foreign policy. Sports still had two important roles to play--one, as a vehicle to implement certain foreign policy goals, the other to maintain and further the prestige of the GDR as a unit and that of the socialist bloc as a whole. East Germans continued to boycott sports events in West Berlin. A series of negotiations in 1973 failed to resolve this problem and eventually both governments had to step in to achieve a settlement. Finally on May 8, 1974 in the Hotel Stadt Berlin in East Berlin, the DSB and DTSB signed an agreement regulating a program of limited sports exchanges between the two nations on the basis of the IOC rules and regulations and the Berlin Four Power Agreement of September 3, 1971. However, four years later, the inner-German sports contacts are still restricted by the DTSB to a few dozen a year. [36] Practice and principle are two different things, and the current East German policy of "Abgrenzung" ("keeping the distance") applies to sports too. [37]

In Montreal at the 1976 Olympics, the GDR proved to be one of the world's superpowers in sports, winning 40 gold medals, which was six more than the United States was able to garner despite the fact that the U.S. had almost 200 million more inhabitants. The GDR won eleven of twelve women's swimming events. Every rower on the GDR team won a medal; five women's crews and three men's crews won gold medals. Udo Beyer beat favored American Al Feuerbach to win the shotput; Waldemar Cierpinski defeated Frank Shorter to win the marathon. In women's track, the GDR won nine events, including a sweep of the pentathlon. The rise of the GDR in Olympic competition was as follows:

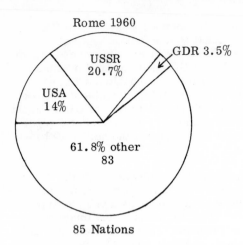

Rome 1960

USSR 20.7%

GDR 3.5%

USA 14%

61.8% other 83

85 Nations

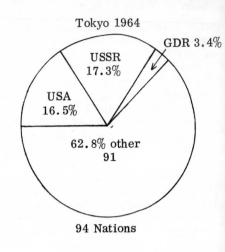

Tokyo 1964

USSR 17.3%

GDR 3.4%

USA 16.5%

62.8% other 91

94 Nations

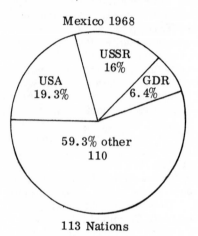

Mexico 1968

USSR 16%

USA 19.3%

GDR 6.4%

59.3% other 110

113 Nations

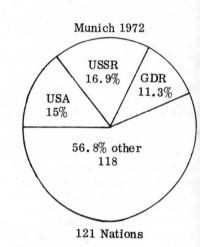

Munich 1972

USSR 16.9%

GDR 11.3%

USA 15%

56.8% other 118

121 Nations

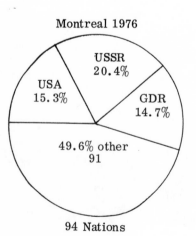

Montreal 1976

USSR 20.4%

USA 15.3%

GDR 14.7%

49.6% other 91

94 Nations

See: Thomas Lempart, "Einige Daten fuer eine Analyse der Ergebnisse der Olympischen Spielen von Muenchen", Leistungssport, Vol. 3, No. 2,(1973), p. 86.

If the results of the women's events are computed from Montreal, the result would show that the GDR is the best nation in the world as far as women's sports are concerned.

Nation	Total medals	Medals (Women)	% of the maximum no. medals that could be won in women's sports (108)
Soviet Union	125	36	33.3%
Ger. Dem. Rep.	90	49	45.4%
U.S.A.	94	17	15.7%
Fed. Rep. Ger.	39	6	5.5%
Rumania	27	8	7.4%
Bulgaria	22	6	5.5%
Canada	11	7	6.5%

A large proportion of the medals won at the Olympics were won by East German women.[38]

In order to understand how the East Germans were able to use sport as a vehicle for their foreign policy, some understanding of the domestic framework and structures in the GDR is necessary. The domestic sports structure in the GDR was shaped very much by the demands placed upon it by the government, which in turn was responding to the international environment. A linkage can be defined as a "basic unit of analysis...any recurrent sequence of behavior that originates in one system and is reacted to in another."[39]

The entire sports system in the GDR is a highly organized, well administered, efficient and well financed network. Until 1948, sports were under control of the Free German Youth and the Free German Labor Federation (FDGB). The DSA (Deutsche Sportausschuss) then replaced the communal sports organizations. Industries were encouraged to form factory sports clubs (Betriebssportgemeinschaften), which after April 3, 1950, were organized along Soviet lines. These BSGs were largely financed by factories and labor unions. Until 1957, they formed the basic unit in the GDR sports program. Each club had several sections, with one section for each sport.

In 1952, the State Committee for Physical Culture and Sport was established along with subcommittees at the various governmental levels. The Committee was responsible for overall coordination and the drafting of legislation, as well as most other activities related to the sports program. The DSA continued to administer the international part of the sports program.[40]

The administrative and coaching positions in the key positions were staffed by graduates of the German University for Physical Culture in Leipsig, which had been established in October of 1950. The university served both as a research institute for sports and sports medicine as well as a training center for coaches, officials, administrators and therapists. The university, known as the DHFK, was responsible for taking the most talented students and ideologically educating them as well as giving them the necessary technical training. The result was a network of schooled cadres who were in turn placed in the school and university system.

Sport was a required course in the schools. There, the cadres had a double job. One task was to supervise the mandatory sport hours which began with the elementary grades at the schools. The other was to uncover talent. The system was designed to uncover talent as early as possible. Even in the pre-school years there were classes stressing physical movement and flexibility. Those children in the elementary schools who showed promise of talent, appeared to have growth potential and did well in flexibility and skill tests, were directed to special schools after conversations with their parents. Each district had these special Kindersportschule and Jugendsportschule. Besides the necessary training facilities, weight rooms, playing fields, swimming pools and medical supervision, the schools had dormitories (Internats) complete with cafeterias. Each pupil or student received a specially designed school plan; special tutors were available. [41]

The GDR leadership realized that if the GDR was to compete effectively, then literally every stone would have to be turned in order to uncover all the available talent in order that the country could compete on an equal par with countries with larger populations. Sport was given a relatively high spot in the leadership's value system in order to encourage as many people as possible to go out for sport. Sport was even mentioned in the new constitution of 1968 as a major factor in the social-economic organization of the socialist system in the GDR. Articles 18.3, 25.3 and 35.1 guarantee every GDR citizen the right to sport and guarantee that the state will undertake every possible measure to provide physical culture and sport facilities and opportunities to its citizens. [42]

The Spartakiade system served as an additional talent funnel. Spartakiades were held for children and youth at every governmental level starting with eliminations in the schools. The winners in the lower levels were sent on to the higher levels, with the central Spartakiade being the last stop. In 1977, for example, some 920,000 children participated, and 13,500 of these qualified to participate in the finals of the Sixth Spartakiada in Leipzig. The planning and organization of these events, which GDR planners boasted was larger than the Olympic Games as far as the program was concerned and was run off in a fraction of the time, was typical of the minute political, economic, technical, scientific and medical planning involved. [43]

This philosophy that sport was not a privilege but rather an essential part of life, combined with the central planning and scientific nature of the sports system, helped produce the GDR athletic explosion. The state was generous with financing in the construction of facilities and the payment of sports instructors and coaches, as well as research assistants and medical personnel. The SED issued periodical "Jugendgesetze" to further the development of sport. This all cost the state quite a sum of money--one estimate in 1970 placed the annual expenditures for sport at 1.4 billion marks a year, or roughly two percent of the total GNP. [44]

Graduates from the school system then either entered the university system, the army, or one of the large state owned industrial programs. All had their own sports clubs, sports centers, sports coaches and sports doctors and therapists. The larger cities had special sports centers for elite athletes. These were identified as such by the SC before their name, such as SC Einheit Dresden. The athlete received a job at the sponsoring firm, where he worked half a day for full pay. Many of the firms had special positions, the so-called "Kaderstelle", which were reserved for the top athletes. These athletes who were delegated to one of these positions did not work in the firm at all, while drawing several hundred marks a month pay.[45] Many received free housing or special meal allowances. Training camps were held at regular intervals.

Those who went into the army entered a similar system, since the army maintained a system of sport clubs (ASKs). In 1974, there were 180,000 members in the ASKs; 54 of the 330 member GDR delegation to the Munich Olympics were from ASKs. The athletes in the army also had relatively few jobs or assignments in order that they would have the necessary time available for training. Another 230,000 athletes belonged to the Dynamo sports clubs, which were formed in 1953 and run by the state police. The SV police clubs were organized on a similar basis to the SC factory and ASK army clubs. There were special sports centers for the Dynamo teams[46]. Being an athlete gave the individual better chances to study at a university, where the sports program continued not only at the DHfK Leipzig, but in numerous smaller institutes around the country.

The DSA was replaced by the DTSB in 1957, which served to streamline and further coordinate sports activities in the GDR system, where nothing was left to chance. In 1970, the State Secretariat for Physical Culture and Sport replaced the State Committee of the same name. It was responsible for drawing up the yearly sport plans. At each level of organization from the national level down to the communal and factory level, SED officials held key positions in the sports organs and bodies. The reorganization of 1957 resulted in a less important role for the factory sports clubs in the overall picture; there have been other minor changes, but the system remains essentially the same.

The GDR leadership did not only rely on the advantages which have been cited. Political personalities were frequent visitors at sports events. Walter Ulbricht and Erich Honecker helped send off and welcome back Olympic and international championship teams. A host of national awards--Fatherland Service Awards, Banner of Labor, Guths Muths Prize, Friedrich Jahn Medal and the Artur Becker Medal, to name a few, were available to be awarded to outstanding athletes. Some of these awards included annual cash pensions or one time monetary bonuses.[47]

Athletes received extra comforts and luxury items such as extra ration cards in the 1950's, extra portions of otherwise hard to get meat, fruits, vegetables, special tickets to theaters and special events, washing machines, cars, radios and other items for which the average worker usually had to wait for several years. More importantly, premiums and cash grants were paid out to teams and individuals attaining certain marks, setting European, world or Olympic records, winning international championships or otherwise distinguishing themselves. Gold medal winners at Rome and Squaw Valley received 7,000 marks; by Munich, the winners were collecting up to 20,000 marks per gold medal.[48] Guenther Perleberg, 1960 Olympic kayak champion, received 5,000 marks in 1960 and averaged around 10,000 marks a year in various premiums for the next three years. Olympic race walker Hannes Koch received 800 marks for qualifying for the all-German team in 1960; a 1,000 for walking 4:19 and 50 kilometers and another 1,000 for the year's best time over 20 kilometers. Max Weber, another walker, received 2,000 marks in 1960 for his time over 50 kilometers. Koch received 1,000 marks when he qualified for the 1962 European championships. Cyclist Dieter Wiedemann reported that he earned around 2,000 marks a year in material goods such as radios which his team won at competitions. A victory in the Friedensfahrt bicycle race brought him 3,000 marks. Smaller competitions could still earn the racers money--the Egyptian tour in 1961 netted the GDR winning team members 500 marks each. The Olympic fourth place finisher in rowing, Hans Joachim Neuling, received 1,500 marks when he qualified for the Olympics in 1960. He and his partner Heinz Weigel both were awarded 2,000 marks for their fourth place. World cycling record holder Juergen Kissner received 1,500 marks for his part in a world record in the 4,000 meter team pursuit; the attainment of various time standards resulted in bonuses of 500-3,000 marks. Every sport had its norms. With athletes signing contracts that they would achieve certain norms within the year, plus the chances to travel outside the GDR and the added financial considerations, the better GDR athletes lived a life which did not begin to compare with that of their Western counterparts, the latter having to struggle along as best they could on under the table payments from promoters and equipment manufacturers. Soccer player Michel Polywka received 400 marks a game for every victory in the Oberliga and if the victory was at an away game, the sum increased to 600 marks.[49]

The size of the grant varied according to the international importance of the sports achievement. The payoff was always delivered by a person the athletes never knew (though they referred to him as Santa Claus, among other terms) and was handed out in an unmarked envelope in cash. Cyclist Hamut Scholz netted 4,000 marks in victory premiums; world champion canoeist Wulf Reinicke would have received around 6,000 marks for his victory except that he decided to remain in the West.

Thus, the GDR athletes who went out in the world to compete for the GDR were well prepared, well trained and highly motivated ideologically as well as materially. Backed up by a team of coaches, sports doctors, physical therapists, psychologists, scientists, and technicians, they were in an excellent position to accomplish exactly what the SED hoped they would do-- gain international prestige and recognition for the GDR. It is interesting to speculate whether, if the Western world had accepted the GDR as a regular member in 1949, the East Germans would have developed such an extensive sports system. Their policy was intransigent from the beginning, at the same time uncompromising and yet innovative. Sports had been used as a vehicle for foreign policy in the 1930's by the Soviet Union, Germany, Italy and Japan, but not on such a scale. Viewed from the position East Germany found itself in the world of 1949, the choice of sports as a method to help force international diplomatic recognition was a stroke of brilliant genius and one for which the West was totally unprepared. Sport brought many benefits to the GDR, but the foremost one was diplomatic recognition.

Footnotes

[1] Bundesministeriumfuer innerdeutsche Beziehungen (ed.), DDR Handbuch. (Cologne: Verlag fuer Wissenschaft und Politik, 1975), pp. 217-218.

[2] Auswartiges Amt der Bundesrepublik Deutschland (ed.), Das Auswartige Politik der Bundesrepublic Deutschland. (Cologne: Verlag Wissenschaft und Politik, 1972), pp. 30; 254.

[3] Ibid., p. 192.

[4] Ibid., p. 3.4. See also Michael Freund, Deutsche Geschichte. (Guetersloh: Bertelsmann, 1975), p. 1599.

[5] H. Bodensieck, Deutschland Politik der Bundesrepublik Deutschland: Gross Berlin, Staatsname, Ansprueche, Realitaeten. (Stuttgart: Ernst Klett, 1972), p. 64.

[6] James Rosenau, The Adaption of National Societies: A Theory of Political System Behavior and Transformation. (New York: McCabeb Seiler, 1970), p. 4.

[7] Thomas Schelling, The Strategy of Conflict. (London: Oxford University Press, 1960), p. 84ff.

[8] "Bei uns ist es immer Olympia", Der Spiegel, Vol. 26, No. 32 (July 31, 1972), p. 72.

[9] Dieter Frenzke, Die Anerkennung der DDR, Voelkerrechtliche Moeglichkeiten und Folgen. (Cologne: Verlag Wissenschaft und Politik, 1970), p. 20.

[10] Ibid., p. 43ff.

[11] Klaus Steinmar, "Friedliche Koexistenz, internationale Zusammenarbeit und Sport", Theorie und Praxis der Koerperkultur, Vol. 24, No. 4 (April, 1975), p. 297.

[12] Guenther Woenneberger (ed.), Die Koerperjultur in Deutschland, 1945-1961. (Berlin: Sportverlag, 1967), pp. 82; 174. See also Heinz Schuffenhauer, "Gedanken zur Rolle von Koerperkultur bei der allseitigen Bildung und Erziehung aus historisch-paedagogische Sicht", Theorie und

Praxis der Koerperkultur, Vol. 24, No. 4 (April, 1975), p. 300; Guenter Starke, "Gesellschaftliche Stellung und gesellschaftliche Funktionen von Koerperkultur und Sport in der DDR", Theorie und Praxis der Koerperkultur, Vol. 24, No. 10 (October, 1975), p. 903ff; Rudi Hellmann, "Koerperkultur in unserer Gesellschaft", Theorie und Praxis der Koerperkultur, Vol. 24, No. 6 (June, 1975), p. 483.

[13] See Handbuch, p. 810 and Woenneberger, p. 144 as well as Der Spiegel, Vol. 26, No. 32 (August 7, 1972), p. 79.

[14] Karl Ihmels, Sport und Spaltung in der Politik der SED. (Cologne: Verlag Wissenschaft und Politik, 1965), p. 58; see also Willi Knecht, "Die Friedensfahrt der Okkupaten", Deutschland Archiv, Vol. 2, No. 5 (May, 1969), p. 546ff. and "28. Friedensfahrt: Ein Rennen mit vierlerlei Eigenarten", Deutschland Archiv, Vol. 8, No. 5 (May, 1975), p. 572ff.

[15] Ihmels, p. 102.

[16] Ihmels, p. 39 from Die Sozialistische Sportbewegung. (Berlin: Sportverlag, 1961), p. 16.

[17] Ihmels, p. 10. Hoenecker made the statement while heading the FDJ (Free German Youth) at a DSA meeting, October 1, 1948.

[18] Ihmels, p. 74 from Deutsche Sportecho, April 15, 1957.

[19] Willi Knecht, Die geteilte Arena. (Nuremberg: Presseverlag Bahr, 1968), p. 33.

[20] Karl Heinz Gieseler, Sport als Mittel der Politik. (Mainz: von Hase und Koehler, 1965), pp. 55-56.

[21] Der Spiegel, Vol. 26, No. 32 (July 31, 1972), p. 81.

[22] Deutsche Sportbund (ed.), Dokumentation on the Political Interference of the East German Sports Organizations. (Frankfurt/M:DSB, n.d.), p. 19.

[23] Ihmels, p. 75 from "Die naechsten Aufgaben der DTSB" in Die Sozialistische Sportbewegung, Vol. 4 (April, 1960).

[24] Ihmels, p. 73 from Die Sozialistische Sportbewegung, Vol. 2 (1957).

[25] Documentation, p. 7. (Rudi Reichert, April 24/25, 1959).

[26] Ibid., p. 7.

[27] Ibid., p. 8. (Alfred Neumann, October 21, 1960).

[28] Ihmels, p. 45 from Sport im Bilde, No. 4 (February 21, 1958).

[29] Bill Henry, "Diplomacy Snarls Squaw Valley", Los Angeles Times, February 19, 1959.

[30] Gieseler, p. 64.

[31] Karl Heinz Gieseler, Memorandum zur Flaggen und Hymnen Frage. (Frankfurt: DSB, n.d.), pp. 6-7.

[32] Der Spiegel, Vol. 26, No. 32 (July 31, 1972), p. 86.

[33] Ihmels, p. 47.

[34] Der Spiegel, Vol. 26, No. 32 (July 31, 1972), p. 68.

[35] Guenther Heinze, "Der DDR Sport--ein anerkannter und geachteter Partner im international en Sportleben", Theorie und Praxis der Koerperkultur, Vol. 22, No. 16 (October, 1973), p. 874; private correspondence with Martin Kramer, DTSB Presschief, December 3, 1976.

[36] Heinze, p. 874.

[37] Rolf Heggen, "Schwierige innerdeutsche Kontakte: Ausser Sport kein Wort", Frankfurt Allgemeine Zeitung, April 6, 1977. See also Willi Knecht, "DTSB/DSB. Auf ungleichen Wegen in die Zukunft", Deutschland Archiv, Vol. 7, No. 7 (July, 1974), p. 725ff. and Knecht, "Beginn des deutschen Sportverkehr", Deutschland Archiv, Vol. 7, No. 6 (June, 1974), p. 568ff.

[38] Tomasz Lempart, Olympische Spiele Montreal, 1976. Vorbereitung-Auswertung. Bundesausschluss Leistungsreport. (Frankfurt: DSB, 1976).

[39] James Rosenau, "Toward the Study of National and International Linkages" in Linkage Politics, edited by James Rosenau. (New York: Free Press, 1969), p. 45.

[40] Ihmels, p. 15.

[41] Ihmels, p. 33.

[42] "Verfassung der Deutsche Demokratische Republik", <u>Deutschland Archiv</u>, Vol. 7, No. 11 (November, 1974), p. 1196ff.

[43] Willi Knecht, "Sportbilanz 69. Der Wettlauf der ungleichen Brueder", <u>Deutschland Archiv</u>, Vol. 2, No. 12 (December, 1969), pp. 1341-2. See also the <u>Frankfurter Neue Presse</u>, July 28, 1977 and the <u>Stuttgarter Nachrichten</u>, July 30, 1977.

[44] <u>Der Spiegel</u>, Vol. 26, No. 34 (August 14, 1972), p. 93; Woenneberger, p. 164; Ihmels, p. 34.

[45] Willi Knecht, <u>Amateur 72</u>. (Mainz: von Hase und Koeller, pp. 178, 199, 215, 221.)

[46] Knecht, <u>Amateur</u>, p. 149ff; <u>DDR Handbuch</u>, pp. 805-6.

[47] Ihmels, p. 36.

[48] Knecht, <u>Amateur</u>, p. 252.

[49] <u>Ibid.</u>, pp. 180, 184, 203, 204, 208, 217, 222.

The author would like to thank officials of the DSB and DTSB for providing literature and information pertaining to this topic. He would especially like to thank Karl Heinz Gieseler, Willi Knecht and Horst Planert for their aid.

February 20, 1978

Apartheid Sport: South Africa's Use Of

Sport In Its Foreign Policy

Richard E. Lapchick

From the moment that the United States team refused to dip the American flag to King Edward VII at the opening ceremonies of the 1908 Olympic Games in London, politics has been inextricably linked with the Olympic Movement in particular and international sport in general.

Since that time, the sports fields of the world have served not only as locations for individual competition between outstanding athletes, but also as testing grounds for the strength of political systems. Richard D. Mandells' The Nazi Olympics concludes that Hitler used the 1936 Berlin Olympics as a key to providing the early success of his Nazi regime. Since World War II, the Olympic Games have served as a showcase for the Cold War. After the unofficial team defeat of the United States in the 1964 Games, Vice-President Humphrey said that we had been, "humiliated as a great nation," by the Soviet Union and that we must conclusively prove that a free society produces better athletes than a socialist society.[1] While numerous examples of Cold War sports politics could be cited, the case of the IOC and the 'two Chinas' incident is as instructive as any.

In 1959 the IOC ruled that Nationalist China was no longer representative of the people of China and had to reapply as Taiwan. The United States State Department immediately took the position that this decision was the result of "communist threats."[2] Two bills condemning the IOC were introduced into Congress and, finally, President Eisenhower intervened and convinced Avery Brundage, the IOC President, to reverse the decision.[3]

However, the most flagrant example of the politics of international sport is the case of South Africa. The controversy surrounding the participation of South African teams in international sport also marked the shift of major concern in the politics of international sport from ideology to a new factor: race and racism. This shift was, to a large extent, influenced by the rise of non-Western nationalism in general, and of African nationalism in particular.

Reprinted by kind permission of the author and the Journal of Sport and Social Issues. Volume I, 1976.

The adamant refusal of the South African Government to permit integrated teams to represent their country, that is, the extension of apartheid into sport, has led to intensive global pressures and protests. In spite of those protests, South Africa was permitted to continue its international competition until 1970 when it was dismissed from almost all of the international sports federations and, most importantly, from the Olympic Movement itself.[4]

Apartheid, as the official Government policy, was introduced by the National Party after its victory in the 1948 election. Laws were gradually introduced to affirm the social system that had already evolved in South Africa since the Union was formed in 1910. Likewise, apartheid in sport only became 'official' after the National Party's victory in 1948. Up to that point, it was the sports bodies themselves that had maintained the social system of segregation in sport.[5] Since 1948, the Government has gradually taken control of sports policy. By the early 1960's, the pretense of independent sports bodies was dropped and policies emanated from the highest governmental offices, including that of the prime minister. In 1966 a ministry of sport was created to handle sports issues as they had become more complex.

When Prime Minister Vorster suggested that an integrated team from New Zealand might be permitted to enter South Africa as part of his 'Outward Policy,' a national election had to be called for in 1970.[6] The issue was that important in South Africa.

Although most observers of South African life were aware of the obvious fact of racial discrimination in South African sport, the international sports decision-making bodies, led by the IOC, chose to allow South African teams to continue to compete. The decisions of these bodies in general, and of individual nations in particular, at times have seemingly been motivated by some means other than strictly sports criteria. In fact, these decisions, as well as internal sports decisions in South Africa, often seem as motivated by racial, economic and political factors as by sports factors.

As sport has become more and more important to the public and to leaders, it has become more and more apparent that politics has become an integral and growing, if unwelcome, part of sports, with significant repercussions both for the future of international sport and for the relations of the nations involved. The question of race and international sport is no small part of the politics of international sport.

The general purpose of this article will be to analyze how South Africa has used sport in its foreign policy and how the international sports community has responded to the reality of apartheid sport. Special attention will be paid to the role of the IOC and its response to apartheid sport.[7]

The subject is made more important by the fact that while the naivete of the American public has gradually been eliminated with regard to the now tarnished axiom that 'sport is above politics,' the majority of Americans still fail to recognize the significance of the racial factor.

In a survey conducted in the Summer of 1972, 68% of all the people interviewed (black and white) felt that politics and sport were thoroughly mixed at the international level. However, only 45% thought that race was a factor in sport.[8] The case of South Africa may demonstrate that it is the racial factor and not the general political factor that has become the most important theme in international sport in the 1960's and 1970's.

The Importance of Sport in South Africa's Foreign Policy

Several factors converge to make South Africa's sports image important to her wider overseas image.

First of all, as South Africa has become increasingly condemned in international political circles because of her apartheid policy, acceptance by the international sports community has become increasingly important to that sports-mad country. Within South Africa the illusion is created - and used by the Government - to tell South Africans that, yes, the international community really does accept us in spite of United Nations resolutions. When South Africa was temporarily accepted for the 1968 Olympics (they had not been allowed to participate in the 1964 Tokyo Games), the reaction in South Africa was one of joy. Frank Braun, the head of South Africa's Olympic Committee, attributed their successful battle for readmittance largely to Nigeria's Sir Ade Ademola.[9] Reg Honey, South Africa's delegate on the IOC, praised South Africa's friends in the international community for their understanding of South Africa's position.[10] These sports leaders were thus able to tell the South African people that the opinion of South Africa, even in black Africa, was not as bad as it was being portrayed in the foreign press.

Internally, the National Party members used the readmittance as a justification for the prime minister's 'Outward Policy.' Part of that policy was the 'concessions' made--which will be described later--to the IOC in Teheran in 1967. One MP said: "nothing succeeds like success. Nationalists are supporting Mr. Vorster enthusiastically now for the simple reason that his politics work. The preliminary reports we have received from the constituencies show that the tide of popular opinion is suddenly swinging strongly behind the outward-looking policies. Our people now know what it all means."[11]

The concessions that were made were as follows: South Africa would send a mixed team to the Mexico Olympics and all would march under the same flag and wear the same colors; South Africans of different racial groups could compete against each other at the Games; a non-white Olympic committee would be formed and each racial group would designate its candidates for selection; and, finally, a liaison committee of whites and non-whites would be formed, under Braun's chairmanship, and would make the final selections.[12]

On the basis of these concessions and the readmittance of South Africa for the Games, The Times (London) emphasized how important sport had become as a lever for diplomacy; that sport was the number one weapon of the outside in its attempt to change apartheid.[13] A New York Times editorial called the concessions "revolutionary."[14]

But a legitimate question would seem to be: did world opinion change South Africa's attitude or did South Africa change world opinion of apartheid? Many South Africans clearly felt the latter was the case. An editorial in Die Volksblad (Bloemfontein) summed up this view of the role of sport in South Africa's foreign policy with its comment that, "Every international sports success of South Africa is a blow against our sports and political enemies."[15] When the South Africans sent their rugby team to Britain in 1969, Die Burger (Cape Town) said that the rugby team had an extraordinary responsibility to influence British public opinion in favor of South Africa.[16] In reality, the answer to the above question would be that there is some truth in both propositions.

The second factor converging to make South Africa's sports image important to her wider overseas image is the factor of non-white South African opinion of the Government's sports policy.

Obviously, if the Government could point to representative groups of non-white athletes and sports officials who adhere to the policy of apartheid sport, then the legitimacy of protests overseas would be seriously diminished.

There had been two important non-racial protest movements in South African sport: the South African Sports Association (SASA), formed in 1959, and its successor, the South African Non-Racial Olympic Committee (SAN-ROC), formed in 1963.[17] Since non-whites were not allowed in any white sports associations, all non-white sportsmen were members of SAN-ROC when the South Africans were banned from the 1964 Olympics.

It was at that point that the Government realized that it had to split the non-racial sports movement. It did this in two ways. First, it arranged for the formation of non-white associations that would be affiliated to the white associations in their respective codes of sport. Although such affiliation was clearly one of a subordinate status (the new non-white bodies never carried more than 10% of the vote), many non-whites joined because of Government promises of international competition--as representatives of non-white South Africans--as well as promises of improved facilities and better coaches. However, it must be made clear that all concessions were strictly within the policies of apartheid at home.

The Government had already imprisoned Dennis Brutus, the inspiration behind the founding of the non-racial movement, for trying to go to Baden-Baden for the IOC meeting while he was under banning orders in South Africa.[18] His successor, John Harris, was arrested for sabotage--unrelated to SAN-ROC activities--in 1964.[19] Harris was convicted and executed. Dennis Brutus maintains that this was the end of the non-racial movement inside South Africa.[20] Indeed, until SAN-ROC was reconvened in 1966 in London, under the leadership of Brutus and Chris de Broglio, white South Africans had a free ride in the international sports community.

But the question still remains: were non-white South Africans who remained behind and joined the affiliated associations allowed any choice, that is, could they demonstrate against sports apartheid without fear of severe reprisals? To answer this, we must look at what the consequences were for those who led the non-racial movement while it existed in South Africa: sports facilities were withdrawn to the point of yielding an effective end of that sport on a non-racial basis--such was the case in football (soccer);[21] non-white athletes were denied the possibility of international competition without first affiliating with the segregated bodies;[22] travel documents were withdrawn from officials who represented non-racial sport;[23] banning orders were issued for some non-racial leaders (Dennis Brutus, Wilfred Brutus and George Singh);[24] some leaders were arrested (Dennis Brutus, Wilfred Brutus and John Harris);[25] and imprisoned (Dennis Brutus and John Harris);[26] or were, finally, forced into exile (Dennis and Wilfred Brutus, Omar Cassem, Chris de Broglio and Reg Hlongwane).[27] In addition, numerous outstanding non-white athletes have been forced to compete overseas as a result of not being able to compete at home.[28] Finally, after non-white spectators began to show their approval for _every_ foreign team competing against white South African teams, they were systematically banned as spectators unless they applied for and received a Government permit to attend a specific event.[29]

It can readily be concluded that non-whites did not, in fact, have the option to protest apartheid sport without very serious personal and collective repercussions. The knowledge of such repercussions severely weakens and, perhaps, destroys the argument of the South African officials that the non-whites who do cooperate with the system are the ones who are representative of the non-white population in South Africa.

This brings us back to the Teheran 'concessions.' For non-white South Africans the only thing that really mattered was what would the concessions do for them INSIDE South Africa? The answer came in no uncertain terms from Prime Minister Vorster in April of 1967 as he explained the concessions to his Parliament: "I therefore want to make it quite clear that from South Africa's point of view no mixed sport between whites and non-whites will be practiced locally, irrespective of the standards of proficiency of the participants . . . we do not apply that as a criterion because our policy has nothing to do with proficiency or lack of proficiency. If any person, locally or abroad, adopts the attitude that he will enter into relations with us only if we are prepared to jettison the separate practicing of sport prevailing among our people in South Africa, then I want to make it quite clear that, no matter how important those sports relations are in my view, I am not prepared to pay that price. On that score, I want no misunderstanding whatsoever . . . in respect of this principle we are not prepared to compromise, we are not prepared to negotiate and we are not prepared to make any concessions."[30] Thus, the internal ban on mixed competition was completed. It meant the effective end of the career of Papwa Sewgolum, the leading Indian golfer, after several years of indecision. He had been the only non-white allowed to compete in white events--although this 'privilege' had been gradually removed since he won the Natal Open over Gary Player and 112 other whites in January of 1963. This was a significant decision as South Africa had received widespread international criticism after it forced Sewgolum to receive his trophy in the rain. The trophy was handed through a window in the clubhouse where the 113 white participants were being served drinks by the Indian servants.[31] This was, perhaps, apartheid sport's most pathetic moment.

Vorster's statement also dashed the newly aroused hopes of other non-white athletes. Vorster then went on to the question of non-white spectators: "In the second place our attitude in respect of sport is that attendance of members of one group takes place by way of permit, if at all . . . provided that separate facilities are available and as long as it does not result in situations which are conducive to friction and disturbance."[32] In light of these two parts of Vorster's speech, it became obvious to all who cared to examine the situation that sports apartheid in South Africa had, in fact, been strengthened. However, because of the international concessions--most notably, the sending of an integrated team to the Olympics--right wing MP's and members of the Opposition in South Africa, as well as several leading South African newspapers, criticized Vorster for making radical concessions. In quick response to such interpretations, Vorster announced on the following day: "If there are people who in any way believe or think that it can be inferred from my speech that all barriers will now be removed, then they are making a very big mistake."[33]

As Frank Braun announced the 'concessions' in Teheran to the IOC, Vorster was telling South Africans, "I feel compelled to warn sports administrators to read my policy statement on sport very carefully and not to raise expectations that cannot be fulfilled."[34]

Four months later, even the matter of sending a mixed team to the Olympics was cast into doubt by Minister of Sport Waring. Even while the IOC investigating team was in South Africa, Waring announced: "Our policy is separate sport and if the demand is made upon us--a political demand--that we must change our pattern of sport and mix it, we are not prepared to pay the price. We are quite prepared that our non-whites should take part in the Olympic Games. We will pick a white team and a black team."[35]

With all of this information in hand, the white-dominated IOC voted to allow South Africa to compete in the 1968 Olympics. The IOC apparently chose to ignore the fact that absolutely nothing had changed for non-whites in South African sport. This decision not only united the African and most other non-white nations in opposition to South African participation, but almost destroyed the Olympic Movement in the process.

The Africans knew that virtually the only place that South Africa was vulnerable was in her international sports relations. An editorial in the Ugandan Government newspaper, The People (Kampala), summed up this position: "Here is a field in which Africa does not need to plead, cajole or threaten other powers to take action against apartheid; we can act decisively ourselves . . . the South Africans do not consider it minor . . . What is our policy toward this infiltration. . . If we wish to accept their offers--baited hooks, they have been called--let us say so openly. . . Unless we face these serious problems, they are going to be a serious threat to the Organization of African Unity (OAU). Once South Africa gets a hold INSIDE the OAU, that is the beginning of the end of our anti-colonialism stand."[36]

The African nations had formed the Supreme Council for Sport in Africa (SCSA) in December of 1966. One of the first things they did was to pass a resolution calling for a boycott of the 1968 Olympics if South Africa was allowed to participate.[37] This boycott threat was reiterated on the day before Vorster's 'concessions' speech in Parliament in April and again in December.[38] Therefore, the IOC had no reason to believe that the African nations would participate if the South Africans were readmitted.

On the eve before the Report of the IOC Commission was published in Grenoble, the African National Congress (ANC) broadcast an appeal on Radio Tanzania about the Olympics: "It is in the sphere of sports, the arts and culture that South Africa can be made to feel the full weight of international moral indignation against apartheid. . . It is a cynical act of hypocrisy even to suggest that they will march under the same flag and sing the same National Anthem when they are prohibited from doing so inside South Africa. The test of whether there is race discrimination or not against the black people in South Africa can only be demonstrated by what happens inside South Africa. . . We appeal to all men of goodwill, fair play and justice to exclude the white South African sports from the Olympic Games."[39]

As the decision neared, Frank Braun was constantly informing the press of how the people of South Africa accept and support the prevailing political and social order in South Africa. This brought on the wrath of the normally agreeable non-white newspaper, Post (Natal). In an editorial, it criticized Braun's statements: "It is an arrogant, incorrect and political assumption to say that the POPULATION of South Africa supports the prevailing political and social order. Mr. Braun might be speaking for the majority of the WHITE population of this country. But he cannot--and should not--pretend to speak for the majority of ALL people here. Non-whites are just as anxious to see the South African flag flying at the Mexico Games--but not at the price of having to say we support apartheid and all the agony it has brought."[40]

In spite of it all, the IOC went ahead and voted South Africa into the 1968 Games. But the IOC got more than they anticipated. They knew that they would be boycotted by the 32 members of the SCSA. However, they apparently did not understand how far politics and race had permeated the sports world.

Nearly one month after the Grenoble decision, the New York Times reported that only ten nations--all white--had agreed to go to Mexico.[41] While the Soviet Union tried to decide if Olympic gold was more important than Third World prestige, The Times (London) reported that Peking was ready to take advantage of a Soviet decision to participate.[42] The remainder of the Eastern European nations waited for the Soviet decision.[43] With South Africa in the Olympics, the promise was of a lily-white Games.

With the full weight of the Supreme Council having been shown, the IOC was forced to reverse its decision. It did so by a wide margin: 47 for South Africa's exclusion, 16 for South Africa's participation, and 8 abstentions.[44]

Prime Minister Vorster underlined the racist attitude that the black African nations had been talking about all along with his reaction to the reversal: "If what has happened is to be the pattern of how world events are going to be arranged in the future, we are back in the jungle. Then it will no longer be necessary to arrange Olympic Games, but rather to have tree climbing events."[45]

But the Africans had already gained a new sense of confidence in their own power. They continued to press. In May of 1970 they were partly responsible for the cancellation of the 1970 South African cricket tour of Britain--along with the militant opposition in Britain itself--by their threat to pull out of the 1970 Commonwealth Games. It was the British Government itself that cancelled the tour as Home Secretary Callaghan called it a threat not only to the Commonwealth Games, but also to Commonwealth relations in general.[46] This was another example of how politics, race and sport had become intertwined.

However, it was the week before that the Supreme Council had its greatest triumph at the IOC meeting in Amsterdam. It had been expected that the IOC would vote to keep South Africa out again in 1972 but would not expel it from the Olympic Movement itself.[47] But the Africans wanted more than this, and they presented 8 charges against South Africa in light of its apartheid sports policy.[48] This, combined with Frank Braun's abrasive presentation to the IOC, finished the South Africans who were expelled from the Olympic Movement by a vote of 35 to 28, with 3 abstentions. All press accounts expressed great surprise that the Africans had gathered such strength.[49]

South Africa's Historical Relationship with the IOC

With all the evidence and, seemingly, the vast majority of world opinion against South Africa, it would almost seem more appropriate to ask why the South Africans were permitted to remain in the Olympic Movement until 1970--even though they completely violated all Olympic Principles on race and sport--rather than how could they be expelled in 1970.

Perhaps the best explanation is that the IOC has been dominated by representatives from white member nations who did not oppose South Africa's continued good standing in the Olympic Movement.[50]

The IOC, according to its own publication, Olympism, is a self-recruiting elite. Membership on the IOC is a result of election by existing IOC members. The statement that, "It is customary to favor nationals of countries with a long Olympic tradition behind them," is reminiscent of the grandfather clause in the post-Reconstruction era of the South in the United States.[51] The custom was a convenient way of excluding representatives from nations that were colonies during the period when 'a long Olympic tradition' could have been formed. In fact, the first two representatives from Africa were white men: Reg Alexander of Kenya and Reg Honey of South Africa.

The 1960's, during which 61% of the representatives from non-white member nations of the IOC were admitted, only meant a minor change in the racial composition of the IOC. The representatives from the non-white countries had only 33% of the voting power on the IOC in 1970. To achieve their 67% control, it was necessary that 11 of the white nations represented on the IOC had two or more representatives.

Moreover, of the National Olympic Committees (NOC's) without an IOC representative--which, in effect, means they are powerless--only 12.4% were from white nations while 87.6% were from non-white nations.[52]

To the idealistic sportsman or woman who might feel that such statistics are meaningless because sport and the Olympic Movement are above politics, race, etc., the results of the following survey should be instructive.

Sixty-eight percent of the white nations polled were not opposed to South Africa's participation. However, 98% of the non-white nations opposed South Africa's participation without complete sports integration in South Africa. Thus, it can be seen that the South African issue developed along strict racial lines.

It is also intriguing to note the exceptions to the more or less strict racial groupings. The full 32% of the white nations who opposed South Africa's participation were from the Socialist Bloc, perhaps implying that their attempted alignment with the Third World extends into the realm of sports. The only non-white country that did not oppose South Africa was Malawi.[53] The implication of economic ties as a balancing factor for racial differences is well worth pursuing in another study, as is the question of Socialist alignments with the Third World.

In any event, it must come as a shock to some naive sports-enthusiasts to recognize the extent to which race and politics have become a part of the world of international sports. However, the world of international sport in the 1970's is a far cry from that envisioned by Baron de Coubertin, the man who rekindled the Olympic Movement to help bring world peace in 1894. It is now much more like George Orwell's view of international sport: "It is bound up with hatred, jealousy, boastfulness, disregard for all rules and sadistic pleasure in witnessing violence--in other words, it is war minus the shooting."[54]

The World Catches up with South Africa

However, the fact remained that in May of 1970 a full two-thirds of the IOC membership came from white nations. Obviously, many of these members had to vote against South Africa in May. What were the factors that caused them to change positions so very dramatically?

Three key factors can be singled out: the militant international opposition to sports apartheid, with its home in Britain, made South Africa's traditional allies less likely to support her due to threats to peace at home; South Africa's refusal to allow Arthur Ashe, the black American tennis star, to compete in the South African Open at least temporarily cost South Africa the support of the United States; and, as has already been pointed out, the African nations, now with the backing of the other non-white nations as well as most of the Socialist Bloc, realized their own power to destroy the system of international sport as it is known and employed it to the fullest extent. A brief explanation of the first two factors is in order, although any brief explanation cannot do justice to the magnitude of the circumstances.

To simplify a very complex story, it took until May of 1970 for the MCC--the body responsible for cricket in Britain--to cancel the 1970 South African cricket tour of Britain. The MCC did this after an incredible amount of mismanagement and under extreme pressure from the Wilson Government. The tour had become a major political issue between Wilson and Opposition leader Heath, and had begun to arouse the passions of Britain's non-white population.

The meaning of the 1970 tour cannot be separated from the meaning of the cancelled 1968 British tour of South Africa. For both, the decisive issue was clearly racial. In 1968 Prime Minister Vorster refused to allow an integrated British team to enter South Africa. Basil D'Oliveira, the Colored South African cricket star then playing in Britain because he was not allowed to play in his own land, was the center of the controversy. As a result of public pressure, the MCC was forced to cancel the tour after they themselves had seemingly tried to exclude D'Oliveira to avoid a confrontation with Vorster. Vorster's decision was clear: "We are not prepared to accept a team thrust upon us by people whose interests are not the game, but to gain certain political objectives which they do not even attempt to hide. The team as constituted now is not the team of the MCC but the team of the Anti-Apartheid Movement, the team of SAN-ROC. . . Leftist and liberal politicians had entered the field of sport and wanted to use it to suit their own purposes and pink ideals."[55]

In spite of this humiliation, the MCC voted to go ahead with plans for the 1970 tour. This resulted in the formation of the Stop the Seventy Tour Committee (STST) under the leadership of a 19-year-old South African exile, Peter Hain. Ironically, it was Peter Hain, then a mere 15, who had delivered the eulogy for John Harris, the executed leader of SAN-ROC.[56] STST spontaneously decided to use the 1969-70 Rugby Tour of South Africa in Britain as a show of strength. It was quite a showing: Hain and STST brought out more than 50,000 demonstrators, resulting in 400 arrests and much panic in Britain.[57]

The MCC finally responded by shortening the tour from 28 to 12 matches 11 instead of 18 weeks.[58] As the date for the tour opening came nearer, many anti-apartheid groups--moderates and radicals--increased their pressure to cancel the tour. As has already been stated, the Supreme Council announced it would boycott the Edinburg Commonwealth Games in July if the tour went on, which could have resulted in an all-white Games.[59]

When the MCC refused to respond to the threats of the demonstrators and the SCSA, the Government moved in, led by then Home Secretary Callaghan, who asked the MCC to withdraw its invitation on behalf of the Government. He explained: "We have particularly in mind the possible impact on relations with other Commonwealth countries, race relations in this country, and the divisive effect on the community. Another matter for concern is the effect on the Commonwealth Games."[60]

Thus, the South Africans virtually forced the British Government to move on this issue instead of cancelling themselves. This entire episode, dragged out over three years with South Africa's staunchest supporter, had a definite effect on the IOC vote in May.

Another factor with a similar effect was what has become known as the Arthur Ashe Affair. The Affair took place at the highest levels of Government in both the United States and South Africa. The facts of the story are quite clear.

Ashe applied for a visa to compete in the South African Open on December 15, 1969. On the same day, Secretary of State Rogers arranged for representations to be made to South Africa's Ambassador in Washington by Assistant Secretary of State Newsom, as well as to South Africa's Foreign Minister in Pretoria by U. S. Ambassador Roundtree. Roundtree later met with Prime Minister Vorster on behalf of Ashe. Vorster assured him that he would take up the matter with his Cabinet, which he did.

On January 27th, Vorster and Foreign Minister Muller summoned Roundtree to tell him that the decision had been reached to deny the visa. They maintained that Ashe had political motives behind his trip.[61]

Ashe later summed up their decision before the United Nations when he told delegates that the South Africans "did not want me because I am not white."[62]

The humiliation, not only of Ashe but of high State Department officials, finally forced the United States to act in leading the move to suspend the South Africans from the Davis Cup. Like the British, the United States was left with no choice as a result of South African actions. The case was so clear-cut that even Australia, which along with Britain and New Zealand were South Africa's principal international supporters, voted against South Africa at the Davis Cup meeting.[63]

By 1970, no less than 89 nations had become actively involved in the dispute over South Africa's right to international competition. As has been noted, many of the decisions on whether or not to compete against South Africa have been made at the very highest levels of Government. Just as international competition has meant success for South Africa, a rejection of such competition has had the opposite effect. This can be judged, in part, by the severity of the verbal attacks levied against those who rejected South Africa in international competition (such as the attacks on the IOC in 1963-64, 1968 and 1970, and those on the British Government in 1970 after the cancellation of the cricket tour). But, more importantly, it can be judged by the calls for change in policy by South African whites as their sports isolation was nearly complete in 1970.

Post-Isolation Blues: A Setting for Change?

Beginning in December of 1969, with total sports isolation in sight, three important South African officials called for major policy changes in sport.[64] When isolation was not only in sight but was a fact in May of 1970, the calls from white sportsmen and officials were not only for reform but for sports integration.[65] It took isolation to get these sportsmen to talk about multi-racial sport. These sportsmen and officials were left with no alternative as a result of the actions of the international sports bodies: if they wanted to resume competition, the cost would clearly be the elimination of apartheid from sport.

Whether or not these calls for integration have led to any significant changes is open to serious debate. Obviously there is importance in the calls themselves. The 1973 South African Games were integrated. In November, Arthur Ashe competed in the South African Open and the black light-heavyweight champ, Bob Forster, fought Pierre Fourie, a white man, in South Africa.

However, integration in sport is far from being a reality in 1976. Until there is a multi-racialism at the club level in sports, any 'breakthroughs' at the national level can only be interpreted as gestures to get South Africa back in the good graces of the international sports world. This is not necessarily meant to belittle the gestures: they are important. But the reality of life in South African society in general, and sport in particular, remains unchanged.

As long as this is true, South Africa's international critics will continue to attack the Government through the field of sports. The essence of that attack was summed up in an editorial in the Sunday Times (Johannesburg) on May 31, 1970, shortly after the IOC decision: "South Africa's critics have simply discovered that sport is the most useful weapon they have yet found with which to beat us and while it is the sportsmen who are the sacrificial victims--they are being ostracized and deprived of the right to participate in world sport--the main target of attack is the racial policy of South Africa, or, to put it more precisely, the racial policy of the Nationalist Party."

This summer we saw a major effort made to complete the isolation of South Africa. The United Nations Special Committee Against Apartheid resolved at its annual conference to impose sanctions against any national team competing with South Africa.

Thus, more than 30 African nations boycotted the Olympic Games in Montreal rather than compete against New Zealand. This was because New Zealand, as a matter of government policy, had sent a rugby team to South Africa this summer.

In August, the Federation Cup tennis series (the women's equivalent of the Davis Cup) was boycotted by several nations as the International Lawn Tennis Federation is essentially the only major international sports body that allows South Africa to compete.

It is simply a reality that the boycotts and threats will continue as long as South Africa practices apartheid in sport. Their choice is clear.

Footnotes

[1] New York Times, May 23, 1966.

[2] Ibid., June 3, 1959.

[3] Ibid., August 1, 1959.

[4] See: The Times (London), May 16, 1970; Guardian (Manchester), May 16, 1970; Sunday Times (London), May 17, 1970; and Observer (London), May 17, 1970.

[5] Based on personal correspondence between Oscar State and T. Rangasamy, May 13, 1946.

[6] It should be noted that South Africa has also prohibited integrated teams from other countries to compete in South Africa. The 1970 New Zealand rugby team was the first integrated team ever to compete in South Africa. Prior to that time, numerous New Zealand rugby teams had come with no Maori players despite large protests in the 1950's and 1960's in New Zealand (see: Richard Thompson, Race and Sport [London: Oxford, 1964]). A British cricket team that included Basil D'Oliveira, a former Cape Colored cricket star, was personally banned by Prime Minister Vorster (see Basil D'Oliveira, The D'Oliveira Affair [London: Collins, 1969], Peter Hain, Don't Play with Apartheid [London: Allen and Unwin, 1971], and Chris de Broglio, South Africa: Racism in Sport [London: Christian Action Publications, 1970]). Finally, Arthue Ashe, the black American tennis star, was also personally banned by Vorster from competing in the 1969 and 1970 South African Opens. Numerous other less publicized examples could be given.

[7] Since the study focused on historical and contemporary phenomena, a combination of documentary sources, newspaper surveys (South African, British and American), personal interviews, and a survey of the attitudes of the National Olympic Committees was used to complete this work.

[8] Survey conducted in August of 1972 in the following cities: New York, Philadelphia, Washington, D.C., Norfolk, Denver and Los Angeles. 78 blacks and 155 whites were interviewed.

[9] Eastern Province Herald (Port Elizabeth), February 16, 1968.

[10] Ibid.

[11] _Sunday Times_ (Johannesburg), February 18, 1968.

[12] _Star_ (Johannesburg), March 22, 1967.

[13] Editorial, _The Times_ (London), February 17, 1968.

[14] Editorial, _New York Times_, February 22, 1968.

[15] J. Drysdale and C. Legum, _Africa Contemporary Record: Annual Survey and Documents_, 1969-70, p. B287.

[16] _Ibid._

[17] Now called the South African Non-Racial Open Committee.

[18] _New York Times_, September 22, 1963.

[19] Muriel Horrell (ed.), _A Survey of Race Relations in South Africa: 1964_, (Johannesburg: Institute of Race Relations, 1965), p. 32.

[20] Statement by Dennis Brutus, personal interview, March 27, 1973.

[21] See: _The World_ (Johannesburg), August 5, 1966; Editorial, _The World_, August 29, 1966; and _Post_ (Natal), November 26, 1967.

[22] See: _Star_ (Johannesburg), August 19, 1963; and _Post_ (Natal), August 25, 1963.

[23] See: Horrell (ed.), _Survey: 1955-56_, p. 227; Thompson, _op. cit._, p. 22; and _The Times_ (London), December 4, 1959.

[24] See: _New York Times_, January 29, 1962; _Cape Argus_ (Cape Town), September 16, 1967; and "The African Football Confederation Memo on South Africa," November 1, 1967.

[25] See: _New York Times_, September 22, 1963; _The Times_ (London), May 31, 1963; _Cape Argus_ (Cape Town), September 16, 1967; and _New York Times_, September 23, 1963.

[26] See: _New York Times_, September 22, 1963; _Cape Argus_ (Cape Town), September 16, 1967; and Horrell (ed.), _Survey: 1964_, pp. 32, 93-94.

27 See: Personal correspondence between Chris de Broglio and Jeremy Thorpe, MP, July 18, 1966; statement by Chris de Broglio, personal interview, March 18, 1970; statement by Omar Cassem, personal interview, March 22, 1970.

28 Richard Lapchick, "The Politics of Race and International Sport: The Case of South Africa," (Westport: Greenwood Press), p. 10.

29 See: The Times (London), September 2, 1955; December 28, 1957; and February 1, 1958.

30 Hansard Report, (Columns 3959-3964), April 11, 1967, in Report of the IOC Commission on South Africa, pp. 67-69.

31 The Times (London), January 29, 1963.

32 IOC Report, p. 69.

33 The Times (London), April 13, 1967.

34 Eastern Province Herald (Port Elizabeth), May 6, 1967.

35 Cape Argus (Cape Town), September 16, 1967.

36 Editorial, The People (Kampala), April 1, 1967.

37 SCSA Resolution Concerning South Africa, Bamako, December 1966.

38 See: The Times (London), April 10, 1967; and Star (Johannesburg), December 14, 1967.

39 ANC, Commentary #12, January 30, 1968.

40 Editorial, Post (Natal), February 11, 1968.

41 New York Times, March 10, 1968.

42 The Times (London), March 6, 1968.

43 SAN-ROC, News and Views, March 20, 1968.

44 IOC, Newsletter #8, May 1968, p. 150.

[45] The Times (London), April 25, 1968.

[46] Guardian (Manchester), May 22, 1970.

[47] Star (Johannesburg), May 14, 1970.

[48] African NOC Charges against SANOC, Addressed to the IOC Amsterdam Session, May 1970.

[49] See: The Times (London), May 16, 1970; Guardian (Manchester), May 16, 1970; Sunday Times (London), May 17, 1970; and Observer (London), May 17, 1970.

[50] See: IOC: Rules and Regulations (Lausanne: IOC, 1972.)

[51] Monique Berlioux, Olympism (Lausanne: IOC, 1972), p. 8.

[52] All figures compiled from the official Olympic Directory, 1969 (Lausanne: IOC, 1969).

[53] The information was gathered in a survey completed in the Spring of 1970 in which the NOC's were asked for their position on South African participation in the Olympics.

[54] New York Times, October 4, 1959.

[55] The Times (London), September 18, 1968.

[56] Statement by Peter Hain, personal interview, April 14, 1970.

[57] The Times (London), January 29, 1970.

[58] Ibid., February 23, 1970.

[59] Guardian (Manchester), April 24, 1970.

[60] Ibid., May 22, 1970.

[61] All facts based on the testimony of Oliver S. Crosby, an official State Department spokesman, before the Sub-Committee on African Affairs of the House of Representatives on February 4, 1970.

[62] UN Unit on Apartheid Papers, April 1970. Hearing of Mr. Arthur Ashe, p. 3.

[63] Rand Daily Mail (Johannesburg), March 24, 1970.

[64] See: Natal Mercury (Durban), December 16, 1969; and Guardian (Manchester), December 16, 1969.

[65] See: Guardian (Manchester), May 25, 1970; and Rand Daily Mail (Johannesburg), May 25, 26, 27, 28, and 30, 1970.

Sport As Transnational Politics: A
Preliminary Analysis Of Africa

Timothy M. Shaw and Susan M. Shaw

The study of "transnational politics" has transformed the analysis of
international relations. Its focus on "unofficial" or informal relations both
between and within states adds a new and fruitful dimension to our view of
the international system.[1] By recognizing a rich diversity of "non-governmental" actors it goes beyond the orthodox "state-centric" perspective and
projects a "mixed actor" model of world politics.[2] The utility of the transnational politics approach for the study in the international system is examined in this essay. We draw on data from Africa to support a very preliminary and tentative analysis. Our concern is, then, with the political aspects
of sport in Africa and with the appropriateness of the transnational perspective in describing and analysing these. We turn first to the concept transnational relations and to a general overview of its relevance to the study of
sport as international politics.

From International to Transnational Sports: A Conceptual
Introduction

Traditional international relations has concentrated on a few interstate
issues such as diplomacy and international law, war and peace. However,
as the international system has become more open to new states and people
and as economics has increasingly become the new "high politics", so such
orthodox concerns have given way to new perspectives.

The transnational politics approach is one of these; it breaks away
from dealing only with intergovernmental and primarily "diplomatic" relations. Rather its focus is on "contacts, coalitions, and interactions across
state boundaries that are not controlled by the central foreign policy organs
of governments."[3] By definition a transnational relationship must be "international" and must involve nongovernmental actors, such as multinational
corporations, trade unions, parties, liberation movements, etc. Transnational structures, then, link particular interests or institutions within states
and give them an external dimension. Such transnational relations include

Reprinted by kind permission of the Journal of Sport and Social Issues. Volume 2, 1977.

exchanges between corporate branches in different countries, international gatherings of socialist or communist parties, and world associations of particular religions or professional associations.

To date, empirical research on transnational organisations has concentrated heavily on the activities of the multinational corporation. Other institutions examined include liberation movements, international labor bodies, international scientific cooperation, international religious movements and international foundations. Because of recent advances in communications technology and because of the imperative of cooperation in a world facing ecological decay and shortages, transnationalism is likely to continue to spread and to detract from the established dominance of the state in international politics; governments may be less ready to control transnational compared with national activities. But, the "transnational organizational revolution in world politics"[5] has not yet included the analysis of sport. This article is an early attempt to discover whether the general transnational approach is appropriate for the study of sport, and to indicate ways in which the analysis of sport suggests revisions to this general perspective.

If we abandon the assumption that states act as if they were a single, consistent actor, then parts of regimes may themselves engage in a form of transnational politics termed "transgovernmental relations."[6] Subunits of government--different ministries or parts thereof, particular state corporations and agencies--may act in relatively autonomous ways without reference to higher authority. Such transgovernmental activity may produce a rather inconsistent or ambivalent foreign policy if different parts of the state bureaucracy are engaged in incompatible pursuits. However, it can also lead to transgovernmental policy coordination and coalition-building in which different agencies or bureaus collaborate on particular issues and exchange support.[7] Such transnational activities can enhance the status of participants within their own national bureaurcracies and increase the influence of each over their own government's decisions (See Figure 1).

Finally, transnational and transgovernmental relations may lay the foundation for the creation of complex international coalitions over particular international issues. Support may be gathered from non-governmental institutions, international organisations as well as from transnational and transgovernmental structures. The existence of such complex and diverse coalitions in the international system over a range of issues--such as conflicts in the Middle East and Southern Africa and the creation of a New International Economic Order or an International Law of the Sea--takes us a long way from state-centric and realist assumptions about international relations.

The Diverse Politics of Sport

The transnational perspective examined here goes beyond the orthodox assumptions either that sport is apolitical or that it is a simple case of interstate power politics. Rather we suggest that politics is a pervasive and characteristic aspect of international sport; it can neither be separated from sport nor can it be regarded simply as something which governments do alone. Rather, its political character is apparent at all levels of sports competition and organisation.

a) <u>International politics: the orthodox paradigm</u>

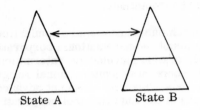

b) <u>Transnational politics: non-governmental interactions</u>

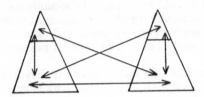

c) <u>Transgovernmental politics: intra-governmental interactions</u>

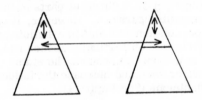

Figure 1.   Transnational and Transgovernmental Politics.

Cf. Kaiser "Transnational Politics: toward a theory of multinational politics" and Nye and Keohane "Transnational Relations and World Politics: an introduction."

In the case of Africa, sport has a particular salience and appeal because of limited resources and visibility in other national attributes. This is even so in domestic competition and organisation, especially in the more populist sports such as soccer and boxing. The political content of sports in Africa is particularly important in international games, whether they be regional, continental or global. African states place a special emphasis on participation in international competition because of limited alternative resources through which to secure international recognition and status. They regard victories as successes for the African continent rather than merely for their own country but international participation by itself is also important. The salience of external sports increases the influence of national sports bodies--both councils for all sports and national organisations for particular sports. Most of these institutions in Africa have close relations with the state, especially with ministries of culture, welfare, youth or recreation, and with the ruling party and the military; indeed the military in some African states--as in the superpowers--is used to subsidise, and act as a patron for, promising sports performers.

In addition to the establishment of national sports bodies, Africa has also created regional and continental institutions to organise and regulate international sports. These are based on national delegations and include the All-Africa Games and the Africa Cup of Nations (Soccer) as well as the East and Central African Games, All-Africa Hockey, Swimming and Handball Championships and All-Africa University Games. Two further continental organisations are the African Amateur Athletics Confederation and the Federation of African University Sports. Finally, national sports councils are represented in the Yaounde-based Supreme Council for Sports in Africa (SCSA) which is designed to develop sport on the continent but has been preoccupied with excluding South Africa and Rhodesia from international competition.[8] It acts as a communications centre and clearinghouse for sport just as the Organization of African Unity (OAU) does for African diplomacy; indeed, it has a formal relationship with the OAU. Its President, Abraham Ordia, and Secretary-General, Jean-Claude Ganga, have been particularly active opponents of racism in sport. Sport in Africa has been underanalysed to date; but it clearly includes a rich diversity of transnational and transgovernmental relations both among independent states themselves and between them and other organisations especially over the issue of Southern Africa. We touch on this briefly here and return to it again in the next section.

All actors attempt to maximise support and visibility through the form of coalitions and alliances, whether these be based on shared ideology, class, race or enemy. The case of South Africa is illustrative of such coalition politics. For example, within the United Nations (UN) the dominant, majority coalition includes the liberation movements, African states (especially the several crucial "frontier" countries), other nonaligned and socialist regimes, and UN agencies and committees.[10] Against this formidable transnational coalition stand the white regimes, their non-governmental associates and (in a somewhat ambivalent way) many of the Western states. The dominant coalition favours majority rule and a rapid redistribution of resources, whereas the minority faction is defensive of the regional status quo and plays an essentially "counterrevolutionary" role.[11]

The dominant coalition has succeeded in mobilising support from a wide range of transnational institutions in favor of political change in Southern Africa including trade unions, political parties and sports bodies. Sport organizations in Africa (i.e., SCSA and others) have strongly endorsed the idea of a sports boycott of South Africa. This boycott has been supported by quite a large number of international sports organisations,[12] although many of these international federations (particularly those whose membership is dominated by West Europeans and North Americans)[13] exhibit an ambivalent attitude towards participation with South Africa. There have been a number of occasions, for example, on which the international sport federation in a particular sport has not definitely banned South Africa from membership, but neither has it resisted the exclusion of South Africa from specific world championships. However, transnational sports organisations have had an inescapable political role to play with regard to South Africa since the idea of a sports boycott developed and became popularized.

It is clear from this brief consideration of sports organisation and practice in Africa that sports and politics are inseparable: indeed, sport is often a form of politics. Sport interacts with politics at several levels--city, provincial, national and international--and probably becomes more politicized at the higher levels. Sport is politics because of the competition for scarce resources--status, finance, skills--which occurs at level both within and between sports teams and sports organisations. Pooley and Webster have asserted that "national governments seek to increase their power through sport in order to achieve their goals."[14] Clearly sport is a form of international politics in which national status and pride are at stake; concern for international sporting image leads to the "development" of national teams. Sport can also be an expression of national unity and ideology.

The rapid expansion of international competition has led to the recent growth of quasi-governmental sports bodies--national Councils of sports or Councils of recreation. These bodies engage in bureaucratic politics within states, seeking to maximize their resources and influence inside the national governmental system; they also correspond with each other to provide mutual support for their common activities--this is clearly a case of "transgovernmental" politics. Further, they encourage the activities of national associations and teams and in turn expect support from them both within the state and in international competition--cases of "transgovernmental" and "transnational" politics respectively.

Perhaps the most obvious and influential transnational sports organization is the International Olympic Committee[15] which acts as a "private" (even aristocratic) institution to organise and regulate Olympic competition; in theory, such competition occurs between individuals under the auspices of National Olympic Committees rather than between states _per se._ In practice, of course, most National Olympic Committees are closely associated with, or are even sections of, national sports bodies or sports ministries. The international Olympic movement has always had an ambivalent-- if not contradictory or hypocritical--attitude towards international politics. The movement seeks to encourage "peace" between nations--which is perceived to be a "nonpolitical" form of idealism--and it tries to exclude any conflict between states because it is "politics," and hence undesirable! This untenable conception of sport as having a pacific and nonconflictual role has, to our knowledge, never been realized, even at the time of the ancient Olympics. Other international sporting associations--for soccer, tennis, cricket, gymnastics, etc.--are further examples of transnational organizations in which national groups promote their common interests while at the same time they compete for positions, resources and status.

The transnational and transgovernmental politics approach, then, may advance our understanding of sport as international politics. Sport is not just international politics between states: the politics of sport is also present within international and national associations and between them and national regimes and, at times, international organizations. The transnational and transgovernmental perspective may provide new insights into the complex network of national and international sports bodies and competitions (See Figure 2) and into coalitions of sports-related institutions mobilised over issues such as the participation of South Africa or Taiwan in the international sporting system. As such, it helps to overcome conservative modes of analysis based on state-centric assumptions.[16]

This perspective, then, focuses on the behavioral aspects of sport as politics by widening the definition of politics to include more than government and formal political institutions. Politics cannot be separated from sport: it is a pervasive and intrinsic aspect of both internal and international sport. To be sure, "the nations of the world rank differently according to the amount of interest their Governments take in the organization of sport."[17] But the degree to which the state controls sport is only one among several indicators of sport as politics. Hopefully, the transnational approach indicates other and diverse forms of sport as politics in the international system. The case of South Africa is illustrative of the complexities of sport as an issue in international politics: both transnational and transgovernmental institutions have been concerned with the exclusion of South Africa from international sport as well as governments and international organisations.

Africa Against Apartheid: Sport as Anti-Racist Ideology

In the case of South Africa it is internal structures and values which profoundly affect its external acceptability as a participant in international sport. As the composition of the community of nations changed after World War II to include a majority of new, non-white, Third World states so apartheid--which includes racial separation and inequality in sport--became increasingly anathema.[18] Apartheid means not only that sport is practised separately by different racial groups but also that sports opportunities and resources for whites are vastly superior to those provided for other races. Sport is almost a religion in white South Africa;[19] meanwhile, non-white facilities are minimal and blacks have been excluded from international teams. The white minority regime claims that sport is private and apolitical in South Africa and that segregation in sport is merely an aspect of a traditional way of life. But, even if this were true, South African sport would inevitably have a political aspect; in the case of South Africa its political and racial content is clearly of great significance. Government legislation, police and uneven distribution of resources combine to effectively exclude non-whites from "South African" sport.

Sports organizations in South Africa have been forced to conform with "separate development" legislation except at the national level where non-white associations could, if they wished, affiliate with their respective white "national" association; but only white national sports associations can affiliate to the South African Olympic and National Games Association--symbolic of white paternalism and supremacy. The administration of sports policy is

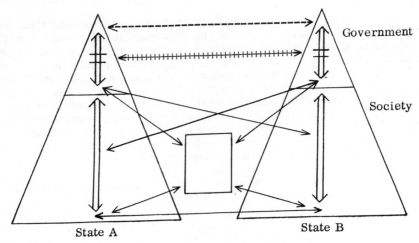

International Sports Institution

$\Longleftarrow\ --\ \Rightarrow$ International (interstate) competition

$\Longleftarrow\!\longrightarrow$ Transnational politics

$\Longleftarrow\!+\!+\!\Rightarrow$ Transgovernmental politics

$\Longleftarrow\!\Longrightarrow$ Intra-national politics (often related to transnational or transgovernmental relations)

$\Longleftarrow\!\Vert\!\Longrightarrow$ Intra-governmental politics

Figure 2. International Politics of Sport.

the responsibility of different departments for different racial groups although the Minister of Sport can intervene, especially in cases involving international or "multinational" sports.[20] There are still no effective multiracial or nonracial sports institutions in South Africa, although any such nonracial sports associations are now grouped in the South African Council of Sport and some are affiliated to all-African federations or the Supreme Council for Sport in Africa.

As South Africa's sports apartheid led to international exclusion, so a nonracial group in exile has been formed as an alternative national association to the established exclusive institutions. At present this non-apartheid group constitutes a transnational organisation but after political change it will presumably become an official institution. The South African Nonracial Olympic Committee (SAN-ROC) has advocated the exclusion of racially-exclusive or -biased South African teams from international sport and has won recognition from the dominant coalition in the UN as the legitimate (if presently non-effective) "national" sports body. The work of SAN-ROC has been opposed and hampered by the white regime but it has nevertheless gradually succeeded in widening the boycott of South Africa in sport.

The UN opposes racial discrimination in South African sports and condemns it as a violation of Olympic principles, although the International Olympic Committee itself has been more ambivalent in its treatment of South African (and Rhodesian) applications for continued participation in the Games. For the last decade, the UN has considered sport to be an additional political weapon through which to oppose the minority regimes. Gradually the acceptance of the idea of sanctions in sport has spread to include the majority of countries, games and competitions, even including some of South Africa's traditional sporting partners.[21]

Most African, Third World and socialist states have ended any sporting ties they had with South Africa; their governments have thus implemented successive UN resolutions on the issue. In general, Western states have been more ambivalent and reluctant, partially because of the inheritance of close sports relations and partially because of their official policies of non-interference in sport. The non-official and "transnational" character of many western sports links with (white) South African clubs and organizations has constrained the implementation of UN policy by western regimes.[22] But as the cost of non-compliance has increased (especially the threat to sports exchanges with black Africa), Western government pressure has also grown to prevent internationally unacceptable sports contacts--intranational politics have had to change even in "plural" western societies to protect most transnational or international sporting relations.

The gradual spread of compliance with UN resolutions has made the sports boycott of South Africa almost comprehensive and universal.[23] This success is attributable to the continued advocacy of the boycott by SAN-ROC within the dominant coalition opposing white rule in Southern Africa. Further, other nongovernmental actors have lent their encouragement--especially the liberation movements and their transnational support groups--and more specific non-state organizations have been formed just to prevent sports cooperation with South Africa. UN organs concerned with Southern Africa along with the OAU and the SCSA have encouraged and provided legitimacy for anti-apartheid sports movements such as the Stop the Seventy Tour Campaign (Britain)[24] and Halt All Racist Tours (HART) and Citizens' Association for Racial Equality (CARE) (New Zealand). The International Campaign Against Racism in Sport (ICARIS) has been established to coordinate and continue the boycott and to intensify South Africa's isolation.[25]

This large and growing transnational and transgovernmental coalition has succeeded in expanding and implementing a comprehensive boycott of South Africa in international sport.[26] The greatest success of the dominant transnational coalition to date has surely been the withdrawal of African states from the Montreal Olympics to protest the New Zealand rugby tour of South Africa,[27] a tour that had become a general election issue in New Zealand and which contributed to the electroal demise of the Kirk government and its replacement by Muldoon as Prime Minister--an advocate of renewal of "noninterference" in international sports.[28] The African boycott which must have caused some understandable disappointment among athletes and sports officials--was almost complete and was secured by the active involvement of SAN-ROC and SCSA officials in Montreal, a clear and successful case of transnational coalition-building based on a variety of national and transnational organisations, even though it did not include many non-African states. Fear of its repetition has produced a flurry of transnational and intergovernmental activity to "save" the 1978 Commonwealth Games in Edmonton from a further African walkout over New Zealand's continued sporting ties with South Africa.

The increasing effectiveness and impact of this boycott has led to some belated changes in South African sports policy, to a vigorous foreign policy campaign to regain acceptability[29] and to increased government activity in the form of officially-approved "multinational" games. Sports cannot be fully integrated and become genuinely nonracial in South Africa without jeopardising the whole edifice of apartheid. However, South Africans, especially white sportsmen, are desperate for international sporting contact. This dilemma has led to a few incremental changes designed to largely preserve internal racial separation and stratification while appearing to satisfy demands for mixed international teams and even national competitions.[30] The "concessions" amount to a reluctant acceptance of "multinational" international and national events and teams combined with a grudging permissiveness towards, but not encouragement of, inter- or nonracial sport domestically. The 1973 "multinational" games in Pretoria were also an attempt to regain external acceptability without implementing any basic structural changes in sports within South Africa.[31]

In September 1976, as part of the Vorster regime's attempt to secure international status by appearing to advance nonviolent change in Zimbabwe and Namibia, the Minister of Sport introduced a new sports "policy." This goes beyond previous attempts at creating external "multinational" teams and competitions and allows "intergroup" competition at all levels for individual sport and for the possibility of team sports in "intergroup" leagues or matches; it also permits integrated spectator arrangements. It does not permit integrated teams at the provincial or club levels. However, given the whole edifice of apartheid it is a permissive decree; it does not advocate or compel interracial sport. Moreover, it has been made compatible with the structure of separate development as each sports-person has to also affiliate with their racially-defined national association before they can play in mixed events. In other words, it is not advancing nonracial sport or undermining apartheid. But it would appear to complicate the stand of groups in opposition to the present regime and its sports policy by allowing for some controlled competition within as well as outside South Africa. So, South Africa can now field racially-mixed groups of players in both team and individual international events; these can use the national flag or colors. However, until all sport in South Africa is deracialized and until black sportspersons benefit from a radical redistribution of resources the boycott is likely to continue. In the present situation of two dialectical international coalitions any breeching of sanctions serves to reinforce apartheid in sports whereas the strengthening of the boycott tends to further advance nonracial sport and contribute to general external pressure on the white regime.[32]

Towards a Political Economy of Sport

The transnational and transgovernmental approaches to international sport may advance our understanding of the complex politics of sport and the potential for coalition formation against unacceptable opponents such as South Africa. However, the issue of race may mask a more important problem in international sport--that of inequalities both within and between states. The issue in the South African case is not simply one of race, but also the related problem of "class." At present, even if blacks had equal rights their sports participation would be limited because of the uneven distribution of resources within that social system.

The problem of inequality is present at all levels of sport interaction-- between individuals, teams, organizations and states. Some sports are more exclusive and expensive than others and so tend to be the preserve of the "transnational elite"--yachting, polo, horse-riding, etc.--whereas others are more populist and open to improvisation--soccer, boxing, track, etc. To date African states have been highly successful in the latter, "la-bour-intensive" sports rather than in the former, "capital-intensive" activi-ties. To broaden and maintain its international sporting achievements Africa needs now to win in a wider range of activities. However, winning at the Olympics and other events is closely related to national wealth and objec-tives.[33]

Inequalities are growing between African states in the increasingly un-even distribution on the continent of wealth, power, resources, etc.[34] This inequality will likely be reflected in the future in unequal sports successes with a few leading African states--Nigeria, Egypt, Kenya--becoming domi-nant. This may cause difficulties for African sports organisations and may threaten African unity in the sports sphere. To date, sport in Africa has been one way to advance Africa's interests, identity, visibility and skills and to bring pressure against the white regimes of Southern Africa. However, if we advance from a transnational perspective and towards a political economy approach to international sports[35] then we would have to recognise the po-tential problem of internal and international inequalities confronting the de-velopment of Africa's sports potential; this is a further illustration of the difficulties arising from Africa's inheritance of dependent development in the world system.

References

[1] This approach originated in the suggestive work of Robert O. Keohane and Joseph S. Nye. See especially their "Introduction" and "Conclusion" in their collection on Transnational relations and world politics. (Cam-bridge, Mass.: Harvard University Press, 1972), pp. ix-xxix and 371-398.

[2] On the implications of this diversity of actors and issues for Africa see Timothy M. Shaw "The actors in African international politics" in Timothy M. Shaw and Kenneth A. Heard (eds.), Politics of Africa: development

and dependence. (London: Longman and Dalhousie University Press, 1977).

[3] Nye and Keohane "Transnational relations and world politics: an introduction," p. xi.

[4] See Nye and Keohane (eds.), Transnational relations and world politics passim. and Gerald A. Sumida, "Transnational movements and economic structures" in Cyril E. Black and Richard A. Falk (eds.), The future of the international legal order, IV The structure of the international environment. (Princeton: Princeton University Press, 1972), pp. 524-568.

[5] Samuel P. Huntington, "Transnational organizations in world politics," World Politics 25(3), April 1973, p. 333.

[6] See Robert O. Keohane and Joseph S. Nye, "Transgovernmental relations and international organizations," World Politics 27(1), October 1974, p. 41.

[7] Ibid., pp. 41-50.

[8] For a refreshingly frank assessment of the obstacles confronting sport in Africa, especially the absence of long-term planning, commitment and organisations, see Stanley Cole, "Towards the Montreal Olympics: why Africa never wins," Afriscope 6(5), May 1976, pp. 6-11.

[9] One hopeful exception is the recent compilation by Ramadhan Ali, Africa at the Olympics. (London: Africa Books, 1976) which is really a history of Africa in international sports.

[10] For a more comprehensive analysis of transnational coalitions over Southern Africa, see Timothy M. Shaw, "International organisations and the politics of Southern Africa: towards regional integration or liberation?" Journal of Southern African Studies 3(1), October 1976, pp. 1-19.

[11] On the common interests of black and white ruling classes in Southern Africa against racial change in the region, see Timothy M. Shaw and Agrippah T. Mugomba, "The political economy of regional detente: Zambia and Southern Africa." Journal of Southern African Studies 4(4), Winter 1977/8.

[12] See Muriel Horrell, "Sport and recreation" in her A Survey of race relations in South Africa, Volume 26, 1972. (Johannesburg: SAIRR, 1973).

[13] On the characteristic and continuing Western dominance of UN agencies see Robert W. Cox and Harold K. Jacobson (eds.), The anatomy of influence: decision-making in international organization. (New Haven: Yale UP, 1973).

[14] John C. Pooley and Arthur V. Webster, "Sport and politics: power play." Journal of CAHPER 41(3), January-February 1975, p. 13.

[15] For a preliminary analysis of the Olympic Movement as a transnational phenomenon, see David B. Kanin, "The role of sport in the international system," International Studies Association Conference, Toronto, February 1976. Kanin suggests that the political content of the Olympic games includes propaganda, recognition and diplomacy. See also Susan M. Shaw, "The organization of the International Olympic Committee," Dalhousie University, December 1975.

[16] See the critical and creative work by Richard W. Mansbach, Yale H. Ferguson, Donald E. Lampert, The Web of world politics: non-state actors in the global system. (Englewood Cliffs: Prentice-Hall, 1976), pp. 2-45.

[17] Alex Natan, "Sport and politics" in John W. Loy and Gerald S. Kenyon (eds.), Sport, culture and society. (New York: Macmillan, 1969), p. 210.

[18] For thorough analysis and history of South Africa's sports policy and its international exclusion, see Richard E. Lapchick, The politics of race and international sport: the case of South Africa. (Westport, Conn.: Greenwood Press, 1975).

[19] See Susan M. Shaw, "Sport and political ideology in South Africa," ARENA, Institute of Sport and Social Analysis, Newsletter 1(2), 1977.

[20] For a more comprehensive analysis of the tortuous "bureaucratic politics" of sport in South Africa, see Susan M. Shaw, "Sport and politics in South Africa," Dalhousie University, March 1975.

[21] See "Exclusion of South African racist sports bodies from international sports." UN Unit on Apartheid, 20/75, May 1975; Racism and apartheid in Southern Africa: South Africa and Namibia. (Paris: UNESCO Press, 1974); and Apartheid: its effect on education, science, culture and information. (Paris: UNESCO, 1972).

[22] On the escalation and widening scope of UN General Assembly resolutions taken each year on "apartheid in sports" and on the official positions of many UN members, see "Against apartheid in sports: actions taken by governments concerning sporting contacts with South Africa," UN Centre Against Apartheid, 3/76, January 1976.

23 On the support of the nonaligned states for a universal sports boycott against South Africa and for an international convention against apartheid in sports, see "Fifth Conference of Heads of State for Government of Non-aligned Countries, Columbo, Sri Lanka, August 1976'," UN Centre Against Apartheid, 23/76, September 1976, pp. 8 and 14-16.

24 See Peter Hain, Don't play with apartheid: the background to the Stop the Seventy Tour Campaign. (London: George, Allen & Unwin, 1971).

25 See Richard E. Lapchick, "Apartheid sport and South Africa's foreign policy: 1976," UN Centre Against Apartheid, SEM/6, June 1976 and Tom Newnham "Apartheid and sports: international boycott of apartheid sports," UN Center Against Apartheid, 15/76, July 1976. Cf. "Sport: a dynamic approach," South African Scope, May 1975, p. 2.

26 On the role of SAN-ROC and the increasing isolation of South Africa in in-ternational sport, see Sam Ramsamy and Chris D. de Broglio, "Isolate South Africa from international sport and support SAN-ROC," UN Centre Against Apartheid, SEM/10, June 1976; "Seminar on South Africa - II: Concerted international action against apartheid in sports," UN Unit on Apartheid, 29/75, August 1975; and Ali, Africa at the Olympics, pp. 40-65 and 130-133.

27 See Peter Osugo, "The black triumph at Montreal Olympics," Africa 61, September 1976, pp. 80-81.

28 On the history of the politics of South African sport in New Zealand, see Richard Thompson, Retreat from apartheid: New Zealand's sporting con-tacts with South Africa. (London: OUP, 1975).

29 See Richard E. Lapchick, "Apartheid Sport: South Africa's use of sport in its foreign policy," Journal of Sport and Social Issues 1(1), 1976, pp. 52-79.

30 On the different faces of South African sport--external and internal--see Peter Hain, "Keeping up the pressure on South African sport," The Times. (London) 24 May 1975, p. 12; reprinted in Sport Sociology Bulle-tin 5(2), Fall 1976, pp. 32-33.

31 On the "multinational" games, see Joan Brickhill, Race against race: South Africa's "multinational" sport fraud. (London: International De-fence and Aid Fund, 1976).

32 See Susan M. Shaw, "Sport and politics: the case of South Africa," Journal of CAPHER 43(1), September-October 1976, pp. 30-38.

[33] On the relationship between several socioeconomic, politico-military and educational factors and winning medals at the Olympics, see Susan M. Shaw and John C. Pooley, "National success at the Olympics: an explanation," International Seminar on the history of Physical Education and Sport, Trois Rivieres, Quebec, July 1976.

[34] On the development and implications of internal and external inequalities on the continent, see Timothy M. Shaw, "The political economy of African international relations," Issue 5(4), Winter 1975, pp. 29-38 and "Discontinuities and inequalities in African international politics," International Journal 30 (3), Summer 1975, pp. 369-390.

[35] Radical, "neo-Marxist" scholars have advocated this perspective on sport within societies; a similar approach to international sport is also needed. For a review of Marxist and other sociological analyses, see Richard S. Gruneau, "Sport, social differentiation and social inequality" in Donald W. Ball & John W. Loy (eds.), Sport and social order: contributions to the sociology of sport. (Reading, Mass.: Addison-Wesley, 1975), pp. 121-184.

Federal Involvement In Sport To Promote American Interest Or Foreign Policy Objectives - 1950 - 1973

Roy Clumpner

Since 1950 the world has become increasingly cognizant of numerous countries using sport[1] for political purposes. Chief targets of attack have traditionally been socialist countries, most notably the Soviet Union, and more recently the German Democratic Republic. What has largely been unrecognized is the fact that so-called capitalist, or "free world" countries have done basically the same thing, but have managed to go unnoticed in this aspect. Chief among these countries has been the United States.

Even though Americans have traditionally abhorred federal involvement in any sphere which they deem to be outside the realm of government,[2] the American federal government from 1950-1973 repeatedly made attempts to aid American amateur sport involved in international competition in order to promote American interests and foreign policy objectives. Two ways[3] in which this was done was to promote and encourage American international athletic success and to sponsor American cultural exchanges with other countries. This latter program had begun on a limited basis after World War II, but was greatly increased following Soviet inroads in this area in the 1950's. In both of these programs, the Cold War instigated their development.

Promoting International Athletic Success: The Rise of Soviet Sport

Today, the Communist aggressor has again forced this Nation into battle--a battle to save the free world. On the wild, inhospitable, rangy hills and mountains of Korea, in bitter cold, sleet, rain and mud, the cream of American youth--the Nation's finest--hold the line against the spread of Communism throughout the world.[4]

So began the infamous decade of the fifties upon which the foundation of American foreign policy was laid for the next two decades. Not only was the struggle between the two ideological camps to take place on the field of battle but also on the field of sport as well.

American international supremacy in amateur athletics, spurred by a decisive victory in the 1948 Olympics, was undaunted and undiminished at the beginning of the second half of the twentieth century. Even when the International Olympic Committee extended an invitation for Soviet representation in 1951, thereby qualifying the Soviets for their first modern Olympics in 1952, American feeling of superiority continued unabated. The only question which stood in the minds of Americans was by what margin Uncle Sam would win the 1952 Games. For the first time since the 1936 Olympics, lines were drawn ideologically between two hostile camps.

> The United States has to have its strongest possible representation just to teach the Red brothers a lesson that can't be excused or concealed. . . . There will be 71 nations in the Olympics at Helsinki. The United States would like to beat all of them, but the only one that counts is Soviet Russia. The Communist propaganda machine must be silenced so that there can't be even one distorted bleat out of it in regard to the Olympics. In sports the Red brothers have reached the put-up-or-shut-up stage. Let's shut them up.[5]

Even though the State Department at this time was taking notice of Soviet athletic exchanges, little thought was given toward government aid for the purpose of sending the American Olympic team.[6] Again, just as in the past, private funds were solicited. This procedure was highlighted by a fourteen and one-half hour telethon during which over 250 celebrities participated, including such celebrities as Bing Crosby, Bob Hope and Frank Sinatra.[7] The American attitude toward federal aid for the U.S. Olympic team was best summed up by sports columnist Arthur Daley:

> Instead of letting our Olympians hold out their hats like beggars every four years, we could let the Government pick up the tab. The federal authorities never would notice a sum like $650,000. But when that time comes, we should quit the Olympics. Sports lovers--and this applies to all sports--want nothing from the Government--money, advice, controls, interference or bureaucrats.[8]

American supremacy in the Olympics was maintained in 1952, but what was not expected was the strong second place Soviet showing. From this point onward American federal concern in American international athletics changed and coincided with the diminishing image of American athletic supremacy in the Olympic games. Americans soon began to take notice of the all-out effort on the part of the Soviet Union and began to ask themselves about the role which sport played in the entire east-west confrontation. Some Congressmen questioned the meaning of the rapid advancement of Russia in the world of sports, and to what extent superiority in competitive athletics was tied in with national success, prosperity, and invincibility of warfare.[9]

Further public recognition of Soviet inroads into international sport occurred in 1955 with the publication of an article in a popular magazine by Avery Brundage, president of the International Olympic Association,[10] and

a speech by William Randolph Hearst, Jr., editor-in-chief of Hearst newspapers, when each returned from trips to the Soviet Union. Both noted the
likelihood that the United States would have a tough time at the 1956 Olympics in Melbourne and expressed concern as to the effect a U.S. loss would
have on its prestige among the sport conscious young people throughout the
world.[11] With the floodgates open, the issue cropped up with increasing
frequency:

> The Russians will knock the ears off the Americans in the
> 1956 Olympic Games in Melbourne, Australia, next year. It
> isn't a pretty fact but it's virtually an inescapable one. . . .
> The Red brothers will scream to the world that this is merely
> one more proof of how decadent the capitalistic system really
> is. . . . They have no intention of missing out on a propaganda
> vehicle as monumental as this one. . . . The embarrassing
> part of it all is that the United States might not be able to out-
> score the Russians even with our best.[12]

Congress also was alerted and the topic was discussed repeatedly.[13]
One of the more vociferous representatives was Senator Butler:

> Are we in the United States--where our record of excel-
> lence in the field of amateur sportsmanship is a byproduct of
> our unique system of government--allowing the Soviet Union to
> pollute the Olympic Games; to use, with diabolic deceit, the
> spirit of sportsmanship itself as a velvet-gloved iron fist to
> ruthlessly hammer out their godless propaganda.[14]

One of the main objections voiced by Americans and their congressional representatives concerning Soviet athletes competing in the Olympics was
professionalism.

> The Soviet Athlete is as much a pawn in the vast Soviet
> mechanism as any other segment of the total Soviet proletariat.
> He is not an individual. He has no independence. He is anything
> but a free agent. His only right is the right to obey. And his
> duty is simple and absolute. He must win. . . . What further
> evidence do we need that the atheistic masters of the Kremlin
> are flagrantly violating the principle of the Olympic Games when
> we consider that these 12 million athletes are trained from
> childhood to adolescence, like performers in a circus, and to
> young manhood and womanhood? The hand of government pos-
> session, direction, compulsion is everywhere. This is clearly
> in violation of Olympic rules.[15]

In 1956 in the Senate, S. Conc. Res. 78[16] was introduced which contained two resolutions calling on Congress to voice opposition to the use of
Soviet professional athletes in the upcoming Melbourne Olympics.

> Resolved. . . . That it is the sense of the Congress that
> American athletic committees should do everything humanly pos-
> sible to effect the disbarment of Russian professional athletes

from the 1956 Olympic Games, and that said committees should
actively solicit in this undertaking the cooperation of all other
participating nations outside the Iron Curtain; and, be it further
Resolved, that it is the sense of the Congress, that in the event
such cooperation of non-Communist nations and/or such disbar-
ment of Russian professional athletes from the 1956 Olympic
Games shall have been found to be unattainable, the athletic
committees of the United States should participate in the 1956
Olympic Games only under official protest of the wanton violation by Soviet Russia of the spirit and rules of the International
Olympic Games. . . .17

Senator Butler's resolution failed to generate public and congressional
backing and died, but in the meantime the controversy continued in Congress.

. . . . when one considers that the Russian Communists
are out to win these Olympic games as an indication of their
superiority over the United States, the seriousness of the situation is apparent. . . . . We must remember that the Russian
Communists have the biggest propaganda machine in history and
that they will pound away at all the people of the world--if they
should win the 1956 Olympics, that our American democracy is
decaying, that our athletic victories of the past will never again
be achieved, that we are a decaying society--like the Roman
Empire in its last days.18

Attitudes, as reflected by some members of Congress, slowly began to
change toward the idea of federal aid to the American Olympic Team. Some
Congressmen suggested the possibility of using the President's emergency
fund to assist the American Olympic Committee in fielding a full United
States Olympic Team.19 To that end Congressman Feighan attempted passage of bill H.R. 6777 in 1955, which would have included within the President's fund provision for assisting the athletic program of the United States
with a view toward aiding American athletes to participate in the 1956 Olympic games. About the same time two other bills, S. 3280 by Senator Butler
and H.R. 9366 by Congressman McDonald, were before Congress. Each
called for a reimbursement to athletes selected by the United States Olympic
Association to represent the United States at the Melbourne Olympics. Needless to say, the passage of these bills would have meant a reversal of past
attitudes toward the federal sector involving itself in sport. Congress was
not swayed. Both bills died in committee and Congress continued to follow
the same path of non-involvement as before. In fact, Senator Butler, author
of one of the above bills, seems to have had a change of heart later in the
session when he spoke about financial support of athletic teams:

I do believe, however, that we are treading on dangerous
ground when we say that it should come from Government by whatever means. And, I say further, that finances are not our most
immediate need. Government subsidization of our athletes would
make them official representatives of the American Government--
which they are not.20

Public and congressional fears came true at the Melbourne Olympics. The United States placed second to the Soviet Union in the unofficial point standings. Despite this, the doomsday warnings forecast by so many never really reached fruition as the public and Congress remained rather unresponsive to the entire matter. Federal interest in the Olympics began to strengthen as the United States prepared for the 1960 Winter and Summer Olympics, and any indication that the Cold War was drawing to an end was surely not evident in Congress:

> Let us not, however, be swept off our feet by any illusion that competition between athletic teams ultimately generates goodwill between us and the people of the Soviet Union. . . . The unfortunate fact is that these Russian athletes competing against our bona fide amateur track stars were, for practical purposes, tools of the Soviet regime being exploited to promote the achievements of Communism.[21]

The news media also continued its assault on the Soviet professionals:

> The Communists are well aware of the great propaganda value of the Olympics. As such, the Kremlin and all its satellites employ the games as a political weapon, an easy and ready-made avenue for penetration of the free world. Their athletes are in reality Communist agents, professionals in every sense.[22]

Some writers, in fact, advocated a revision in the Olympic rules:

> There is a solution, as bold as the first sputnik--just stop kidding ourselves and drop that old-fashioned term, "amateur." Why not let pros, as well as amateurs, enter the Olympics? No more our amateurs against their professionals.[23]

Possibly to soften the blow of what appeared to be an imminent defeat, President Eisenhower, at a press conference in February of 1960, declared that in his view it was not necessary to keep up with the Soviet Union in all areas, including sports.[24] Fears of Soviet sport domination were well founded as the Soviet Union doubled the medal total of its closest rival in the Winter Games of 1960, causing Congressman Stratton to remark:

> Mr. Speaker, does this not look like the same thing that we seem to be running into also in the race for space and the construction of superior military power? Have we Americans indeed lost the old competitive spirit? Is it true that in space and in the race for military superiority and in the competition to produce the best educated engineering and scientific brains, just as in the competition for gold medals in the Winter Olympics, "they're eager and we're not"?[25]

The Soviet Winter Olympic victory was followed by yet another Summer Games defeat for the United States, this time by a greater margin than the Melbourne Games. Less than a year later, the White House released a report known as the "Conclusions and Recommendations of the President's

Committee on Information Activities Abroad," headed by Mansfield D. Sprague. Of the approximately twenty pages in the report, two paragraphs were devoted to sport. While admitting that some Soviet sporting victories had certain propaganda value, the Sprague Report stated that the problem didn't justify any fundamental departure from the established American practice of participating in the Olympic games and other international competitions on a private and amateur basis.[26] The committee's report in this regard came under heavy criticism from at least one writer, John J. Karch:

> This shows pathetic complacency and indifference to an important American activity and an almost appalling lack of appreciation, or knowledge, of Soviet propaganda efforts in sports. It leads one to realize that our situation is serious and calls for much self-evaluation and an examination of Soviet philosophy, aims, and programs in this significant field in which impact is made upon many millions of people in all nations.[27]

Karch outlined fifteen steps which the United States needed to take to remedy the situation, some of which were quite antithetical to America's past:

> Adequate expenses should be provided--by government and private sources--to obviate the necessity of door-to-door begging for transportation and living expenses. . . . We should stress victory, not merely participation. Our children are taught that it isn't important whether you win or lose, but how you play the game. Nothing could be more nonsensical. In reality, teams and individuals play to win. The millions of spectators in the United States and throughout the world attend sports events and exhort their teams to win. In the Olympics and international meets, only the winners are honored.[28]

Wilkinson's National Foundation Plan

Possibly unknown to Karch and others, something was being done at the federal level by Bud Wilkinson, director of the President's Council on Physical Fitness and special consultant to President Kennedy. As a result of his discussions with President Kennedy, the Attorney General and various sports groups, Wilkinson proposed the creation of a national foundation to increase participation in sports and fitness activities, broaden recreational activities, and to strengthen United States representation in the Olympic games and other international athletic competitions, especially in thirteen underdeveloped sports and women's sports.[29]

The proposed foundation was to be administered by a ten or twelve man board of trustees and was to be financed from a privately obtained endowment fund. Besides giving financial support to worthwhile fitness, recreation, and sports development projects, the foundation was to encourage municipalities and states to build facilities for underdeveloped sports, to promote an annual national sports festival comprising all Olympic events, and encourage high school and college conferences to adopt and emphasize, on an interscholastic or intercollegiate basis, underdeveloped sports.[30] In addition, an attempt

s made to enlist the cooperation of the military to train and develop teams
r rowing, water polo, rifle and pistol competition, equestrian events and
alking. The proposed foundation would also have been responsible for pro-
oting competitive Olympic programs for women, obtaining the use of
chool and college facilities when not in use, stimulating an international exchange of athletes and coaches, encouraging the development of comprehensive sport film libraries emphasizing training films, and establishing a national awards system for Olympic sports.[31]

Apart from the typical advantages of an overall national program with
the possibility of future success, Wilkinson noted two additional features
which he felt were advantages:

> [It] would avoid dampening--by Government subsidy--pri-
> vate initiative and support, and making presently self-support-
> ing activities reliant upon such subsidies . . . would reinforce
> the U.S. tradition of relying on private action and support for
> sports development.[32]

In discussing this aspect several years later, V. L. Nicholson, Director of
Information for the President's Council on Physical Fitness, stated that
Wilkinson's reasons for private financing of the foundation were based on his
belief that schools, colleges, and the amateur sports-governing bodies would
not accept federal subsidies for sports development, the fact that government
subsidization of athletics was a ticklish matter internationally, and his feeling that funds could be obtained from private sources.[33]

Wilkinson and President Kennedy discussed the problems of launching
the foundation, and the President indicated that he would be willing to call together ten or twelve influential and interested men and urge them to get the
foundation started. Kennedy also stated that he would speak at a dinner to
inaugurate a fund-rasiing drive.[34] Neither the kick-off dinner nor the foundation went beyond the planning stage. John F. Kennedy was assassinated in
1963 and Wilkinson subsequently resigned to run for political office.

Humphrey's Fitness Program

While Wilkinson was busy with his proposal for a national foundation,
Senator Hubert Humphrey was on the floor of the Senate extolling the need
for a coordinated fitness program for the nation. Humphrey's five-point fitness plan was not limited solely to physical fitness, for one major point was
aimed at increasing United States Olympic performance:

> Third, we should encourage civic and sports leadership
> throughout the land to establish--voluntarily--a national goal, a
> national plan and program for American participation in the in-
> ternational competition, particularly in the Olympics.[35]

To do this Humphrey proposed a national foundation not unlike that of Wilkinson's:

A private U.S. Olympic foundation, or its equivalent, should, in my judgment, be established. . . . On the board of the private U.S. Olympic foundation should serve the greatest civic, sports, and professional leadership in our land. To the foundation should come generous donations from business, labor, philanthropy, and private groups and citizens. . . . With the proposed foundation's money there should be devised a permanent, voluntary, National Olympic plan. Its goal should be to field the strongest possible Olympic team--representative of the best talent that the 50 States of the Union can offer. Such a private foundation, representing all interested U.S. groups, would raise money to assist in the training, the transportation, and the temporary housing of our Olympic contestants.[36]

Humphrey made repeated reference to this topic in the Senate,[37] and also published an article in a national magazine in January, 1963.[38]

You may ask what the Olympics have to do with international politics. Make no mistake about it, the relentless struggle between freedom and Communism embraces almost every level of life from spacemen to sprinters. Because the Russians understand this, they have converted the once-idealistic Olympic games into an ideological battlefield. They sneer at the "AMERIKANSKIS" as a nation of softies and portray the United States as a "tired, decadent, declining power." Once they have crushed us in the coming Olympic battle, the Red propaganda drums will thunder out a worldwide tattoo, heralding the "new Soviet men and women" as "virile, unbeatable conquerors" in sports--or anything else.[39]

In the article Humphrey proposed a ten-point plan, salient among which were items that called for an increase in the fitness level of American youngsters, a nationwide junior Olympics, an emphasis on obscure Olympic sports with appropriate facilities, the adoption of Olympic rules and standards and more encouragement to American girls to participate in sport.[40]

As for the federal government's role:

Uncle Sam should do more to stimulate enthusiasm in the Olympics. The government could help conduct a nationwide publicity campaign, could also help by picking up more of the tab for the international travel and expenses of the coaches and teams.[41]

Possibly unknown to Humphrey, events were taking place within the federal government on this matter.

At this time the NCAA-AAU feud was at its peak, and as it continued it became evident that if the United States was to assume world leadership in the field of athletics, something had to be done.

The situation in 1963 left much to be desired. The comparative position of the United States in international athletics had actually been declining for some years, relative to other nations that had previously embarked on national programs to encourage the development of athletic talent. A number of nations had established cabinet or sub-cabinet positions and devoted considerable resources to those programs. . . . To restore and maintain our national position in this field would, in the opinion of international sports experts, require a substantial long-range national effort to encourage the development of athletic talent. Such an effort, it appeared, could probably not be launched and continued effectively by athletic leadership excessively preoccupied with the AAU-NCAA conflict.[42]

As a result, exploratory talks between government officials and sports leaders were made in the spring of 1963, and in mid-1963 an informed task force was developed within the federal government to consider the problems affecting amateur athletics and to assess the contribution the government might make in helping find solutions to those problems. Members of this task force consisted of representatives of the Department of State, Department of Justice, and the President's Council on Physical Fitness.[43]

At the outset, the task force recognized that amateur athletics in the United States must remain under the control of private organizations. At the same time, it was clear that the government had a legitimate interest in American sports, particularly as they relate to international competiton, and that this interest called for more national attention to the development of our international athletic capabilities.[44]

Feeling that the government's attention should be steady and not spasmodic, the task force accordingly recommended that a permanent interagency committee be established which could serve as a clearinghouse for information on amateur athletics which would give private organizations the means for better developing the athletic potential of the United States.[45] On August 6, 1963 President Kennedy took the Task force's advice and issued Executive Order 11117, which established an interagency committee on international athletics.

Whereas it is vital that the United States be constantly informed concerning all events, activities, and conditions that might have a potential effect upon the foreign relations of this Nation and the well-being of its people; and
Whereas international amateur athletic competitions and related activities conducted by private individuals and organizations free from Government sponsorship, interference, or

control frequently make significant contributions to international goodwill and elevate standards of physical welfare throughout the world; and

Whereas these activities merit sympathetic attention and encouragement by the United States; and

Whereas it would be advantageous for the Department of State to have the advice and assistance of other departments and agencies in discharging its responsibilities in this regard; . . . There is hereby established . . . .[46]

Generally, the committee's functions concerned four areas:

(1) To provide continuing attention to athletic problems at the staff level in order to supplement the attention of top level officials . . . (2) To coordinate the interests and activities of its member agencies--State, Defense, Interior, Justice, the President's Council on Physical Fitness, the U.S. Information Agency, and the Peace Corps--all of which are concerned in some respect with athletics and its problems; (3) To act as a clearinghouse for the exchange and review of sports information of special interest to Government agencies and sport organizations; and (4) To make reports and recommendations to the President and Secretary of State, as appropriate.[47]

Membership of the committee was to be varied but nonetheless restricted to individuals already within the offices of the federal government. It was to be composed of representatives to be designated by the Secretary of State, the Attorney General, the Secretary of Health, Education, and Welfare (in his capacity as Chairman of the President's Council on Physical Fitness), and the heads of such other departments and agencies.[48]

Continued Proposals to Aid Amateur Sport

During this same time span events were taking place pertaining to the funding of United States international athletic teams. In 1961 the federal government broke all precedent when the State Department helped defray the travel costs of the United States Nordic Ski Team which was sent to compete in Poland. The rationale was that under federal laws competition behind the "Iron Curtain" qualified for federal funding.[49] Although this direct payment was precedent-setting, it did little to alter the existing private funding of amateur athletics. As the 1964 Olympics drew closer, articles again began to appear calling for some type of national plan with, in some cases, federal funding: "Adequate expenses should be provided--by government and private sources--to obviate the necessity of door-to-door begging for transportation and living expenses."[50] Senator Humphrey took to the Senate floor to exhort his fellow congressmen to action in both July and November of 1963.[51] On the latter date he introduced a seven-point program which repeated many of the earlier programs he had put forth, mainly the need for a national foundation, an Olympic development program and the development of amateur sport facilities, plus the creation of an appropriate presidential symbol for American Olympic participants in the form of an Olympic participation medal.[52]

During the same year Senator Humphrey received a proposed plan from the Amateur Athletic Union by which the United States Government would appropriate $500,000 to eighteen sports-governing bodies to financially assist with travel expenses for various national championships. [53]

While Humphrey did not openly condone or condemn the idea, he did broach the subject of federal involvement while warning the amateur feuding bodies to patch up their differences:

In this country, athletics are overwhelmingly nongovernmental in nature; that's the way they should be kept. None of us wants the U.S. Government to intervene, if it doesn't have to. The Government has enough of its own problems to attend to. . . . Nevertheless, the U.S. Government does have a legitimate interest in fostering a sound solution. The U.S. Olympic Committee was chartered by the U.S. Congress. If the goal of Public Law 805 is not being achieved, then, the Congress has little alternative but to review that law and make whatever changes are necessary in it. [54]

Several congressmen meanwhile were attempting to pass various pieces of legislation to aid, in some manner, amateur athletics. Congressman Wilson introduced H. Res. 5807 in 1963, which was designed to grant federal personnel leave with pay if they were engaged in international athletic competition.

Mr. Speaker, the honor and prestige of the United States of America becomes a matter of great concern whenever a team from this country enters an international amateur athletic tournament. Whatever the semantics of discussion on sportsmanship may entail, the fact remains that our Nation is judged by people all over the world on the success or failure of our amateur athletes. [55]

This bill was followed one year later by H. Res. 10539 by Congressman Morse "to authorize the appropriation of funds to pay certain expenses of the U.S. Olympic Team that will participate in the 1964 Olympic games to be held in Tokyo, Japan."[56]

Congressman Morse, possibly influenced by the poor U.S. showing in the 1964 Winter Olympic games in Innsbruck, Austria, reversed his past stand against federal involvement in sport.

It may be time, however, to reconsider our traditional reluctance to provide Government support to U.S. Olympic teams. The present situation is humiliating for the athletes involved and destructive of team performance and morale. . . . The argument that we do not want to make our athletes political minions or adopt the practices of the Soviet Union does not reflect the realities of the situation. Many free world nations provide governmental financial support for participation in the Olympic games --notably the Western Europe nations. In my view the support of a group of outstanding amateur athletes carries with it no greater political overtones than any other program of cultural or educational exchange.[57]

Whether the situation was humiliating or not, Congress failed to act on either piece of legislation.

In February Senator Humphrey again came to prominence on the issue of American athletic performance in international competitions. He cited the poor United States showing in the Olympics and proposed that President Johnson appoint a White House commission on sports to outline a nationwide program dedicated to improving American performances in international competition.[58] Reiterating what he had repeatedly called for in the past, Humphrey notes that the responsibilities in this area "rest fundamentally on private shoulders, but the United States Government cannot ignore the fact that Communism has gained tremendous propaganda mileage out of Eastern bloc sports victories."[59] Humphrey's ideas were backed in principle by Senator Keating: "Mr. President, whether we do it through a Congressional study, a White House Commission, or amateur groups throughout the country, it is imperative that the United States start planning for the 1968 Olympics."[60]

Attention was focused on the President as Humphrey waited for a response.

Although the President has not publicly responded to the senator's proposal, some administration officials say that Mr. Johnson already has approached several business and industrial leaders and retired military officers about the idea.[61]

Gavin's Report to the President

Behind the scenes the Interagency Committee on International Athletics adopted Bud Wilkinson's concept of a sports foundation and encouraged President Johnson to consider it. President Johnson turned to General James W. Gavin to consider the possibility of such a foundation and, after discussions with sports and other national leaders and with the Interagency Committee, General Gavin agreed to consider the problems of organizing a foundation.[62]

On June 12, 1964 General Gavin met with the President and at the President's request agreed to make a detailed study of the problem.[63] Gavin's approach to the study was threefold: "(1) To evaluate the present status and future plans of competitive amateur sports in the United States and in selected foreign countries; (2) to analyze data and opinion on scale and need for additional or improved administration, facilities, equipment, training, finance and research; and (3) to determine the organization, staff, program, budget, and financial plan for a new national institution designed to meet identified needs."[64]

The study, while it had federal backing, was not federally financed but rather financed privately through a donation by the Fuller Foundation, Inc. of Boston and Arthur D. Little, Inc. From the beginning Gavin ran into a problem which was to persist throughout the study in that little comprehensive information of national scope was available on the status, problems, and developmental needs of amateur sports in the United States.[65]

On January 25, 1965, six months after it was initiated, General Gavin presented his report to President Johnson.

Responding to your request for a review of the status of amateur sports in the nation today, I have the honor to recommend to you the establishment of a new institution, the National Amateur Sports Foundation. . . . As a result of my review of this subject, I am convinced that a vigorous national program of amateur sports can contribute to the solution of the social problems of underprivileged young people, strengthen the position of the United States in international sports competition, enrich education at all levels, and encourage the achievement of excellence in the field of physical endeavor commensurate with achievement in other cultural fields.[66]

Gavin's report listed several observations and in particular pointed out the value of sport in developing the individual and strengthening the fabric of society, and the fact that other nations were recognizing physical fitness and amateur sport as public responsibilities to be supported by public funds while the United States failed to have a comprehensive amateur sports program.[67] Gavin then noted the only way to remedy the problem:

None of these problems is likely to be resolved satisfactorily in the absence of a new organization of appropriate scale and quality; and, as a consequence, the United States in the long run risks falling behind other nations of the world in the quality of its performance in competitive amateur sports.[68]

The report proceeded to recommend the creation of a new institution to be called the National Amateur Sports Foundation, which was to plan, coordinate, promote and support the conduct and development of amateur sports throughout the United States.[69] The functions of the foundation were to study advise, formulate and maintain a national policy relating to amateur sports, to coordinate the activities of national sports associations, to strengthen and expand the development of competitive amateur sports in the United States and to carry out activities that extended knowledge or facilitated the practice of amateur sports.[70] (See Table 1.)

As to the foundation's makeup and creation:

Because the Foundation should represent a unique fusion of the public interest and private initiative in an activity traditionally free from Government control, we recommend its organization as a private body corporate under Congressional charter, and that the President of the United States bestow upon it the prestige of his office by appointing the initial board of trustees and a minority of successor trustees as vacancies occur.[71]

Table 1. American Tours – 1954-1972.

July 1 – June 30		Total Number of American Tours*
1954 – 1955	(2)	2
1955 – 1956	(10)	10
1956 – 1957	(8)	8
1957 – 1958	(7)	7
1958 – 1959	(6)	6
1959 – 1960	(3)	3
1960 – 1961	(11)	11
1961 – 1962	(10)	10
1962 – 1963	(7)	7
1963 – 1964	(10)	10
1964 – 1965	(7)	7
1965 – 1966	(17)	17
1966 – 1967	(10)	10
1967 – 1968	(14)	14
1968 – 1969	(10)	10
1969 – 1970	(3)	3
1970 – 1971	(3)	3
1971 – 1972	(2)	2

* Tours scheduled to visit more than one area are listed as one tour.
(See original dissertation for complete tabloid analysis of sport by country visited by year.)

Financing the foundation was to be a combination of private and public moneys, with an initial federal grant of three million dollars for each of the first three years of its existence, to be matched by private donations. Eventually the foundation was to operate on the income from an endowment fund.[72]

In closing, General Gavin emphasized the need for the President's help in establishing the foundation and called upon the President to give the matter his closest attention.[73]

In spite of the fact that the report was requested by the President, no public statement or written document was released by President Johnson after reception of Gavin's report. Later, in reflecting on this aspect, General Gavin remarked:

> President Johnson, when he received our report on a proposed national amateur sports foundation, just pigeonholed it, and, despite several calls at the White House, I never could get anything done about it.[74]

Possibly affecting the President's lack of action was the attention the Chief Executive was giving at the time to the Vietnam War and, as a result, the idea for the foundation was retired--at least for the time being.

Coinciding with Gavin's report, the United States Olympic Committee, which had been under criticism for its organizational structure, authorized a similar study of its own by the Arthur D. Little Company in which some reorganizational recommendations were made.[75] In it, Gavin's idea of a national amateur sports foundation was only referred to lightly, although the U.S.O.C. had previously gone on record in support of the idea at its 1963 meeting.

Interagency's First Report

Meanwhile, the Interagency Committee on International Athletics was at work preparing its first official report to the President. Late in January of 1965 the committee presented a summary of its efforts and future concerns along with reporting that it was in the process of conducting a survey with all diplomatic and consular posts concerning the organization of sports in each individual country and the effect of American sports performance on the attitudes of the people in that particular country.[76] In addition, the committee noted it had appointed a facilities subcommittee to gather information on the type of facilities needed for Olympic and other international sports, the availability of such facilities, and the steps which the federal government might properly take to encourage expanded availability of such facilities.[77] The committee disclosed that it envisioned four areas of new business. One area was to review the results of the 1964 Olympic games in terms of long-range trends, underlying factors and overall international impact. Another was to explore whether community action supporting the United States national position in international athletics could be linked to comprehensive programs to eliminate social problems. Also, the committee was to explore whether the existing programs of other federal agencies could be conducted in a manner that would encourage the improvement of amateur athletics in the United States. Finally, the committee was to consider the stimulation of research into the subject of amateurism and professionalism in sports in order to better understand their national and international significance.[78] As far-reaching as these undertakings and these future plans were, little was heard publicly from the committee after 1965 as it maintained an extremely low profile through the second half of the 1960s. Nothing was ever published or announced on these four topics, and except for a published report on the impact of sports on the achievement of United States foreign policy objectives in 1965, little was heard again from the committee.

Continued Interest in American International Success

The issue of American international athletic success remained, however, and was again brought to the attention of the public by Vice President Humphrey in a television program on the Russian sports revolution in the summer of 1966,[79] and an article by Irving Jaffee in the American Legion Magazine in September of 1967.[80] In both cases the need for a national program was again emphasized.

Vice President Humphrey also became somewhat involved in 1968 when Black American athletes threatened to boycott the 1968 Summer Olympic games in Mexico City because of racism in America. The possibility of such an action would have greatly decreased American chances of surpassing the performance of Soviet athletes, and Vice President Humphrey obviously knew this when he appealed to the boycotters: "I can't emphasize too strongly what it is like to win an Olympic medal. It is hard to argue with a champion; he is a winner, not a talker."[81]

Boycott or not, the American Olympic team proceeded to upend the Soviet Union in the Summer Olympics of 1968, the first time since 1952. As in the past, the American Olympic team went to the games without federal aid, although unsuccessful attempts were made in Congress in 1966 (H. Res. 17068) and 1967 (H. Res. 633) to authorize the issuance of Olympic stamps to assist in financing American participation in the Olympic games, thereby ensuring a stronger American effort. Attempts were also made in 1967 (H. Res. 13062) and 1969 (H. Res. 443) to provide matching grants for the construction of athletic facilities along Olympic standards, but they too met with failure. Thus, promotional interest by the federal government in the second half of the 1960s generated very little in the way of concrete results, if public interest can be gauged by congressional action.

Except for a few forays into minor matters pertaining to international sport in which Congress voiced its opposition to allowing Moscow to host the Olympic games[82] and a one-day Senate hearing on Cuba's use of sport for political purposes,[83] congressional involvement to promote American interests and foreign policy objectives was relatively dormant until 1972. At that time the ire of Congress was aroused, not only by the massacre of eleven Israeli athletes at the Munich Olympic games by Arab terrorists,[84] but also by the poor U.S. showing, due in part to organizational blunders of U.S. officials and seemingly biased judgments of officials favoring Communist countries. This resulted in calls once again for the creation of a national amateur sports foundation much like that proposed by General Gavin in 1965.[85]

At the same time, the executive branch of the government, working behind the scenes, attempted to find a remedy to the amateur athletic problems which were highlighted in the 1972 Olympics. Two members of the White House staff, Steve Mead and Mike Harrigan, were assigned to look into the entire problem with hopes of finding a solution amenable to all parties involved so that the United States could field its best team in the 1976 Montreal Olympics. In 1973 their recommendation for solving the internal amateur athletic organizational struggle was cited in a research paper aimed at breaking up the AAU's control over the USOC.

It should be clear from the foregoing data that the necessary solution is to reorganize the USOC so that no one body controls the USOC and no one body controls each of the federations governing international competition.[86]

As for Congress and its involvement in these matters, it was their opinion that:

Congress seems content to react to the kind of hassles resulting from USOC ineptitude at Munich and the recent Russian basketball series, but it doesn't seem to have the patience for the kind of painstaking research and investigation necessary to develop sound legislation. Barring positive leadership by the President, most members of the Congress probably will continue to use the problems in amateur athletics merely as a convenient vehicle for getting their names on the sports pages.[87]

To them the answer to the situation lay in an investigation of the United States Olympic Committee as called for in the bill presented in late 1973 by Congressman Mathias and which had the backing of the executive branch. By the end of 1973 no visible results were forthcoming in this area, possibly due to the preoccupation of the President and Congress with the Watergate scandal which was just surfacing at that time.

In spite of repeated attempts to promote American international success in the face of possible Soviet Cold War athletic gains, very few concrete results were forthcoming. True, an interagency Committee on International Athletics had been created and numerous attempts were made to establish a National Amateur Sports Foundation. However, all these efforts proved futile in the face of issues which the federal government deemed to be more important, specifically Vietnam and Watergate. Coinciding with this was the continued opinion by a majority in Congress that aid to sport should be left up to private agencies, not the federal government.

Sponsorship of Athletic Exchanges

The 1950s began with the State Department using two vehicles, the Fulbright Act of 1946 and the Smith-Mundt Act of 1948 (U.S. Information and Educational Exchange Act), to implement cultural exchanges with other countries. At this time the idea of using American athletic representatives as political emissaries was very limited, and when a sport exchange did take place, it usually concerned physical educators sent to various countries.

Characteristic of these exchanges were the three specialists who were invited to Thailand in the early 1950s to assist in curriculum development changes at a training school.[88] By and large, however, these programs were quite small and were generally considered of secondary importance.

A definite change in the attitude of the State Department occurred in the early part of the decade. As with so many policy changes that occurred during this period, a key factor which yielded the change in policy was the Cold War. Up to this juncture, sport as a method of gaining inroads into various countries for political propaganda purposes had largely been ignored by most countries. However, in 1951 a State Department official, speaking before the Amateur Athletic Union's National Convention, noted a new tactic which was being used by the Soviet Union:

> Reports from our embassies during recent months afford positive proof that the Kremlin has mounted a gigantic cultural offensive. It is designed to prove the Soviet line of supremacy in the arts as well as in the athletic field. During 1951 they have sent a greatly increased number of artists, musicians, and athletes into competitions of one sort or another.[89]

By adding sport as one weapon in their arsenal, the Soviet Union mounted a significant cultural "offensive." They sent groups on tours of various countries in an attempt to generate a favorable image of Soviet life and the Communist system. Reaction to this "offensive" in the United States was slow. By 1953 Soviet athletic teams sent on visitations to foreign countries had increased from twenty-nine in 1950 to sixty-eight teams, and foreign sport teams visiting the U.S.S.R. had similarly increased from twenty-one to sixty-four.[90] No organized program for athletic exchanges to offset this Soviet program, other than the Fulbright and Smith-Mundt Acts were in existence in the United States in the early decade. Van Dalen cited two programs which could have been organized by the State Department at that time, although available State Department records fail to verify their existence.

Outstanding track performers were sent to all corners of the globe to compete and give exhibitions. Penn State's excellent soccer team was flown by the State Department to the troubled Near East early in 1951 for a series of games. A swimming team from the University of Michigan, headed by its veteran coach, Matt Mann, toured the British Isles in 1951 and gave exhibitions and coaching clinics.[91]

Left uncontested, Soviet sport cultural exchanges at the close of 1954 had grown to an annual sum of eighty-eight.[92]

By 1954 it had become apparent that unless strong and well-organized counter-measures were taken by the United States, this important field of action would continue to go by default. Unopposed, the flood of cultural delegations from the Communist States and the attraction of items exhibited at trade Fairs could not fail to make their inevitable impact upon the peoples of other countries.[93]

Reacting to the problem, President Eisenhower, in 1954, requested and received from Congress five million dollars in funds to be appropriated to the President's emergency fund for international affairs for a special international program for cultural presentations. Designated as one segment of these cultural presentations was sport, which included both competitions and demonstrations. By the end of 1955 nine State Department supported teams had traveled on goodwill tours overseas--the majority to the Near East, South Asia, Western Europe and Latin America.[94] At the same time Soviet cultural and sport delegations increased from 88 in 1954 to 148 in 1955.[95]

Increasing pressure began to mount in Congress to place the program on a permanent and more active basis. This idea was reinforced when William Randolph Hearst, noted newspaper owner, returned from the Soviet Union and reported what he had seen. Speaking about the sending of Soviet athletes abroad to The People's Republic of China and India, Hearst remarked: "It stands to reason that such extensive wooing of impressionable minds is likely to pay dividends, unless we compete vigorously with the Communist effort and even surpass it."[96] Hearst then outlined to the press, and later in private consultation with Eisenhower, his plan for combating the Soviets in this area.

What I would like to advocate here today, is the establishment of a permanent board commissioned to formulate a strategy on all fronts for meeting the challenge of this intellectual, competitive coexistence. It should survey the whole global scene and develop plans for the future for getting the peoples of the world on our side. Sports, theater, educational exchanges; no field should be neglected in the competition of the two conflicting systems.[97]

A similar proposition was advanced to President Eisenhower in April of 1955 by General David Sarnoff, chairman of the Radio Corporation of America.[98]

In Congress several bills were introduced to establish the program on a permanent basis.

I have come to the conclusion that the battle of competitive coexistence has entered a new phase that calls for a quietly aggressive presentation of all the good things America has to offer and stands for. By this I mean by word, by picture, by exhibit, by groups of artists, and athletes to spread the story that this is indeed a land of plenty in industry, culture, sports--these are, after all, products of freedom. I, therefore, join with my colleagues by introducing a bill which will make a permanent part of our national life the program which has been developed and supported by the President's emergency fund.[99]

Congressional praise of the program flowed. Several members of Congress commended sport exchanges in particular as having an especially powerful impact. Congressman Mundt inserted into the Congressional Record, for the information of his colleagues, a newspaper article extolling the virtues of one sport tour:

- 418 -

In this global struggle for the minds of men, with democracy arrayed against communist, the State Department sought to
impress our Pan-American neighbors by sending them a young
man who was representative of the highest type of sportsman. A
gifted extemporaneous speaker and world famous athlete, Dillard
filled the bill so well that United States Embassies in the countries he visited have been deluging the State Department with
praise for his work.100

Hearings were held in both the House and Senate, in 1955 and 1956, on
the concept of establishing the cultural exchange program on a firmer and
more permanent basis. In some cases athletic exchanges in particular were
cited for their possible effect.

. . . almost the most effective thing we are doing in the
Orient is sending over these American individuals and groups,
especially our athletes. They bring just fabulous rewards. I
don't think Americans generally appreciate that one of the greatest contributions we have made to the world is the code of sportsmanship that has developed here, with mass participation in
sports, competing hard and being a good loser. One essential in
a democracy is not what you do when you win, but how you behave
when you lose. In many countries to lose is regarded as a personal insult to be avenged. You have to challenge somebody to a
duel or find some other way to overcome him. Our sports activities do more than anything we have done to help these people get
the fundamental American idea that in a democracy you do your
best; if you lose, you still belong to the country and work in cooperation until the next opportunity comes. The mind of the youth
of Asia, which is the No. 1 target of the Communist, is something that we have neglected too long.101

Possibly influenced by the revelation that in 1955 Soviet sport exchanges with the free world had risen to 239,102 Senate Bill 3116--known as
the "International Cultural Exchange and Trade Fair Participation Act of
1956"--was passed by Congress and became Pub. Law 860. This established
the cultural presentations program on a permanent basis within the Department of State, with the United States Information Agency in charge of the
tours within the country visited. As a result, athletic tours for fiscal 1956
were increased to fifteen. Soon afterward the number of tours decreased to
a mere six in 1957, seven in 1958, two in 1959, and seven in 1960.103 It
was, in sum, a minimal program compared to the 239 sport exchanges generated by the U.S.S.R. in 1955 alone.

At this juncture another exchange program was inaugurated. In 1957
arrangements were made for the first time for direct exchanges of athletic
teams between the United States and the U.S.S.R., with exchanges set to begin the following year.

Another change took place within the State Department's Athletic Exchange Program in 1958. Coaches were sent overseas to several countries
to aid the national teams of other nations and to give demonstration clinics.104

By this time the program was an integral part of American foreign policy, even though this fact was not outwardly acknowledged by State Department officials.

These goodwill tours will continue to be effective as long as the governing bodies of amateur athletics in the United States continue to show the leadership and supervision they are now displaying, and as long as we in the Government recognize that our role is merely one of assistance and facilitation and not that of control or supervision. In a word, amateur sport belongs to the people of the world and not to governments. We must exercise every care to see to it that sports in our country are not employed for political or propaganda purposes. On the other hand, the fact that great athletes have enhanced the prestige of our country through their great sense of fair play and good sportsmanship is most gratifying to us, and I ask "Would any loyal American, in or out of Government, want it otherwise?"[105]

As the decade of the sixties began there was no overt evidence that intensity of the Cold War was declining. For example, the American Embassy in Helsinki, Finland, issued a request to the State Department for an American tour and spiced their request with Cold War rhetoric:

The Embassy believes the project is admirably suited to make the greatest impact on the Finns and to help bolster the morale of a people being subjected to strong pressures in all phases of their national life from the neighboring Soviet Union and from their own domestic Communists. The Finns are perhaps the most sport conscious people in Europe and their appreciation of leading track and field athletes is based upon a long tradition. Hence, the Embassy would propose that a group of some dozen American track and field athletes, following the Olympic competitions in Rome, come to Helsinki to compete in a dual meet with the Finns for a period of one or two days before an undoubtedly filled stadium of over 50,000 spectators.[105]

Available State Department records fail to mention if the request was granted

In 1961 further consolidation of the exchange program was made with passage of H. Res. 8666, the Mutual Educational and Cultural Exchange Act of 1961, which became Pub. Law 256. This act consolidated and superseded most of the previous legislation in the area [Smith-Mundt Act - Pub. Law 860 in 1955] and authorized the Bureau of Educational and Cultural Affairs (CU) to formulate broader programs:

The Act, in effect, restored international educational and cultural exchange programs as a recognized area of our official foreign relations, parallel with overseas information programs, technical assistance, and other programs.[107]

Within the bureau, the worldwide athletic program was administered by the Office of Athletic Programs with three officers. The overal responsibility of this office was to formulate the Department's athletic program policies relative to group and team tours to other nations, and to advise and assist the State Department's Advisory Panel on International Athletics.108 Individual tours by American coaches, however, came under the State Department's American Specialists Program and its staff, who worked in close cooperation with the Office of Athletic Programs.

From 1960 to 1964 the intensity of program operation increased in comparison to its level of operation during the late fifties. Seven tours were arranged in 1960, sixteen in 1961 (seven to Eastern European countries), ten in 1962, and eight in 1964.109 During the ten-year period from 1952 to 1962 the annual budget for the athletic programs averaged approximately $100,000 per year and was steadily increased afterwards so that by 1967 the budget was set at approximately $300,000 per year, the highest level it was ever to attain.110

Throughout, congressmen continued to assail Communists who had made substantial inroads in this area. To offset the international thrust of their continuing to push for exchange programs, several congressmen felt it was mandatory to develop more American programs:

It was no accident that the Soviets are sending their best coaches to developing countries; that they are importing hundreds of athletes from Latin American, Asian, and other lands. . . . All over Latin America and Asia, Soviet coaches and teams are having a field day with the athletes and crowds of emerging countries. Red propaganda is brain-washing millions of people in the new nations with an image of a so-called Soviet superman. . . Red sports stars give a decidedly different image to people throughout the world than Red soldiers who patrol the Wall of Shame in Berlin. A massive increase in the U.S. Athletic exchange program is essential. We have been sending over too few sports leaders and, often, teams of too modest caliber. And we have been inviting too few athletes from abroad in our exchange program.111

In April of 1963 a report was released on the impact of the Exchange of Persons Program on the United States, the countries involved, and American foreign policy.

There is no doubt in the minds of most of our informants, or in the minds of the Commission itself, that the exchange program has in fact served the broad interests of the United States in its relations with other countries. To the extent that it has increased mutual understanding, it has certainly served those interests. To the extent that it has dispelled misconceptions about America and Americans it has, in a very important way, served our total international objectives. It has served them also to the extent that it has demonstrated favorably, as we have just seen, American character and achievement. . . . Thus, the

- 421 -

relation of the exchange program to the conduct of America's foreign policy is inevitably a close one.[112]

The report, however, failed to specifically analyze the impact of sport exchanges. Further, hearings held in 1963 and 1964 on the cultural exchange program failed to focus on the impact of sport exchanges, although attention was paid during the hearings to other areas such as musicians and actors.[113] Whether or not this neglect by the State Department and Congress to discuss sport exchanges reflects a lesser degree of value placed on sport exchanges by these organizations is difficult to ascertain with the present evidence.

Those in charge of the athletic programs in the State Department, however, continued to extol the virtues of sport in this context:

> Sport offers a nation a remarkable opportunity to excel, to work together at something enjoyable and rewarding to national human feelings of pride and excellence. Sports will tie a group of people together faster than many other ennobling principles. We believe that what is good for a new or developing country is good for the peace and stability of the world. And we see our faith in this proven time and again as American athletes spread out around our world teaching other people how to excel in various sports, how to compete to the best of their abilities, how to distinguish themselves in whatever sport they are most adept.[114]

Whether or not goodwill resulted from all programs sponsored is questionable. For example, in 1964 a State Department-sponsored team of National Basketball All-Stars traveled throughout Poland, Rumania, Yugoslavia and Egypt, and trounced all opponents by at least twenty points. In one country a minor incident occurred:

> In Yugoslavia we were supposed to play in a place, and I didn't see an American flag anywhere. I demanded they put up a flag. Somebody said something about me not following protocol and I said protocol my eye--no flag, no ball game. The flag went up.[115]

Study of the Achievement of U.S. Foreign Policy Objectives

Any indications that the Department of State was not involved in sport for American foreign policy objectives were dashed in 1965 when the Interagency Committee on International Athletics released to the State Department its study of the impact of sports on the achievement of United States foreign policy objectives:[116]

> The United States' foreign policy objectives can be achieved to some extent through the medium of sports: this is an assumption implicit in the very existence of Government sports programs. The purpose of this study was to explore the premise, to see whether in fact attainment of foreign policy objectives through sports

can be demonstrated on a worldwide level and substantiated by actual information from our diplomatic posts.[117]

The information gleaned from all diplomatic posts was based on a questionnaire to determine whether sport was emphasized in that particular country, if it was affected by the sports performance of other countries, the sports image of the United States in that country, to what extent Eastern bloc countries participated in athletic activities in that country, and whether sport provided an opportunity to reach young potential leaders through contact or with a message that would result in better understanding of United States policies.[118]

Some of the more general conclusions of the study revealed that the world was quite sport conscious and that athletic activities were the least suspicious approach to youth throughout the world.[119] Additionally, it was discovered that nations which did not have a strong political prominence in the world scene often sought such pride through recognized excellence in sports, and often succeeded.[120]

The main genesis of the study dealt with the role which sport played and could play with reference to American interests in five areas or continents of the world. It was found that of the five areas, Africa was most influenced by sport and that sport exchanges there would favorably affect the United States' image. " . . . it would be to the advantage of the United States to increase diplomatic efforts in this direction."[121]

Africa was followed by Eastern Europe:

In bloc countries where an outside presence is automatically viewed with suspicion, the U.S. might wisely take advantage of the entree into certain leader and potential leader circles which only sports can provide.[122]

And Latin America:

With the widespread interest in sports evidenced throughout Latin America, with sports having a hold on all segments of the population for one reason or another, and with the climate generally favorable toward approach to youth through athletic activities, the United States has an excellent opportunity to further its foreign policy objectives through the use of sports.[123]

According to the report, the Near East and South Asia were not as susceptible.

The overall picture in the Near East and South Asia suggests that the United States would be able to make diplomatic strides but that a concerted effort is essential in order to overcome a widespread passiveness toward athletics.[124]

Leading all others as the area least susceptible to sport was Western Europe:

The prevailing level of sophistication in most European countries is such that the national images of foreign countries are not likely to be colored by sports performances of those countries.[125]

To what extent this report influenced the sending of State Department-sponsored American teams, athletes and coaches cannot be totally ascertained. When all the tours are graphed according to areas from fiscal 1955 to 1972 (the last year information was available) and then compared, pre-1965 and post-1965, the following changes seem to have taken place.[126] (See Tables 2 through 9.)

Table 2. Athletic Tours - Pre- and Post-Fiscal, 1965.

	Average Number of Tours	
	1954/55-1964/65	1965/66-1971/72
Africa	1.2	2.7
Western Europe	1.4	1.0
Eastern Europe	1.7	1.1
East and West Europe	3.1	1.4
Far East	1.1	1.2
Latin America	1.0	2.4
Near East - South Asia	2.5	2.2

Table 3. Athletic Tours - Africa.

	Number of Tours							
	1	2	3	4	5	6	7	8
1954-1955								
1955-1956	■							
1956-1957								
1957-1958								
1958-1959	■							
1959-1960	■	■						
1960-1961	■	■						
1961-1962	■	■						
1962-1963	■	■						
1963-1964	■	■	■					
1964-1965	■	■	■					
1965-1966	■	■	■					
1966-1967	■	■	■	■	■			
1967-1968	■	■	■	■				
1968-1969	■	■	■	■				
1969-1970	■	■	■					
1970-1971	■	■	■					
1971-1972	■							

Table 4. Athletic Tours - Western Europe.

	Number of Tours							
	1	2	3	4	5	6	7	8
1954-1955								
1955-1956	■	■	■	■	■			
1956-1957	■							
1957-1958	■	■						
1958-1959								
1959-1960								
1960-1961	■							
1961-1962								
1962-1963	■	■						
1963-1964	■							
1964-1965	■							
1965-1966	■	■	■					
1966-1967	■	■						
1967-1968	■	■						
1968-1969								
1969-1970	■							
1970-1971								
1971-1972	■							

Table 5. Athletic Tours – Eastern Europe.

	Number of Tours							
	1	2	3	4	5	6	7	8
1954–1955								
1955–1956								
1956–1957	■							
1957–1958	■							
1958–1959								
1959–1960								
1960–1961	■	■	■	■				
1961–1962	■	■	■	■	■	■		
1962–1963	■	■						
1963–1964	■	■	■					
1964–1965	■	■	■					
1965–1966	■	■	■					
1966–1967	■	■						
1967–1968	■	■						
1968–1969	■	■						
1969–1970								
1970–1971								
1971–1972	■							

Table 6. Athletic Tours - East and West Europe (Combined)

	Number of Tours							
	1	2	3	4	5	6	7	8
1954–1955								
1955–1956	■	■	■	■	■			
1956–1957	■	■	■	■	■	■		
1957–1958	■	■						
1958–1959								
1959–1960								
1960–1961	■	■	■	■	■			
1961–1962	■	■	■	■	■			
1962–1963	■	■	■	■				
1963–1964	■	■	■	■				
1964–1965	■	■	■	■	■			
1965–1966	■	■	■	■	■	■		
1966–1967	■	■	■	■				
1967–1968	■	■	■					
1968–1969	■	■	■					
1969–1970	■	■						
1970–1971								
1971–1972	■	■						

Table 7. Athletic Tours – East Asia.

	Number of Tours							
	1	2	3	4	5	6	7	8
1954–1955								
1955–1956	█	█	█					
1956–1957	█	█	█					
1957–1958	█	█						
1958–1959								
1959–1960								
1960–1961	█	█	█					
1961–1962								
1962–1963	█							
1963–1964	█							
1964–1965								
1965–1966	█	█						
1966–1967	█	█	█					
1967–1968	█							
1968–1969	█	█	█					
1969–1970								
1970–1971								
1971–1972								

Table 8. Athletic Tours – Latin America.

	Number of Tours							
	1	2	3	4	5	6	7	8
1954–1955	■	■						
1955–1956	■							
1956–1957	■	■						
1957–1958	■							
1958–1959	■							
1959–1960								
1960–1961								
1961–1962	■							
1962–1963	■							
1963–1964	■							
1964–1965	■	■						
1965–1966	■	■	■	■	■			
1966–1967	■	■	■	■				
1967–1968	■	■	■	■	■			
1968–1969	■	■	■					
1969–1970								
1970–1971	■							
1971–1972	■							

Table 9. Athletic Tours – Near East/South Asia.

	Number of Tours							
	1	2	3	4	5	6	7	8
1954–1955								
1955–1956	■	■	■	■	■	■		
1956–1957	■	■	■					
1957–1958	■	■	■					
1958–1959	■	■	■					
1959–1960	■		■					
1960–1961	■	■	■					
1961–1962	■	■	■					
1962–1963	■	■						
1963–1964	■	■	■					
1964–1965	■	■	■					
1965–1966	■	■	■	■	■			
1966–1967	■	■	■	■	■			
1967–1968	■	■	■					
1968–1969	■	■	■					
1969–1970								
1970–1971								
1971–1972	■							

Except for Eastern Europe, most of the other areas which the 1965 report advised to be emphasized were emphasized accordingly. The report outlined the susceptibility of Africa to sport and sport exchanges, and, as a consequence, this area received the greatest emphasis in the following year. Likewise, a reduction of exchanges occurred in areas in which the report noted that inroads would be difficult to make. The most notable example here was Western Europe. Thus, it does seem that the Department of State was at least partially influenced by the Interagency's 1965 report.

Athletic exchanges by 1967 roughly accounted for 10 percent of the annual cultural presentations budget, while 27 percent of the funds for the Department's American Specialists Program (later changed to STAGS--Short-Term American Grantees) went to sending athletic coaches and individual athletes overseas.[127] The program at this time was funded at its highest level and was running smoothly as is seen in this 1967 report to Congress:

> In the conduct of our foreign affairs, sports and physical education are effective instruments in presenting the U.S. image abroad, in improving communications within the international community (particularly the younger generation) and in helping other nations improve the physical well-being of their societies. To accomplish these ends the athletic programs of the Department of State comprise a threefold operation. First, specialists are sent, upon request, to other countries to aid them in the development of their sports and physical education programs. Second, foreign specialists are brought to the United States for educational and training purposes. Third, teams and groups are sponsored on tours to exhibit, demonstrate, or compete as a part of the Department's Cultural Presentation Program.[128]

The programs themselves during this period varied, according to the area visited. For example:

> In the more industrialized regions of the world athletic presentations units are normally involved in exhibitions and competitions, whereas in the developing areas emphasis is placed upon training and development of foreign athletes, coaches, administrators, and youth groups. In the latter cases demonstrations, clinics, workshops and similar activities have proved especially productive.[129]

Of significant impact on many countries were the number of coaches and physical education specialists sent upon request. For example, in fiscal years 1964 through 1969 forty-eight specialists received partial or full grants to visit some twenty countries in Central and South America, plus Mexico. In addition, ten United States coaches were sent between 1966 and 1968 to help train Mexican athletes.[130]

> The Embassy reported that the U.S. coaches registered outstanding successes in training Mexican athletes and that there was widespread belief in Mexico that our coaches contributed significantly to the showing oy Mexican athletes in the Olympic Games.[131]

After 1967 a noticeable drop occurred in the number of exchanges operated by the State Department and in State Department-sponsored tours, due directly to reductions in funding.[132] As the director of International Athletics Programs described it: "The period from 1967-1971 was a dormant, indecisive period where the program had a low profile and thus stood relatively still."[133]

Harris/Ragan Management Report

In 1971 another study was published, known as the Harris/Ragan Management Report, which was undertaken to see how the Department of State could maximize the effects of the sports exchange program of the Bureau of Educational and Cultural Affairs. Unlike the one undertaken in 1965, this report was conducted by a private management corporation outside sport. In the study forty-four individuals, ranging from sports administrators, observers, commentators and participants to government administrators, were approached on the topic of sports exchanges. The results of the report indicated that sport had largely been ignored by the Department of State, probably due to certain stereotypes associated with it, chief among which was the belief that sports were said by many to have a negligible impact on international relations, that they were too ephemeral and would lose their purity if they were tied more closely to United States international interests and the belief that they appealed generally to baser states.[134] The impression gained by the researchers, however, was much different.

> . . . the evidence gathered in the course of this study suggests that these are erroneous impressions. Sports can be employed as a consistent and potentially useful factor in the planning and implementation of U.S. foreign policy.[135]

Citing that each country was different in its appeal for sport, with some totally unaffected by it, the report went on in a convincing manner as to sport's importance:

> Whatever the ends served by international sports activity, there is little doubt that sports have almost universal appeal. Appreciate it or not, understand it or not, sports are said to be read and discussed more knowledgeably by more people than almost any other single subject.[136]

The report then suggested that three potential options were available to the Department of State: one was for the Department of State to act as a facilitator, another the promoter, and the third as a programmer of sport.

As a facilitator, the program was to remain basically as it was, playing an insignificant role in international sports. The Department of State would continue to aid American teams wishing to tour abroad, fill the requests of foreign embassies for coaches and athletes, or accept and help establish an itinerary for any foreign sports visitor.

> It is a reactive and non-directive approach and has had notable success. Even if the Department of State rejects a more

expansive role in international sports, the facilitator role is valuable and, with improvement, should be continued.[137]

Suggestions also were offered for improving the State Department's role as
facilitator. It was suggested that the department concentrate on STAGS in
order to maximize exposure and opportunities for contact, that it should
cease rendering endorsements for tours that the State Department did not financially support, and that seed money be provided to groups instead of paying the entire cost of a sport tour, which in turn would increase the number
of tours offered. It was also felt that sport tours should concentrate on
American sports, especially swimming, track and field, and basketball.[138]

Two additional suggestions were made, both of which pertained mainly
to Africa and Eastern Europe.

Geography: the Department should concentrate on Africa
and Eastern Europe where sports are an integral part of our cultural affairs program. . . . Program Content: In Africa, competitions between American and African teams should be minimized in favor of exhibitions, demonstrations, and clinics. . . .
No one likes losing. Eastern Europeans, on the other hand,
might only be satisfied with competitive action.[139]

Thus, to continue in the role of the facilitator would mean that the State Department would maintain the program at its present level with a few changes.

The report went on to say that if the Department of State felt that the
recent American setbacks in international competition, its failure to obtain
the 1976 Summer Olympics, and the ongoing NCAA-AAU squabble were coun-
terproductive to promoting mutual understanding and peace, then perhaps
the State Department should become an active promoter of the United States
participation in international sports. This role would require much more
money to subsidize United States athletic participation in international competitions and numerous other programs. It would also require that United
States sport organizations be represented before foreign governments and
other international organizations, that it sponsor and endorse specific activities promoting United States strength in international sports, and become a
coordinator and mediator between sporting organizations.

It you decide to become a Promoter, you need to determine
what most effectively promotes U.S. participation in international sports, and how the Department can best contribute to it; and
you need the commitment of U.S. sports groups and the Congress
in this role.[140]

Finally, if the department chose the role of a programmer, the Bureau
of Educational and Cultural Affairs would have to act as the coordinator of
the State Department and the private sector in packaging sports activities,
meeting a defined United States national need in specific countries.[141]

If you decide to become a Programmer, you need the
understanding of policy and program planners·in the Department

of State to consider fully the potential role of sports activities in the achievement of foreign policy objectives.[142]

Summing up all three programs, the report stated that the facilitator and promoter roles placed the emphasis on sports as an important field of endeavor and a significant part of life requiring the department to largely serve sports, whereas the programmer role would use sports activities as they existed rather than foster them in new areas.[143]

The report concluded by leaving the final decision entirely up to the State Department, without giving endorsement to any course of action.[144]

The Harris/Ragan report was sent to the various foreign post directors throughout the world and, as a result of the study and foreign-post feedback, the facilitator program for the most part was maintained and continued to be the major emphasis in the State Department's athletic program through 1973.[145]

State Department Conferences

One noticeable change in the State Department athletic program was the increased involvement by the International Athletic Programs Division in organizing conferences with the private sector on sport and the emphasis away from attempting to influence countries along Cold War lines to the idea of mutual international understanding through sport. In December of 1971 the Bureau of Educational and Cultural Affairs Advisory Panel on International Athletics recommended that a conference take place between representatives of national amateur athletic associations and other organizations having programs in international athletics.

The Panel believed that a conference of this kind should be convened for the purpose of exploring how the private sector and the government working together might increase international understanding through sports.[146]

On May 22, 1972 twenty-eight representatives from twenty national athletic associations and other organizations in international athletics met for a round-table conference of the State Department in Washington, D.C. At the conference a variety of topics were discussed. Chief among these were the organization programs and interests of the participants, opportunities and needs overseas, and increasing the range of athletic exchanges. At the conference it was disclosed that in preparing for the discussion on opportunities and needs overseas, the State Department had conducted another survey with its overseas posts, much like the one done in 1965 by the Interagency Committee on International Athletics.

Responses to these queries . . . were unanimously enthusiastic about the contribution to international cooperation and understanding that is established through athletic exchanges. They promote friendship, bring about increased knowledge of other nations and peoples, open up new contacts and generally lead to greater appreciation of one people by another.[147]

A list of each nation's sport interests had been tabulated for the conference, and some general suggestions about the International Athletic Exchange Program were formulated, such as making small supplementary grants to cover the costs of visiting an area or country not originally included in the travel plans of privately sponsored teams and reciprocal exchanges so the United States would profit from knowledge in unfamiliar fields such as soccer. By and large, the conference was mainly a brain-storming session with different views taken on a variety of issues. For example, on the topic of federal aid to sport, some of the participants failed to take any interest in seeking governmental funding for athletes while others deemed such funding essential despite the long tradition to the contrary in the United States.[148]

This was not the last conference sponsored by the State Department during this period. In December of 1973 another conference was convened in which twelve outstanding American scholars, representing such disciplines as political science, law, physical education, sports psychology, philosophy, communication, black cultural studies, international or intercultural relations, development psychology, and social psychology, took part. They met in Washington, D.C. for a one-day symposium to discuss issues surrounding sport competition and other mediums of sport as means for enhancing international relations, and to identify and discuss possible activities that might be promoted in academic or program-development oriented organizations to gain optimum value from international sport involvement.[149] Using again a brain-storming approach, various topics were discussed, chief among which were the types of sports mediums to be used and their potential impact on international relations; organization, management and the funding process for international exchanges; public affairs and the media; and behavioral and social science involvement in the program.[150] Activities were suggested which could be pursued by the academic community or by organizations geared for program development to increase mutual understanding between nations and to improve international relations through sport mediums. These included exchanges, research and activities in direct support of exchange of athletes.[151]

Throughout the symposium numerous ideas and suggestions were forthcoming which had great implications for the program, although a great many of these suggestions had already been put into operation before the symposium was convened. Sport had been used as a vehicle to foster international friendship between two unfriendly powers in 1972 when President Nixon accepted an invitation for U.S. table tennis players to tour the People's Republic of China. This was the so-called "Ping Pong Diplomacy" which, after the invitation was accepted, did not involve the federal government to any further extent as the tour was organized and paid for by a private table tennis organization.

In 1973 the International Athletics Programs Branch of the State Department did take an active role in amateur athletics when it became embroiled in a confrontation with the Amateur Athletic Union over the invitation of American swimmers to tour the People's Republic of China, an action which marked a definite change from the past. As a member of the International Aquatics governing body (FINA), the AAU was required to take action against swimmers and coaches going on the tour because the People's Republic of China was not a member of the international body. As a result, the first coach of the team was forced to resign and any swimmer wishing to participate was threatened by suspension from the AAU.

Fearing a possible affront to the Chinese, since the invitation had already been accepted, the State Department organized the tour rather than allowing the AAU to do so. Swimmers on the tour allowed their AAU membership to expire. The tour was quite successful, due mostly to the fact that no direct interaction competition was involved. Rather, the State Department implemented the policy of only giving demonstrations and coaching clinics, mainly with the idea of fomenting friendship and understanding. Upon their return the athletes and team officials were greeted with notices of AAU suspensions, which prompted Senator Pearson to admonish the two governing organizations:

> I find this arbitrary action by the AAU and FINA not only deplorable but incredible. These organizations have attempted to usurp the authority of the U.S. Government to conduct foreign policy. They have punished athletes, including six Olympic medalists and three members of the board of the U.S. Olympic Committee, for their participation in a program designed to achieve an important foreign policy objective.[152]

By the end of 1973 the International Athletics Programs branch of the Bureau of Educational and Cultural Affairs had directed their program toward three objectives: (1) the teaching team concept where sports teams of two to fifteen people were sent to a particular country to address unique problems in sports development; (2) the providing of seed money to sports organizations which, if unaided, would not have the means to extend their involvement into the international arena; and (3) the assistance to groups conducting projects totally funded from the private sector.[153]

Additionally, the department also facilitated sports fund raising by endorsing a sports group wishing to travel overseas at their own expense. By the end of 1973 the future plans of the department were to emphasize more activities in a less competitive atmosphere, feeling that the end result of fostering goodwill and understanding between countries could be much better achieved than by intense competition.[154] As a result, the department's presentations were projected to consist more and more of teaching activities in the area of track and field, swimming, diving and gymnastics, a far cry from the early days of the program during the initial phase of the Cold War.[155] The Deputy Assistant Secretary of State for Educational and Cultural Affairs best summed up the change in policy and direction: "Our interest is in furthering international mutual understanding and communication through sports."[156]

Peace Corps and the People-to-People Sports Committee

Two additional programs which concerned overseas sports exchanges must be mentioned when discussing federal programs involving the use of sport for American interests or foreign policy objectives. One was the use of sport by the Peace Corps (a direct federally funded program) and the other was a private organization known as the People to People Sports Committee which, although it was not a federal program, was given federal encouragement and executive backing.

Established by Executive Order 10924 on March 1, 1961, the Peace Corps was a pool of trained men and women, particularly schooled in the areas of health, education, agriculture and skilled labor, who were sent to aid various foreign countries who requested their aid. Originally, the only sport-affiliated part of the overseas program took place within the various schools in which Peace Corpsmen found themselves teaching. Sport oftentimes was a secondary activity and an additional part of a worker's job.[157] In many cases such instructors were physical educators who were trained for the program by the American Association for Health, Physical Education and Recreation (AAHPER), which had a contractual agreement with the Peace Corps since the organization's creation in 1961. Many countries, especially the emerging countries in Africa, began to request specific coaches to train their national teams. In such cases a specialist from inside the program was provided and, with the help of AAHPER, an advertising campaign was enacted to bring more of this type of specialist into the program.[158] An example of this campaign is typified by a mid-1960s poster which read:

PHYSICAL EDUCATORS
ATHLETIC COACHES

Your skills are needed in developing nations around the world. . . . Those interested in helping to develop, expand, and strengthen physical education and athletic programs in other lands have an opportunity to use their special skills in the AAHPER Peace Corps Projects. All levels of professional ability can be utilized. Assignments include instructing in secondary and university physical education programs and coaching of club, regional, and national athletic teams.[159]

While a Peace Corps assignment usually meant two years in the field, in some cases there were coaching specialists assigned for an unusual one-year assignment.[160] This was the exception rather than the rule in that the majority of sport coaching was done by physical educators. A change took place in 1969 when the Peace Corps began to train a special group of nineteen coaching specialists whose only job was to coach in schools, clubs or national teams.[161] From this evolved a permanent program known by many as the "Sports Corps."

In the early 1970s Bill Toomey, Olympic decathlon champion and world record holder, was sent by the Peace Corps to Venezuela, Ghana, Honduras, Ethiopia and Kenya to test out the idea of the so-called "Sports Corps."[162] Toomey found the countries he visited responsive to the idea and a second tour—this time to nineteen Asian countries—was organized, where the idea met with similar approval. As a result, the program begun in 1969 continued. By 1972, 283 American coaches were serving in twenty-five countries, and fifteen national teams were being coached by these Americans at the 1972 Olympics.[163]

Throughout the program sport was used as an important adjunct by the Peace Corps, which in itself was an important means by which the United States gained entry into foreign countries: " . . . we are one of the few Arms of the Peace Corps that is immediately accepted and appreciated by all countries. And with no suspicion and more of that Big Brotherism."164 While it did play a significant role, the importance of sport should not be exaggerated, for within the Peace Corps structure the priority of sport programs was not high. Services such as food supply and health understandably came first.165 Small or not, sport did play a part within the total Peace Corps program, which was in turn one aspect of American foreign policy.

The other organization which should be mentioned in the area of the use of sport for American interests or foreign policy objectives was a nongovernmental agency known as the People-to-People Sports Committee. This organization was one of forty-one committees of the People-to-People Foundation, an organization whose creation was stimulated by President Eisenhower. In 1956 Eisenhower called a People-to-People Conference which he hoped would lead to an organization which would help to create a climate in which governments could work more effectively for peace.166

Throughout the years the foundation has had as its honorary chairman the President of the United States, thereby adding a sense of importance to its actions. Although outside government auspices, it indirectly was linked to the federal government by such endorsements and the support of Washington,167 and in many ways was a propaganda tool for the United States at the nongovernmental level. In 1968 it almost became directly involved with the federal government when Congressman Dooley introduced H. Res. 11252 to amend the International Cultural Exchange and Trade Fair Participation Act of 1956 by providing for exchanges of athletes. Dooley's bill called for the authorization of two million dollars so the program could be expended by the President through the People-to-People Sports Committee. Obviously, some close links had already been established with the federal government.

Some of the activities envisioned by the Sports Committee in the early years of the program were to function as a liaison and organizer in promoting sport exchanges between the United States and other countries, and to act as a domestic and international clearinghouse for information on American sport.168

By 1968 the organization was well established and recognized, and its efforts lauded, even in Congress:

Mr. Speaker, today I would like to commend an organization that is making a major contribution to our society. . . . Its program utilizes the universal interest in sports and the understanding of good sportsmanship as a base from which to begin. It is truly the American people's program, not a commercial organization for profit or a Government-sponsored agency, although it has the support of official Washington. The committee cooperates with existing sports organizations. It encourages those which have no international exchange program to launch one. It stimulates those which have one to expand it. It provides funds and other types of assistance to them. It brings into the international sports exchange movement delegations drawn from schools, clubs, colleges, and universities, both amateur and professional. It cooperates closely with governmental agencies both domestic and foreign.[169]

In addition to sport exchanges, the committee operated hospitality centers for athletes and officials from numerous nations at the 1960 and 1964 Olympic games, and the 1963 and 1967 Pan-American games.[170] It also distributed what was known as sport kits to the young people in the emerging countries of the world and to Peace Corps volunteers at no cost. Each kit contained equipment to pursue one particular sport, which was customarily presented by the United States ambassador in that country.[171]

By the end of 1971 the Sports Committee had programmed twenty-four major sports exchanges involving fifty different countries in activities ranging from sailing to golf. Upon the advice of President Nixon in 1972, the committee became especially interested in including exchanges and competitions with Communist countries.[172]

Thus, what had begun early in the 1950s as a haphazard program of international athletic exchanges had by 1973 expanded to include other areas within the State Department, most notably the Peace Corps, and even included exchanges with Communist countries whose own programs early in the 1950's had spurred American interest.

Conclusion

In conclusion, the use of sport for foreign policy objectives has not been restricted solely to Socialist countries, but has been used by the American federal government as well. Generally speaking, the promotion by the federal government for American international athletic success and the sponsoring of athletic exchanges were reactions to Soviet movements in these areas and were not initiated by the American government.

Traditionally, Americans have always felt an anathema toward federal intrusion into what they deem to be a private sector, and sport was no exception. However when it seemed the existence of democracy was at stake during the Cold War feelings against federal involvement in sport were brushed aside. Even then, a low profile was kept with the amount of emphasis on this aspect largely dependent upon the interest of the administration at the time and not dependent upon congress for implementation.

In spite of these forays, American federal involvement in sport to promote American interests and foreign policy objectives was miniscule when compared to the Soviet Union from 1950-1973. The importance which socialist countries, in particular the Soviet Union, placed on sport for political purposes far overshadowed that stressed in the United States. When this attitude was coupled with the age-old American belief that "the less government the better," little federal involvement could be expected in the United States.

Footnotes

[1] Sport in this context entails organized games, contests and matches at the amateur and professional levels in addition to physical education and fitness.

[2] Traditionally the powers entrusted to the federal government by the Constitution consisted of the authority to levy taxes, duties and imports, coin money, fix weights and measures, grant patents and copyrights, establish post offices, post roads, raise and maintain an army and navy, regulate interstate commerce, manage Indian relations, international relations and war, pass laws for naturalizing foreigners, control public lands and admit new states to the union.

[3] A third method which will not be discussed here was the granting of financial aid to enable sport associations to host prestigious international athletic events on American soil (Olympic and Pan-Am games).

[4] Congressman Dewey Short, Address before the National Rifle Association, 82nd annual convention, U.S. Congressional Record, Vol. 99, 83rd Congress, 1st session. (Washington, D. C.), 27 March 1953, p. A1862.

[5] Arthur Daley, "Sports of the Times," New York Times, 10 June 1952.

[6] Richard B. Walsh, "The Soviet Athlete in International Competition," U.S. Department of State Bulletin, 24 December 1951, pp. 107-10.

[7] Jeffrey Chase, "Politics and Nationalism in Sports: Soviet and American Government Involvement in Amateur Sports as an Aspect of the Cold War." (Masters thesis, San Jose State University, 1973), p. 80.

[8] Arthur Daley, op. cit.

[9] Congressman Philbin, Remarks, U.S. Congressional Record, Vol. 100, Pt. 10, 83rd Congress, 2nd session, 1954, p. 13763.

[10] Avery Brundage, "I Must Admit Russian Athletes are Great," Saturday Evening Post, 30 April 1955.

[11] William Randolph Hearst, Jr., Speech before the National Press Club, Washington, D.C., 28 February 1955, audiotape (National Archives, Washington, D.C.).

[12] Arthur Daley, "Will the Soviet Union Sweep the Olympics?" American Legion, June 1955, pp. 16, 53.

[13] U.S. Congressional Record, Vol. 101, 94th Congress, 1st session, 1955, pp. 5169, 5907, 11213.

[14] Ibid., p. 8209.

[15] Ibid.

[16] Concurrent resolutions must be passed by both houses of Congress and do not require the signature of the President and do not have the force of law. They are generally used to make or amend rules applicable to both houses or to express the sentiment of the two houses.

[17] U.S., Congress, S. Conc. Res. 78, 84th Congress, 2nd session, 1956.

[18] Congressman Feighan, Remarks, U.S. Congressional Record, Vol. 102, Pt. 3, 84th Congress, 2nd session.

[19] Ibid., p. 3789.

[20] U. S. Congressional Record, Vol. 102, 84th Congress, 2nd session, p. 8834.

[21] Congressman Derwinski, U.S. Congressional Record, Vol. 105, Pt. 11, 86th Congress, 1st session, 1959, p. 14026.

[22] Constantine Brown, "New Olympic Victory for Reds," Washington Evening Star, 15 June 1959.

[23] Irving Jaffe, "Why America Can't Win the 1960 Olympics," American Weekly, 17 January 1960.

[24] John J. Karch, "How the Soviet Union Exploits Sports," American Legion, February 1962.

[25] U.S. Congressional Record, Vol. 105, 86th Congress, 2nd session, 1960, p. A 1827.

[26] John J. Karch, op. cit.

[27] Ibid.

[28] Ibid.

29 U.S. Congressional Record, Vol. 110, 88th Congress, 2nd session, 1964, p. A 1451.

30 Ibid.

31 Ibid.

32 Ibid.

33 V. L. Nicholson, Letter to Honorable Leon K. Sullivan, House of Representatives, in U.S. Congressional Record, Vol. 110, 88th Congress, 2nd session, 16 March 1964, p. A 1451.

34 Ibid.

35 U.S. Congressional Record, Vol. 108, 87th Congress, 2nd session, 1962, p. 19186.

36 Ibid., p. 19188.

37 U. S. Congressional Record, Vol. 108, 87th Congress, 2nd session, 1962, pp. 20670-71; 22488-92.

38 Hubert Humphrey, "Why We Must Win the Olympics," Parade, 6 January 1963.

39 Ibid.

40 Ibid.

41 Ibid.

42 Draft of a Report of the Interagency Committee on International Athletes to the President and the Secretary of State, January 1965, p. 4.

43 Ibid.

44 Ibid.

45 Ibid., p. 5.

46 Executive Order 11117, 16 August 1963.

[47] Nicholas Rodis, Chairman, Interagency Committee on Athletes, Department of State, Hearings before the Committee on Commerce, U.S. Senate, "The Controversy in Administration of Track and Field Events in the United States," Serial No. 89-40, 89th Congress, 1st session, 1965, p. 514.

[48] Executive Order 11117, op. cit.

[49] Irving De Koff, "The Role of Government in the Olympics." (Ph.D. Dissertation, Teachers College, Columbia University, 1962), p. 74; see also "Fund Reaches Goal," New York Times, 11 January 1962, and "Ski Team to Get Government Aid, First of Its Kind," New York Times, 10 December 1961.

[50] John J. Karch, "How Soviet Union Exploits Sports," American Legion, op. cit.

[51] U.S. Congressional Record, Vol. 109, 88th Congress, 1st session, 1963 pp. 12392-12400; 22402-3.

[52] Ibid., pp. 22402-03.

[53] Ibid., pp. 12396-97; see also Amateur Athlete, April 1963.

[54] U.S. Congressional Record, Vol. 109, 88th Congress, 1st session, p. 22403.

[55] Ibid., p. 6867.

[56] U.S., Congress, House Bill 10539, 88th Congress, 2nd session, 1964.

[57] U.S. Congressional Record, Vol. 110, 88th Congress, 2nd session, 1964, p. 5904.

[58] C. P. Trussel, "Humphrey Urges White House to Help Raise U.S. Sport Level," New York Times, 14 February 1964.

[59] Ibid.

[60] U.S. Congressional Record, Vol. 110, 88th Congress, 2nd session, 1964, p. 5579.

[61] "Olympic Post-Mortem: Pay More and Play Better," National Observer 24 February 1964.

[62] Draft of a Report from the Interagency Committee on International Athletics, January 1965, p. 7.

[63] Ibid.

[64] James M. Gavin, Report to the President of the United States, "Amateur Sports in America: An Appraisal and a Proposal," prepared by Arthur D. Little & Co., 25 January 1965, p. 1.

[65] Ibid.

[66] James M. Gavin, Letter to the President of the United States, 25 January 1965.

[67] James M. Gavin, Report, op. cit., p. 1.

[68] Ibid.

[69] Ibid., p. 3.

[70] Ibid., pp. 3-4.

[71] Ibid., p. 39.

[72] Ibid.

[73] James M. Gavin, Letter, op. cit.

[74] U.S., Congress, Hearings before the Committee on Commerce, United States Senate, "Amateur Sports," 93rd Congress, 1st session, on S. 1018, S. 1192, S. 1580 and S. 1690, Serial No. 92-23, 1973, p. 119.

[75] "Toward a More Effective United States Olympic Effort," Report to the U.S. Olympic Committee, Arthur D. Little & Co., 1965.

[76] Draft of Report from Interagency Committee on International Athletics, op. cit., p. 10.

[77] Ibid.

[78] Ibid., pp. 13-14.

[79] Amateur Athlete, August 1966, p. 10.

[80] Irving Jaffe, "A Plan to Rescue Our Olympic Beggars," American Legion, September 1967.

[81] "Humphrey Urges U.S. Athletes Not to Boycott Olympic Games," Washington Post, 30 March 1968.

[82] U.S. Congressional Record, Vol. 116, 91st Congress, 2nd session, pp. 14547, 1458-82.
U.S. Congressional Record, Vol. 119, 93rd Congress, 1st session, p. H 7919.

[83] U.S., Congress, Hearings before the Subcommittee to Investigate the Administration of the Internal Security Act and Other Internal Security Laws of the Committee on the Judiciary, United States Senate, Pt. 25, 92nd Congress, 1st session, October 1971.

[84] The following resolutions of protest were introduced, all of which were unsuccessful in passage: S. Res. 358, H. J. Res. 1294, House Resolutions 1106, 1107, 1109, 1110.

[85] H. Res. 17192 and S. 4038 (1972); H. Res. 3441 and S. 169 (1973).

[86] White House Staff, Research Paper, 21 May 1973, p. 14.

[87] Ibid., p. 13.

[88] Charley Dailey, "Physical Education in Thailand," Physical Education Around the World, Monograph No. II, (ed.) William Johnson. (Indianapolis, Ind.: Phi Epsilon Kappa Fraternity, 1968), pp. 70-72.

[89] Richard B. Walsh, "The Soviet Athlete in International Competition," Department of State Bulletin, Vol. xxv, No. 652, Pub. 4441, 24 December 1951, p. 1007.

[90] Press Release, U.S. Information Agency, 21 May 1956.

[91] Deobold Van Dalen, Elmer Mitchell, and Bruce Bennett, A World History of Physical Education. (New Jersey: Prentice-Hall, 1953), p. 491.

[92] U.S., Congress, Senate Report 1664, "International Cultural Exchange and Trade Fair Participation Act of 1956," 84th Congress, 2nd session, 1956, p. 2.

[93] Ibid.

94 Department of State Cultural Presentations Program, "Tours Completed from Beginning of Program in 1954 through June, 1958, FY-1955 through FY-1958." (Mimeo paper.)

95 U.S., Congress, Senate Report 1664, op. cit.

96 William Randolph Hearst, Jr., Speech before the National Press Club, Washington, D. C., 28 February 1955, audiotape (National Archives, Washington, D. C.).

97 Ibid.

98 General David Sarnoff, "A New Plan to Defeat Communism," U.S. News and World Report, 27 May 1955.

99 Congressman MacDonald, Remarks, U.S. Congressional Record, Vol. 101, 84th Congress, 1st session, 1955, p. 8203.

100 U.S. Congressional Record, Vol. 101, 84th Congress, 1st session, p. 5057; see also "Dillard Wins Praise as United States 'Ambassador,'" Cleveland Press, 16 February 1955.

101 Congressman Judd, Statement, U.S. Congress, House Hearings, Committee on Foreign Affairs on Draft Bills proposed in Executive Communications No. 863, No. 953 and No. 1061, Amending the United States Information and Educational Exchange Act of 1948, and No. 1409, Providing for Cultural and Athletic Exchanges and Participation in International Fairs and Festivals, 84th Congress, 2nd session, 1956, p. 9.

102 Press Release, U.S. Information Agency, 21 May 1956.

103 Department of State Cultural Presentations Program, op. cit. (Mimeo paper.)

104 Jeffrey Chase, op. cit., p. 94.

105 Address before the Amateur Athletic Union by Harold E. Howland, International Exchange Service, U.S. Department of State, Amateur Athlete, January 1958.

106 American Embassy (Helsinki), letter to Department of State, 9 May 1960.

107 Department of State, Bureau of Educational and Cultural Affairs (CU), "Landmark Events in the History of CU," 1973.

108 Bureau of Educational and Cultural Affairs, Department of State, "The Department's Athletic Exchange Program, 1965-1970," 1970.

109 Department of State Cultural Presentations Program, op. cit. (Mimeo paper.)

110 Interview with Walter Boehm, Director of International Athletic Programs, Bureau of Educational and Cultural Affairs, Department of State, Washington, D.C., 25 February 1974.

111 Senator Hubert Humphrey, Remarks, U.S. Congressional Record, Vol. 108, 87th Congress, 2nd session, p. 20671.

112 U.S. Advisory Commission on International Educational and Cultural Affairs, Report, "A Beacon of Hope--The Exchange-of-Persons Program," April 1963, p. 28.

113 U.S., Congress, House Hearings, "Winning the Cold War," U.S. House of Representatives, Hearings before the Subcommittee on International Organizations and Movements of the Committee on Foreign Affairs, 88th Congress, 1st session, 1963.

114 Nicholas Rodis, "The State Department's Athlete: A New Look to Foreign Policy," Amateur Athlete, August 1964.

115 "Red Auerbach, Expert on Subject, Lectures on Diplomacy at Tufts," Washington Post, 7 February 1965.

116 Interagency Committee on International Athletics, "A Study of the Impact of Sports on the Achievement of U.S. Foreign Policy Objectives," 5 November 1965.

117 Ibid., p. 1.

118 Ibid.

119 Ibid., pp. 1-2.

120 Ibid.

121 Ibid., Pt. 1, pp. 1-5.

122 Ibid., Pt. 2, pp. 1-4.

123 Ibid., Pt. 4, pp. 1-3.

124 Ibid., Pt. 5, pp. 1-4.

125 Ibid., Pt. 2, pp.

126 These figures were compiled from U.S. State Department semi-annual and annual reports of the International Educational Exchange Program, from "The Department's Athletic Exchange Program, 1965-1970," Xeroxed U.S. State Department Report: 1970, and U.S. Department of State Cultural Presentations Program, "Tours Completed from Beginning of Program in 1954 Through June 1968." They are to be considered only as indicators and not as complete and final statistics on exchanges.

127 U.S. Department of State, Annual Report of the Bureau of Educational and Cultural Affairs, FY-1967.

128 Advisory Committee on the Arts, report to Congress and the Public, "Cultural Presentations USA--1966-67," p. 57.

129 Ibid.

130 J. Manuel Espinosa, Bureau of Educational and Cultural Affairs, Latin America, letter to Jerome B. Speers, Bureau of Educational and Cultural Affairs. (Washington, D.C.: Department of State, 18 December 1969) 1969).

131 Ibid.

132 Chase, op. cit., p. 96.

133 Walter Boehm, op. cit.

134 Harris/Ragan Management Corporation, "International Sports Policies for the Department of State," a presentation of options, 24 September 1971, p. 2.

135 Ibid.

136 Ibid., p. 4.

137 Ibid., p. 6.

138 Ibid., pp. 11-13.

139 Ibid., pp. 11-12.

[140] Ibid., pp. 15-16.

[141] Ibid., p. 18.

[142] Ibid., p. 23.

[143] Ibid., p. 26.

[144] Ibid., p. 28.

[145] See letters:
To Alan A. Reich, Deputy Assistant Secretary of State, Bureau of Educational and Cultural Affairs, by Owen W. Roberts, Staff Officer, Bureau of Educational and Cultural Affairs, African Program, 12 October 1971;

To Alan A. Reich, Deputy Assistant Secretary of State, by Stephen A. Comiskey, Staff Officer, Bureau of Educational and Cultural Affairs, Latin American Program, 20 October 1971;

To Alan A. Reich, Deputy Assistant Secretary of State, by Francis B. Tenny, Staff Officer, Bureau of Educational and Cultural Affairs, East Asian Program, 13 October 1971;

To Mr. Lewis, Bureau of Educational and Cultural Affairs, by Francis B. Tenny, Staff Officer, Bureau of Educational and Cultural Affairs, East Asian Program, 6 January 1971;

To Alan A. Reich, Deputy Assistant Secretary of State, by Arthur B. Allen, Staff Officer, Bureau of Educational and Cultural Affairs, Near Eastern and South Asian Programs, 19 October 1971;

To Alan A. Reich, Deputy Assistant Secretary of State, by Guy E. Coriden, Staff Officer, Bureau of Educational and Cultural Affairs, Eastern Europe Program, 20 October 1971.

[146] "Round-Table Conference on International Athletic Exchanges," Department of State, International Conference Room, 22 May 1972, p. 2.

[147] Ibid., p. 5.

[148] Ibid., p. 9.

[149] Robert N. Singer, "Multidisciplinary Symposium on Sport and the Means of Furthering Mutual International Understanding," U.S. Department of State, Bureau of Educational and Cultural Affairs, 4 December 1973. (Tallahassee: Florida State University, February 1974), p. ii.

[150] Ibid.

[151] Ibid., p. iii.

[152] U.S. Congressional Record, Vol. 119, 93rd Congress, 1st session, 1973, p. S 13199.

[153] Robert N. Singer, op. cit., pp. 4-5.

[154] Walter Boehm, interview, op. cit.

[155] Ibid.

[156] U.S. Congressional Record, Vol. 119, No. 95, 93rd Congress, 1st session, 19 June 1973.

[157] Robert B. Cooney, Press Officer, Peace Corps, telephone interview, Washington, D.C., 24 April 1974.

[158] Ibid.

[159] AAHPER Peace Corps Project, Advertising Poster, 1960s.

[160] Robert B. Cooney, telephone interview, op. cit.

[161] Robert Gillham, member of the First Sports Specialist Program, personal interview, San Jose, California, 17 June 1975.

[162] Tom Quinn, "Sports Corps Builds Teams--And Nations," Washington News, March 1972, article inserted into U.S. Congressional Record.

[163] Ibid.

[164] Ibid., quote of Glenn Randall, director of Sports Corps, p. E 2856.

[165] Robert B. Cooney, telephone interview, op. cit.

[166] New York Times, 15 June 1957.

[167] U.S. Congressional Record, Vol. 114, 90th Congress, 2nd session, 1968, p. 22975.

[168] U.S. Congressional Record, Vol. 103, 85th Congress, 1st session, 1957, pp. 9430-31.

[169] Congressman Meeds, Remarks, <u>U.S. Congressional Record</u>, Vol. 114, 90th Congress, 2nd session, <u>op. cit.</u>, p. 29975.

[170] <u>Ibid</u>.

[171] "Round-Table Conference on International Athletic Exchanges," <u>op. cit.</u>, pp. A 9-10.

[172] <u>Ibid</u>.

Legal Aspects Of A United States

Foreign Sports Policy

James A. R. Nafziger

I. Introduction

The father of the modern Olympic Games, Baron Pierre de Coubertin, envisaged international athletic exchange as the "free trade of the future."[1] No nation would regulate this trade to its political advantage. The Olympic Games, as well as other international political arenas, would be unpolluted by political currents. To a remarkable extent, considering the course of twentieth century history, these aspirations have been met.[2] But athletic exchange, like other forms of human interaction, nevertheless remains exposed to sovereign intervention; a measure of politics is inevitable in any transnational activity, whether in the United Nations or a global convention of medieval musicologists.[3] Effective management of any transnational human activity is, therefore, a matter of regulating rather than eliminating political intervention. Within the nation-state system, such regulation depends heavily upon harmonious laws and policies of participating governments.

National sports laws and policies vary in scope and kind. Governmental support of athletic programs and exchange is all but universal, ranging from the employment by Scandinavian governments of cross-country skiing competitors and border guards to the massive programs of national aggrandizement exemplified by those of the People's Republic of China and East Germany. The "college-bonus" system of support is used in the United States, and the "cash-bonus" and pervasive military service ·system is employed by the Soviet Union.[5] Rule 26 of the Olympic Games, which governs the important question of "amateur" status, was recently reformed after years of controversy to respond to the trend away from rigid amateurism.[6] Rewritten Rule 26, and more particularly its implementing by-laws, offers greater opportunity for governmental assistance to amateur Olympic aspirants. Such governmental support presupposes the efficacy of keeping the home folks happy while impressing one's neighbors by setting a world record on some foreign athletic track. After all, the theory goes, athletic competition offers a relatively inexpensive and humane way of flexing the national muscles; presumably, athletic prowess serves the national interest.[7]

Reproduced by kind permission of the author and the Vanderbilt Journal of Transnational Law, 8(4):837–855, 1975.

Whether, and if so how, international athletic success serves the national interest, are questions of considerable importance to the United States Government as it considers whether it should exercise greater legal control over amateur athletics. Indeed, insofar as amateur sport involves international exchange, should this country further develop a foreign sports policy?[8] To do so might seem on first impression to require this country not only to modify its traditional laissez-faire approach toward participation by its nationals in transnational sports, but also to reinterpret the free-trade vision of Baron de Coubertin, the Olympic Rules,[9] and other Grundnorms of sports, so as to rationalize a seemingly further politicization of the athletic arena.

The times do not generally favor entry by the United States Government into a new arena of potential international conflict, especially one created for its own sake, such as sports competition.[10] But sport is no longer simply isolated, private activity; it is now a popular movement. Not only are governments and politics involved in sports, but governments harness the popularity of sports activities for diplomatic purposes.[11] Moreover, the spectacular expansions of media coverage of transnational athletic competition brought all the glory, humanity, organization, administrative bungles, and ultimate horror of the 1972 Games in Munich into the United States living room so graphically as to firmly establish, if it was not already, the important role of sports in public international affairs. The involvement of this country's athletes in global competition is now of major public interest, if not concern. With Munich behind, we wrestle with such questions as the freedom of United States athletes to compete against both white and racially mixed teams of Rhodesians and South Africans. Answers to such questions cannot arise strictly from the private sector, for they relate to substantial matters of foreign and civil rights policy. If, then, sports competition is inextricably entangled in a burgeoning popular movement and in politics, it may be time for the adoption of some further policy to guide participation by United States nationals in transnational sports.

Within a transnational setting, the relationships between "nationalism and sports" and between "politics and sports" historically have been viewed in this country as disjunctive. Until recently, any official United States intervention into transnational athletic exchange has been regarded adversely. Now, however, with an emerging Realpolitik recognition of the inevitability of governmental involvement in sports, and even its peace-making merit, it is important to distinguish among the levels of such possible involvement:

Level I--simple governmental financial assistance, either by direct appropriations, use of revenue from governmental lotteries, or other means. Such assistance is not only acceptable, but encouraged, as an international practice;[12]

Level II--direct governmental supervision and control over the administration of domestic sport, a widespread practice which is at least symbolized, if not manifested, in some countries by a cabinet-level Minister of Sports;

Level III--diplomatic exploitation of sports in the external affairs of the government.

A United States foreign sports policy might exist at any or all three levels of governmental involvement. This article however, will be concerned primarily with the special problems related to the possibility of United States involvement in sports at Level III.

II. Current United States Governmental Involvement in Sports

The current involvement of the United States Government in sports activity is modest and generally free of comprehensive policy restraint. Already discernible, however, are the outline of a domestic sports policy that bears some incidental transboundary implications, and certain international policies identified primarily with a facilitative program administered on a shoestring budget by the Department of State. This article will briefly examine each of these.

A. Domestic Involvement

Domestic sports policy[13] barely qualifies as such, but one can discern a pattern of involvement at Levels I and II that includes oligopolistic protection from antitrust laws for baseball (but generally not for other sports); congressional chartering of the United States Olympic Committee (with indirect transnational implications); laws and regulations governing the broadcasting and televising of sports; allocations of military security appropriations for sports in the armed services; support of a Sports Corps within ACTION; state and local governmental support of physical education and individual athletes; and a growing presidential role, which until recently was limited to presiding over the Council on Physical Fitness and, of course, when politically feasible, tossing out a baseball on opening day.

Recently, by executive order, the President established an ad hoc 18-member Commission on Olympic Sports.[14] Its purpose is, partly through hearings, to study the United States Olympic Committee (USOC) on a sport-by-sport basis, examine allegations of mismanagement by the USOC of its responsibilities during the 1972 Olympic Games,[15] determine factors which impede or tend to impede the United States from fielding its best amateur athletes in transnational competition, and study measures for financing and otherwise assuring more effective United States participation in the Olympics. The Commission is charged with the responsibility of submitting two reports of findings and recommendations to the President.

As against these few instances of governmental involvement in sports, passage of the proposed Amateur Athletic Act[16] would be of profound significance. The Act is designed to strengthen United States athletic activity and programs at home and abroad, and to settle disputes between competing amateur sports organizations,[17] which are apparently immune to internal, private reform.[18] Actually, two proposals were introduced unsuccessfully in the 93rd Congress and will likely be put before the 94th Congress. The first proposal, with several variations, would refer all internal jurisdictional disputes to the American Arbitration Association.[19] An alternative proposal—the Amateur Athletic Act—is more far-reaching and controversial. It would create a five-member, independent United States Sports Board, one member of which must be an amateur athlete, with broad authority to issue and revoke charters of sanctioning bodies for athletic competition, subject both to the Board's regulations and court review. Each chartered body would govern at least one, and up to three, sports, if the other two could benefit from common administration. This second bill contained an earlier provision, later eliminated, to create a national sports development foundation to enrich and enlarge amateur athletics in this country.

B. Transnational Involvement

The scope of the proposed Amateur Athletic Act is explicitly international. Indeed, it is illuminating to note that of four "findings" articulated in Section 101 of the Act, two are explicitly and one implicitly addressed to world order and foreign commerce considerations. The international implications of the Act are underscored by the serious reservations toward it which have been expressed by the International Olympic Committee,[20] presumably under Rule 25 of the Olympic Rules and Regulations.[21]

Even without the Act, politics color United States athletic participation in international competition and other forms of exchange. All levels of the government may be called upon to support the convening of transnational competition in this country. The role of the public taxpayer in this support became poignantly clear when Denver voters rescinded an invitation to hold the 1976 Winter Games there. The international ramifications of governmental support of military participation in international shooting and swimming meets and the extraterritorial effect given to United States artitrust laws governing professional sports not only in the United States but in Canada exemplify political involvement. San Francisco Seals, Ltd. v. National Hockey League (NHL),[22] for example, considered the antitrust implications of an NHL refusal to grant the plaintiff a franchise in Vancouver, British Columbia. The court noted in dicta that major-league professional hockey extending to Canada was subject to federal antitrust laws and that the relevant geographical market for professional hockey before live audiences, under sections 1 and 2 of the Sherman Act,[23] encompassed the United States and Canada. The court concluded that territorial restraints imposed by the NHL did not restrain trade or commerce within the language of the Sherman Act. But such international ramifications of domestic laws and policy are of little significance.

Of greater significance to a discussion of United States foreign sports policy is the program administered by the Department of State to facilitate athletic exchange. That program includes sponsorship and administration of visits by foreign sports administrators and an outbound program consisting of 10-20 coaches a year, a small number of outstanding athletes to conduct demonstrations, several teachers of sports organization and administration, and a few teams to participate in goodwill tours. Between 1952 and 1973, 531 coaches and 117 teams were sent abroad. The Department of State also provides seed money to enable select organizations to raise private funds to carry out their programs more effectively, and assists athletes and coaches with briefings and other diplomatic support while they are abroad.[24]

III. Preliminary Legal Aspects of a United States
Foreign Sports Policy

Let us return to the central question, "What are the salient legal aspects of a United States foreign sports policy?" More broadly stated, what, if any, are the authoritative restraints on the achievement by the United States Government of all levels, particularly Level III, of political involvement in transnational athletic exchange?

A. Domestic Law

As a matter of domestic law, the executive branch of the federal government may, under the foreign relations power[25] or under delegated congressional authority,[26] employ amateur athletics as another tool of foreign policy. Passage of the Amateur Athletic Act would offer the executive branch appointive and supervisory discretion of a sort that would at least indirectly bear foreign policy considerations. More ambitious extensions of the foreign relations powers to athletic competition invite questions not of domestic law, but of transnational law and of domestic political efficacy and feasibility, as defined by a formulation of the "national interest."

B. Minimal Options and Authoritative Objectives Within the National Interest

The national interest underlying current United States international sports programs "is in furthering mutual understanding and communication through sports."[27] Accordingly, the government has strengthened its role in sports by committing further resources to facilitate people-to-people communication and public diplomacy conducted by private individuals and groups.[28] It is accepted that transnational athletic exchange has served as a useful symbol, signal, and catalyst for the improvement of a nation-state's international relations. Moreover, even limited athletic exchange serves to make those relations less artificial and more socially anchored.

A study undertaken for the Department of State in 1971, which observed that "sports has largely been ignored"[29] by Foggy Bottom, identified four reasons for this deficiency[30] and suggested two options in addition to the present one of facilitation:

(1) As an active promoter the Department would work to increase the stature of United States participation in international sports programs as a primary means of achieving the objectives of the Fulbright-Hays Act;

(2) Alternatively, the Department could become a programmer of United States participation in international sports, viewing sports as a foreign affairs resource which, when balanced with other such resources, might be important to the achievement of foreign policy objectives.[31]

The study recommended that the government's choice between these options be made by balancing the attendant risks and benefits. As to risks, the facilitative role seemed the safest; the promoter role, though more attractive, was riskier as it depends upon sufficient funding; the programmer role seemed even riskier, as foreign affairs officials might deny its usefulness and the participants themselves might disparage its political implications. As to benefits, the promoter and programmer roles offered greater assurance of effective participation in international competition where the United States has been poorly represented in the past; and the programmer role would recharacterize the government as a consumer rather than a handmaiden of sports activities, and would, therefore, tend to recharacterize the overall role of sports in domestic social life.[32] In considering which option to pursue, the study concluded that "the Department must first decide the objective of its sports activities and have a cogent plan for achieving that objective before very strong feelings, either way, emerge."[33]

The State Department's Bureau of Educational and Cultural Affairs seeks to achieve three objectives: (a) to enlarge the circle of those able to serve as influential interpreters between this and other nations; (b) to stimulate institutional development in directions which favorably affect mutual comprehension; and (c) to reduce structural and technical impediments to the exchange of ideas and information.[34] Within this framework, the Bureau has conducted a limited program of facilitating athletic exchange, while eschewing direct sponsorship of athletic exchange.[35] No definitive policy can be drawn from these broadly stated objectives.

Were the facilitative role of the State Department's Bureau of Educational and Cultural Affairs expanded, so would be its implications for United States foreign policy. But whatever the role to be performed by the Bureau, the increased capacity and current use of sport as a diplomatic tool suggest the importance of a more operational statement of objectives--indeed, of a comprehensive foreign sports policy. For instance, when, for foreign policy reasons, State X is boycotted by States Y and Z, how should United States participants respond? How, if at all, should the Government formally respond? Should United States teams be advised against engaging in competition against teams of states, or indeed, liberation movements, which the government does not recognize? Such questions abound.

It is in the United States' interest to resolve such questions coherently and consistently. It is time for a foreign sports policy transcending the sporadic and incidental governmental intervention and the facilitative activities of the Bureau of Cultural and Educational Affairs. A comprehensive national policy could be largely shaped by such transnational bodies as the International Olympic Committee and its 26 constituent sports federations.

IV. Toward an Authoritative Process to Shape
United States Policy

A. A Unilateral Framework: Its Pitfalls

Should the United States Government look upon sport simply as a diplomatic tool to serve the exigencies of the times, or perhaps more generously

as a tool for unilateral promotion of world order? Either perspective is
deficient because of the degree of ambiguity and complexity inherent in unilateral decisions and policy. It would be ill-advised for the United States
any longer to "go it alone." Although athletic exchanges organized by the
United States do generate some goodwill, there is little agreement on the efficacy of sports as an instrument of world order.[36] The ritual or cathartic
role of sports as an agent in conflict resolution, or as a socializing model
for the development of self-control, seems to be ambiguous. Considered
globally, the cultural contexts and the athletic activities themselves are apparently too diverse to permit any useful conclusions, unless simply that
sport represents a microcosm of human society--to recall Baron de Coubertin's metaphor, trade in sports, like material goods, will neither save the
world nor, by itself, further threaten world order.

To add to the uncertainty and complexity of unilateral decision-making,
sport operates in different ways in different contexts. National athletic interests differ.[37] Individuals may be culturally conditioned to participate actively or passively for a variety of diverse reasons: for aesthetic pleasure
related to the beauty of controlled body movement, for dramatics and strate-
gy-interplay, for the sheer excitement of competition, for the thrill of physical exertion or even violence within the rules, or for the experience of
learning. The controlling perspectives will depend on the sport, the age,
sex, and other characteristics of the participants, the level and intensity of
competition, the type of exchange, and, most importantly, the cultural context. A few examples of divergent perspectives may be useful. Current evidence suggests that the interest of the People's Republic of China in participation in international competition is prompted by the desire for friendship,
to learn good techniques, and only peripherally to vanquish competition.[38]
The exquisite manner in which the Chinese have conducted "ping-pong diplomacy," involving a careful selection of team members on a par with foreign
visitors but capable of rewarding competition with friendship and new skills,
testifies to this distinctive perspective.[39] In parts of the Middle East and
Middle Asia, participation in sports is overwhelmingly limited to men and
quite frequently to the military, the affluent, and the professional elite. In
Africa, contemporary nation-building sensitivities may be so strong as to
preclude bilateral competition with United States athletes; in Eastern Europe,
competition may be the only avenue of athletic communication; and so on.

Therefore if the United States is to adopt a unilateral role in world
athletic exchange, it must deftly unravel a plethora of factors that will affect
administrative decision-making in a particular political/cultural situation.
This may be too much to expect. Thus, given our limited resources of time
and administration, there appears to be a clear need to develop more comprehensive, overreaching policies to organize decision-making over the long
haul. Because it seems clear that we shall have to make a variety of decisions related to the participation of our nation in transnational sports, a coherent foreign sports policy would be greatly assisted by recourse to international norms and rules.

B. A Multilateral Framework: Its Promise

A purely unilateral framework is clearly inadequate to guide decision-making if sport is regarded not simply as an activator and amplifier of international discourse and rapport, but, more ambitiously, as a means of managing crises, accommodating social change and, in general, improving the lot of man. To elevate sport to a policy level that entails these latter considerations is not premature; the fact is that sports "are there" already. High-level United States-Canadian security planning to combat the terrorist threat to the 1976 Montreal Games that crippled the 1972 Munich Games underscores the political vitality of transnational sports competition.[40] Quite often sports activity has operated to mitigate international tension in more important contexts--United States relations with the Soviet Union and the Peoples Republic of China, and perhaps soon with Cuba--and those in which the artificial conflict of sport has itself directly generated further conflict--Central American soccer skirmishes. Sport has encouraged recognition of governments--East Germany and China--and it has encouraged social progress, if only gradually and spasmodically--South Africa[41] and the Soviet Union.[42] Policies of communication and cooperation seem preferable to those of confrontation.

The Kheel Commission, which attempted unsuccessfully to resolve the dispute between the Amateur Athletic Union and the National Collegiate Athletic Association, emphasized the importance of United States adherence to international rules in its involvement in international sports.[43] Since those international rules are becoming better articulated, better understood, and more authoritative, adherence will be simpler. In this development, the Olympic Movement is by far the leading instrumentality. The installation of Lord Killanin as President of the International Olympic Committee (IOC) has brought a growing appreciation within the Olympic Movement of the need not only for reform of the nature of the Games, but for the strengthening of commitments to an open, precedent-based process of decision-making to afford an enlarged measure of predictability to constituent federations and, most importantly, to individual teams and athletes. Especially since its 1973 Varna Congress--and no doubt haunted by remembrances of Munich terrorism--the IOC has sought to operationalize its accepted peacemaking role.[44]

Rule 3, the _Grundnorm_ of the Olympic Rules and Regulations, recites a realistic and empirically justifiable statement of organizational aims:

> . . . to promote the development of those fine physical and moral qualities which are the basis of amateur sport and to bring together the athletes of the world in a great quadrennial festival of sports thereby creating international respect and goodwill and thus helping to construct a better and more peaceful world.

The detailed Rules and Regulations define the Olympic Movement as an institution and serve externally to define more pervasive norms related to transnational athletic exchange. Without attempting to describe and analyze the legal aspects of the Movement, it suffices here to note two recent instances by which nettlesome questions of foreign affairs have been resolved by explicit procedures and decision-making under the Rules.

1. Diplomatic recognition is often a thorny problem for international non-governmental organizations.[45] China's ping-pong diplomacy presented a recent challenge to the skill of IOC decision-makers. Responding to this challenge in meticulous accordance with its Rules,[46] the IOC moved from a distinctly hostile position towards the People's Republic of China to one of gradual inclusiveness.[47] The new position has in turn engendered a pattern of invitation and response throughout the transnational sports arena.

2. Another recognition problem is that of Rhodesia, the credentials of whose athletes were rejected by the IOC at the last minute prior to the opening of the 1972 Olympic Games.[48] Debate persists whether, in protecting fundamental human rights, it is more constructive to involve or bar nationals of wayward countries. Clearly, despite the concomitant tension, the ongoing diplomatic and international organizational effort to employ sports competition as a means of elmininating state-sanctioned racial cleavage in Rhodesia and South Africa has worked better than other techniques;[49] and these efforts can be made to work without self-detriment to the competition itself so long as political pressures are either sublimated or expressed in accordance with well-articulated rules and principles, as they regrettably were not in the instance of the IOC decisions to bar Rhodesian participation in the Munich and Montreal Games. These decisions were particularly ironic because Rhodesian teams are racially mixed.[50] Moreover, in the instance of the decision to bar Rhodesia from the 1976 Games, the IOC declined to follow the recommendations of its own three-man investigatory commission on the status of the Rhodesian National Olympic Committee (RNOC).

On February 11, 1975, the IOC issued the report of the Commission (consisting of a Brazilian, a Canadian and a Pakistani), which determined that Rhodesia was a geographical and political entity and that it was therefore competent to confer citizenship and issue passports. The Commission recognized that a restrictive de facto discrimination, particularly in educational development, existed in Rhodesia, but it concluded that the constitution and the rules and practices of the RNOC were neither racially discriminatory nor violative of IOC rules. Moreover, the RNOC was deemed independent of the Rhodesian government, in accordance with Olympics Rule 26.[51] The report of the Commission seemed to confirm the commitment of the IOC to the concept of social change through inclusion, rather than exclusion.[52] Although its 1972 decision, taken in a mood of great pressure, if not coercion, seemed exceptional, the IOC nevertheless decided in May 1975 to extend that decision to the 1976 Games.

Whatever the substantive merits or deficiencies of its decisions, the IOC increasingly manifests a reliance upon prescribed procedures. In view of this evolving, lawyerly process--only suggested by these two examples-- it is not unlikely that a pattern of decision-making will develop within the Olympic Movement with some resemblance to a jurisprudence to guide future athletic change. The International Olympic Committee has become more inclined to make its decisions public and is pointedly offering guidance in shaping domestic policies and organization.[53] Increasingly, then, transnational sports competition can be expected to generate debate and inform the public of certain norms within the international legal framework that can be applied to defining United States foreign sports policy. Moreover, a deference to the value structure premised in Rule 3 of the Olympic Rules would relieve private and public policymakers alike of the kinds of political choices that have given sports organizations a bad name when they have made unpopular decisions, and which have raised the "bug-bear" of a politically polluted sports arena.

V. Conclusion

In light of the foregoing analysis, the United States Government clearly should develop a comprehensive and coherent foreign sports policy, rooted in the values and norms of the Olympic Movement. Good policy can mean an end to bad politics. Although Rules 8 and 25 of the Olympic Rules[54] as well as related injunctions may be read to discourage further involvement by the government in athletic matters, that interpretation seems inaccurate. What is important is not the quarantine of governments and politics from international athletic exchange, but the channeling of governmental decisions and politics along acknowledged lines of world ordering. Here is a golden opportunity for the United States to establish constructive policy, not simply on the basis of bureaucratic interplay, political expediency, ideological constraints and pluralistic pressures, but upon the basis of emerging global values. A foreign sports policy seems the best means of protecting individual athletes from political injury, while guiding governmental and nongovernmental decision-making along lines consistent with emerging world community norms. Policy is, after all, a kind of fiberglass pole which need not supplant the vaulter.

Footnotes

[1] P. Coubertin, Une Campagne de Vingt et Un Ans 1887–1908 90 (1908). Coubertin's statement, made during the Sorbonne Conference of November 25, 1892, not surprisingly was met by indifference and misunderstanding. See Lucas, Olympic Genesis: The Sorbonne Conferences of 1892 and 1894, 85–86 Olympic Rev. 607 (1974).

[2] See J. Meynaud, Sport et Politique (1966) [hereinafter cited as Meynaud].

[3] Note two recent statements by Lord Killanin, President of the International Olympic Committee (IOC): "It is not possible to divorce sport and politics, but it must be possible to protect sport from political exploitation. . . ." Address by Lord Killanin, Official Opening of the 75th Session of the IOC, Oct. 21, 1974, in 85–86 Olympic Rev. 572, 573 (1974); "It is inevitable that . . . sport must be affected by politics." Address by Lord Killanin, Winnipeg, Canada, Nov. 1, 1974, Id. at 579.

[4] See, e.g., 41 Sports Illustrated, Sept. 16, 1974, at 32.

[5] See, e.g., Washburn, Soviet Amateur Athlete: A Real Pro, N.Y. Times, July 21, 1974, § 5, at 2, col. 4.

[6] The rewritten eligibility rule, in contrast to its complicated predecessor, simply requires Olympic competitors never to have received "financial rewards or material benefits" from sport, and to abide by the rules of their international sports federations. 85-86 Olympic Rev. 585 (1974). See also N.Y. Times, Oct. 22, 1974, at 51, col. 8.

[7] There is considerable evidence that it does. See, e.g., Meynaud, supra note 2; H. Morton, Soviet Sport (1963); S. Sieniarski, Sport in Poland (1972). Aside from the most obvious examples of sovereign intervention in sports, evidence of the apparent importance attached to a national identification with athletic competition may be seen in the periodic contests among national proposals for the site of forthcoming Olympic Games. The time and money expended on the concomitant lobbying and public relations effort is staggering. See Washington Post, Oct. 23, 1974, § D, at 7, cols. 3, 4-5.

[8] The Department of State has convened two non-governmental conferences in order to elicit opinion on this subject--the Round-Table Conference on International Athletic Exchanges (May 22, 1972), and the Symposium on Sport and the Means of Elevating International Understanding (Dec. 4, 1973).

[9] Insofar as a foreign sports policy would reach Olympic participation, as it almost certainly would, Rule 25 of the Olympics is directly implicated:

National Olympic Committees must be completely independent and autonomous and must resist all political, religious or commercial pressure.

National Olympic Committees that do not conform to the Rules and Regulations of the International Olympic Committee forfeit their recognition and consequently their right to send participants to the Olympic Games.

Rule 8 also declares that "the Games are contests between individuals and not between countries or areas." International Olympic Committee, Olympic Rules and Regulations (1972).

[10] Public and professional opinion on this subject is ambiguous. A 1971 sampling of 44 sports administrators, government administrators, sports commentators, government observers, and sports participants revealed mixed attitudes towards expansion of the government's role in sports including federal financial support for sports and, indeed, the efficacy of a sports policy; most of those surveyed did, however, agree on the need to keep "politics" aloof from sports and to improve the program administered by the Department of State. Harris/Ragan Management Corporation, International Sports Policies for the Department of State: A Presentation of Options 25 (unpublished, Sept. 24, 1971) [hereinafter cited as Harris/Ragan Report]. Bearing in mind that this survey was taken prior to the Munich Olympic Games and the demise of plans for the Denver Winter

Games, arguably today the public would be more inclined to accept, or even call for, a more active governmental role in sports. A Harris Sports Survey taken after Munich disclosed considerable public disenchantment with the administration, and particularly with the rule enforcement of international competition, and indicated considerable public support for official protection by the government of U.S. interests in the Games. Sports Fans Assess '72 Olympics, in The Harris Survey (Oct. 5, 1972).

11 The press has frequently reported on international politics in sports. E.g., N.Y. Times, Oct. 25, 1974, at 49, col. 4; Washington Post, Oct. 30, 1974, § F, at 1, col. 8 (refusal of India to participate against South Africa in Davis Cup competition); Washington Post, Feb. 7, 1975, § A, at 14, col. 1; and 42 Sports Illustrated, Feb. 24, 1975, at 18 (refusal of India, contrary to commitment, to allow participation by South Africa and Israel in world table tennis championships held in Calcutta, together with simultaneous invitation of participation to the Palestinian Liberation Organization). Indian teams in particular appear to be "guided by the rules and regulations of the State." Washington Post, Feb. 7, 1975, § A, at 14, cols. 1, 5; Washington Post, March 20, 1975, § E, at 4, col. 5 (refusal of the Mexican Government to grant visas to South African Davis Cup tennis team to play in Mexico and directive to Mexicans not to compete with South Africans elsewhere); 42 Sports Illustrated May 12, 1975 at 15 (same, with respect to World Championship Tennis Competition in Mexico); Washington Post, May 7, 1975, § D, at 2, col. 3 (French exclusion of Rhodesian tennis team). On the politicization of the International Chess Federation see Oregonian, March 20, 1975, § A, at 10, col. 1 (on rule-changing proposals by the United States Chess Federation: "The voting Wednesday went generally by blocs, with East and West European and Arab federations siding with the Russians, and Asian and Latin American federations lining up with the United States.")

12 The IOC favors governmental assistance to amateur sport, so long as it is confined to financial and "non-political" support of programs. Lord Killanin, President of the IOC recently expressed his gratification "to see how much Governments are encouraging the development of sport in their countries and with a few exceptions they have given their support without any political ties. I cannot overemphasize the importance and desirability of Government aid, and reconfirm the dangers of Government interference of a political nature in the running of sport in any country." 84 Olympic Rev. 490 (1974). See also, Letter from Lord Killanin to President Gerald Ford, in 41 Sports Illustrated, Sept. 2, 1974, at 12.

13 See generally Weistart, Athletics, 38 Law & Contemp. Prob. (1973); Koppett, Sports and the Law: An Overview, 18 N.Y.L.F. 815 (1973); Hochberg, Second and Goal to Go: The Legislative Attack in the 92nd Congress on Sports Broadcasting Practices, 18 N.Y.L.F. 841 (1973); Samuels, Legalization of Gambling on Sports Events, 18 N.Y.L.F. 897 (1973); Carolson, The Business of Professional Sports: A Reexamination in Progress, 18 N.Y.L.F. 915 (1973).

14 Exec. Order No. 11868, 3 C.F.R. 26,225 (Supp. 1975). See Washington Post, June 20, 1975, § D, at 1, col. 1. Cf., Olympic Sports Commission Act of 1974, S. 1018, 93rd Congress, 2nd Session (1974); H. R. 15241, 93rd Congress, 2nd Session (1974).

15 For details of these allegations see Scannell, note 18 infra: Scannell, '76 Montreal Olympics Could Be Another Munich, Washington Post, Oct. 23, 1974, § D, at 1, col. 1.

16 Amateur Athletic Act of 1974, S. 3500, 93rd Congress, 2nd Session (1974) (1974). Cf. H. R. 10190, 93rd Congress, 1st Session (1973).

17 Primarily the "infuriating fratricidal feuding" between the Amateur Athletic Union (AAU) and the National Collegiate Athletic Association (NCAA), which have engaged for seventy years in jurisdictional warfare that has jeopardized both individual athletes and the representation of this country in international competition. For a succinct history of this dispute see 120 Cong. Rec. 58,780 (daily ed. May 21, 1974) (remarks of Senator Pearson). Cf. Koch, A Troubled Cartel: The NCAA, 38 Law & Contemp. Prob. 135 (1973). The probable effect of the proposed Act on this dispute has been summarized as follows:

> Ostensibly, the bill cuts the power of the AAU off at the knees by limiting the number of sports that can be controlled by a single organization to one (or at the most three when it can be demonstrated that the other two would benefit from common administration). Right now the AAU governs 11 international sports and has voting control over all 26 sports that come within the purview of the U.S. Olympic Committee.
>
> Under the terms of the bill, the status of the NCAA is unaltered except in one important respect--it cannot arbitrarily prohibit athletes from competing in open events. Such prohibitions have been the NCAA's primary weapon in its long power struggle with the AAU. 41 Sports Illustrated, July 22, 1974, at 14.

18 A proposal for structural reform of the AAU has been rejected by its leadership. The reform would entail the election of AAU directors, not at-large according to current practice, but by the individual sports committees which would be recognized by the United States Olympic Committee (USOC) independently of the AAU itself. Scannell, IOC Shambles Through the 1976 Olympic Countdown, Washington Post, Oct. 24, 1974, § D, at 1, col. 1.

19 E.g., S. 3273, 93rd Congress, 2nd Session (1974).

20 IOC President, Lord Killanin, publicly remarked that "the legislation in the Tunney Act--I have heard different versions--is implemented with a

board of five people, then the U.S. would risk putting itself not only out of the Olympic Movement but also out of the international federations. There is much to be done in this country to improve sport and develop sport. Most of us are fed up reading about rows between the AAU and NCAA. The strong likelihood of a presidential commission on sport is a healthy sign." Washington Post, Feb. 23, 1974, § C, at 1, col. 5; in a later letter to President Ford, Lord Killanin wrote that "S-3500 would violate the I.O.C. rules." 41 Sports Illustrated, Sept. 2, 1974, at 12.

21 See note 9 supra. However, the chartering of the United States Olympic Committee evidences governmental intervention which, though minimal, has been acceptable to the IOC. Because of its acceptance of such governmental intervention in national committees, the IOC may be stopped from challenge, under the Olympic Rules, of greater United States legal control over the operations and structure of the USOC.

22 379 F. Supp. 966 (C.D. Cal. 1974).

23 15 U.S.C. §§ 1, 2 (1971).

24 See transcript of the speech delivered by Alan A. Reich, Deputy Assistant Secretary of State for Educational and Cultural Affairs, before the Central Assembly of International Sports Federations, in 119 Cong. Rec. 95 (daily ed. June 19, 1973); remarks of Walter Boehm, in R. Singer, Multidisciplinary Symposium on Sport and the Means of Furthering Mutual International Understanding (U.S. Dept. of State, Bureau of Educational and Cultural Affairs, Dec. 4, 1973) (1974).

25 U.S. Const., art. II, §§ 1-3.

26 United States v. Curtiss-Wright Export Corp., 299 U.S. 304 (1936).

27 See note 24 supra.

28 See Reich, New Role for Associations in Promoting World Understanding, Assn. Management, Feb. 1973, at 32.

29 Harris/Ragan Report, supra note 10, at 2.

30 Identified as these:

Sports are said to have negligible impact on international relations; sports are believed to be too ephemeral; sports apparently would lose their purity if tied more closely to U.S. international interests; sports are thought to appeal generally to baser tastes . . . . Id.

31 Harris/Ragan Report, supra note 10, at 7.

[32] Id. at 25-26. Criteria for judging the efficacy of a United States foreign sports effort under the auspices of the State Department will vary according to the intensity of governmental involvement. Low-level policies will be concerned with more or less immediate returns on each dollar invested. For example: what works at a clinic in a particular country? What doesn't? Should we have sent the Kansas basketball coach to Mauretania after his visit in Dakar? If the government sees itself as a facilitator, the exposure which the United States receives and the contacts which the activity generates will be critical at this low level of policy. If, however, the government's role extends to that of a promoter or programmer, then the success of its athletes in competition abroad, the degree to which a foreign country adopts a newly introduced American sport, or the accomplishment of some other major objective, will dominate our evaluation of governmental performance.

[33] Id. at 28.

[34] U. S. Dept. of State, Bureau of Educational and Cultural Affairs, the CU Program Concept (Oct. 1, 1973).

[35] See, e.g., U.S. Dept. of State, Report of Round-Table Conference on International Athletic Exchanges 4 (May 22, 1973) (reference to a successful program of the Partners of the Americas). See Moes, Inter-American Program: Building Good Sportsmen, Washington Post, Oct. 14, 1972, § D, at 14, col. 5.

[36] The relevant socio-psychological and philosophical literature is voluminous. See, e.g., Slusher, Sport: A Philosophical Perspective, 38 Law & Contemp. Prob. 129 (1973); Nafziger, The Regulation of Transnational Sports Competition: Down from Mount Olympus, 5 Vand. J. Transnat'l. L. 180, 181 nn.3-4, 182 nn.6-8, 183 n. 10 (1971).

[37] For instance, note the summary of responses from United States Embassies as to national athletic interests in respect of United States assistance. Report of Round-Table Conference, supra note 35, at B1.

[38] See, e.g., Johnson, Faces on a New China Scroll, 39 Sports Illustrated, Sept. 24, 1973, at 86; Underwood, And the Yu-I Flowed Like Wine, 42 Sports Illustrated, June 2, 1975, at 24.

[39] See Nafziger, supra note 36, at 205.

[40] See Washington Post, May 12, 1974, § D, at 10, col. 1.

[41] See, e.g., Washington Post, Oct. 29, 1974, § A, at 19, col. 1.

42 "There are even reports from diplomatic sources in Geneva that the Soviet Union has softened its stand on human freedom issues at the European security conference to demonstrate there will be freedom of movement for everyone at the Olympics, should it be awarded them." N.Y. Times, Oct. 20, 1974, § 5, at 3, col. 5.

43 See S. Rep. No. 93-380, 93rd Congress, 1st Session (1973).

44 See, for example, the recent statement of Lord Killanin, President of the IOC, that, "Whilst the motto of the IOC is 'Citius, Altius, Fortius', there is no doubt that the demonstration of goodwill shown at the Varna Congress and subsequently confirms that there is a subsidiary motto--'Sport for a World of Peace,'" 84 Olympic Rev. 490 (1974).

45 Newly adopted Olympic Rule 25 provides that "[r]ecognition of an NOC [National Olympic Committee] in a country does not imply political recognition of that country. Recognition of an NOC is dependent on that country having enjoyed a stable government for a reasonable period of time."

46 See Closing Speech of Lord Killanin, 1973 Olympic Congress in Varna, Bulgaria, in 72-73 Olympic Rev. 471, 473 (1973).

47 See, e.g., Washington Post, Feb. 15, 1974, § D, at 8 (initial exclusion of the People's Republic of China by the International Amateur Athletic Federation (IAAF) from track-and-field participation in the 1974 Asian Games Games); Washington Post, June 12, 1974, § D, at 6, col. 1 (vote by the International Football Federation (FIFA) against Chinese membership); 41 Sports Illustrated, Oct. 21, 1974, at 18 (membership vote by the International Volleyball Federation to replace Taiwan by the People's Republic of China). The evolution of the People's Republic of China's readmission into the global sports arena is fascinating. In 1958, the People's Republic withdrew from all international athletic federations. With the exception of a few exhibition tours, principally of its table tennis team, China was isolated from transnational competition until 1974. The 1974 Asian Games provided a major boost to renewed involvement by the People's Republic in transnational competition. An excellent account of the politics involved in the invitation to the People's Republic of China appears in Putnam, A Great Plung Forward for China, 41 Sports Illustrated, Sept. 16, 1974, at 33:

> [w]hen the Iranians were awarded the Asian Games for 1974, they made it clear that they wanted the People's Republic, not Taiwan, to represent China. By an overwhelming margin, the Asian Games Federation agreed, threw out the Taiwanese and invited the mainlanders to replace them. The International Olympic Committee, which has a long history of supporting Chiang Kai-Shek at the expense of all the Chinese athletes who do not live on his island, threatened to withdraw its sanction for the Asian Games. Numerous federations sait they would boycott the Games and the generalissimo sulked.

Undaunted by the threats, the Iranians began quiet negotiations with IOC members, who finally agreed to approve the
Games if the federations of the various sports would go along
with the new China policy. After more negotiations, the federations slowly began unloading Taiwan to make room for the
People's Republic. FINA, the federation that controls swimming, diving and water polo, proved the toughest group to
crack. The mainland Chinese applied for membership, but
stipulated that if Taiwan was not ousted from FINA, the federation could forget their application. By a two-vote margin,
the 30 members of FINA's executive committee voted to forget
it. Following 11th hour negotiations with FINA President Dr.
Harold Henning of the United States, the Chinese dropped the
offending clause from their application, and the day before the
Asian Games opened approval was granted for them to participate in the water-sports events as nonmembers.

In its statement on the matter, which foreshadowed its newly formulated
position toward the People's Republic of China, the IOC stated that it
". . .deplore[d] the fact that the Asian Games Federation ha[d] decided
not to invite one of the recognized NOC's, which was a member of the
Asian Games Federation."

Nevertheless, noting precedent, and "[i]n view of these facts, it has been
decided unanimously that in the interests of the development of sport in
Asia, the IOC should continue to give its recognition and patronage to the
Asian Games Federation, which automatically goes to the Games." 76-77
Olympic Rev. 103 (1974).

[48]
See Nafziger, On the Rules of the Games, 70-71 Olympic Rev. 449, 451
(1973). More recently, the IOC voted to exclude Rhodesia from the 1976
Games. U.S. Press Release, WS/715, at 3 (June 20, 1975) (noting approval of the decision by the Security Council Committee on Sanctions
against Southern Rhodesia).

[49]
See Nafziger, supra note 36, at 207. For a more detailed history and
analysis of the interrelationship between sport and apartheid in South
Africa see Lapchick, South Africa's Use of Sport in Foreign Policy and
the International Response, March 23, 1974 (unpublished paper presented
at the 15th Annual Convention, International Studies Association). Note
in particular the concluding paragraph of that paper: "As long as this is
true, South Africa's international critics will continue to attack the government through the field of sports. The essence of that attack was summed up in an editorial in the Johannesburg Sunday Times on May 31, 1970,
shortly after the IOC decision:

South Africa's critics have simply discovered that sport is
the most useful weapon they have yet found with which to beat us
and while it is the sportsmen who are the sacrificial victims--
they are being ostracized and deprived of the right to participate
in world sport--the main target of attack is the racial policy of

South Africa, or, to put it more precisely, the racial policy of the Nationalist Party."

[50] In an exercise of reverse ping-pong diplomacy, as indicated, supra note 11, India recently refused to allow teams from Israel and South Africa to compete in the 1975 World Table-Tennis Championships. Ironically, the South African team was racially mixed. Washington Post, Feb. 7, 1975, § A, at 14, col. 1.

[51] See note 9 supra; Excelsior (Mexico City), Feb. 12, 1975, at 7, col. 1.

[52] See the recent statements of Lord Killanin, antagonistic toward national policies of boycott and exclusion, supra note 3, at 580. See N.Y. Times, Oct. 22, 1974, at 51, col. 1.

[53] Note, for example, the discussion in note 20 supra.

[54] See note 9 supra.

Section 5

SPORT COMMUNICATION FOR

DEVELOPMENT AND EDUCATION

Introduction

In the arena of international sport competition, the fact that athletes from the People's Republic of China are unable to compete in the Olympic Games has given rise to the "China (Peking) Question," a sobriquet coined by the International Olympic Committee. The National Olympic Committee to serve all Chinese athletes, as recognized by the I.O.C., is resident in Taiwan and is known as the Republic of China Olympic Committee. The All-China Sports Federation serves the needs of all Chinese athletes, but itself is not recognized by the I.O.C.

Sport communication is a force to be developed. People have little difficulty in appreciating and acknowledging the non-verbal components, but the verbal interactive elements need to be explored further. For example, the Centre for International Sport Studies (CISS) reports that it has received requests from different parts of the non-English speaking world to develop special courses "built around sports subjects and covering the special registers of sport terminology." The easy manner in which politicians apply sport terminology to their polemics might be of interest here, but more significant than this facetious observation is the role that sport is made to play in propaganda. Goodhart and Chattaway (1968) cite a report from Pravda in 1958 which announced: "A successful trip by the sportsmen of the U.S.S.R. or the People's Democratic countries is an excellent vehicle of propaganda in capitalist countries. The success of our sportsmen abroad helps in the work of our foreign diplomatic missions and of our trade delegations." (p. 17). Sport communication is an open construct, the nature of which is only just being explored and developed for its potential for international understanding.

Sport can be seen as a form of conflict resolution, a "blowing off of steam", an outlet for aggressive impulses, a diversion of man's inherent violent tendencies into the more peaceful and socially acceptable arena of sports. Konrad Lorenz in his work On Aggression argues for this theory.

The theory of functionalism is very much the guiding philosophy behind the cultural programs of the U.S. State Department. Functionalism postulates a basic and growing interdependence in the world. The form of contact between nations is seen as being more important than their governmental structures. The interaction between hundreds of organizations, groups and individuals in areas of "low politics" such as cultural affairs, business and sports, creates thousands of cross-cultural, transnational linkages between towns, cities, professional groups, labor unions, universities, business firms, sport federations and individuals. Loyalties and dependence on a state theoretically have diminished. Dependence on a multiplicity of organizations for the satisfaction of daily needs is increased. Theoretically, then, economic, cultural and physical interdependence result in such a widespread web of contacts between different societies that the resort to physical violence decreases. War becomes too costly for the individual units, i.e., dysfunctional. Such is the theory: "International competition between amateur athletes contributes to international peace and understanding", according to the Amateur Athletic Act of the AAU (USA) of 1973.

The idea of furthering world peace was one of the underlying motives of Baron Pierre de Coubertin's plan for reviving the Olympics. Athletic contests would become the free trade of the future.

> Should this institution prosper...it may be a potent if indirect factor in securing universal peace. Wars break out because nations misunderstand each other. We shall not have peace until the prejudices which not separate the different races shall have been outlived. To attain this end, what better means than to bring the youth of countries periodically together for amicable trials of muscular strength and agility? The Olympic Games with the Ancients controlled athletics and promoted peace. Is it not visionary to look to them for similar benefactions in the future? (cited in Richard Mandell, The First Olympics, p. 72.)

This idea of using sports as a diplomatic tool has been evident in the U.S. State Department. Since 1952, the Department has sent over 120 teams and 540 coaches abroad in various exchange programs in an effort to bring people together and thereby further international understanding. Alan Reich, Deputy Assistant Secretary for Educational and Cultural Affairs has stated: "Diplomacy has gone public...People to people communication has become a dominant force in the international relations throughout the world." Sports exchanges are seen as enhancing the understanding of another nation's values and culture. Sports provide a way for "friendly give and take interchange" which can lead to other types of friendly relations. "A sense of commonness of interest shared with other peoples across political boundaries" is conveyed by such sports events. Over 10,000 Americans are annually involved in international sports competitions, clinics, tournaments, meets and exhibitions.

> When people to people bonds and communications networks are more fully developed, there will be a greater readiness to communicate, to seek accommodation, to negotiate. The likelihood of international confrontation will diminish and prospects for peaceful solutions will be enhanced. (Congressional Record, June 19, 1973.)

Whether sports events on an international level serve to further understanding and reduce conflict has never been adequately studied. Sports can create conflict as well as dissipate it, but they may also rechannel conflict from higher levels of confrontation in politics and armaments, to playing fields, where it can be better regulated and controlled. More study is needed to establish whether this is the case. As with other transnational processes, sport has only come in for significant academic attention since the technological revolution in communications and transportation following World

War II. Although, as has been demonstrated, sport was an organized international process well before the contemporary era, it is only since about 1960 that it has been considered as such. Both the social science of sport and sport medicine have been developing with greater interest and concentration since 1960. However, the last twenty years has shown that not enough is known about the social dynamics of sport. As a consequence of this ignorance, several colleges and universities around the world have concentrated educational efforts towards the better understanding of sport.

The first four sections of this anthology, Sport and International Relations, have been attempts to define "the state of the art." Now we will take a look at approaches to future study. In the first place, the question of "sport for all" will be examined. To what extent are states interested in sport as a means of physical education as well as a tool in national policy?

A corollary issue to the "sport for all" question involves some of the political considerations of preceding sections, is "sport for all" still beneficial if used for the purposes of inculcating the masses with state propaganda? Can mass sport become a tool of repression when used to control the leisure life of people whose regular pursuits are already under government (or corporate) control? What about dual sport systems - those where mass sport is merely a basis for culling élite athletes from the populace? Sport itself may be a right, but the standard of living to be won through athletic endeavor can remain a privilege granted only to the sporting elite. The extent of "sport for all" may, in this context, vary in qualitative as well as quantitative terms from state to state.

The issue becomes especially important as the United States looks to East German gold medals and wonders if its own training methods are antiquated. Is "Socialist" sport really "sport for all?" Should national training centers be created in the United States and elsewhere in order to create international champions? Is this issue of such importance that federal money be allocated for such centers? Instead of "sport for all," will we take money from all in order to train an athletic élite?

Sport can also be used as a cohesive agent. It can become a unifying agent for many of those societies with a multiplicity of languages, tribal factions and ethnic groups. Many African heads of state place an importance on attending national and regional sports events as a means of building adhesion in the state system. President Sekou Toure of Guinea, President Houphouet-Bolgny of the Ivory Coast and President Leopold Sedar Senghor were all enthusiastic sports fans.

Along with political education, other problems are introduced here. Commercialization is another multinational concern which is intrinsic to modern sport. How does it affect the conduct of sport? How does it influence the politics of sport? Can sport remain an educational process when material enrichment becomes the prime result of sport achievement? Is there still any distinction between "amateur" and "professional?" Coubertin felt that ancient sport declined when it became specialized and profitable. Has the health process been hurt by concentration in specific sports? If the enlargement of a tennis player's forearm or of a swimmer's shoulders indicate specialization, do they also show deformity or portend general decay? If sport is supposed to be a process which teaches maturity and basic social value to participants, why is it that many of the most accomplished athletes seem to care for nothing except for the money they make, or for the number of products they can endorse? Or are these basic social values? If not, we return to the basic question of whether or not athletic achievement really means anything at all. Perhaps the educational value of sport is itself a myth. Or perhaps there is a need for better use of sport, through sport academies which will use sport as it can be used.

And what of the spectator? The ideology of sport, including the Olympic myth, stresses the direct participant in sport action. There is little attention paid to fans except in terms of whether or not spectating, like participating, can serve to release pent-up aggression (or rather, whether it can focus it at a specific time and place). Since spectators are the most numerous actors in the sport process, since they are the targets of state sport propaganda and the source of funds which guarantee Olympic prosperity, should not consideration of their role be expanded to include the political effects of mass sport spectating, as well as the organization of mass leisure? It should be remembered that, among other things, sport supplemented religion as an American national pastime. Sunday baseball put an end to Sabbath blue laws in many states. The Argentine government was so concerned with fan violence that, at one time, all soccer matches were scheduled for 7:00 A.M. Several countries have considered banning "instant reply" in order to prevent riots from developing after bad calls by referees.

Clearly, the issues raised by the study of sport must be considered in their larger cultural context. Does sport have a greater educational role than, say, dance or meditation? Why do sport ideologists see this series of competitive activities as special? Perhaps, rather than altering the political use of sport, sport itself should be de-emphasized. Perhaps sport only serves a useful social role for certain individuals whose particular characteristics are suited to it. If so, then the educational benefits of everything from knitting to camping should be examined in order to determine their social values. If different leisure pursuits help different people, should they be encouraged as much as sport is now?

These issues can only be dealt with if investigators of sport know a great deal more about the societies they are concerned with than they do about the rules of the games they like to play. In the future, if "sport studies" are to earn academic respect, researchers will have to be acquainted with a range of cross-disciplinary concerns. Sport scholars must learn to deal with sport as a political, cultural, economic, and social process. Perhaps the understanding of the role of sport in society will only come after a new generation of researchers are trained in a range of subjects heretofore ignored in the simple concentration on one physical category of social activity.

In Section 5 commentary is made on the efforts of some nations to organize the role of sport on a general health-participatory level. One model, "Sport for All" is tested empirically, and draws attention to difficulties and deficiencies encountered in other spheres of international communication through sport. In the opening reading, Lowe provides a brief examination of differing national models of participatory sport--Sport for All; Participaction; Trimm dich durch Sport--and future directions and developments in spectator sport. An analysis of leisure models and how sport is perceived as a functional subsystem of leisure is offered, and future values attaching to competition are explored.

In the presentation, "Sport for All," Jackson offers an empirical test of national and international perceptions of "Sport for All." He gives a historical overview of the inception of the construct and its permeation throughout nations, cites the interplay between politics and "Sport for All," and explores this movement in both Western and Eastern European nations. The Council of Europe cited significant dangers in "Sport for All" as being commercialization, regimentation and productivism. These challenges are discussed. For Ostermann, the separate development of sport facilities and education and participation in West and East Germany is not only rooted in the different ideologies that they adopted, but also on different patterns of social behavior and intercourse based on broad cultural changes and new culture perspectives in Europe since World War II. East Germany instituted compulsory training in athletics and developed means of involvement in sport in the entire educational system so that sport and athletics came to play a basic function in the cultural development of East Germany. Extensive sport facilities were of course also developed in West Germany and the population was offered ample opportunity to participate in sport and athletics. But this effort was not as comprehensively developed and implemented in the cultural matrix of West Germany. In West Germany involvement in sport and athletics plays essentially a more professional social role on a voluntary basis on the part of the public.

Kanin draws a distinction between intergovernmental organizations (I.G.O.) and transnational organizations (T.N.O.). The Keohane/Nye model of transnational politics if introduced and how this model can be applied to cultural exchange is explored. Sport is a form of cultural exchange which is particularly vulnerable to political interaction, and this tests the Keohane/Nye model. An analysis of how the International Olympic Committee, the International Sports Federation and similar groups interrelate to function as transnational organizations is offered to show that political content is explained within a conceptual framework relating political sport to public diplomacy.

The two contributions on the concept of "nation-building," presented by Uwechue and Sie respectively, are parallel in their thesis, but point to differing cultural perspectives, responses to colonialism, and subsequent outcomes. Independence is a dominant theme in Uwechue's contribution, and this reading should be studied alongside the Shaws' presentation "Sport as Transnational Politics: A Preliminary Analysis of Africa," in Section 4. National development is the dominant theme of the Sie contribution with emphasis on the development of national identity through sport.

The contribution by Haag traces the development of sport studies as a function of an increasing international awareness of sport in society. He defines the international role of sport and focuses on efforts by educators and other professionals to bring a better understanding to colleges and universities by reference to leading conferences of international value. Sport education and sport sciences are highlighted through the categorization of available texts. The concluding contribution, "Educational Directives for International Sport Studies" complements the Haag statement and gives background on the interface between culture and politics (recall the question raised in the Introduction to Section 1). The way in which sport meshes with each component is suggested through a discussion of "symbol and prestige," and the concept of a "sport academy" is introduced and several examples given. A precipitating force in the United States would be the President's Commission on Olympic Sports. Educational forces are at work in the American Youth Sports Center (U. of Illinois), and the United States Sports Academy (U. of South Alabama), and the Center for International Sport Studies (University of Sussex).

When Huizinga wrote of the sterility of sport forty years ago, he was asserting this judgment in light of his prediction that government control of sport would reduce it of all cultural components which are ascribed to it through its derivation from play. Governments, he suggests, make sport too serious, thereby robbing it of potential "culture-creating activity." The root cause, in Huizinga's opinion, is overemphasis of the principles of agonism. In the same breath, so to speak, he indicates that communications--dramatically expanded over the past forty years--may be the saving function. In this manner, Huizinga predicted the potential force of sport communication.

Sport Beyond The Age Of

High Mass Consumption

Benjamin Lowe

To ensure success the Native should sport.
From <u>Murphy</u>, by Samuel Beckett

Introduction

In 1956 the Ad Hoc Committee on the Triple Revolution presented the
argument that, although there was a fundamental mutually reinforcing interrelationship between the Cybernation, the Weaponry, and the Human Rights
Revolutions, the primary moment of concern rested with the Cybernation
Revolution. While the argument of the Committee centered on the effects of
the Cybernation Revolution in terms of the production and consumption of
material resources, the main questions raised by the Cybernation Revolution redirect the emphasis to <u>social</u> resources. This is best illustrated by
quoting the question asked by the Ad Hoc Committee: "What is man's role
when he is not dependent upon his own activities for the material basis of his
life?"--a question which, clearly enough, cannot be answered in material
terms.

It is tempting to equate the Cybernation Revolution with Rostow's (1961)
"age of high mass consumption," except that Rostow does not dwell upon the
dubious benefits of computerization. But, whatever the similarities of the
two perspectives, the questions remain the same for the period beyond, a
time we can loosely call "the future."

Except during periods of war and revolution, social change takes place
at a comprehensible pace for most people. The mechanisms of social insti-
tutions--and sport can be so classified--are cumbersome and unwieldly, and,
for change to be incurred, long hours of planning and projection must be encountered not without equal time having been spent on assessing progress to
date. This theorem applies equally for both material and social change.
Thus Rostow and other economists may estimate conditions for the future as
a balance of production and consumption, but they must rely on social and behavioral scientists for estimates of the human response to those conditions.

First published in <u>Society and Leisure,</u> 7(4):155-165, 1975.

This becomes no more significantly apparent than in the prediction of man's future in leisure.[1]

The question is moot whether man will be beyond devoting his time to the production and consumption of material goods in the future, but whether he will employ some of his time in sports pursuits as active release for his energies can be taken for granted. What needs to be examined is whether these forms of sport pursuit will change and take new forms or remain much as we know them today. Some would argue that changes in patterns of sports involvement depend on a vicissitudinous value system.

Sport and Value

The relativity of values across cultures is as diverse as interpretations given to the term "sport" by different nationalities. Similarly, scales of values fluctuate in their relative valencies between nations to much the same degree that sport assumes levels of significance (and therefore, value) within these nations. Those nations which historically set "leisure" high in the scale of values have come to realize, from the unilateral pursuit of that objective, that a very real and pragmatic reassessment of the use of time imposes a reflection on that original value-scale. Thus, the traditional view of the nobility of physical effort in work becomes reinterpreted in the language of the leisure age as the gracious pursuit of physical activity for aesthetic experience. What was formerly regarded as trivial and time-wasting becomes valuable and time-worthy. This latter argument for the constructive and worthy use of time in leisure through sports owes its foundation to the origins of sport in modern society, devised in part by the necessity of a leisure-class to find full and fruitful use merely for the "passage" of time. To validate this argument beyond the age of mass consumption involves a re-education of the masses towards a value emphasis held traditionally by the classes.

Sport as Value

Traditionally, sport has been held in esteem for military preparation, for national health and fitness purposes, as a medium for the inculcation and transmission of cultural norms (ideal behavior patterns and beliefs), as a psychological counterbalance to periods of "book-learning" throughout the history of education, and, in more recent collegiate history, as a catalytic element in bonding the community. There is no reason to doubt that some of these values attaching to sport will prevail beyond the age of mass consumption, but equally, there will be reemphasis on the valencies of the particular values, just as it is fairly well predictable that some of those mentioned will no longer be held. In an age when sophisticated communications transcend all possibilities for warmaking, a militaristic interpretation of sport might be sustained in the mythic superstructure of society (culture) and thus still be positively valued, but within the qualifications and limitations imposed on all values in mythology.

The interpretation of the term "sport" in Europe takes on a more diverse meaning than is typically held in North America. The participatory and recreational discussion epitomized in "sports club" life can be found in ethnic pockets of America and Canada, but more importantly, "sport" serves to mean "fitness for life." Hence, the belief held by Europeans that sport beyond the age of mass consumption must be more spontaneously participatory is given substance in their efforts to realize the objectives underlying the slogans "Sport for All" and "Trimm Dich Durch Sport."[2] In Canada, this movement is labelled "Participaction," the code word for "the Canadian movement for personal fitness."[3] The parallel concern of the United States is embodied in the concept of "lifetime sports," but the emphasis is obliquely related and incipiently leisure- or recreation-directed rather than fitness- or health-sponsored. Two unique developments in the United States, which come close to the "Sport for All" idea, are "Sports for the People" and the Esalen Sports Program. The growth of the "sports-club" cult in the United States is seen as a manifestation of exigencies for high level sports performance within the university, but extraneous of Intercollegiate Athletics. This reflection of increased initiatives towards more active participation in sports need not necessarily reduce (or replace) the fervor held by large crowds for attendance at grand sports spectacles. Trends in stadium construction in recent years suggest no slackening of interest in the major league sports.

Hitherto not considered, sport as the medium for the transmission of values (sport as education), yet traditionally seen as the vehicle for inculcating the standard of ideals associated with the Nineteenth Century, developments in sport reflect more basic values than conceptual abstractions. Typically, and most forcefully demonstrated, are latter-day innovations of competitive pursuits employing competition between man's ingenuity and the fickle forces of nature. These directions are substantively locked into changing value-orientations, such as environment-consciousness and pollution abatement. Consciousness III, if it prevails beyond the age of mass consumption, mitigates against further developments in motorized sports (or those remaining being fitted with anti-pollution devices), while sponsoring the creation of such pursuits as wind-surfing, ice-boating, land-sailing, wind-sailing and rapids-skiing with pontoons on the feet. The increasing popularity of such sports as white-water canoeing and sculling, sailing, crew, archery, cycling and the like, and a continued excitement generated by membership in small group sports (football, soccer, baseball, etc.), realigns or redefines the education that sport provides. Sky-diving must go the way of water-skiing, since the cost to the environment by aircraft and motorboat emission is levied against the "harmlessness" of such events.

Speaking of leisure in the future, Kaplan states: "...the new leisure, because it is more than a recuperation from work, can become a potential source of the deepest values..." (p. 297). Marxists would argue that the very conceptual use of the term "leisure" is outdated and indeed that "recuperation from work" is negatively inspired. Their idea of the expression of the "deepest values" attaching to sport in leisure rests with a dialectic interpretation of sport as "reproduction."[4] Sport as "reproduction" transcends all other value-attachments, taking it out of the realm of justification for militaristic health and fitness, and educative purposes, or even ideological purposes.

Pursuing Kaplan's thought on an occidental plane, and with sport as the focus of attention within leisure, trends indicate that one of man's most fundamental values, that of beauty, is attaching to sport. The aesthetics of sport promise to be better understood in the future. At present, this is a misty area of inquiry, necessarily so due to the fact that there is a lack of informed opinion on the subject.[5] When there is a more substantive comprehension of the aesthetics of sport, there will be an enrichment of man's total experience in sports endeavor, both from a participatory as well as a spectating viewpoint.

Sport and Role

Kenyon's (1969) paradigm of sport involvement is useful as a conceptual schema delineating what is meant by role in relation to sport. The paradigm distinguishes between primary and secondary levels of involvement, the former category being essentially and exclusively the domain of the athlete, whereas secondary involvement can mean (i) attendance at a sport event (direct consumption); (ii) watching sport on television and reading about sport in the newspaper (indirect consumption); and (iii) coaching and managerial (leadership) roles.

Participation

The position which an athlete holds in the realm of sport will depend as much on the role he sees himself playing as upon the value structure to which he attaches. Society, or that fickle segment of it which identifies itself as "the fancy" (fans), will continue to place its demands on him and influence his role accordingly, particularly in the professional (league) ranks or "haute competition" (high level competition). The blending of the professional ranks and high level competition describes the setting of "open" sport, and it is more appropriate in non-league situations (tennis, skiing, swimming, etc.). League performance, the "spectacle" of sport, is its own reward for the athlete, and the win-loss record is compensated in the economics of the game (championship winners get bonus paychecks). The Olympic athlete spurns financial reward today in preference for social reward (prestige) which will find its own fiscal watermark (job security) later in life.

A return to the original concept of amateur is highly likely in sport by those who seek high level performance for its own sake. For those athletes, sport will be its own reward in aesthetic experience. The extrinsic (trophy) trappings of heights, weights, distances and times (records) and scoring (win-loss), and the intrinsic subtleties associated with amassing social capital, are extraneous to the experience when sport is an art and the athlete styles himself an artist.

Spectating

The spectator of the future can be seen as a better educated man than heretofore. The mystery of "crowd contact", the need to be among others in an essentially non-threatening group experience, may never be properly understood, and this should hold true in spite of the educational progress assigned to the typical person who seeks sports events as his mode of satisfying such a "need." <u>Sport education</u>, a programmatic concept derived out of physical education, serves the purpose of educating the spectator as much as facilitating sports participation. The latter is traditional, the former innovative.

But what of the stadia in which the educated spectator will witness sports competition? The development and design of new stadia provide for a multiplicity of visual and auditory stimulations. The suspension of huge television screens over the domed playing area promises intensity-focused instant replays of the more spectacular highlights of the game. Eighty foot high computerized scoreboards promise a circus display of festival pyrotechnics recording the "great play", and reinforcing the lightness of spirit attaching to the true experience of sports action perceived.

Trends in stadium construction are geared towards a more total life experience. The stadium becomes increasingly a part of the grander metropolitan plan encompassing a theater, a convention center, an art gallery, and a pedestrian shopping mall, as part of the revitalization of a formerly decayed city center reborn in urban regeneration. The deeper cultural embodiment of sport thus becomes manifest, and the closer relationship of sport and the arts finds a realization to be taken for granted in the future.

Concluding Notes

It serves the purpose of this essay, in the concluding notes, to cite Kaplan (1960) once again. Here, Kaplan is quoted for his observations on leisure (free-time), and several of the ideas presented in this essay are tested against "models" he has drawn. Firstly, his "essential elements of leisure" are presented, and latterly his "three issues" in the future of free-time. The only concern registered here is that "sport", even in its widest interpretations of the term, does not account for all free-time.

Essential Elements of Leisure

Kaplan (1960) states:

> The essential elements of leisure, as we shall interpret it, are (a) an antithesis to "work" as an economic function, (b) a pleasant expectation and recollection, (c) a minimum of involuntary social-role obligations, (d) a psychological perception of freedom, (e) a close relation to values of the culture, (f) the inclusion of an entire range from inconsequence and insignificance to weightiness and importance, and (g) often, but not necessarily, an activity characterized by the element of play. (p. 22).

In (a) the economic function of work is crucial in the realignment of concepts structuring time-passage. Whether sport is seen as "production" or "reproduction" hinges on the cultural heritage providing the initial dimensions of perspective. It is not too far-fetched to envision "sport", "participaction", "trimm", and "fitness" taking the primary role of work in substantiation of (as well as a substitution for) the economic wealth of all citizens in society. Certainly, if space travel becomes commonplace in the future, the "work" of sport/fitness guarantees the wealth (economics) of personal health.

The pleasant expectations and recollections (b) of sport, by our present-day value system, goes without saying. The pain of effort is recalled as the joy of effort, and the spectacular play relived in imagination excites in the retelling. Social-role obligations (c), in satisfying demands placed on non-voluntary sports participation and spectating, restate what is, and what is not, leisure. Recuperation or rehabilitation are not currently regarded as leisure, but the restatement of prerogatives demanding physical and psychological output by the body could lead to redefinition in the future.

Pursuing the foregoing argument, the perception of freedom (d), will be exclusive of sport from any role standpoint, as will the relation to values (e), except for the limitations and possibilities expressed earlier under "Sport and Value."

Finally, with the passage of time, sport becomes of more consequence and significance (f) in the greater leisure spectrum. This holds true regardless of a Utopian or an Orwellian turn of events in the future. And, while ever play is an element of the culture (g), the greater emphasis on sport-role must perforce be Utopian.

Three Issues in the Future of Free-time

Kaplan asks:

1. To what extent do persons relate themselves to other persons as values, as distinct from interests held in common with other persons?

2. To what degree do they require activities that are fixed by rules and well-ordered traditions, as distinct from creative or relatively free activities?

3. To what degree do they seek to go to the world for direct and new experiences, as distinct from leisure experiences in which the world is brought to them? (p. 25).

Regarding "persons as values" focuses rather abruptly on the issue of competition in sport in the future. An implicit philosophy of excellence mitigates for high level competition, and the message that the future holds for consideration must be that the value of competition be a common interest subservient to the values held for other persons. As for watching others engaged in competition, this should become less partisan. Hence, the real existence of fair play (the embodiment of sportsmanship) comes to be taken for granted.

The rule-boundedness of sport characterizes its reality, and people will recognize this or forfeit sport to a large degree. Such traditions as scorekeeping need not necessarily persist, logically making record-breaking irrelevant, but some alternatives would have to be found to compensate for box scores statistics upon which those who earn their living by sport come to depend as a measure of their worth. Federal or municipal sponsors of sport would be as dependent as are the owners of today. High level competition in sport is creative and will continue to be; the relative freedom prevailing in mass sport is not at odds with rule-boundedness.

The polarity provided by "going to the world" and "having the world brought in" touches upon the difference between participating and spectating. Furthermore, this polarity reflects the trend hinted earlier which lends some credence to the search for new experience through sport created in counterthrust to the limitations imposed by consideration for ecological concern. If the media is seen as a force in bringing the world of sport in, then it can also be seen as a motivating force for the populace to be stimulated to go out and try some of what it sees.

In Reflection

Revolutions come and go, their impacts reflected only in the amount of social change they effect, measured in short-term or long-term consequences. Man's kinetic impulses seek outlet on more consistent and persistent levels than his creative powers can match. Were it not so, sport would be a transient idea, culturally recorded as having taken place only in a given time and place. The cycles of time since the earliest recorded games of Babylon, Hellas and China suggest a counter-argument to the concept of transience. Equally, there are "lost" games, evidence of which is seen in courtyard paving stones of Minoan palaces, and of which the artifacts alone do not relate how they were used: similarly, there will be in the future many "found" games, new discoveries and innovations in game playing developing along with the progress of man. The people of the future will be no less resourceful than those of the past in adapting games to sport—presuming what is meant by sport today does not undergo the same transfiguration of meaning that it has undergone over the past few centuries.

Footnotes

[1] See "Leisure and Recreation Futures: Life Styles Analysis." Volume 3 of Opportunities in the Leisure Industry. Kansas City: Midwest Research Institute, 1972.

[2] More information on these movements can be obtained from: Clearing House, rue des Minimes 21, B-1000 Bruxelles, Belgium.

[3] Further details can be obtained from: Sport Participation Canada, P.O. Box 1148, Montreal 101, Quebec.

[4]
The highest ideals (values) of Marxist thought attach to work, labor or "production." The interpretation of sport as "reproduction" places it in the highest category of value, and thus of human inspiration and aspiration, according to Reiner Bussek and the sport theorists of the University of Hamburg. See also, Niwa, T., "The Function of Sport in Society Today," International Review of Sport Sociology, 8(1):53-68, 1973.

[5]
By virtue of (i) the complex relationship between (and separating) subjective and objective aesthetic perceptions, (ii) a traditionalist philosophic approach, as opposed to a behavioral and empirical approach, and (iii) the cultural separation of "sport" and "the arts", fundamental inquiry into the aesthetics of sport remains a thing of the future.

References

[1]
Ad Hoc Committee on the Triple Revolution. The Triple Revolution. Reprinted in W. E. Moore and R. M. Cook (eds.), Readings in Social Change. Englewood Cliffs, N. J.: Prentice-Hall, Inc., 1967.

[2]
Canning, J. E. (ed.)., Values in an Age of Confrontation. Columbus, Ohio: Charles Merrill Publishing Co., 1970.

[3]
De Grazia, S., Of Time, Work and Leisure. New York: Doubleday and Co., Inc., (Archer Books), 1964.

[4]
Glasser, R., Leisure: Penalty or Prize? London: Macmillan, 1970.

[5]
Kaplan, M., Leisure in America: A Social Inquiry. New York: John Wiley, 1960.

[6]
Rostow, W. W., The Stages of Economic Growth. Cambridge: University Press, 1961.

Sport For All

*John J. Jackson**

Having studied this topic from a wide variety of angles this writer's
first impression is to feel like Per Hauge-Moe (1975) reported feeling when
he introduced "Sport For All" to a television audience in Olympia, Greece.
He likened himself to the man who had listened to a very learned discourse
on a classical problem. When asked if he was more enlightened he replied,
"Frankly, no. But, I now feel confused on a much higher level."

What Is "Sport For All"?

In 1949, ten European countries founded the Council of Europe with the
broad aim:

> To achieve greater unity between its Members for the pur-
> pose of safeguarding and realizing the ideals and principles
> which are their common heritage and facilitating their
> economic and social progress (Council for Cultural Coop-
> eration, 1964:1).

By 1964, the Council of Europe had seventeen member countries and had
established the Council for Cultural Cooperation (CCC) in 1962 which had a
Committee for Out-of-School Education and Cultural Development (CCC,
1964:1). It was the latter body which adopted the slogan "Sport For All" as
the appropriate expression to cover a long-term European aim. At the tenth
session of the CCC (June 6-10, 1966) a "Declaration of principle" was made
which asserted that it lay with institutions concerned with sport to help "all
citizens, irrespective of age, sex, occupation or means, to understand the

* The author is gratefully indebted to the following experienced individuals
who contributed background information for the preparation of this essay:
John Bloomfield (University of Western Australia), Robert Buckley (County
Cork Education Committee), Gerald Carr (University of Victoria, Canada),
Roy Clumpner (Western Washington State College), Carson Conrad (PCPFS)
Gerald Glassford (University of Alberta), Wolf Lyberg (Swedish Sports
Federation), Peter McIntosh (University of Otago), Per Hauge-Moe (Nor-
wegian Confederation of Sports), Ernie Nicholls (University of Alberta),
Jürgen Palm (Deutscher Sportbund), Bengt Sevelius (Swedish Sports Feder-
ation), Uriel Simri (Wingate Institute for P.E. and Sport), Jörg Stäuble
(Swiss National Association for P.E.), Geoffrey Stretton (The Sports Council), George Walker (Sport Section, Council of Europe), Cor Westland (University of Ottawa), Walter Winterbottom (The Sports Council).

value of sport and to engage in it throughout their lives". (Council of Europe, 1971:2). The Council of Europe defined "sport" as "free, spontaneous physical activity engaged in during leisure time: its functions being recreation, amusement and development". (Council of Europe, 1971:5-6).

Different countries have placed slightly varied interpretations on this definition of "Sport For All". In fact, it means what it says in the above definition. Thus, everything from the highest élite sport to the most casual effort demanding physical activity is included. However, for the purpose of this chapter, élite sport will not be discussed further and only mass sport will be given particular attention. Further, this literal meaning is applicable anywhere in the world.

The Growth of European "Sport For All"

By 1970, six countries (Norway, Sweden, The Netherlands, Iceland, West Germany and Denmark) had established national campaigns intended to increase mass participation in sport, as a result of Council of Europe promptings. Credit must go to Norway for introducing a novel campaign under the slogan "Trim" for Trim has a similar meaning in most European languages and evokes the idea of fitness, neatness, well-being and smartness. The Council of Europe has expressed the hope that the word "Trim" might become synonymous with fitness campaigns throughout, and beyond member countries while countries adopting such campaigns should, through the Council of Europe, cooperate with each other by exchanging views and knowledge gained from experiences (Barry, 1970).

Conferences (Trim and Fitness International) to enable intercountry exchange of ideas began on a biennial basis in Norway in 1969. In 1971 it was held in the Netherlands and, by the time of the 1973 Frankfurt-on-Main conference, nineteen countries* were showing active interest in cooperating to achieve the objective "Sport For All". This cooperation took the form of each country's delegate explaining what his country had done and was doing regarding administration, personnel, finance and communication methods. When the 1975 Conference was held in Washington, D. C., Australia was added to the list of participating countries while Denmark, Finland, Iceland, Ireland, and Yugoslavia were not represented (Report of the Fourth International Conference on Trim and Fitness, 1975). Full details of the 1977 Paris Conference are not available yet but Brazil was represented and Per Hauge-Moe (1977) said it was, " ... by far the best of all five . . . bon voyage, et bienvenne à Portugal [1979]".

Definitions Relating to Politics

For the purposes here, view "political" structure within any one country as being that country's organized polity (condition of civil order; form,

---

* Austria, Belgium, Canada, Denmark, Federal Republic of Germany, Finland, France, Iceland, Ireland, Japan, Mexico, Netherlands, Norway, Poland, Sweden, Switzerland, United Kingdom, U.S.A., Yugoslavia.

process of civil government; organized society, state). Consider "political process" as referring to the events which are involved in the determination and implementation of organizational goals and/or the differential distribution and use of power within the country or countries concerned with the goals being considered.

European "Sport For All" Charter

In March 1975 a conference of European Ministers Responsible for Sport was held in Brussels and draft recommendations for a "European Sport For All Charter" were drawn up (CMS (74) 10, 1975 and CMS (75) 15, 1975). This "charter" was officially adopted by the Council of Europe Committee of Ministers on September 24, 1976 under the heading "On The Principles For A Policy of Sport For All". The Council of Europe is an international political group and this "charter" document clarifies this connection between politics and "Sport For All":

> (1) Recognizing that the aim of the Council of Europe is the achievement of greater unity between its Members for the purpose of safeguarding and realizing the ideals and principles which are their common heritage and of facilitating their economic and social progress, in particular by pursuing common objectives designed to protect and promote European culture;
>
> (2) Recalling Recommendation 588 (1970) of the Consultative Assembly on the development of sport for all and the creation of coordinating structures, and Recommendation 682 (1972) on a European Sport for All Charter;
>
> (3) Aware of the diverse contributions which sport can make to personal and social development through creative activities and recreational pursuits and of man's need for physical exercise for both his physical and his mental well-being;
>
> (4) Acknowledging the universal appeal of sport and its particular value in a rapidly changing world which is characterized on the one hand by increasing leisure and on the other by urbanization and technological development that tend to isolate man from his natural environment;
>
> (5) Emphasizing that the concept of sport for all, first formulated by the Council of Europe in 1966 to promote cultural development, relates to policies which seek to extend the benefits of sport to as many people as possible;

(6) Stressing the comprehensive nature of this concept which embraces sport in many different forms, from recreational physical activity to high level competition;

(7) Realizing that sport for all raises problems which cannot be satisfactorily solved within a purely national framework;

(8) Maintaining in this context that the formulation of common principles would enable national policies to be progressively harmonized;

(9) Welcoming the work already done by the Council for Cultural Cooperation and various other international bodies in establishing common principles;

(10) Recalling the Conference of European Ministers responsible for Sport held in Brussels (1975);

(11) Considering that a text defining these principles, as retained by that Conference of European Ministers responsible for Sport under the title of the "European Sport for All Charter", might provide a common basis for the actions of governments and other authorities concerned, Recommends to member governments:

    a. to base their national policies as far as possible on the principles contained in the "European Sport for All Charter" appended to this resolution;

    b. to distribute the "Charter" as widely as possible among interested persons and bodies within their territory. (Council of Europe, Resolution (76) 41).

    (Emphasis added.)

Appendix to Resolution (76) 41

PRINCIPLES FOR A POLICY OF SPORT FOR ALL

(Defined by the Conference of European Ministers
responsible for Sport in Brussels (1975) under
the title "European Sport for All Charter")

Article I

Every individual shall have the right to participate in
sport.

Article II

Sport shall be encouraged as an important factor in human development and appropriate support shall be made available out of public funds.

Article III

Sport, being an aspect of sociocultural development shall
be related at local, regional and national levels to other areas
of policy-making and planning such as education, health, social
service, town and country planning, conservation, the arts and
leisure services.

Article IV

Each government shall foster permanent and effective
cooperation between public authorities and voluntary organizations and shall encourage the establishments of national machinery for the development and coordination of sport for all.

Article V

Methods shall be sought to safeguard sport and sportsmen from exploitation for political, commercial or financial
gain, and from practices that are abusive and debasing, including the unfair use of drugs.

Article VI

Since the scale of participation in sport is dependent,
among other things, on the extent, the variety and the access-
ibility of facilities, the overall planning of facilities shall be
accepted as a matter for public authorities, shall take account
of local, regional and national requirements, and shall incorporate measures designed to ensure full use of both new and
existing facilities.

Article VII

Measures, including legislation where appropriate, shall be introduced to ensure access to open country and water for the purpose of recreation.

Article VIII

In any programme of sports development, the need for qualified personnel at all levels of administrative and technical management, leadership and coaching shall be recognized.

European "Sport For All" As A Political Instrument

The efforts to develop "Sport For All" in Council of Europe member countries, and in countries across the world with similar democratic ideals, reflects an attitude of the wider functions of sport in a dynamic society. "Sport For All" is "a discovery" - not that there has been a change in sport itself, but in its social setting. No longer is sport a pastime of a minority of enthusiasts or of a favoured class - recreational sport is an essential part of the lives of the inhabitants of all industrialized countries (Council of Europe, 1971:6).

> Having become "Sport For All", sport is not, however, simply a form of entertainment for the masses. . . It can also be regarded as a factor capable of changing society; in other words, it can be a political instrument (Council of Europe, 1971:7).

Thus, in this Council of Europe setting, sport is a means of attaining peaceful aims - its biological function is vital in an automated society and it meets man's need for communication, participation and self-expression (sport's sociocultural function). Hence, it is claimed it is no longer a luxury for a country to have a sports policy for it is an integral part of sociocultural policy and an "overriding need" (Council of Europe, 1971:7). The Council of Europe's (1971:8) document states:

> Man should not have to adapt himself to living conditions which degrade him. He must dominate the world around him and make it a more habitable place, more worthy of him.

"Play" was seen as an integral part of culture and a means to satisfy self-expression needs.

In making its case for "Sport For All" the Committee for Out-of-School Education and Cultural Development (Council of Europe, 1971:9) saw threats in "commercialization," "regimentation", and "productivism". Commercialization could be "either positive or harmful" - for example, sports industry benefits or exploitation of individuals. "Regimentation" must be carefully guarded against whilst "productivism" would be equally intolerable and "Sport

For All" should not be merely regarded as a factor in productivity - it would be an instrument of alienation if a law made sport compulsory for all employees.

The concerns were addressed more fully in "Background and Comments" to the "Sport For All" Charter (CMS (74) 10, 1975:16):

> ... sport has such appeal and such power to influence human behaviour ... it is increasingly urgent in all countries to safeguard the integrity of sport and to protect sport against any encroachment by powers and influences (commercial, financial, political, etc.) seeking to subordinate it to aims that negate the intrinsic values of sport ... sport should help to liberate man, not to subjugate or debase him ... governments must protect sport and sportsmen ...

The Secretary General (1973) summarised these views when he said:

> The Council of Europe is a political organisation. Sport - especially "Sport For All" - occupies a special place ... has a profoundly human significance. Its raison d'etre is to contribute to the happiness and fulfillment of the individual. It is up to all those who carry responsibility for their countries' sports policies to see to it that this lofty purpose is safeguarded.

The Scale of Mass Sport in "Western" Countries

Table 1 gives a brief overview of how governments of countries with proclaimed Western European "Sport For All" ideals were making provision in 1975 (Report of the Fourth International Conference on Trim and Fitness, 1975).

Table 1.

Country	Name of "Sport For All" Campaign	Organizational Structure	Annual Finance*
Australia	"Life. Be In It" Began in the State of Victoria and four other states plan to adopt it (Hauge-Moe, 1977) (Bloomfield, 1977)	National Fitness Councils in States with the Australian Government coordinating.	Joint responsibility of Australian and State Governments. Australian Government: $A 11.5 million for facilities, $A 950,000 for programs, $A 100,000 for developing a national approach.
Belgium	"Sport +" means more sport for an increasing number of people in more places. (Flemish-speaking region).	National "Sport +" Committee plus Secretariat in the Dutch Culture Ministry of Sports Administration (BLOSO).	Government: 24,400,000 BF sponsor (A.S.L.K.): 1,500,000 BF
Canada	"Participaction" A part only of Recreation Canada	Private, non-government with funding.	$5,676,000 plus sponsorship.
The Republic of Germany	"Trim-Aktion"	German Sports Federation (DSB)	None from Government. Sponsors: 400,000 DM. Franchise: 250,000 DM. Donated publicity: DM 10 million.
Japan	"Trim, Fitness and Mass Sports"	Agency embodying 11 ministerial offices and 200 non-governmental organizations. Coordinated by Prime Minister's Office.	Y300 million (U.S. $1 billion) for Trim projects. Y140 billion (U.S. $467 million) on enterprises and facilities for mass sport.

Table 1 (Continued).

Country	Name of "Sport For All" Campaign	Organizational Structure	Annual Finance*
Mexico	"Deportito"	The Mexican Sports Confederation.	Not stated. All children of primary school age contribute 20 centavos a week to pay for sports.
The Netherlands	"Trim"	Netherlands Sports Federation - private and non-governmental	None stated. Main sources of income are from football pools and a national weekly "lotto-game".
Norway	"Trim"	The Norwegian Confederation of Sports - based on 7,000 sports clubs with a total membership of one million.	U.S. $5 million (Government grants and football pool profits).
Poland**	"Physical recreation is an essential part of Polish social policy"	State institutions. Trade unions.	1,000,000,000 z.
Sweden	"Trim"	Swddish Sports Federation - 23 District Federations and 53 Special Sports Associations.	U.S. $16.5 million (State funds).
Switzerland	"Trim"	Swiss Federation for Physical Fitness - "Umbrella" of 66 Sports Organizations.	SFr 583,000. From Federal Government, States, Sports Lottery and own means.
United Kingdom	"Sport For All"	The Sports Council Independent Royal Charter Body.	1976 Income - Mainly from the Department of the Environment. ₤8,899,595 (The Sports Council, 1976)

Table 1 (Continued).

Country	Name of "Sport For All" Campaign	Organizational Structure	Annual Finance*
United States of America	No comprehensive national program in the European sense.	The nearest body is The President's Council on Physical Fitness and Sports (PCPFS).	PCPFS operating budget $575,000. Private groups and other agencies of government invest $40 million per year PCPFS in cooperating programs.

* These figures in no way indicate the total spending on mass sport.
** Poland's political philosophy differs from that of most Western European countries but a Polish representative plays an active part in the "Trim and Fitness International" Meetings.

"Sport For All" Political Activity Within Countries

Having investigated political activity relating to "Sport For All" from a broad perspective the political activity within example countries will be discussed. This cannot be all-encompassing but serves to demonstrate that, indeed, such political activity is extant.

Canada. Though "Participaction" (Sport Participation Canada) is Canada's closest body to a European "Sport For All" type organization it should be noted that most provision of mass sporting opportunities is provided by other agencies. Similarly is the case in other materially advanced countries. Thus, in Canada, there is involvement by the federal government, by all ten provincial governments, and by municipal governments. Indeed, it is at the local level where most actual provision for mass participation in sport is made.

To illustrate this point, the City of Edmonton (Alberta) spends approximately $17 million per year on its Parks and Recreation Department. This vast sum of money must be found in taxes and, therefore, the Parks and Recreation Department "competes" with other claims on the municipal purse. As broad spending policy is determined by City Council and Aldermen have to get elected, the provision for mass sport can easily be affected by these politicians. Thus, recreationally worthy programs can often be "cut" from the budget so that a program which makes politicians look good is kept in.

On a different aspect of political involvement at this level of government is the issue of capital grants. In Alberta, the Provincial Government makes capital grants for recreational facilities to municipalities on a per capita basis. From this source Edmonton receives $4.5 million annually and administers the disposal of the money. However, when the grant cheques are actually handed over, Provincial Members of the Legislative Assembly insist on doing so themselves in their own districts. In that way, they receive media publicity and, perhaps, something of what Petrie (1975: 192) has called a "beneficial and saleable image". Similarly, in New Zealand, the Minister for Sport personally signs all letters to local voluntary bodies telling them that their application for funds has been granted by a generous government – this, despite the fact that he has an advisory sports council with a supposedly independent chairman.

The Federal Republic of Germany. The largest organised group in the Federal Republic of Germany is that of sports people. In 1976, 14,194,344 citizens were members of 45,518 sports clubs – representing 22 percent of the total population (Scala, 1977a:39). Thus, though there is no direct co-ordination with the government or political parties, the Deutscher Sportbund (DSB) is able to function as a "pressure group". For example, DSB has involved the President of the country in a Trim campaign and gained special grants for projects such as "Trim For The Aged". From a different perspective:

> Sport may not be used to hide the regressions of an
> industrialised society nor to make light of social and
> other defects ... many people believe a society is work-
> ing towards its improvement when it gives sport its due
> place and accepts it as a correcting factor in life (Scala,
> 1977b:42).

United Kingdom. The provision of facilities and the development of "Sport For All" is of great interest to central government and local authorities in the U.K. As far as possible the government tries not to interfere with the organisation of sport and the Sports Councils, set up by Royal Charter, are given the responsibility of spending government funds for the development of sport. A Royal Charter body is "chartered" to work independently of government and, therefore, not have to change sport policy if the political party in power happens to change. The present government (Labour) stated its sports policy in a 1975 White Paper (H.M.S.O., 1975) which concluded:

> Where the community neglects its responsibilities for
> providing the individual with opportunities and choice in
> the provision of sports and recreational facilities, it
> will rarely escape the long-term consequences of this
> neglect. When life becomes meaningful for the individ-
> ual then the whole community is enriched.

The situation then, broadly in the U.K., is closely allied to the ideals of Western European "Sport For All" and, generally, that is the way it works.

However, such policy does not prevent political strife among the parties concerned. From 1935 until 1972, the Central Council of Physical Recreation (C.C.P.R.) provided national support services for the development of mass sport, mainly through sports governing bodies. After much deliberation prior to 1972 it was decided that the C.C.P.R. would merge with the then Advisory Sports Council to form the Executive Sports Council under a Royal Charter. Within this arrangement the C.C.P.R.'s staff and assets would be transferred to the Sports Council and all the work previously done by the C.C.P.R. staff would continue under the new body.

At the time this first became public knowledge Miss Phyllis Colson, the founder of the C.C.P.R. and then the retired General Secretary, removed from her will a bequest of ₤1,000 to the C.C.P.R. She said, " ... sacrilege! ... Too political. Bang goes a life's work ..." (Evans, 1974: 185). Within a year she was dead but then events took an ironical turn. At the 1971 A.G.M. of the C.C.P.R., Prince Philip (President of the C.C.P.R.) said he found it difficult to accept the proposal that the C.C.P.R. should commit "voluntary hari kiri" (Evans, 1974:224). Thus, as McIntosh (1975:49) stated:

> The C.C.P.R. was preserved and reconstituted only to be used by <u>some of its honorary officers</u>* as a political instrument to belabour both the government of the day [conservative] and the Sports Council which was being loyally and efficiently served by the former staff of the C.C.P.R. (Emphasis added.)

An Extraordinary General Meeting of the new C.C.P.R. held on April 9, 1973 elected a new Central Committee and, the same day, that committee chose as its chairman <u>Labour</u> M.P. Mr. Denis Howell (Evans, 1974:229). The chairman of the Sports Council, Sir Roger Bannister, soon resigned (related?) and Mr. Howell became Minister of Sport and Recreation when the Labour party returned to power in 1974 (Evans, 1974:229). However, he was not able to resume Chairmanship of the Sports Council. More could be written about this but the "skullduggery" is locked up in the archives of the Sports Council and as McIntosh's review concluded, " ... that is another story yet to be told." (McIntosh, 1975:49). So, what started as a sensible rationalization idea which was agreed to by both parties did not work out that way (except in Scotland where the Scottish Council of Physical Recreation did "merge" with the Scottish Sports Council). Since 1972, the C.C.P.R. has risen like a phoenix from the ashes in such a way that the power of the Sports Council must have been emasculated.

<u>United States of America</u>. The U.S.A. does not have a comprehensive national "Sport For All" program in quite the same way that some Western European countries have. The President's Council on Physical Fitness and Sports (PCPFS) was established by Presidential Executive Order which has been slightly amended from time to time. The latest one (United States, 1976) begins:

> The Secretary of Health, Education, and Welfare ... shall, in carrying out his responsibilities in relation to education and public health, develop and coordinate a national program for physical fitness and sports.

Importantly, however, it has absolutely no authority to dictate or regulate the activities of schools, colleges, clubs, recreation departments, or other institutions that conduct sports and fitness programs. Furthermore, the Council does not make grants of money for facilities, equipment, staff, or any other purpose. What it does do is work closely with the communication media and in 1977 will spend about $150,000 to develop advertising materials which will be distributed to 900 television stations, 8,000 radio stations, 1,800 daily newspapers, and 3,000 magazines. In this way 220 million Americans can receive the message which would cost $30 million dollars if the PCPFS had to pay for it.

The Consultant to the President on Physical Fitness and Sports (Chairman of the PCPFS), 14 members of the PCPFS, the 100 members of the President's Conference, and the four top people on the national staff all serve at the pleasure of the President. However, positions have not changed drastically in the way some political appointments change in the U.S.A. For example, Captain James Lovell (Chairman) was originally appointed by President Johnson in 1967 and Mr. C. Carson Conrad (Executive Director) was first appointed Special Advisor on Physical Fitness by President Kennedy in 1961 and served in that position until he assumed his present title under President Nixon in 1970. Obviously, the PCPFS is not <u>seen</u> to be political for the National College Physical Education Association for Men passed a motion at its 1977 annual conference in Orlando which began:

> Whereas the President's Council on Physical Eitness
> and Sports in a non-political agency ... (NCPEAM,
> 1977).

Strictly, however, it is political in that it is working under Presidential Executive Order using public funds to explain and develop physical fitness. Also, the PCPFS has used figureheads, such as sports stars and an astronaut in top positions, and Presidents have been aligned with the Council for what Petrie (1975:192) has called a "beneficial and saleable image".

Some Communist Countries

The main purpose of this paper is to discuss "Politics and 'Sport For All'" of the Western European type but mass sport provision in some communist countries will be briefly outlined from a political viewpoint. Ulbricht (1969:14-15) of the German Democratic Unity Party was cited by Carr (1972: 150):

> We are of the opinion that the harmonic development of
> man's mental and physical capacities, particularly in
> the youth, is necessary so that they can master all the
> skills required to fulfill the important goals of socialist
> production. This means high morals, socialist ethics,
> and the consciousness and capacity of defending the
> achievements of the working class, the people, and the
> homeland. If these are our goals, then it's necessary
> that sport and physical education become truly an affair
> of the <u>whole population</u>*. Under capitalistic conditions
> this is not possible but under provisions of the Worker's
> and Peasants' State it's not only possible, it's necessary
> ... (*Emphasis added.)

As Carr (1972:149) has further pointed out, communist sport has a strong association with labour. A basic physical relationship is seen between work and sport in that fundamental forms of work activity are repeated in the motor movements of sport. Communist sport historians support this view by claiming that old cave and rock paintings showing paleolithic man running, jumping, and throwing in relation to hunting are essential proofs of the unity of the original relationship.

Marx, himself, drew on the ideas of a British socialist who had combined elementary education with manual training and gymnastics in the factory schools of New Lanark (1839-1849) (Bernett, 1968:93 cited by Carr, 1972: 147). Subsequently Marx (1959:483-484) wrote in Capital:

> From the factory system budded, as Robert Owen has shown us in detail, the germ of education of the future, an education that will, in the case of every child over a given age, combine productive labour with instruction and gymnastics not only as one of the methods of adding to efficiency of production, but as the only method of producing fully developed human beings.

In reinforcing Marxist philosophy, Lenin saw a need for citizens of "an extraordinarily high and well-rounded education". He particularly favoured sport and physical education as a "preparation of the proletariat for revolutionary war". Also, as preparation for defense against capitalist imperialism and aggression (Eichel, 1970:295 cited by Carr, 1972:153).

The Marxist-Leninist philosophy as it relates to mass sport may be summarized from within the German Democratic Republic's stated "truly humanistic mission" (Eichel, 1970:307 et passim cited by Carr, 1972:153-155):

1. Physical education and sport is considered as a birthright of all socialist citizens. Through striving, creativity, and initiative, sportspeople are considered as important contributors to the national culture.

2. Physical education contributes effectively towards increasing the total work output of the socialist community.

3. Sport provides a good medium for the development of political conviction because of the possibilities it provides for "collective" training.

4. Sport and physical education aids in preparing the citizens for the defense of socialism and their homeland against capitalism.

These basic philosophies pervade in the major developed communist countries. Since 1930-31 the Russians have urged masses of people to work for G.T.O. ("Ready for Labour and Defense") Badges (McIntosh, 1968:192).

In 1972 the tests were revised to include people from age ten to sixty years and in fact, during the years 1965-1975, 86 million people passed the test (Bennett, 1975:197).

In the People's Republic of China, the Marxian dialectical materialism philosophy pervades the whole state including the mass sport programs. The revolutionary committees of the various communes and work brigades speak very strongly to their colleagues with respect to the need for fitness and health through participation in "Sport For All" type programs. Their badges, which parallel the G.T.O. badge system, are aimed at improving the health of workers and thereby enhancing the production capabilities of the nation. According to Bennett (1975:191) China has de-emphasized competitive sports and the pursuit of world records ever since the Cultural Revolution. Having seen excellent Chinese badminton teams in Canada and the U.K., this writer finds that "Friendship First" idea not totally explicit of the real situation. This is not to say the teams were not friendly, for they were, but the standard of badminton they played could hardly have been achieved by de-emphasizing excellence!

Summary

"Sport For All" was originally conceived in the Council of Europe as a means of achieving greater unity between its member countries for safeguarding their common ideals and principles to facilitate economic and social progress. Thus, "Sport" as "free, spontaneous physical activity engaged in during leisure time: its functions being recreation, amusement and development" should be made available to "all citizens, irrespective of age, sex, occupation or means".

After having six European countries propagating "Sport For All"/Trim programs in 1970, there were nineteen countries showing active participation of some form in the concept by 1973. By then the idea had spread across the world to include Canada, Japan, Mexico, and the U.S.A.

In 1976, a formal "Sport For All" Charter was officially adopted by the Council of Europe Committee of Ministers which set out the part "Sport For All" would play to protect and promote European culture so as to, among other things, contribute significantly to individuals' self-actualization type benefits. It was seen to have a biological function, a social communication function, and a self-expression function. By such means man would dominate his world and make it a more habitable place which would be worthy of him.

Dangers in "Sport For All" were seen by the Council of Europe to be in commercialization, regimentation, and productivism.

After outlining the scale of Western European type "Sport For All" the political activity within example countries was discussed. Generally, it was demonstrated that each country's broad "Sport For All" policy bore close resemblance to that of the Council of Europe. There was, however, other political activity such as that described at the local level of government in Canada, by the political pressure of the Deutscher Sportbund, by the political party differences in the U.K., and the use of "Sport For All" as a political saleable image in the U.S.A.

Mass sport was seen also to be an objective of major communist countries where the reasons for it included harmonic development of man's physical capacities, high morals, productivism, defense, and collective training.

Discussion

Broad View. From what has been written it is evident that "Sport For All" type programs are politically motivated whether from Eastern or Western bloc countries. Each basic philosophy points to a personal benefit for man himself. The West wants man to use the benefit freely and as he chooses for the betterment of mankind. The Communists want the benefit to increase productivism and improve defense capability.

Commercialization. Even the Council of Europe saw "Sport For All" dangers in commercialization, regimentation, and productivism. Some of these fears appear to have been well-founded by subsequent events. There are many examples of commercialization resulting from the spread of "Sport For All". Three forms of this commercialization serve to demonstrate the point. One, where individuals or groups are commercialized by sponsorship arrangements such as in straight advertising of products or when commercial businesses sponsor sporting events. Such activity is very widespread in the West. The sponsors mainly support events for advertising reasons and would not do so if there was no financial profit in it for them. The sportsperson, or group, accepts sponsorship for economic reasons and also for sports development reasons. The sportsman may not necessarily like the product he's helping to sell but he subjugates that feeling and takes the money. Indeed, sponsorship has done a great deal in the West to promote "Sport For All" during economically stringent times. So, whether such sponsorship is right or wrong does not matter as far as the objective fact is concerned--the institution "sport" is used for commercial reasons. The second major way the phenomenon of "Sport For All" is used commercially is when, for example, a cigarette brand is advertised which just happens to picture a happy tennis couple. This does not even cost the sponsor anything other than the cost of advertising but he certainly uses tennis (a "Sport For All") to help sell his product. The third of these forms of commercialization comes in terms of market moulding and planned obsolescence - suddenly tennis clothes are pastel colours and not white so everybody buys coloured tennis clothes. Then it changes again - solid deep stripes across one shoulder so, again, everyone must buy a new stripe! This point has been exaggerated here but only slightly. Widespread related aspects of the economics of sport consumerism have been described fully by McPherson (1975:238-275). To illustrate further the vastness of leisure spending, figures show that Americans will spend $160 billion on leisure and recreation in 1977 and by 1985 the figure is expected to be $300 billion (U.S. News and World Report, 1977:62).

However, having said this about commercialization in the West, it may well be what the mass of people want. The jobs provided help the free enterprize economy and the bright tennis clothes and cigarettes make life fun.

Regimentation. There is little evidence of regimentation of "Sport For All" in countries with Western European ideals. It does exist in some Communist countries where calisthenics are performed before or during work in factories and other places of employment. Similarly, it has occurred in the West but to a very limited extent and it rarely appeals for long.

Productivism. At present the West does not ostensibly propagate "Sport For All" for reasons of productivism but there are signs of trends in that direction.

In 1976, for example, the Government of Canada sponsored a study on "Employee Fitness" and in 1977 published a book under the same title (Collis, 1977). The book points out the benefits to firms of having fit workers and tells them how to operate programs. Indeed, several companies have programs in many parts of North America but will only provide them when they can see a financial advantage.

Another specific example is seen in the Presidential Executive Order 11562 which legalizes the PCPFS:

> The Secretary shall:
>
> ... (i) assist business, industry, government and labour organizations in establishing sound physical fitness programmes to elevate employee health and to reduce the financial and human costs resulting from inactivity (United States, 1976:2).

Conclusions

This essay demonstrates that politics and "Sport For All" are closely related and very widespread in "Western" and Communist countries. It is recognized that vast portions of the world have been omitted from discussion. However, it is known that such programs are closely related to politics in Israel, for example, and that no similar programs exist extensively in Arab countries. Developments are taking place in many parts of South America, Africa, India, and Asia. At the recent 1977 Commonwealth Prime Ministers' Conference in England, the British Prime Minister stated that 650 million people in the world have to live on less than $50 per year. In areas where such poverty exists "Sport For All" is farthest from people's thoughts and will remain so at least until the sine qua non of hunger has been satisfied.

References

Barry, Jack. "Sport For All--National Campaigns." Paper read at Central Council of Physical Recreation Annual Staff Conference, Lilleshall National Sports Centre, England, December 3, 1970.

Bennett, Bruce L., Maxwell L. Howell and Uriel Simri. Comparative Physical Education and Sport. Philadelphia: Lea and Febiger, 1975.

Bernett, Hajo. "Sozialistische Körperkultur," in Einführung in die Theorie der Leibeserziehung. Schorndorf bei Stuttgart: Verlag Karl Hofmann, 1968, cited by Carr, Gerald Anthony. "The National Socialist Programme of Sport, Physical Education and Recreation and That of the German Democratic Republic." Unpublished Doctoral dissertation, The University of Stellenbosch, 1972.

Bloomfield, John. Personal correspondence from Professor Bloomfield of The University of Western Australia to the writer. '

Carr, op. cit.

Collis, Martin L. Employee Fitness. Canada: Health and Welfare, n.d. [1977].

Council of Europe [Strasbourg, France].

> Committee of Ministers. "On the Principles for A Policy of Sport For All." Resolution (76) 41. September 24, 1976.
> Council of Europe. Planning the Future (VIII). Strasbourg: CCC/EES (71) 22, 1971.
> Council for Cultural Cooperation. Training the Trainer. Strasbourg: CCC, Section III, Out-of-school Education, No. 3, 1964.
> CMS (74) 10. Draft Recommendation on the European Sport for All Charter. Conference of European Ministers Responsible for Sport, Brussels, March 20-21, 1975.
> CMS (75) 15. Background Paper: The Public Authorities and Sports For All: Areas For Cooperation: Machinery For Cooperation. Conference of European Ministers Responsible For Sport, Brussels, March 20-21, 1975.
> Secretary-General of the Council of Europe. Speech at the ceremony organised in his honour by Panathlon International, Rome, November 9, 1973.

Eichel, Wolfgang and Others. "W. I. Lenin und die Verwirklichung seiner Lehre auf dem Gebiet von Körperkultur und Sport in der DDR," in Theorie und Praxis der Körperkultur. Staatliches Komitee fur Körperkultur und Sport beim Ministerrat der Deutschen Demokratischen Republik, 1969, Vol. 4, April, 1970, cited by Carr, op. cit.

Evans, H. Justin. Service to Sport: The Story of the CCPR - 1935 to 1972. London: The Sports Council, 1974.

Hauge-Moe, Per. "Sport For All: On Its Way Toward Reality?" TV Seminar, Olympia, Greece, October 20-27, 1975. [Mimeographed].

_____. "The Last Words," Paper read at Fifth Trim and Fitness
International Conference, Paris, Mary 5, 1977.

H.M.S.O. Sport and Recreation. [White Paper]. London: Department of
the Environment, August, 1975.

Ibid. Citing Professor Grupe, University of Tübingen, 1977b.

Kramer, Hermann J. Körpererziehung und Sportunterricht in der DDR.
Schorndorf bei Stuttgart: Verlag Karl Hofmann, 1969, cited by Carr,
op. cit.

Marx, Karl. Capital: A Critical Analysis of Capitalist Production, Volume
I. Moscow: Foreign Languages Publishing House, 1959. [Translated
from the third German edition by Samuel Moore and Edward Aveling -
edited by Frederick Engels].

McIntosh, P. C. Sport in Society. London: Watts, 1968.

_____. "Vision Splendid." Book review of Evans, op. cit. in
Sport and Recreation. [London: The Sports Council]. Spring, 1975.

McPherson, Barry D. "Sport Consumption and the Economics of Consumerism," in Sport and Social Order, (eds.) D. W. Ball and J. W. Loy.
Reading, Massachusetts: Addison-Wesley, 1975.

National College Physical Education Association for Men. "Resolutions
Passed at Orlando Meeting". [1977]. Newsletter. Vol. 17, No. 1,
1977.

Petrie, Brian M. "Sport and Politics," in Ball and Loy, op. cit.

Report of the Fourth International Conference on Trim and Fitness.
Washington, D. C.: [PCPFS] May 19-24, 1975.

Scala. [Federal Republic of Germany]. Nr. 3, 1977a.

The Sports Council. Annual Report 1975-6. London: The Sports Council,
1976.

[Ulbricht, Walter]. "20 Jahre DDR - 20 Jahre Korperkultur des Volkes," in
Theorie und Praxis der Korperkultur. op. cit., cited by Carr, op. cit

U.S. News and World Report. "How Americans Pursue Happiness," May 23,
1977.

United States of America. The White House, Executive Order 11562, Physical Fitness and Sports, October 25, 1976.

Sport In The Cultural And Educational Development Of Post-War Germany

Waldemar Ostermann

In the immediate wake of World War II, a unified perspective of sport in Germany appeared to prevail over politics, as the defeated nation was fully engaged in the process of reconstruction. This post-war reconstruction was under the coordination of the United States occupying West Germany with the other two victorious Allied Powers, Great Britain and France, and the Soviet Union occupying East Germany. The issuance of licenses to sport and athletic associations that survived the war was exercised by the occupying powers who also advised regarding effective developmental strategies of various sport and athletic plans. The unified viewpoint concerning the development of a comprehensive system of sport and athletics in Germany is reflected in the meeting of the International Olympic Committee in Lausanne, Switzerland, in 1951, where the delegates from divided Germany agreed that one united team should represent Germany in the Olympiad. But the socialist regime in East Germany, becoming firmly established under Soviet coordination, refused to accept a united German team. Avery Brundage succeeded in persuading the East German regime to accept the Lausanne agreement, and a united German team participated in the 1956 Winter Olympics in Cortina d'Ampezza, Italy.

Thereafter the view urged by Brundage that sport as a transnational effort should prevail over political and national orientations lost its impetus. The political developments in West and East Germany became significantly polarized, and similarly the role of sports in society developed independently with different perspectives. The social role of sport can clearly not be separated from general political developments. Arnd Kruger in Sport und Politik (Sport and Politics) elaborates how sport and politics are interdependent as social phenomena. He portrays how sport has played the social role in the service of politics since ancient times. Accordingly, the interaction in sport between the Federal Republic of Germany (West) and the German Democratic Republic (East) became almost entirely disrupted by the time the wall appeared separating West and East Germany. The GDR incorporated sport and athletics much more comprehensively into the social and political matrix and into the educational system than did the FRG. The GDR further utilized sport as an effective instrument in intercultural communication in its efforts to establish international recognition.

Based on the pioneering efforts of Friedrich Ludwig Jahn who established the norm of "athletics of the German people," which was effectively
implemented outside the educational system and also as a pre-military service activity, the perspective of sport was thereafter more comprehensively
developed in terms of the introduction of various national sport events, and
of extensive training in athletics and gymnastics which efforts were also in
time incorporated in the educational system. Participation in some form of
sport has thus nearly become universal in Germany. Almost every town,
however small, has its own swimming pool, gymnasium and outdoor sports
grounds. With this historical development the structure of sports and gymnastics and relevant training were rapidly developed separately in the FRG
and the GDR. This commitment to sports is specified in the Charter of German Sports established by the German Sport Alliance on the FRG in 1966,
and similarly for European Sports by the European Council in 1975, and for
World Sports by UNESCO in 1977 which proclaims that "sport is available to
all people." This ethos affirms that all people should have equal opportunity
to participate competitively in sports to enhance their well-being and
achievements. But unfortunately this ethos is by no means realized in international sport events where the political dimension has come to play a dominant role. The political weight is well reflected in sport interactions between the FRG and the GDR.

Within the political framework of the Allied Powers, development of
the structure of sports in the FRG took place in a balanced fashion according
to the political monition of Adenauer to avoid experiment. This perspective
was firmly implemented by the coordination of Willi Daume who also became
President of the German Sport Alliance. Restoration and consolidation of
sport and athletic associations in the provinces (Lander) and the nation were
performed also with a focus on Germany as a whole (West and East Germany). The role of sport in society is couched in a free sport organization
with democratically drawn up associations. The functions of the many sport
groups in the FRG are not mutually coordinated, they function independently
with their particular individual goals. And achievements in sport depend on
the voluntary commitment of athletes, coaches and trainers.

In 1956, the German Sport Alliance realized the significance of a federal initiative in the improvement of education in sports and athletics, which
was found to be quite inadequate. A recommendation with four demands was
submitted to improve education and training in this vital area. The four demands indicate:

1. Increase in the current scope of education in sport;

2. More extensive training of instructors in sports;

3. Increase of sport facilities in schools;

4. Cooperative development in schools and sport associations of more
    extensive sport facilities and sport programs.

These recommendations did have a beneficial impact in that sport facilities
and programs were indeed enhanced. In 1958, a growing discrepancy in

activities and policies of local and national sport associations became evident, for the sport facilities were not equitably available to all citizens. They failed to foster a comprehensive development of sport and athletics and good health of the German people.

The federal diet of the FRG propagated in 1959 the "second course" policy (Zweite Weg) for equitable provision of facilities and services to satisfy the needs in sport, recreation and health of the entire population. The German Olympic Committee dismissed, however, in the same year the "Golden Plan" which delineated the assessed deficiency in sport facilities. Plans were formulated to rectify this lack of sport facilities and the need of 6.3 billion marks was indicated to bridge this gap. As the "second course" policy presupposed the implementation of the "Golden Plan," all political parties, in preparation for the upcoming elections in 1961, promised the realization of the "Golden Plan." Sport activities continued to develop without signifiaant federal aid and without effective intervention of the sport associations who lacked the necessary authority for such a comprehensive effort in the organization of sport in the FRG. In 1960, the dialogue continued with political parties underlining the responsibility of the federal government to provide the necessary funds for the sport needs of the nation.

In spite of various deficiencies in the organization of sport and lack of supportive federal influence in the FRG, the Olympic achievements of the FRG were superior to those of the GDR until 1960 just prior to the construction of the wall. The German Sport Association failed both to analyze the basis for this superiority and to establish plans to improve performance in sport. It must not be overlooked that the general social welfare conditions in the GDR were inferior to the significant recovery of the FRG, and, under the oppression of the Soviet military and political influence, a significant recovery without abundant aid as the FRG received under the Marshall Plan required much longer time. In contrast, the GDR was fully involved in reorganizing its sport system with the aim of advancing beyond the achievements of its more populous neighbor.

Olympic Records of the FRG and the GDR

Medals	Gold FRG	Gold GDR	Silver FRG	Silver GDR	Bronze FRG	Bronze GDR
Oslo (Winter 1952)	3	–	2	–	2	–
Helsinki (Summer 1952)	--	–	7	–	17	–
Cortina d'Ampezzo (Winter 1956)	1	–	--	–	--	1
Melbourne (Summer 1956)	5	1	9	4	6	2
Squaw Valley (Winter 1960)	2	2	2	1	1	–
Rome (Summer 1960)	10	3	10	9	6	7

Since the earliest stages of development of the GDR the role of sport comes to play a basic function in the cultural development. The importance of physical culture and sports in the lives of the citizens of the GDR is demonstrated by a government bill of February 8, 1950 for the promotion of youth and sports which was passed into law by the People's Chamber, the highest representative organ of the Republic. Its members represent workers, farmers, employees, intellectuals, craftsmen and tradesmen, private businessmen, and 25% of the deputies are women. The Republic provides sufficient funds for the development of sport facilities and programs for children and young people, and for mass sport events on the national and international scale.

The socialist perspective was officially introduced into the government of the GDR in 1952 and the structure and functions of the system of sport were also incorporated into the socialist matrix. Walter Ulbricht, chief of the Communist Party in the GDR, firmly stated at the conference of ministers of culture from the German provinces (West and East Germany), in Koblenz (West Germany), April 4, 1955:

> "Of special importance is the development of physical culture. Socialist Germany is in need of healthy, decisive, educated, and goal-oriented citizens. The Politbureau (in GDR) has considered the criticism and proposals of sport experts concerning the improvement of sport activities and facilities and finds it necessary to establish a Federal Department for Sport and Physical Culture and a corresponding administrative organization in divisions or districts. The Department will be mandated to exercise the important task of providing guidance and facilities for the development of our sports people so that they can also adopt and share the valuable experience of the Soviet Science of Physical Culture."
> (Cited in Sport and Politik and translated by the author).

The sport structure as stated by Ulbricht was developed and implemented rapidly. Not to neglect the defensive component of sport, the "Society for Sport and Technique" was established after the Soviet paradigm. And in all districts "Sportclubs" were established which one does not join voluntarily but to which one is delegated via state-oriented channels. Activities and programs of all athletes and sportspeople are coordinated by the German Association of Gymnastics and Sports which was established in 1957. Athletic and sport programs in schools and outside the educational system are more closely coordinated, incorporating also the two national groups of youths, the "Young Pioneers" and the "Free German Youth." Schools for sport for children and the German University for Physical Culture in Leipzig were opened, and the extensive programs of physical education are supported by sophisticated and refined scientific research studies. To facilitate efficient and effective functioning of the extensive sport structure, a scientific council was established to coordinate research projects and report results to the Department of Sport and Physical Culture. Based on the conveyed information more extensive programs are developed and implemented. The extensive effort in developing an all-inclusive sport system was pursued with two central themes: 1) international recognition of the sport establishment of the GDR, and 2) incorporation of educational and non-educational sport programs for effective education of the youth in physical culture which has become a vital obligatory component in the educational program.

A sense of democratic patriotism began to accompany the extensive program in sports as more and more professional people escaped from the GDR to the FRG in the late 1950's. The GDR became very concerned about the growing exodus and the wall was considered the effective measure to stop it. More extensive programs in sports and athletics were developed on the basis of three methodological-didactic demands:

1) The main goal of basic training in athletics and sports is to increase productivity of the labor force as well as boost performance in sports;

2) The time of education must be utilized optimally in order to develop interest in instruction and practice of sports and athletics;

3) Specialization and differentiation in sports should occur as early as possible in order to determine and more fully develop talents for particular sports according to relevant scientific examination.

Only after the wall was built and a significant degree of social regimentation was established could the above demands be effectively met.

Sport communication in Germany prior to the wall confronted the problem of international recognition of the GDR. In the Olympic games in Helsinki only the FRG participated. The German Sport Alliance decided in Oberwesel in 1952 (West Germany) to discontinue communication with sport organizations in the GDR. The reason for the discontinuance was in fact delivered by the GDR in a complaint that sportsmen from West Berlin who participated in sport events in the GDR posed political questions and even engaged in political dialogue. The German Sport Alliance in the FRG was insulted by this GDR assertion and decided to terminate interaction with its neighbor. But shortly thereafter in a meeting in West Berlin a compromise was reached and a unified effort in sport, in the sense of participation in the Olympic games, was reconsidered. The delegates, however, from the two Germanys had different notions concerning such a unified effort with respect to their different political perspectives.

The provisions which focused on success in the agreements reached were interpreted differently by the two groups of delegates in light of their different political concepts. The propagandists of the GDR praised the notions of "love of freedom" and "love of nations" in the sense of the Soviet embracing political strategies, and they argued that their proposals concerning a unified German sport program were just and equitable for the freedom loving workers, farmers, and professional people in Germany. The West German delegates refused to accept most of the offered proposals of the GDR as they were considered basically an expression of the posture of the political (Communist) party. But for the time being, the perspective of a unified German posture in sport was mutually accepted despite many disagreements.

After extensive negotiations athletes from the FRG and the GDR participated together in one unified team in the Summer Olympic Games in Melbourne and the Winter Olympic in Cortina d'Ampezzo. The German Olympic team was of course under the management of the FRG utilizing uniforms and the emblem of West Germany. But the Olympic team was unstable, laden with deep mutual suspicion and distrust. Teams from the FRG and the GDR arrived and left independently. And at a meeting in Dortmund (West Germany) in 1957, the sovereignty of the GDR was announced by the sport representatives from East Germany. As the FRG did not recognize the sovereignty of the GDR, the unified sport effort remained unresolved and it was agreed upon tentatively that sport teams from both sides were to be labelled "Deutsche Meisterschaften" (German championship teams). Some sport events continued between West and East Germany, but they came to a halt when the wall appeared in 1961. The emblem and the flag of the GDR were now recognized by the International Olympic Committee. And it is of interest to note the significant advances that the GDR achieved in the 1960 Olympic games based on extensive preparations.

The situation of sport in the FRG social matrix was significantly improved in the 1960's also in terms of a new committee established by the National Olympic Committee and the German Sport Alliance. The new committee (Bundesausschuß für Förderung des Leistungssports) coordinates advanced seminars for trainers in Olympic sports, plans more extensive sport programs, and manages a comprehensive program in sport medicine. This committee was initially directed by the physiologist, Dr. Nöcker, who escaped from Leipsig and who previously also served as Chef de Mission of the formerly unified German Olympic team. He affirmed the vital importance of the mission of this committee to sustain the West German Olympic team at a high level in expertise and achievement. And Dr. Nöcker was also active in developing a comprehensive scientific and medical program to support the sport system and the Olympic team of the FRG similarly to what was developed in the GDR. But lack of funds and personnel did not render this committee very effective. And as the results of the Olympic games in Mexico indicate, the pragmatic efforts pioneered by Dr. Nöcker are essential for the FRG to surpass the GDR in Olympic achievements.

Olympic Results in Rome, Tokyo and Mexico

| | Rome | | Tokyo | | Mexico | |
	Medals	Points	Medals	Points	Medals	Points
FRG	23	167	34	219	26	182.5
GDR	19	114	16	119	25	240

As the GDR began to surpass the FRG in Olympic achievements, the West German government made more funds available for the Olympic efforts. Sport and athletic programs were also improved outside of schools and in the school systems where they have reached a very unacceptable condition. But despite the improvements of the national and local sport and athletic programs that the German Olympic Committee and the German Sport Alliance as well as the newly established committee proposed and had implemented to improve the expertise and performance of West German athletes, the GDR does have an advantage in terms of its previous development of a comprehensive sport program which was fully incorporated into the educational system and into the social, political, and cultural matrix.

The GDR continued vigorously the development of sport and athletics on a priority basis. The financial and material resources were adequately provided from a central source in contrast to the FRG where relatively insufficient financial support came from local, regional and federal sources. The sport system in the GDR has now become a comprehensively closed system. Sport programs in schools and outside of schools have been interlocked facilitating efficient and effective utilization of available sport talent and facilities. Instruction in sport has been quite systematically developed in the educational system. Instructors in physical education and trainers remain in close contact and closely monitor development of sport skills and sport achievements. Talents in sport are carefully assessed in schools, particularly in sport schools. And workers competent in sport are released from their professional work for special training in sport and for sport events.

Motivation to participate in sport is also effectively generated. At first popularization of the GDR regime was involved. According to the principle of recruitment, the more frequently one is observed with popular phenomena, the more readily one becomes identified with them. Achievement in sport involved identification with the state for which awards and social advantages are also provided. Creation of a GDR national consciousness was achieved by making available objects with which citizens are proud to identify related to the state's activities. Thus achievement in sport can be more easily attained according to measurable objectives identified with the state as "socialist achievements."

After the 1968 Olympic Games it became obvious that the GDR had developed an articulately planned sport system whereby the physical and human resources of the nation of a population of 18 million were quasi-optimally utilized for achievements in sport. The FRG had no comparable sport system, and the many subsystems of sport functioned not in coordination and frequently in mutual conflict. In light of this unfortunate situation, Willi Daume, President of the German Sport Alliance and of the National Olympic Committee, exclaimed at the Munich Olympic games: "We accept the challenge of the GDR."

Daume's thesis was supported by the federal government and reinforced by beneficial changes in sport organizations after 1968. But leftist sport ideologists in the FRG declined the thesis and, in place, referred to a perspective of sport for the workers which had its origin in 1933. The advent of implementation of Daume's thesis occurred at the extraordinary sport conference, in 1969, in which the national committee dealing with the development of sport was reorganized and strengthened. Comprehensive organization and planning of a national sport system and sport performance was now more coherently executed in conjunction with the many sport organizations.

This effort was also reflected in the development of a more comprehensive program of sport and athletics in the educational system in coordination with established programs outside of the educational system dealing with administration, a commission in training, a technical commission, and a scientific commission for the general sport system in the FRG.

The tradition of Olympic sport in Germany serves as an effective incentive for younger people to become involved in sport. But the FRG with a democratic social environment and a democratic government is dependent on the voluntary initiative of athletes and trainers for achievements in sport. No compulsive measures with potential rewards are available, as is the case in various degrees in the GDR. And no system of scholarship or student aid for college students is available as in the United States. In the traditional "Prussian" perspective, achievement in sport, be it in the Olympic Games, in national events, etc., is still viewed essentially as a private pleasure.

If the "Prussian" oriented perspective is considered to basically characterize the orientation of sport in the GDR, solution to various problems discussed above must be sought in sport itself as it is supported by the current measures to raise the level of sport achievements. The following items are necessary in this pursuit:

1. Effective structure of the organization of sport;

2. Methods and forms of education in sport;

3. Motivation of athletes to perform achievements in sport;

4. Cooperation of sport and science;

5. Rationalization of planning methodologies of training processes.

Compared to the previous progressive Olympic achievements of the FRG, a sudden decline occurred in the FRG results in the Olympic Games in Mexico. Exhaustive analysis of this situation revealed the following external factors necessary for improvement in sport achievements: Confidence in sport, joy and pride in (Olympic) sport achievements and sympathy toward losses on the part of the federal government, the sport associations, and the people. As the federal government became more involved in supporting the sport system in the FRG, the social function of sport was more comprehensively considered in making efforts to develop young people for major sport achievements in conjunction with their education and their professional involvement.

Further development of socialist society in the GDR demands constant realization of the productive and creative potential of the people. The social role of sport as considered in the FRG is indeed compatible with the function of sport in the GDR society where the principle of performance or production is to better serve satisfaction of the material and cultural needs of the citizens. Sport is considered to satisfy in a special way, within the framework of the scientific and technological revolution, the necessities of higher development of productive capacity and skills of people to more effectively control the natural environment and society. The role of sport thus takes on a growing important function as socialist society more fully and extensively develops.

In contrast to the growing development of a more comprehensive sport system in the FRG, sport in the GDR now plays a prominent developmental role. The basic functions of sport and physical culture in the GDR socialist environment are stated below.

1) Sport contributes significantly to the development of a well-rounded educated socialist personality and fosters the development of a firm state consciousness. The highest sport accomplishments are considered a quintessential expression of great physical and moral achievements in character, effort, etiquette, and self-control.

2) Performance in sport spurs the young generation to consistent and regular training patterns. The social impact of this commitment draws more and more of the population to involvement in physical culture and sport. This relationship was already realized by the founder of modern Olympic games, Pierre de Coubertin, expressed in his Olympic Recollections. He formulated that "in order that a hundred people develop their bodies, fifty people must be involved in sport; and in order that fifty people participate in sport, twenty must specialize in sport; and in order that twenty specialize, five must be capable of prominent achievements in sport."

3) Participation in sport is an important factor in the state and utilization of leisure time. It provides an opportunity for people to actively and independently develop competencies in sport through training and public contests.

4) The sport system in the GDR is considered to promote the perspective of friendship and freedom between nations and support the esteem of the GDR, a socialist state of workers and farmers. Achievement in sport is considered to express the cultural capacity of the Republic and the commitment of the GDR citizens to sport. The problems of GDR development and achievement in sport agree with the Olympic concept and humanistic orientation of the founder of the modern Olympic movement. The GDR problems in the sport system focus on the physical and cultural education of the youth in order to develop character, good health, and a firm national spirit in the maturing youth.

5) The modern sport orientation offers insight into the physical development of the human individual, and also indicates the optimal way for the development and enhancement of physical capabilities of people. By means of training and contests the limits of physical and psychical capabilities are extended, which upon scientific analysis shed light on their developmental phase.

Achievement in sport thus plays a primary role in the GDR system of sport and physical culture. This orientation is supported by the following reasons.

1) Sport achievements express in a concentrated manner the ideological, political, economic, and social and educational questions concerning the relationships of social class and social power.

2) The political impact of the sport system in terms of models of achievement in sport influences significantly the standards of sport, especially for children and youth.

3) The conscious demands of discipline, achievement, courage, endurance, readiness to accept risks in confronting responsible challenges help foster a sound socialist personality.

4) The effective contribution of sport achievements strengthens GDR socialist society and comes to terms with the class conflict of imperialism.

The legal basis for the comprehensive system of sport and physical culture which is fully incorporated in GDR society was firmly established in the 1968 federal resolution dealing with problems concerning the role of sport and physical culture in the social development of the Republic. This resolution focused on the involvement of the citizens of the GDE in sport, athletics, and physical development to promote joy and recreation for the people, as well as good health and good education, competition and achievement, adequate national defense, and freedom and friendship among nations.

The above perspective is effectively disseminated by means of GDR sport communication. It is also reflected in intercultural communication that the GDR shares with many "socialist" nations, especially in the Third World. The ultimate goal of the extensive international and intercultural communication activities of the GDR is to enhance the prestige of the German Socialist State and to promulgate the strength and effectiveness of the socialist ideology on the international scale.

The Olympic System: Transnational Sport Organization And The Politics Of Cultural Exchange

David B. Kanin

The study of international organization has always been laced with a great deal of hope. The revulsion with World War I was translated into a disgust with the international system which was believed to have created it. Neo-Kantian legalism expected so much from the League system that it was more believed in than understood.

Although the Second World War dimmed some of the expectations for political organizations, the factor of faith remained strong. If political bodies did not perform as expected, technical and economic organizations would. With sovereignty discredited, functional interdependence would make it obsolete. It was not enough that these organizations did their tasks, they were charged with remaking the system as a whole.

As Mitrany gave way to Haas, the role of the state in the process was rehabilitated. Integration was still the rallying cry, but now it was to take place on all levels simultaneously. The problem seemed to be one of synchronization in some brighter future.

This concentration on belief has spilled over into the area of humanitarian and cultural international organization as well. The former can claim to provide a service recognized by all as universally desirable. Neither politics nor economics can be satisfactory excuses for denial of aid to victims of natural or man-made disasters.

Cultural organizations do not have the same self-evidence of humanitarian purpose as do such groups as the Red Cross. Cultural exchange does not involve the repairing of bodies or the elimination of disease. It does involve programs designed to strengthen patterns of communications in ways which will favorably influence relations between states and peoples.[1] It is assumed to provide aid to socialization, defined as "recurrent face-to-face contact which imparts to each participant an increasing awareness, understanding, and perhaps even a sympathetic appreciation of the position or point of view of the other."[2] Psychological empathy and aesthetic appreciation are expressly the purposes of such transactions.[3]

Implicitly, the "theory" of the benefits of intercultural transactions is a loose application of the Deutsch socio-causal paradigm of political integration.[4] Political integration is to follow a socialization process leading to the creation of a homogenous transnational population.

Such interchanges, however, also involve a conscious policy of political influence, much as in other forms of transnational relations.[5] The study of transnational organizations with cultural exchange functions should concentrate on political content as much as on cultural education, particularly when those organizations are based on units which correspond to those of the international political system.

This problem is approached by the Keohane/Nye model of transnational relations[6], but also in relation to the kind of socialization described above. "Attitude change" is described as one of the primary effects of the explosion in transnational relations, but the input of political units regarding this process is largely relegated to that of purposeful increase in transgovernmental communication.[7] Part of the difficulty relates to Huntington's organizations to the principle of nationality; IGO's are said to embody it, transnational organizations (TNO's) are believed to ignore it.[8] In fact, however, even such organizations as the International Olympic System*, which expound a disgust for international politics, are themselves used for the purposes of national prestige and policy, Indeed, it is quite possible that these TNO's thrive on their own political content, and that it is to the advantage of states to permit these TNO's ideological freedom, while exercising enormous political influence.

The artificial distinctions concerning politics and transnational relations are compounded by the "issue area" conceptualization of Keohane and Nye.[9] While it is true that variations in the process of international politics leads to doubt in the homogeneity, conceptually and politically, of the international system,[10] rigid compartmentalization of transnational processes threatens oversimplification of transnational concepts. Nye, for instance, split his perception of international socialization into mass (SIm) and elite (SIe) parts. His charting of these concepts was dominated by SIe. SIm was relegated to the conceptual wilderness of "other."[11]

There has been a relative paucity of consideration of the effects of SIm and especially of the organizations with this as their function. The exception, UNESCO, is a perfect illustration of the problems inherent in such compartmentalization. UNESCO has been plagued by the same "Hope" which has been the millstone of all international organizations. Niebuhr noted that, from the beginning, UNESCO was a disappointment to the great expectations of its creators.[12] Since wars started in the minds of people, this organization was to build defense of peace through understanding. The resulting policies of the states represented in UNESCO reflected the prevailing political system, rather than the one UNESCO was to help create. Sathyamurthy complained that political debate tinged all discussions within the

---

* International Olympic System comprises four units, see p. 521).

- 516 -

organization,13 and implied the prevailing view that such considerations were intrusions on the UNESCO process.

The assumption that "politics" can only intrude on ideally apolitical organizations needs to be reexamined. Cultural exchange is perceived to work best when it serves the cause of social integration despite political differences between the states involved. It is my contention that political issues are as much to the heart of such interchanges as is social integration. The international system cannot be categorized into rigid political or social issue areas. The system is too complex for such academic management to work. If international organizations are to grasp hold of the political environment, they must first be understood in light of their own intrinsic political content.

The results of the lack of such conceptual unity can be demonstrated using the example of a transnational organization older and more complex than UNESCO. Like the International Red Cross,14 the International Olympic system strives for international recognition of its importance. The IOS does not have the benefits of disaster relief as evidence, but it does have a claim regarding the heritage of ancient Greece to give it legitimacy. Aron, in his initiation of the term "transnational," invoked the heroic image of sport as an example of the phenomenon.15 Few have since, because (1) sport is not supposed to be "political," i.e., Olympic ideology is believed, (2) many observers are unaware of the existence of an old and complex transnational organization dealing with sport, and (3) sport, as SIm, is relegated to the conceptual wasteland reserved for such international transactions.

The Olympic Games, World Cup Soccer, Thomas Cup Badminton, and "Ping Pong Diplomacy" are all part of the same subsystem of international politics. Sport is a rulebound, competitive set of activities with uncertain outcomes engaged in for non-occupational purposes. Sports have histories, rules, and traditions attached to them resulting from their organization into bureaucratic administrative structures. Agreed upon measures of performance increase the international unity of sport tradition. Statistics serve as the unity of sport activity through time and space. Professional sport is a contradiction in terms for athletes, but still falls within the definition for spectators. The activity need not be physical (chess is a sport).16

As an international process, sport can be understood within the following conceptual framework:

International sport is a form of cultural activity which attracts the attention of, and is understood by, a mass public. Most of those involved in sport transactions are indirect participants; spectators who have their "contact" with athletes and fans from friendly or hostile states second hand, via the mass media. The "face-to-face" aspect of the socialization process is not a factor for most of those involved in sport. Athletes and officials do have personal contact, but need not wait to return home to relate the details of their experiences. Modern communications technology makes matches of national interest immediately available to anyone who wants to watch or listen. It enables this mass public, which tends to identify with the athletes, to take instant notice of contests against representatives of other states. Governments can use this identification when sporting events are staged to demonstrate the temper of international relations. The cancellation of such an event can also be useful in public diplomacy. It is a safe way (in terms of the risks of war or diplomatic rupture) of expressing displeasure with another country.

Sport is safe in this way because it is <u>peripheral</u> to the international system. Sporting events are not as vital to the state as are economic, legal, or diplomatic relations. A defeat in a match will not normally be avenged by the use of force by the state whose athletic representatives have lost.* Although, as shall be seen, sport is organized into units corresponding to states, governments have little control over the rules, equipment, standard of play, or outcome of sport. Yet, even without the direct application of state power, the public can be made aware of state moods and policies toward other states. It is somewhat misleading to insist, with Keohane/Nye, that the more transnational a system is, the more likely that non-governmental units will be the basic initiating and compelling forces.[17]

Unlike many forms of intercultural transactions, sport is competitive in nature. Art works can be exchanged without necessarily leading to a "zero-sum" comparison of national heritages. Comparisons between cultures are common, but they are not required by the mechanism of most cultural activity.

Such comparisons are intrinsic to the workings of international sport. If the staging of a sporting event can be a sign of socialization, the event itself is a direct comparison of the physical and human resources of the societies involved. States, and the IOS as well, may try to use sport to represent international goodwill, but the mechanism of sport makes it a potential forum for interstate competition as well.

If sport is a useful instrument in public diplomacy because of its public, politically peripheral nature, and unusual in intercultural relations because it is intrinsically competitive, it is also important in international relations because, as an activity, sport has no intrinsic political value. Sport can be used by any state to demonstrate the prowess of the human resources of any ideology or value system. The activity has no political content in itself, therefore the organized sport process can be given any political or ideological interpretation imaginable. Sport organization provides an arena for the direct comparison of athletes representing different social systems by spectators who can understand the rules which are common to most of the world. This has been called the "liquid" quality of sport.[18]

When a sporting event is arranged between representatives of adversary states, the result is as often a focus of international rivalry as it is a

---

* The so-called Soccer War between El Salvador and Honduras in 1969 was <u>sparked</u> rather than <u>caused</u> by the football series. Sport rivalry focused the effects of other problems in a compact time and space for the attention of spectators and governments.

forum for peaceful contact between peoples. Sometimes this aspect of sport affects the athletes themselves. Decathalon champion Bob Mathias described hatred for the "Russians" as a primary motivation behind the achievements of American athletes in the 1952 Helsinki Olympics, the first Olympic contended by both superpowers.[19]

Athletes and sport officials do often become good friends with their counterparts from even the most hostile of states. It is not the athlete, however, who is the most important actor in the process, but rather the spectator. Spectators are targets for the national and ideological comparisons intrinsic to the process. It is in this atmosphere that many states have set up government bodies to coordinate sport activity.

The use of sport to convey a diplomatic message or to promote identification between citizen and state is now a regularized and systematic phenomenon. This is true even though the organs of international sport remain functionally autonomous. Questions relating to the conduct of sport are dealt with inside the organization of sport. The latter is a self-contained mechanism when it comes to rival claims made by the direct participants of sport competition.

International sport relations generally fit the Keohane/Nye transnational model (Figure 1).[20] Since this model does not include consideration of such NGO's as the organs of international sport, it must be adapted to accommodate these actors, as pictured in Figure 2, via ISO's.

The international sport system is divided along two rival lines, splitting on the question of credentials for participation. Athletes are defined as "professional" or "amateur" depending, roughly, on whether or not they take money directly for their sporting endeavors. There is no single institution in control of all professional athletes. International amateur sport, however, is largely under the jurisdiction of the Olympic system.

The amateur-professional distinction has always been a fine one, and the growing interest of corporations and states has made it even more so. Many states now subsidize their best athletes, and there are companies which use athletes as human billboards. Some components of the IOS, such as the International Association Football (soccer) Federation (FIFA), allow professionals to compete in some of their activities. Only "amateurs" can take part in Olympic soccer matches, but professionals are allowed to compete on national teams in the World Cup series. The latter is an example where non-Olympic competition is more prestigious than the Olympic counterpart because spectators perceive that only the former involves the best athletes. Victory in the World Cup is often the cause of virulent patriotic outbursts.[21]

Despite the World Cup, and the recent growth of such activities as the Canada Cup ice hockey matches, the amateur based Olympic system remains the chief source of transnational sport interchanges. Its organization and sociocausal ideology provide the main focus for the activity of sport in international politics. States reinforce the advantages inherent in the peripheral political status of sport by permitting the Olympic system to retain control

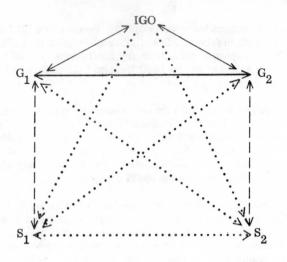

Figure 1.

IGO = Intergovernmental organization

G   = Government

S   = Society

——————— Classic interstate politics

— — — — Domestic politics

•••••••• Transnational interactions

of its activities. Governments often base domestic sport programs on some version of the Olympic ideal, amended to correspond to stated national goals.

Interstate sport does not always depend on components of the Olympic system for promotion and execution. Bilateral sport exchanges are often arranged through the same channels as other forms of political transactions. But even such events as "Ping Pong Diplomacy" take advantage of the fact that the Olympic system provides a forum for the alteration of mass perceptions of international relations. The 1971 visit of the United States table tennis team to China received the kind of publicity which enabled the event to serve as a major development in public diplomacy (Figure 3). This transaction involved government, business, and sport organizations in a fashion which blurs the definition of transgovernmental offered by Keohane/Nye.[22]

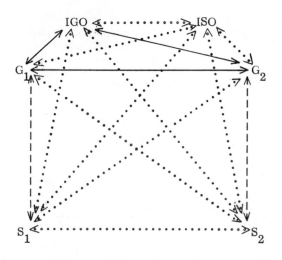

Figure 2.

IGO = Intergovernmental organization

ISO = Intersocietal organization

G   = Government

S   = Society

——————— Classic interstate politics

– – – – – – Domestic politics

•••••••••• Transnational politics

Their concept is useful in dealing with the problems in Huntington's transnational framework,[23] but their earlier work is more useful as far as the phenomenon itself is concerned.[24]

The International Olympic System (IOS) is made up of four parts:

(1) The International Olympic Committee (IOC)

(2) National Olympic Committees (NOC's)

(3) International Sport Federations

(4) Regional Games Federations

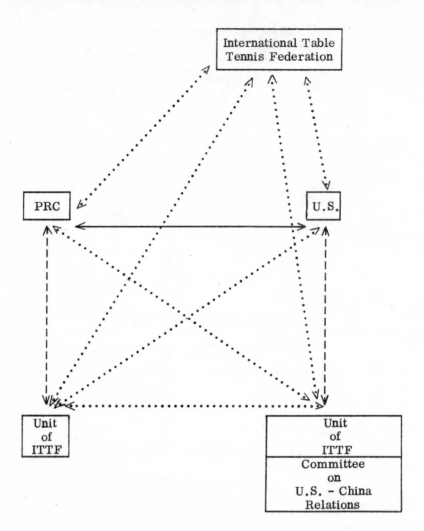

Figure 3. Example of Sport Transaction: "Ping Pong Diplomacy".

These organs have jurisdiction over the following events:

(1) The Olympic Games. These have been held every four years
since 1896. Each four year cycle is called an "Olympiad," with
the Games celebrated at the end. The Moscow Olympics will be
the Games of the XXIInd Olympiad. Winter Olympic Games, held
in the same year, do not have such a designation, since the
ancient Greeks had no winter sport festivals. Since World War II,
the Winter Games have been awarded separately.

(2) Regional Games. These are celebrated at four year cycles as well. Each region has its Games in a non-Olympic year, in the tradition of other ancient Games.

(3) World, Regional and National Championships in each sport. These are held at varying intervals under the control of the federations, or of their sanctioned national units.

The International Olympic Committee, founded in 1894, is still the centerpiece of the Olympic Movement (made up of the IOC, NOC's, and those federations in control of Olympic sports). Its founder, Baron Pierre de Coubertin, set its purpose at running the Olympic Games and at preserving the Olympic ideal of international goodwill and sportsmanship.[25] Coubertin perceived the need for a unifying ideology for all sportsmen (female competition came later, in stages) in order for the activities of the IOC to serve a socializing function.[26] He was also concerned that each of his countrymen become physically fit enough to hold off their more numerous enemies from across the Rhine. He found his mythology in the ancient Olympic tradition which had received attention of modern Philhellenes. The philosophical unity of body and spirit was to be the model for future social man. Coubertin's program focused on individual athletes, rather than on any state or organization. In order to make his ideas practical, however, he had to construct an organization which could satisfy the desires for prestige held by the states at which he preached. Coubertin favored a system under which each country had an opportunity to host the Games, rather than one which would have awarded the Games to Greece in perpetuity.[27] The honor of holding the Games became one of the earliest forms of international sport dispute. Its latest manifestations were the American failure to win the 1976 award for the bicentennial, and the Soviet success, after twenty years, in planning the first Socialist Olympics for 1980.

As the system of sport federations grew, the functions of the IOC became reduced to the selection of Olympic sites and the perpetuation of its own membership. Since the federations have taken over the actual mechanism of organized sport, the IOC has evolved into a body largely concerned with its own ideology.* The decline in the functional importance of the IOC can be seen in the marked decrease in the incidence of General Congresses of the Olympic Movement, over which the IOC presides. To date there have been ten such conclaves:

1894, Paris	1914, Paris
1897, Le Havre	1921, Lausanne
1905, Brussels	1924, Prague
1906, Paris	1930, Berlin
1913, Lausanne	1973, Varna, Bulgaria

---

* It can be argued that, as the functions of the IOC have declined, and deviations from the amateur idea have increased, the IOC has had to defend its ideology with ever greater force. The mythology becomes increasingly important as fewer and fewer believe it. Robert Tucker noted the same phenomenon with regard to the Soviet Communist Party. R. C. Tucker, The Marxian Revolutionary Idea. (New York: Norton, 1969), 192.

In lieu of these meetings, the IOC has had to rely on various liaison committees to keep it informed of the workings of the NOC's and federations.

Lausanne was chosen as the site for IOC headquarters in 1913. Members of the Executive Board sit there for four year terms. The IOC President is elected for eight years and is expected to be the leading spokesman for the Olympic Movement.

IOC members are not official representatives of their states to the Olympic body; they are to be ambassadors of the Olympic ideal to their homelands. Yet, from the beginning, the IOC has reflected the political situation around it. The IOC was born in the area of the "Great Powers," and more members were on it from those countries than from the others. Neither the subsequent League or United Nations Assembly models led to any change in that system; Olympic demography continues to reflect, more or less, the political power balance.[28] This means that the IOC has a sort of weighted voting system, as has been suggested for the United Nations General Assembly.

The popularity of intergovernmental organization following World War I resulted in a subtle alteration of Olympic Ideology. The terminology used to explain the purpose of the Olympic Movement was altered to step into line with the prevailing "internationalist" mood. The IOC was said to go beyond the function of aiding in the moral development of individual athletes; it was now excepted that these athletes were representatives of states, and that these representatives would be useful in the struggle to spread desirable internationalist values.[29]

State athletes were to be accepted as "peaceloving" as long as they came from countries which were part of the victorious coalition. Germany was barred from the 1920 and 1924 Games. German athletes were allowed back in Olympic competition only after their country had entered the League and the rest of the European system under the aegis of "Locarno Diplomacy."

The IOC changed its ideology in order to graft itself onto the League system. Coubertin put this directly in a letter to the President of the League Assembly shortly after the 1920 Olympics, in which he welcomed the League to the ranks of international organization.[30]

The decline of the League brought an end to the IOC attempt to obtain a role in the political system surrounding it. Since then, the IOC has limited its ideology to the moral development of youth, and to the good feelings athletic contests could create. The IOC has repeatedly insisted that it is independent of UN interference over such issues as South African sport participation. The question of how independent the law of an international organization can be has never been definitely approached in terms of the IOC.[31]

The National Olympic Committees are composed of local Olympic officials, representatives of various national sporting bodies (state organs or the local units of sport federations), and persons from other interested government and business agencies. The NOC's are the national representatives of the IOC and act for it on all domestic matters. As long as they recognize the supremacy of the IOC and of Olympic ideology, NOC's are granted considerable autonomy over national sport affairs. In order for a national Olympic committee to be recognized by the IOC, it must represent a country which the latter decides is a viable political unit with a stable government.[32] The NOC must be granted IOC sanction before the state can be celebrated in the Olympic Games. Sport federations have the same powers over the units of their competitions.

In effect, recognition of a national Olympic committee is tacit recognition of the jurisdiction of the state within its boundaries. The name and territorial limits of each state are reflected exactly in the units of transnational sport. The term state, in fact, was once defined in terms of the presence on its territory of a recognized NOC.[33]

The IOC insists that NOC's be structurally separate from the state, but makes little complaint if the NOC is under de facto control of political authorities. The 1936 Olympic arrangements were acceptable to the IOC despite the domination of the German Olympic Committee by a "Reichssportfuhrer."[34] Today most NOC's are under government subsidy or influence. The United States Olympic Committee, while functionally independent, is governed by a Congressional charter which can be revoked or altered.

NOC's, when controlled by states, still do not fit easily under the label "transgovernmental." They do much of their international business outside of regular diplomatic channels, but this is because of the perception of sport as "apolitical," rather than because of any functional considerations. NOC's do not relate only to counterparts in other countries; much of their role is possible only in conjunction with the IOC and the federations.

If a group objects to a certain state, a boycott of the athletes who represent it provides a means of expressing policy. Representative assaults on the legitimacy of states are possible because the Olympic system provides a forum for the expression of the political status quo. States may have the weapon of sovereignty to ward off transnational organization, but non-state actors do not.[35] The publicity surrounding transnational sport serves as a magnet for dissidents because it celebrates the political units these people oppose.

No city can submit a bid to host an Olympic celebration except through its NOC. The latter chooses the national team which represents its country in the Games. NOC's are allowed wide latitude regarding methods of team selection.

When an Olympic member state receives the award of the Games, the NOC forms, along with local federation units, government and business agencies, a Games Organizing Committee. The organizing committee is responsible for preparation of the Olympic site. This body manages the Olympics themselves, but must conform to federation rules concerning the equipment and conduct of each sport.

The organizing committee must also finance Olympic preparation, and is subject to IOC overview during the long period required to create an Olympic site (the Games are usually awarded six years in advance). The organizing committee can adjudicate disputes which cannot be settled under specific IOC guidelines, and can sometimes add sports to the Olympic program which have not been there before.

The NOC's serve to guard the purely national character of the Olympic Movement. Only those wearing state colors may participate in the Games, and NOC's often see to it that these teams consist only of state citizens. The teams, once chosen march in the opening Olympic ceremony behind the national flag. Victors are saluted to the strains of their national anthems.

Each sport is under the control of an <u>International Sport Federation</u>. Some of these are older than the IOC itself, but all have grown along with the Olympic system. At first, responsibility for judging and rulemaking was left to the athletic bodies of host states. After disputes between American and British officials at the 1908 London Olympics, pressure increased in favor of more central standardization of these processes. Some IOC members[36] felt that the administration of individual sporting events should be removed from the national sport organs.

At Paris, in 1914, the IOC met with representatives of the federations and gave over to them the right to control their individual sports in Olympic competition. The federations were lifted to a status equal with the IOC. From then on, they had a voice in the planning of all sporting events, no matter where they were staged. This grant of Olympic legitimacy led as well to centralization of the control of each sport in the hands of its federation.

In the contemporary era, federations legislate standards for equipment and athletic programs. In addition, they choose all referees and control participation by defining the term "amateur" as they wish (this word has been as difficult to decipher as "aggression"). While the IOC and the federations disagree over the precise meaning of this term, and despite the fact that some federations allow professionals in their activities, all federations continue to agree that only "amateurs" may participate in the Olympic Games.

The federations are represented on IOC liaison committees (dealing with such topics as sport medicine, drugs and ideology), and meet together in a General Assembly of Sport Federations. Each federation must give its approval to the Olympic program in its sport fifteen days before it is contested in the Games.

The federations also take an active role in <u>Regional Games Federations</u>. Regional Games can be as much a political showcase as the Olympics, since regional powers can display their athletic talent without competition by the rest of the world's athletes. Cuba has made skillful use of the Pan-American Games in overcoming the psychological effects of hemispheric isolation. Cuban victories make an impression on the rest of the region, while showing the spectators at home how much the Revolution affects its athletic beneficiaries.*

Those federations which govern sports not on the Olympic program can still be in the Olympic system, as long as they are administered like Olympic sports and maintain some definition of "amateur." Some federations parallel the Olympic Movement in the hope of eventual Olympic participation. Some groups, on the other hand, have given up any Olympic connection. The International Lawn Tennis Association is dominated by professionals. The Davis Cup competition, unusual in tennis in that it has an Olympic-like concentration on state units, also has dropped any "amateur" pretense.

The division of power within the Olympic system is charted in Figure 4. Power is distributed in such a way as to maintain an equilibrium between organs which were created independently, and which are jealous in their regard for their own place in the system.

The functions of that system (Figure 4) determine the political content of sport, as well as the power structure of the Olympic system. Each event under Olympic or federations auspices enables states to use their athletic champions any way they choose.

The membership function is therefore perhaps the most important. Claude's description of this process in the United Nations also applies to the Olympic system.[37] Collective legitimization is a much sought after Olympic commodity. As in the UN, members can become non-participants. South Africa was thrown out of the Olympic Games in 1964, but remained a member of the system until the 1970's. There are no actors such as the Palestine Liberation Organization, which participates in United Nations functions without the status of full membership. There would be little point in allowing athletes to come to the Olympics as "observers," and such status at IOC headquarters would do little more, since they are not nearly as significant as UN headquarters are to the UNO.

Membership has been a cause of constant Olympic turmoil. Before World War I, Czechs sought to take advantage of a strong athletic tradition[38] in order to achieve Olympic recognition. Bohemia had both an IOC member and a separate Olympic committee.[39] Austria-Hungary recognized the political importance of such participation, and blocked recognition of Bohemia after 1908. Finland and Tsarist Russia had a similar relationship at the Stockholm Games of 1912.[40]

At times, sport has provided a means for carrying out policy which could not be put into practice elsewhere. The United States found a rare

---

* The ongoing use of sport in Cuban-American relations is interesting, but conceptually different from "Ping Pong Diplomacy." The former was the first public demonstration of a diplomatic revolution. The South Dakota basketball trips to Cuba were, on the other hand, preceded by Senators Javits, Pell, and McGovern, and were, therefore, somewhat less significant.

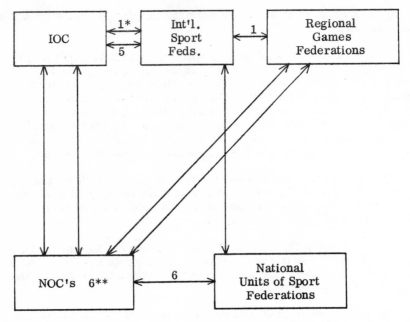

Figure 4. Olympic Functions.

Functions

1. Membership in Olympic Movement

2. Rules of Sport

3. Judging

4. Choice of Site for Olympic or Regional Games

5. Olympic Program

6. National Team Selection Process

---

* Each applicant must join at least 5 federations and form an NOC in order to qualify for Olympic participation.

** Often an NOC will grant jurisdiction on team selection to national bodies in specific sports.

application of the Stimson Doctrine of non-recognition at the 1932 Los Angeles Olympics. Japan tried to get "Manchukuo" in the Games, and the Americans took the lead in refusing such an extension of tacit legitimacy.[41]

German participation after World War II presented a special problem. There was only one NOC for "Germany." The Feeeral Republic sought to keep the situation as it was, since it meant that the unification of Germany could be stressed in a public political forum.[42] The DDR tried to achieve separate representation, in order to press its claims to be a separate political unit. From 1952-1964 a single German team marched behind a compromise flag and had its victors saluted by a Beethoven hymn, rather than either national anthem. The DDR was given "provisional" NOC status in 1955, and achieved separation in several federations before competing in the 1968 Olympics. Each federation is as much an arena for this type of membership battle as is the IOC.

The federations are still important in the "China" issue, as the PRC is still not in the Olympic Games. In each federation, as well as on the IOC, a "Two China" policy has been as impossible as in the United Nations. Both Chinas agree on two things: there is only one China, and Taiwan is part of it. The Canadian refusal to permit Taiwan athletes from attending the 1976 Montreal Olympics was simply an extension of its relationship to "China." To permit athletes traveling under a passport it did not recognize to represent "China" in a representative international event would have been a breach of Canadian foreign policy.

Either "China" might provide problems for the USSR if present at the Moscow Olympics. The Soviets have promised to admit all recognized NOC teams to their Games, but to do so in regard to Taiwan would raise the same problem faced by Canada.

The presence of athletes from Peking would mean that the representatives of these two quarreling states would be thrown together in the most public of political arenas. The Olympics could be used to demonstrate either hostility or improved relations. The politically peripheral nature of sport would enable "friendship" to serve the same purpose as in U.S.-China relations. "Ping Pong Diplomacy" involved a fast shift in the popular perception of "Red China," but did not necessitate definite political commitments. The two Communist states could demonstrate "normal" state-to-state relations without initiating any change on the Party level.

Another recognition question involves the United States and the Helsinki Agreement. The Final Act did not involve a complete recognition of post-war boundaries, according to President Ford. He asserted that the United States did not recognize Soviet occupation of Esthonia, Latvia and Lithuania. The yachting competition in 1980 will be based off Soviet Esthonia. If this country permits participation by its athletes in events in that area under Soviet jurisdiction, the United States will be extending unprecedented diplomatic approval of the situation, and will be reversing an aspect of foreign policy in practice since 1940.

A final consideration involving collective legitimacy is the case of Puerto Rico. That island is the only sub-sovereign actor in the Olympic Movement. Independence forces have been unsuccessful in their attacks on the mainland. If they can recruit sympathetic athletes, future Olympic and Pan-American competition might become the most significant forum for public separatist pressure yet. Incidents in this vein might be called "intrusions," but they would be direct applications of political consideration inherent in transnational sport organization.

The collective legitimacy granted by Olympic membership extends to two other areas, domestic legitimacy and foreign policy reinforcement. Olympic hosts in particular seek to use the award to socialize their publics. The first Olympiad provided the Greek royal family with an opportunity to tie its shaky popularity to the glory of the ancients. This imported German dynasty took over the organizing committee, and involved itself in judging.[43] Greek publicists[44] used appeals to "Olympism" to focus Greek claims regarding Crete. Greece was portrayed in the light of defending European civilization from the Turks, just as its ancestors had held back Persia in heroic times. Calling the most prestigious event in 1896 a "marathon" had some political significance.

The 1936 Games were awarded before Hitler came to power. The Weimar Republic hoped to celebrate the return of Germany to equal status in the European community; the Nazis used the Games as a festival marking the ongoing destruction of that system.[45] The original recipients of the 1936 award thus had very similar goals to those who planned the Munich Olympics of 1972.

In 1968 Mexico became the first "Third World" country to host an Olympic Games. While the government sought to demonstrate a progressive image, certain students staged riots timed to coincide with the Games in order to challenge the claim to stability and revolutionary heritage.[46]

The independence of "Third World" states in the past two decades has created a plethora of NOC's determined to press the use of sport in both domestic integration and foreign policy expression. Transnational sport is one arena where they can compete on equal terms, both on the playing fields and in Olympic councils. These states have achieved the goal of removing South Africa and Rhodesia from significant parts of organized sport.

The IOC, opposed in principle to such "intrusions" of politics, can do little about it. It cannot even discipline the NOC's it is angry at. Not even this basic disagreement over "politics" allows the IOC the option of challenging the jurisdiction of NOC's. The IOC threatened to discipline states and NOC's which had pulled out of the Montreal Olympics over New Zealand participation (New Zealand maintains sport ties to South Africa).[47] After the Games, however, no action was taken against these NOC's, it was merely promised that any repetition of such actions would be punished.[48]

One athlete tried to compete in Montreal as an individual after his NOC had pulled out, only to be turned down by the IOC. Even when in sympathy with such athletes, the IOC cannot challenge NOC control over team selection, and therefore cannot alter the political character of its own organization.

Rulemaking and judging questions can cause different sorts of political problems. The rules of sport are as open to conflicting interpretation as are the tenets of international law. Such disputes can be as difficult to settle as cases before the World Court, because of their cultural depth. Even though most rules are universally accepted, standards of play can be very different from region to region. Cultural differences on such issues as the acceptability of violence can cause significant asymetries of perception in international matches. Judges and referees from one area are often sent to another to function, and may have an imperfect view of their host's perception of the activity they are to mediate. European soccer referees, in particular, have had some difficulties when working Latin American matches.

At times, officials themselves may quarrel during competition. Many have complained that there is no "referee" in the anarchic international political system, but in the Olympic Games there are sometimes too many. The 1908 London Olympics were the scene of so many disputes between American and British officials that recriminations continued into the next Olympiad.[49]

In all sports requiring decisions which are both subjective and definitive, special problems persist. Diving, boxing, gymnastics and figure skating are plagued by incidents involving national judging idiosyncracies. In any sport where victory is not decided by time or distance, the progress of an athlete may depend on where the judges come from.

When spectators perceive a "bad" judgement, their "attitude change" may not be positive in nature. The same people who might accept public policy on the grounds that their leaders know more than they do will not accept such positions in international sport. The "fan" can verbalize why he or she thinks a call is "bad," or why his or her favorite athlete is being cheated. When such frustrations are on a national level, such as in the United States following the 1972 Soviet-American Olympic basketball match, outbursts can have a political expression. The Soviet team was brought to the U.S. the next year, and its matches were witnessed by the most fervently nationalistic audiences this author has ever seen.

Organized sport can be a specific outlet for political frustration. Soviet and Czech ice hockey teams played for the world championship a few months after the Soviet invasion of Czechoslovakia. Czechoslovakians saw their representatives defeat the Soviets for the first time in several years. The reaction in Prague was a riot against Soviet offices and individuals. This release of emotion was echoed in the Czechoslovak press, causing the Soviets to repeat charges that the Czechoslovaks had failed to control their newspapers. This breach of the peace resulted in the final demotion of Alexander Dubcek, and the final muzzling of the offending newspapers.[50]

The Olympic system, in its function and its organization, is a part of the international political system it claims to transcend (Figure 5). Its

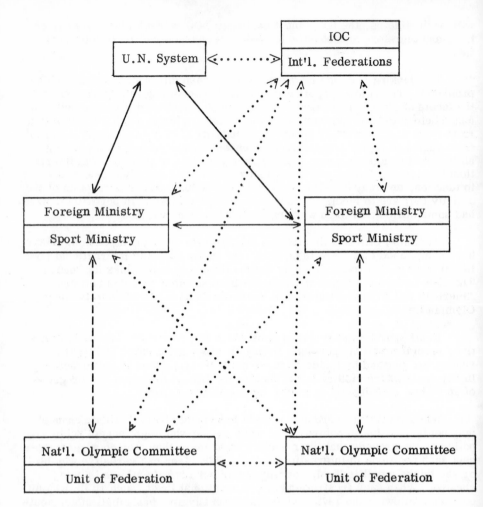

Figure 5. The Olympic System in International Relations.

relationship to state units permit it to reflect the political environment of the day. What is still difficult to define, at this time, is its relation to other international organizations, particularly IGO's. While multi-national corporations are content to use the organs of sport for publicity and advertising, the U.N. finds the system difficult to relate to.

In 1975, the U.N. Special Committee to Combat Apartheid and Racism urged the General Assembly to take up the question of South African participation in international sport. The result was UNGA Resolution 3324, urging that all such ties between member states and South Africa be cut off.[51] IOC reaction was to tell the U.N. that sport was none of its business, and to urge its member NOC's to ignore political pressure. The Davis Cup organization, of which South Africa was a member, found itself a battleground between that country and those opposed to it. South Africa urged that countries defaulting matches against South Africa be expelled, while some of those countries demanded the same fate for South Africa, in support of the U.N. position.[52]

The Special Committee supported the "Third World" walkout from the 1976 Olympics over the New Zealand issue.[53] It also supported further General Assembly action on the subject, and called for an international conference to consider the subject.[54]

Whether or not this conference will have any practical result will depend on how it approaches the question of sport in relation to the rest of international organization. A better understanding of the issue will emerge only if it is examined in the light of the political content of sport organization.

Such study may be of benefit to other organizations as well. It may be that the ineffectiveness of UNESCO stems from its failure to deal with organizations controlling educational, scientific, and cultural functions on the basis of how they work, instead of what they "should" do. UNESCO, for instance, is on record as accepting traditional assumptions concerning the "benefits" of sport transactions.[55] If "cultural exchange" is to be understood, much less applied to the "cause of peace," it may be necessary for each organization concerned with these functions to take another look at each other, and at themselves.

In the contemporary era, international relations have moved more into the realm of public scrutiny than ever before. Intercultural relations should be subject to careful study as integral parts of the international system. An analysis of the process that goes into any interchange is more important in the determination of the political, as well as humanitarian or cultural, significance of a transaction, than are traditional distinctions between those activities which are considered "important" and those which are not.

Footnotes

[1] Department of State, Bureau of Educational and Cultural Affairs, "The CU Program Concept," March 12, 1974.

[2] Peter Wolf, "International Organization and Attitude Change: A Reexamination of the Functionalist Approach," International Organization, XXVII, 3 (1973), 369.

[3] Robert O. Jones, "International Sports Communication: The Public and Private Sectors." Paper presented to the convention of the International Studies Association, February, 1976.

[4] K. Deutsch, "Integration and Arms Control in the European Political Environment: A Political Report," American Political Science Review, LX, 1 (1966), 354-65.

[5] Wolf, op. cit.

[6] R. Keohane and J. S. Nye, Transnational Relations and World Politics. (Cambridge: Harvard University Press, 1972).

[7] See Keohane and Nye, "Transgovernmental Relations and International Organizations," World Politics, XXVII, 1 (1974), pp. 39-62.

[8] Samuel Huntington, "Transnational Organization in World Politics," World Politics, XXV, 3 (1973), p. 339.

[9] Keohane and Nye, Transnational Relations and World Politics, pp. 169-71.

[10] See Keohane and Nye, "Transgovernmental Relations and International Organization," p. 55.

[11] J. S. Nye, "Comparative Regional Integration," International Organization, XXII, 4 (1968), p. 875.

[12] Reinhold Niebuhr, "The Theory and Practice of UNESCO," International Organization, IV, 1 (1950), pp. 3-5.

[13] T. V. Sathyamurthy, "Twenty Years of UNESCO: An Interpretation," International Organization, XXI, 4 (1967), p. 617.

[14] D. P. Forsythe, "The Red Cross as a Transnational Movement: Conserving and Changing the Nation-State System," International Organization, XXX, 4 (1976), pp. 617-620.

[15] Raymond Aron, Peace and War. (New York: Praeger, 1968), p. 105.

[16] D. B. Kanin, "The Role of Sport in International Relations." (Ph.D. dissertation, Fletcher School of Law and Diplomacy, 1976), p. 313.

[17] Keohane and Nye, "Transgovernmental Relations and International Organizations," p. 55.

[18] Harry Edwards, The Sociology of Sport. (Homewood, Illinois: Dorsey Press, 1968), p. 88.

[19] W. O. Johnson, All That Glitters is not Gold: The Olympic Games. (New York: G. P. Putnam's Sons, 1972), p. 221.

[20] Keohane and Nye, Transnational Relations, xiv.

[21] Janet Lever, "Soccer: Opium of the Brazilian People," Transaction, VIII, 2 (1969), pp. 37-38.

[22] Keohane and Nye, "Transgovernmental Relations and International Organizations," p. 42.

[23] Huntington, op. cit., pp. 333-368.

[24] Keohane and Nye, Transnational Relations, pp. ix-xxix.

[25] T. E. Sullivan, The Olympic Games of 1912. (New York: American Sports Publishing Company, 1912), p. 27.

[26] Baron Pierre de Coubertin, "The Olympic Games of 1896," The Century Magazine, LIII, 1 (1896), pp. 39-53.

[27] Central Committee in Athens, The Olympic Games: B.C. 776-A.D. 1896. (Athens: Charles Beck, 1896), II, p. 8.

[28] See IOC, Olympic Directory. (Lausanne: IOC, 1973), pp. 61-69.

[29] American Olympic Committee, Report of the American Olympic Committee, VII Games, 1920. (AOC, 1920, p. 78.

[30] Journal of the First League Assembly, #8 (December 23, 1920), p. 67.

[31] See J. L. Kunz, "General International Law and the Law of International Organization," American Journal of International Law, XLVII, 3 (1953), pp. 456-461.

[32] IOC President Avery Brundage in The New York Times, July 19, 1952.

[33] British Olympic Council, The Fourth Olympiad. (British Olympic Association, 1908), p. 29.

[34] Richard Mandel, The Nazi Olympics. (New York: Macmillan, 1971), p. 62.

[35] Keohane and Nye, "Transgovernmental Relations and International Organization," p. 58.

[36] W. M. Sloane, "The Olympic Idea," The Century Magazine, LXXIV, 2 (1912), p. 411.

[37] I. L. Claude, "Collective Legitimization and the United Nations," International Organization, XX, 3 (1966), pp. 367-79.

[38] L. Jandacek, "The Sokol Movement in Czechoslovakia," The Slavonic Review, XI, 31 (1932), pp. 65-80.

[39] IOC, Olympic Directory, p. 61.

[40] Swedish Olympic Committee, The Games of Stockholm. (SOC, 1912), Plate 108.

[41] The New York Times, May 26, 1932.

[42] The New York Times, May 10, 1951.

[43] Central Committee in Athens, The Olympic Games, B.C. 776-A.D. 1896. (Athens: Charles Beck, 1896).

[44] See D. Kalopothakes, "The New Olympic Games," Harper's Weekly, September 25, 1895, pp. 919-924.

[45] Richard Mandel, The Nazi Olympics. (New York: Macmillan, 1971).

[46] James Coote, Olympic Report, 1968: Mexico and Grenoble. (London: Robert Hale, 1968), p. 22.

[47] The New York Times, July 20, 1976.

[48] The New York Times, June 12, 1977.

[49] T. A. Cook, The Olympic Games of 1908, A Reply to Certain Criticisms. (London: British Olympic Association, 1908).

[50] See E. Taborsky, "Czechoslovakia: The Return to Normalcy," Problems of Communism, XIX, 6 (1970), p. 32.

[51] The New York Times, March 11, 1975, March 16, 1975, April 29, 1975.

[52] Ibid.

[53] The New York Times, July 26, 1976.

[54] The Boston Globe, November 10, 1976.

[55] UNESCO, *Sport, Work, Culture: Report of the International Conference on the Contribution of Sports to the Improvement of Professional Abilities and to Cultural Development*. (Helsinki, 1960).

Nation Building And Sport In Africa

Raph C. Uwechue

The struggles for independence in many African countries were regarded as a force heralding positive development because they were opposing
colonialism, a repressive and negative force.[1] However, no sooner had independent states been established than disillusionment set in. It became
painfully clear that African states lacked the capability to solve problems of
disease, illiteracy, poverty and backwardness in general. Above all they
were incapable of uniting all their people into a coherent community with disastrous consequences in Nigeria, Burundi, Congo and others.

What were the causes of this? Many see the cause in so-called tribal-
ism. Others assert that for all their nationalist mobilization during the fight
for independence, virtually all former colonies never succeeded in becoming
independent in the true sense of the word. As most states resulted from a
negotiated process involving the former colonial masters, no real change in
the power relationship took place.[2] "The resultant weaknesses", states one
writer, "tend to reduce whatever modest degree of independence an individual state may attain from time to time. All attributes of statehood are adversely affected and their political potency is reduced internally as well as
externally".[3] The internal powerlessness evidences itself in the countries'
inability to mobilize their own people towards such desired goals as economic and political development.

What solutions have been offered? A few states such as Tanzania have
chosen the African socialist way--Ujamaa--in the belief that a system which
is closely connected with the culture of the people is the surest way of mobilizing them. Others believe that an unhesitating sortie into full capitalism is
the answer.[4] Others still have advocated a mixture of the two. All of them
agree that the people must be mobilized if the developmental process is to be
meaningful. But how? Tanzania, as we have said, chose Ujamaa. Others
argue indirectly for the military that "frequent coups are a sign of change
and progress".[5] Increasingly many people are pointing to physical education
and sport as the media most suited to mobilize the people.[6]

In examining the role of sport in the nation building process in Africa,
I shall deal with three periods: pre-colonial, colonial and post-independence
periods. Besides affording a history of the topic, such a classification may
enable us to gauge the importance which was attached to sport in the various
periods.

Materialien zum Internationalem Kulturaustausch, Institut fur Auslandsbeziehungen, Stuttgart, Vol. 5/1978.

Pre-Colonial Period

Physical education formed part of the overall traditional education, the aim of which was to prepare the young for life as adults.[7] Adults also engaged in sport both for personal as well as for political, social and religious reasons. Among the Ibo of Nigeria, wrestling was engaged in by adults as a religious activity whose aim was the strengthening of crops.[8] In this sport, it was not uncommon for someone from among the spectators to step forward and take over from either a tired or irate participant, "so that no ill effect should be produced on the reproductive forces of nature".[9]

Different games were played for different purposes such as creating skills or imparting endurance. In all cases the games were closely related to the age and sex of the participants as well as to location and season. Other distinctions were as to outdoor, indoor, daytime or moonlight. For instance during festivals and ceremonies in many parts of Africa, the predominant form of sport is dancing. Sport also depended on what the community based its subsistence. For instance among the Luo of Nyanza, where fishing is the way of life, canoe paddling is the main form of sport.[10]

The physical training of boys and girls in traditional society began at the age of about ten or twelve years. Before that, they were "free to play about" although invariably they imitated what they saw of the realities of adult life.[11] As such they began to condition themselves towards adult life by recreating such activities as hunting, farming, marrying, fishing, building, cooking, worshipping and so on. As the boys and girls became older, they were gradually integrated into the economic, social and political life of their societies according to their age-sets. Besides determining what games were played by what age-group, age-sets helped to inculcate the significance of a particular game on a particular age-group. Boys or girls in a given age-group always had the opportunity to assess the meaning of a game in terms of their own group. The value of group life, the idea of leading or being led, the sense of fair play, invariably sank deeper when members of an age-group played together as this tended to reinforce the reality of social interaction.

An enduring aspect of traditional education was its functionalism. As such physical education in the form of games and play bore a close relation to the culture of the society. The games reflected adult life and gradually increased in their reality as the children became older until their eventual integration into adult life.[12]

Colonial Period

The introduction of colonialism and its institutions brought about a partial eclipse of traditional culture. With the advent of western education, whether sponsored by missionaries or the colonial administration, came the first appearance of Western sport. Many aspects of traditional culture were suppressed if found to be inconsistent with the new norms. For instance the British doctrine of repugnancy permitted the overriding of African tradition in the interests of "natural justice, equity, and good conscience".[13] In East Africa the cattle rustling sport engaged in by the Suk, Masai and the Turkana was proscribed during colonial days because it interfered with the smooth running of the colonial administration.[14] Others were encouraged if they either did not adversely affect the administration or tended to support it such as the regatta on Lake Nyanza in which some ethnic communities were invited by the British to join.

In the schools which they started, missionaries soon introduced such games as football, hockey, cricket and others. In many cases, the introduction of a particular game was evidence of the class origin of the Europeans.[15] In Nigeria, sport was soon made to conform to the colonial norm, with the institution of Empire Day celebrations in 1893. The day was chosen "as a time for remembering and showing loyalty to the British Crown".[16] It was a day on which the various ethnic groups in the country came together in sporting and gaming activities.

The introduction of western games was not a widespread phenomenon indicating an awareness on the part of missionaries and colonial administrators for the physical well-being of the Africans. In the report of the Phelps-Stoke Commission of the early 1920s, it was found that African education was steeped in the tradition of the four "Rs"--including religion.[17] The Commission restated the importance of physical education in the molding of such virtues as honesty, fair play, generosity, courage, purity and love of the beautiful.[18] It recommended the adoption by the colonial authorities of African music, dance and other indoor games in a report which was remarkable for its foresight. Many African boys and girls who had been to a mission school were beginning to despise African dances and music.

Colonialism brought with it new centres of sport such as the army, police and other institutional sponsors. These developed to such an extent in many countries that they formed the nucleus of the modern sports movement. In Nigeria, the first modern athletic grounds were erected at police and army posts.[19] Besides the need to socialise its members to its goals, these institutional sport centres existed because Africans lacked individual resources to support their games. This fact helped to reinforce the colonial system in many ways. Those recruited into the police and army soon internalized the norms and group solidarity of their institution. In the cities, clubs belonged to elites who were well placed economically in the colonial society. They needed to do this in order to be able to attract good players. Their ability to attract and retain the players depended on the rewards they could offer to the players.[20]

The colonialists in the main allowed the participation of Africans in games where the Europeans themselves were too few to play by themselves. In the cities where they were numerous enough, there was a strict segregation of teams and spectators.[21] However, in the smaller communities of places where seclusion was dangerous or impracticable, the colonialists enthusiastically joined the indigenous people in sporting and other activities.

The indigenous people who came into contact with western sport whether in schools, army, police or clubs in the city were a tiny fraction compared to the whole population. For those that did actually come into contact with them, leaving school or the city invariably meant the end of the experience. For many they could not rejoin the socializing process of their ethnic groups, either.

Post-Independence Period

In 1964 the International Council of Sport and Physical Education (ICSPE) sent out a questionnaire to various countries to elicit information about their sport structures, sport participation and leadership training programmes for teachers, coaches and officials. When the findings were related to African countries, it was found that the sports movement was not new in Africa.[22] Basing their examination on traditional Africa and ignoring the colonial era, the analysts stated that what was new in Africa "is the introduction on a large scale of modern sports in their western form of a competitive character".[23]

This is not quite correct as the colonial period familiarized many an African area with western sports and the concept of competition in sport is not unknown in Africa. However the statement is important in implying the need to examine and conceptualise sport in the new phenomenon of the African nation-state.

An important distinction needs to be made between the meanings of state and nation although many would justifiably argue that the two are synonymous. State-building has been seen primarily as a process emphasizing "efficient administration, economic development, further specialization and expansion of the civil service".[24] In short, the emphasis is on bureaucracy. When talking about nation building, the subject is the "inculcation of political loyalties to the system as a whole, transcending the bounds of kinship, language and locale".[25]

When discussing nationhood, one would thus deal with the forces which unite or divide the people. In this connection sport and nation building is a topic which calls for the examination of how sport can engender forces which unite the nation.

It must be pointed out at the outset that protagonists of sport as a developmental medium do not claim that sport directly brings about development. They argue that its importance lies in its capacity to predispose people towards change. Sport's ability to "capture the interest of people in almost all countries no matter what their stage of development" makes it the most suitable medium through which to inculcate desired goals.[26]

Sport has been defined as "any physical activity which has the character of play and which involves a struggle with oneself or with others, or a confrontation with natural elements. . . . If this activity involves competition it must then always be performed in a spirit of sportsmanship. There can be no true sport without the idea of fair play..."[27] Speaking during the Rabat Seminar on sport[28] M. P. Vagliani of UNESCO said: "The qualities of loyalty, generosity, disinterestedness, and respect for others which the young sportsman derives from sport in school, place of work and the stadium are destined to be practiced in his social and professional life if he remains faithful to the ideals of fair play. Emulation does not mean, for him, hostile opposition; the dialogue prevails over the struggle, tolerance over contempt; love of the country does not degenerate into an exaggerated nationalism; egoism gives way to solidarity. <u>We thus see in sport an ethical quality which can transfer itself to real life</u>." (emphasis added).

Is there evidence in Africa that sport as stated above is well understood? Do African governments share a belief in the importance of sport? In one sense the answer is yes. In many countries in Africa, there are ministries of youth and sport or a sport office attached to the ministry of labour, education, social affairs and so on.[29] Outside government are sport federations for the various games such as football, boxing and so on which are in turn affiliated to their international sports federations. Many countries have national sports councils in which government and voluntary organizations coordinate sport among schools, the armed forces and civil organizations. There are also regional sports organizations and of course the Supreme Council of Sport in Africa. Thus in terms of structures, there does appear to be a realization in Africa of the importance of sport.

The question--is there a realization in Africa of the development value of sport?--is harder to answer. Sport does not appear to be receiving as widespread support in Africa as it does in the west or the east. Some observers think that because sport does not bear a direct relationship with development, it being only indirectly related, African countries do not see it as deserving immediate attention. Rather questions of hunger, poverty and even state security tend to receive first priority. The proper role of sport in the social milieu of Africa does not seem to be quite clearly appreciated. The emphasis of sport administrators appears to be directed away from mass participation. In Ghana for instance, the full-time sports organizers of all the regional councils "have the responsibility of spotting and developing the talents of promising sportsmen and women".[30] The reason behind this trend was once stated by Professor J. A. Laoye of Nigeria thus: "The people of every country would very much like their country to rank high in the field of sports and the name of their country written in the World Book of Sports... The production of national and international champions in different sporting activities is in fact one of our main objectives because we believe that such champions are ambassadors of the country".[31]

Needless to say, the effort to produce international athletes and champions diverts resources away from sports for all. This failure to appreciate the need to involve the whole people also evidences itself in other respects.

In many African countries today, many games are permitted which trace their origin to colonial times and belong to a socially differentiated society. Games such as horse riding, golf, lawn tennis and others which involve an inordinate amount of skill and expense are unsuited for popular mobilization. In some countries lawn tennis receives equal ranking with such mass sports as soccer. The reason for this is that countries are anxious to win international contests. "These two activities", states one country's development plan, "have been singled out for early attention because of their popularity and primacy (soccer and tennis) in the world of sports".[32] The concern with building the national image through sport is the form in which attempts to use sport for nation building exists today in Africa. However, as President John F. Kennedy discovered in 1960, the physical fitness of a few individuals says nothing about the whole country. "Never in history," said he, "has the United States been represented by a more vigorous group of athletes in national and international competition. Yet we must not allow our pride in these few men to obscure the fact that over the past decades the level of physical fitness of much of our citizenry has been far below any reasonable national standard".[33]

The failure to emphasize people-oriented sport evidences itself in the provision of facilities such as stadia. Because they offer opportunities for mass participation, stadia are important as environments for socialisation.[34] Many African countries are only beginning to construct them.

In the African context, stadia are especially important in that they offer the opportunity of preserving African culture in sport. Many aspects of African sport are mass-oriented such as dances and stadia constitute the best mechanism for integrating African tradition in modern sports, a process which is beginning in some schools syllabi. The idea has never been lost sight of although during colonial days attempts were made to suppress traditional sports in favour of western sports. The move was not quite successful given the nature of the African environment which made the impact of colonialism uneven. In East African schools many teachers were incorporating African choreography in their syllabi and "it is quite remarkable to see the change of tempo which results. A dull lifeless lesson is transformed into something live and active when a local dance-game is played."[35]

However factors are legion which militate against the adoption of Africanness in physical education and sport in schools and adult life. To begin with, the move to traditional games is counteracted and frustrated by the urge to compete and win championships in international games. As a result, foreign games form part of the culture of many African countries. Africa has succeeded in having countries with racist systems expelled from the international forum. It should be able to use its sporting strength to persuade the international community to offer championships in games which originate from Africa.

In case the introduction of African sports on the international arena is opposed as being impracticable, the Africans can begin the process themselves on a continental basis. This is where the Supreme Council of Sport in Africa (SCSA), formed in 1965, could perform a vital function.

The SCSA has already begun to move in this direction. In April 1971 it and the ICSPE organized the first seminar in Africa on the contribution of sport to the construction of modern Africa.[36] One of the aims of the seminar was to formulate a "persuasive statement concerning the role of sport in development". Its emphasis was to be on suggestions "which blend properly into African culture".

The problems of sport in nation building in Africa are many. First of all, even the most ardent protagonists of sport will be the first to admit that

the ethics learnt in participation and fair play do not automatically get transferred to real life.[37] Many of them express only the hope that a true sportsman or sportswoman will not abandon the ethics of the game in everyday life
This to some extent takes the wind out of sport advocates. If the chances of
sports causing people to act fairly and ethically are not that preponderant,
what assurance is there that they will be beneficial? The argument which
sport advocates usually use is one based on the cost-benefit syndrome. They
argue that the enormous amounts of money which are expended to build the
image of the country could usefully be used on the training of sport stars who
bring instant recognition to a country. They point to Abebe Bikila and Mirus
Yifter of Ethiopia, Kipchonge Keino of Kenya and Filbert Bayi of Kenya.

Although the capacity for instant fame rightly belongs to international
athletes, the argument for training them takes away some of the force out of
the overall argument. The point is not to emphasize the image of the country, but the health of the people and as such it must be mass sports which is
at issue and not the training of a few athletes.

The claim that sportsmen and sportswomen will be likely to practice
the ethics of their games in real life overlooks the fact that these people have
to exist in a definite environment. As any aspect of social interaction, sport
is governed by the prevailing social and political conditions of a country.[38]
One of these conditions is the ubiquitous malady of corruption which in Africa, as everywhere else, dissipates scarce resources. The provision or
lack of facilities is itself determined by the prevailing condition in any country.

This leads to a most important consideration on the relation of sport
and politics. The need to mobilize the whole population is a political decision which must be implemented for the whole nation if it is to succeed. It is
futile to harp upon the advantages to be had from the introduction of sport-
for-all if the powers that be do not wish to see the full implications of the
process. One of those implications may be that a successful mobilization of
the people may result in the demand for more resources which the state as
currently constituted is unable to satisfy. In other words, the total mobilization of the people may in the eyes of some authorities carry within it the
implication of radical change.

Another way in which politics affect sport is in regional cooperation.
During the Rabat seminar, Colonel H. E. O. Adefope, then chairman of the
National Sports Council of Nigeria called on governments to promote region-
al sports "within areas prescribed rationally by geographical convenience".
The recent break-up of the East African Economic Community demonstrates
that geographical rationality is not the end of the story.

Colonial history may also militate against the promotion of interregion-
al sports. As is well-known, cricket is popular in former British colonies
and cycling in former French colonies. To get the two to cooperate in these
sporting events demands major adjustments.

Some educators have recently spoken against physical education as a
concept. They argue that it is "an unnecessary European import; that sports

and games are a waste of energy when physical energy is urgently needed for nation building".[39] To my mind, this is evidence of the lack of a proper understanding of the role of sport in development. It is an undisputed fact that in many countries, especially those which take the socialist path, physical education and sport are accorded a most important place in their developmental process.[40] For instance Article 18 of the East German constitution guarantees the right of physical culture and sport to all its citizens.[41] "The vigour of the citizens today", stated one official, "creates the vigour of the state tomorrow".

Delegates to the Rabat seminar also learnt the seriousness with which sport is regarded in West Germany. Through its Sports Academy, established in 1920 in Cologne, Germany offers a full-fledged sports programme to its citizens in the form of sports medicine, sports physiology, bio-engineering, psychology, sociology, traumatology, pedagogics and research into a host of other related topics. On the international level, the Academy works in close contact with the German government, German dipolmatic representatives abroad, diplomatic representatives of other countries inside West Germany and other relevant institutions.

The lack of effective governmental backing for sport in Africa results in the absence of money, the root of the majority of sport's troubles. Many solutions were suggested during the Rabat seminar such as that the Organizations of African Unity must absorb the SCSA and that way help to influence African governments. Others said that the SCSA should buy sport equipment in bulk and resell it at a profit. This is believed to lead to the strengthening of the SCSA and the provision of badly needed equipment. Some have called on governments to lift duty on sporting goods or to establish industries in Africa which would make sports goods from local raw materials. The advantage of this is that while it helps to foster local games since only those goods to be used in mass games would be worth the trouble, it also makes it possible for traditional choreography to be incorporated in modern sports.

Some officials have instituted sports pools and lotteries to create badly needed money for the provision of such facilities as swimming pools and soccer fields. Although obviously welcome, these attempts are usually a drop in the ocean if there is no support coming from the government.

Knowledge of the role which sport can play in the developmental process of a nation exists in Africa. Speaking to the Rabat seminar in 1971, Mr. T. Kankasa, then Minister of State for Labour and Social Service said: "Progress in a nation depends on the active contribution of the individuals who make up that nation, and a nation of healthy and fit individuals is more likely to produce more for the benefit of the nation. A country's greatest asset is its human resources and since sport helps to stimulate people, mentally and physically, the development of sport leads to the development of human-resources." Thus although knowledge exists of the role of sport in development, no government in Africa has as yet launched sport on a developmental course on the same scale or magnitude as in the eastern countries. Ghana, Malawi and Guinea have used youth brigades but these have tended to be for specific political goals rather than as part of a long-term process of mobilizing the people.[42] Studies have been made on the role of sport, but no follow-up measures have been made.[43]

The lethargic manner in which African countries view sport is in marked contrast with the practice of other countries. As Reet Howell observes, the status which physical culture and sport occupy in many western and eastern countries is the result of conscious efforts on the part of the political authorities.[44] Such a conscious effort must bear a relation to the life of the nation as a whole. As Mr. Akililu Habte of Ethiopia once said: "No amount of physical exercise or sports or athletics is going to help the African child to be physically fit if he is undernourished or malnourished."[45]

What most countries need in Africa today was spelt out clearly by a former athlete. "The first advice one can offer ... is the establishment of a State Research and Planning Unit which will discover exactly what facilities, leadership cadres, and organizational structures exist and how they might be better coordinated. Secondly, it is to recommend the importance of an efficient communications system which will explain to people the purposes of the sports movement. Thirdly, it is to devise a national program of physical education and sports which utilizes the indigenous activities, involves the youth actively and imaginatively, and is so structured that it can rapidly continue to work on local effort alone."[46]

All this presupposes a political will on the part of the powers that be.

Inter-Africa Games

Sport assumes a totally different dimension when inter-African competition is involved. The move to involve all the African nations in the sports movement has been more resolute and successful than the efforts to involve the people in the individual countries in the sport movement. One reason may be the strength of the Pan-African sentiment to assert the identity of being African, which has so long been suppressed. Inter-African cooperation is also simpler and more manageable than national sports because the existence of trained athletes makes the job of competition easier. In other words, inter-African sports does not involve the drudgery of training, but only the testing of the efficiency already gained.

Before the coming of independence to many African countries, Africans had participated in international competitions as members of the countries which were the colonial masters over them. Even after some countries had become independent, the initial tendency was to depend on regional competitions among countries with similar colonial histories. The exception to this was the Africa Cup of Nations football contest, first held in Khartoum in 1957.

The first sign of change came in 1960 when Nigeria decided to host the West African Games in Lagos as part of her independence celebrations. She opened the competition to all West Africans, French- and English-speaking. A year later, Nigeria along with Liberia were invited to Abidjan to join in the previously all-French "Games of Friendship". In April 1963 the third "Games of Friendship" in Dakar brought together 24 countries, five of whom,

Gambia, Ghana, Liberia, Nigeria and Sierra Leone, were English-speaking. Although the games were still largely a West African phenomenon, there were some positive developments already, one of which was the first involvement of women athletes.[47]

It was during the Dakar games that a decision was taken to ask Congo-Brazzaville to host the first All-Africa Games, to which all independent African states would be invited to send athletes with the exception of South Africa and Rhodesia. Not only would Africa unite in friendly competition, but also in the desire to assert its freedom from oppression. The games would be conducted in the same spirit of political unity as the Organization of African Unity.

On 18 July, 1965 the first All-Africa Games were opened by Alfonse Massamba Debat, then president of the Congo Republic. "The torch of African sport", he said, "will not fade out. On the contrary, its flame has today reached every corner of our continent ... it is a privilege for Brazzaville to be able to brandish this torch on this historic occasion, when the whole of Africa is declaring and celebrating its entity."[48]

More than 3,000 sportsmen and women from 28 independent African states attended the games. After the event, it was decided to establish the SCSA with headquarters in Yaounde, Cameroun. Andre Hombassa was elected president, Jean Claude Ganga, also of the Congo Republic, secretary-general, Abraham Ordia of Nigeria, first vice-president and Badara Sow of Mali, second vice-president. In 1967 the OAU officially recognized the SCSA.

At the Second All-Africa Games in Lagos in 1973, 37 independent African states participated and for the first time no foreign assistance was involved unlike in the past when French help had been solicited. With more than 1,500 athletes from all over Africa, this was the largest gathering of sportsmen and women. They competed in track and field, soccer, boxing, basketball, volleyball, tennis, swimming, cycling, table tennis, handball and judo. The competitions were preceeded by a show of African traditional culture in the form of African dances and movements.

Based on the model of the OAU the All-Africa Games which can be regarded as detracting from the Africanness of the whole event are the games themselves, some of which trace their origin from the colonial period. With the exception of soccer, boxing and swimming, most games have a regional bias. However, it is important that the games are taking place at all. It will not be long before the unity forged through constant contact is utilized for the creation of other stronger ties. The games are essentially a reflection of the political climate of the continent and as new levels of understanding are reached, these will be reflected also on the games.

Footnotes

[1] Michael F. Lofchie (ed.)., The State of the Nations. (University of California Press; Berkeley, Los Angeles, 1971), p. 9.

[2] Claude E. Welch, Jr. (ed.)., Soldier and State in Africa. (Northwestern University Press, Evanston, 1970), p. 3; Ruth First, Power in Africa. (Panthenon Books, New York, 1970), p. 27.

[3] Henry L. Bretton, Patron-Client Relations: Middle Africa and the Powers. (General Learning Press, New York, 1971), p. 1.

[4] Peter Enahoro, "The Tolbert Years", Africa No. 71, July 1977, p. 59.

[5] Samuel P. Huntington (ed.)., Changing Patterns of Military Politics. (Free Press: New York, 1962), p. 40.

[6] In this paper, physical education and sport will be used interchangeably

[7] E. Y. Egblewogbe, Games and Songs as Education Media. (Ghana Publishing Corporation, 1975), p. 27.

[8] John Ademola Adedeji, The Role of Physical Education in the Nation Building of Nigeria. (Unpublished Ph.D. thesis, The Ohio State University, 1972), p. 71.

[9] Ibid.

[10] Sidney Owen Hall, The Role of Physical Education and Sport in Kenya. (Unpublished Ph.D. thesis, The Ohio State University, 1973), p. 136.

[11] E. Y. Egblewogbe, op. cit., p. 27.

[12] John Ngara, "Games..." (Review article). Africa Woman No. 7, November/December 1976, p. 67.

[13] Henry L. Bretton, Power and Politics in Africa. (Longman: London, 1973), p. 123.

[14] Sidney Owen Hakl, op. cit., pp. 134-136.

[15] Rémi Clignet and Maureen Stark, "Modernization and Football in Cameroun", Journal of Modern African Studies, 12, 3, 1974), p. 411.

[16] John Ademola Adedeji, op. cit., p. 90.

[17] Sidney Owen Hall, p. 138.

[18] Ibid., p. 139.

[19] John Ademola Adedeji, p. 93.

[20] Rémi Clignet and Maureen Stark, p. 444.

[21] Ibid.

[22] D. W. J. Anthony, The Role of Physical Education and Sport in Developing Countries. (Unpublished Ph.D. thesis, University of Leicester, 1971), Chapter 11.

[23] Ibid.

[24] Claude E. Welch (ed.), p. 4.

[25] Ibid.

[26] D. W. J. Anthony, "The Role of Sport in Development", International Development Review, December 1969, p. 10.

[27] ICSPE/UNESCO, Declaration on Sport. (UNESCO House, Paris, 1969).

[28] ICSPE/SCSA, The Contribution of Sport to the Construction of Modern Africa. April 1971, Rabat (hereafter The Rabat Seminar).

[29] Africa Yearbook and Who's Who 1977. (Africa Journal, Ltd., London, 1977).

[30] Ghana 1976: An Official Handbook. (Ghana Information Services, Accra), p. 419.

[31] Sports facilities for schools in developing countries. UNESCO, Paris 1973, p. 15.

[32] Nigeria, Third National Development Plan 1975-80. (The Central Planning Office, Federal Ministry of Economic Development, Lagos, 1975), p. 286.

[33] Sport facilities for schools in developing countries, p. 15.

[34] D. W. J. Anthony, The Role of Physical Education, p. 20.

[35] J. W. Owen, "Physical Education in East African Schools, Oversea Education, v; 28 (January 1957), p. 174.

[36] The Rabat Seminar.

[37] D. W. J. Anthony, The Role of Physical Education, p. 4.

[38] Marie-Therese Weal, "Sport: The Opium of the People", Red Mole v. 1, No. 5 (14 May, 1970), p. 5.

[39] Sport facilities for Schools in Developing Countries, p. 19.

[40] D. W. J. Anthony, The Role of Physical Education and Sport, p. 32.

[41] Albert P. Glanstein and Gisbert H. Flanz (eds.), Constitutions of the Countries of the World. (Oceans Publications, Inc., New York, Dobbs, February 1975), p. 14.

[42] John Ademola Adedeji, p. 223.

[43] Ghana: White Paper on the Report of the Committee appointed to review the Organization of Sport in Ghana, Accra, 1968.

[44] Reet Howell, "The USSR: Sport and Politics Intertwined", Comparative Education, Volume 11, No. 2, June 1975, p. 137.

[45] Sport facilities for Schools in Developing Countries, p. 20.

[46] D. W. J. Anthony, The Role of Sport in Development, p. 11.

[47] Ramadhan Ali, Africa at the Olympics. (Africa Books: London, 1976), p. 117.

[48] Ibid., pp. 118-119.

The Problem Of Sport And Nation Building In Southeast Asia

Swanpo Sie

General Background

Southeast Asia is defined here as Burma, Cambodia, Indonesia, Laos, Malaysia, the Philippines, Singapore, Thailand and Vietnam. These countries have a total land area of about 1.8 million square miles and a population of approximately 250 million. Of these nations, Indonesia has the most territory and the largest population, encompassing almost half the land mass and half the population of Southeast Asia.

Before the second World War the countries of Southeast Asia, with the exception of Thailand, were under the colonial rule of Western Europe and the U.S.A. During the second World War the countries of Southeast Asia were under the rule of the Japanese military government; after the War they struggled for independence from their colonial rulers.

Geographical conditions and historical development are partial reasons for the great variety of ethnic and linguistic differences and cultural patterns among and within the nations of Southeast Asia. Despite their differences, however, these countries share many characteristics and common interests. They were dominated for years by Western powers, they became members of the developing and newly emerging nations following independence, and most of them still face problems of national development and political stabilization. In almost all of the countries of Southeast Asia, the military forces are of political importance directly and/or indirectly. All of these countries have problems of population growth, minority difficulties of varying seriousness, high illiteracy rates, and have lived through years of political and economic difficulties.

Southeast Asia is traditionally a meeting place of cultures and religions. Religious beliefs range from animism through the world religions of Islam, Christianity, Buddhism and Hinduism, and include Confucianism, Taoism and ancestor worship. Sometimes the people practice a mixture of several beliefs.

Zeitschrift für Kulturaustausch, Institut für Auslandsbeziehungen, Stuttgart, Vol. 4/1977.

Western social, political, economic and cultural influences, including the ideologies of socialism and communism, came by way of the Portuguese, the Spanish, the Dutch, the British, the French and the North Americans.

As a result of West European and North American colonialism in Asia, the cultures of most Southeast Asian nations have been changed to varying extents by the outside forces of Western influence. Since independence they have been seeking their own identities as nations. Political and economic forces, including the war in Vietnam, foreign aid programs from the U.S.A. and Europe, and tourism are other factors which have profoundly influenced the development of the nations of Southeast Asia. In some areas the result is a mixture of acculturation and artificially created identities.

Nation building in Southeast Asia with its complex problems of political stabilization, national integration and economic, social and cultural development is an immense challenge which the nations of Southeast Asia are attempting to meet using all possible means, including sport.

Brief Historical Background of Sport Movements

Prior to independence, sport activities in the Southeast Asian colonies reflected the philosophies and policies of their colonial rulers. In the Philippines, schools gave more emphasis to competitive sport than sport-for-all, which reflected the practices in the U.S.A. In Cambodia, Laos and Vietnam, sport movements were modeled after those of France, tempered by the influence of mainland China. Burma, Malaysia and Singapore were under British influence, while Indonesia was Dutch oriented. Those Chinese in Southeast Asia who considered themselves to be Chinese nationals overseas and who called themselves Hua Chiao (literally, overseas Chinese) had their own sport movements with certain goal oriented philosophies and policies patterned after their homeland China.

Among the colonial rulers, the U.S.A. was the most liberal, which explains why the Philippines moved into the international world of sport relatively early. In fact, the Philippines was one of the initiators of the Oriental Olympic Games held in 1913 in Manila. These Games later became the Far Eastern Championships which were held regularly every two years, and which the Philippines hosted several times. The Far Eastern Championships and its representing organization, the Far Eastern Athletic Association, were terminated in 1934 due to a political issue concerning the representation of Manchuria in the Games. An attempt was made to prepare another sport meet for the Asian nations, to be called the Oriental Championship Games. The first Games, which were to be held in Tokyo in 1938, did not take place due to the political developments in Asia and the political tensions in the world on the eve of the second World War.

Although not stated officially, these sport movements in Southeast Asia were indirectly oriented towards political and nationalistic goals. The colonies were striving for more social, cultural and political freedom from their rules and for the development of nationalism and national integration among their populations. Sport was viewed as an indirect means to these ends.

Not long after the outbreak of World War II, Southeast Asia was occupied by Japan. During the Japanese occupation sport movements were strictly guided by the Japanese military government. Participation in military drill exercises was compulsory among school children and youth. Throughout Southeast Asia the Japanese introduced morning physical exercise by radio, called "Radio Taiso." The goal was to develop militancy among the populations, especially the youth, so they would serve as a reserve army to fight side by side with the Japanese against their common enemies at the time--the Western European and North American colonial rulers.

Sport movements during the short occupation period had little effect on the course of sport development later; however, they did contribute to strengthening the Southeast Asian nations in their efforts to instill nationalistic feelings, national integration and a fighting spirit in their populations, particularly the youth.

After the War, in 1947, when the nations of Southeast Asia were struggling for independence from colonial rulers, a Conference on Asian Relations was held in New Delhi. Representatives to the Conference agreed that sport competition among Asians would encourage Asian unity. Such unity was aimed at strengthening friendship and relations among Asian nations for common social, economic and political interests and for approaching national and international problems with a base of Asian solidarity. The proposal to hold sport competitions among the Asian nations was accepted. As a follow-up to this proposal, and with the support of the late Indian Prime Minister Jawaharlal Nehru, a regional Olympic Games in Asia known as the Asian Games was agreed upon. The first Asian Games, originally planned for 1950, was held in New Delhi, India in March of 1951. The Philippines again was the first nation in Southeast Asia to host the Games when the second Asian Games was held in Manila in 1954.

Following independence, sport movements in Southeast Asia grew rapidly. A unique development occurred in Indonesia under the late President Soekarno, who officially declared sport movements to be an important part of Indonesia's nation building.* A special chair for sport was established in Soekarno's cabinet in 1962 with the instituting of the Ministry for Sports.

Among other developments, Soekarno personally requested the late President John F. Kennedy of the U.S.A. to send Peace Corps volunteers in sport to Indonesia. Although the Peace Corps did not have a sport program at that time, Soekarno made it clear that sport was the one area in which volunteers would be welcome. Sport was the logical choice for Peace Corps involvement since it was the least politically volatile and most politically acceptable area to the various ideological factions of the time, and because it enjoyed great popularity among the population. With Kennedy's help sport was accepted into the Peace Corps program and volunteers in sport were sent to Indonesia in 1962. Many other Southeast Asian countries quickly followed suit and requested sport volunteers also.

---

* Address by President Soekarno to Indonesian athletes in Bandung on April 9, 1961.

The Indonesian government called the U.S. Peace Corps volunteers Sukarelawan Pembangunan, which translates as "Volunteers for Development." Since volunteers in sport were the only Peace Corps volunteers ever admitted to Indonesia, the choice of name seems to indicate an emphasis on the role of sport in nation building; however, another reason this name was chosen was to sidestep propaganda arising from the anti-Peace Corps campaign launched by the Indonesian Communist Party.

In support of Indonesian strategies in international relations, Indonesia's activities in the international sport movements were intensified. In 1961 Indonesia hosted the Thomas Cup Badminton World Championships. Indonesia was considered as one of the candidates to host the 1963 Summer Universiade as well. Due to the political situation--especially the relations between Indonesia and the European countries--the General Assembly of the International Federation of University Sports held in Sofia, Bulgaria in 1961 voted in favor of Brazil as host of the 1963 Universiade. In 1962, Indonesia hosted the fourth Asian Games, which entailed political issues when the Indonesian government refused to grant visas to the teams from Israel and Taiwan. This political interference during the fourth Asian Games resulted in the censure of the International Olympic Committee and the withdrawal of Indonesia from the Committee.

Following Indonesia's break with the International Olympic Committee, Soekarno initiated the Games of the New Emerging Forces (GANEFO) in Jakarta in 1963. It was declared that the GANEFO proposed to strengthen all nations of the world who considered themselves anti-imperialists, thus condemning past colonial rule in Southeast Asia. The underlying idea behind the GANEFO, which was strongly supported by the People's Republic of China, was to set the stage for a Conference of the New Emerging Forces to be held in Jakarta a few years later. The Conference was to establish a "Third World" United Nations organization composed primarily of Asian, African and Latin American countries. The cooperative aspects of GANEFO were intended to foreshadow--actually to facilitate--a parallel alliance in the political arena, which would have had profound effects on international relations and the course of national development in the Southeast Asia countries. Had this plan been realized, the political and economic shape of the world today might well be substantially different, since the resource-rich Third World countries would have had a unified political power base from which to bargain with the technologically advanced countries. Furthermore, the prospect of two United Nations organizations had political ramifications which threatened to disturb, if not alter, the existing world balance of power.

Although the GANEFO was successful in the realization of its aims, with most of the Southeast Asian countries and numerous others represented, a combination of forces and historical events prevented realization of the far-reaching political plan. Strong opposition from the U.S.A. and Western European countries, exploitation of the situation by socialist countries, political developments in Asia and Africa, and the fall of Soekarno in Indonesia resulted in the discontinuation of the GANEFO, and the Conference of the New Emerging Forces was never held. Interestingly enough, the Federation of the Games of the New Emerging Forces, which was the representing organization of the GANEFO, still exists officially since its members never met to dissolve the organization.

Indonesia's relations with the International Olympic Committee were subsequently normalized and Indonesia's re-entry as a member of the International Olympic Committee was granted. Soekarno's fall also resulted in termination of the Ministry of Sport, which was degraded to a Directorate of Sport in the Ministry of Education and Culture.

Meanwhile, Thailand and neighbouring countries initiated a sport competition among the countries in the Southeast Asian Peninsula, called the Southeast Asia Peninsular (SEAP) Games. It was stated that the purpose of the Games was to strengthen the existing bonds of friendship among the nations of Southeast Asia. The first SEAP Games was held in Bangkok, Thailand in December, 1959, and the Games have continued to the present. It is unclear whether the SEAP Games originated as a maneuver of the Southeast Asia Treaty Organization (SEATO) established in 1954 as an anti-communist alliance with headquarters in Bangkok.

In spite of national independence and efforts to promote national identities, Southeast Asia remains attracted to Western influences in sport, in part because of the historical domination of the colonial powers. Recent American and European military, political and economic intervention in Southeast Asia and the rapid growth of tourism are other factors which have profoundly influenced the Southeast Asian countries in their efforts to build nations with their own national, cultural, social and economic identities. Sport movements have been likewise affected.

Sport, Nation Building and Problems

Although the countries of Southeast Asia have their own specific difficulties, broad problems of nation building generally involve such elements as traditional, cultural and social barriers within societies. Differences of religion, ethnic group, language, customs, and economic and political interests may become obstacles to national integration and national development. Sport, with its broad relevance to education, social welfare, culture, politics and health, if adequately planned, may serve the purposes of nation building and foster national integration. It should not be the purpose of nation building to destroy traditional mores, but rather to transform them into broader social group functions which are better adjusted to a new, modern environment. Sport has a significant role to play in such transformations.

It is evident that sport movements in Southeast Asia have been influenced by the attitudes and policies of governments and political leaders directly and indirectly. Indonesia's late President Soekarno declared sport movements an official part of the Indonesian revolution building a new Indonesian nation. Cambodia's Prince Norodom Sihanouk believed that sport could promote unity among people. To his own countrymen he stated that the prestige of the nation could be elevated through improvement in sport competition, since the real world often judges the strength and value of a nation in terms of its performances in sport. Southeast Asian top political leaders

--including Cambodia's Prince Sihanouk, Indonesia's late President Soekarno and the present Vice President Hamengkoe Boewono IX, Malaysia's former Prime Minister Tengku Abdul Rachman, and the Philippines' President Marcos--have been very enthusiastic and personally involved in sport movements at the national and international levels. Furthermore, a review of reports and articles on the development of sport movements in the various Southeast Asia countries shows that almost all sport movements in these countries depend on government financing for support.

Despite fine plans and programs and despite keen interest in sport on the part of the population, very little real progress has been made, especially in the implementation of sport movements in the interests of nation building. Leaders and government authorities have frequently complained about shortages of facilities and experts. Governments and national sport organizations have often invited foreign coaches and experts from the U.S.A., the U.S.S.R. and other Eastern and Western European countries; however, most of these foreign experts have been invited to improve the performance of competitive athletes rather than to assist in the implementation of sport for nation building and national development.

It is a fact that too much stress has been put on high performance competitive sport. There seems to be a vast gap between theoretical understanding and practical implementation of sport for nation building in Southeast Asia. Indonesia is a prime example of actual government priorities in this area. The best sport facilities in Jakarta, the finest in Southeast Asia, are used for developing top performance athletes. Foreign sport coaches and experts are almost always invited for the upgrading of competitive sport.

Among the Southeast Asian nations, Indonesia has the most training schools for physical education and sport experts, at both high school and university levels. Two decades ago the quality of these training schools was high. Standards are now questionable due to ignorance and to the low priority budget allocated to this area by the Indonesian government. Many graduates from these training schools have difficulty finding jobs, yet foreign coaches are invited to Indonesia and paid salaries twenty to forty times that of local experts. This is because priority is given to top performance sports which need top international coaches.

Recognizing the urgent need for upgrading the quality of teachers at the training schools for physical education and sport, the Indonesian Sports Science Center and the Indonesian Coordinating Body for Physical Education, Health and Recreation attempted to attract technical assistance from the U.S.A. and the Federal Republic of Germany. It was hoped that this upgrading could be extended to other interested nations in Southeast Asia. The U.S.A., as indicated by U.S.A.I.D. officials and the Cultural Affairs office of the U.S. Embassy in Jakarta, was assigning a low budget priority to the field of physical education and sport; however, a favourable reaction was shown by the government of the Federal Republic of Germany. With the strong support and involvement of the Goethe Institute in Jakarta, a government grant from the Federal Republic of Germany was allocated for a two week Workshop in Concepts of Sports Sciences in Indonesia, specifically designed for the upgrading of deans and instructors of the Colleges for Physical

Education and Sport throughout Indonesia. The Workshop was held in Bandung in September of 1975, with main lecturers in the fields of sport science and related areas, from well-known German institutions of higher learning. This was the first time in the history of the Colleges for Physical Education and Sport that instructors had the opportunity to receive quality instruction from foreign experts. Enthusiasm was high and workshops were expected annually for succeeding years; however, the Indonesian government and national sport authorities expressed such a lack of interest that a second workshop planned for 1976 failed to be realized. Plans were not made to continue such upgrading workshops, despite a minimal effort needed on the Indonesian side. The upgrading of college instructors is not directly related to producing top performance athletes and therefore is of low priority in the sport development program of the nation.

Discussions with teachers and government authorities in physical education from various nations of Southeast Asia have revealed similar situations in those countries. The biggest handicaps are the lack of funds, facilities and qualified experts. Yet the limited funds and facilities available are used for promoting the development of an elite group of national top athletes rather than for the development of the entire nation. The few experts these nations have are not used to their full potential, yet experts are imported from abroad.

In order to promote national identities, some governments are encouraging the development and promotion of indigenous sports and dances among their populations. Examples are the Sepak Takraw in Malaysia and Singapore, the incorporation of the basic movements of Pencak Silat in the morning exercise program of Indonesia, and the re-creation of indigenous dances for tourists in most of the countries of Southeast Asia. While of unquestionable value in the cultural sphere, many of these indigenous activities are not particularly supportive of national integration and national identity objectives, in part because of the way they are handled. The popularity of many indigenous activities is limited to certain regions because they are bound to local traditions and cultural patterns. Those sports and dances which are of wider interest pose certain problems when manipulated for purposes of national development. Many of these problems are directly related to the powerful and inexorable force of Western ideas. By the time an indigenous sport or dance has been standardized, divorced from its religious and/or cultural context, glamourized, shortened and simplified for mass consumption and tourist tastes, it often has lost its relevance to the vast majority of the national population from which it sprang. Sport has been fortunate in that it has been somewhat less subject to loss of integrity than indigenous dance, which is sometimes totally artificial in manufacture.

All governments of Southeast Asian countries are interested in promoting sport activities among their populations, especially among youth and school children. They understand the importance of integrating sport with education, health and culture and its role in economic development and social life. They recognize the value of sport for the harmonious development of body and mind, health, ethical values, worker efficiency, social consciousness, relaxation, and for the intellectual, moral, aesthetic and emotional development of the individual. Sport is viewed as useful for the promotion of national integration and the facilitation of international relations and international recognition. The governments have fine programs and plans aimed at the educational, cultural, health and welfare aspects of nation building; they have well stated aims and objectives for sport and other areas--on paper-- and little else.

When national development is concentrated heavily on industrial, agricultural and economic factors, little or no priority is usually given to long-term and intangible investments such as education, health and welfare. Investment in sport development, as is the case with education, health and welfare, is not only expensive, but also does not bring about an immediately profitable economic return. National and international sport competition, on the other hand, is of great government interest because of its high visibility and relatively quick returns in the form of national recognition and political support. In the context of contemporary Western development theories, sport development, although recognized as important, receives little attention in national development plans as long as the economic situation of a country remains unstable. When sport development does receive attention on the national level in Southeast Asia, as was the case in Indonesia under Soekarno and in other emerging nations during the GANEFO movement, it is usually to gain political ends and thus has been essentially temporary in character and short-range in impact.

Although improvements have been made in the area of economic stabilization in some of the nations of Southeast Asia, particularly in Singapore and Malaysia, most of the countries of Southeast Asia are still far from stable. Mismanagement, internal political struggles and corruption in the government are problems which the nations of Southeast Asia have to face and to solve. Other problems such as the population explosion, unemployment, food supplies and the plague of communicable diseases, surely need immediate attention and priority in the national development plans. Only the future will reveal whether long-term, intensive educational and social welfare reforms can be postponed indefinitely without risk of national collapse.

In the same way that sport movements can be supportive and useful for a nation's development plan, they also can be damaging. Sport movements can be very expensive and can be manipulated for political, business, and personally corrupt purposes. In most of the nations of Southeast Asia--where there is a lack of experts, where sport movements are run by professional amateurs and/or amateur professionals, where high performance competitive sport is the priority effort--the role of sport movements in nation building is questionable in light of current practices.

Theoretically sport could play a unique and perhaps unmatched role in the fostering of national integration, national cohesion, national spirit and national identity in Southeast Asian countries. Unlike any other area, it cuts across social, economic, educational, ethnic, religious and language barriers. Unlike any other area, it elicits massive enthusiasm and support among populations and offers a key for the development of cooperation on local, national and international levels. Furthermore, it is easily adapted to support of educational, health and social welfare objectives. Unfortunately, current government attitudes among both the Southeast Asian countries and their Western supporters make the realization of the potential of sport for nation building in Southeast Asia unlikely within the foreseeable future.

Bibliography

Ahmad, A. Bakar, "The Elementary School Physical Education Programme in Singapore," Proceedings of the Sixteenth International Congress of the International Council on Health, Physical Education, and Recreation. (Swanpo Sie and Mary Windorski Sie, Editors). Jakarta: Directorate General of Sports and Youth, Republic of Indonesia, 1973, pp. 106-108.

Aquino, Francisca R., "Current Trends of Physical Education in the Philippines," Official Report of the Asian Congress on Physical Education, Jakarta, August 21-23, 1962, p. 41-45.

Dewan Olahraga Republik Indonesia, Mengapa Indonesia Menarik Diri dari Olympic Games Tokyo? Jakarta: Dewan Olahraga Republik Indonesia, Siaran No. 1, 1964.

Games of the New Emerging Forces, Documents of the First GANEFO Congress. Jakarta: Panitya Kongres GANEFO, 1963.

Games of the New Emerging Forces, Documents of the Preparatory Conference for the GANEFO. Jakarta: Panitya Persiapan Kongres GANEFO, 1963.

Grueninger, Robert W., "Physical Education in Indo-China," Physical Education Around the World (W. Johnson, Editor), Monograph No. 5, Phi Epsilon Kappa Fraternity. Indianapolis, Indiana, U.S.A., 1971, pp. 23-24.

Hanna, W. A., "The Politics of Sports," American University Field Staff, Southeast Asia Series, Vol. X, No. 19, October 1962.

Indonesia, Embassy of, Washington, D.C., Report on Indonesia, 12 (August 1963), pp. 18-19.

Indonesia, Republik, Departemen Olahraga, Meresapi Makna dan Tudjuan Revolusi Olahraga. Jakarta: Departemen Olahraga, Siaran Chusus No. 1, 1963.

Indonesia, Republik, Departemen Olahraga, Revolusi Keolahragaan Melaksanakan Amanat Penderitaan Rakjat. Jakarta: Departemen Olahraga, Siaran No. 1, 1964.

Indonesian Olympic Committee, Indonesia and the International Olympic Committee. Jakarta: Komite Olympiade Indonesia, 1963.

Keputusan Presiden Republik Indonesia, No. 94, Tahun 1962. (Presidential Decree.)

Keputusan Presiden Republik Indonesia, No. 176, Tahun 1964. (Presidential Decree.)

Keputusan Presiden Republik Indonesia, No. 57, Tahun 1967. (Presidential Decree.)

Komite Olahraga Nasional Indonesia, "Keputusan Sidang KONI PARIPURNA I, tanggal 26 s/d 29 Pebruari, 1968." Jakarta: Komiet Olahraga Nasional Indonesia, 1968. (Mimeographed.)

Manusama, J. L., "Physical Education in Indonesia," Official Report of the Asian Congress on Physical Education. Jakarta, August 21-23, 1962, pp. 24-31.

McCollum, Robert H., Josefina J. Ruiz and Candido C. Bartolome, "Physical Education in the Philippines," Physical Education Around the World (W. Johnson, Editor), Monograph No. 5, Phi Epsilon Kappa Fraternity. Indianapolis, Indiana, U.S.A., 1971, pp. 59-68.

Organizing Committee of the 1961 Universiad, "Address by Sie Swanpo, President of the All Indonesian University Students Sport Union, to the Ordinary General Assembly of the FISU, held at Sofia, Bulgaria, on September 4-5, 1961." Sofia: The Press Centre of the Organizing Committee of the 1961 Universiad, 1961. (Mimeographed.)

Sie, Swanpo, Administrasi Keolahragaan dan Masyarakat di Indonesia. Jakarta: Pusat Ilmiah Keolahragaan, 1975.

Sie, Swanpo, "Dari IOMA sampai B.K.M.I.," Mahasiswa dan Masjarakat, No. 6: 19-32, Mei 1972. (Publication of the Department of Education and Culture, Republic of Indonesia, Jakarta).

Sie, Swanpo, "Recent Development of Physical Education and Sports in Indonesia," Proceedings of the Eighteenth International Congress of the International Council on Health, Physical Education, and Recreation (D. Schmull, J. Groenman and J. W. de Vries, Editors). Zeist: The Jan Luiting Foundation, 1975, pp. 248-251.

Sie, Swanpo, "Historical Development of Physical Education and Sports in Indonesia," Proceedings of the Pre-Olympic Seminar on the History of Physical Education and Sport in Asia (Uriel Simri, Editor). The Wingate Institute for Physical Education and Sport, Israel, 1972, pp. 143-167.

Sie, Swanpo, "Social and Political Aspects of Physical Education and Sports in the Framework of Indonesia's National Development," Proceedings of the Sixteenth International Congress of the International Council on Health, Physical Education, and Recreation (Swanpo Sie and Mary

Sie, Swanpo and Nicolaas J. Moolenijzer, "Physical Education in Indonesia," Physical Education Around the World (W. Johnson, Editor), Monograph No. 5, Phi Epsilon Kappa Fraternity. Indianapolis, Indiana, U.S.A., 1971, pp. 35-48.

Sie, Swanpo and Mary W. Sie (Editors), Concepts of Sports Sciences. Jakarta: The Indonesian Sports Science Center, 1975.

Singapore, State of, Ministry of Education, "Physical Education in Singapore Schools 1962," Official Report of the Asian Congress on Physical Education. Jakarta, August 21-23, 1962, pp. 45-48.

Somboonsilp, Punya, "The Role of Health, Physical Education and Recreation in Rural Development in Thailand," Proceedings of the Sixteenth International Congress of the International Council on Health, Physical Education, and Recreation (Swanpo Sie and Mary Windorski Sie, (Editors). Jakarta: Directorate General of Sports and Youth, Republic of Indonesia, 1973, pp. 112-114.

Toh, Boon Huah, "School Sport Councils in Federation of Malaya Physical Education Programme," Official Report of the Asian Congress on Physical Education. Jakarta, August 21-23, 1962, pp. 39-40.

Visudharomn, Kong, "Physical Education in Thailand," Official Report of the Asian Congress on Physical Education. Jakarta, August 21-23, 1962, pp. 48-53.

International Dimensions Of Sport

Education And Sport Science

Herbert Haag

The examination of the international dimensions of sport, sport education and sport science will be approached in three major ways. In the opening remarks, sport, sport education and sport science are explained as a theoretical framework for analysis of international relations. A justification of international relations is given drawing upon the three phenomena of sport, sport education and sport science. In the second major part of this presentation, different types of associations are reported, emphasizing the role played in inaugurating, helping and improving international relations. Up to the present day, quite a diversity of associations and organizations have been developed at the international level.

The knowledge of models and concepts used in other countries, a favorable attitude towards the international exchange of ideas and transnational relationships, as well as efficient actions, have to be taken into account in order to ensure that international relations are developed and constantly improved in the field of sport, sport education and sport science (Zeigler, 1968). Thus, the third major part of this paper explores the exchange of information on the international level as a function of keeping international relations alive. In recognition of the information "explosion" of recent years, it is specifically important to make provisions for appropriate transmission of information at the international level; otherwise, misconceptions may arise, and time-consuming procedures be employed in order to keep open international discourse.

1. The concepts of sport - sport education - sport science

These three basic terms have to be seen closely interrelated and yet clearly distinct. The basic phenomenon would be sport. This phenomenon could be used in order to pursue educational aims and objectives. Thus, sport education is a process-oriented kind of action. Sport science finally is the overall scientific field dealing with the social phenomenon called sport.

1.1 The notation of sport as an international endeavor

Although the word sport is taking on international meaning as being all-inclusive for any kind of physical activity which is done in one's free time, the word is used in the English speaking countries in a rather narrow sense, namely as competitive sports.

Sport is seen as a basic pattern of culture, which has reached great importance in most societies today. Movement behavior as related to sport is showing many similarities but also differences in regard to the cross-cultural perspective. Sport, however, is a subject which lends itself for investigations on an international scale. Outcomes of such research could be a better understanding of each other, the willingness to learn from alternatives and by this process, enlarging one very important worldwide communication system not limited by race, creed or political beliefs. Sports have become a widely used "international language".

1.2 Sport education as part of education based on human movement

The social phenomenon sport is taken as a means in order to reach certain educational objectives. Furthermore the importance of this social reality sport requires that pupils are prepared in an educational process to cope with this phenomenon and its different aspects. Again an international dimension seems to be available since sport in the form of physical education is an educational process requiring not too many verbal cues in order to be realized. Cross-cultural and international perspectives can be considered, to a great extent, to be a function of non-verbal communication. Education in general means desired change of behavior. Thus, it is only logical to base education first on the fundamental behavior dimensions of the human being. These major dimensions would be: movement-, speech-, thinking-, and feeling-behavior. Therefore sport education is based on one behavior dimension, which is characteristic for the human being. Furthermore, it has to be taken into consideration that there is also a relationship between the different behavior dimensions incorporating a mutual influence.

1.3 Sport science--a problem-oriented scientific field and its international research dimension

The field of sport science has undergone a tremendous development during the last few years. The following aspects help to verify this development:

a. There are an increasing number of scientific journals devoted specifically to sport.

b. There has been an enlargement of the number of book series related to topics in sport science.

c. The number of single books dealing with sport science has increased.

d. An increasing number of meetings, symposia, and congresses dealing with sport science are being held.

e. Associations and organizations devoted to different aspects of sport science are being established.

f. In graduate schools, new programs of study leading to master's and doctoral degrees in sport science are being offered.

g. Separate organizational units for sport science are being organized at institutions of higher learning.

These developments are noticeable on both a national and an international level. This means that the development of sport science can be observed all around the world, which is indicative of the increasing importance of science in our lives in general. Within the realm of science, an interesting development has been seen during recent years. In addition to the so-called traditional sciences, such as philosophy, law, medicine, history, etc. a new category of sciences is forming. These new sciences could be characterized as theme or problem-oriented sciences. They come into existence when urgent problems within our social life call for answers through scientific investigations. Examples of such areas of social concern today are: nutrition, information, environment, and also sport. This new category of sciences is also interdisciplinary, because it depends upon many of the various traditional sciences.

The construct of this new science--sport science or sport sciences-- is an example of this relationship (Haag 1978, 9).

The subfields of this new scientific field can be exemplified in the following pattern:

a. Anatomical-physiological and biomechanical foundations

a.1 Sport medicine
a.2 Sport biomechanics

b. Social-behavioral foundations

b.1 Sport psychology
b.2 Sport pedagogy
b.3 Sport sociology

c. Historical-philosophical foundations

c.1 Sport history
c.2 Sport philosophy

Besides the clarification of the body of knowledge of a certain scientific field, it is also important to consider the dimension of research methodology. Three basic research design patterns can be distinguished: historical, status quo (descriptive), and experimental design. The intention of this research can be to deal with a single situation, to compare at least two aspects or to compare with a criterion (e.g. norm); this means that the comparative research dimension can be implied in every research design. It is quite understandable that comparison is most likely to be implied in pedagogical, sociological or historical research. However, it has to be mentioned that the number of theories proven by research in regard to the comparative aspect is still very limited. Research on the international level however is necessary according to sport and sport education being a phenomenon and an educational approach with international character (Bennett, 1975, Vendien and Nixon, 1968).

2. Organizations on the worldwide level--an international meeting place

The world of sport is characterized in different countries by a wide variety of organizations, federations and associations at the national level. Mostly, this is a very extensive network from local and state, up to the level of the whole nation. Tendencies towards bureaucracy can be observed associated with sport as a social phenomenon. Most of these organizations and associations are also represented on the international level, thus speaking the international language of sport, sport education and sport science.

Klan Rijsdorp, professor for physical education in Holland and former president of ICHPER, has developed an excellent scheme and structure by which the many international organizations can be categorized and explained (Rijsdorp 1973, 38-39). In this model he is distinguishing general organizations (ICSPE, ICHPER, FIEP) and categorical organizations (sport disciplines, specific themes or groups, and theory fields of sport sciences). The general organizations are described in the following in connection with the organizations dealing with specific themes.

2.1 Organizations for sport disciplines

Every sport discipline has at least a national association or federation as long as the respective sport is part of a nation's sport program. Very often there are also organizations for the different political subunits of the country, if it has a federal political structure. Beyond the national scenery, there often is an international organization taking care of international rules and competitions, mainly world championships and Olympic Games in cooperation with the "International Olympic Committee." Sometimes there are even organizations on a continental level like European federations or associations for certain sports. This international network of organizations is a mighty power to control, develop and coordinate sports all around the world and by this one major component of international relations.

Examples for this type of organization are:

- "Federation International de Ski" (FIS)
- "Federation International de Football Association" (FIFA)
- "Federation International de Natation Association" (FINA)

2.2 Theme oriented scientific organizations

In relation to sport - sport education - sport science, there are many themes, topics or problems which are the major concern of specific organizations. In most cases they have an equivalent organization in different countries, sometimes even a further substructure. They either have personal or institutional membership. Some examples for this type of organization are common task, organization of congresses, and publications (Table 1).

Table 1.

Title	Function
a. "International Council on Health, Physical Education, and Recreation" (ICHPER)	representation of teaching professions
b. "International Council of Sport and Physical Education" (ICSPE)	research in sport science
c. "Federation International d'Education Physique" (FIEP)	representation of teaching professions
d. "International Association of Physical Education and Sports for Girls and Women" (IAPESGW)	representing girls and women, working in the field and dealing with these specific questions
e. "International Association for Sports Information" (IASI)	documentation and information on the international level, development of retrieval systems
f. "Association International de la Presse Sportive" (AIPS)	mass media and sport, sport education, sport science
g. "Internationaler Arbeitskreis Sportstaettenbau" (IAKS)	facilities and equipment for sport, development and research
h. "International Olympic Committee" (IOC)	dealing with the Olympic idea, Olympic Games
i.. "Internationaler Skilehre verband"	teaching skiing (example, for an organization dealing with the teaching aspect in one sport)
j. "International Olympic Academy"	promoting and maintaining the true Olympic ideology

2.3 Scientific organizations for the theory fields of sport science

According to the concept of sport science as developed in part 1.3 there are existing organizations on the international level which deal with the specific theory fields of sport science. There are often developed regional units like in sport history for North America or in sport psychology for Europe. In several countries there are even working groups for specific theory fields of sport science on the national level (Balz et al. 1975). By these patterns it is possible that information on different aspects of sport science is transmitted from local up to international units. Examples for this type of international organizations are found in Table 2. (the respective journal is mentioned too).

Table 2.

Sport-medicine	Federation International de Medicine Sportive (FIMS)	Journal of Sports Medicine and Physical Fitness
Sport-biomechanics	International Society for Biomechanics	Journal of Biomechanics
Sport-psychology	International Society of Sport Psychology	International Journal of Sport Psychology
Sport-pedagogy	International Council on Health, Physical Education, and Recreation (ICHPER)/"Federation International d'Education Physique" (FIEP)	International Journal of Physical Education Bulletin of FIEP
Sport-sociology	Committee for the Sociology of Sport of ICSPE	International Review of Sport Sociology
Sport-history	International Association for the History of Physical Education and Sport (HISPA)	Journal of Sport History
Sport-philosophy	Philosophic Society for the Study of Sport	Journal of the Philosophy of Sport

3. Avenues for exchange of information on the international level

International relations can only develop and be fruitful if the informa-tion basis is sufficient for all participating partners. In this world of over-whelming information, it is often very hard to have an adequate set of infor-mation, especially at the international level. It also seems to be more and more important to have a so-called "instrumental knowledge," and this means to know how one can help oneself with a certain problem which has to be solved. Therefore the question of international relations in regard to sport, sport education, and sport science is regarded in the following under the as-pect of various kinds of available information.

3.1 Journals for theory and practice

Within the publications in the field of sport, scientific and nonscientific literature can be distinguished. With regard to the scientific literature, journals play an important role in addition to that of books. Various categor-izations of the scientific journals can be made:

a. Journals covering aspects of various sport disciplines (e.g., The Athletic Coach).

b. Journals for a specific sport discipline (e.g., Swimming World).

c. Journals of national organizations for sport, sport education, and sport science (e.g., JOHPER Journal).

d. Journals dealing with sport science as a whole, covering themes of different theoretical fields (e.g., Quest).

e. Journals dealing with a specific theme of sport science (e.g., Journal of Motor Behavior).

f. Journals dealing with a specific theoretical field of sport science (e.g., International Journal of Physical Education for Sport Peda-gogy).

With regard to the last group of journals, dealing with a specific theo-retical field of sport science, one can observe that, at least on the interna-tional level, every theoretical field thus far has its own journal for the publi-cation of themes and topics that are specific to the respective fields. The development of sport science as a scientific discipline has been so rapid that even on the national level this differentiation of journals according to the various fields of sport science is already beginning. (e.g., Canadian Jour-nal of History of Sport and Physical Education for sport history in Canada, or Zeitschrift für Sportpaedagogik for sport pedagogy in the Federal Republic of Germany).

1. Sport Medicine--Journal of Sport Medicine and Physical Fitness. (Editor-in-Chief: Dr. G. La Cava Rome, Via Flaminia Nuova, 270-00191, Italy.)

2. Sport Biomechanics--Journal of Biomechanics. (Editor-of-Chief: Verne L. Roberts, Head, Bioscience Division, Highway Safety Research Institute, Huron Parkway and Baxter Road, Ann Arbor, Michigan, 48105, USA, and F. Gayner Evans, Department of Anatomy, University of Michigan, Ann Arbor, Michigan 48104, USA.)

3. Sport Psychology--International Journal of Sport Psychology. (Editor-in-Chief: Ferruccio Antonelli, Via della Camilliccia 195 - 00 135, Rome, Italy.)

4. Sport Pedagogy--International Journal of Physical Education. (Editor-in-Chief: Herbert Haag, Institut für Sport und Sportwissenschaften, Abt. Sportpaedagogik, 23 Kiel, Olshausenstrasse 40 - 60. Federal Republic of Germany.)

5. Sport Sociology--International Review of Sport Sociology. (Editor-in-Chief: Andrzej Wohl, Akademia Wychowania Fizycnego, Warszawa, ul. Marymoncka 34, Poland.)

6. Sport History--Journal of Sport History. (Editor-in-Chief: A. Metcalfe, Department of History, Radford College, Radford, Virginia 24147, USA.)

7. Sport Philosophy--Journal of the Philosophy of Sport. (Editor-in-Chief: H. J. Van der Zwaag, Department of Sport Studies, Curry Hicks Building, University of Massachusetts, Amherst, Massachusetts 01002, USA.)

This description of the journals for certain fields of sport science on the international level uses a specific model for explaining sport science that implies seven theoretical fields. It is recognized that there are other models available; however, the one given seems to sufficiently analyze and describe sport science (Hoag, 1978, 261-267).

3.2 Books and book series

Besides the journals, books and book series are getting more and more recognition also on the international level. In relationship to this information possibility the following categories can be distinguished:

a. Lexica, dictionaries (e.g., Roethig, P. (ed.): Sportwissenschaftliches Lexikon. 4. Aufl. Schorndorf (Hofmann) 1977).

b. Handbooks (e.g., Hubbard, A. W. (ed.): Research Methods in Health, Physical Education, and Recreation. 3rd edition. Washington, D.C. (AAHPER) 1973).

c. Reports from congresses and symposia (e.g., Grupe, O. et al. (ed.): Sport in the Modern World - Chances and Problems. Berlin (Springer Verlag) 1973).

d.   Readers (e.g., Haag, H. (ed.): <u>Sport Pedagogy: Content and Methodology</u>. Baltimore (University Park Press) 1978).

A very important category is books which appear in a book series. There are more and more series developed in this field, concentrating on certain aspects, or considering a certain type of literature. In the Federal Republic of Germany there are presently existing, for example, about thirty different book series. Within this investigation an example is given for a book series, which just has been developed on an international scale.

International Series on Sport Sciences. (Editors: Richard C. Nelson and Chauncy A. Morehouse, Pennsylvanis State University.)

The principle focus of this series is on preference works primarily from international congresses and symposium proceedings. Each volume in the series is published in English, but is written by authors of several countries. The series therefore is truly international in scope, and because many of the authors normally publish their work in languages other than English, the series volumes are a resource for information often difficult if not impossible to obtain elsewhere.

Thus, books and book series as one information dimension have grown tremendously and have to be seen in a very differentiated way.

3.3 Various information media

There are various kinds of information possibilities, besides journals and books, which can be mentioned briefly within this investigation for the purpose of completeness:

a.   Films and slides on specific sport disciplines.

b.   Problem-oriented films and videotapes.

c.   Information retrieval systems for documentation and information.

d.   Newsletters, press reports, etc.

e.   Microcard- and microfihe systems.

f.   Different other audio-visual material (e.g., overhead transparencies).

Along with the further development of technology there will be another and probably more sophisticated possibilities for information media. On the international level the "International Association for Sports Information" (IASI) is especially dealing with these information issues.

Concluding Comments

The late president of ICSPE, Philip Noel-Baker, wrote in 1962 "Sport and physical education have been an active civilizing force in the 20th century, and now play on active part in the educational system of almost every country. It has created a new link between nations, a new means of communication between people who live for sport, who too often have been barely conscious that they are all members of one great human family." (Noel-Baker 1962, 183).

This perception from 1962 is still valid; it even has obtained a new meaning through the challenge by the countries of the Third World and the necessary help which they have deserved in order to develop sport - sport education - and sport science in accordance with their specific sociocultural needs. One big challenge has to be met in this regard. Every aspect of human culture has a tendency to professionalization, bureaucratization, scientific explanation, and perversion. Another challenge especially for international relations lies in the possibility of understanding and properly guiding these tendencies so that one basic philosophic idea could be better fulfilled: "The greatest happiness of the largest amount of people on this world."

Literature

Balz, F., Bernett, H., Beyer, E., Haag, H., and Jonas, B. (Eds.): Information on Sport in the Federal Republic of Germany: Sport Organization - Sport Education - Sport Science. Schorndorf (Hofmann) 1975.

Bennett, B. L., et al.: Comparative Physical Education and Sport. Philadelphia (Lea and Febiger) 1975.

Grupe, O., et al. (Ed.): Sport in the Modern World - Chances and Problems. Berlin (Springer) 1973.

Haag, H. (ed.): Sport Pedagogy: Content and Methodology. Baltimore (University Park Press) 1978.

Noel-Baker, Ph.: "Sport and International Understanding," in: International Journal of Adult and Youth Education. UNESCO 14 (1962) 4:183.

Rijsdorp, K.: "Memo Concerning the Cooperation Between International Organizations on Physical Education and Sports," in: International Journal of Physical Education 10 (1973) 4:38-39.

Roethig, P. (Ed.): Sportwissenschaftliches Lexikon. 4. Aufl. Schorndorf (Hofmann) 1977.

Vendien, C. L./Nixon, J. E. (Eds.): The World Today in Health, Physical Education, and Recreation. Englewood Cliffs (Prentice Hall) 1968.

Zeigler, E. F.: Problems in the History and Philosophy of Physical Education and Sport. Englewood Cliffs (Prentice Hall) 1968.

Educational Objectives For

International Sport Studies

Benjamin Lowe

> ...sports, as one kind of cross-cultural
> transnational interaction and communication,
> become a significant force for international
> understanding.

> Congressional Record, Vol. 119, No. 95,
> Tuesday, June 19, 1973, "Sports--Gate-
> way to International Understanding."

In common with the thinking that there should be established a national academy of international relations (Center for World Studies; National Academy for Peace and Conflict Resolution), there exists current opinion that a similar focus of attention should be found in an academy of international sports studies. This thinking is not limited to the United States, for the United Kingdom has initiated such a move with the intention of setting up a "Centre for International Sport Studies" at the University of Sussex. Part of the thinking in the U.S.A., however, stems from the recommendations made by the past administration's President's Commission on Olympic Sports. (The supporting rationale in each national case is not identical, and part of this difference will be discussed here.) But, first, how important is sport? Petrie (1975) states:

> Sport is an element of social reality, strongly anchored to the
> political-economic system in which it is placed, that has sig-
> nificance far beyond the trivial. It provides a means of under-
> lining and exhibiting the major elements of the ideological base
> of the power structure of society. (p. 190)

In an article for the Department of State publication International Educational and Cultural Exchange, entitled "International Exchange and National Development," T. A. Lambo (1977) states:

> International educational and cultural exchange is one of the
> most powerful vehicles that exists to promote international
> understanding, reorientation and reeducation of national

> leaders, and sensitization to, and appreciation of, other
> problems and their dimensions, thereby promoting national
> development. (p. 25)

The axiomatic nature of this statement is then explored from the African standpoint in respect to underlying values, alternative states of consciousness, and within a framework of spatio-temporal elements normally foreign to the thinking of cultures drawing their origins from the European nexus of civilization. Beyond this first point, Lambo states that such conditions separating "Western" from African thought present a "difficult task of harmoniously reconciling our new science and technology to our traditional attitudes and belief systems." The difficulty, as Lambo sees it, lies between the rational materialism of the West and the basic African philosophies in which existence (process) is more significant to life than events (product). Human spontaneity is one of the cornerstones of the unitary experiencing process ("human beings participate with all capacities--feeling, thinking, willing, action."), and the way in which the life of a person fits into a cosmology of existence is more valid than how (or whether) it fits into a story sequence. Fundamentally, there exists a contradiction between the African cultures that are qualitatively-oriented and those of the West that are quantitatively-oriented. The major lesson that Lambo is teaching us is that the super-imposition of the European heritage on the development of the African university system "failed in fashioning innovative methods and techniques of education relevant to local needs." The lesson is salutory only insofar as it focuses attention on alien outcomes resulting from well-intentioned motives. Alternatives, flexibility, openness, creativity--the underlying motives for innovative education and change-oriented social priming, acculturation responsive to multifaceted planes and vectors of human behavior, contribute to the formulation of educational directives for international sports studies.

The symbolic role of sport as a cultural force in modern society has been given greater and greater attention by nations of the world, to the extent that in some countries, it has come to serve a prestige function for national identity in spheres of international communication. The extent to which the symbolic cultural force of sport has been employed beyond merely acting as a scale for measuring prestige cannot be estimated at this point in time--althought there exist unverified reports that the carryover influence enters political as well as commercial enclaves. On the purely symbolic plane, there are mutually reinforcing references from both sides of the argument. This is curious, for one would expect antagonistic (or at least, conflicting) statements, yet agreement suggests clearly that sport is a non-threatening subject in any language, rather like music and the arts. Unlike music and the arts, however, sport symbolizes alternative forms of warfare and overt conflict. Thus, in respect of potential for national development (cultural ideology), sport presents a Janus image.

Symbol and Prestige

The claim is not one-sided. "Holier-than-thou" accusations are neither disputed nor contradicted by those for whom the recognition of sport as prestige carries real significance. The judgment by Georg von Opel, member of the International Olympic Committee (German Federal Republic -

West Germany), is borne out by official opinion stated by Erich Honnecker, Party Secretary of the German Democratic Republic (East Germany). Opel, (1971), states:

> The participation of Socialist countries in the Olympic Games has given national prestige a leading role, and the Communist states value Olympic victories as proof of their better socialist system. (p. 104)

Honnecker, in his Report of the Central Committee to the 9th Congress of the Socialist Unity Party of Germany (Berlin, 1976) stated categorically: "Our State is respected in the world because of the excellent performances of our top athletes." The complementary statements made by the two spokesmen for a divided Germany find parallel agreement between spokesmen for the United States and the U.S.S.R., the two nations most typically associated with the symbolic perpetration of the "cold war." The United States Representative to the 1973 World University Games in Moscow, Roswell Merrick, stated: "The Soviets regard athletics as a continuation of politics by other means," and as if to underscore the truth of this observation, S. L. Axelrod of the Soviet Union wrote: "...the triumph of our athletes...is proof of the superiority of the Soviet socialist culture over the rottenness of the culture of capitalist countries." (Quoted in Henry W. Morton, Soviet Sport, p. 18). The "truth" of what Axelrod said for the U.S.S.R. could be applied to the German Democratic Republic for, besides earning high honors in the Olympic Games (1972 and 1976), the G.D.R. actually surpassed Great Britain in Gross National Product for the year 1976. Great Britain, it is recalled, holds the position of being one of the original five "super-powers" in the United Nations, a carryover from immediate post-World War II recognition of former Imperial supremacy.

The German Democratic Republic is a modern country caught in the "struggle for independence" syndrome. Achievement and mastery (the mystique of a successful society) are shown in no better light than in physical success--"winning" or "record-breaking" in sport being a primary media example in terms of communication between groups (and nations). There is no doubt that the "collective identity" of a group (or nation) finds symbolic reference in such successes, and it can be seen as merely a marginal leap to speculate that the increment in the Gross National Product of the G.D.R. might be a function of the way in which the population emulated or responded to the "vision" provided by her athletes. Perhaps this "leap" is not so great as simplistic criticism would suggest for as Murray (1976) states of Australia (a "relatively homogeneous body"): "Sport has been regarded, and still is, as one form of symbolic dialogue for this collectivity...It's appeal has long been acknowledged as universal and its power to communicate as significant." To what extent the German Democratic Republic ever "lost" her fundamental German identity as a result of partition is beyond discussion here, but what is certain is that the world knows about G.D.R. sovereignty principally through the performance of her athletes, rather than through the expression of her inalienable right to exercise closing the Berlin corridor (historically an internationally explosive situation).

President's Commission on Olympic Sports

In September, 1975, President Ford initiated his Commission to study the status of "amateur/Olympic" sport in the United States. The funding for this task was $596,000, and the job was to be completed by January, 1977. The composition of the Commission included U.S. Senators, Congressmen, athletes (former and current Olympians), persons holding executive office in national sports associations, and others "from the world of sport."

The "First Report to the President" issued by the Commission appeared on February 9, 1976. Broadly, the First Report approached such areas of discussion as (i) the current amateur sports system, (ii) amateur sports systems in other countries, and (iii) reorganization of the current amateur sports structure. Parenthetically, the second of the just-mentioned areas deserves immediate reflection because implicitly in the final outcome (namely, stated in the Final Report) is the assumption that "other countries do it better than in the U.S.A.," a dangerous assumption in light of differing cultural objectives for sports participation. The First Report also offered a draft model of a national "highest sports authority," and recommended alternatives (private sector; governmental; quasi-governmental corporation; federated association) for its implementation. As Gerald B. Zornow, Chairman of the Commission stated in his opening letter to the President: "...the most important idea contained in this report concerns the needs to reorganize the current structure for amateur sports in this country."

Several considerations are worth comment here, not the least of which is the constant use of the term "amateur sports." "The structure of American amateur sports...is an anomoly to other nations," states the opening sentence of Chapter III, "Amateur Sports Systems in Other Countries." The difference between the U.S.A. and the European National Sports Systems is that the U.S.A. lacks what the others all have--"a highest authority for sport." The First Report suggests that there are distinct advantages in this European system which includes: "A continuing dialogue between government officials and designated sports spokesmen," and, "Amateur sports, speaking as a single voice, can command greater response from the public and the government." It points out that the government role is well-defined in most countries, and that such nations support the employment of full-time professional administrators for sports. (Again parenthetically, the worst side of this argument was admirably illustrated by the black African nations who pulled their athletes out of the XXI Olympiad in Montreal in a demonstration of political effectiveness at the government level.) Underpinning popular interest in sport in the European nations, the First Report notes, is the involvement of political leaders personally concerning themselves with amateur sports, and: "This is even more true of developing countries, where international sports are viewed as a relatively fast way to garner world prestige and recognition," it adds. Athletic success in Europe and developing countries is recognized as coming from (i) the support given by industry "... companies readily support athletes by providing them with jobs--and many donate the athlete's salaries for broken-time support when they are away training and competing," and (ii) governmental sports development wherein facilities are coordinated and use-maximized, and in which government and private funding can be made directly to clubs for specific program support.

Incentive to athletic success is stimulated in the former case (industrial support) because international success is viewed with corporate pride, but more pragmatically, for the athlete: "Outstanding achievements in competition are rewarded in some cases with promotions for athletes within their companies." The implications for upward social mobility are clear to the athlete coming from a lower socio-economic stratum of society, and record-breaking (world standards) must be all that much more appealing and rewarding. (The logical pursuit of this philosophy is becoming identified as a cornerstone for re-evaluating sports participation in some circles of academic inquiry.)

While the First Report appraises the scene of "amateur sports" and recommends the ensuing seven months be devoted to further research and exploration of the "highest sports authority" concept, the Final Report, January, 1977, reflects a growth in the whole concept of the way international sport should be viewed today. Primarily, the fact that top level performance athletes of today constitute an elite group is recognized as being dependent upon high level organization centrally structured and maximally financed. This lesson appears to have been learned from Europe. More specifically, the free enterprise system of the U.S.A. finds closer parallel with Western European and Commonwealth countries where industrial corporations sponsor the major funding, facilitated by government sanction and marginal political interference (or dependency). Within the spirit of the underlying philosophy of industrial society: "The development of elite athletes from the level of national recognition to international caliber may be considered an end product of competition." The assumption that competition is both sacrosanct and inviolable in principle is not questioned, except when it applies to factional disputes between National Governing Bodies of sport. Thus, the resolution of franchise disputes is a major topic to which the recommendation of the Central Sports Organization (CSO) addresses itself. Concordant with the latter, a bill of athletes' rights is proposed, the arbitration of such a bill to fall within the CSO where, presently, franchises disputing over an athlete are referred to the American Arbitration Association under an amendment to Article II, Sections 6 and 7, of the U.S. Olympic Committee. A parallel between "athletes' rights" and "human rights" is intimated in the opening graphs of the Final Report (Overview), in which it is stated: "The state of amateur sports in the United States today is comparable to the condition of the nation itself in the years following the Revolutionary War." A salutory comment might be added in reflection of the way in which black American athletes organized to boycott the XIX Olympiad in Mexico City, in 1968, in the name of "human rights"--no less significant than the efforts of athletes to bring human rights to the suppressed people of South Africa.

In the world of modern elite athletes, the anachronism of "amateur" is addressed by the Final Report of the President's Commission on Olympic Sports. Curiously, the concept is sustained in fundamental value terms, evidently out of deference to the codes prescribed by the International Olympic Committee. However, the recommendation for clarity and uniformity in respect of financing as it affects non-professional (contracted/league) athletes is a worthy exercise. Beyond this, the question of developing world class athletes is posed. "The status of sport in modern society is changing," states the Final Report, emphasizing that "sport on the international level has ceased to be the exclusive domain of the leisure classes (yet) the opportunity to take part is still tempered by one's ability to pay various costs, access to coaching, facilities and equipment." Part of the change in the status of sport in society is attributed to the international shift of emphasis from sport as an avocation to sport as s serious full-time pursuit. Once the subject of world class performance is entered, sociological and cultural criteria arise particularly in respect to such issues as the "National Sport" and differential media coverage of professional (as opposed to "amateur") sport.

The point to which we arrive in this overview of the President's Commission on Olympic Sports is contained in one of the major "objectives that would begin to solve the plight of many U.S. athletes;" namely--

> Regional training centers to provide easy access and prime coaching to all athletes; and sports institutes to serve as centers for training and developing coaches and officials.
> (p. 99)

As long as this recommendation is seen as being couched in an educational (institutional) context, few can entertain dispute with its intention. The hallmark of approval for supporting the recommendation depends for its integrity upon an ethic which presupposes that elite performance is for expressive or artistic purposes rather than for prestige or social reward purposes.

Profit-motivated or self-serving agencies are free to misinterpret the intent of the President's Commission on Olympic Sports. One danger lies in the good intentions of corporations to support athletics on a national scale. When the resulting mandate of the Commission is understood to mean that industry can pursue in the name of Olympism a sales strategy exploiting association with Olympic endeavor on the part of the youth of the nation, then the time has come to reassess fundamental principles which the Commission may have missed in its work. Hence, the likelihood that the Sears sponsorship of the Junior Olympic could be turned into a crass campaign of sales promotion reinforcing the worst principles of free enterprise becomes fair warning. Doubtless the Sears Foundation (the sponsoring agent of the Sears, Roebuck Corporation) would consider its motives misunderstood by the public and the American Athletic Union (under whose aegis the Junior Olympics program is conducted) if, in fact, "Junior Olympics" become a sales slogan. The irony of this image is made clear by other messages in this paper which remind us of the inviolable sanctity of the true amateur athlete who does not wish to make a penny from his performance.

ACADEMY OF INTERNATIONAL SPORTS STUDIES

Once in awhile a discussion will center on the role and function that a National Institute of Sports would serve, and suggestions are tendered that technical and coaching provisions should be made for countries outside the United States wishing to build national sports teams of Olympic age-group representation. To a broad extent, this is the mission and mandate of the existing United States Sports Academy which recently negotiated a $10 million scheme to assist the Arabian oil emirate of Bahrain in its sports endeavors. In other countries (France, German Democratic Republic, Finland,

Nigeria), National Institutes of Sport have been built and funded from the highest federal level of government, thereby intimating to the U.S. that the idea is not new. Great Britain, too, is still talking about a National College of Sport to oversee the six "Centers of Excellence" that are currently being established around the country (Bond, 1976).

High level performance sport is not purely physical (physiological/biomechanical), for psychological and sociological variables enter with equal weight under all conditions of sports encounter. The academic study of the sports sciences has sound theoretical support knowledge to integrate with the technical knowledge of high performance sport. Sport, at any level of performance can be defined as self-induced stress, for physical and sociopsychological factors of stress are prevalent whenever the athlete enters the sport domain. The definition of sport in terms of stress factors has yet to be fully explored--this comment serves only to pinpoint how much still remains to be accomplished by virtue of the fact that "sport" still lacks adequate definition.

Drawing together the advances in technical knowledge with advances in social scientific knowledge to show the inextricable integration of these developments for high performance sport, Hatfield (1976) states:

> Scientific and medical advances have supplied athletes with highly sophisticated training techniques which involve not only a profound knowledge of exercise physiology, but sociopsychological considerations as well. (p. 34)

An Academy of International Sport Studies recognizes this integration, even rests upon it as a basic mandate for its existence. Yet, functionally, technical aspects in the realm of competitive performance (the demonstration of human physical skill potential) demand superlative equipment and facilities employed under the guidance of highly trained staff with specialized technical knowledge. On this level, the educational experiences offered make no greater claim than the development and acquisition of high-level technical competitive performance. Satisfying the academic, theoretical aspects of the educational process, resource staff specialized in the sports sciences instruct in advances in psychology, sociology, medicine, law, history, philosophy and policy as these apply to the role of sport as social phenomenon. Clinical and laboratory experiences provide the primary locus of interface between the academic and the technical. This interfacing resolves the conflict engendered by the separation of science for sport from science of sport for man.

Technological innovations typify science for sport, only placing limitations on the athlete when ethical principle or risk of harm are encountered. In the case science of sport for man, self-improvement rather than productivity underpins the major objective for sport-knowledge and the role of the person is valued more highly than the result he achieves. (This can be challenged by reference to Popular Culture alternatives accounting for the role of the sport-hero in society.) The Academy, however, cannot afford to be product-oriented in promoting skilled technical performance goals; more significantly, principle educational objectives must prevail in a framework of human rights legislation. This puts the Academy in line with the recommendations of the Helsinki accord. Top level athletes from around the world comprise an elite group whose human rights supersede national frontiers and circumscribe the globe. As an elite group, they cannot afford to be elitist in any other form of behavior than their athletic performance. This lesson, also, is fundamental to the mandate for the Academy of International Sports Studies.

American Youth Sports Center

The proposal to establish an American Youth Sports Center at the University of Illinois reflects the recognition (by educators and social scientists) of the gap between the cultural activity of sport and what is known about sport from research. A fundamental communication link is to provide information both to community sport youth leaders and to sport scientists about the activities of each other. The knowledge explosion about sport has been recorded in a number of articles (Lowe, 1974; Lowe and Walsh, 1976), and this information now seeks application in positive youth sports experience.

A major objective of the AYSC is to maximize the benefits of sport participation and research, the one complementing the other, and the other the one in two-way interactive effect. Six major functions of the AYSC are listed as:

1. To develop an information storage and retrieval system for collecting all available information about youth sports.

2. To identify, promote, and initiate needed research on priority problems in youth sports programs.

3. To synthesize and translate research into meaningful generalizations for coaches and youth sport administrators.

4. To evaluate the strengths and weaknesses of existing sports programs.

5. To provide a consulting service for youth sports leaders and sport scientists.

6. To create an experimental coaching development program and evaluate its impact on the quality of youth sports programs.

The interdisciplinary nature of sports studies is highlighted by the first major function--"information storage and retrieval." There already exists a number of such systems around the world. The United States Department of State funds the "International Sports and Physical Education Data System" housed at the University of California - Santa Barbara. In Canada, at the University of Waterloo can be found the "System for Information Retrieval in Leisure and Sports;" and at the University of Birmingham, in England, there is the "Documentation Centre for Sports and Physical Education." Among others around the world, there exists in Germany, at the Bundesinstitüt für

Sportwissenschaft, Cologne, what is known as "Sportdokumentation." (The significance of the international proliferation of such functions really will be discovered only when each is linked to the others in a formalized international communications network.)

Within the American Youth Sports Center, nine divisions are identified for information storage, and these are representative of the sub-categories found in most systems. These are: exercise physiology; biomechanics; motor development; sport sociology; sports organization and administration; sports medicine; motor learning; sport psychology; and, sports facilities and equipment. The AYSC consulting service will draw from this system as required, and it will be equally accessible to coaches and researchers.

Three other national American developments peripherally similar to the AYSC include the New England School of Athletic Training (housed at the Massachusetts Maritime Academy); the United States Sports Academy, located at the University of Southern Alabama; and the Center for International Sport and Physical Education, part of the Department of Physical Education at the University of California, Long Beach. (Long Beach is self-styled: "International City.") As is noted elsewhere many College and University Departments of Physical Education are instituting sub-departments specified as "Sports Studies," but, to date, there does not appear to be a College or University department exploring the mode of inquiry which would propel an International Program of Sports Studies. A composite picture appears to be forming, based on levels of academic interests and inquiry, to suggest that the time is ripe for the formulation of such a Program.

Centre for International Sports Studies

The Centre for International Sports Studies (CISS) is a child of ITEX—International Training Exchange, a proposal drafted by the British government sponsored Central Bureau of Educational Visits and Exchanges (CBEVE) in June, 1976. One month later, in July 1976, the CBEVE issued a personalized invitation/proposal entitled: "Centre for International Sports Studies," which was sent to a "number of distinguished administrators in community recreation, physical education and sport." The proposal indicated that the most appropriate site for the CISS would be "within the framework of the Institute for Development Studies at the University of Sussex." The CBEVE is a government agency, therefore, government funding will support the CISS once it is instituted.

The objective of the CISS is to cooperate with and provide services to the developing countries and Third World nations, with special reference to sport and recreation. In order to initiate the idea, participants were invited to meet at the University of Sussex on Friday, September 3, 1976, a time chosen to coincide with the prestigious International Olympic Committee Solidarity Course for Sports Administrators, being held August 23-September 17, 1976, and organized by the British Olympic Association in conjunction with the University of Sussex. The CISS seminar lasted for two days, and the level of discussion was primarily exploratory and informational. Participants of the Solidarity Course, all of whom were representatives of Third World (developing) nations, were invited to share in the discussions.

The major outcome of this meeting was the resolution for the Steering Committee to meet again in January, 1977, in order to draft a more substantive proposal for CISS with the objective of pushing for its inception in September, 1977.

To all intents and purposes, the first few years of activity of the CISS will be coordinated by two officers. Their primary function will be to develop and implement short courses for visiting groups of students and field technicians. There does not appear to be any "educational" incentive behind the CISS beyond a technical assistance level, thereby suggesting that little integration of CISS activities with existing degree programs at the University of Sussex is envisaged. Thus, the title of the Centre may turn out to be a misnomer in the short term. This would change if, as is being speculated, the United Kingdom Documentation Centre for Sport and Physical Education were to be transferred to the University of Sussex in 1979 (when current funding expires and new funding is to be negotiated). Ultimately, it is difficult to imagine the rationale for the continued existence of a center for international sports studies which does not integrate its activities with a degree program.

A footnote to the inaugural discussions on the Center for International Sports Studies is worth comment on account of the objectives of CISS being to serve Third World and developing countries. All the participants in the Olympic Solidarity Seminar were from developing and Third World nations, and in the report of the course prepared by the British Olympic Association (the chief sponsor), the opinions of the participants were solicited as to their satisfactions and dissatisfactions with the way it had gone and how well it had served them. Their primary complaint was that they would have liked a greater involvement of sports administrators representing developed nations of the world. The good intentions of the International Olympic Committee in granting scholarship assistance to the participants had misfired inadvertently, at least insofar as the mix of the seminar participants was concerned. In most other instances, the participants were happy that the opportunity had been given to them, and they recommended further annual seminars be sponsored by the IOC to be located in other developed countries of the world.

International Olympic Academy

In 1960, the International Olympic Committee founded the International Olympic Academy at Olympia under conditions characterized as: "life under the tents, the penury of resources, the time of construction," and during "times without heart and perhaps without soul." It was their belief that sport would bring harmony to fulfill the "true meaning of human existence." The Academy was established to hold fourteen-day meetings each year, and it has done so on an uninterrupted basis to date. The Report of the 11th Session reflected on the first decade of activity:

> ...at the end of the first decade it has been proved that the aims for which the Academy was founded have been fulfilled.

> The way has now been opened and paved for the new decade. A cultural centre has been founded in the place which

is the heart of the international Olympic Movement. Ancient Olympia, where adequate facilities have been built and where work progresses under international cooperation and assistance. Efforts may now tend at making the I.O.A. a bright beacon which will illuminate, with almost blinding intensity, the ideals of modern athletics, the pure conscience and honest values on which they are based and their achievements in our times, so that today's youth may profit from them in the near future.

All efforts of the I.O.A. will aim at teaching persistence, honesty, justice and love for human beings and the real need for good and progress and for the smooth and normal evolution which comes smoothly and effortlessly just as spring descends every year from the mountain tops to cover the whole earth with its kindness, its colours and scents. Finally, all our efforts will be aimed at teaching all people how to live in a genuinely competitive way, not submitting to their fate, but guiding and shaping their fate for a better future.

We believe that the attitude of the civilized human being towards the various acute social problems is dictated, to a great extent, by his ideological attitudes towards sports. Sports have thus become an essential and important factor of culture and learning, if we take present tendencies into consideration. (pp. 11-12).

This expression of conviction, admittedly from men and women devoted to sport as a primary source of inspiration, states the case equally for the establishment of an Academy of International Sports Studies. The strength of argument presented here indicates that the annual fourteen-day event held at Olympia more than justifies founding an institution dedicated to international sports studies on a continuing basis.

Conclusion

In a world of fanciful "fantastic" ideas, the "sport-alternative" can be considered for the surrogate role that it might play in situations identified as "the major trouble spots" of the world--Israel and the Arab states; Greece and Turkey (Cyprus); Southern Africa; and elsewhere. It is the viewpoint of Petrie (1975) that it is possible to "transfer aggressive nationalism from direct conflict on the battlefield to symbolic conflict between the representatives of rival political-economic systems at major international sporting events". Let us look at the Israeli/Arab case. In Israel, the Maccabiah Games are held every two years, and in the Arab world, there exists the Pan-Arabian Games, held quadrennially. The "fantastic" suggestion (and facetious, at this stage) is that one major sports festival be organized in substitution for both existing Games as a means of bringing the two "warring" factions together in the spirit of quadrennial antagonism. The symbolic effect reduces the true spirit of sport to the level of farce the more seriously the contest is taken as symbolic of true conflict. Thus, the ethical lesson is both good for sport and good for community (international) relations. Far too often, the role of sport is given serious sanction in support of national prestige characteristics. (Do the Arabs and Isarelis flaunt their Olympic success at each other in post-Olympian reflection of their relative world esteems?) When sport is seen for what it is, it serves admirably in its symbolic role--when it is imbued with other characteristics, it fails. Sport is a sensitive social symbol and needs to be better understood for its frailty and potential strength.

On the basis of national concerns for sport in the health of a nation, as well as for the functional social role that it plays in international affairs, some countries have accorded sport greater attention than has been given in the past. As subject of interest, sport has shaken off the stigma of "unworthiness." The Council for Cultural Cooperation of the Council of Europe made the following statement at Strasbourg in 1975:

> Lastly, sport--an activity often regarded (wrongly) as incidental to culture. At a Conference of European Ministers responsible for Sport, meeting in Brussels in March 1975 at the invitation of the Belgian Government, a recommendation was made to the Committee of Ministers of the Council of Europe concerning the adoption of a European "Sport for All" Charter. This Charter defines the fundamental principles of Sport for All and provides the basis for closer cooperation between member states of the CCC in matters of sport. It also proclaims the importance of sport in contemporary European society and emphasizes the protection and support that it must receive if it is to fulfill its acknowledged mission. (p. 85)

The "Sport for All" movement was perhaps the first major international ministerial thrust in recognition of the role of sport in the life of man. Coincidental with the European "Sport for All" movement there exists in Canada "Participaction," and while there is no slogan title in the United States, the principle of "life-time sports" has taken hold in the educational system from high school through university levels of instruction (Lowe, 1975). "Sport for All" has nothing to do with "prestige-sport." This basic fact is at the crux of the difficulties faced by Great Britain in establishing "Centres of Excellence." International sports studies suggests that the world is big enough for both elements of sports-pursuit. People recognize and extoll high performance sport, they seek to witness it, speak about it, and regard its phenomenal existence from a variety of entertainment modalities (beauty of action, contained violence, shared social experience, etc.). For those people who participate, they may do so from purely expressive (artistic) perspectives, or they may find in sport an avenue to social rewards such as higher status living, personal prestige, or other social accolades. The fact that these views speak to people of all nationalities restates the central claim for the foundation of an Academy of International Sports Studies. Such an Academy will provide the surroundings and conditions within which a better understanding of people in educational and cultural interaction behave towards each other, for within sports action and its observation there can be found the seeds of all human nature.

References

Bond, Clive
1976

"A National College of Sport."
British Journal of Physical Education, 7(4):168-169.

1977

Final Report of the President's Commission on Olympic Sports, 1975-1977, Washington, D.C.

Goodhart, Phillip
Chattaway, Chris.
1968

War Without Weapons.
London: W. H. Allen.

Hatfield, F. C.
1976

"Ethnocentrism and Conflict in Olympic Competition: Parallels and Trends". Review of Sport and Leisure, I:32-44.

Lambo, T. A.
1977

"International Exchange and National Development".
International Educational and Cultural Exchange, XII, No. 3, 25-33.

Lowe, Benjamin
1974

"Sport Sociology: The First Ten Years."
Journal of the New Zealand Association of Health, Physical Education and Recreation, 7(3):32-38.

Lowe, Benjamin
1975

"Sport Beyond the Age of High Mass Consumption."
Society and Leisure, 7(4):155-165.

Lowe, Benjamin
Walsh, Joseph
1976

"Comparative Sport Psychology: British and American Developments."
Paper presented to the Bicentennial meeting of the American Studies Association, Philadelphia, April 1.

Morton, Henry W.
1963

Soviet Sport.
New York: Collier Books.

1974

Multidisciplinary Symposium on Sport and the Means of Furthering Mutual International Understanding. United States Department of State Bureau of Educational and Cultural Affairs.

Murray, Louis
1976

"Some Ideological Qualities of Australian Sport."
Australian Journal of Health, Physical Education and Recreation, 73:7-10.

Petrie, Brian
1975

"Sport and Politics."
In D. W. Ball and John W. Loy (Eds.), Sport and Social Order.
Reading, Mass.: Addison-Wesley Publishing Co.

1976

President's Commission on Olympic Sports.
First Report to the President, Washington, D.C.

1976   Social Sciences of Sport.
                        BETS No. 3, ERIC Clearinghouse, Washington, D.C.

von Opel, Georg   "The Future of the Olympic Games."
     1971   Report of the Eleventh Session of the International
                        Olympic Academy at Olympia, Athens.

Bibligraphic References

(The purpose of this extensive reference list is to assist researchers in the field of sport and international relations. Most references are English, with a few in other languages. For a fuller list of French and German references, the reader is directed to the UNESCO journal Cultures, Volume IV, No. 2, 1977, pp. 154-165.)

Acheson, Dean. "Morality, Moralism and Diplomacy" in Dean Acheson, Grapes From Thorns. New York: W. W. Norton, 1972.

_____. The Struggle for a Free Europe. New York: W. W. Norton, 1971.

Adam, Karl. Leistungssport - Sinn und Unsinn. Muenchen: Nymphenburger, 1975.

Adelbeck, Gert, et al. Sport in the Federal Republic of Germany. Hassfurt: Verlag für Zeitgeschichtliche Documentation, 1972.

Aflalo, P. G. Sport in Europe. New York: E. P. Dutton and Co., 1901.

Akselrod, S. L. Fizicheskaia Kultura i Sport v USSR. Moscow: Fizkultura i Sport, 1954.

Allardt, Erik, "Basic Approaches in Comparative Sociological Research and the Study of Sport" in Guenther Lüschen, Cross Cultural Analysis of Sport and Games. Champaign, Ill.: Stipes Publishing Company, 1970.

_____ and Stein Rokkan. Mass Politics. New York: Free Press, 1970.

All-China Athletic Federation. Sport Flourishes in New China. Peking: Foreign Languages Press, 1955.

Anderson, Helga. "Sports and Games in Denmark in the Light of Sociology." Acta Sociologica, II, #2 (1956):1-27.

Anderson, M. S. The Eastern Question. London: Macmillan, 1966.

Arnakis, George. The Ottoman Empire and the Balkan States to 1900. Austin, Texas: Pemberton, 1959.

Auf der Maur, Nick. The Billion-Dollar Game: Jean Drapeau and the 1976 Olympics. Toronto: Lorimer, 1976.

Auswaetige Amt der Bundesrepublik Deutschland (Ed.). Die Auswaetige Politik der Bundesrepublik Deutschland. Köln: Verlag der Wissenschaft und Politik, n.d.

Avedon, Elliot M. and Brian Sutton-Smith. The Study of Games. New York: John Wiley, 1971.

Baden-Powell, Maj. Gen. Robert. Sport in War. New York: Frederick A. Stoke Co., 1908.

Baker, Philip J. "Olympiads and Liars." The Outlook, CII (October 19, 1919): 355-360.

_____. "The Olympic Games," The Independent, CXIII, #3875 (August 16, 1924): 96-98.

Baley, James A. "Suggestions for Removing Politics from the Olympic Games." Journal of Physical Education and Recreation 49(3):73, 1978.

Ball, Donald W. "A Politicized Social Psychology of Sport: Some Assumptions and Evidence from International Figure Skating Competition." International Review of Sport Sociology. 8(3/4):63-68, 1973.

_____. "Olympic Games Competition: Structural Correlates of National Success." International Journal of Comparative Sociology, 13(304):186-200.

Barnes, H. and Ruedi, O. M. The American Way of Life. New York: Prentice Hall, 1950.

Becker, Helmut. "Die Olympische Aufsteig der DDR". Deutschland Archiv, 7(2):157-165, Feb. 1974.

Bedecki, Thomas G. Modern Sport as an Instrument of National Policy with Reference to Canada and Selected Countries. (Ph.D. dissertation, Ohio State University, 1971.)

Beisser, Arnold. The Madness in Sports. New York: Appleton-Century-Crofts, 1967.

Bend, Emil. Some Functions of Competitive Team Sports in American Society. (Ph.D. dissertation, University of Pittsburgh, 1970.)

Bennett, Bruce L., Maxwell L. Howell and Uriel Simri. Comparative Physical Education and Sport. Philadelphia: Lea and Febiger, 1975.

Berelson, Bernard. Content Analysis in Communication Research. Glencoe, Ill.: The Free Press, 1952.

Berg, W. "Fuer Gesundheit, Lebensfreude, Erholung and Leistungsfaehigkeit aller Buerger," Theorie und Praxis der Korper-Kultur 22(11):969-970, Nov. 1973.

Berkowitz, Leonard. <u>Aggression: A Social Psychological Analysis</u>. New York: McGraw-Hill, 1962.

Berlioux, Monique. <u>Olympism</u>. Lausanne: IOC, 1972.

Bernett, Hajo. <u>Untersuchungen zur Zeitgeschichte des Sports</u>. Schorndorf bei Stuttgart: Hoffman, 1973.

_____. <u>Nationalsozialistische Leibeserziehung, Eine Dokumentation ihrer Theorie und Organisation</u>. Schorndorf bei Stuttgart: Hoffman, 1966.

_____. <u>Sportpolitik im Drittenreich. Aus den Akten der Reichkanzlei</u>. Schorndorf bei Stuttgart: Hoffman, 1971.

Birnbaum, Karl. <u>East and West Germany. A Modus Vivendi</u>. Lexington, Mass.: D. C. Heath.and Company, 1973.

_____. <u>Peace in Europe: East-West Relations 1966-1968 and the Prospects for a European Settlement</u>. London: Oxford University Press, 1970.

Bloss, Hans. "Sport Development Assistance under Educational and Political Aspect." <u>International Journal of Physical Education</u> XIV (3):21-23, and XIV (4):9-12-1977.

Boasson, Charles. <u>Approaches to the Study of International Relations</u>. Assen, Netherlands: Van Gorcum and Co., N.V., 1972.

Boehm, Walter. "Who Wins?" <u>International Education and Culture Exchange</u>, IX, #4 (Spring, 1974):10-14.

Boigey, Maurice. "The Olympic Games Today and Yesterday," <u>The Living Age</u>, CCCXXI, #4167 (May 17, 1924):949-952.

Bouet, Michel. "The Function of Sport in Human Relations." <u>International Review of Sport Sociology</u>, 1:137-140, 1966.

Bowra, C. M. <u>Pindar</u>. London: Oxford University Press, 1964.

Boyle, R. H. <u>Sport - Mirror of American Life</u>. Boston: Little, Brown, 1963.

Brasher, Christopher. <u>Mexico, 1968</u>. London: Stanley Paul, 1968.

Breitmeyer, Arno and P. G. Hoffman. <u>Sport und Staat</u>. 2 vols. Hamburg: Broschek, 1934.

Brickhill, Joan. <u>Race Against Race: South Africa's Multi-national Sport Fraud</u>. London: International Defense and Aid Fund, 1976.

Britain in the World of Sport. London: Physical Education Association, 1956.

British Olympic Council. The Fourth Olympiad. London: British Olympic Association, 1908.

Broom, Eric F. A Comparative Analysis of the Central Administration Agencies of Amateur Sport and Physical Recreation in England and Canada. (Ph.D. dissertation, University of Illinois, 1971.)

Brown, N. O. Love's Body. New York: Vintage, 1966.

Brown, Seyom. New Forces in World Politics. Washington, D.C.: Brookings Institute, 1974.

_____. The Faces of Power: Constancy and Change in United States Foreign Policy From Truman to Johnson. New York: Columbia University Press, 1968.

Brundage, Avery. "Principles of the Olympic Movement." Journal of Health, Physical Education and Recreation, 30(8):25-26, 54, 1959.

_____. The Speeches of President Avery Brundage, 1952 to 1968. Lausanne: IOC, 1969.

Buhkarin, Nikolai. Economic Theory of the Leisure Class. New York: Monthly Review Press, 1972.

Buxton, Anthony. Sport in Peace and War. London: Arthur D. Humphreys, 1920.

Caillois, Roger. Man, Play, and Games. Glencoe, Ill.: Free Press, 1961.

Callaghan, John L. An Analysis of the Role of Sport in England and the United States. (Ph.D. dissertation, University of Southern California, 1971.)

Cantelon, Hartford A. The Political Involvement in Sport in the Soviet Union. (M.A. Thesis, University of Alberta, 1972.)

Carolan, P. The History, Development and Evaluation of a Federal Emphasis on Physical Fitness in Civilian Defense, 1940-1945. (Ph.D. dissertation, Columbia University, 1952.)

Carr, Albert. Truman, Stalin and Peace. Garden City, New York: Doubleday, 1950.

Carr, Gerald. "The Use of Sport in the German Democratic Republic for the Promotion of National Consciousness and International Prestige." Journal of Sport History, 1(2):123-136, 1975.

Central Committee in Athens. The Olympic Games: B.C. 776 – A.D. 1896. 2 vols. Athens: Charles Beck and Co., 1896.

Cheffers, John T. F. A Wilderness of Spite: or, Rhodesia Denied. New York: Vantage Press, 1972.

Chester, David. The Olympic Games Handbook. New York: Scribners, 1971.

Cistriano, John J. "The 1977 International Olympic Academy." Journal of Physical Education and Recreation 49(3):69-70, 1978.

Ciupak, Zofia. "Sports Spectators--An Attempt at a Sociological Analysis." International Review of Sport Sociology, 9(2):89-102, 1974.

Clark, E. H. "The Olympic Games and their Influence upon Physical Education." Journal of Health, Physical Education, and Recreation, 35(6): 23-25, 1964.

Clignet, R. and Stark, M. "Modernization and the Game of Soccer in Cameroun." International Review of Sport Sociology, 9(3/4):81-98.

Connally, Olga. The Rings of Destiny. New York: David McKay Co., 1968.

Conrad, Wolfgang. Frisch, Fromm, Froehlich, Frei Sport und Gessel-schaft. Reinbek bei Hamburg: Rowohlt, 1971.

Cook, T. A. The Olympic Games. London: Archibald Constable and Co., 1908.

_____. The Olympic Games of 1908: A Reply to Certain Criticisms. London: British Olympic Association, 1908.

Cooper, J. Ashley. "An Anglo-Saxon Olympiad." The Nineteenth Century XXXII, #187 (September, 1892):380-388.

_____. "Olympic Games." The Nineteenth Century and After, LXIII, #376 (June, 1908):1011-1021.

Coote, James. Olympic Report 1968: Mexico and Grenoble. London: Robert Hale, 1968.

Cozens, F. W. and Stumpf, F. Sports in American Life. Chicago: University of Chicago Press, 1953.

Crase, Darrell. "The Domination of American Track and Field by Foreign Athletes." Sport Sociology Bulletin 6(2):1-14, 1977.

Curtis, William B. "By-Gone International Athletic Contests: What Americans Have Accomplished." The Outing, XXXVI, #4 (July, 1900):350-357.

Czwalina, Klemens. Der Beitrag der Leibesuebunger und des Sports zur politischen Erziehung. Ahrensburg g. Hamburg: Czwalina, 1970.

Dahrendorf, R. Class and class conflict in industrial society. Palo Alto, California: Stanford University Press, 1959.

Daley, Arthur and Kieran, John. The Story of the Olympic Games, 776 B.C. to 1972. Philadelphia: Lippincott, 1972.

Daley, Robert. The Bizarre World of European Sports. New York: William Morrow, 1963.

Danford, Howard G. Recreation in the American Community. New York: Harper Brothers, 1953.

Daniels, A. B. "The Study of Sport as an Element of Culture." International Review of Sport Sociology, 1:153-165, 1966.

Daume, Willi. Deutscher Sport, 1952-1972. Frankurt am Main, 1973.

Davenport, Joanna. "The Women's Movement into the Olympic Games." Journal of Physical Education and Recreation, 49(3):58-60, 1978.

Davidson, Gary. Breaking the Game Wide Open. New York: Atheneum, 1974.

De Broglio, Chris. South Africa: Racism in Sport. London: International Defense and Aid Fund, 1970.

De Coubertin, Baron Pierre. "The Olympic Games of 1896." The Century Magazine, LIII, #1 (November, 1896):39-53.

_____. "The Meeting of the Olympian Games." North American Review, CLXX, #523 (June, 1900):802-811.

De Grazia, Sebastian. Of Time, Work and Leisure. Garden City, New York: Doubleday, 1962.

De Koff, Irving. The Role of Government in the Olympics. (Ed.D. dissertation, Columbia University, 1962.)

Demmert, Henry G. The Economics of Professional Team Sports. Lexington, Mass.: D. C. Heath and Co., 1973.

Denney, Reuel. The Astonished Muse. Chicago: University of Chicago Press, 1957.

Denning, Michael. The Role of Government of Canada and the Province of Ontario in the Implementation of the Fitness and Amateur Sport Act. (M.A. Thesis, University of Western Ontario, 1974.)

Doerry, Kurt and Wilhelm Dorr. Das Olympia Buch. Munich: Olympia Verlag, 1927.

"Do International Sports Help the Cause of Peace?" American Review of Reviews, LXXI, #3 (March, 1925):27-328.

D'Oliveira, Basil. D'Oliveira: An Autobiography. London: Colliers, 1968.

Draper, Mary. Sport and Race in South Africa. Johannesburg: South African Institute of Race Relations, 1963.

D. S. B. Dokumente zum Thema Sport und Politik. Frankfurt-an-Main; D. S. B., 1961.

_____. Die gesellschaftlichspolitische Rolle des Sport. Kundgebund ges Bundestages 1974 des Deutschen Sportbundes am 25 Mai 1974 in Essen mit Ansprachen. Frankfurt: DSB, 1974.

_____. Documentation on the Political Interference of the East German Sport Organizations. Frankfurt am Main: DSBm 1967.

_____. Grundsatzerklaerung des Praesidenten des DSB anlaesslich des Gespraechs des DSB mit dem DTSB am 7 Juli 1970, Halle. Frankfurt am Main: DSB, 1970.

D.T.S.B. Die geschichtliche Aufgabe des DDR Sports und die zukunft des deutschen Sports. Argumente, East Berlin: DTSB, 1962.

_____. Das olympische Spiel. Dokumentation, East Berlin: DTSB, 1963.

_____. Das war der Weg nach Tokyo. Dokumentation, East Berlin: DTSB, 1964.

_____. 20 Jahre DDR. 20 Jahre Koerperkultur des Volkes. Dokumentation zum Thema 20 Jahre erfolgreiche Entwicklung von Koerperkultur und Sport. Reden, Gesetze, Beschluesse, Erlasse, Verordungen. Berlin: Sportverlag, 1969.

Duhu, Robert. Sport and International Relations. (M.S. Thesis, University of California, 1967.)

Dulles, Foster Rhea. America Learns to Play. New York: Appleton-Century, 1940.

Dumazedier, Joffre. Toward a Society of Leisure. New York: Free Press, 1967.

Dunning, Eric (Ed.). The Sociology of Sport. London: Frank Cass and Co., 1971.

Eckhardt, Fritz. Friedrich Ludwig John: Seine Politische Würdigung im Dritten Reich. Berlin: Limpert, 1937.

Edwards, Harry. The Revolt of the Black Athlete. New York: Free Press, 1969.

_____. The Sociology of Sport. Homewood, Ill.: Dorsey Press, 1973.

Eichberg, Henning. Der Weg des Sports in die industrielle Zivilisation. Baden-Baden: Nomos Verlags-gessellschaft, 1973.

Eggleston, John. "Secondary Schools and Oxbridge Blues." British Journal of Sociology, XVI, #3 (September, 1965):232-242.

Elias, Norbert and Dunning, Eric. "The Quest for Excitement in Unexciting Societies" in Guenther Lüschen, Cross Cultural Analysis of Sport and Games. Champaign, Ill.: Stipes Publishing Company, 1970, pp. 31-51.

Enos, Ed. "An Analysis of Sport and Physical Education in the Union of Soviet Socialist Republics." Swimming World, 16(11):13-17, Nov. 1975.

Erbach, G. "Die Beduetung des 30. Jahrestages der Befreiung vom Faschismus durch die Sowjetunion fuer die Entwicklung der sozialistischen Koerperkultur in der DDR", Theorie und Praxis der Koerper-Kultur, 24(3):193-210, March 1973.

Feld, Werner. Reunification and West German Relations. The Hague: Martinus Nijhoff, 1963.

Filatov, Lev. USSR Hockey. Moscow: Novosti, 1967.

Fox, William T. R. (Ed.). Theoretical Aspects of International Relations. Notre Dame, Indiana: University of Notre Dame Press, 1959.

Frank, Jerome D. Sanity and Survival: Psychological Aspects of War and Peace. New York: Vintage Books, 1967.

Frankel, Joseph. Contemporary International Theory and the Behaviour of States. London: Oxford University Press, 1973.

Friedland, Edward, Seabury, Paul and Wildavsky, Aaron. The Great Detente Disaster. Oil and the Decline of American Foreign Policy. New York: Basic Books, 1975.

Fuoss, Donald E. An Analysis of the Incidents in the Olympic Games from 1924 to 1948 with Reference to the Contribution of the Games to International Goodwill and Understanding. (Ed.D. dissertation, Columbia University, 1951.)

Furber, Henry J. J. "Modern Olympic Games Movement." The Independent, LIV, #2776 (February 13, 1902):384-386.

Gallico, Paul. A Farewell to Sport. New York: A. A. Knopf, 1950.

Games Committee. The Interallied Games, 1919. Paris: Publications Periodique, 1919.

Gardiner, E. Norman. Athletics of the Ancient World. Oxford: Clarendon Press, 1930.

Gardner, Lloyd, Schlesinger, Arthur Jr., and Morgenthau, Hans. The Origins of the Cold War. Waltham, Mass.: Ginn-Blaisdell, 1970.

Gennadius, J. "The Revival of the Olympic Games." Cosmopolis, II, #4 (April, 1896):59-74.

Gesellschaft zur Forderung des Olympischen Gedankens in der DDR. Nationalismus und Sport. Eine Dokumentation ueber den beabsuchtigten Missbrauch der Spiele der 20. Olympiade 1972 in Muenchen fuer nationalistisches Prestigestreben durch die herrschenden Kreise der BRD. Berlin: Gesellschaft zur Foerderung des Olympischen Gedankens in der DDR, 1972.

Gesellschaft zur Foerdung des olympischen Gedankens (Ed.). Revanchismus und Sport vor den Spielen der 20. Olympiade 1972. Muenchen und Kiel--Residenzen der Revanchismus? Ostlandritt als olympische Disziplin? East Berlin: Gesellschaft zur Foerderung des olympischen Gedankens in der DDR, 1970.

Gieseler, Karlheinz. Sport als Mittel der Politik. Mainz: von Hase und Koehler Verlag, 1965.

Gieseler, Karlheinz and Blank, Eberhard. Der Sport in der Bundesrepublik Deutschland. Bonn: Boldt, 1972.

Gillett, Charlie. All in the Game: The Function and Meaning of Sport. Middlesex: Penguin, 1971.

Glader, Eugene. A Study of Amateurism in Sports. (Ph.D. dissertation, University of Iowa, 1970.)

Glass, Bill and William M. Pinson, Jr. Don't Blame the Game. Waco, Texas: Word Book Publishers, 1972.

Gloom, John. "Functionalism and World Society", in John Gloom and Paul Taylor (Eds.), Functionalism: Failure and Practice in International Relations. London: University of London Press, 1975.

Gluckman, Max. "Football Players and the Crowd." The Listener, LXI, #1560 (February 19, 1959):331-332.

Goelher, Josef. Oelbaumzweig und Goldmedaille. Geschichte und Geschichten der antiken und modernen Olympischen Spiele. Wuerzburg: Arena Verlag, George Popp, 1968.

Goldstein, R. and R. Arms. "Effects of Observing Athletic Contests on Hostility." Sociometry, XXXIV, #1 (March, 1971);83-90.

Golombek, Harry. Fischer v. Spassky. London: Barrie and Jenkins, 1973.

Goodhart, Philip and Christopher Chataway. War Without Weapons. London: W. H. Allen, 1968.

Graebner, Norman (Ed.). The Cold War: Ideological Conflict or Power Struggle. Boston: D. C. Heath, 1963.

_____. Cold War Diplomacy. Princeton: D. van Nostrand, 1962.

Grapentin, Oscar. Die Olympischen Spiele in Deutschland, 1936. Halle: Padogogischen Verlag von Herman Schroedel, 1936.

Green, Arnold. Recreation, Leisure and Politics. New York: McGraw-Hill, 1964.

Grix, Arthur E. Japans Sport in Bild und Word. Berlin: Wilhelm Limpert Varlag, 1937.

Groll, H. and H. Strohmeyer (Eds.). Jugend und Sport. Vienna: International Seminar on the Sociology of Sport, 1970.

Grube, Frank and Gerhard Richter. Leistungssport in der Erfolgsgesellschaft. Hamburg: Hoffman and Campe, 1973.

Grundgeiger, Klaus (Ed.). Sport in Deutschland 1973. Die neutrale Bilanz. Stuttgart: Deutsche Sportbibliothek Verlag, 1973.

Grupe, Ommo (Ed.). Sport in the Modern World: Chances and Problems. New York: Springer, 1973.

G.S.G.T. Sport et Progres de l'Homme. Paris: Les Editeurs Francais Reunis, 1976.

Hain, Peter. Don't Play with Apartheid. London: George Allen and Unwin, Ltd., 1971.

Hall, Sidney O. The Role of Physical Education and Sport in the Nation-Building Process in Kenya. (Ph.D. dissertation, Ohio State University, 1973.)

Halle, Louis. The Cold War as History. New York: Harper and Row, 1967.

Hanna, W. R. The Politics of Sport. New York: American Universities Field Staff, 1962.

Harbott, R. Olympia und die Olympischen Spiele von 776 B.C. bis Heute. Berlin: Wilhelm Limpert Verlag, 1935.

Harder, Heize. Unternehmen Olympia. Cologne: Kiepenheuer und Witsch, 1970.

Harlan, Hugh. History of Olympic Games Ancient and Modern. Los Angeles: Bureau of Athletic Research, 1932.

Harris, H. A. Greek Athletes and Athletics. London: Hutchinson, 1964.

_____. Sports in Greece and Rome. London: Thames and Hudson, 1972.

Hart, M. Marie (Ed.). Sport in the Socio-Cultural Process. Dubuque, Iowa: William C. Brown, 1973.

Harvey, Charles (Ed.). Sport International. New York: A. S. Barnes, 1960.

Heinila, Kalevi. Leisure and Sports. Helsinki: University of Helsinki Institute of Society, Publication 5, 1959.

_____. "Notes on Inter-Group Conflicts in International Sport." International Review of Sport Sociology, I (1966):31-38.

Heinz, Guenter. "Auf dem Wege der sich vertiefenden Zusammenarbeit im europaeischen Sport." Theorie und Praxis der Körper-Kultur, 24(4): 289-291, April 1975.

_____. "In the Sign of Olympic Solidarity," Sports in the GDR, No. 3, 1976, pp. 17-23.

Helanko, R. "Sports and Sociolization." Acta Sociologica, II, #3 (1957):229-239.

Hellman, R. "Koerperkultur und Sport in unserer Gesellschaft," Theorie und Praxis der Körper-Kulter, 24(6):483-491, June, 1975.

Henry, Bill. An Approved History of the Olympic Games. New York: G. P. Putnam's Sons, 1948.

Hertz, Frederick. The German Public Mind in the Nineteenth Century. London: George Allen and Unwin, 1975.

Hille, Barbara. "Zum Stellenwert des Sports bei Jugendlichen in der Bundesrepublik und in der DDR, Deutschland Archiv, 9(6):592-601, June, 1976.

Hoch, Paul. Rip Off the Big Game: The Exploitation of Sports by the Power Elite. Garden City, New York: Doubleday, 1972.

Hoffman, Stanley. The State of War. New York: Praeger, 1965.

Holmes, Judith. Olympiad 1936. New York: Ballantine, 1971.

Horton, George. "Revival of Olympic Games." North American Review, CLXII, #472 (March, 1896):266-273.

Howard, G. E. "Social Psychology of the Spectator." American Journal of Sociology, XLIII, #1 (July, 1912):33-50.

Hughes, W. L. and J. F. Williams. Sports, Their Organization and Administration. New York: A. S. Barnes and Co., 1944.

Huizinga, Johan. Homo Ludens: A Study of the Play Element in Culture. Boston: Beacon, 1955.

Huntington, Samuel. "Transnational Organization in World Politics." World Politics, XXV, #3 (April, 1973):309-368.

Ibrahim, Hilmi. Sport and Society. Long Beach, Calif.: Hwong Publishing Co., 1976.

Ihmels, Karl. Sport und Spaltung in der Politik der S.E.D. Köln: Verlog Wissenschaft und Politik, 1965.

Indrapana, Nat. Sport and Physical Education in Thailand, 1932-1966. (Ph.D. dissertation, University of Alberta, 1973.)

International Olympic Committee. Olympic Directory. Lausanne: International Olympic Committee, 1973.

Izenberg, Jerry. How Many Miles to Camelot? New York: Holt, Rinehart and Winston, 1972.

Jackson, Walter. A Study of the Recreational Pursuits of American Presidents. (M.A. Thesis, University of Maryland, 1962.)

James, C. L. R. "Cricket in West Indian Culture." New Society, XXXVI, #1 (June 6, 1963):8-9.

Johnson, William O. Super Spectator and the Electric Lilliputians. Boston: Little, Brown and Co., 1971.

_____. All That Glitters is Not Gold: The Olympic Games. New York: G. P. Putnam's Sons, 1972.

Jokl, E. (Ed.). Sports in the Cultural Pattern of the World. Helsinki: Institute of Occupational Health, 1956.

Jones, J. M. and A. R. Hocher. "Racial Differences in Sports Activities: A Look at the Self-Paced vs. Reactive Hypothesis." Journal of Personality and Social Psychology, XXVII, #1 (1973):86-95.

Jones, R. W. "Sport and International Understanding," in Sport-Work-Culture. (Helsinki), Paris: U.N.E.S.C.O., 1959.

Kahn, Roger. "Let's Pull Out of the Olympics." Saturday Evening Post, CCXXXVII (October 10, 1964):8-10.

Kaiser, Ulrich. Zahlt sich Muenchen aus? Ideen Investitionen fuer 1972. Frankfurt am Main: Limpert, 1970.

Kalopothakes, D. "The New Olympic Games." Harper's Weekly, XXXIX (September 25, 1895):919-924.

Kamen, Richard. The Morality of Amateurism in a World of Free Enterprise: A Survey and Investigation. (M.S. Thesis, Brooklyn College, 1956.)

Karbe, Wolfgang. Sports from 1938 to 1956 in East and West Germany. (M.A. Thesis, University of California, Berkeley, 1958.)

Keating, James W. "Sportsmanship as a Moral Category." Ethics, LXXV, #1 (October, 1964):25-35.

Kennedy, Edward. "Beyond Detente." Foreign Policy, 16:3-29, (Fall, 1974).

Keohane, R. and J. S. Nye. Transnational Relations and World Politics. Cambridge: Harvard University Press, 1972.

Kerestes, Alexander. Sport and Physical Education in Hungary. (M.A. Thesis, University of Alberta, 1967.)

Keri, Hedvig. "Ancient Games and Popular Games." American Image, XV, #1 (Spring, 1958):41-89.

Kidd, Bruce. "Olympics, '76." Canadian Dimension, 11(5):15-25, 1976.

_____. "Run, Run, Run, Run, Run, Runnnnnn". Weekend Magazine of the Montreal Star, July 31, 1975, pp. 14-16.

Kiernan, John and Arthur Daley. The Story of the Olympic Games: 776 B.C. - 1968. New York: Lippincott, 1969.

Kingsmore, John. The Effect of a Professional Wrestling and Professional Basketball Contest upon the Aggressive Tendencies of Male Spectators. (Ph.D. dissertation, University of Maryland, 1968.)

Kiviaho, Pekka. "The Regional Distribution of Sport Organizations as a Function of Political Cleavages," International Review of Sport Sociology, 10(1):5-14, 1975.

Klapp, O. E. "The Creation of Popular Heroes." American Journal of Sociology, LIV, #2 (September, 1948), 135-141.

Knecht, Willi. Die geberstenen Ringe. Eine Betrachtung zur sportpolitischen Situation in Deutschland am Vorabend der Olympischen Spiele, 1964. Frankfurt-am-Main: Hassmuller, 1964.

_____. Nach Tokio und zurück: Sportpolitik in Deutschland. Diessen, Ammersee: Tucher-Verlog, 1965.

_____. Die geteilte Arena. Nürnberg: Bahr, 1968.

_____. "Muenchen 1972 und die olympische Anerkennung der 'DDR'," Deutschland Archiv, 1(9):1009-1010, Sept. 1968.

_____. Verschenkter Lorbeer. Deutsche Sportler zwischen Ost und West. Koeln: Kiepenheur and Witsch, 1969.

_____. "Laufen Sozialisten schneller." Deutschland Archiv, 9(1): 1-9, Jan. 1969.

_____. Partnerschaft auf Raten. Wersaumnisse und Perspektiven bundesdeutschen Sportpolitik. Frankfurt am Main: Limpert, 1970.

_____. "Die Basis der sozialistischen Koerperkultur," Deutschland Archiv, 2(3):240-251, March 1969.

_____. " 'DDR' Fahnen an bundesdeutschen Masten," Deutschland Archiv, 2(4):438-439, April 1969.

_____. "Der CSSR Sport: Reflexionen einer verhinderten Reform," Deutschland Archiv, 2(8):881-889, August 1969.

_____. "DDR Sport als Wegbereiter der Weltgeltung," Deutschland Archiv, 2(9):953-957, September 1969.

_____. "München 1972. Modell für olympische Erpressung," Deutschland Archiv, 2(11):1221-1227, November 1969.

_____. "Medaillen '69. Der Wettlauf der ungleichen Brueder," Deutschland Archiv, 2(12):1338-1346, December 1969.

_____. "München 1972--Schicksalspiele," Deutschland Archiv, 3(5): 540-545, May 1970.

_____. "Innterdeutscher Sportverkehr--Aktion gebremster Schaum," Deutschland Archiv, 3(6):663-687, June 1970.

_____. "Die Isolation des West-Berliner Sports." Deutschland Archiv, 4(1):48-53, January 1971.

_____. Die ungleichen Brüder. Fakten, Thesen und Kommentore zu den Beziehungen zwischen den beiden deutschen Sportorganizationen D.S.B. and D.T.S.B. Mainz: Von Hase und Koehler Verlag, 1971.

_____. Amateur 72. Mainz: Von Hase und Koeller Verlag, 1971.

_____. "Steht West Berlin dem Sport im Wege?" Deutschland Archiv, 4(6):561-564, June 1971.

_____. "Die Sportpolitik der Amateure," Deutschland Archiv, 4(7): 684-687, July 1971.

_____. "Muenchen sehen und siegen. Der DDR Sport vor den Olympischen Spielen 1972," Deutschland Archiv, 4(12):1292-1301, December 1971.

_____. "Sportpolitik in der Phase der Entscheidung," Deutschland Archiv, 4(4):337-343, April 1973.

_____. "Manfred Ewald--Sportfuehrer der DDR," Deutschland Archiv, 6(5):468-472, May 1973.

_____. "Kommt der sowjetische Sport an Berlin vorbei," Deutschland Archiv, 6(9):905-910, September 1973.

_____. "Sowjetsport beharrt auf Sonderreglung fuer Berlin," Deutschland Archiv, 8(3):233-236, March 1975.

_____. "DDR ruestet zur groessten Sportschau der Welt," Deutschland Archiv, 8(5):451-455, May 1975.

_____. "28. Friedensfahrt. Ein Rennen mit vielerlei Eigenarten." Deutschland Archiv, 8(6):572-575, June 1975.

Kokusai bunka shinkokai. Sports Second Impression, Tokyo. Kokusai bunka shinkokai (Society for International Cultural Relations), 1939.

Kolatch, Jonathan. Sport, Politics and Ideology in China. Middle Village, New York: Jonathan David, 1972.

Komorowski, Manfred. "Cuba's Way to a Country with Strong Influence in Sport Politics--The Development of Sport in Cuba since 1959." International Journal of Physical Education, XIV (4):26-32, 1977.

Kraemer, Gerd. Wie fern ist uns Olympia? Osnabrueck: Fromm, 1971.

Kramer, Hermann Josef. Koerpererziehung und Sportunterricht in der DDR. Schorndorf bei Stuttgart: Hoffman, 1969.

Kramp, Brigette (Ed.). Sport in der DDR. Berlin: Sportverlag, 1971.

Krockow, Christian von. Sport und Industriegesellschaft. Muenchen: Piper, 1972.

_____. Sport: Eine Soziologie und Philosophie des Leistungsprinzips. Hamburg: Hoffman-Campe, 1974.

Krueger, Arnd. Die Olympische Spiele 1936 und die Weltmeinung. (Ph.D. dissertation, University of Cologne, 1972.)

_____. Die Olympische Spiele und die Weltmeinung. Ihre Aussen-politische Bedeutung unter besondere Beruecksichtigung der USA. Berlin: Bartels and Wernitz, 1972.

_____. Sport und Politik. Von Turvater Jahn zum Staatsamateur. Hannover: Fackeltraeger, 1975.

_____. "Sport und Politik," Neue Zuricher Zeitung, Oct. 24, 1975, #247, p. 53.

_____. "Der Leistungssport als Subsystem der Gesellschaft," Leistungssport 6(1):4-11, 1976.

Kyuzo, Takenoshita. "The Social Structure of the Sport Population in Japan." International Review of Sport Sociology, 2:5-18, 1967.

Labedz, Leopold. "The International Scene in the Seventies." Survey, 19 No. 2 (87):1-10, Spring, 1973.

LaFeber, Walter. America, Russia, and the Cold War, 1945-1971. New York: John Wiley and Sons, 1967.

Lapchick, Richard E. The Politics of Race and International Sport. West-port, Connecticut: Greenwood Press, 1975.

Larrabee, Eric and Rolf Meyersohn (Eds.). Mass Leisure. Glencoe, Ill.: Free Press, 1958.

Lenk, Hans. Werte-Ziele-Wirklichkeit der modernen Olympischen Spielen. Schorndorf: Hoffmann, 1964.

_____. Leistungssport: Ideologie oder Mythos? Zur Leistungskritik und Sport-philosophie. Stuttgart, Berlin, Mainz: Kohlhammer, 1972.

Lever, Janet. "Soccer: Opium of the Brazilian People." Trans-Action, VII, #2 (December, 1969):36-43.

Lineberry, William P. The Business of Sports. New York: H. W. Wilson, 1973.

Lorenz, Konrad. On Aggression. New York: Bantam, 1971.

Lowe, Benjamin. The Beauty of Sport: A Cross-disciplinary Inquiry. Englewood Cliffs, New Jersey: Prentice-Hall, Inc., 1977.

_____. "The Ballet of Action, the Champion of England, and the Fancy: the Social Matrix of Pugilism in Eighteenth Century England." Paper presented before the 7th International HISPA Congress, Paris, April, 1978.

Lowe, Benjamin and Richard P. Borkowski. "Reflections on Sport as Mythology in Industrial Society." Paper presented before the Third Canadian Symposium on the History of Sport, Halifax, Nova Scotia, August, 1974.

Lowe, Benjamin, Peter Hill and Jean Roberts. "A Cross-cultural Study of Athletes Representing Four Countries in the Commonwealth Games." Australian Journal of H.P.E.R. 70:22-26, December, 1975.

Loy, John and G. S. Kenyon. Sport, Culture, and Society. New York: Macmillan, 1969.

Lucas, John A. Baron Pierre de Coubertin and the Formative Years of the Modern International Olympic Movement. (Ed.D. dissertation, University of Maryland, 1962.)

Lüschen, Günther. "Cooperation, Association, and Contest." Journal of Conflict Resolution, XIV, #1 (1970):21-34.

_____. Cross Cultural Analysis of Sport and Games. Champaign, Ill.: Stipes Publishing Company, 1970.

_____. "The Sociology of Sport." Current Sociology, XV, #3 (1967):1-140.

MacArthur, Douglas. "Education in America." Saturday Evening Review, (October 16, 1961), p. 3g.

_____. A Soldier Speaks. Public Papers and Speeches of General of the Army MacArthur. Edited by Major Vorin Whan, Jr. New York: Praeger, 1965.

Mandell, Richard D. The Nazi Olympics. New York: Macmillan, 1971.

_____. The First Modern Olympics. Berkeley: University of California Press, 1976.

Marquand, Allen. "The Old Olympic Games." The Century Magazine, LI, #6 (April, 1896):803-816.

Martin, A. R. "Self-Alienation and the Loss of Leisure." American Journal of Psychoanalysis, XXI, #2 (1961):156-165.

Mathews, Joseph. "The First Harvard-Oxford Boat Race." The New England Quarterly, XXXIII, #1 (March, 1960):74-82.

Mayer, Otto. A Travers les Anneaux Olympiques. Genova: Cailler, 1960.

McIntosh, Peter C. Sport in Society. London: C. A. Watts and Co., 1963.

_____. "Historical View of Sport and Social Control." International Review of Sport Sociology, 6:5-16, 1971.

McNeil, Larry. The Development of a Theory of Sports Competitiveness. (Ed.D. dissertation, North Texas State University, 1971.)

McPherson, Barry D. Socialization into the Role of the Sport Consumer: The Construction and Testing of a Theory and Causal Model. (Ph.D. dissertation, University of Wisconsin, 1972.)

Meade, G. P. "The Negro in Track Athletics." Scientific Monthly, LXXV, #6 (December, 1952):366-371.

Meier, Marcel, Anotol Michailowsky and René Schaerer. Sport zwishen Ost und West. Bern: Buechler, 1962.

Meinberg, Eckhard. Leistung in Sport und Gesellschaft. Duesseldorf: Bagel, 1975.

Mějo, Ferenc. The Modern Olympic Games. Budapest: Pannonia Press, 1956.

Melik-Chakhnazarov, Achot. Le Sport en Afrique. Paris: Presence Africaine, 1970.

Meynaud, Jean. Sport et Politik. Paris: Payot, 1966.

Milne, Armour. Czechoslovak Sport, 1945-1955. Prague: Orbis, 1955.

Mitchell, Brian (Ed.). Today's Athlete. London: Pelham Brooks, 1970.

Molyneuz, Dennis D. Central Government Aid to Sport and Physical Recreation in Countries of Western Europe. University of Birmingham, 1962.

Montagu, Ivor. East-West Sport Relations. Peace Aims Pamphlet No. 52. London: National Peace Council, 1951.

Morse, Edward. "The Transformation of Foreign Politics: Modernization, Interdependence and Externalization." World Politics, XXII:371-392, 1970.

Morton, Henry. Soviet Sport, Mirror of Soviet Society. New York: Collier, 1963.

Murray, Gilbert. "Olympic Rediviva." The Living Age, CCLVII, #3347 (August 29, 1908):572-574.

Natan, Alex (Ed.). Sport and Society. London: Bowes and Bowes, 1958.

Neumann, Hannes. Die deutsche Turn bewegung in der Revolution 1848-49 und in der amerikamischen Emigration. Schorndorf: Hoffman, 1968.

Neville, R. Play Power. London: Paladin, 1971.

Newsweek. "Diplomacy Through Sports," Newsweek 80:42, Sept. 4, 1972, p. 41.

_____. "The Olympics: 'Political Blackmail', Newsweek 80/42 (Sept. 4, 1972), pp. 41-42.

Nikiforov, I. I. "Physical Culture and Sports in the USSR!'" New World Review 24/7 (July 1958), p. 27.

Noll, Roger E. (Ed.). Government and the Sports Business. Washington, D.C.: Brookings, 1974.

Norton, D. J. A Comparison of Political Attitudes and Political Participation of Athletes and Non-Athletes. (M.A. Thesis, University of Oregon, 1971.)

Novikov, A. D. and A. M. Maximenko. "The Influence of Selected Socio-Economic Factors on the Level of Sports Achievements in the Various Countries." International Review of Sport Sociology, 7:27-40, 1972.

Olsen, Jack. The Black Athlete: A Shameful Story. New York: Time, Inc., 1968.

"The Olympic Games at Athens in 1896." The Nation, LXI, #1579 (October 3, 1908):237-238.

Organizationskomiee fur die IV Olympischen Winterspiele. Amtlicher Fuhrer zur Feier der IV Olympischen Winterspiele zu Garmisch-Partenkirchen 1936. Berlin: Reichsportverlag, 1936.

Organizing Committee for the XIV Olympiad. Official Report. London, 1948.

Organizing Committee for the Games of the XV Olympiad. Official Report. Helsinki, 1952.

Organizing Committee. The Games of the XVII Olympiad. Rome, 1960.

Organizing Committee. The Games of the XVIII Olympiad. Tokyo, 1964.

Palmer, Norman D. and Howard C. Perkins. International Relations: The World Community in Tradition. (Third Edition). Boston: Houghton-Mifflin Company, 1969.

Pauker, Ewa T. G.A.N.E.F.O.: Sports and Politics in Djakarta. Santa Monica, Calif.: Rand, 1964.

Pausanis. Descriptions of Greece. Trans. and ed. by J. G. Frazer. London: Macmillan, 1913.

Perry, Gertrude V. History and Development of the Sokol Movement in Czechoslovakia. (M.A. Thesis, George Peabody College for Teachers, 1936.)

Petrovsky, Evgeny. Sport in the Soviet Union. London: Soviet News, 1946.

Pfetsch, Frank. Leistungssport und Gesellschaftssystem. Socio-Politische Faktoren im Leistungs-Sport. Die BRD im internationalen Vergleich. Shcorndorf: Hoffman, 1975.

Physical Education and Sport. Strasbourg: Council of Europe, 1964.

Physical Education and Sport in Finland. Helsinki: Werner Soderstrom Osakeyhitio, 1969.

Physical Education and Sport in Japan. Tokyo: Physical Education Bureau in the Ministry of Education, 1970.

Pickford, R. W. "Aspects of the Psychology of Games and Sports," British Journal of Psychology, XXXI, #4 (April, 1941):279-293.

_____. "The Psychology of the History and Organization of Association Football." British Journal of Psychology, XXXI, #2 (October, 1940):80-43, 129-144.

Pindar. The Isthmian Odes. Edited by J. B. Bury. Amsterdam: Adolf M. Hakkert, 1965.

_____. The Nemean Odes. Edited by J. B. Bury. Amsterdam: Adolf M. Hakkert, 1965.

_____. The Olympian and Pythian Odes. Edited by Basil L. Gildersleeve. New York: Harper Brothers, 1885.

Pipes, Richard. "Operational Principles of Soviet Foreign Policy," Survey 19, No. 2 (87) (Spring, 1973), pp. 41-61.

Planning for Sport. London: Sports Council, 1968.

Pooley, John and Arthur V. Webster. "Sport and Politics: Power Play." Journal of the Canadian Association of Health, Physical Education and Recreation 41(3):10-19, 1975.

Possekel, Horst and Guglielmi, Gerhard. Koerperkultur und Sport im sozialistischen Industriebetrieb. East Berlin: Tribune, 1971.

Powell, John T. "Sport and World Society." Address before the Bicentenniel Conference of the National Association of Physical Education for College Women, Asilomar, Calif., June, 1976.

Prokop, Ulrike. Soziologie der Olympischen Spiele. Sport und Kapitalismus. Muenchen: Hanser, 1971.

Pudelkiewicz, E. "The Socio-Historic Background of the Ideology of Racism in Sport." International Review of Sport Sociology, 7(3-4):89-113, 1973.

Radetz, Walter. Werner Seelenbinder: Leben, Haltung, Wirkung. Berlin: Sportverlag, 1969.

Reich, Alan. "Sports-Gateway to International Understanding." Congressional Record, 93rd Congress, 1st Session (June 19, 1973), Vol. 119, No. 95.

Remley, Mary Louise. Twentieth Century Concepts of Sport Competition for Women. (Ph.D. dissertation, University of Wisconsin, 1970.)

Report of the Department of Sport and Recreation. Pretoria, South Africa: Government Printer, 1968.

Report of the Inquiry into Crowd Safety at Sports Grounds. London: Her Majesty's Stationery Office, 1972.

Richard, D. J. Soviet Chess. Oxford: Clarendon Press, 1965.

Richter, Joerg. Die vertrimmte Nation oder, Sport in rechter Gesellschaft. Reinbek bei Hamburg: Rowohlt, 1972.

Riordan, James. "Soviet Sport and Soviet Foreign Policy." Soviet Studies, 26(3):322-344, 1974.

_____. "The Russian Formula." Swimming World, 16(11):14, 97, November, 1975.

_____. Sport in Soviet Society. Cambridge: Cambridge University Press, 1977.

_____. "Why Sport Under Communism," Anglo-Soviet Journal, 37 (1):8-17, 1976.

Roberts, Michael. "The Vicarious Heroism of the Sports Spectator." The New Republic, CLXXI, #22 (November 23, 1974):17-20.

Roesch, Heinz Egon. Ist das noch Sport? Kritische Anmeringen zum Sport und zu den Olympischen Spielen. Freiburg i, Br.: Herder, 1972.

Rosecrance, R. and A. Stein. "Interdependence: Myth or Reality." World Politics, 26:1-27, 1973.

Rosenau, James N. (Ed.). International Politics and Foreign Policy. New York: The Free Press, 1969.

_____. The Adaptation of National Societies: A Theory of Political System Behavior and Transformation. New York: McCaleb-Seiler, 1970.

_____. "Adaptive Policies in an Interdependent World." _Orbis_ 16:153-173, 1972.

_____. _International Studies and the Social Sciences_. London: Sage Publications, 1973.

_____. _Linkage Politics: Essays on the Convergence of National and International Systems_. New York: The Free Press, 1969.

_____. _The Scientific Study of Foreign Policy_. New York: The Free Press, 1971.

Rowell, Henry T. _Rome in the Augustan Age_. Norman, Oklahoma: University of Oklahoma Press, 1962.

Roxborough, Henry. _Canada at the Olympics_. Toronto: Ryerson Press, 1969.

Ruiz, R. "Die Mittelamerikanischen und Karibischen Spiele--ihre Entstehung und Entwicklung unter besonderer Beruechtigung der Teilnahme des sozialistischen Kuba?" _Theorie und Praxis der Korper-Kultur_, 24(6):559-563, 1975.

Sage, George (Ed.). _Sport in American Society_. Reading, Mass.: Addison-Wesley, 1970.

Sandilands, C. S. _Atalanta, or the Future of Sport_. New York: E. P. Dutton and Co., 1928.

Sands, Robert. "International Sport is Politics." _Australian Journal of Health, Physical Education and Recreation_, 72:7-10, 1976.

Schelling, Thomas. _The Strategy of Conflict_. Cambridge, Mass.: Harvard University Press, 1960.

Scherer, Georg and Norbert Wolf. _Sport zwischen Spiel und Leistung_. Essen: Fredebeul and Koenen, 1972.

Scherer, Karl A. _Der Maennerorden. Eine Geschichte des Internationalen Olympischen Komitees_. Frankfurt: Limpert, 1974.

Schmalenberger, Herbert. The Reflection of Nationalism in the U. S. and the USSR in the Sports News. (M.A. Thesis, University of California, Berkeley, 1958.)

Schmidt, Bodo. "Towards the Promotion of Sport in Developing Countries, _International Journal of Physical Education_, XIV (4):19-22, 1977.

Schmidt, E. "Koerperkultur und Sport--Mittel zur sozialistischen Erziehung und Bildung der Lehrlinge," _Theorie und Praxis der Körper-Kultur_, 23(3):211-213, 1974.

Schnepel, Emil P. The Life and Work of Friedrich Ludwig Jahn. (M.A. Thesis, Ohio State University, 1935.)

Schöbel, Heinz. Olympia und Seine Spiele. Berlin: Sportverlag Berlin, 1965.

_____. The Four Dimensions of Avery Brundage. Leipzig: Edition Leipzig, 1968.

Scholer, Elmer A. A Public Recreation System of Norway. (Ph.D. dissertation, University of Illinois, 1960.)

Schroeder, W. "Zum Problem der Traditionen in der sozialistischen Koerperkultur in der DDR," Theorie und Praxis der Körper-Kultur, 24(6):540-550, 1976.

Schulke, Hans Juergen (Ed.). Sport, Wissenschaft und Politik in der BRD. Koeln: Pahl, Ruegenstein, 1975.

Schulte, Dieter. The Role of Sport in the German Democratic Republic--Its Social, Cultural and Political Values. (M.A. Thesis, UCLA, 1975.)

Schwank, Willi. Sport und Gewerkschaft in der Bundesrepublik. Eine historische Bestandsaufnahme zur Wertung des Sports durch den Deutschen Gewerkschaftbund und seine Organe zwisschen 1949 und 1975. Ahrensburg bei Hamburg: Czwalina, 1975.

Schwartz, J. Michael. "Causes and Effects of Spectator Sport." International Review of Sport Sociology, 8(3-4):25-42, 1973.

Scriven, F. B. Sports Facilities for Schools in Developing Countries. Paris: UNESCO, 1973.

Semotiuk, Darwin M. The Development of a Theoretical Framework for Analyzing the Role of National Government Involvement in Sport and Physical Education and its Application to Canada. (Ph.D. dissertation, Ohio State University, 1970.)

Sessons, H. Douglas. "An Analysis of Selected Variables Affecting Outdoor Recreation Patterns." Social Forces, 42(1):112-115, 1963.

Shih, Chi-wen. Sports Go Forward in China. Peking: Foreign Languages Press, 1963.

Shipman, Samuel. "Sports in the Soviet Union." Current History, 47:81-85, 1937.

Sie, Swanpo. The Place of Health Education, Physical Education, and Sports in Educational Planning for National Development in Indonesia. (Ph.D. dissertation, University of Missouri, 1971.)

Sieniarski, Stefan. Sport in Poland. Warsaw: Interpress Publishers, 1972, 180 pp.

Silverman, A. The World of Sport. New York: Holt, Rinehart and Winston, 1962.

Simri, Uriel (Ed.). Proceedings of the Pre-Olympic Seminar on the History of Physical Education and Sports in Asia. Netanya, Israel: Wingate Institute, 1972.

Sipes, Richard. "War, Sports, and Aggression: An Empirical Test of Two Rival Theories." American Anthropologist, 60:64-80, 1973.

Siska, Heinz. Volkerkampf Olympia. Berlin: Willi Bischoff, 1936.

Skorning, L. "Chronik unserer Sportbeziehunger zur UdSSR," Theorie und Praxis der Körper-Kultur, 24(3):206-224, 1975.

Sport and Physical Education in Israel. Natanya: Wingate Institute, 1974.

Sport in Britain. London: H.M.S.O., 1972.

Sport in Korea. Seoul: Korean Amateur Sports Association, 1972.

Sport in the Seventies. London: H.M.S.O., 1972.

Sport Organization in Austria. Vienna: Austrian Documentation Service, 1965.

Starbuck, Eric. Soviet Sports. New York: National Council of American-Soviet Friendship, 1945.

Starke, G. "Geselischaftliche Stellung und gesellschaftliche Funktionen von Koerperkultue und sport in der DDR," Theorie und Praxis der Körper-Kultur, 24(10):901-909, 1975.

Starosta, W. "Some Data Concerning Social Characteristics of Figure Skaters." International Review of Sport Sociology, 2:165-175, 1967.

Stavrianas, L. S. The Balkans Since 1453. New York: Holt, Rinehart and Winston, 1968.

Stern, B. C. "Socialization and Political Integration through Sports and Recreation." Physical Education, 25(3):29-30, 1968.

_____. The Relationship Between Participation in Sports and the Moral and Political Socialization of High School Youth in Chile. (Unpublished doctoral dissertation, Stanford University, 1972.)

Stoltz, Otto and Willy Wange. Sprung über den Vorhang? Sport und Politik. Nöln: Mittelrheiniseke Drücken v. Verlogsanstalt, 1953.

Strutt, Joseph. The Sports and Pastimes of the People of England. London: Chatto and Windus, 1898.

Strych, Edward. Der westdeutsche Sport in der Phase der Neugrundung 1945-1950. Schorndorf: Hoffman, 1975.

Sullivan, J. E. "The Olympic Games of 1906 at Athens." Spaulding Athletic Library, XXIII, #273 (July, 1906).

_____. The Olympic Games of 1912. New York: American Sports Publishing Company, 1912.

Sussman, M. "Leisure: Bane or Blessing?" Social Work, I(3):11-18, 1956.

Swedish Olympic Committee. The Olympic Games of Stockholm, 1912. Stockholm, 1913.

Talamini, John and Charles Page (Eds.). Sport and Society, An Anthology. New York: Little, Brown, 1973.

Tanter, Raymond and Richard H. Ullman. Theory and Policy in International Relations. Princeton, N. J.: Princeton University Press, 1974.

Tarasov, Nikolai. Soviet Sport Today. Moscow: Novosti, 1964.

Tetsch, Ernst J. (Ed.). Sport und Kulturwandel. Stuttgart, Institut fur Auslandsbeziehungen, 1978.

Third Winter Olympic Games Committee. Official Report. Third Winter Olympic Games Committee, 1932.

Thompson, Richard. Race and Sport. London: Institute of Race Relations, 1964.

Thompson, William and T. W. Lawson. The Lawson History of the America's Cup. Boston: Lawson, 1902.

Turner, Thomas E. The Effects of Viewing College Football, Basketball, and Wrestling on the Elicited Aggressive Behavior of Male Spectators. (Ph.D. dissertation, University of Maryland, 1968.)

Ulam, Adam. Expansion and Coexistence. Soviet Foreign Policy 1917-1973. New York: Praeger, 1974.

_____. The Rivals. America and Russia since World War II. New York: The Viking Press, 1971.

UNESCO. Sport, Work, Culture: Report of the International Conference on the Contrubitons of Sport to the Improvement of Professional Abilities and to Cultural Development. Helsinki, 1960.

United States Olympic Committee. <u>Proceedings: National Conference on Olympic Development</u>. Washington, D. C.: American Association for Health, Physical Education, and Recreation, 1966.

Vanderzwaag, Harold. <u>Toward a Philosophy of Sport</u>. Reading, Mass.: Addison-Wesley, 1972.

Veblen, Thorstein. <u>Theory of the Leisure Class</u>. New York: The Modern Library, 1934.

Vernacchia, Ralph A. "Problems of Modern Olympism." <u>Journal of Physical Education and Recreation</u>, 49(3):70-72, 1978.

Veto, Joseph (Ed.). <u>Sports in Hungary</u>. Budapest: Corvina Press, 1965.

Vican, Sidan. "A Sociologist's Look at the Phenomenon of Soccer." <u>Sociologica</u>, 13:5-20, 1971.

Vinnai, Gerhard. <u>Football Mania</u>. London: Ocean Books, 1970.

Waller, Klaus and H. Michels. <u>Sport - Profit - Politik</u>. Frankfurt a. M: Verlag Marxistische Blatter, 1974.

Walsh, Richard. "The Soviet Athlete in International Competition:" <u>U.S. State Department Bulletin</u> 25/652 (Dec. 24, 1951), pp. 1007-1008.

Washburn, Melvin. "Sport as a Soviet Tool." <u>Foreign Affairs</u>, 34(3):490-499, 1956.

Watkins, Glenn G. The Law and Games in Sixteenth Century England. (M.A. Thesis, University of Alberta, 1969.)

Watman, Melvin. <u>History of British Athletics</u>. London: Robert Hale, 1968.

Webster, F. A. M. <u>The Evolution of the Olympic Games, 1829 B.C. - 1914 A.D.</u> London: Heath, Cranton, and Oureley, 1914.

Weir, L. S. <u>Europe at Play: A Study of Recreation and Leisure Time Activities</u>. New York: A. A. Barnes and Co., 1937.

Weiss, Paul. <u>Sport: A Philosophic Inquiry</u>. Carbondale: Southern Illinois University Press, 1969.

Wenkart, Simon. "The Meaning of Sports for Contemporary Man." <u>Journal of Existential Psychiatry</u>, 3(12):397-403, 1963.

Weyand, Alexander M. <u>The Olympic Pageant</u>. New York: Macmillan, 1952.

Weyer, Willi. <u>Sport und Staat</u>. Bonn: Liberal Verlag, 1972.

White, C. M. D. An Analysis of Hostile Outbursts in Spectator Sports. (Ph.D. dissertation, University of Illinois, 1970.)

Wiehl, Jeski von, Olympische Spiele wozu? Muenchen: Schneekluth, 1972.

Winkler, Hans Joachim. Sport und Politische Bildung. Modell-fall Olympia. Opladen: Leske, 1972.

Wohl, Andrzej. "Competitive Sport and Its Social Function." International Review of Sport Sociology, 5:117-126, 1970.

Wright, F. A. Greek Athletics. London: Jonathon Cape, Ltd., 1925.

Wu, Kuei-Shon. Physical Education in the Republic of China from 1880 to 1965. (M.A. Thesis, University of Alberta, 1965.)

Zeigler, Earle, Maxwell L. Howell and Marianna Trekell. Research in History, Philosophy and International Aspects of Physical Education and Sport. Bibliographies and Techniques. Champaign, Ill.: Stipes Publishing Company, 1971.

Zenter, Kurt. Pierre de Coubertin. Leipzig: University of Leipzig In-augural Dissertation, 1935.

Zingale, Donald P. A History of the Involvement of the American Presidency in School and College Physical Education and Sports During the Twenti-eth Century. (Ph.D. dissertation, Ohio State University, 1973.)

Zinkewych, Osyp. Ukranian Olympic Champions. Baltimore: Ukrainian Information Service, 1972.

Index

sport politics (see also
  "political sport")   201, 298,
      303, 334, 352, 387ff.,
          380, 474
sport psychology   564, 567, 580
sport relations   253,
      333-339, 354
sport science (see social
  science of sport)   578
sport sociology   564, 567, 580
sports foundation   411ff.
sports movements (see
  also international
  sport movements)   552
sportsmanship   ix, 8, 46,
      114, 135ff., 143, 234,
      273, 402, 483, 541
sportswriters (see
  publicity, press)   150, 273
squash   244, 327
Squaw Valley   303, 323,
      355, 507
status (see prestige)   204, 214,
      243, 259, 318, 380,
          412, 530
Stockholm   118, 130, 147, 527
Stop the Seventy Tour
  (STST)   378, 393
strength   132, 209, 236, 249,
      266, 270, 335, 369,
          434, 583
Strenk, Andrew   302, 347-368
subsidization   194, 203, 207,
      312, 362-364, 389,
      406, 453, 474, 575
Sudan   333
Supreme Council for
  Sport in Africa
  (SCSA)   111, 303, 375,
      389ff., 542-543
survival   281
Sweden   134, 137, 337,
      487, 494
swimming   36, 132, 244,
      264, 266, 273, 282,
      328, 351, 389, 417,
          434, 456, 547
Switzerland   38, 133, 164,
      356, 487, 494
symbol (symbolic
  dialogue)   242
Syria   175, 293, 333

System for Information
  Retrieval in Leisure
  and Sports (SIRLS)   579
System Idolatry   205

table tennis   271ff., 351
Taipei   274
Taiwan   2, 110, 174, 205,
      260, 264, 268ff., 283ff.,
          336, 369, 472, 529
Talamini, John
  (and Page, C.)   vii, 260
Tanzania   111, 204, 538
technological
  innovation   149, 192-193,
      230, 247, 578
tennis   132, 244, 255,
      282, 328, 377, 390, 474
terrorism (terrorists)   302, 415
Thailand   165, 280, 285,
          293, 551
Third World   3, 7, 205,
      270, 288, 292, 324, 333,
      375, 377, 391, 530, 580
Thirer, Joel   153-159
Thomas Cup
  (badminton)   517, 554
Tibet   266
Tokyo   137, 280, 323, 371, 510
totalitarianism   136ff., 156
tourism   300ff., 552, 555
trade unions (labor
  unions)   386, 472
transnational analysis   303,
          386-399, 516ff.
transnational organi-
  zations (TNO)   476, 515-537
transnational
  politics   386, 516ff.
transnational sports
  competition (see also
  international sport
  competition)   160-190,
      200-206, 270, 298,
          454, 456ff.
transnational sport
  system (see sport
  as system)   273, 298,
          304, 515-537
Tunisia   204, 293, 301, 333
Turkey   7, 116, 337, 582